NEGOTIATIONS IN THE CASE LAW OF THE INTERNATIONAL COURT OF JUSTICE

Negotiations in the Case Law of the International Court of Justice

A Functional Analysis

KAREL WELLENS

Radboud University, The Netherlands

Routledge
Taylor & Francis Group
LONDON AND NEW YORK

First published 2014 by Ashgate Publishing

Published 2016 by Routledge
2 Park Square, Milton Park, Abingdon, Oxfordshire OX14 4RN
711 Third Avenue, New York, NY 10017, USA

First issued in paperback 2016

Routledge is an imprint of the Taylor & Francis Group, an informa business

British Library Cataloguing in Publication Data
A catalogue record for this book is available from the British Library

Library of Congress Cataloging-in-Publication Data
Wellens, Karel, author.
Negotiations in the case law of the International Court of Justice : a functional analysis / By Karel Wellens.
p. cm.
Includes bibliographical references and index.
ISBN 978-1-4094-1045-4 (hardback)
1. International Court of Justice. 2. Pacific settlement of international disputes. 3. Arbitration (International law) I. Title.
KZ6275.W45 2014
341.5'52--dc23

2014018648

ISBN 13: 978-1-138-70075-8 (pbk)
ISBN 13: 978-1-4094-1045-4 (hbk)

Contents

Acknowledgements

The idea behind this study is that doctrine on the law of peaceful settlement of disputes mostly deals with either negotiations or adjudication, but hardly with the functional interaction between these two mechanisms.

The author is indebted to former undergraduate students Anouk de Bruijn and Dominique Arntz for their assistance in acquiring and checking material that was helpful in the research and writing of the text.

Others to whom I owe a special vote of thanks include Charo Huesa Vinaixa, Mariano Aznar-Gómez and Fay Pazartzis, who share with me the wonderful experience of having been visiting fellows at the Lauterpacht Centre for International Law and whose continuous friendship and support has been a source of inspiration throughout this exercise.

My sincere thanks go also to the members of the editorial team of Ashgate Publishing: Alex Buckley, Carolyn Court, Elaine Couper and Celia Barlow. I wish also to thank Maria Anson for her immaculate proofreading. I am deeply grateful to Alison Kirk: her cooperation, support and understanding have not only been tireless but also went well beyond any line of duty.

The skilful assistance provided at the last hour before my final deadline by Boris Heim of the Information Department of the International Court of Justice was highly appreciated.

Last but not least I would like to thank my wife Chris for her love and tolerance during this journey; without her I would not have been able to write this book.

This book is dedicated to my mother, who passed away during the drafting process, and to my granddaughter Penelope who, intermittently, was successful in making me leave my study.

Introduction

For the first time in the history of the World Court a dispute has been brought before the Court, the subject-matter of which exclusively consists of positively opposing views on the existence – under various sources of international law – of the obligation to negotiate, its alleged violation and the remedy requested to perform that obligation 'in good faith, promptly, formally, within a reasonable time and effectively'.[1] The topic of our study has finally and in an unequivocal way reached the Peace Palace.

A Provisional Conceptual Background

Article 1, para. 1 of the UN Charter defines 'adjustment *or settlement*' of disputes to be one of the purposes of the United Nations.

Chapter VI of the Charter deals with Pacific Settlement of Disputes. Article 33, para. 1 provides that:

> the parties to any dispute, the continuance of which is likely to endanger the maintenance of international peace and security, shall, first of all, seek a solution by negotiation, enquiry, mediation, conciliation, arbitration, judicial settlement, resort to regional agencies or arrangements, or other peaceful means of their own choice.

Although the role of the UN Security Council in promoting the peaceful settlement of disputes is undeniable and it may also investigate 'any situation which might lead to international friction or give rise to a dispute' (Article 34),[2] this study will not go into its role with regard to negotiations on the subject-matter of any dispute pending before

1 Application Bolivia, dated 24 April 2013, instituting proceedings before the International Court of Justice (ICJ) against Chile with regard to a dispute concerning the obligation of Chile 'to negotiate in good faith and effectively with Bolivia in order to reach an agreement granting Bolivia a full sovereign access to the Pacific Ocean', I, § 1 and IV, § 32 (text available on the Court's website). When this book was going to press the Republic of the Marshall Islands, on 24 April 2014, submitted separate Applications against nine States regarding the alleged past and continuing breach of their customary international law obligation to pursue in good faith negotiations to cease the nuclear arms race at an early date and conclude negotiations leading to nuclear disarmament in all its aspects under strict and effective control. Pursuant to Article VI of the Nuclear Non-Proliferation Treaty (NPT) the second obligation is not only one of both conduct and result as declared by the Court in 1996, but it also has, according to the Applicant, an *erga omnes* character.

The UK as a nuclear-weapon State and a party to the NPT, and India and Pakistan as nuclear weapon States not parties to the NPT, are allegedly also in continuous breach of their general obligation to fulfil their customary international law obligations in good faith.

The Applicant *inter alia* requests the Court to order the Respondents to comply with their obligations 'within one year of the Judgment, including the pursuit, *by initiation if necessary*, of negotiations in good faith aimed at the conclusion of a convention on nuclear disarmament in all its aspects under strict and effective international control' (emphasis added). The other remedies requested are adapted to the respective nuclear policies and approaches to the negotiations on nuclear disarmament of the three Respondents (text of the Applications available on the Court's website).

Because the basis for the Court's jurisdiction in the Applications against the Democratic Republic of China, the Democratic Republic of North Korea, France, Israel, the Russian Federation and the United States of America, asserting similar claims, is Article 38, para. 5 of the Rules of Court, there is no case entered in the General List until consent is given to the Court's jurisdiction (Press Release No. 2014/18 of 25 April 2014).

2 Statement by Judge Owada, President of the ICJ, to the Security Council on 27 October 2010, pp. 3 and 5 (text available on the Court's website). On the conciliatory responsibilities of the Security Council see *inter alia* C. Murphy, 'The Conciliatory Responsibilities of the United Nations Security Council' (1992) 35 *German Yearbook of International Law*, 190–204.

the Court or on the use of Article 36, para. 3 of the UN Charter, a provision which, together with article 94, para. 2, reflects the constitutional functional links between the two organs.[3]

Neither will we look into the way, pursuant to Article 14 of the Charter, the General Assembly has recommended measures 'for the peaceful adjustment of any situation, regardless of origin, which it deems likely to impair the general welfare or friendly relations among nations'.

It is sufficient to acknowledge that when exercising some of their powers and competences under the Charter, 'both the General Assembly and the Security Council become engaged in negotiations'.[4]

The Court's Registrar has aptly observed in a paraphrase of Article 24 of the Charter that the Court has 'the primary responsibility for the settlement of international disputes by law'.[5]

Article 1 of the Charter defines '*adjustment or settlement*' of international disputes to be one of the purposes of the United Nations provided this is being done 'in such a manner that international peace and security, and justice, are not endangered'.[6] These are fundamental principles under the Charter and general international law and should be respected by parties to any dispute.[7] Hence, 'the progress of international law, in its efforts to prevent war and promote international cooperation, is above all directed to the pacific settlement of disputes',[8] which can be considered to be 'the fundamental mission of international law'.[9]

Because 'peaceful settlement of international disputes is the most critical issue of our time',[10] it is unsurprising that we witness a change of international law itself, which from a fundamentally doctrinal law it used to be is becoming more and more jurisprudential.[11]

In this study by an academic observer, the term 'settlement of disputes' means the 'efforts made by parties or a third party to solve the state of dispute that arose between States' and is distinguished from 'solution of a dispute being the dissolution of the dispute itself', whereas 'dispute settlement method' means an individual settlement procedure that parties choose and 'dispute settlement process' means the process towards the settlement of a dispute through a dispute settlement procedure of choice.[12]

We will come back to the Court's approach to the definition of a dispute, but at this stage it is sufficient to refer to Merrills' description of a dispute as 'a specific disagreement concerning a matter of fact, law or policy in which a claim or assertion of one party is met with refusal, counterclaim or denial by another'.[13]

The 'final resolution' of a dispute 'implies that the underlying circumstances giving rise to the dispute have been satisfactorily addressed so that they no longer exist whereas settlement implies that the parties

3 On the practice and legal effects of Security Council referral to the ICJ see *inter alia* G. Distefano and E. Henry, 'The International Court of Justice and the Security Council. Disentangling Themis from Ares', in K. Bannelier, T. Christakis and S. Heathcote (eds), *The ICJ and the Evolution of International Law: The Enduring Impact of the Corfu Channel Case* (London and New York, 2012), pp. 60–75. See also more generally N. White and M. Saul, 'Legal Means of Dispute Settlement in the Field of Collective Security: The Quasi-Judicial Powers of the Security Council' in D. French, M. Saul and N. White (eds), *International Law and Dispute Settlement: New Problems and Techniques* (Oxford and Portland, 2010), pp. 191–224.

4 A. Lall, *Modern International Negotiation: Principles and Practices* (New York and London, 1966, p. 21.

5 Ph. Couvreur, 'A propos de l'effecitvité de la Cour Internationale de Justice dans le règlement pacifique des différends internationaux' (1996) 4 *African Yearbook of International Law*, 103–34 at 105: 'la responsabilité principale du règlement des différends internationaux par le droit'.

6 *Request for the Interpretation of the Judgment of 15 June 1962 in the Case concerning the* Temple of Preah Vihear (Cambodia v. Thailand) *(Cambodia v. Thailand), Provisional Measures, I.C.J. Reports 2011, Order of 18 July 2011*, p. 537, at p. 554, para. 66.

7 *Ibid.*

8 *Ambatielos case (jurisdiction), Judgment of 1 July 1952: I.C.J. Reports 1952*, p. 28, Individual opinion by Judge Carneiro, at p. 54.

9 L. Delbez, *Les principes généraux du contentieux international* (Paris, 1962), p. 11: 'la mission fondamentale du droit international'.

10 J. .Merrills, *International Dispute Settlement* (5th edn, Cambridge, 2011), p. 308.

11 C. Apostolides, 'Preface' in C. Apostolides (ed.), *Les arrêts de la Cour Internationale de Justice* (Dijon 2005), p. 5. See also generally Sociéte Française pour le Droit International, *Colloque de Lille. La juridictionnalisation du droit international* (Paris, 2003).

12 S. Sakamoto, 'Revaluation of "Decisions Ordering the Duty to Negotiate" by the International Court of Justice' (1997) 96 *Journal of International Law and Diplomacy*, 3, 1–24; and (2000), vol. 98, 6, 35–63, at 9–10, note 1.

13 J. Merrills, *International Dispute Settlement*, p. 1.

have reached a binding agreement whether or not the underlying issues remain'.[14] Although it has to be acknowledged that while 'it is tempting to believe that there ought to be ways of resolving disputes once and for all, partial or step-by-step solutions may often be the best that can be managed'.[15]

Inter-state disputes are 'delicate affairs';[16] they may be inevitable, but they certainly are *dysfunctional for the society* of States.[17] 'The resolution of disputes is a *function* which, first and foremost, serves the interest of maintaining international peace and understanding.'[18]

Negotiations basically consist 'of discussions between the interested parties with a view to reconciling divergent views, or at least understanding the different positions maintained'.[19] It has also been pointed out that in general 'a negotiation brings about a decision'.[20] Indeed, negotiations may bring a State to withdraw its claim, or at least part of it; to renounce the exercise of a particular right; to dissipate a misunderstanding; and to bring about a compromise between the parties to the dispute.[21]

Negotiations, as a diplomatic means to settle disputes, and their judicial settlement are at both ends of the spectrum. Both means of pacific settlement have been the subject of extensive legal writing since the adoption of the World Court's Statute in 1922. Judicial settlement of international disputes 'has *come to be seen* as retaining a superiority, at least at the conceptual level, in relation to political means of settlement, to the extent that the solution reached is based on the rule of law'.[22]

The Purpose of this Study

Writing almost 40 years ago, Paul Reuter was able to acknowledge that negotiation 'is little known by lawyers' and 'almost ignored by law',[23] and that still seems to be the case today; indeed, given 'the importance of negotiation in international relations, the dearth of literature on the subject is surprising'.[24]

Diplomatic negotiations between States do constitute an important aspect of the overall background to cases before the ICJ. In many cases negotiations have been conducted but have finally turned out to be (partially) unsuccessful, thereby bringing the parties to the Peace Palace. Doctrine has analysed the interaction between these two means, but to a much lesser extent than their respective role and functioning.

This study brings to the fore the way negotiations have been playing a multifunctional role in the Court's jurisprudence: a condition of jurisdiction and/or admissibility for the submission of the dispute; a potential and parallel role during the course of the proceedings, sometimes forming part and parcel of the judicial settlement even in the post-adjudicative phase; and eventually in case of failure of such negotiations, bringing the parties back before the Court.

---

14 A. Spain, 'Examining the International Judicial Function: International Courts as Dispute Resolvers' (2011) 34 *Loyola of Los Angeles International and Comparative Law Review*, 5–31, at 5.

15 J. Merrills, *International Dispute Settlement*, 81.

16 R. Kolb, *The International Court of Justice* (Oxford and Portland, 2013), p. 12.

17 L. Prott, 'The Role of the Judge of the International Court of Justice' (1974) 10 *Revue Belge de Droit International*, 437–507 at 476.

18 R. Kolb,*The ICJ*, p. 1139.

19 M. Shaw, 'Settling Territorial Disputes' in *Liber Amicorum Jean-Pierre Cot. Le procès international* (Brussels 2009), pp. 255–81, at p. 258.

20 E. Nys, *Le Droit International. Les principes, les théories, les faits* (3 vols, Brussels, Paris, 1906) vol. 3, p. 12: 'une négociation aboutit à une décision'.

21 A. Rivier, *Principes du Droit des Gens* (2 vols, Paris, 1896), vol. 2, Livre VIII, pp. 152–3.

22 A. Trindade, 'The Relevance of International Adjudication Revisited: Reflections on the Need and Quest for International Compulsory Jurisdiction' in R. MacDonald and D. Johnston (eds), *Towards World Constitutionalism: Issues in the Legal Ordering of the World Community* (Leiden and Boston, 2005) pp. 515–42, at p. 515 (emphasis added). For the purpose of our study there is no need to ascertain whether this perception is fully justified.

23 P. Reuter, 'De l'obligation de négocier' (1975) 14 *Communicazioni e studi*, 711–33, at 714: 'est peu connue des juristes' and 'presque ignorée par le droit'.

24 M. Waibel', The Diplomatic Channel' in J. Crawford, A. Pellet and S. Oleson (eds), *The Law of International Responsibility* (Oxford, 2010), pp. 1085–97, at p. 1086.

Recourse to the Court may be initiated by (one of) the parties as part of their negotiation process, while the Court itself may function as a catalyst for negotiations.[25] The Court itself recognized that its function is 'to resolve any legal questions that may be in issue between parties to a dispute; and the resolution of such legal questions by the Court may be an important, and sometimes decisive, factor in promoting the peaceful settlement of the dispute'.[26]

In sum it is wholly appropriate to consider 'judicial intervention as an element of a diplomatic process'.[27]

The analysis will provide us with an insight into the way the complementarity between the two mechanisms works in their daily functioning. Indeed, 'their relationship is much more rich and nuanced that may appear at first sight'[28] as part of the 'mosaic of international dispute settlement procedures'.[29]

We will be able to put the functional interaction[30] between the diplomatic and judicial settlement of inter-state disputes in the right perspective in light of the analysis of the Court's jurisprudence spreading over more than six decades.[31]

The growing importance of the functional interaction has been amply illustrated by some recent cases before the Court.[32]

This study's aim is to uncover possible trends in the Court's jurisprudence – 'a trend in jurisprudence is the reflection of a trend in society, and has no direct link with the way in which the courts handle their work'[33] – with regard to the functional interaction between the diplomatic and judicial component, a question which until recently has attracted 'relatively little attention'.[34]

Case-law will enable us to ascertain the Court's 'judicial policy' in the narrow sense: namely 'the general orientations which underlie the jurisprudence of the Court with regard to some basic legal issues connected with the way the Court understands its judicial function';[35] in other words the evolutionary trajectory – sometimes only to be detected through slight changes – of the functional interaction as handled by the Court. Our analysis will then enable us to identify a number of structural trends.

The Court's jurisprudence will perhaps provide us with principles that govern not only the direction but also the outcome of negotiations between parties as a means to peacefully settle disputes between them as

25 B. Ajibola, 'Dispute Resolution by the International Court of Justice' (1998),11 *Leiden Journal of International Law*, 1, 123–30, at 126.

26 *United States Diplomatic and Consular Staff in Tehran, Judgment, I.C.J. Reports 1980*, p. 3, at p. 22, § 40.

27 G. Giraudeau, *Les différends territoriaux devant le juge international. Entre droit et transaction* (Leiden, Boston, 2013), Titre 1, p. 27: 'l'intervention du juge en tant qu'élément d'un processus diplomatique'.

28 L. Boisson de Chazournes, 'Introduction' in L. Boisson de Chazournes, M. Kohen and J. Vinuales (eds), *Diplomatic and Judicial Means of Dispute Settlement* (Leiden, Boston, 2013), p. 7.

29 J. Merrills, 'The Mosaic of International Dispute Settlement Procedures: Complementary or Contradictory?' (2007) 54 *Netherlands International Law Review*, 2, 361. On the functional interaction between negotiation and non-adjudicative means of settlement of disputes see *inter alia* J. Merrills, *International Dispute Settlement*, p. 125: 'methods of dispute settlement are interconnected'.

30 See on the topic of our study also V. Lowe, 'The Interplay between Negotiation and Litigation in International Dispute Settlement' in N. Tafsir Malick (ed.), *Law of the Sea, Environmental Law and Settlement of Disputes: Liber Amicorum Judge Thomas A. Mensah* (Leiden, 2007), pp. 235–47. See also N. Ghozali, 'La négociation diplomatique dans la jurisprudence internationale' (1992) 25 *Revue Belge de Droit International*, 323–50.

31 Unless indicated otherwise, when the party or the judge presenting a particular argument has been identified, excerpts are referring to Court's pronouncements, rulings and *dicta*. This study takes account of the Court's jurisprudence up to 15 Augusr 2014.

32 A reference to an early example of functional interaction, almost *avant la lettre*, was made by Judge Jessup in his dissenting opinion to the South West Africa cases: *South West Africa, second phase, Judgment, I.C.J. Reports 1966*, p. 6 at p. 423.

33 H. Thirlway, 'Some Observations on Recent Trends in the Work of the International Court of Justice' (2012) 55 *Japanese Yearbook of International Law*, 4–30, at 5.

34 L. Boisson de Chazournes, 'Introduction', p. 2.

35 P.-M. Dupuy, 'The Judicial Policy of the International Court of Justice' in F. Salerno (ed.), *Il Ruolo del Giudice Internzaionale Nell'Evoluzione del Diritto Internazionale e Comunitario. Atti del Convegno di Studi in memoria di Gaetano Morelli* (Milan 1995), pp. 61–82, at p. 62. On the *various modes* of the Court's judicial functions see *inter alia* S. Wittich, 'The Judicial Functions of the International Court of Justice', in I. Buffard, J. Crawford, A. Pellet and S. Wittich (eds), *International Law between Universalism and Fragmentation: Festschtift in Honour of Gerard Hafner*(Leiden, Boston, 2008), pp. 981–1000.

well as with general trends in the way the Court has been dealing with negotiations in the performance of its functions, notwithstanding the fact that undoubtedly it 'is difficult to identify literature dealing with general trends in international litigation'.[36]

The Georgian racial non-discrimination case against the Russian Federation (hereinafter referred to as the *CERD case*) is a landmark case on the interpretation of compromissory clauses in general and the precondition of prior negotiations more in particular. It is the first case ever for the Court to decline jurisdiction on the sole basis of a prior negotiation condition not being fulfilled – and which did entail (new) rigid requirements 'as to the existence of a dispute' and 'the condition of negotiations sufficient for the seisin of the Court'.[37] Separate and dissenting opinions in that case reflect the concern of judges that as a result parties to future cases will find themselves in a straitjacket.[38]

We will assess the potential influence on the functional interaction of the formalistic approach adopted by the Court in this case.

From the judgments, advisory opinions and positions taken by individual judges it will be possible to piece together a view of the Court's general attitude towards the functional interaction between the two modes of peaceful settlement of disputes (PSD).

An important *caveat* applies: when we determine 'the conclusions reached by the ICJ' we must 'be careful not to ascribe conclusions to the *Court* that it did not itself advance'. There 'is always a danger of

---

36 P. Sands, 'Introduction and Acknowledgements' in R. Mackenzie, C. Romano, Y. Shany and P. Sands (eds), *The Manual on International Courts and Tribunals* (2nd edn, Oxford, 2010), p. xvii.

37 *Case concerning Application of the International Convention on the Elimination of All Forms of Racial Discrimination (Georgia v. Russian Federation), Preliminary Objections, Judgment of 1 April 2011, I.C.J. Reports 2011*, p. 70 (hereinafter referred to as the *CERD case*), Separate opinion by Judge Simma, at p. 191, para. 7. The case has recently been described by a former President of the Court as 'a very, very difficult case for the Court': R. Higgins, 'Shabtai Rosenne and the International Court of Justice' (2013) 12, 2, *The Law and Practice of International Courts and Tribunals*, 163–75, at 174.

38 *CERD case, I.C.J. Reports 2011*, Separate opinion by Judge Simma, at p. 191, para. 7. As a majority judgment 'inevitably must take account of different judicial views and will reflect the lowest common denominator of the majority' (*Sovereignty over Pedra Branca/Pulau Batu Puteh, Middle Rocks and South Ledge (Malaysia/Singapore), Judgment, I.C.J. Reports 2008*, p. 12, Dissenting opinion by Judge *ad hoc* Dugard, at p. 133, para. 2) it is 'prone to represent a negotiated result rather than the product of completely articulated reasoning process' (L. Boisson de Chazournes and S. Heathcote, 'The Role of the New International Adjudicator', *Proceedings of the American Society of International Law* (2001), 129–35, comments by K. Griffith, at 136). The Court's deliberations 'consistent plus à tenter de trouver un compromis satisfaisant entre les juges, plutôt qu'à appliquer un syllogisme classique à partir de la base du droit applicable'. Indeed, 'les "négociations" ainsi réalisées en faveur d'une solution emportant le plus large soutien possible sont essentielles … une solution qui consacrerait un compromis entre les intérêts des parties peut aussi constituer une solution capable de rallier une majorité suffisante au sein de cultures et d'opinions juridiques différentes': G. Giraudeau, *Les différends territoriaux*, p. 243. Individual 'opinions provide a comprehensive reasoning based on the diverse judicial and ethical views of the individual judges': A. Paulus, 'International adjudication', in S. Besson and J. Tasioulas (eds), *The Philosophy of International Law* (Oxford, 2010), pp. 207–24, at p. 220. Moreover, not every dissenting judge is necessarily and in all cases 'obliged to attack at the very heart of the judgment': *Maritime Delimitation and Territorial Questions between Qatar and Bahrain, Merits, Judgment, I.C.J. Reports 2001*, p. 40, Joint dissenting opinion by Judges Bedjaoui, Ranjeva and Koroma, at p. 153, para. 15.

One should note in passing that recently a Declaration may constitute a 'partly concurring and partly dissenting opinion': *Case concerning Maritime Dispute(Peru v. Chile), Judgment, I.C.J. Reports 2014*, Declaration by President P.Tomka, para. 1. In the same case Judge *ad hoc* Orrego Vicuña appended a separate, partly concurring, partly dissenting opinion: *ibid.*

We will not address the question of the decision-making process within the Court and whether and to what extent the diplomatic training of several members of the Court drive them towards consensus (L. Reed, 'Observations on the Relationship between Diplomatic and Judicial Means of Dispute Settlement' in L. Boisson de Chazournes, M. Kohen and J. Vinuales (eds), *Diplomatic and Judicial Means of Dispute Settlement* (Leiden, Boston, 2013), pp. 291–306, at p. 291); neither will we explore the question whether some of its decisions 'conceal a hint of expediency' (M. Bedjaoui, 'Expediency in the Decisions of the International Court of Justice' (2000) LXXI *British Yearbook of International Law*, 1–17. 'La prise en compte de l'opportunité des solutions prononcées n'est pas contraire à l'office du juge, si elle reste la conséquence d'un raisonnement juridique': G. Giraudeau, *Les différends territoriaux*, p. 273.

misinterpretation, or of reading too much into the text of a judgment' when we examine 'what the Court *appears* to have done'. The study hence 'constitutes an *interpretation* of' the approach employed by the Court.[39]

States involved in disputes might find our concluding assessment of the Court's approach towards the functional interaction helpful when designing their participation in a process of negotiations, preceding or taking place in parallel with or after the end of the proceedings before the Court.

The Methodology of the Study

The study will consist of a detailed and critical analysis of the Court's case-law through the prism of the functional interaction between negotiations and the performance by the Court of its functions. 'Settlements in international affairs follow their own patterns and laws, based on the premises of each case. In spite of similarities, each international issue tends to be *sui generis*.'[40]

Notwithstanding that this certainly also applies to inter-state disputes, the purpose of this study does not require a description or an analysis of the 'history' of the cases and for which one can turn to the wide array of authoritative comments on each case.

The focus will thus not be on the merits of each individual judgment, order or advisory opinion, but on their contribution to and clarification of this functional interplay. Hence, whether the Court has accepted in an individual case particular arguments of the parties on the merits will not be a matter for analysis or reference. Case-law merely provides the framework for our functional analysis.

A number of issues and questions – such as the existence of a dispute, its subject-matter, the failure of negotiations – will reoccur throughout the book in a manner which at first glance might entail a perception of repetitiveness. This can be explained by the colour of the functional interaction changing through the prism of the time factor involved prior to, during and after the proceedings.

For most of the aspects which will present themselves we will also briefly turn to what negotiation scholars of the international relations discipline can offer us as background for our functional analysis.

The Scope of the Study

Outside the scope of this study will be the important role of negotiations as part of the *travaux préparatoires* in the Court's interpretative work on treaties[41] as this role of negotiations is clearly distinct from their settlement of disputes function. It is sufficient to recall that 'the only major limitation' the ICJ has placed on resorting to *travaux préparatoires* 'is when negotiations were confidential or *between States other than those parties to the dispute*'.[42]

What really matters for the Court is the 'final outcome of the negotiations, however difficult of achievement'.[43]

Negotiations may take place in 'private bilateral exchanges', in 'large multilateral conferences' – referred to by Lall as the 'Wider Forums'[44] – or 'in many diplomatic encounters falling between these two ends of a continuum'.[45]

39 J. Green, 'Fluctuating Evidentiary Standards for Self-Defence in the International Court of Justice' (2009) 58 *International and Comparative Law Quarterly*, 163–79, at 172.

40 A. Lall, *Modern International Negotiation*, p. 9.

41 See on this role for instance H. Thirlway, 'The Law and Procedure of the International Court of Justice 1960–1989. Supplement 2006: Part Three (2006) 77 *British Yearbook of International Law*, 1–82 at 23–4.

42 D.P. O'Connell, *International Law* 2 vols (London, New York, 1965), vol. 1, p. 282 (emphasis added).

43 *Legal Consequences for States of the Continued Presence of South Africa in Namibia (South West Africa) notwithstanding Security Council Resolution 276 (1970), Advisory Opinion*, I.C.J. Reports, 1971, p. 16 at p. 30, § 50.

44 A. Lall, *Modern International Negotiation*, p. 101.

45 T. Hopmann, *The Negotiation Process and the Resolution of International Conflicts* (Columbia, SC, 1996), p. 4. Wider Forums could be utilized 'with the traditional forms sometimes simultaneously, sometimes consecutively, and sometimes alternatively': A. Cordier, 'Foreword' in A. Lall, *Modern International Negotiation*, p. vii. A fine example of

We will only deal with inter-state negotiations in the jurisprudence of the ICJ, which is a traditional state-only court 'where diplomacy and sovereignty play important roles';[46] but this should not obscure the fact that an initiative by private parties – commercial companies affected by a particular policy or act of one government (*Anglo Iranian Oil, Interhandel, Barcelona, ELSI cases*) – or individuals who have become victims of such a policy or omissions (*Genocide cases, Belgium Senegal case*) has induced a Government to institute proceedings. The interest of these non-state actors may then actually trigger the bringing of a claim and co-determines the scope of the action before the Court,[47] although the Court can only take into account acts and attitudes of governments in order to establish the existence of understanding between States Parties to a litigation.[48]

A government may be expected to encourage attempts to exhaust local remedies, thereby eliminating the possibility of a corresponding preliminary objection; the 'delay resulting from any such attempt would have been relatively small in comparison with the long period of years consumed by the protracted negotiations on the subject'.[49]

Whether and to what extent the content and scope of the obligation to negotiate, outside the peaceful settlement of dispute context, varies between different branches of international law is also a question beyond the scope of this study.

We will not address the *impact of negotiated settlements on the law* – reflecting another aspect of the multifunctionality of negotiations; neither will we deal with *the use of law by parties during negotiations* aimed at the peaceful settlement of a dispute between them.[50] We will not deal either with the general question of the *development of international law by the Court*,[51] or with the potential, direct impact of the Court on the future of negotiations *within the UN*.

Doctrinal views on more general matters relating to the process of negotiation or on rather procedural aspects of adjudication as a mechanism for the peaceful settlement of disputes will only be referred to in order to contribute to the rather general perspective or background against which the functional analysis will be made.

Whether the exercise by the Court of its advisory jurisdiction will provide us with a different picture altogether remains to be seen, but it is self-evident to include the functional interplay between negotiations and the performance of this particular judicial function.[52]

---

the functional interaction between bilateral negotiations and conference diplomacy can be found *inter alia* in the *Fisheries Jurisdiction (United Kingdom v. Iceland), Merits, Judgment, I.C.J. Reports 1974*, p. 3, Separate Opinion by Judge Waldock, at p. 112, §§ 17–19.

46 D. Terris, C. Romano and L. Swigart, *The International Judge: An Introduction to the Men and Women who Decide the World's Cases* (Oxford, 2007), p. 7.

47 *Interhandel (Switzerland v. United States), Judgment of 21 March 1959, I.C.J. Reports 1959*, p. 6, at p. 29.

48 *Barcelona Traction, Light and Power Company, Limited, Preliminary Objections, Judgment, I.C.J. Reports 1964*, p. 6, at p. 23.

49 *Case of certain Norwegian Loans, Judgment of 6 July 1957, I.C.J. Reports, 1957*, p. 9 at 41: Separate Opinion of Judge Hersch Lauterpacht, p. 41.

50 See on this aspect *inter alia* C. Hutchinson, 'Coming in from the Shadow of the Law: The Use of Law by States to Negotiate Environmental Disputes in Good Faith' (1963) 43 *Canadian Yearbook of International Law*, 101–43.

51 See most recently C. Tams (ed.), *The Development of International Law by the International Court of Justice* (Oxford, 2013).

52 On the Court's advisory function see *inter alia* M. Aljaghoub, *The Advisory Function of the International Court of Justice 1946–2005* (Berlin, 2006) and M.-C. Runavot, 'La fonction consultative de la Cour Internationale de Justice' in A.Ondua and D. Szymczak (eds), *La fonction consultative des juridictions internationales* (Paris, 2009), pp. 21–45. See further also F. Pazartzis, 'The Ambit and Limits of the Advisory Function of the International Court of Justice' in E. Rieter and H. de Waele (eds), *Evolving Principles of International Law: Studies in Honour of Karel C. Wellens* (Leiden, Boston, 2012), pp. 265–80 and M. Wood, 'Advisory Jurisdiction: Lessons from Recent Practice' in H. Hestermeyer (ed.), *Coexistence, Cooperation and Solidarity: Liber Amicorum Rüdiger Wolfrum* (2 vols, Leiden, 2012), vol. 2, pp. 1833–49.

On the pacificatory impact of the Court's advisory function see M. Bedjaoui, 'Les ressources offertes par la fonction consultative de la Cour Internationale de Justice: bilan et perspectives' in UN *Law: International Law as a Language for International Relations* (New York, 1996), pp. 117–43.

The Structure of the Study

This monograph consists of three main parts which present themselves in an almost natural way as negotiations do play their role in the pre-adjudicative phase (Part I), as there is functional interaction between negotiations and judicial settlement during the adjudicative phase (Part II); and again in the post-adjudicative phase (Part III).[53]

In a preliminary chapter we will pay a brief visit to the dynamics of negotiations as a process from an international relations perspective.

Chapter 1 reviews in general terms the multifunctionality of negotiations as a means for the pacific settlement of disputes and their status under public international law. Chapter 2 introduces the functional interaction between negotiations and adjudication as mechanisms of PSD. For instance the identification and more precise description of the legal issues in controversy will have an impact on the judicial task the Court is asked to perform. The clarification role of prior negotiations has the potential of rendering the judicial settlement (slightly) easier.

Chronologically the first role negotiations may be called upon to play as far as the ICJ is concerned is as a precondition for the submission of the dispute. As by the nature of things prior negotiations have not fully successfully played their role when States do conclude a Special Agreement, Chapter 3 briefly surveys the manner in which negotiations have found their found way in compromissory clauses, to be followed by a similar exercise with regard to optional clauses. This chapter also looks into the material and temporal scope of an obligation to negotiate, which perhaps is not unlimited.

Chapter 4 is situated at the doorstep of the adjudicative phase and is devoted to the seisin of the Court.[54]

Irrespective of whether negotiations are a precondition for the submission of a dispute to the ICJ, the existence of a dispute and, in appropriate cases, the failure of prior negotiations are the key to the Great Hall of Justice. Who will decide whether proper negotiations have taken place, and in the relevant circumstances, whether they have failed? Can this decision be left to the parties or is it solely within the Court's power to make that determination: who is the key-holder is the central question in Chapter 5.

Parties may have been negotiating during a long period of time before their dispute ends up before the Court. The adversarial nature of the proceedings does not prevent the parties, once they are before the Court, to start or to resume in parallel negotiations in order to find perhaps at least a partial settlement of the dispute. On the other hand, ongoing negotiations may have an impact on the Court's handling of a dispute or the delivery of an advisory opinion. Chapter 6 will be devoted to these issues.

Prior or ongoing negotiations will always play a role in the judicial settlement of the dispute at hand. Chapter 7 will contribute to clarifying the role of negotiations in the judicial settlement. Negotiations may find their way into the judicial reasoning and be part *of* the basis for the Court's ruling or they may take place *on* the basis for instance of provisional measures indicated by the Court.

The judgment rendered by the Court does not offer any guarantee that the dispute is finally over. Operative clauses may just require post-adjudicative negotiations or they may prove to be necessary anyway, involving

53 'A phase is a particularly troublesome form of concept because a time dimension is added to its other elusive qualities and because other relational questions are raised': W. Zartman, *Negotiation and Conflict Management: Essays on Theory and Practice* (London, New York, 2008), p. 125. For our topic each phase 'is part of subsequent phases' and 'the sequence of phases' is certainly not 'a one-way street' as there will be 'backtracking' in the way the functional interaction operates, as this study will demonstrate.

54 The Court's President pointed out that there has been an important increase in cases brought before the Court under a compromissory clause: 1 per cent in the 1980s, 40 per cent by 2000 and more than 50 per cent in the first decade of the twenty-first century (speech by Judge Owada, President of the ICJ to the Sixth Committee of the General Assembly, 30 October 2009; text on the Court's website) – a trend also confirmed by doctrine. C. Tams, 'The Continued Relevance of Compromissory Clauses as a Source of ICJ Jurisdiction' in T. Giegerich (ed.), *A Wiser Century? Judicial Dispute Settlement, Disarmament and the Laws of War 100 Years after the Second Hague Peace Conference* (Berlin, 2009), pp. 462–92, at p. 486. This incisive study not only provides remarkable statistics (pp. 470–71), a 'black list' of important multilateral treaty-making treaties bypassing the ICJ (at p. 472), but it also shows that 'compromissory clauses establish the Court's jurisdiction in important areas of international relations' (at p. 476). Existing compromissory clauses appear to remain, in general, 'unchanged forever', although nowadays States are 'extremely reluctant to conclude new compromissory clauses' (at pp. 479 and 480).

perhaps more parties than just the parties to the case. The focus in Chapter 8 will not be on the downstream line of compliance with judgments in the sense of what has been the result of such negotiations, or on the effectiveness of the ICJ in solving the dispute.[55]

Whatever the legal basis for such post-adjudicative negotiations, they may eventually fail perhaps also because pre-adjudicative negotiations have not taken care of all relevant legal issues of the dispute and bring the parties back to the Court, as Chapter 9 will demonstrate.

The conclusion revisits the functional interaction between the diplomatic and the judicial component and makes an attempt to carry out a tentative functional mutual impact assessment.

55 See Y. Shany, *Assessing the Effectiveness of International Courts* (Oxford, 2014). One should observe with regard to the Court's performance that a 'list of withdrawn cases, or cases that did not go past the provisional measures stage, may be a sign' of the Court being 'vigorous and creative' in 'finding an optimal role in the complex business of settling international disputes': V. Lowe, 'Interplay', p. 247.

See also A. Pellet, 'Remarques sur l' (in)efficacité de la Cour internationale de justice et d'autres juridictions internationales' in *Liber Amicorum Jean-Pierre Cot. Le procès international* (Brussels, 2009), pp. 193–213, at p. 193 on the difficult question of identifying the criteria by which an international tribunal's efficiency should or could be measured.

See also Ph. Couvreur, 'The Effectiveness of the International Court of Justice in the Peaceful Settlement of International Disputes' in A. Muller, D. Raic and J. Thuransky (eds), *The International Court of Justice: Its Future Role after Fifty Years* (The Hague, 1997), pp. 83–116.

Preliminary Chapter

The Dynamics of Negotiations as a Process from an International Relations Perspective: A Brief Visit

Object and Purpose of this Chapter

The purpose of this chapter is to identify from an international relations perspective some major aspects of the dynamics of *negotiations as a process*. This will allow us to better understand and more properly assess the functional role of negotiations in their interaction with adjudication prior to, during and after the proceedings before the Court. Accordingly, attention will only be paid to those aspects, issues and factors which we believe could be instrumental for the functional legal analysis to follow in providing the more general *theoretical* framework against which the topic of our study has to be placed.

The dynamics of negotiations as a process will permeate the functional analysis in the various parts of the study and also finally when we revisit the functional interaction in our conclusions.

Given the recognition and admission by international relations scholars that there 'is as yet no satisfactory theory of negotiation',[1] it seems reasonable for international lawyers to attempt only to get more insight into those scholars' approaches and findings, and this in order to see whether and how these approaches and findings have eventually found their way, perhaps even their counterpart, in the manner the ICJ has dealt with the process of negotiations in the performance of its judicial function.

One of the leading writers in this field has argued that the main reason for negotiations to have been 'thus far resistant to theory' is 'because their dynamic pattern has not been fully apprehended'.[2]

The 'simple factual questions that can be answered in any set of negotiations' – namely who, what and when[3] – are bound to resurface when the process is being looked at from an international legal perspective.

The State of the Research

> Although negotiation has been discussed in academic texts for centuries, there has been little systematic analysis of this topic until the 1960s. Since that time a substantial set of academic literature and systematic studies has been created and a coherent and cumulative picture of the negotiations process and its effect on the resolution of international conflicts *is beginning to form*.[4]

However, 'the state of research in this field is still too primitive to present a single theory that can explain the impact of the negotiations process on outcomes in all classes of international negotiation' as 'we are still at an early stage in defining the criteria for selecting among the various kinds of theories that might be applicable to any particular case'.[5] Many more case studies are needed 'in order to refine and deepen the theoretical framework' so far presented.[6]

'A theory of negotiations is a set of general interrelated causal statements which explain how and which outcomes are chosen. To be satisfactory, a theory must be coherent, applicable and real.'[7]

---

1 W. Zartman, 'Negotiations: Theory and Reality' (1975) 29 *Journal of International Affairs*, 1, 69–77 at 69 and 70.
2 W. Zartman, 'Negotiations: Theory and Reality', 70.
3 W. Zartman, *Negotiation and Conflict Management*, p. 16.
4 P. Hopmann, *The Negotiation Process*, p. 24 (emphasis added).
5 P. Hopmann, *The Negotiation Process*, p. 32.
6 P. Hopmann, *The Negotiation Process*, p. 313.
7 W. Zartman, 'Negotiations: Theory and Reality', 70.

The deliberate purpose of one theory is 'to provide sound prescriptive advice to policy makers and diplomats interested in resolving conflicts and improving the outcomes of negotiated settlement of disputes',[8] but 'it cannot completely replace the intuitions of the experienced negotiator'.[9]

Following 'the realistic traditions of international politics' providing the framework for early work on the negotiating process, the arrival of a 'more liberal paradigm of international politics' has contributed, with other factors, 'to a substantial reconceptualization of the international negotiation process. In this new light negotiation is increasingly viewed as a tool in which conflicts may be resolved in such a way as to produce mutual benefits for the parties rather than exclusive benefits for one at the expense of others.'[10]

Almost five decades after its publication, Arthur Lall's 1966 book still is the valuable reference work to turn to for a proper understanding of 'how, when and why concessions are made within the process of negotiation to achieve results, and the factors that sometimes obstruct progress'.[11]

The Need to Define 'Negotiations'?

Although 'any attempt at a systematic study begins with precise use of terms',[12] on the preliminary question of defining international negotiations some *prima facie* observations may suffice, as indeed we will return to this question within the international law context.

A certain variety of tentative definitions is common to the fields of international relations and international law. The link between an international relations and an international law approach towards the question of defining negotiations is provided by Article 33 of the UN Charter, as pointed out by Lall.[13]

Given the aim of this chapter and the overall purpose of our study we will limit ourselves to list some of the most well-known definitions international negotiation scholars have to offer. According to one definition negotiation consists of 'a *joint decision-making process* involving *interactive communication* in which parties lack identical interests but attempt to reach agreement'.[14]

Although the definition given by Zartman – negotiation 'is the process of combining divergent viewpoints to produce a common agreement'[15] – appears at first glance attractive by its simplicity, the definition most likely to turn out to be useful for an international legal approach is given by Lall: 'international negotiation is the process of consideration of an international dispute or situation by peaceful means, other than judicial or arbitral processes, with a view to promoting or reaching among the parties concerned or interested some understanding, amelioration, adjustment, or settlement of the dispute or the situation'.[16]

Although *consultations* are more often aiming at the avoidance or prevention of potential disputes, they can operate concurrently with negotiations, consultations 'gradually merging' into negotiations 'where the discussion and conversations expose underlying differences of view between the parties'.[17] The distinction, 'whilst functionally and operationally correct, should not be stretched too far'. Indeed, the 'process of consultations and negotiations are seldom straightforward going clearly from one stage to the next'.[18]

8 P. Hopmann, *The Negotiation Process*, p. 5.

9 P. Hopmann, *The Negotiation Process*, p. 314.

10 P. Hopmann, *The Negotiation Process*, pp. 24–5. A short but illuminating overview of the various theories and ensuing definitions is given by Hopmann when defining the negotiating process at pp. 25–7.

11 A. Cordier, 'Foreword' in A.Lall, *Modern International Negotiation*, p. viii.

12 W. Zartman, *Negotiation and Conflict Management*, p. 13.

13 A. Lall, *Modern International Negotiation*, p. 17. On the various other means of peaceful settlement of disputes see *inter alia* pp. 13–15 and pp. 84–100.

14 G. Blum and R. Mnookin', When *Not* to Negotiate' in A. Schneider (ed.), *The Negotiator's Fieldbook* (Washington, 2006), pp. 101–12, at p. 102.

15 W. Zartman, *Negotiation and Conflict Management*, p. 14.

16 A. Lall, *Modern International Negotiation*, p. 5.

17 C. Fombad, 'Consultation and Negotiation in the Pacific Settlement of International Disputes' (1989), *African Journal of International and Comparative Law*, 707–24, at 709.

18 C. Fombad, 'Consultation and Negotiation', 711–12.

Some Preliminary Observations at the Crossroads of International Relations and International Law

The range of potentially relevant aspects, many of which will return later in our functional analysis, includes the following.

- In the first place parties should accept peaceful methods to settle a dispute or resolve a situation; they should agree on (the) objectives of the process they have expressed willingness to embark upon.[19]
- Which are the most elementary and primary requirements in order to get a process of negotiations really started and in case of deadlock to bring about a revival or resumption of the process?
- What kinds of reasons could contribute to a party's refusal to merely enter into the process?
- How do the factors and causes underlying a party's decision to negotiate relate to the legal obligation for States to embark upon a process of negotiation?

Some minimal requirements are determining the outcome of the process.[20] It is perhaps here that some convergence may be found with the classic Permanent Court of International Justice (PCIJ) and ICJ requirements about how parties should conduct themselves during and even prior to the process of negotiations: movement from original positions[21] apparently being considered the most basic requirement for any process to have a proper and realistic chance to ultimately lead to a successful outcome.

As individual judges will rightly observe, the personal factor should not be underestimated either.[22] Failure or success of negotiations is dependent upon a wide variety of factors and combination of factors which are sometimes difficult to identify and give their proper weight. Some of the factors can be more or less clearly labelled as impediments to the process, while others are more 'underlying inhibitory' ones.[23]

For our perspective negotation scholars have identified the following relevant questions.

> What motivates international negotiators to take justice or fairness into account? How do they understand those concepts in the particular circumstances of particular negotiations? How do they deal with competing conceptions of justice or fairness? How do negotiators' concerns with justice or fairness interact with considerations of power, self-interests, or domestic policies, to what extent, and in what ways, is it important to satisfy negotiators' concerns for justice or fairness if the agreements they reach are to be effective?[24]

Justice and fairness influence the positions taken by the parties, the proposals they table and the exchange of concessions, and they facilitate progress but may also cause deadlocks.[25] Negotiators are:

> more likely to be motivated by concern for justice and fairness and to abide by the terms of the agreements they reach, if they feel that others take their concerns seriously, negotiate in good faith, and demonstrate a willingness to compromise for the sake of reaching an agreement, even if the end result does not quite satisfy some *ex ante* set of abstract principles or demands.[26]

'If two states accept the jurisdiction of the ICJ how does this influence their bargaining behaviour? Conversely, how do expectations about bargaining influence a unilateral state decision to accept or not accept the ICJ's jurisdiction?'[27]

---

19 A. Lall, *Modern International Negotiation*, Chapters 5 and 6.

20 A. Lall, *Modern International Negotiation*, Chapter 21.

21 A. Lall, *Modern International Negotiation*, Chapter 22.

22 A. Lall, *Modern International Negotiation*, Chapter 24.

23 A. Lall, *Modern International Negotiation*, Chapters 10 and 17.

24 D. Welch, Review of *Justice and Fairness in International Negotiation* by C. Albin (New York, 2001), (2002) 117 *Political Science Quarterly*, 3, 524–25.

25 D. Welch, Book review, 525.

26 D. Welch, Book review, 525.

27 E. Powell and S. McLaughlin Mitchell, 'The International Court of Justice and the World's Three Legal Systems' (2007) 69 *Journal of Politics*, 2, 397–415 at 398.

How do international negotiation scholars look at the element of good faith on both sides of the negotiating table? Judicial assessment of the parties' conduct prior and during the process of negotiations may comprise taking into account nonverbal conciliatory signs, a 'firm but conciliatory' stand of each party in a 'pattern of mutual responsiveness' and an 'unconditionally constructive' approach to be followed by both parties.[28]

Which role could an 'international forum' such as the Security Council or the principal judicial organ of the UN play 'to induce countries to take bilateral diplomacy much more seriously than they ever did'?[29]

To what extent are we really confronted with third party 'intrusion'?[30]

Which role has to be or is being assigned to third parties in the various stages of a negotiation process, and what can we learn with regard to the impact of multiparty involvement?

Should the process of negotiations, for instance over a legal dispute, be considered to be an 'incremental one of concessions and counter concessions, in which the gap between the two parties' positions is gradually narrowed until a single point of convergence is reached', involving 'much more a search for agreeable referents of a joint decision than the usual image of a search directly for a jointly agreeable outcome'?[31]

The *convergence approach* in fact consists in isolating 'those points where changes in positions occurred' and it 'tells what to look for and where to look, and it flags the important procedural element of the negotiation process. It recognizes the "process", nature of negotiations, rather than focusing on single-session confrontations or simply final results.'[32]

The so-called *referents* are 'principles of justice' on which both parties can agree, for instance 'special rights', which are 'the major subject of negotiations'.[33]

Does such an approach tie in with what parties and the Court have in mind when they respectively engage in the process and attach judicial weight to the course and the outcome?

International relations scholars willingly admit that it is not possible to state whether 'the search for referent principles and details is the key to negotiations in general' and although 'there is certainly nothing intrinsic in the process that would prohibit incremental negotiations', the 'real world does not proceed ' in the way of incremental negotiations.[34]

They have identified several turning points in a negotiation 'which are not simply conceptual moments' but 'real events', namely:

- 'both parties' expectations are perceived to be within range of each other, hence the chances of a 'jointly agreeable outcome' are seen as 'realistic';
- the 'moment when agreement has been reached on the image or formula to the interpretation of the problem and its solution';
- when each party decides that 'benefits from the items agreed on thus far outweigh the likely costs of the items still left under discussion'.[35]

Both the parties themselves and the Court in carrying out the tasks the parties have entrusted it with are obliged at the various stages of the functional interaction to assess the progress made, or lack of it during the process of negotiations, to determine whether there has been a deadlock which in turn may result in complete failure or provide a new opportunity to restart the process, for instance in light of interlocutory Court decisions.

The way negotiation scholars define the outcome of the process – the mere fact of an agreement having been reached, the efficiency of the outcome, the stability of the outcome and the distribution of the benefits[36] – is not fundamentally different from the manner in which international law assesses the result of the process.

28 T. Hopmann, *The Negotiation* Process, pp. 184, 192 and 193.

29 A. Lall, *Modern International Negotiation*, p. 1.

30 A. Lall, *Modern International Negotiation*, Chapter 12 (emphasis added).

31 W. Zartman, 'Negotiations: Theory and Reality', 71.

32 W. Zartman, *Negotiation and Conflict Management*, p. 24.

33 W. Zartman, 'Negotiations: Theory and Reality', 71.

34 W. Zartman, 'Negotiations: Theory and Reality', 73–4.

35 W. Zartman, 'Negotiations: Theory and Reality', 74–5.

36 T. Hopmann, *The Negotiation Process*, pp. 28–30. Parties to a negotiation 'may apply very different criteria for evaluating their fairness of alternative outcomes', which can be arranged along 'a continuum from symmetrical, where the

It is undoubtedly necessary, as our study will also demonstrate, to duly take into account the time factor in dealing with and allegedly to assess a particular process of negotiations between two disputant parties, be it only for the fact that 'in many disputes, including some of the most serious ones, *until the time is ripe*, negotiation can have little to offer'.[37]

It is quite obvious that the importance and length of the time factor involved in proceedings before the Court will render the instrumental use of these benchmarks with regard to prior negotiations, those conducted during the proceedings and, in cases of request for interpretation, in the post-adjudicative phase, by both Court and parties relatively more difficult.

A number of *explanatory factors* have been added to the complexity of the process of negotiations.[38]

The Pre-Negotiation Phase

It is a wrong assumption 'that entering into negotiation is always the right thing to do' as 'there will be cases where the costs of entering the negotiation plainly outweigh the potential benefits'.[39]

International lawyers tend to approach the process of negotiations as suitable to have started at a particular *critical date*, namely when both parties actually came together at the negotiating table. As a result the important functional role of the pre-negotiation phase is often underestimated or neglected altogether.

International relations discipline is there to adjust a rigid approach taken by lawyers. Indeed, the decision whether or not to open formal proceedings is of paramount importance and constitutes the very heart of the pre-negotiation phase: laying 'the groundwork for deciding whether or not to open formal negotiations, decide on the timing for opening negotiations, and begin to establish an agenda to guide them'.[40]

Pre-negotiation is a 'purposive period of transition that enables parties to move from conflicting perceptions and behaviours (unilateral attempts at solutions) to cooperative perceptions and behaviours'.[41]

Reality prevents drawing a sharp, and thus potentially also legally relevant line dividing the negotiations from the pre-negotiations phase, as this latter process 'may be quite formal and actually constitute a negotiation in itself'.[42]

A distinction appears to impose itself depending on the *integrative* or *distributive approach* towards the negotiations. Indeed, in the first case parties will try to use the pre-negotiation phase 'to their advantage in structuring the ensuing formal negotiation' such as 'control over the agenda-setting elements': including those items 'over which they believe they can exercise the greatest tactical control during the negotiations' and by excluding 'those items over which they stand to lose a great deal and from which they can gain little'. In the second scenario 'parties are likely to use it extensively for diagnostic purposes ... to come to understand more about one's own needs and interests, the needs and interests of the other party, and ways in which those needs and interests do or do not coincide'.[43]

---

benefits to the parties are approximately equal, to asymmetrical, in which one or more parties gain a great deal of benefits while others benefit less', at p. 30.

37 J. Merrills, *International Dispute Settlement*, p. 22 (emphasis added).

38 T. Hopmann, *The Negotiation Process*, p. 31.

39 G. Blum and R. Mnookin', When *Not* to Negotiate', p. 112.

40 T. Hopmann, *The Negotiation Process*, p. 174.

41 W. Zartman, *Negotiation and Conflict Management*, p. 120. For the various functions of pre-negotiations see in more detail at pp. 121–7: 'lower the risk associated with cooperation'; 'allows the parties to assess and come to terms with the costs of concessions and agreement, and also with the costs of failure, before firm commitments are made'; enables or obliges the parties 'to sort out their *own* motives for negotiating in the given context'; 'time to convince the other party that concessions will be required ... such exchanges and assurances are less risky during this phase because they are indicative of future behaviour rather than commitments'; prepare the home front 'for an accommodative policy'; 'turning the problem into a manageable issue susceptible of a negotiated outcome'; deciding on to include or exclude certain participants; 'to build bridges from conflict to conciliation' setting up 'temporary mechanisms that provide for the change itself on a transitional and provisional basis' and functional relation to regimes and crisis.

42 T .Hopmann, *The Negotiation Process*, p. 174.

43 T. Hopmann, *The Negotiation Process*, pp. 177–8.

From our functional interaction perspective the utilization of the pre-negotiation phase is actually quite relevant given the various functions it is expected to perform: 'significant function in reducing uncertainty prior to entering into formal negotiations'. Ideally 'parties should be able to enter into a negotiation with a clear and more shared understanding of the issues and their interests', although such an understanding:

> may not always facilitate convergence in the negotiation phase, especially if it clarifies the differences that may exist between the parties, but it at least increases the chances that the subsequent negotiations will be based on a realistic assessment of the problem rather than on mutual misconceptions and misunderstandings of one another and of the fundamental issues being negotiated.[44]

The consideration of litigation as one of the alternatives to negotiations may take place even during the pre-negotaiton phase.[45] The importance of this aspect for the functional interaction between negotiations and adjudication needs hardly to be underlined. The pre-negotation phase:

> may also help the parties separate issues that are potentially negotiable from those that are not, so that progress can be made during the actual negotiations on solvable problems, while time is not wasted and emotional tensions are not exacerbated by trying to negotiate problems that are largely incapable of being solved at a particular time or in a specific negotiating context.

It is then not surprising that an effective 'use of prenegotiating preparations may significantly differentiate successful from unsuccessful negotiations. They form part of the larger diplomatic context for negotiation.'[46]

The Various Kinds of Relationships between Parties to a Dispute

They are to be found at various points of a continuum ranging from a conflictual end to the most cooperative end, namely integration: intense hostility and almost complete opposition of interests; the use of coercive diplomacy; 'significant, but non-violent conflicts of interests' manageable by negotiations as a common tool; rapprochement and development of 'common understandings about how to deal with some of the major issues that affect their relationship'; extensive policy coordination; and finally integration.[47] These interactions may change over time, alternate – and not only as a result of complete transformation of the international system.[48]

Traditional relationships of friendship between States as compared to one of traditional rivalry and adversary are of course determining factors for the start, course, progress and outcome of a process of negotiation.[49] Moreover, a 'number of empirical studies of negotiation have suggested that the negotiation process directly mirrors what is occurring in the overall political relationships among the parties, so that breakthrough in negotiations may depend on a general improvement in the political relations among adversaries'.[50]

Forward- and Backward-Looking Approaches

Although the aim of negotiation is to end conflict, this result may take many forms – for instance negotiating *forward- and backward-looking outcomes*, meaning in fact to put an end to a particular dispute and also involving measures in order to prevent its recurrence.[51]

44 T. Hopmann, *The Negotiation Process*, pp. 179–80.
45 W. Zartman, *Negotiations and Conflict Management*, p. 118.
46 T. Hopmann, *The Negotiation Process*, pp. 179–80.
47 T. Hopmann, *The Negotiation Process*, pp. 197–8.
48 T. Hopmann, *The Negotiation Process*, p. 218.
49 T. Hopmann, *The Negotiation Process*, p. 199.
50 T. Hopmann, *The Negotiation Process*, p. 200.
51 W. Zartman, 'Negotiating Forward- and Backward-Looking Outcomes' in W. Zartman and V. Kremenyuk (eds), *Peace versus Justice: Negotiating Forward- and Backward-Looking Outcomes* (Lanham, MD, 2005), p. 1.

When we look at the judicial function one could be tempted to rapidly agree that both aspects – forward- and backward-looking – can also be found in the Court's performance of the task it has been given by the parties, in the sense that the binding nature of a judgment on the merits of the case, enshrined in Article 59 of the Statute, puts an end to (part of) the legal dispute as submitted, and this coupled with the judicial presumption that no State will in the post-adjudicative phase conduct itself in such a way as to bring the settled dispute back to life, exception made of course for the situation envisaged in Article 60 providing for a request for interpretation when a dispute arises in the post-adjudicative phase 'as to the meaning or scope of the judgment'.

However, the intrinsic link between the subject-matter of the dispute and negotiations (see Chapter 1), inevitably reappears once the dispute is before the Court. In this regard the subject-matter of the dispute and the corresponding submissions co-determine the backward- and/or forward-looking approach and outcome of the judicial intervention. Indeed, for instance judicial determination of state responsibility for an internationally wrongful act will in most cases be accompanied by the imposing of guarantees and assurances of non-repetition as requested.

In case for instance of territorial and maritime delimitation disputes the judicial fixing of the disputed boundary may, depending on the submissions, be accompanied by an obligation for the parties to put in place, through a process of post-adjudicative negotiations, a detailed regime of cooperation, those negotiations thus not merely aiming at implementing the judgment.

Doing justice to (past) legal claims and the construction of future peaceful relations are not mutually exclusive aspects of international adjudication.

As far as the parties' submissions are concerned, 'les prétentions des gouvernements montrent que ces derniers élaborent leurs stratégie argumentative en anticipant le caractère transactionnel de la solution qui sera prononcée'.[52]

In a broader sense international litigation's 'prospective function' involves the articulation of 'legal principles applicable in the future', hence parties are having 'considerable interest not only in whether they win or lose a particular case, but also in *how* they win or lose it – in the rule that emerges from the decision in the case'.[53]

Negotiation is a Process

'Negotiation is a process and its outcome can only be explained by process analysis: where you get is a function of how you get there',[54] namely through three consecutive stages:

1. *diagnosis* 'sometimes termed pre-negotiation', requiring 'each party to ask a number of questions', *inter alia* 'specify the issues to be covered, separating those that can be negotiated from those that must be left out';
2. *formulation*, search for 'either a common understanding of the problems and its (type of) solution' and establishing a 'principled basis of their search for a joint solution'; and
3. *specification*, the 'translation of the formula into detailed terms'.[55]

Moreover the process itself may be transformative on parties' priorities and interests, although it also 'may inflame conflicts'.[56]

52 G. Giraudeau, *Les différends territoriaux*, p. 69.

53 V. Lowe, 'The Function of Litigation in International Society' (2012) 61 *International and Comparative Quarterly* 209–22, at 213.

54 W. Zartman, 'Process and Stages' in A. Schneider ed.), *The Negotiator's Fieldbook* (Washington, 2005), pp. 95–8, at p. 95.

55 W. Zartman, 'Process and Stages', pp. 96–7.

56 G. Blum and R. Mnookin, 'When *Not* to Negotiate', p. 108.

Deadlock of the Process

What can we lawyers learn from the negotiation scholars with regard to this phenomenon? Is it possible to identify a set or a mix of various causes that may trigger a deadlock? And which incentives are at the disposal of the parties, third States, or the Court for that matter, to break a deadlock? Is it here that we can situate *the facilitative aspect of the Court's judicial function* when for instance using it 'judiciously' the Court by issuing recommendations is stressing the parties 'wider responsibilities' and is ' putting their dispute in context with a view to encouraging a peaceful settlement'?[57]

When do we consider a deadlock to happen, and is it always leading to a complete failure of the process or is there room for a *functional* role of deadlock, for instance in setting in motion the interaction between negotiation and adjudication?

On the other hand, it has rightly been pointed out that failed negotiations:

> do not, as might be thought, simply leave a dispute where it was to begin with. On the contrary, although they can sometimes improve matters by demonstrating that the parties are slowly moving closer together, they can also have the opposite effect. Indeed, because negotiations involve exploring the possibilities for resolving a dispute peacefully, lack of progress may encourage the use of force by seeming to eliminate every alternative.[58]

> The existence of inclusive negotiations by no means guarantees movement towards a political settlement. Indeed, particularly if there is little likelihood, in the absence of a settlement, of a return to violent conflict on a scale unacceptable to both sides, the process itself may come to be seen as almost a substitute for a settlement, an attitude encapsulated in a long-standing Turkish Cypriot aphorism that 'no solution is a solution'.[59]

57 J. Merrills, *International Dispute Settlement*, p. 152.

58 J. Merrills, *International Dispute Settlement*, p. 23.

59 A.Guelke, 'Negotiations and Peace Processes' in J. Darby and R. MacGinty (eds), *Contemporary Peacemaking: Conflict, Peace Processes and Post-War Reconstruction* (New York, 2008), pp. 63–77, at p. 71.

PART I
Negotiations in the Pre-Adjudicative Phase

Chapter 1
The Multifunctionality of Negotiations as Means for the Peaceful Settlement of Disputes and their Status under International Law

Introduction

A preliminary question that immediately presents itself is a definitional and conceptual one. The various options of approaching this issue are almost unlimited. Different disciplines and branches will produce a variety of doctrinal definitions, as already indicated in the preliminary chapter.

As far as international law is concerned we could turn to the renowned classical international law dictionaries in order to compare their definitions of negotiations.

It is sufficient at this stage to recognize that negotiation 'is a process which at many points not only has significant international legal implications' but 'is itself also an institution of international law. Negotiation is, indeed, at the crossroads of international law and diplomacy';[1] as to the latter, negotiation is its central function.[2]

How would one define in more precise terms this instrument of *negotiations* : exploratory talks[3] of a non-committal nature, a mere exchange of views, diplomatic correspondence (the object of this daily practice between governments is to solve problems arising from opposite views and opinions)[4] and exchanges, disputations, consultations, high-level meetings, conference diplomacy ? Is there room to make a distinction between 'direct' and 'indirect' negotiations ?[5]

With regard to 'parliamentary diplomacy' we could already note that 'the negotiation of solutions of international problems within the framework and through procedures of an organized body acting under established rules of procedure, such as the General Assembly of the United Nations'[6] has been recognized by the Court 'as one of the established modes of international negotiation'.[7] Moreover, if 'the question in issue is one of mutual interest to many States, there is no reason why each of them should go through the formality and pretence of direct negotiation with the common adversary State, after they had participated in the collective negotiation with the same State in opposition'.[8]

---

1 A. Watts, 'Negociation and International Law' in P. Borba Casella (ed.), *Dimensao Internacional do Direito. Estudos em Homenagem a G.E.do Nascimento e Silva* (Sao Paulo, 2000), pp. 519–36, at p. 519.

2 G. Geamanu, 'Théorie et pratique des négociations' (1980) 166 *Recueil des Cours Académie de Droit International* 369–447, at 373. Diplomacy 'has withstood the test of centuries and proved to be an instrument essential for effective co-operation in the international community, and for enabling States, irrespective of their differing constitutional and social systems, to achieve mutual understanding and to resolve their differences by peaceful means': *United States Diplomatic and Consular Staff in Tehran, Provisional Measures, Order of 15 December 1979, I.C.J. Reports 1979,* p. 7, at p. 19, para. 39.

3 Which should be distinguished from *in meriti* negotiations: P. Kovacs, 'Article 7' in P. Klein and O. Corten (eds) (2 vols, Oxford, 2011), *The Vienna Convention on the Law of Treaties: A Commentary,* vol. 1, pp. 125–44, at p. 132, para. 29.

4 R. Chayes as referred to by C. Van Assche, 'Article 13' in P. Klein and O. Corten (eds), *The Vienna Convention on the Law of Treaties,* vol. 1, pp. 246–85, at p. 262, para. 37.

5 *Pulp Mills on the River Uruguay (Argentina v. Uruguay), Judgment, I.C.J. Reports 2010*, p. 4, at p. 52, para. 84 (Argentina).

6 *South West Africa cases (Ethiopia v. South Africa; Liberia v. Union of South Africa), Preliminary Objections, Judgment of 21 December 1962: IC.J. Reports 1962*, p. 319, Separate opinion by Judge Jessup, at p. 434.

7 *South West Africa cases, I.C.J. Reports 1966*, p. 6, Dissenting opinion by Judge Padilla Nervo, at p. 452.

8 *Ibid.* The South West Africa cases and the Northern Cameroons case did provide a unique opportunity for judges to elaborate on this new form of diplomacy and negotiations. Judges Spender and Fitzmaurice considered the exchange of arguments across the floor of an international assembly as 'disputation' and not as 'negotiation', and that even if those exchanges could be considered to have failed, there was still the need for direct discussions between the parties: *Case*

In assessing the real potential of conference diplomacy in terms of its contribution to the peaceful settlement of disputes (PSD) one has to be aware of 'an aspect of propaganda and an element of rigidity which may be harmful to sound negotiation'.[9]

'Informal negotiations' do ' imply that statements made by one or the other party are non-committal and should not be taken as final'.[10] The non-committal nature carries with it the possibility that such statements or positions taken could later be used in proceedings before the Court.

Furthermore, the 'borderline between negotiations, consultations and more general diplomatic representations is not at all well-defined, although one generally recognizes that negotiations involve the bringing of discussions into a sharper focus and more adversarial posture than was the case previously',[11] a characteristic feature which is particularly relevant for the functional interaction with adjudication.

The object and purpose of this study, however, appear to justify postponing the question of a judicial definition until a later stage as the analysis of the Court's case law will gradually reveal how the ICJ itself has been struggling with the issue. Perhaps the Court has used various definitions, albeit not always in a consistent manner; approaching the issue maybe on an *ad hoc* basis, that is until its recent judgment in the *CERD case.*

Revisiting the functional interaction in the concluding observations will allow us to follow the winding road the Court has been following until in its 2011 judgment it was bound to rule not only on the threshold to find the existence of negotiations, but also to consider 'their adequate form and substance' and to determine 'to what extent they should be pursued before it can be said the precondition [of prior negotiations] has been met',[12] issues we will deal with in following chapters of this study.[13]

The functional role of international law within the process of negotiations, both within and outside the context of PSD, has been succinctly and very aptly described by Arthur Watts. At the very least international law 'forms the unavoidable background to international negotiations, standing as the silent witness to diplomatic transactions; at the other extreme, where the difference between the parties involves a dispute as to their rights and obligations, international law will be in the forefront of the negotiations'.[14] According to Bilder, States will in the latter scenario bargain merely 'in the shadow of the law'.[15]

To the extent that international law is seen by the parties 'as a body of binding rules ultimately enforceable through a third party arbiter', 'parties negotiate "in the shadow of the law", *meaning their prospects of success should the matter be litigated*'.[16]

---

concerning the Northern Cameroons (Cameroon v. United Kingdom), Preliminary Objections, Judgment of 2 December 1963: I.C.J. Reports 1963, p. 15, Separate opinion by Judge Fitzmaurice, at p. 123; *South West Africa cases, I.C.J. Reports 1962*, Joint dissenting opinion by Judges Spender and Fitzmaurice, at p. 562.

9 H. Darwin, 'Negotiation' in H. Waldock and C. Meredith (eds), *International Disputes: The Legal Aspects*. Report of a Study Group of the David Davies Memorial Institute of International Studies (London, 1972), pp. 77–82 at p. 79. On this particular form of negotiations see more generally J. Kaufmann, *Conference Diplomacy: An Introductory Analysis* (3rd edn, Basingstoke, 1996).

10 A. Davérède, 'Negotiations. Secret' in *Max Planck Encyclopaedia of Public International Law* (Oxford, 2012), § 2.

11 A. Watts, 'Negociation and International Law', p. 520. For a general model of the process of negotiations covering the various stages see *inter alia* P. Gulliver, 'Negotiations as a Mode of Dispute Settlement: Towards a General Model' (1972–73) 7 *Law and Society Review*, 667–91 at 689; and G. Geamanu, 'Théorie et pratique des négociations', 401–2.

12 *CERD case, I.C.J. Reports 2011*, at p. 132, para. 156.

13 It is sufficient at this stage simply to recall that the Court had no difficulty in recognizing and admitting that 'the issue of negotiations between Georgia and the Russian Federation is complex' (Judgment, § 179) and that, given the practice of States themselves, it is not surprising that also the Court has been facing the difficulty of sometimes sharply distinguishing the various procedures especially when a particular regional process such as the Contadora process is involved (*Border and Transborder Armed Actions (Nicaragua v. Honduras), Jurisdiction and Admissibility, Judgment, I.C.J. Reports 1988*, p. 69, at p. 99, para. 75) and which 'appears to comprehend a protean amalgam of elements of negotiation, good offices, mediation and possibly conciliation, the proportionate weight of each element varying from phase to phase' (Separate opinion by Judge Sahabuddeen at p. 154). The case has been described as 'one of the most far reaching judicial cases for the American States as a whole': Santiago Torres Bernardez, 'Are Prior Negotiations a General Condition for Judicial Settlement by the International Court of Justice?' in C. Barea et al. (eds), *Liber Amicorum 'In Memoriam' of Judge José Maria Ruda* (The Hague, 2000), pp. 507–25 at p. 507, para. 2.

14 A. Watts, 'Negociation and International Law', p. 523.

15 R. Bilder, 'An Overview of International Dispute Settlement' (1986–1987) 1 *Emory Journal of International Dispute Resolution*, 1–32 at 31.

16 C. Hutchinson, 'Coming in from the Shadow', 114–15 (emphasis added).

Proliferation of international law rules 'accompanied by a legalization of international discourse' and a 'trend toward the "judicialization" of the conduct of diplomacy', 'bearing witness of the improvements in the modalities of peaceful settlement of disputes'[17] is bound to have an impact on the role of law during negotiations as a means of peaceful settlement of disputes.

The unifying tread of our study is limited to exploring the judicial approach by the ICJ towards the functional interaction between negotiations and resort to the Court.

A brief look at the role of negotiations outside the context of peaceful settlement of disputes may provide us with useful elements for the subsequent analysis.

1.1 The Role of Negotiations outside the Context of Peaceful Settlement of Disputes

Although '[t]here is never complete equality of will or pressure from two parties in the direction of negotiations between them',[18] '[s]hifts in the balance of power between parties may exert significant influence on a decision to open negotiations, on the process of negotiations, and on the frequency and substance of agreements reached'.[19]

Negotiations do play an important role in relations between States as a mechanism to produce instruments governing their respective and collective conduct as members of the international community.[20] If negotiation is 'to be compulsory' then 'the circumstances in which the obligation arises, as well as its content, need careful definition, or an allegation of a failure to carry out the agreed procedure may itself become a dispute issue'.[21]

The Legal Basis of the Obligation to Negotiate

A conventional basis

Although negotiation may still 'widely [be] regarded as essentially a voluntary process',[22] the duty to negotiate has gradually evolved in becoming 'one of the general principles of contemporary international law'[23] – although perhaps not as a matter of customary international law,[24] and which may of course be incorporated in treaty provisions.

The intention expressed by certain powers to continue to administer particular territories 'until other arrangements had been agreed' with the UN imply that negotiations will have to take place. Attempts by one

---

17 L. Boisson de Chazournes and S. Heathcote, 'The Role of the New International Adjudicator', at 132 and *Accordance with International Law of the Unilateral Declaration of Independence in Respect of Kosovo, Advisory Opinion, I.C.J. Reports 2010*, p. 403, Separate opinion by Judge Cançado Trindade, at p. 535, para. 28.

18 A. Lall, *Modern International Negotiation*, p. 65.

19 T. Hopmann, *The Negotiation Process*, 196. Whether 'issues of trust and good faith have an importance in negotiations to end violent political conflicts that they do not have in limited international negotiations, between adversaries where the complications are often largely technical in character' – as pointed out by A. Guelke, *Negotiations and Peace Processes*, p. 76 – remains to be seen.

20 *Armed Activities on the Territory of the Congo (New Application: 2002) (Democratic Republic of the Congo v. Rwanda), Jurisdiction and Admissibility, Judgment, I.C.J. Reports 2006*, p. 6, at p. 27, para. 46. The Court did acknowledge that the mere risk of a Foreign Secretary being exposed to 'legal proceedings' could deter the Minister from travelling for the performance of his duties, such as representing his government in negotiations: *Arrest Warrant of 11 April 2000 (Democratic Republic of the Congo v. Belgium), Judgment, I.C.J. Reports 2002*, p. 3, at pp. 21–2, paras. 53–5. It should be noted that the degree of interference on the Minister's capacity to conduct negotiations abroad was not relevant to the assessment of the violation by Belgium of its obligations: at pp. 29–30, para. 71. A Foreign Secretary unable to travel as result of an international warrant for his arrest is allegedly unable 'to carry out his duties in a proper manner': Arrest *Warrant of 11 April 2000 (Democratic Republic of the Congo v. Belgium), Provisional measures, Order of 8 December 2000, I.C.J. Reports 2000*, p. 182, at pp. 187–8, para. 20 (DRC).

21 *Mutatis mutandis* J. Merrills, *International Dispute Settlement*, p. 6 on consultations.

22 A. Watts, 'Negociation and International Law', p. 525.

23 *North Sea Continental Shelf, Judgment, I.C.J. Reports 1969*, p. 3, Dissenting opinion by Judge Lachs, at p. 219; see also Separate opinion by Judge Padillo Nervo, at p. 98.

24 M. Rogoff, 'The Obligation to Negotiate in International Law: Rules and Realities' (1979) 16 *Michigan Journal of International Law*, 141–85, at 153.

party to modify, directly or indirectly, the terms of an existing legal situation requires and is conditioned by the consent of the other party, thus implying negotiations.[25]

Article VI of the NPT provides us with the best-known example of a *pactum de negotiando* and of a distinct *pactum de contrahendo* as each State Party 'undertakes to pursue negotiations in good faith on effective measures relating to the cessation of the nuclear arms race at an early date and to nuclear disarmament, and on a treaty on general and complete disarmament under strict and effective control'. Both *pacta* are distinct in terms of the subject-matter and of the timing.[26]

In its 1996 *Nuclear Weapons Advisory Opinion* the Court stressed that the legal importance 'of that obligation goes beyond that of a mere obligation of conduct; the obligation involved here is an obligation to achieve a precise result – nuclear disarmament in all its aspects – by adopting a particular course of conduct, namely the pursuit of negotiations on the matter in good faith'.[27] The Court left no doubt that the vast majority of the international community is facing in this regard a twofold obligation, namely to pursue and to conclude the negotiations.[28]

General obligations, to be interpreted in light of the object and purpose of a bilateral treaty, 'have to be transformed into specific obligations of performance through a process of consultation and negotiation',[29] whereas the nature of *specific obligations* may in a number of situations endow this duty with a continuous and semi-permanent character, to bring about harmonious development in specific fields.[30]

Once a treaty has been concluded to govern inter-state relations, 'it is always for the parties concerned to decide, by agreement, in what conditions their mutual relations can best be balanced'.[31] That is the very object and purpose of the exercise of diplomatic negotiations.

The agreement of both parties – as subsequent practice as a rule of treaty interpretation – 'may be expressed through their joint or parallel positive activity', which could consist of negotiations on the modalities of application.[32]

An obligation of cooperation entails first a duty to consult in good faith and then later on 'to negotiate the various arrangements needed'.[33]

Different declarations and commitments by one party may finally result in the exchange of notes containing an offer and its acceptance to negotiate regarding an agreement.[34]

---

25 *South West Africa, I.C.J.Report 1966*, at p. 10 (Ethiopia and Liberia).

26 With regard to the end objective of a *pactum de contrahendo* it is important to be aware that the character of an international agreement or undertaking is not determined by the terminology; in practice there exists a great variety in usage and the character of treaty stipulations has been attached to many different types: *South West Africa cases, I.C.J. Reports 1962*, at p. 331.

27 *Legality of the Threat or Use of Nuclear Weapons, Advisory Opinion, I.C.J. Reports 1996*, p. 226, at pp. 263–4, para. 99.

28 *Nuclear Weapons Advisory Opinion, I.C.J. Reports 1996*, at p. 264, para. 100. That a *pactum de contrahendo* 'is *prima facie* evidence, a necessary but not sufficient condition for successful negotiations' to follow (W. Zartman, 'Negotiating Forward', p. 289) is amply illustrated by the nuclear disarmament negotiations. On the notion of *pactum de contrahendo* more generally see L. Marion, 'La notion de "Pactum de Contrahendo" dans la jurisprudence internationale' (1974) 78 *Revue Générale de Droit International Public*, 351–98 and U. Beyerlin, 'Pactum de contrahendo und pactum de negotiando' (1976) 36 *Zeitschrift für ausländsiches öffentliches Recht and Völkerrecht*, 407–43. On the operational aspects of both notions with regard to an important international conflict see A. Cassese, 'The Israel-PLO Agreement and Self-Determination' (1993) 4 *European Journal of International Law*, 4, 564–71.

29 *Gabcikovo-Nagymaros Project (Hungary/Slovakia), Judgment, I.C.J. Reports 1997*, p. 7, at p. 68, para. 112.

30 *Oil Platforms case, I.C.J. Reports 1996*, p. 803, at p. 813, para. 26 and at p. 814, para.28.

31 *Maritime Delimitation in the Area between Greenland and Jan Mayen, Judgment, I.C.J. Reports 1993*, p. 38, at p. 77, para. 86.

32 *Kasikili/Sedudu Island (Botswana/Namibia), Judgment, I.C.J. Reports 1999*, p. 1045, Dissenting opinion by Judge Parra-Aranguren, at p. 1213, para. 17.

33 *Interpretation Agreement between the WHO and Egypt, Advisory Opinion, I.C.J. Reports 1980,* at p. 95, para. 49. Judge Lachs doubted whether 'there is an obligation of, or even call for, negotiations with the host State': Separate opinion, at p. 111.

34 Application by Bolivia instituting proceedings before the International Court of Justice against the Republic of Chile, III, paras. 16 and 17–18.

General obligations under international law may provide an additional legal basis for the obligation to negotiate, together with 'agreements, diplomatic practice and a series of declarations attributable to the respondent's highest-level representatives'.[35]

The Particular Nature of the Subject-Matter

In some branches of international law the concept of reaching an agreement as the outcome of successful negotiations may be underlying the history and status of a particular subject, such as the delimitation of the continental shelf.[36]

In international fisheries law the *compelling need of conservation* has resulted in a duty for States to examine *together* the measures required, which may not be taken unilaterally under international law, but only on the basis of an agreement, thus implying negotiations 'either bilaterally or within a multilateral framework'.[37] The Court did agree with this reasoning, but added that in case of disagreement the methods for peaceful settlement of disputes of Article 33 have to be implemented.[38]

With regard to *preferential rights*, a party may, during a first phase of discussions be prepared to recognize preferential rights invoked by the other party, but basic differences may remain as to the extent and scope of those rights and as to the methods of their implementation and enforcement.[39]

Hence their very nature makes it necessary for States to reach an agreement by negotiations in order to make it possible for the holder to exercise those rights: 'It is implicit in the *concept of preferential* rights that negotiations are required in order to define or delimit the extent of those rights.'[40] Hence the Court was right in pointing out that 'the obligation to negotiate thus flows from the very nature of the respective rights of the Parties'.[41]

As any unilateral delimitation of the continental shelf effected unilaterally by one State regardless of the views of the other State or States concerned is in international law not opposable to those States, this entails the 'application of the *related duty* to negotiate with a view of reaching an agreement and to do so in good faith with a genuine intention to achieve a positive result'.[42] The Court rightly added that there is no room for unilateral maritime delimitation.[43]

The argument parties have been taking from this approach is rather straightforward: in situations of delimitation, international law prescribes agreement as the primary method; hence it would be normal for parties to negotiate and it is only when such an agreement does not come about that the parties should turn to procedures of pacific settlement.[44]

35 Application by Bolivia instituting proceedings before the International Court of Justice against the Republic of Chile, IV, para. 31.

36 *North Sea Continental Shelf case, I.C.J Reports 1969,* at p. 33, § 47. See also *Continental Shelf (Tunisia/Libyan Arab Jamahiriya), Judgment, I.C.J. Reports 1982,* p. 18, at pp. 66–7, para. 87.

37 *Fisheries Jurisdiction (Federal Republic of Germany v. Iceland) Jurisdiction, Judgment, I.C.J. Reports 1973,* p. 49, at p. 52, para. 5 (b) (FRG).

38 *Fisheries Jurisdiction (United Kingdom v. Iceland), I.C.J. Reports, 1974,* p. 3, at p. 26, para. 57.

39 *Ibid.,* at p. 16, para. 32.

40 *Ibid.,* at p. 32, para. 74 (emphasis added).

41 *Ibid.,* at p. 32, para. 75.

42 *Delimitation of the Maritime Boundary in the Gulf of Maine Area, Judgment, I.C.J. Reports 1984,* p. 246, at p. 292, para. 87 (emphasis added).

43 *Gulf of Maine case, I.C.J. Reports 1984,* at p. 299, para. 112 (1). There is also a treaty-based obligation to do so contained in Articles 76 and 83 of UNCLOS: *Land and Maritime Boundary between Cameroon and Nigeria (Cameroon v. Nigeria: Equatorial Guinea intervening), Judgment, I.C.J. Reports 2002,* p. 303, at p. 323, para. 26 (5) (b) (Nigeria). For a recent overview of the Court's contribution to the law governing maritime delimitation see the Court President's speech to the Sixth Committee of the General assembly on 2 November 2012, which exclusively dealt with this topic (text available at the ICJ's website).

44 *Continental Shelf (Libyan Arab Jamahiriya/Malta), Application to Intervene, Judgment, I.C.J. Reports 1984,* p. 3, at p. 14, para. 19 (Libya).

One could add that 'within the context of conventional delimitation of territories, the frontiers drawn by States have [a] tendency to situate themselves geographically between the respective claims of the Parties, so as to find a pacificatory equilibrium'.[45]

An Obligation Not to Negotiate?

In particular situations States may be under an obligation *not* to negotiate, such obligation originating from general international law, previously having been agreed upon by States Parties to a treaty or imposed judicially.

Rather exceptional and almost unprecedented is a situation where a party is able to argue that the very fact of the negotiations having taken place constitutes conduct which is in breach of general international law and requests the Court to impose upon the Respondent an injunction to refrain from any further negotiations.[46]

Examples of a pre-existing understanding that no negotiations would be conducted without consent of a particular Power could be found under colonial rule, an obligation *not even to enter into negotiations* without the consent of the colonial Power.[47]

A State may also be under the obligation not to enter into and thus not to embark upon negotiations aiming at the conclusion of any particular agreement concerning an international river without consulting with its neighbour.[48]

The Court's 1971 *Namibia Advisory Opinion* provides us with an example of a judicially imposed *pactum de non contrahendo* and thus also *de non negotiando* when it ruled that there is an obligation for States not to enter into treaty relations with South Africa 'in all cases in which the government of South Africa purports to act on behalf of or concerning Namibia'.[49]

1.2 The Multifunctional Role of Negotiations within the Context of Peaceful Settlement of Disputes

Multifunctionality from an International Relations Theory Perspective

Within the context of PSD negotiation 'is a process whereby the parties directly communicate and bargain with each other in an attempt to agree on a settlement of the issue'.[50] However, in case parties 'are at odds to the fundamental basis on which the process rests'[51] no negotiation process can be successful.

Acceptance of negotiations as a method for PSD might 'fluctuate in degree' but 'must be dominant for negotiations to get underway'[52] – although acceptance 'may mean substantially different things to the parties

45 G. Giraudeau, *Les différends territoriaux*, p. 47: 'dans le cadre de la délimitation conventionnelle des territoires, les frontières tracées par les Etats vont avoir tendance à se situer géographiquement entre les revendications respectives des parties, de manière à y trouver un équilibre pacificateur'.

46 *East Timor (Portugal v. Australia), Judgment, I.C.J. Reports 1995*, p. 90, at p. 101, para. 25 (Portugal) and at p. 95, para. 10, (5) (a) (Portugal).

47 *Case between Qatar and Bahrain, I.C.J. Reports 2001,* p. 40, at p. 56, para. 44 and at p. 57, para. 48; see also Dissenting opinion by Judge *ad hoc* Torres Bernardez, at p. 412, para. 440. Another example of a *pactum de non contrahendo/non negotiando* can be found in the Land *and Maritime Boundary case, I.C.J. Reports 2002,* at p. 404, para. 203. That delimitation resulting from negotiations between Colonial Powers dividing their respective spheres of influence may lie 'at the heart of' contemporary cases, is not surprising: *Case between Botswana and Namibia, I.C.J.Reports 1999,* p. 1045, at p. 1054.

48 *Dispute regarding Navigational and Related Rights (Costa Rica v. Nicaragua), Judgment, I.C.J. Reports 2009*, p. 213, at p. 229, para. 19.

49 *Namibia Advisory Opinion, I.C.J. Reports 1971,* at p. 55, para. 122. A rather exceptional example in the case law of a non-judicial exclusion from participation in negotiations could be found in the *Bosnian Genocide case* as a result of a General Assembly Resolution: *Application of the Convention on the Prevention and Punishment of the Crime of Genocide, Provisional Measures, Order of 8 April 1993, I.C.J. Reports 1993*, p. 3, at p. 13, para. 17.

50 R. Bilder, 'An Overview', 22.

51 *Namibia Advisory Opinion, I.C.J. Reports 1971,* Separate opinion by Judge Dillard, at p. 160.

52 A. Lall, *Modern International Negotiation*, p. 37.

involved'[53] and in a number of cases parties have different opinions on the selection or priority of one of the two modes of settlement. They rarely share 'precisely the same goals', but when coming to the negotiating table 'they impliedly declare their willingness to search for various peaceful ways of *accommodating each other*'.[54]

Negotiations 'would hardly serve any real purpose' in the parties' perception if their objectives cannot 'at least be brought to a state of common understanding'.[55]

Third parties may have assisted or influenced the initiating by the parties of the process of negotiations.[56]

In 'order to promote progress towards a settlement it is more conciliatory to describe even a fairly clear dispute as a situation, if at all possible'.[57] Indeed, when circumstances are such as to permit this approach, it will then only gradually become obvious to the parties that the situation which they have been willing to address at the negotiating table is related to and covers an (underlying) dispute: that is when the *crystallization* of the dispute occurs.

An 'operative desire to clarify, ameliorate, adjust, or settle the dispute or situation' is a decisive factor: 'there must be a will to move from the *status quo*'; if that is absent, 'there cannot be a negotiation'.[58] That is exactly where the legal obligation to negotiate (its nature, legal basis, scope and content) enters the stage to perform its functional role.

Multifunctionality from an International Law Perspective

International law does impose certain conditions to the process of negotiations and attaches legal consequences on negotiations within the framework of PSD. The legitimacy of a resolution of a dispute through a process of negotiations is drawn from consent, 'but this legitimacy is tainted by power disparities'.[59]

The international law of dispute settlement[60] consists of a network of cooperational duties for both the Court and for the parties, and to which we return in subsequent chapters. It is sufficient at this stage to mention that the three stakeholders – 'Applicant, Respondent and the Court itself – should take part in a sort of dialogue in order 'to make an effort *in bona fide* to resolve the dispute through the judicial system'.[61]

The General Obligation to Settle Disputes and the Obligation of Good Faith

In contemporary international law 'there is no doubt that *the peaceful settlement of disputes* is a general obligation independent of the importance or the possible consequences of a dispute'[62] – for instance the likely impact of its continuance on international peace and security; it is 'one of the principles basic to the whole

53 A. Lall, *Modern International Negotiation*, p. 40.

54 A. Lall, *Modern International Negotiation*, p. 40 (emphasis added).

55 A. Lall, *Modern International Negotiation*, p. 47.

56 See *inter alia* D. Frazier and W. Dixon, 'Third-Party Intermediaries and Negotiated Settlements, 1946–2000' in J. Bercovitch and S. Gartner (eds), *International Conflict Mediation: New Approaches and Findings* (London and New York, 2009), pp. 43–66.

57 A. Lall, *Modern International Negotiation*, p. 24.

58 A. Lall, *Modern International Negotiation*, p. 31.

59 A. Peters, 'International Dispute Settlement: A Network of Cooperational Duties' (2003) 14 *European Journal of International Law*, 1, 1–34 at 5.

60 For use of this terminology see for instance P. Bastid, *Cours de Droit International Public* (Paris 1963–64), Part 8: Le droit relative au règlement des différends internationaux. See also C. Santulli, *Droit du contentieux international* (Paris, 2005) and C. Brown, *A Common Law of International Adjudication* (Oxford, 2007). This area of international law, which perhaps is only *emerging* at present (R. Kolb, *The ICJ*, p. 7), is at the same time particular and overarching and consists of principles, rules, rights and duties relating to peaceful settlement of disputes. A different study altogether would consist in analyzing 'the degree to which the parties cooperate with the Court and the impact this has on the efficiency of the Court's procedure and ability to settle disputes': C. Schulte, *Compliance with Decisions of the International Court of Justice* (Oxford, 2004), p. 14.

61 H. Sakai, '*La Bonne Administration de la Justice* in the Incidental Proceedings of the International Court of Justice' (2012), 55, *Japanese Yearbook of International Law*, 110–33, at 125.

62 K. Oellers-Frahm, 'Nowhere to Go? The Obligation to Settle Disputes Peacefully in the Absence of Compulsory Jurisdiction' in T. Giederich (ed.), *A Wiser Century? Judicial Dispute Settlement, Disarmament and the Laws of War 100 Years after the Second Hague Peace Conference* (Berlin, 2009), 435–53 at 436.

structure of international society'.[63] Parties 'are obliged, by the Charter and general international law, to respect these fundamental principles of international law'.[64]

Although the 'possibility of a dispute remaining unsettled does not amount to a violation of the obligation to settle disputes peacefully',[65] however leaving a significant dispute unresolved because 'any conceivable settlement or even attempt of settlement is likely only to exacerbate the sense of grievance of one or another party and increase tensions' and hence 'simply to leave the dispute to simmer, hoping that someday, somehow, it will go away'[66] does not seem in compliance with the general obligation to *at least attempt* to settle the dispute peacefully.

Pursuant to the Manila Declaration, if a dispute cannot be settled States must at least manage it and keep it under control,[67] and this is in line with Article 1, para. 1 of the Charter: partly failing negotiations may indeed bring about *an adjustment*.

Depending on the *petita* of the parties the Court's judgment may not really solve the dispute, but it may result in a temporary adjustment.

This general obligation does not, however, affect the freedom of the parties, as expressed in Article 33 of the Charter, to choose one of the mechanisms listed there; there is 'some support for the view' that in case of disputes 'the States concerned are under an obligation under customary international law to seek to settle the dispute *through negotiations*',[68] although there is no customary-law stepladder of settlement procedures giving priority to negotiations.[69]

The Court has made it perfectly clear that the obligation to negotiate an agreement as a means of dispute settlement is a 'principle which underlies all international relations'.[70]

Conversely, 'it is not a legal rule that a dispute exists only if it is reflected in a formal exchange of representations. If the subject of a disagreement is perfectly clear, then a dispute may exist, even if there has been no official contact.'[71]

The *obligation to settle disputes* 'is an obligation to reach a particular and measurable outcome: the disposal of the dispute'.[72] Inherent in the *obligation to settle disputes peacefully* is a 'general, customary law-based duty of cooperation with a view to a settlement'.[73]

Absent a general or conventional obligation for States to negotiate, the principle of good faith does not seem to exclude the discretionary power of States to refuse to enter into the (pre)negotiation phase, although in such a situation 'the international community may not only condemn its unwillingness to seek peaceful settlement but will draw adverse inferences as to the merits of its position with regard to the dispute'.[74]

The similar absence of a general or conventional obligation for States to settle their disputes by adjudication equally affects the scope of application of the principle of good faith.

Optional or compromissory clauses excluding from the jurisdiction of the Court disputes for which other means of peaceful settlement had been or will be agreed is part of the functional tension between adjudication and negotiation.

63 D. Bowett, 'Developments in the Settlement of Disputes' (1983) 180, *Académie de Droit international. Recueil des Cours*, 177.

64 *Request for Interpretation of the Judgment of 15 June 1962 in the Case concerning* The Temple of Preah Vihear (Cambodia v. Thailand) *(Cambodia v. Thailand), Provisional Measures, Order of 18 July 2011, I.C.J. Reports 2011*, p. 537, at p. 554, para. 66.

65 K. Oellers-Frahm, 'Nowhere to Go?', 451.

66 R. Bilder, 'An Overview', 6–7.

67 J. Merrills, 'The Means of Dispute Settlement' in M. Evans (ed.), *International Law* (3rd edn, Oxford, 2010), pp. 559–81, at p. 560.

68 A. Watts, 'Negociation and International Law', p. 525 referring to Fitzmaurice (emphasis added).

69 A. Peters, 'International Dispute Settlement', 14.

70 *North Sea Continental Shelf case, I.C.J. Reports 1969*, p. 3, at p. 48, para. 86.

71 J. Merrills, 'The Mosaic', 367.

72 A. Peters, 'International Dispute Settlement', 9.

73 A. Peters, 'International Dispute Settlement', 9.

74 R. Bilder, 'An Overview', 12.

However, once either of the two mechanisms has been embarked upon, the principle of good faith fully and unreservedly governs the conduct of both parties prior to, during and after the proceedings before the Court, as this study will further demonstrate.

Both the obligation to settle disputes peacefully and the obligation of good faith are dispute *driven* but aiming at different objectives. Peaceful settlement of disputes 'is concerned only that the dispute is peacefully diffused, perhaps even on a temporary basis'. In this way the concept is 'generally agnostic about the result of the settlement *vis-à-vis* the problem it attempts to solve'. The duty to negotiate in good faith, on the other hand, is 'very much concerned that agreement achieves, or helps to achieve, a certain result', meaning that the outcome should reflect a certain substantive objective.[75]

The principle of good faith requires parties to start the process of negotiations – one of the main functions of the pre-negotiation phase being 'to establish an agreed classification of the dispute in order to decide the best way of handling it'[76] – with sincerity, to conduct the discussions meaningfully; not to prematurely abandon the process; in case of an objective failure of the process to attempt to resolve the dispute with another mode – and requires parties to implement the judgment in good faith.[77] We will come back to these good faith consequences to find out how the Court has approached and assessed them.

The Value of Procedural Arrangements

A State depositing a declaration accepting the compulsory jurisdiction of the Court 'indicates thereby that it considers judicial settlement as the most appropriate method of third party settlement for legal disputes if such disputes cannot be solved amicably'.[78]

At the intersection between a political and legal approach it has to be duly acknowledged that 'the value of arrangements for dispute settlement is not to be judged solely by the cases decided under those arrangements: a provision for compulsory arbitration, by its very existence, can discourage unreasonable behaviour' during the process of negotiations, and 'so may be useful even if it is never invoked'.[79]

From a functional perspective parties do have at their disposal a number of ways to avoid an impasse or a deadlock: they may consider splitting the core issue 'in such a way as to enable each side to obtain satisfaction'; they may use a procedural agreement 'to compensate one side for yielding on the substantive issue'.[80]

Furthermore one should be aware that the practice 'of setting aside a legal problem in order to make progress towards a desirable goal is a familiar one in international relations'.[81] Such '"[w]ithout prejudice" arrangements should be thought of less as a means of settling disputes by negotiation than as a way of managing them. By allowing attention to be focused on those matters which can be negotiated, they allow progress to be made until such time as other more intractable issues can be addressed.'[82]

---

75 C. Hutchinson, 'The Duty to Negotiate International Environmental Disputes in Good Faith' (2006) 2 *McGill International Journal of Sustainable Development Law and Policy* 117–53 at 134. One of the 'peculiar features of modern peace agreements' which make them 'much more difficult to adjudicate than ordinary treaties' is that they 'are process-oriented because they frequently contain obligations for the parties to negotiate a political settlement of the conflict, but do not dictate the outcomes'. The 'non-binary nature' of some types of provisions makes it difficult to adjudicate when there has been compliance with a specific provision, as well as *when a party has breached a duty to negotiate in "good faith"*': A. Lang, '"Modus operandi" and the ICJ's Appraisal of the Lusaka Ceasefire Agreement in the *Armed Activities Case:* The Role of Peace Agreements in International Conflict Resolution' (2007–08), 40 *New York University Journal of International Law and Politics*, 107–69, 129 and 130 (emphasis added).

76 J. Merrills, *International Dispute Settlement*, p. 289.

77 A. Peters, 'International Dispute Settlement' 15–16.

78 *Fisheries Jurisdiction (Spain v. Canada), Jurisdiction of the Court, Judgment, I.C.J. Reports 1998*, p. 432, Separate opinion by Judge Kooijmans, at pp. 492–3, para. 13. A different matter altogether is if 'two States accept the jurisdiction of the ICJ how does this influence their bargaining behaviour? Conversely, how do expectations about bargaining influence unilateral state decision to accept or not accept the ICJ's jurisdiction?': E.Powell and S.McLaughlin Mitchell', The International Court of Justice and the World Three Legal Systems'(2007) 69 *Journal of Politics*, 2, 397–415 at 389.

79 J. Merrills, *International Dispute Settlement*, p. 112.

80 J. Merrills, *International Dispute Settlement*, p. 12.

81 *Nuclear Weapons Advisory Opinion, I.C.J. Reports 1996,* Dissenting opinion by Judge Sahabuddeen, at p. 423.

82 J. Merrills, *International Dispute Settlement*, p. 14.

'Because the costs of a dispute end with its settlement, the fact that a dispute has been settled peacefully can itself be treated as an achievement, regardless of the terms obtained. This is often the key in promoting the peaceful settlement of disputes.'[83]

The Multifunctionality of Negotiations to Settle a Dispute

In contrast to their rather monofunctional convention-oriented counterpart, negotiations as a mechanism for PSD are multifunctional. This multifunctionality is conditioned by the specific factual legal and time context in which various actors operate. For instance, the process may not always be open-ended as the element of time may step in to impose upon the parties a maximum duration to the efforts to find a negotiated solution to a dispute.

In its second Advisory Opinion the ICJ has succinctly but aptly described the multifunctionality of negotiations when it affirmed that negotiation is one of the methods 'recognized by international law for the *establishment, presentation and the settlement of claims*'.[84]

From the perspective of the parties to a dispute negotiations may be considered to perform one or more of the following functions, in most cases in a more or less chronological order.

Negotiations may be conducted to depolitize a dispute, i.e. by 'isolating the legal elements'.[85]
Negotiations may be conducted in order to clarify the legal positions of each party with regard to a pre-existing dispute.
Negotiations may be conducted in order to find out whether a real dispute has arisen between the parties and to determine its nature and subject-matter.
Negotiations may be conducted to isolate minor issues over which a consensus is possible, while at the same time freezing more important and sensitive issues which constitute the core subject-matter of the dispute.[86]
Negotiations may be conducted in order to clarify and to determine the legal issues which later may be submitted to the Court.
Negotiations may be conducted in order to prevent the lapse of a claim by the passage of time.[87]
Negotiations may be conducted in order to conclude the actual compromis for submission of the dispute to the Court.
Negotiations may be conducted in order to solve the dispute either prior or during the course of the proceedings before the Court.
Negotiations may be conducted in order to implement the judgment rendered by the Court.

From the perspective of the Court negotiations between the parties to a dispute have also been dealt with in their multifinctionality. The Court may examine such negotiations prior and/or subsequent to the institution of proceedings for a variety of reasons.[88]

For the purpose of determining questions relating to the existence of the dispute.;
For the purpose of the definition of its subject-matter;
For taking evidence or proof of a specific allegation of a party;

83 J. Merrills, *International Dispute Settlement*,p. 36.

84 *Reparation for injuries suffered in the service of the United Nations, Advisory Opinion: I.C.J. Reports 1949*, p. 174, at p. 177 (emphasis added).

85 J. Merrills, 'The Means of Dispute Settlement', at p. 574.

86 See also for instance *Case concerning right of passage over Indian territory (Preliminary Objections), Judgment of 26 November 1957: I.C.J. Reports 1957*, p. 125, at p. 151.

87 M. Waibel, 'The Diplomatic Channel', p. 1096.

88 Torres Bernardez, 'Are Prior Negotiations' p. 508, para. 7: the assumptions of the references made, 'must, however, be clearly distinguished from cases in which the absence of or failure to exhaust diplomatic or direct negotiations is presented as an objection to the jurisdiction of the Court or as a plea of inadmissibility of an application' (at p. 508, para. 7), issues to which we return later.

For the purpose of providing information about the opposing legal position of the parties;
For the purpose of assessing the conduct of the parties during the negotiations;
For the purpose of evaluating whether the circumstances require the indication of provisional measures;
For the purpose of deciding upon a request by a third State to intervene;
For the purpose of formulating the operative clause of its judgment.

Negotiating and Unilateral Recourse to the Court

'It is no secret that when States undertake negotiations, they often envisage, in a spirit of caution and realism, other solutions should the negotiations fail.'[89] There is no reason to assume things to be different when negotiations aim at the solution of a dispute.

The prospective functional interaction between the two modes of PSD already announces itself here as it 'may therefore be said that envisaging a unilateral substitute solution must necessarily be part of the customary strategy and tactic of negotiation, sometimes in order to put more pressure on the negotiating partner'.[90]

A unilateral recourse to the Court may then perfectly function as a substitute solution in the minds of those taking part in the negotiating process. But it is equally true that the 'contrary can only be asserted if the State has *shown bad faith* and if it has been demonstrated beyond doubt that it only pretended to negotiate, whereas *its firm intention was to sabotage the seeming negotiations in order to impose at all costs a unilateral solution already decided on*'.[91] In this scenario a unilateral recourse to the Court may perfectly function as the solution already decided on.

However, if a process of negotiations is being conducted by both parties in good faith and meaningfully, 'seizure of the Court may appear as an abuse of the Court procedure'. In such a situation 'a court may be obliged to decline jurisdiction in order to encourage a diplomatic settlement'.[92]

The analysis of the case law will demonstrate this bipolar multifunctionality of negotiations as a mechanism towards the peaceful settlement of inter-state disputes, an 'élément du contentieux international'.[93]

Our journey through the Court's jurisprudence from this perspective will also require a constant awareness of this multifunctionality over and above the particularities of each individual case, and this in order to finally asses the functional interaction between negotiations and judicial settlement.

The status under public international law of dispute settlement negotiations is bound to have an impact on both the parties' performance in this regard, and on the Court's assessment of that performance and the role it wishes to attribute to negotiations in its judicial settlement of the dispute, and to which we turn in Chapter 7.

1.3 The Nature of the Obligation to Negotiate

What can be said at this stage of our enquiry about the nature of an obligation to negotiate towards a peaceful settlement of a dispute?

It entails parties to embark upon a process of negotiations 'pour partie liée' as it has to take place 'dans un cadre déterminé'[94] – namely to solve the dispute.

Does it always have to be a *mutual obligation* as pronounced by the Court[95] or is there room, in case of premature or unjustified rupture of negotiations, for a *unilateral obligation* of the other party because this party has maintained its readiness to continue the negotiations?

89 *Gabcikovo case, I.C.J. Reports 1997*, Separate opinion by Judge Bedjaoui, at p. 128, para. 33.

90 *Ibid.*

91 *Ibid.*, Separate opinion by Judge Bedjaoui, at p. 128, para. 34.

92 A. Peters, 'International Dispute Settlement', 15.

93 J. Soubeyrol, 'La Négociation diplomatique elément du contentieux international' (1964) 2 *Revue Générale de droit International Public*, 319–49.

94 P. Reuter, 'De l'obligation de négocier', 720.

95 *Fisheries Jurisdiction (United Kingdom v. Iceland, I.C.J. Reports 1974*, at p. 34, para. 79 (3).

The Court has made it perfectly clear that the obligations under Article 33 of the UN Charter are not only mutual but also 'imperative'.[96] The principle enshrined in Article 33 is according to the Court 'complementary' to principles of a prohibitive nature such as the non-use of force, and it is a principle of customary international law.[97] Hence the Court may, in its operative paragraphs, recall to both parties 'their obligation to seek a solution to their disputes by peaceful means in accordance with international law'.[98]

Would it, given the Court's judgment in the *Pulp Mills case* – where the parties fundamentally disagreed on the *functional role* of the negotiations envisaged in the 1975 Statute[99] – be correct to qualify the obligation to negotiate, contained in a compromissory clause, as *a merely procedural obligation* rather than *a substantive one*? Perhaps the duty to negotiate belongs to both categories at the same time. We will return to this question in Chapter 3.

The dispute in the *Pulp mills case* concerned compliance with both procedural and substantive obligations.[100] A Respondent may contend that the Applicant was claiming 'a procedural right' to 'engage in good faith negotiations'.[101]

Could it be concluded from the divergent views taken by the parties in this case that the duty of negotiation in its *procedural function* is to be considered as a means to bring about the peaceful settlement of a dispute which is *a substantive obligation* under both general and conventional international law?

1.4 Unilateral Stumbling Blocks towards the Negotiating Table

Several unilateral actions or attitudes may constitute sometimes even successive stumbling blocks on the road towards the negotiating table.

The Functional Role of Preliminary Steps

> If a party has an alternative that is clearly superior in terms of its expected value to any possible negotiated settlement, it typically would not make sense to negotiate, although there may be cases in which the decision-maker would find it beneficial to negotiate, even if conscious of the low probability of a better negotiated outcome, in order, for instance, to prove that all 'peaceful' methods have been exhausted prior to using coercive means.[102]

The decision to go to the negotiating table may be taken 'separately, differently and not concomitantly' by the parties leaving 'their previously exclusively unilateral strategy' which may be perceived as 'blocked or overly costly' or when 'the alternative track of negotiating is more promising or comparatively cheaper'.[103]

96 *Aegean Sea Continental Shelf, Interim Protection, Order of 11 September 1976, I.C.J. Reports 1976*, p. 3, at p. 11, para. 35 and at p. 13, para. 41.

97 *Military and Paramilitary Activities in and against Nicaragua (Nicaragua v. United States of America), Merits, Judgment, I.C.J. Reports 1986*, p. 14, at p. 145, para.291.

98 *Ibid.*, at p. 149, para. 292 (12).

99 According to Argentina the negotiations are a 'procedural machinery' which if disregarded would 'undermine object and purpose of the treaty' entailing 'automatically a breach of substantive obligations' since the two categories are indivisible': *Pulp Mills case, I.C.J. Reports 2010*, at pp. 47–8, paras. 71 and 72. According to Uruguay the procedural obligation to negotiate is 'intended to facilitate the performance of substantive obligations' and in this way they are 'a means rather than an end', as the alleged indivisibility of both categories of obligations is artificial: at p. 48, paras. 73–4.

100 *Pulp Mills case, I.C.J. Reports 2010*, at p. 40, para. 46.

101 *Pulp Mills on the River Uruguay (Argentina v. Uruguay), Order of 13 July 2006, I.C.J. Reports 2006*, p. 113, at pp. 123–4, para. 43

102 G. Blum and R. Mnookin, 'When *Not* to Negotiate', p. 103.

103 W. Zartman, *Negotiation and Conflict Management*, pp. 119–20.

Although 'diplomatic *démarches*', unilateral by nature, may have proven to be ineffective[104] and are not part of negotiations they could, in the end, trigger the start of a negotiation round, which in other cases may be triggered for instance by domestic lawsuits against companies possessing the Applicant's nationality.[105]

This political cost-benefit approach may then be joined, converge and be subsumed by a pre-existing legal obligation to negotiate which is derived from the principle of peaceful settlement of disputes as confirmed by the Court's case law.[106]

Whether mere protests can or cannot amount to negotiations proper was already an issue in the *DRC Rwanda case*,[107] but it was brought to the fore by the parties in the *CERD case*[108] where the Court indeed affirmed that the mere fact that a State claims that the other party is in breach of substantive treaty obligations is perfectly possible without initiating the settlement of dispute mechanism provided for in that treaty.[109]

An Offer to Negotiate

Do we have 'an affirmative obligation on a State to seek actively negotiations' with other interested States, or does 'it simply require' States 'to respond favourably when asked by other States to enter into negotiations'?[110]

An offer to negotiate for the purpose of reaching a settlement or of concluding a special agreement certainly testifies to the good will of the party extending such an invitation. It is a unilateral act, but does it entail legal consequences?[111]

For present purposes it is important for any party to a dispute to be well aware of the Court's reassurances in this regard. Indeed, such an offer cannot be interpreted as 'consent to participate' or 'actual participation', nor as implying 'the abandonment of any defence' or 'acceptance of any claim' unless this has been clearly expressed or follows undisputedly from the attitude adopted by that party.[112] Otherwise, such an interpretation would not only seriously hamper the use of the means of settlement provided for in Article 33 of the UN Charter, but it would also constitute an obstacle to the opening of negotiations at all.[113]

It is clear that a widely publicized announcement of an offer by a party to start negotiations – certainly when this has not (yet) been made through the normal diplomatic channels – calls for some reaction within a reasonable period of time on the part of the other party if it wishes to accept such an offer.[114] A State extending an offer to negotiate may expect the other party, while formally accepting the invitation, to take further action to restart the process it had previously unilaterally abandoned.[115]

---

104 *Request for Interpretation of the Avena Judgment, I.C.J. Reports 2008*, at p. 314, para. 7 (Mexico).

105 *Jurisdictional Immunities of the State (Germany v. Italy: Greece intervening), Judgment, I.C.J. Reports 2012*, p. 99, Dissenting opinion by Judge Trindade, at pp. 272–3, para. 261 (referring to Italy's argument).

106 *Pulp Mills case, I.C.J. Reports 2010*, Separate opinion by Judge Cançado Trindade, at p. 145, para. 25 and at p. 202, para. 178.

107 *DRC v. Rwanda case, I.C.J. Reports 2006*, at pp. 40–41, para. 91.

108 *CERD case, I.C.J. Reports 2011*, at p. 131, paras. 151–2.

109 *Ibid.*, at p. 102, para. 69.

110 M. Rogoff, 'The Obligation to Negotiate', 149.

111 Although there is generally 'very little information concerning the process of negotiating special agreements'. *A Dialogue at the Court: Proceedings of the ICJ/UNITAR Colloquium Held on the Occasion of the Sixtieth Anniversary of the International Court of Justice, at the Peace Palace on 10 and 11 April 2006*, UNITAR 2006, at p. 15. For an interesting example of a process of negotiations leading to a Special Agreement see S. Yayakumar, *Pedra Branca: The Road to the World Court* (Singapore, 2009), pp. 35–43, involving four years to settle the agreement between Singapore and Malaysia and another five years to sign and to ratify the Agreement. For an incisive insight into the purpose and structure of a Special Agreement as a way of submitting a dispute to the Court see P. Tomka, 'The Special Agreement' in N. Ando, E. McWhinney and R. Wolfrum (eds), *Liber Amicorum Judge Shigeru Oda* (2 vols, The Hague, 2002), vol. 1, pp. 553–65.

112 *Nottbehom Case (second phase), Judgment of 6 April 1995: I.C.J. Reports 1955*, p. 4 at p. 20.

113 *Nottbehom Case, I.C.J. Reports 1955*, at p. 19.

114 *Case concerning the Temple of Preah Vihear (Cambodia v. Thailand), Merits, Judgment of 15 June 1962: I.C.J. Reports 1962*, p. 6, at p. 23.

115 *Maritime Delimitation case between Costa Rica and Nicaragua*, Application of Costa Rica, dated 25 February 2014, Press Release no. 2014/11 of 24 February 2014 (text available on the Court's website).

On the other hand once a State has made a commitment to enter into negotiations, 'it is not the Court's function to contemplate that it will not comply with it'.[116]

A Memorandum sent in order to invite another State to agree an international maritime boundary may be rejected by the addressee as an 'attempt to renegotiate the existing maritime boundary'.[117]

In the *Interim Accord case* the Court was criticized for not having pointed out one of the procedural conditions of taking countermeasures as provided for in Article 52 of the International Law Commission (ILC) Articles on state responsibility, notably the duty to offer to negotiate,[118] which under customary law requires that 'an attempt should be made to resolve the difference by friendly means – and the failure of negotiations'.[119]

Countermeasures 'may lawfully be adopted while negotiations continue, provided the injured state has complied' with the procedural safeguards expressed in Article 52, 'though their imposition will rarely create a positive atmosphere for negotiation'.[120] In case the responsible State has suspended the ensuing negotiations indefinitely, countermeasures may be reactivated.[121]

The Decision (Not) to Start the Process Because There is No Dispute

A party may reject and deny 'the existence of any obligation between the parties concerning the subject' of an Application,[122] a position which even precurs a potential disagreement over the very existence of a dispute relating to the subject-matter.

In spite of mutual commitments during meetings of a bilateral mechanism for political consultations that 'the bilateral dialogue had to give rise to concrete, appropriate and feasible solutions' on the subject-matter of an existing difference[123] to be followed by a unilateral suspension of a scheduled meeting, negotiations may never have resumed.[124] A request 'to draft a written and concrete proposal to carry forward the process' may be met with the denial of any legal basis as to the subject-matter at hand.[125]

The Applicant's statement before the General Assembly that 'the channels for a bilateral negotiation' in order 'to find a solution' remain open, may encounter a response that 'there are no pending issues between the two countries'[126] and 'that there is no dispute'.[127]

---

116 *Nuclear Tests (New Zealand v. France), Judgment, I.C.J. Reports 1974*, p. 457, at p. 477, para. 63.

117 *Case concerning Maritime Dispute (Peru v. Chile), Judgment, I.C.J. Reports 2014*, para. 136. The invitation was subsequently not renewed (para. 140), perhaps because the instrument may in fact not have been 'a diplomatic intiative' of the government concerned, but a proposal advanced 'on a personal basis' by an Ambassador to 'sound out the feasibility of certain thoughts': *ibid.*, Separate, partly concurring, partly dissenting opinion by Judge *ad hoc* Orrego Vicuña, para. 24.

118 *Application of the Interim Accord of 13 September 1995 (the Former Yugoslav Republic of Macedonia v. Greece), I.C.J. Reports 2011*, Declaration by Judge Bennouna, at p. 710.

119 *Ibid.*, Dissenting opinion by Judge *ad hoc* Roucounas, at p. 747, para. 72. One should note that the original French version reads 'et non l'épuisement des négociations', which does necessarily in all circumstances come down to a failure as such, for instance when a (temporary) deadlock is reached. See generally the recent study by M. Dawidowicz, *Third Party Countermeasures in International Law* (Cambridge, 2013). For an in-depth review of the ILC's work and subsequent developments see J. Crawford, *State Responsibility: The General Part* (Cambridge, 2013).

120 M. Waibel, 'The Diplomatic Channel', p. 1096.

121 For an analysis of the status and scope of the obligation to negotiate in case of unilateral countermeasures see *inter alia* Kwei-jung Ni, 'Redefinition and Elaboration of an Obligation to Pursue International Negotiations for Solving Global Environmental Problems in Light of the Two Shrimp/Turtle Compliance Adjudication between Malaysia and the United States' (2009) 14, *Minnesota Journal of Global Trade*, 111–39. On the place of negotiations within the state responsibility regime when the injured State is considering taking countermeasures during earlier drafts of the ILC see Symposium Countermeasures and Dispute Settlement: The Current Debate within the ILC (1994) 5 *European Journal of International Law*, 1, 20–119.

122 Application by Bolivia instituting proceedings before the International Court of Justice against the Republic of Chile, I, para. 3.

123 *Ibid.*, I, para. 26.

124 *Ibid.*

125 *Ibid.*, III, para. 27.

126 *Ibid.* I, para. 28.

127 *Ibid.*, III, para. 29.

As a party may just refuse any suggestion to seek an agreement by friendly negotiations with the other party or even other interested nations for that matter,[128] political willingness to enter into negotiations is the primordial prerequisite for giving this mechanism any chance to solve a particular dispute. When several countries involved deny the very existence of a dispute, this may result in their absolute refusal 'to take part, in any manner whatsoever, in the procedure provided for in the' relevant dispute clauses.[129]

In another context a Host State may still evaluate a particular situation and may not have concluded that a dispute existed as a controversial legislation had not yet been implemented; as a result it may be not in a position and unwilling to enter formally into a PSD procedure.[130] The State may eventually be willing to enter into 'technical discussions regarding the establishment of an arbitral tribunal' but 'only on an informal basis'.[131]

It should be noted that although disagreement on the existence of a dispute or its justiciability could be qualified as unreasonable behaviour on the part of one of the parties, this does not *ipso facto* prove bad faith.[132]

The Security Council may in vain have called upon the parties to take steps to resolve peacefully remaining issues between them; but, as the Court noted, 'a refusal to enter into any discussion of the matter with the other Party' rules out '*in limine*, any question of an *agreement* to resort to' for instance arbitration or some other pacific means.[133]

This may take the form, envisaged beforehand in a treaty, of one party failing to agree on the selection of a third member of a Treaty Commission, considered by the Court to be less serious than 'a complete refusal of co-operation' in case one party refuses to appoint its own Commissioner.[134]

Because a Mere Request for Information is Not a Real Negotiation

A party convinced that there is no dispute will consider an Application inadmissible because procedural conditions of prior negotiations are not fulfilled, as a mere request for information 'cannot be regarded as real negotiations',[135] whereas the Applicant maintains that negotiations did actually take place but 'did not allow the dispute to be settled'.[136] The most recent and important example of such a situation is of course the *CERD case*, and to which we return later in more detail.

Because There is No Agreement in Principle on the Subject-matter or the Objectives of the Process

An agreement in principle on the subject-matter of forthcoming negotiations is another prerequisite for negotiations to start. An offer to negotiate on a particular aspect of a dispute may be followed by a counterproposal to conduct negotiations on a broader range of subjects, which in turn is not acceptable to the other party.[137]

---

128 *Fisheries Jurisdiction (Federal Republic of Germany v. Iceland), I.C.J. Reports 1973*, at pp. 56–7, para. 19 (FRG).

129 *Interpretation of Peace Treaties (second phase), Advisory Opinion: I.C.J. Reports 1950*, p. 221, at p. 228.

130 *Applicability of the Obligation to Arbitrate under Section 22 of the United Nations Headquarters Agreement of 26 June 1947, Advisory Opinion, I.C.J. Reports 1988*, p. 12, at p. 13, para. 1 and at p. 19, para. 17 (UN Secretary-General).

131 *PLO case Advisory Opinion, I.C.J. Reports 1988*, at p. 20, para. 18 and at p. 33, para. 54.

132 E. Zoller, *La bonne foi en droit international public* (Paris, 1977), p. 131. The writer denies the legal nature of the principle of good faith, although she accepts that it has some legal content (pp. 350–52).

133 *Hostages case, I.C.J. Reports 1980*, p. 3, at p. 26, para. 49 and at p. 27, para. 52. On state preference for arbitration rather than adjudication see *inter alia* L. Malintoppi, 'Methods of Dispute Resolution in Inter-State Litigation: When States Go to Arbitration Rather than Adjudication' (2006) 5 *Law and Practice of International Courts and Tribunals*, 1, 133–62.

134 *Interpretation of Peace Treaties (second phase), Advisory Opinion, I.C.J. Reports 1950*, p. 221, at p. 227.

135 *Questions relating to the Obligation to Prosecute or Extradite (Belgium v. Senegal), Provisional Measures, Order of 28 May 2009, I.C.J. Reports*, p. 139, at p. 148, para. 45 (Senegal).

136 *Belgium v. Senegal case, I.C.J. Reports 2009*, at pp. 147–8, para. 44 (Belgium).

137 *Oil Platforms (Islamic Republic of Iran v. United States of America), Counter-Claim, Order of 10 March 1998, I.C.J. Reports 1998*, p. 190, at pp. 193–4, para. 5.

The *Gabcikovo case* illustrates the importance of stating clearly in advance the subject-matter and the aim of negotiations.[138]

It will ultimately be for the Court to decide whether the negotiations that allegedly took place did cover the subject-matter falling under the compromissory clause invoked by the Applicant in order to determine whether any condition of prior negotiations has been fulfilled so that it could be seised of the dispute.[139]

Whether the Court could or should take into account the position of a party towards negotiations on a different but related dispute when ascertaining that party's attitude towards the subject-matter that actually reached the Court is a different question altogether.

A genuine effort to negotiate implies that parties have to realize that even 'something as close as impossible to full satisfaction' of their demands is 'most unlikely'. What is important is that 'the irreducible objectives' – the identification of which may require 'several rounds of consideration' – 'should not be incompatible'.[140]

In spite of sharing the necessary political willingness, parties may hold divergent opinions as to the desirable outcome and ultimate objective of the negotiations they are embarking upon: in such a situation, reserving one's rights while seeking a solution in conformity with the rules of international law does not strictly coincide with reference to the duty of both parties to bring about an agreed solution.[141]

Whether parties are at liberty to derogate from treaty-based obligations and procedures of consultation and negotiation is a question to be discussed later in relation to the divergent opinions held by parties and some judges in the *Pulp Mills case*.

Because There is No Genuine Prospect that the Process Could be Useful

The well-known legal positions of the parties with regard to the broader dispute dividing them may be such that an attempt to negotiate on a particular issue deriving from or linked to that dispute would seem to be pointless, as the *Right of Passage case* has illustrated.[142]

The extent to which the absence of a genuine prospect that the process could at least be useful, let alone potentially (partially) successful, has a bearing on the Court's assessment of the fulfilment of a prior negotiation condition will be addressed in Chapters 3 and 7.

In a different context a State may as a result of the constitutional division of powers be unable to negotiate on a decision taken by its judiciary and which has been challenged by the other party.[143]

1.5 The Scope of the Obligation to Negotiate

> The obligation to be ready to negotiate with a view to concluding an agreement 'today still represents' the minimum of international-co-operation.[144]

The Court may review the history of the negotiations in order to assess whether the instruments agreed upon 'were freely negotiated by the interested parties on the basis of perfect equality and freedom of decision on both sides'[145] as enduring principles forming the basis for relations between countries.[146]

---

138 *Gacikovo case, I.C.J. Reports 1997*, at pp. 33–4, para.37 and at p. 34, para. 38.

139 *CERD case, I.C.J. Reports 2011*, at p. 136, paras. 170 and 169.

140 A. Lall, *Modern International Negotiation*, p. 50.

141 *Aegean Sea Continental Shelf (Greece v. Turkey), Judgment, I.C.J. Reports 1978*, p. 3, at p. 8, para. 16.

142 See note 86. M. Kohen, 'Interaction between Diplomatic and Judicial Means at the Initiation of Proceedings' in L. Boisson de Chazournes, M. Kohen and J. Vinuales (eds), *Diplomatic and Judicial Means of Dispute Settlement* (Leiden, Boston, 2013), pp. 13–24 at p. 16.

143 M. Kohen, ' Interaction', p. 17.

144 *International status of South West Africa, I.CJ. Reports 1950*, Dissenting opinion by Judge De Visscher, at p. 189.

145 *Fisheries Jurisdiction (Federal Republic of Germany v. Iceland),I.C.J. Reports 1973*, at p. 59, para. 24.

146 *Certain Questions of Mutual Assistance in Criminal Matters (Djibouti v. France), Judgment, I.C.J. Reports 2008*, p. 177, Separate opinion by Judge Koroma, at p. 253, paras. 6–7.

The scope of the obligation has been defined by the ICJ, as it was done by its predecessor, as 'not only to enter into negotiations but also to pursue them as far as possible with a view of concluding an agreement even if an obligation to negotiate did not imply an obligation to reach agreement'.[147]

Individual judges may put forward the view that parties may be under an obligation 'to negotiate in a reasonable manner and in good faith in order to achieve a result acceptable to both Parties, but without being obliged to reach an agreement *at any price*'.[148]

Pactum de Negotiando and Pactum de Contrahendo: Obligation of Conduct and Obligation of Result

When a multilateral treaty such as the UN Charter in Articles 75 and 77 provide that territories may be placed under the trusteeship system by subsequent agreements, the notion of an *agreement* implies 'consent of the parties concerned', but also that they 'must be free to accept or reject the terms of a contemplated agreement'.[149]

That the next paragraph of Article 80 provides that the first paragraph 'shall not be interpreted as giving grounds for delay or postponement of the negotiations and conclusion' of such subsequent agreements does not justify the contention that there exists 'a duty to negotiate *and* conclude Trusteeship agreements'.[150] Article 80 thus contains neither a *pactum de negotiando* nor *a pactum de contrahendo.*[151] The Court rejected as unconvincing the argument that both such *pacta* do impose themselves upon the Powers concerned in order to give the trusteeship system a more than theoretical existence, 'since an obligation to negotiate does not of itself assure the conclusion of' such agreements.[152] But the Court added that the 'normal course indicated by the Charter' is to conclude such agreements.[153]

In 1950 dissenting judges held diverging views as to the existence of both a legal obligation to negotiate and to conclude an agreement[154] or merely 'an obligation *to take part* in negotiations', and this 'at the earliest possible opportunity' with a view of concluding an agreement.[155]

In 1971 Judges Dillard and Padillo Nervo pointed out that South Africa 'was under a duty to negotiate in good faith and even *reasonably* with the UN' and that it 'should have been willing to *negotiate* with the UN an agreement to that effect, as was contemplated by the Charter'.[156]

Is the (post-adjudicative) obligation to negotiate then an obligation of conduct and not of result,[157] unless both States are parties to a *pactum de contrahendo*? Is the distinction more valid in other areas of international relations, and does it belong 'to a time past, when diplomacy was first and foremost an exercise in, or art of, intelligence, deceit, semantic subtlety and prevarication'?[158]

---

147 *Railway Traffic between Lithuania and Poland, Advisory Opinion, P.C.I.J. Series A/B, No. 42, 103*, at p. 116 as cited in *North Sea Continental Shelf case, I.C.J. Reports 1969*, at p. 48, para. 87.

148 *Continental Shelf case between Tunisia and Libya, I.C.J. Reports 1982*, Dissenting opinion by Judge Gros, at pp. 144–5, para. 3 (emphasis added).

149 *International status of SWA, I.C.J. Reports 1950*, at p. 139.

150 *Ibid.* (emphasis added).

151 *Ibid.*, at p. 140.

152 *Ibid.*

153 *Ibid.*

154 *Ibid.*, Dissenting opinion by Judge Krylov, at p. 191; Dissenting opinion by Judge Alvarez, at p. 183.

155 *Ibid.*, Dissenting opinion by Judge De Visscher, at pp. 186 and 187 (emphasis added).

156 *Namibia Advisory Opinion, I.C.J. Reports 1971*, p. 16, Separate opinion by Judge Dillard, at p. 159 (emphasis added) and Separate opinion by Judge Padilla Nervo, at p. 124. Another Charter-based example may be found in Article 43 with this judicial proviso that in this particular situation when negotiating such agreements the Security Council enjoys discretion with regard to who should bear the expenses of an international peace and security operation: *Certain Expenses of the United Nations (Article 17, paragraph 2, of the Charter), Advisory Opinion of 20 July 1962: I.C.J. Reports 1962*, p. 151, at p. 166.

157 *Request for Interpretation of the Judgment of 31 March 2004 in the Case concerning* Avena and other Mexican Nationals (Mexico v. United States of America), (*Mexico v. United States of America), Provisional Measures, Order of 16 July 2008, I.C.J. Reports 2008*, p. 311, at p. 314, para. 9 (Mexico).

158 *Interim Accord case, Judgment, I.C.J. Reports 2011*, p. 644, Dissenting opinion by Judge *ad hoc* Roucounas, at p. 730, para. 27.

International jurisprudence has demonstrated an extreme reserved position, if not hostility, as a matter of principle towards the argument that a *pactum de contrahendo* would imply an obligation of result.[159] Although a judicial decision could serve as a basis for a *pactum de contrahendo*, this is not the case when parties ask the Court to identify the legal principles which later on would provide the framework for their post-adjudicatory negotiations as anticipated in their Special Agreement.[160]

The distinction between *obligations of conduct and of result* is 'unsatisfactory', 'particularly in domains of *protection*',[161] and the peremptory nature of for instance the prohibition of torture, and the human rights nature of the Convention against Torture as such entails that States Parties are under obligations of result.[162]

When the fundamental objective of a primary rule is aiming at the protection of especially vulnerable (non)renewable resources in light of ever-changing scientific information, the obligation to (re)negotiate acquires a *continuous nature*.[163] We will later briefly touch upon the question how and to what extent this will affect the corresponding process of negotiations.

No Room to Settle the Dispute

A Respondent State may claim that the dispute pertaining to the exercise of its sovereign rights is exclusively within the State's national jurisdiction and 'thus not subject to the methods of settlements specified in the Charter';[164] but a refusal to accept arbitration provided for in a concession agreement would constitute a denial of justice according to the Applicant.[165]

Sometimes there is no room to solve a controversy by negotiations to find a compromise and to follow that path, for instance when the disagreement concerns the validity of an arbitral award because of alleged obscurities and contradictions making its execution impossible,[166] or if the difference between parties consists of a claim by one party that the other party would terminate a particular action which it refuses to halt;[167] there is not much of a subject-matter to have negotiations in a proper sense about.

The Court itself has cited its predecessor's famous pronouncement in the *Mavrommatis Palestine Concessions case* that the nature of previous discussions may have been such as to render superfluous renewed discussions, while the PICJ also stressed that no 'general and absolute rule can be laid down in this respect. It is a matter for consideration in each case.'[168]

Provisional Arrangements

In case various attempts to resolve a dispute have failed, parties may reach a *modus vivendi*, pending for instance the adoption by the UN General Assembly of a report of the ILC.[169] Although 'a *modus vivendi* implies

159 L. Marion, 'La notion', 356.

160 E.g. the *1969 North Sea Continental Shelf Case*: L. Marion, 'La notion', 358, notes 19 and 356. The *Lake Lanoux case* perfectly illustrates how the positions of the parties may fundamentally diverge on the mere existence of a *pactum de negotiando* or *de contrahendo*: 376.

161 *Pulp Mills case, I.C.J. Reports 2010,* Separate opinion by Judge Cançado Trindade, at p. 201, para. 174.

162 *Questions relating to the Obligation to Prosecute or Extradite (Belgium v. Senegal), Judgment, I.C.J. Reports 2012*, p. 422, Separate opinion by Judge Cançado Trindade, at p. 505, para. 43 and at pp. 505–08, paras. 44–51.

163 *Fisheries Jurisdiction (United Kingdom v. Iceland), I.C.J. Reports 1974*, at p. 35, para. 79 (4) (e).

164 *Anglo-Iranian Oil Co. Case, I.C.J. Reports 1951*, p. 89 at p. 92.

165 *Ibid.*, at p. 93.

166 Case *concerning the Arbitral Award made by the King of Spain on 23 December 1906, Judgment of 18 November 1960: I.C.J. Reports 1960*, p. 192 at p. 197 (Nicaragua). On the ICJ's attitude towards questions concerning different aspects of the international arbitration process see *inter alia* S. Rosenne, 'The International Court of Justice and International Arbitration', (1993) 6 *Leiden Journal of International Law*, 297–322.

167 *Nuclear Tests (Australia v. France), Interim Protection, Order of 22 June 1973, I.C.J. Reports 1973*, p. 99, at p. 104, para. 25 (Australia).

168 *Mavrommatis Palestine Concessions, P.C.I.J. Series A, No. 2, 1924*; *South West Africa Cases, I.C.J. Reports 1962*, at p. 346.

169 *Fisheries Jurisdiction (United Kingdom v. Iceland), I.C.J. Reports 1974*, at p. 11, para. 22.

the reservation and preservation of the legal positions of both Parties to the controversy',[170] it is 'an arrangement of a temporary and provisional nature concluded between subjects of international law which give[s] rise to binding obligations on the parties'.[171]

But even then when after a series of negotiations parties may have finally been able to conclude an interim agreement, this outcome does not exhaust their obligation to negotiate,[172] as is it '*provisional* pending the solution of the disagreement'.[173]

The Scope of the Obligation and the Functional Interaction

In some cases, 'an agreement includes concessions which are not motivated by reliance on international law',[174] while in other situations concessions may be made because of fear of 'possible further claims' and in return for a presumed guarantee that such claims 'could not be made unless the International Court found that they were legally warranted',[175] another indication of the functional interaction between the two modes of settlement.

Reasonable offers during negotiations may be followed by the insistence on more concessions by the other party and even a unilateral termination of the process by instituting proceedings before the Court, but this 'does not mean that agreement by negotiation was impossible and that all efforts in that direction should be abandoned'.[176]

An Application coupled with a request for the indication of provisional measures may reflect the Applicant's expectation that the Respondent would give way to its demands.[177]

The *Belgium Senegal case* illustrates the potential *functional role* of international negotiations as a mechanism to assist one party to a dispute to comply with the obligation which is at the very heart of the dispute between the parties.[178]

1.6 Content of the Obligation: Conduct of the Parties Prior to and During the Process of Negotiations

Conduct of the Parties Prior to the Start of the Process of Negotiations: The Functional Role of 'Pre-Negotiations'

International law, as other fields of study in international relations, can benefit from the attention paid in recent studies to pre-negotiation.[179]

---

170 *Fisheries case, I.C.J. Reports 1951*, Dissenting opinion by Judge Read, at p. 203.

171 W. Rudolf, 'Modus Vivendi' in R. Bernhardt (ed.) 1997, *Max Planck Encyclopaedia of Public International Law*, 442–4, at pp. 442–3.

172 *Fisheries Jurisdiction (United Kingdom v. Iceland), I.C.J. Reports 1974*, at p. 32, para. 76.

173 *Continental Shelf case between Tunisia and Libya, I.C.J. Reports 1982*, Dissenting opinion by Judge *ad hoc* Evensen, at p. 306. On the functional role of interim arrangements reached during the course of the proceedings see Chapter 6. The expression 'during the course of the proceedings in the case' means 'the period commencing at the moment on which a party files a valid document instituting the proceedings in the Registry and the case is entered in the General list, and ending with the final decision of the Court terminating the proceedings and removing the case from the General List': S.Rosenne, *Provisional Measures in International Law: The International Court of Justice and the International Tribunal for the Law of the Sea* (Oxford, 2005), p. 149.

174 *Gulf of Maine case, I.C.J. Reports 1984*, Dissenting opinion by Judge Gros, at p. 370, para. 16.

175 *Fisheries Jurisdiction (Federal Republic of Germany v. Iceland), I.C.J. Reports 1973*, Separate opinion by Judge Fitzmaurice, at p. 74, para. 10.

176 *Fisheries Jurisdiction (United Kingdom v. Iceland), Jurisdiction of the Court, Judgment, I.C.J. Reports 1973*, p. 3, Dissenting opinion by Judge Padilla Nervo, at p. 45.

177 *Fisheries Jurisdiction (United Kingdom v. Iceland), I.C.J. Reports 1973*, p. 3, Dissenting opinion by Judge Padilla Nervo, at p. 46. See generally K. Oellers-Frahm, 'Use and abuse of Interim Protection before International Courts and Tribunals' in H. Hestermeyer (ed.), *Coexistence, Cooperation And Solidarity: Liber Amicorum Rüdiger Wolfrum* (2 vols, Leiden, 2012), vol. 2, pp. 1685–705.

178 *Belgium v. Senegal, I.C.J. Reports 2009*, at p. 145, para. 29 (Senegal).

179 W. Zartman, *Negotiation and Conflict Management*, p. 127.

Essentially, 'prenegotiation is the span of time and activity in which the parties move from conflicting unilateral solutions for a mutual problem to a joint search for cooperative multilateral or joint solutions'.[180]

Pre-negotiations 'may often begin as part of the general activity of day-to-day diplomatic, interaction', diplomatic démarches, protests etc.; they may be performing a sequence of functions: first to 'identify a problem that needs to be solved', then 'to determine whether or not the time is ripe to open formal negotiations' and 'to refine the joint definition of the problem to be solved'. Thus formal *negotiations* may be 'preceded by *informal explorations* that lay the foundation for negotiations'.[181]

Negotiations often collapse 'because the parties have not prepared sufficiently ahead of time during the pre-negotiation stage'.[182] Hence, 'effective use of *prenegotiation* preparations may significantly differentiate successful from unsuccessful negotiations'.[183]

The absence of normal diplomatic and consular relations may in the view of one party render any proposal for negotiation futile, but this state of affairs may not have prevented regular and frequent meetings between the representatives of the two countries at all levels, as part of a regional peace process.[184]

The Court may very well assess the conduct of parties during a short period of time until one of them proposed negotiations on maritime delimitation.[185] The proposal to start negotiations brings to an end a period of time during which conduct of the parties could have been relevant to some extent but in the end the period was too short and not sufficient for the Court to conclude that there was an established international maritime boundary between the two States.

Conduct of the Parties during the Process of Negotiations

The content of the obligation to negotiate is not uniform but varies in its consistency and volume of ensuing duties depending on the circumstances of each particular situation.[186]

When States have committed themselves to negotiate they have taken upon themselves an obligation to open the process and to conduct themselves accordingly as negotiators. That is what Reuter called *the minimum content*, whereas the *maximum limit* of the obligation is that the parties are not obliged to conclude a treaty.[187]

In contrast to negotiations aiming at the codification of international law, where attempts may not have gone 'beyond the stage of proposals',[188] negotiations as a mechanism for the peaceful settlement of disputes do imply a similar stage of tabling various proposals, but the overall process is even more rigorously subject to the conditions the ICJ has determined with regard to *the proper conduct of negotiations in general* and which have become classical now: *the content of the obligation* for States is that they have to:

> enter into negotiations with a view to arrive at an agreement, and not merely to go through a formal process of negotiation ... they are under an obligation so to conduct themselves that the negotiations are meaningful, which will not be the case when either of them insists upon its own position without contemplating any modification of it ... .[189]

---

180 W. Zartman, *Negotiation and Conflict Management*, p. 119.

181 T. Hopmann, *The Negotiation Process*, p. 175 (emphasis added).

182 W. Zartman, 'Process and Stages', p. 96.

183 T. Hopmann, *The Negotiation Process*, p. 180 (emphasis added).

184 *Armed Activities on the Territory of the Congo (New Application: 2002) (Democratic Republic of the Congo v Rwanda), Provisional Measures, Order of 10 July 2002, I.C.J. Reports 2002*, p. 219, at p. 236, para. 44 (Rwanda's reply to an argument of the DRC).

185 *Territorial and Maritime Dispute between Nicaragua and Honduras in the Caribbean Sea (Nicaragua v. Honduras), Judgment, I.C.J. Reports 2007*, p. 659, at p. 736, para. 256.

186 P. Reuter, 'De l'obligation de négocier', 715.

187 P. Reuter, 'De l'obligation de négocier', 716 and 719.

188 *Fisheries case, Judgment of 18 December 1951, I.C.J. Reports 1951*, p. 116, at p. 131.

189 *North Sea Continental Shelf case, I.C.J. Reports 1969*, at p. 47, para. 85. The argument that a party is entitled to maintain by means of negotiations what it considers to be its right (Colombian-*Peruvian Asylum case, Judgment of 20 November 1950: I.C.J. Reports 1950*, p. 266, Dissenting opinion by Judge Badawi Pasha, at p. 315) seems at first glance

The Court may not fail to observe that a party was 'consulted during the negotiations for its independence ... and [that at] no time did it suggest ... that the frontiers there remained to be delimited'.[190] Thus there certainly is a high duty of vigilance for any party when during negotiations it is being consulted to express its opinion on all relevant matters and issues before it, as this case further illustrates.[191]

Unless the (legal) framework for the process has been established by an agreement between the parties or by the Court they are free to decide on the *format and content* of the process, the *object and purpose* of which 'must be fully compatible with the principles and norms of international law'.[192]

Apart from the obligation to negotiate in good faith, and to which we turn shortly, relevant duties for the parties include engaging 'the States whose vital interests are directly affected by the matter in question'.[193] When obligations *erga omnes* are at stake, this means taking into account the legal interests of the other members of the international society of States. These principles and guidelines as formulated by the UN General Assembly and the doctrinal views on the principle of good faith to be discussed shortly will find their judicial expression in the Court's case law.

One should also be aware that the '"correct" solution of a dispute normally exists independently of, and is unaffected by the conduct of the parties in the course of reaching a settlement of it'.[194]

We will address the impact of the position of third States when parties are negotiating during the course of the proceedings (Chapter 6), and we will review the (dys)functional role for actual or potential future negotiations with third States on both the judicial settlement of the pending dispute (Chapter 7) and in the post-adjudicative phase(Chapter 8).

It is sufficient at this stage to recall that during a 'bargaining process' States 'seek to recruit supporters for their various claims'.[195] States 'may try to raise third party interests that will be affected by the outcome of their dispute to add weight to their own claims'.[196] However, 'when the decision is made to resort to adjudication or arbitration these third party interests are minimized, and the dispute is presented before the tribunal as bilateral'.[197]

One should acknowledge three different categories of *third parties to a case*, or *le tiers à l'instance.*

There is first of all, and rather important from the negotiation part of the functional interaction perspective, '*le tiers cooperative* lorsqu'il propose ses services et "tiers *coopérant*" lorsque son offre est acceptée'.[198]

Secondly there is, from the adjudication part of the fonctional perspective '"le *tiers intervenant*" qui vient ... *devant* la juridiction internationale solliciter ou revendiquer le droit d'intervenir et puis, le cas échéant, faire valoir des "vues" qu'il faudra qualifier juridiquement, en bref, un intérêt juridique'.[199]

And finally there is, from both aspects of the functional interaction perspective, '"*le tiers absent"* qui est directement ou indirectement, juridiquement intéressé au différend et à la solution du litige'.[200]

---

rather difficult to reconcile with the Court's *dictum*, but will almost certainly be put forward when the very existence of a right is the heart of the matter between the parties.

190 *Land and Maritime Boundary case, I.C.J. Reports 2002*, at pp. 341–2, para. 52.

191 *Ibid.*, at p. 408, para. 210 (Cameroon). See also *Land, Island and Maritime Frontier Dispute (El Salvador/Honduras: Nicaragua intervening), Judgment of 11 September 1992, I.C.J. Reports 1992*, p. 351, Separate opinion by Judge *ad hoc* Torres Bernardez, at p. 708, para. 167.

192 General Assembly Resolution 53/101, Principles and Guidelines for International Negotiations, para. 2 (c).

193 Ibid., para. 2 (b).

194 H. Thirlway, 'The Law and Procedure of the International Court of Justice 1960–1989: Part Four' (1992) 63 *British Yearbook of International Law*, 1–96, at 7.

195 C. Chinkin, *Third Parties in International Law* (Oxford, 1993), p. 148.

196 C. Chinkin, *Third Parties*, p. 148.

197 C. Chinkin, *Third Parties*, p. 148. On the role of third parties see generally also H. Ruiz-Fabri and J.-M. Sorel (eds), *Le tiers à l'instance devant les jiuridictions internationales* (Paris, 2005).

198 E. Lagrange, 'Le tiers à l'instance devant les juridictions internationales à vocation universelle (CIJ et TIDM)', in H. Ruiz-Fabri and J.-M. Sorel (eds), *Le tiers à l'instance devant les juridictions internationales*, pp. 9–72, at p. 10.

199 E. Lagrange, 'Le tiers', pp. 10–11.

200 E. Lagrange, 'Le tiers', p. 11.

The Decision to Start the Process

Although 'negotiations must be carried out in good faith' once such an obligation exists, the 'principle of good faith alone does not impose an obligation to enter into negotiations'.[201]

Factors that may 'change [a] state's perception of when it might benefit from negotiating [an] agreed solution to a problem' could include 'an event in the international environment', 'a domestic change', being locked in a 'hurting stalemate' and recognition of non pre-existing opportunities.[202]

There certainly 'is a threshold beyond which a conflict reaches such an intense and painful level that it becomes obvious to everyone that a compromise has to be found',[203] especially in conflict situations where considerations of 'legitimacy and morality underlie the decision to negotiate'.[204]

The turning point when the parties decide 'that negotiations towards a jointly agreeable outcome are realistic' may present itself 'before formal negotiations even begin, and often takes the form of a declaration or commitment to succeed in coming to an agreement, even before any details of that agreement are known'.[205]

The decision to start the process consists of a formal and public gesture indicating by the same token that a successful outcome is possible.[206]

It may happen that a party considers that negotiations on maritime delimitation should be undertaken through mixed commissions, but that in the 'interest of avoiding frictions between [the] two countries' such discussions should be 'postponed, in order to [a]wait the adequate moment to proceed with negotiations',[207] a point of view which was shared by the other party.[208]

Parties may subject the start or the resumption of negotiations to the fulfilment of particular preconditions such as, respectively, the implementation or the suspension of particular works.[209] The question may be raised whether the putting forward of such preconditions which one party must be aware are not acceptable to the other one does not come down, in practical if not in legal terms, to a refusal to enter into negotiations.

The 'Process' Nature of the Negotiations Influences the Parties' Conduct

States are under a dual duty: a positive one 'to maintain a constructive atmosphere' and a negative one 'to refrain from any conduct which might undermine' the process and its progress.[210] The seizure and detention of documents and data allegedly relating to one party's positions and strategies regarding a future process of negotiations 'manifestly distorts the character' of this process by placing that party 'at a considerable negotiating disadvantage'.[211]

The initial attitude taken by each of the parties from the moment they decide to enter into negotiations is not only of crucial importance for the chance of a successful outcome later on, but also when after a long period of negotiations still no agreement has been reached; this is bound to have an impact on their respective conduct.

Given the *time element* involved in any process of negotiation it cannot come as a surprise that States' attitudes may change during the course of the process. However, just 'as a shifting balance of power may affect the durability of any negotiated settlement, so too may changes in norms',[212] as the *Gacbcikovo case* has amply demonstrated.

---

201 M. Rogoff, 'The Obligation to Negotiate', 155.

202 T. Hopmann, *The Negotiation Process*, p. 177.

203 G. Faure, 'Deadlocks in Negotiation Dynamics' in W. Zartman and G. Faure (eds), *Escalation and Negotiation in International Conflicts* (Cambridge, 2005), pp. 23–52, at p. 37.

204 G. Blum and R.Mnookin, 'When *Not* to Negotiate', p. 106.

205 W. Zartman, 'Negotiations: Theory and Reality', 74.

206 P. Reuter, 'De l'obligation de négocier', 717.

207 *Territorial and Maritime Dispute between Nicaragua and Honduras, I.C.J. Reports 2007*, at p. 679, para. 53.

208 *Ibid.*, at pp. 679–80, para. 54.

209 *Gabcikovo case, I.C.J. Reports 1997*, at pp. 57–8, para. 90.

210 General Assembly Resolution 53/101, Principles and Guidelines for International Negotiations, para. 2 (e).

211 *Questions Relating to the Seizure and Detention of Certain Documents and Data (Timor-Leste v. Australia)*, CR 2014/1, pp. 16–17, para. 3 (Timor-Leste).

212 A. Guelke, 'Negotiations and Peace Processes', p. 76.

The suggested weakness of a process approach towards rival territorial claims – implying an 'evolution' in the attitude of the rival 'claimants',[213] does not seem to apply more generally to dispute settlement oriented negotiations.

A State may, for instance, give the impression that, 'subject to minor modifications', a draft was acceptable while subsequently asking 'for a number of fairly substantial alterations' touching fundamental points of principle and therefore being unacceptable to the other party.[214]

It remains to be seen when perhaps unexpectedly a deadlock or failure of the process occurs if the Court will, unless explicitly invited to do so by the submissions of (one of) the parties,[215] see a need to explore whether such conduct by either of the parties was the direct cause of the (temporary) unsuccessful outcome of the process.

The perception that both parties 'are within range of each other' may arise 'during the negotiations after the sessions have already begun with' no guarantees 'between the parties'; this turning point is the 'threshold of seriousness'.[216]

Negotiations do not take place in splendid isolation from the overall international relations between the parties – such as 'deep mutual mistrust' between them 'for may years'[217] – and are (constantly) being influenced by developments and events occurring in related areas of interest; for instance a formal meeting of a Mixed Commission of delimitation for the purpose of winding up its work may not be held because the attention of both countries was directed towards the conclusion of another treaty which in fact situates former frontier areas wholly in the territory of one party.[218]

Making 'acceptance of an agreement contingent upon some change in the behaviour of the other parties with regard to issues having no direct bearing on the negotiations'[219] does not seem to be in conformity with the good faith requirement governing the process from start to finish.

Once a dispute has been resolved through a successful process of negotiations, parties 'often express regret that it took them so long to get to the bargaining table',[220] but of course the 'mere existence of normative elements as part of a negotiated settlement does not guarantee their success, as the examples of Rwanda and Sierra Leone in the 1990s underline'.[221]

Negotiate in Good Faith: What Does it Require from the Parties?

In international law good faith is 'a normative and general principle of international law'.[222] Hence the presumption and the requirement of good faith are the basis for both the negotiation process and the implementation of the agreement reached to such an extent that it has to be acknowledged that 'to negotiate otherwise than in good faith is surely not to negotiate at all',[223] and good faith is 'consubstantial with the idea of negotiations'.[224]

---

213 H. Thirlway, 'The Law and Procedure of the International Court of Justice 1960–1989. Supplement, 2009: Parts Seven and Eight' (2009) 80 *British Yearbook of International Law*, 10–216, at 37.

214 *Interpretation Agreement between the WHO and Egypt, Advisory Opinion, I.C.J. Reports 1980*, at p. 83, para. 24.

215 Application by Slovakia to request an additional judgment after the Gabcikovo 1997 judgment: ICJ Press Release 1998/28, para. 1.

216 A. Lall, Modern *International Negotiation*, pp. 74 and 76.

217 *Gabcikovo case, I.C.J. Reports 1997*, Separate opinion by Judge Bedjaoui, at p. 134, para. 53. See further on the various factors here R. Bilder, 'An Overview', 18, note 30. The impact and effect of the seizure and detention of certain documents and data allegedly relating to one party's positions and strategies for future negotiations on that process is clear: 'Trust is lost, relations are poisoned'. *Case between Timor Leste and Australia*, CR.2014/3, p. 12, para. 3, Timor-Leste replying to a question raised by Judge Cancado Trindade.

218 *Temple of Preah Vihear case, I.C.J. Reports 1962*, at p. 20.

219 T. Hopmann, *The Negotiation Process*, p. 209.

220 G. Blum and R. Mnookin, 'When *Not* to Negotiate', p. 110.

221 A. Guelke', Negotiations and Peace Processes', p. 67.

222 *Interim Accord case, I.C.J. Reports 2011*, Dissenting opinion by Judge *ad hoc* Roucounas, at p. 730, para. 28.

223 *Ibid.*, at p. 731, para. 28 (referring to Thirlway).

224 *Ibid.* (referring to Kolb).

The duty of good faith under general international law may require parties to conduct themselves in relation to a disputed area in such a manner as to avoid causing harm to the interests of each other.[225]

It is interesting to note that such duty also flows from the duties of good faith and cooperation owed by States before the Court, the cooperational duties mentioned earlier.[226]

The duty to negotiate in good faith is 'firmly rooted in general international law'.[227] Hence, an express requirement of good faith is not necessary as this obligation may be implicit in a particular provision on negotiations between the States Parties.[228]

Necessary Preconditions

The evident precondition for any round of negotiations to be potentially successful is that the parties have to take the necessary measures in order to create a climate that is conducive to the holding of the negotiations in the first place. This is for instance confirmed by the Security Council when acting under Chapter VI of the Charter it urges two governments 'to do everything in their power to reduce the present tensions in the area so that the negotiating process may be facilitated'.[229] Conversely, parties may expect a Security Council resolution to 'clear away the obstacles to a resumption of the dialogue'.[230]

According to negotiation scholars, State practice confirms the 'view that renunciation of the use of force is not [a] necessary prerequisite for negotiations, nor does the absence of such a renunciation necessarily nullify the willingness of countries to negotiate'.[231]

Notwithstanding their obligations under the Charter, 'parties (may) feel they should have recourse to arms at any moment in the event that negotiations prove unsuccessful'.[232]

'The determination to use force unless the other side shows some signs of submission does not, therefore, preclude negotiation', but it cannot be 'total or exclusive adherence' to such determination.[233]

From an international law perspective, although situating itself in the process of negotiations between a State and a non-state entity[234] and taking place under the aegis of the UN with a third State as *facilitator*, a commitment by both parties 'not to use force or the threat of force during the peaceful settlement negotiations'[235] is an imperative pre-existing *ius cogens* obligation when it comes to inter-state negotiations.

When during periods of bilateral negotiations over a dispute accusations and counter-accusations over incursions are being exchanged,[236] the question may be raised whether the mere occurrence of such incidents is compatible with the duty of conducting the negotiations in good faith and the generally desirable conduct by both parties during such a period of negotiations.

Although 'accusations and replies' on particular issues could 'attest to the existence of a dispute' between the parties 'on a subject-matter capable of falling' within the scope of the treaty concerned, the Court made it perfectly clear that they do not necessarily demonstrate 'an attempt at negotiating these matters'.[237]

---

225 *Questions of the Delmitation of the Continental Shelf beyond 200 Nautical Miles from the Nicaraguan Coast (Nicaragaua v. Colombia),* Application of Nicaragua, dated 16 September 2013, p. 6, para. 11 (e) (text available on the Court's website).

226 *Ibid.*

227 *Pulp Mills case, I.C.J. Reports 2010*, Separate opinion by Judge Greenwood, at p. 225, para. 16.

228 *Interim Accord case, I.C.J. Reports 2011*, at p. 684, para. 131.

229 *Aegean Sea Continental Shelf case, I.C.J. Reports 1976*, p. 3, at p. 12, para. 38.

230 *Ibid.*, at p. 12, para. 40 (Greece).

231 A. Lall, *Modern International Negotiation*, p. 41.

232 A. Lall, *Modern International Negotiation*, p. 44.

233 A. Lall, *Modern International Negotiation*, p. 41. We will return to prior negotiations in times of armed conflict in Chapter 3.

234 Scheduled meetings may be cancelled 'due to differences between the parties on the mode of negotiations', more in particular the precise moment of a non-state party becoming involved in the process: *CERD case, I.C.J. Reports 2011*, Separate opinion by Judge Simma, at p. 205, para. 33.

235 *CERD case, I.C.J. Reports 2011*, at p. 91, para. 46.

236 *Territorial and Maritime Dispute between Nicaragua and Honduras, I.C.J. Reports 2007*, at p. 681, para. 58.

237 *CERD case, I.C.J. Reports 2011*, at p. 139, para. 181.

Parties' Perception of Changing Attitudes

It may be useful for parties 'to be clear and firm about one's commitments and fundamental interests at the outset, and then to remain flexible and even soften one's position during the course of negotiations through various concessions'.[238] Furthermore, 'concessions are most effective if they are reciprocated immediately, producing a sequence of mutual concessions that tends to converge towards the middle of the available bargaining space between the resistance points of the two parties'.[239]

The 'key to problem solving' and the best approach to the negotiating process is for each party to 'be unconditionally constructive', 'firmly but conciliatory', and this in a 'pattern of mutual responsiveness'.[240]

Although 'movements and reversals of positions' could be 'expressions of attempts by the two sides to maximize the response of the other side' and such 'tactics are of the essence of negotiation' they may lead 'to accusations of bad faith' and doubts 'about the sincerity of the negotiating process'.[241]

A party's announcement at a press conference that 'its approaches toward the negotiation process will undergo substantial change'[242] may constitute an expression of that party's subsequent unwillingness to continue negotiations on particular matters.

Conduct of one party may be considered by the other party not only as destroying the 'existing format of negotiations' but also as 'irresponsible actions' which are 'capable of ruling out any possibility of peaceful settlement of conflicts'.[243]

A response calling a domestic parliamentary initiative 'provocative' and 'counter-productive' is likely to be seen as an indication 'that there is no political will to "defreeze" the conflict resolution process'.[244]

In a maritime delimitation dispute, a party may decide to 'not publicly assert or enforce its claim' beyond a previously published line 'pending the then current negotiations' as a gesture of good will in order not to endanger the ongoing negotiations, in spite of the fact that as a result of an arbitral award rendered in a completely different case between two different parties it had decided to adjust its original claim.[245]

Making this claim public just under a year later may then give rise to the objection by the other party that 'expansion' of the claim 'in the midst of negotiations was not in keeping with' pre-existing conventional obligations.[246]

Some Doctrinal Views on the Good Faith Requirement

As soon as parties have taken the decision to start negotiations towards the conclusion of a treaty and from the moment they actually enter into the process, their conduct carries with it certain legal effects,[247] as the pre-conventional contacts are governed by the principle of good faith.[248]

They not only have to accomplish in good faith the series of acts which together constitute the agreements' conclusion, but they also have to abstain from any action which later on would prejudice the execution of the envisaged treaty,[249] for instance by defeating its object and purpose.

238 T. Hopmann, *The Negotiation Process*, p. 188.

239 T. Hopmann, *The Negotiation Process*, p. 188.

240 According to Pruitt and Rubin Fischer referred to by T. Hopman, *The Negotiation Process*, p. 192 and according to Fischer referred to at p. 193.

241 A. Lall, *Modern International Negotiation*, p. 299.

242 *CERD case, I.C.J. Reports 2011*, at p. 138, para. 177.

243 Russian letter sent to the President of the Security Council as cited by Judge Simma in his Separate opinion, *CERD case, I.C.J. Reports 2011*, at p. 202, para. 27.

244 Georgian letter sent to the President of the Security Council as cited by Judge Simma in his Separate opinion, *ibid.*, at pp. 206–7, para. 35.

245 *Gulf of Maine case, I.C.J. Reports 1984*, at p. 284, para. 71.

246 *Ibid.*, at p. 286, para. 74.

247 J.-P. Cot, 'La bonne foi et la conclusion des traités' (1968) 4 *Revue Belge de Droit International* 1, 140–59, at 141.

248 R. Kolb, 'Aperçu sur la bonne foi en droit international public' (2001) 54 *Revue Hellénique de Droit International* 1, 1–42, at 22. See also note 82, at 22 for the Swiss amendment to that effect during the Vienna Conference on the Law of Treaties.

249 J.-P. Cot, 'La bonne foi', 141.

The ILC's recommendation 'extending the obligation to refrain from acts which would defeat the object and purpose of an eventual negotiated agreement to the negotiating phase'[250] and not requiring States to take positive action[251] was not adopted at the Vienna Conference.[252] This does not rule out that substantive obligations on negotiating States may nevertheless 'be imposed by customary international law or by general principles of law applicable to the relations between States'.[253]

The principles of good faith and of abuse of rights are prime candidates in this regard; rules sanctioning violations of these principles during the process of negotiations would suffice.[254]

The general law principle of good faith requires States first to conduct themselves in a loyal and reasonable manner; secondly they should not hide behind equivocal formulations in order later to benefit from the text's ambiguity.[255] Furthermore, abuse of rights 'may be seen as precluding a State from taking any action which would frustrate the *purposes of negotiations*'.[256]

Giving serious consideration to proposals tabled by the other party is an important part of the loyal and reasonable conduct required by '*substantive good faith*'[257] whereas '*procedural good faith*'[258] requires *inter alia* the willingness to compromise[259] and in case of deadlock further negotiation.[260]

State practice gave rise to a number of directives or guidelines parties to the process should endeavour to follow, 'such as to honour partial agreements, to maintain flexibility, to be willing to make concessions on basis of reciprocity'.[261]

It is indeed 'simple-minded to imagine that one can receive concessions in a negotiation to settle a dispute without giving something in return'.[262] However, in this last respect it should be recalled that the 'norm of reciprocity fails to consider the relative fairness of the initial positions of the parties'.[263]

It is well recognized that negotiations 'require more than a mere exchange of information or even consultation'. Indeed, it is only 'if the two sides submit statements as to the merits of the dispute [that] can one speak of negotiations in the sense contemplated' in Article 33 of the UN Charter. The duty to negotiate 'with an open mind cannot be equated with a duty to abandon one's own position if that position is firmly grounded on law'.[264]

---

250 M. Rogoff, 'The Obligation to Negotiate', 146.

251 J.-P. Cot, 'La bonne foi', 155.

252 On the ILC's initial draft proposals see *inter alia* E. Zoller, *La bonne foi*, pp. 54–7 and T. Hassan, 'Good Faith in Treaty Formation' (1981) 21 *Virginia Journal of International Law* 1, 443–81 at 467–76.

253 M. Rogoff, 'The Obligation to Negotiate', 146.

254 J.-P. Cot, 'La bonne foi', 158. A State may start arbitration proceedings in order 'to set aside, avoid or have declared invalid or otherwise not binding upon it' a treaty which it has concluded 'on the ground, in substance, that' the other State Party 'was obliged to, but did not negotiate the treaty or treaties in *good faith*': *Questions Relating to the Seizure and Detention of Certain Documents and Data (Timor-Leste v. Australia), Request for the Indication of Provisional Measures, Order of 3 March 2014, I.C.J. Reports 2014*, Dissenting opinion by Judge *ad hoc* Callinan, para. 5 (emphasis added).

Interestingly enough, the example given by the Special Rappporteur Sir Humphrey Waldock with regard to Article 18 as it stands now did refer to action undertaken 'during the negotiation': L. Boisson de Chazournes, A. La Rosa and M. Mbengue, 'Article 18' in P. Klein and O. Corten (eds), *The Vienna Convention on the Law of Treaties: A Commentary* (2 vols, Oxford, 2011),, vol. 1, pp. 369–404, at p. 383, para. 24. It should be added that 'good faith (sometimes) prompt[s] the States to act positively to uphold the object and purpose of the treaty concerned' already during the preceding negotiations: at p. 398, para. 62 (brackets added).

255 J.-P. Cot, 'La bonne foi', 146.

256 T. Hassan, 'Good Faith', 449 (emphasis added).

257 T. Hassan, 'Good Faith', 476.

258 T. Hassan, 'Good Faith', 478.

259 T. Hassan, 'Good Faith', 479.

260 T. Hassan, 'Good Faith', 480.

261 G. Geamanu, 'Théorie et Pratique', 412–13.

262 R. Kolb, *The ICJ*, p. 537.

263 Icklé as referred by C. Hutchinson, 'The Duty to Negotiate', 148, note 135.

264 C. Tomuschat, 'Article 33 UN Charter', in A. Zimmermann, C. Tomuschat, C. Tams and K. Oelllers-Frahm (eds), *The Statute of the International Court of Justice: A Commentary* (Oxford, 2012) Statute 2012, pp. 119–33, at p. 124, MN 17.

Observing the principle of good faith does not seem to entail that a particular position taken during a process of negotiations has to be maintained unchanged throughout the whole process; quite the contrary, as the judicial requirements will demonstrate. However, a certain degree of consistency will be necessary in order to prevent the invocation by the other party of estoppel, provided the other conditions for estoppel are being fulfilled (effective and good faith reliance by the other party on a particular declaration which has incited it to a particular conduct or position taken, a prejudice which would result from the first party modifying its initial position and a causal link between the initial position, the resulting action and the prejudice).[265]

Nevertheless, one of these conditions failing the position taken by one party 'may still be adduced in evidence as an admission to show a lack of consistency or weakness in a party's position'.[266] This may be called estoppel '*minus quam perfectum*'.[267]

An understanding between the parties that they will not invoke positions they have taken during the process of prior negotiations, especially in cases where the records are not in the public domain, to some extent rests on the same basis of public interest as the claims of non-disclosure of relevant material before the Court.[268]

Requirements According to Negotiation Scholars

Vague articulation of the duty to negotiate in good faith may have resulted in disputes having been protracted or having gone unresolved.[269] It is sufficient 'to acknowledge here that the more authoritative body of rules is available, in a particular branch of law, the more narrow the bounds within legal discourse can take place in *good faith*'.[270]

In fact at this point the two functions of negotiations do meet and inevitably interact: the creation of (new) primary rules for state conduct and the peaceful settlement of disputes.

Whether international law as such 'functions to facilitate or frustrate dispute resolution'[271] is a legitimate question, but it does not really concern us here.

Negotiation scholars may have identified some basic requirements for negotiations which taken as a whole may be described as 'ethics of dispute management';[272] the Court's approach by formulating judicial requirements for parties'conduct during the process undoubtedly has brought that basic code of conduct into the realm of law.[273]

Some of the 'many tactics available to negotiators to influence the process of bargaining' are in fact part of the conduct the ICJ requirements are aiming to govern: 'offers, demands, concessions, retractions, threats and promises'.[274]

---

265 R. Kolb, 'Aperçu sur la bonne foi en droit international public. Deuxième partie' (2001) 54 *Revue Hellénique de Droit International* 1, 383–428, at 387 and 389.

266 D. Bowett as cited by R. Kolb, 'Aperçu sur la bonne foi', 388.

267 R. Kolb, 'Aperçu sur la bonne foi', 388.

268 K. Keith, 'Naval Secrets, Public Interest Immunity and Open Justice' in K. Bannelier, T. Christakis and S. Heathcote (eds), *The ICJ and the Evolution of International Law: The Enduring Impact of the Corfu Channel Case* (London, 2012), pp. 124–46, at pp. 144–5. See further on this aspect Chapter 7.

269 C. Hutchinson, 'Coming in from the Shadow', 101.

270 C. Hutchinson, 'Coming in from the Shadow', 104.

271 C. Hutchinson, 'Coming in from the Shadow', 102.

272 K.Oellers-Frahm, 'Nowhere to Go?', 451.

273 By the same token, the Court's case law also seems to be able to dispel the unclarity about the distinction between good faith and a spirit of understanding and cooperation signalled by H. Thirlway, 'The Law and Procedure of the International Court of Justice 1960–1989: Part One' (1989), 60 *British Yearbook of International Law* 1–157, at 24, note 60. The judicial formulation of the basic requirements for parties to conduct themselves in such a way during the process of negotiations that they comply with their obligation to negotiate in good faith finds its counterpart, as indicated in this subparagraph, and to a surprisingly large extent in what negotiation scholars call 'minimum requirements': A. Lall, *Modern International Negotiation*, p. 288.

The checklist of 'seven precepts that should be followed in the pre-negotiation phase' does seem to apply to negotiations proper as well (Zartman and Berman as referred to by T. Hopmann, *The Negotiation Process*, pp. 178–9) and are in fact underlying the ICJ requirements.

274 T. Hopmann, *The Negotiation Process*, p. 180.

Running counter to this fundamental requitement is *inter alia* an attitude of obstruction: 'for example, by interrupting communications or causing delays in an unjustified manner[275] or [*unilaterally*] disregarding procedures agreed upon (*Lake Lanoux*)'[276] or insisting on their own positions, refusing to compromise on any point[277] or 'acts calculated to frustrate the object and purpose of the treaty' (containing the obligation).[278]

Also according to negotiation scholars, '[s]ome movement from original positions is necessary if there is to be even a measure of success in negotiation'.[279] In case 'moves are insufficient in relation to fundamental issues involved, there is no immediate possibility of *real* negotiations'.[280]

Although for a proper understanding of 'the processes and principles which underlie the movement of parties' one has to 'take into account the obvious tendency to maintain original positions as firmly as possible',[281] in a *bona fide* process of negotiations 'concessions are made, facts are accepted, compromises are worked out, admissions and apologies are offered. Documents embodying such acts may well be exchanged'; but it is important that 'all this should take place on a footing of openness and equality'.[282]

'Negotiation does not involve simply receiving the other party's output and sending back his new input in return.'[283] Parties 'must give evidence at some stage of the negotiations of a degree of willingness to make some movement, either apparent or real, from their original or starting positions'.[284]

Importantly, 'when one party continues adamant in spite of the movement of the other, the issue passes beyond the realm of negotiation, and conflict becomes a likely alternative'.[285]

Judicial Requirements of Good Faith as Reflected in the Court's Case Law

We are interested in the way judicial intervention by the Court actually provides parties to a process of negotiation with benchmarks, directions and guidelines on how to conduct themselves, irrespective of the subject-matter of the dispute dividing them.

Is it true that pursuant to the principle of good faith '[l]ittle substantive guidance has been offered beyond the concept of reasonableness'?[286]

The fundamental requirement is that parties should conduct themselves in such a way throughout the process, upon which they should embark without *a priori*,[287] that the negotiations are meaningful[288] – i.e. that parties 'are expected to negotiate with a view to reaching a settlement'[289] 'without however being obliged to reach an agreement' or 'to lead to a particular outcome'[290] as in international law, 'the commitment to negotiate does not entail an obligation to reach an agreement'.[291]

275 Although 'answers to proposals that are delayed far beyond what one would reasonably expect do not necessarily mean a refusal to move', they 'may indicate that the other party may face a lengthy decision-making process' (G. Faure, 'Deadlocks', 30).

276 *Interim Accord case, I.C.J.Reports 2011*, at p. 685, para. 132 (first emphasis added).

277 *Ibid.*, Dissenting opinion by Judge *ad hoc* Roucounas, at p. 730, para. 27 citing G. White.

278 *Pulp Mills case, I.C.J. Reports 2010*, Separate opinion by Judge Keith, at p. 127, para. 17. Parties disagreed on whether such an obligation of abstention from particular activities did exist under general international law or was a particular conventional one under their bilateral treaty: *I.C.J. Reports 2010*, at p. 68, para. 152 (Uruguay) and at p. 69, para. 153 (Argentina).

279 A. Lall, *Modern International Negotiation*, p. 288.

280 A. Lall, *Modern International Negotiation*, p. 288 (emphasis added).

281 A. Lall, *Modern International Negotiation*, p. 299.

282 *Land and Maritime Boundary between Cameroon and Nigeria, Preliminary Objections, Judgment, I.C.J. Reports 1998*, p. 275, Dissenting opinion by Judge Weeramantry, at p. 376.

283 A. Lall, *Modern International Negotiation*, p. 76.

284 A. Lall, *Modern International Negotiation*, p. 297.

285 A. Lall, *Modern International Negotiation*, pp. 296–7.

286 C. Hutchinson, 'Coming in from the Shadow', p. 103.

287 *Pulp Mills case, I.C.J. Reports 2010*, Separate opinion by Judge *ad hoc* Torres Bernardez, at p. 261, para. 92.

288 *Pulp Mills case, I.C.J. Reports 2010*, at p. 67, para. 146.

289 *Interim Accord case, I.C.J. Reports 2011*, Dissenting opinion by Judge *ad hoc* Roucounas, at p. 730, para. 27.

290 *Pulp Mills case, I.C.J. Reports 2010*, Separate opinion by Judge Greenwood, at p. 226, para. 16.

291 *Ibid.*, Separate opinion by Judge *ad hoc* Torres Bernardez, at p. 261, para. 92. In Chapter 3 we will address the question whether the obligation of (prior) negotiations is (un)limited.

According to negotiation scholars the intended impact of the Court's well-established requirements does form part of the 'effect of international law on the negotiating postures of countries'.[292]

We will see and find whether and how the Court's approach to the fundamental requirements it imposes, and which at the time of writing Lall detected as 'certain incipient trends', did indeed develop 'into principles which will sufficiently affect international relations'.[293]

Part of this development may be found in the Court finding it useful to recall that once negotiations were actually underway a recurring element in Security Council resolutions has been the emphasis on the crucial *importance of progress* in the negotiations and the call upon the parties 'to intensify their efforts to achieve an early and comprehensive political settlement'.[294]

Conversely, within the performance of its role in the peaceful settlement of a dispute between a State and a non-state entity such as a breakaway part of its territory the SC may in Guiding Principles addressed to an International Contact Group not only stress that a negotiated solution should be an international priority, but it may also add that once the process has started it cannot be blocked and must be brought to a conclusion, the final decision – i.e. the outcome of the negotiations to be endorsed by the SC. The Council may refer to Guiding Principles of a Contact Group which in turn call upon the good faith and constructive engagement of the parties.[295] In doing so the SC rallies itself with the content of the obligation to negotiate as confirmed by the ICJ. Furthermore, it not only determines in a non-flexible way the substantive parameters for the negotiations or the nature of the desirable outcome, but it also retains the final control of approval.

Further elaboration and refinement by the Court of its requirements in that the parties should duly take into account the legitimate interests and rights of the other party involved in the dispute perfectly reflects the cooperative approach towards dispute resolution when it takes place outside the courtroom, and seems to be based on what the negotiation scholars call the 'convergence approach'[296] through simple coincidence of initial positions, concessions, counter-concessions and compromise.[297]

Although in particular circumstances the principle of good faith 'may also require the temporary non-exercise of the rights asserted' or 'at least restraint in their exercise' this does not apply more generally.[298]

In 'the absence of the element of potentially irreversible damage, good faith may restrain only acts of deliberate provocation or attempts to establish a *fait accompli* capable of prejudicing the outcome of the negotiations'.[299]

The Court made it perfectly clear, admittedly at the stage of the indication of provisional measures, that if 'a State is engaged in the peaceful settlement of a dispute with another State through arbitration or negotiations, it would expect to undertake these arbitration proceedings or negotiations *without interference* by the other party in the preparation and conduct of its case'.[300]

---

292 A. Lall, *Modern International Negotiation*, p. 345.

293 A. Lall, *Modern International Negotiation*, p. 354.

294 *CERD case, I.C.J. Reports 2011*, at pp. 91–93, para. 48. For an early example of the Court referring to the General Assembly reminding parties of their obligation under peace treaties to cooperate in 'the settlement of the question' see *Interpretation of Peace Treaties, Advisory Opinion, I.C.J. Reports 1950*, p. 65, at p. 66.

295 *Kosovo Advisory Opinion, I.C.J. Reports 2010*, p. 403, at p. 431, para. 66.

296 W. Zartman, *Negotiation and Conflict Management*, p. 20.

297 W. Zartman, *Negotiation and Conflict Management*, pp. 21–22. Negotiation scholars have identified several ways of arriving at convergence: simple coincidence of initial positions, concessions, counter-concessions, compromise (pp. 21–2), although in analysing the progress or lack of it in a negotiating process, the Court, for obvious reasons, has to look at the *substantive arguments* parties have been putting forward during that process and to which they may have been referring during the proceedings, and this apart from their cooperational duties mentioned earlier.

The adversarial nature of adjudication – which varies of course depending on the way of seisin of the Court – is to some extent mitigated by the cooperation the parties have to exercise in order to contribute to an orderly progress of the proceedings, and this as part of the same cooperational duties.

298 H. Thirlway, 'The Law and Procedure of the International Court of Justice 1960–1989: Part One', at 23–4 referring to the *North Sea Continental Shelf case* and the *Fisheries Jurisdiction case* between the UK and Iceland.

299 H. Thirlway, 'The Law and Procedure of the International Court of Justice 1960–1989: Part One', at 23–4.

300 *Seizure of documents case, I.C.J.Reports 2014*, para. 27 (emphasis added). The use of the word 'interfere' in an operative paragraph of the Court's Order was considered problematic because of 'its breadth and unspecific nature': *ibid.*, Dissenting opinion by Judge *ad hoc* Callinan, para. 32. The Court will address this in more detail when dealing with the merits of the case.

A party is well justified to consider the seizure and detention of documents and data relevant to future negotiations as 'a violation of its right to communicate with its counsel and lawyers in a confidential manner with regard to issues forming the subject-matter' of that process.[301]

As far as post-adjudicative negotiations are concerned 'the readiness of the Parties to accept' assistance of a third party 'would be evidence of the good faith with which they conduct bilateral negotiations in order to give effect to the judgment of the Court'.[302]

Judicial Assessment of the Performance of the Good Faith Obligation

Although it is in most cases 'unlikely that issues involving the obligation to negotiate will be resolved by a judicial body'[303] the question still arises about the Court's assessment of the performance of the good faith obligation.

'En interprétant la portée de la négociation, le juge doit tenir compte des usages de la diplomatie, de ses préoccupations et de ses méthodes.'[304]

In examining a prior negotiation condition the Court's approach is not one of deference granting 'a certain margin of appreciation to a state within which the dispute resolver does not scrutinize the state's decision' and thus of judicial restraint.[305]

On the contrary, the Court while admitting that it is in the first instance for the parties to assess the need for and the (lack of) progress of their prior negotiations, in a judicially active way examines whether and to what extent the parties have fulfilled a conventional prior negotiation condition while maintaining, however, its unwillingness to determine whether the State invoking the clause had fulfilled that condition in good faith.

As to a claim that the other party has failed to comply with the legal obligation to negotiate, the Court will require 'a lower standard of proof for State responsibility to be incurred' because such an alleged violation originates in an omission.[306]

In the Great Hall of Justice parties will argue that they have shown 'openness to compromise' and that the other party has been 'intransigent'.[307]

It is not within the inherent jurisdiction of the Court to make *motu proprio* a judicial assessment of the parties' performance of this obligation. The jurisdictional clause must have endowed the Court with jurisdiction to examine the question whether the parties were engaged in good faith negotiations.[308]

In general with regard to good faith review the Court is not going beyond a 'touch and feel' type test.[309] The Court 'will be slow to assume an abuse of right in other than flagrant cases',[310] an abuse of right to be distinguished from good faith *stricto sensu*.[311]

301 *Ibid.*, para. 27 (Timor-Leste).

302 *Gabcikovo case, I.C.J. Reports 1997*, at p. 79, para. 143.

303 M. Rogoff, 'The Obligation to Negotiate', 172.

304 M. Bourquin, 'Dans quelle mesure le recours à des négociations diplomatiques est-il nécessaire avant qu'un différend puisse être soumis à la juridiction internationale?', in H. Accioly (ed.), *Hommage d'une génération de juristes au Président Basdevant* (Paris, 1960) pp. 43–55 at p. 52.

305 M. Schill and R. Briese, 'If the State Considers: Self-Judging Clauses in International Dispute Settlement' (2009) 13, *Max Planck Yearbook of United Nations Law*, 61–140, at 74. Judicial self-restraint has recently been described as 'l'art de ne rien faire': *Certain Activities carried out in the Border Area (Costa Rica v. Nicaragua); Construction of a Road in Costa Rica along the San Juan River (Nicaragua v. Costa Rica), Order of 16 July 2013, Provisional Measures, I.C.J. Reports 2013*, p. 230, Dissenting opinion by Judge Cançado Trindade, at p. 244, para.4.

306 Katherine del Mar, 'The International Court of Justice and Standards of Proof' in K. Bannelier, T. Christakis and S. Heathcote (eds), *The ICJ and the Evolution of International Law: The Enduring Impact of the Corfu Channel Case* (London, 2012), pp. 98–123 at p. 108.

307 *Interim Accord case, I.C.J. Reports 2011*, at p. 684, para. 129 (Macedonia).

308 *Ibid.*, at p. 684, para. 130.

309 M. Schill and R. Briese, 'If the State Considers', at 118.

310 H. Thirlway, 'The Law and Procedure of the International Court of Justice 1960–1989: Part One', at 28.

311 H. Thirlway, 'The Law and Procedure of the International Court of Justice 1960–1989. Supplement, 2005: Parts One and Two' (2005) 76 *British Yearbook of International Law*, 1–119, at 8.

It is however a sensible general point that 'a higher standard of good faith than normal is required when a sophisticated European State is engaged in negotiations with a newly independent State'.[312]

In order to find 'the existence of bad faith' on part of (one of) the parties '(a circumstance which would justify either party in claiming to be discharged from performance)' 'something more must appear than the failure of particular negotiations'[313] even after a period of 16 years.[314]

The Court made it perfectly clear that the (lack of) result obtained through the process of negotiations is not the standard to measure whether the obligation to negotiate has been undertaken in good faith.[315]

The Court must indeed 'consider whether the Parties conducted themselves in such a way that negotiations may be meaningful'[316] and this depends on the course of the negotiations, the abstention from actions which frustrated the process[317] and on the (lack of) contributions made by either of the parties to the process.

The seizure and detention of documents and data allegedly relating to one party's positions and strategies regarding a future process of negotiations 'violates fundamental principles governing the conduct of negotiations and litigation'.[318]

A letter by one of the parties claiming that the process had failed and that henceforth a dispute settlement procedure should become operational is important for determining when the process was effectively deadlocked and whether actions taken thereafter should not be taken into account in the judicial assessment about the obligation to negotiate in good faith: the end of the process also terminates the prohibition on frustrating actions.[319]

Circumstantial evidence could be submitted, but it should be 'supported' not by disputable inference but by clear and convincing evidence which compels 'a conclusion of bad faith'.[320]

Turning to the records, the Court may find that public statements by political leaders of both parties did raise concerns as they suggested 'an inflexible position', concerns which (may) have been alleviated by the view of a UN mediator that the parties were negotiating 'in earnest'.[321] The Court may duly note a degree of openness to and indication of an apparent change from proposals that differ from the initial positions taken by the parties.[322]

In the circumstances of the case the Court may conclude that the Respondent 'has not met its burden that the applicant breached its obligation to negotiate in good faith'.[323] The Court then may finally (re)emphasize that the governing accord 'places the Parties under a duty to negotiate in good faith' on the fundamental initial difference.[324]

The Court may come under criticism when its reasoning and conclusions give rise to the perception that it rewards the party who allegedly negotiated in bad faith.[325]

---

312 H. Thirlway, 'The Law and Procedure of the International Court of Justice 1960–1989. Supplement, 2005: Parts One and Two', at 8, commenting on Libya Chad 1994, p. 20, para. 36.

313 *Interim Accord case, I.C.J. Reports 2011*, at p. 685, para. 132.

314 *Ibid.*, at p. 685, para. 134.

315 *Ibid.*

316 *Ibid.*

317 *Pulp Mills case, I.C.J. Reports 2010*, Separate opinion by Judge Keith, at p. 130, para. 24.

318 *Seizure of documents case,* CR 2014/1, p. 25, para. 17 (Timor-Leste).

319 *Pulp Mills case, I.C.J. Reports 2010*, Separate opinion by Judge Keith, at pp. 130–31, para. 25.

320 *Interim Accord case, I.C.J. Reports 2011*, at p. 685, para. 132. See also in the same sense but in different circumstances *Whaling in the Antarctic (Australia v. Japan:New Zealand intervening), Judgment of 3 March 2014, I.C.J. Reports 2014*, Dissenting opinion by Judge Owada, para. 22 and Dissenting opinion by Judge Abraham, para. 29. In his Separate opinion Judge Greenwood did not consider that the Respondent 'has been shown to have acted in bad faith', as the statements invoked for that purpose by the Applicant did 'not suffice to make out a case of bad faith': para. 29. In passing, one could note that New Zealand's Declaration of intervention under Article 63, para. 2 is the first one which has been successful in the Court's case law: paras. 8 and 12.

321 *Interim Accord case, I.C.J. Reports 2011*, at p. 686, para. 135.

322 *Ibid.*, at p. 685, para. 135. See contra on this point Dissenting opinion by Judge *ad hoc* Roucounas, at p. 725, para. 11.

323 *Ibid.*, at p. 686, para. 138.

324 *Ibid.*, at p. 692, para. 166.

325 *Pulp Mills case, I.C.J. Reports 2010*, Dissenting opinion by Judge *ad hoc* Vinuesa, at p. 272, para. 20 and at pp. 274–5, para. 33. In different circumstances the Court may have been be criticized for seeing no need to address other

On the other hand the international society should not accept that bad faith of one of the parties during a process of negotiations could prevent an agreement intended to establish an important international status for a particular territory.[326]

As the process of negotiations is extending over a period of time, all kind of factors and events are most likely to influence the parties' conduct, and this works in diverging directions. So after years of negotiations a party may decide not to enforce a particular domestic law, 'in order to improve the prospects of negotiations'.[327]

It is also true that particular events or incidents are capable of enlarging the initial dispute to include other issues which 'only made the negotiations between the two Parties more arduous'.[328] The Court did not elaborate on whether such an impact would run counter to the good faith requirement.

Judges took divergent positions on the conformity with the duty to negotiate in good faith of actions undertaken by one of the parties during the course of the process.

Whereas 'the extremely *advanced preparation* of a "substitute solution" as leverage on negotiations with the partner' may 'not in itself in any way (be) unlawful',[329] steps taken by one party to carry out or authorize works which are the very subject of the ongoing negotiations, during a particular stage of a procedure provided for in a treaty, 'may be contrary to that duty'.[330]

One of the parties may however opt 'for a policy of "faits accomplis", having recourse to unilateral measures when the negotiations were still under way' and there was still an opportunity of an agreed solution.[331] In that respect the distinction between the construction of such a solution and its operation 'is purely artificial in the context of the pressure/negotiations relationship game'.[332]

Under the requirement of good faith parties should abstain from 'creating faits accomplis' which 'cannot but prejudice the outcome' of negotiations.[333]

Even when the breakdown of the negotiations is being invoked as a reason for substituting the final settlement through the resolution of the dispute by an agreement between the parties for a unilateral action,[334] the 'notion of a "final settlement" cannot mean anything else than the resolution of the dispute between the parties … either by an agreement reached between them. But the notion of a settlement is clearly incompatible with the unilateral step-taking by one of the parties aiming at the resolution of the dispute against the will of the other.'[335]

1.7 Inherent Link between the Subject-Matter of the Dispute and the Process of Negotiations

There is a clear connection between the quality, content of rights and obligations which are the subject-matter of a dispute and the appropriate means for their enforcement and settlement of a dispute, negotiations being only one of the means parties are free to choose.

The different nature of the issues involved flowing from a variety of subject-matters of various cases before the Court may require, for instance, a different approach of facts and evidence[336] and 'the nature of the legal problems which are to be solved' is one of the 'factors' which may 'have some impact on the

arguments invoked by the Applicant *inter alia* accusations of bad faith: *Whaling in the Antarctic (Australia v. Japan:New Zealand intervening), Judgment of 3 March 2014, I.C.J. Reports 2014*, Dissenting opinion by Judge Abraham, para. 28. The Court's review of a Respondent's conduct and the conclusions of its judgment may however 'entail a finding of bad faith which is not explicitly expressed': Dissenting opinion by Judge Yusuf, para. 54.

326 *International status of SWA, I.C.J. Reports 1950*, Dissenting opinion by Judge Alvarez, at p. 184.

327 *Gulf of Maine case, I.C.J. Reports 1984*, at p. 282, para. 66.

328 *Gulf of Maine case, I.C.J. Reports 1984*, at p. 283, para. 68.

329 *Gabcikovo case, I.C.J. Reports 1997*, Separate opinion by Judge Bedjaoui, at p. 132, para. 47 (emphasis added).

330 *Pulp Mills case, I.C.J. Reports 2010*, Separate opinion by Judge Greenwood, at pp. 225–6, para. 13.

331 *Gabcikovo case, I.C.J. Reports 1997*, Dissenting opinion by Judge Herczegh, at p. 191.

332 *Ibid.*, Dissenting opinion by Judge Ranjeva, at p. 173.

333 *Legal Consequences of the Construction of a Wall in the Occupied Palestinian Territory, Advisory Opinion, I.C.J. Reports 2004*, p. 136, Separate opinion by Judge al-Khasawneh, at p. 239, para. 13.

334 *Kosovo Advisory Opinion, I.C.J. Reports 2010*, Dissenting opinion by Judge Bennouna, at p. 509, para. 44.

335 *Ibid.*, Declaration by Judge Tomka, at p. 462, para. 28.

336 A. Riddell and B. Plant, *Evidence before the International Court of Justice* (London, 2009) p. 411.

orientation or on the contents of the decisions taken by the Court'[337] – but perhaps also on the functional role of negotiations.

During the phase of *diagnosis* (see Preliminary Chapter) the parties must 'consider and specify the issues to be covered, separating those that can be negotiated from those that can or must be left out'.[338] Conversely, during negotiations parties may focus on broader issues, but this does not exclude (one of) the parties to regard the issues which came before the Court as important.[339]

The almost unlimited variety of matters which constitute the daily areas of concern between States obviously implies that not all topics are of equal importance to them. It is inevitable that when issues in controversy belong to a 'very sensitive area of international relations' such as the one diplomatic protection has to deal with,[340] this may have an impact on the unfolding of the negotiation process. Examples clearly belonging to this rather sensitive area include territorial questions, use of force and exercise of criminal jurisdiction.

Given 'the potential for such disputes to escalate with destructive consequences for the States concerned',[341] subject areas such as territorial and maritime delimitation inherently carry with them the primordial need for a process of negotiation, the outcome of which 'is dictated by the relative bargaining power of the parties'.[342] Conversely, maritime disputes 'count, without doubt, amongst the most sensitive issues submitted by States to international adjudication'.[343]

However, one must duly note that although object and purpose of a bilateral treaty often 'follow clearly from its text' this should not be 'understood as meaning a comprehensive settlement of all questions regarding the actual course of the delimitations it establishes. In certain places, it sets forth only in broad lines where the delimitation of spheres of interests run but leaves the fixation of its course in detail to the future application of the Treaty.'[344]

With regard to the inherent link between the subject-matter and the process of negotiation, in the field of international relations, the word '"nonnegotiable" does not exist'. The 'word may correspond to the facts and circumstances at a given time' or 'to approaches toward one or another possible form of negotiation'.[345]

However, in international law some questions do have implications going far beyond the scope of any particular dispute (between two states), and therefore as being incapable of independent settlement between States.[346] Indeed, the high-ranking nature of particular subject-matters entails that they are considered to be *non-negotiable* and/or that a pre-existing obligation to negotiate has to be considered one of result and not merely of conduct. For instance, the 'discharge of international obligations, including *erga omnes* obligations cannot be made conditional upon negotiations'.[347]

In the punishment of genocide the Court has been endowed by the international community 'with a key role'. Hence, neither 'negotiation nor arbitration would be appropriate mechanisms for dealing with a dispute between States in this regard'. Indeed, the Court 'represents the only means of recourse against violations of a treaty'[348] and the admissibility of reservations to Article IX of the Convention cannot be regarded 'as a private affair to be settled between a pair of States'.[349]

---

337 P.-M. Dupuy, 'The Judicial Policy', p. 64.

338 W. Zartman, 'Process and Stages', p. 96.

339 *CERD case, I.C.J. Reports 2011*, Separate opinion by Judge Owada, at p. 177, para. 21.

340 *Barcelona Traction, Light and Power Company, Limited, Judgment, I.C.J. Reports 1970*, p. 3 at p. 33, para. 37.

341 *Land and Maritime Boundary case, I.C.J. Reports 2002*, Dissenting opinion by Judge Koroma, at p. 473, para. 1.

342 *Ibid.*, Declaration by Judge Oda, at p. 467, para. 26.

343 *Maritime dispute between Peru and Chile, I.C.J. Reports 2014*, Declaration by Judge Sepulveda-Amor, para. 18.

344 *Case between Botswana and Namibia, I.C.J. Reports 1999*, p. 1045, Dissenting opinion by Judge Fleischhauer, at p. 1200, para. 5.

345 A. Lall, *Modern International Negotiation*, p. 131.

346 *South West Africa cases, I.C.J. Reports 1962*, Joint dissenting opinion by Judges Spender and Fitzmaurice, at pp. 551–2.

347 *Wall Advisory Opinion, I.C.J. Reports 2004*, Separate opinion by Judge Al-Khasawneh, at pp. 238–9, para. 13.

348 *DRC v. Rwanda case, I.C.J. Reports 2002*, Separate opinion by Judge *ad hoc* Mavungu, at pp. 287–8, para. 58 (citing Imbert).

349 *Reservations to the Convention on Genocide, Advisory Opinion, I.C.J. Reports 1951*, p. 15, Joint dissenting opinion by Judges Guerrero, McNair, Read and Hsu Mo, at p. 45 (iv). Negotiations taking place during the proceedings in the *Pakistani POW case* and giving rise to the postponement of the request for provisional measures were focused on the

Other closely related matters also possessing a paramount human dimension may still, for the time being, be suited for a process of negotiation but not without the modifications required, such as the States concerned acknowledging 'the human dimension' of a contentieux between them.[350]

As a result of the humanization of the international legal order this will increasingly become the case affecting the way negotiations have to be conducted, for instance by demanding an extra effort of the parties with regard to their willingness to find a compromise, although certainly not necessarily a longer period to find a solution.[351]

In a number of cases the 'concrete situation of the individuals directly affected' is one of predominant elements, and 'not merely abstract issues of exclusive interest of the litigating States in their relations *inter sese*'.[352]

The lack of *locus standi in judicia* for individuals[353] could then be an additional factor ideally affecting the functional interaction as a whole. That is to say, during inter-state negotiations States cannot waive claims on behalf of human beings as they are the bearers of the rights allegedly violated.[354] Such a waiver would be 'against the international *ordre public*' and would, in case of crimes against humanity committed by States, be 'in breach of *ius cogens*'.[355]

Under treaties of this kind, 'singling out the predominance of considerations of general interest(or even *ordre public*), transcending the individual interest of States Parties there 'is no space' for 'unilateral state action, or even for bilateral reciprocal concessions'.[356]

A matter of jurisdictional immunities finding its factual origin in violations of human rights and international humanitarian law cannot be approached from a strictly inter-state dimension:[357] the regime of reparation 'would exhaust itself at the inter-state level'.[358]

Although the 'existence of a wider dispute between the parties' must be borne in mind, proposals on that dispute does not rule out the 'possibility that it may also (perhaps even in the same document) be offering to negotiate' on the narrower dispute, but such an offer must be clearly discernible.[359] That during negotiations parties may focus on broader issues does not exclude (one of) the parties regarding the issues which came before the Court as important.[360]

---

question of the exercise of jurisdiction under Article VI, and not on matters of substance in connection with accusations of genocide. Because of the lack of urgency the Court held that there was no longer a request for provisional measures; later on the case was removed from the docket in order to facilitate negotiations.

350 *Belgium v. Senegal case, I.C.J. Reports 2009*, Dissenting opinion by Judge Cançado Trindade, at p. 177, para. 31.

351 *Belgium v. Senegal case, I.C.J. Reports 2012*, Dissenting opinion by Judge Cançado Trindade, at pp. 505–8, paras. 43–51; at p. 519, para. 83; and at p. 550, para. 159.

352 *Judgment No 2867 of the Administrative Tribunal of the International Labour Organization upon a Complaint filed against the International Fund for Agricultural Development, Advisory Opinion, I.C.J. Reports 2012*, p. 10, Separate opinion by Judge Cançado Trindade, at p. 57, para. 19.

353 *ILOAT Judgment Advisory Opinion, I.C.J. Reports 2012*, Separate opinion by Judge Cançado Trindade, at pp. 87–8, paras. 102–3.

354 *Jurisdictional Immunities of the State (Germany v. Italy), Counter-Claim, Order of 6 July 2010, I.C.J. Reports 2010*, p. 310, Dissenting opinion by Judge Cançado Trindade, at p. 373, para. 114.

355 *Germany v. Italy case, I.C.J.Reports 2010*, Dissenting opinion by Judge Cançado Trindade, at p. 377, para. 124 and at p. 396, para. 178.

356 *Whaling in the Antarctic (Australia v. Japan), Declaration of Intervention of New Zealand), Order of 6 February 2013, I.C.J. Reports 2013*, p. 3, Separate opinion by Judge Cançado Trindade, at p. 34, paras. 56–7.

357 *Jurisdictional Immunities of the State (Germany v. Italy), Application for Permission to Intervene, Order of 4 July 2011, I.C.J. Reports 2011*, p. 494, Dissenting opinion by Judge Cançado Trindade, at p. 530, para. 60.

358 *Germany v. Italy case, I.C.J. Reports 2012*, Dissenting opinion by Judge Cançado Trindade, at p. 269, para. 252. See also for instance H. Moser, 'Restitution Negotiations: The Role of Diplomacy' (2002), 20 *Berkeley Journal of International Law*, 196–201 at 200.

359 *CERD case, I.C.J. Reports 2011*, Separate opinion by Judge Greenwood, at p. 328, para. 13.

360 *Ibid.*, Separate opinion by Judge Owada, at p. 177, para. 21.

Chapter 2
A First Visit to the Functional Interaction between Negotiations and Adjudication by the Court as Mechanisms for the Peaceful Settlement of Disputes

Introduction

The focus in recent legal writings on peaceful settlement of disputes (PSD) has been shifting from a rather piecemeal approach of every single method towards the interaction between the various modes and mechanisms.[1] But also state practice indicates that certain categories of disputes such as territorial ones may require 'an approach that brings together a number of' various methodologies of peaceful settlement,[2] while the Court itself has clearly stated that for parties there is always the possibility 'to have recourse to a conjunction of judicial determination and settlement by agreement'.[3]

The President of the Court has persuasively made the point that 'the adjudication method is not necessarily an independent one and can very well be used as a complement to others such as negotiation'.[4] Indeed, settlement of a dispute does not necessarily constitute a 'single operation' but may be or become a process of which adjudication is part.[5] Indeed, the Court's procedure:

> is beginning to be seen as a resort to be employed in a closer relationship with normal diplomatic negotiation. No longer is resort to the International Court of Justice seen, to use the traditional phrase, as a 'last resort' when all negotiation has finally failed. Rather, it is sometimes now to be seen as a recourse that might usefully be employed at an earlier stage of the dispute.[6]

The case law since President Jennings' speech seems to confirm this trend.

This way, 'judicial findings of fact and rulings of law may define the bounds of constructive negotiation'. That is also the reason why in assessing the Court's work also those cases 'which, at a certain stage of the proceedings, have become ripe for and resulted in negotiated settlements' should be taken into account.[7]

---

1 J. Merrills, *International Dispute Settlement*, p. 125. Also the continuum and integrated approach are manifestations of this recent development.

2 M. Shaw, 'Settling Territorial Disputes', p. 256.

3 *Application for Revision and Interpretation of the Judgment of 24 February 1982 in the Case concerning the* Continental Shelf (Tunisia /Libyan Arab Jamahiriya) *(Tunisia v. Libyan Arab Jamahiriya), Jugdment, I.C.J. Reports 1985*, p. 192, at p. 218, para. 47.

4 Judge Robert Jennings writing in his scholarly capacity in 1993, as cited in *East Timor case, I.C.J. Reports 1995*, Dissenting opinion by Judge Skubizewski, at p. 259, para. 111. For instance Ecuador and Colombia did reach an agreement which 'fully and finally resolves all of 'the Applicant's claims (*Aerial Herbicide Spraying (Ecuador v. Colombia), Order of 13 September 2013, I.C.J. Reports 2013*, p. 278, at p. 279), both parties acknowledging that 'reaching a settlement would have been difficult, if not impossible, but for the involvement of the Court' (Judge P. Tomka, President of the ICJ in his speech before the Sixth Committee of the UN General Assembly on 1 November 2013; text available on the Court's website).

5 *East Timor case, I.C.J. Reports 1995*, Dissenting opinion by Judge Skubizewski, at p. 259, para. 112.

6 Judge R. Jennings, President of the ICJ, in his speech before the UN General Assembly on 15 October 1993, *International Court of Justice Yearbook*, 1992–93, p. 218, at p. 220. Recently the President of the ICJ expressed the still more traditional view on the Court's role: Judge Tomka, President of the ICJ in his speech in Bucharest on 16 May 2013 (text available on the Court's website).

7 Judge S. Schwebel, President of the ICJ in his speech before the UN General Assembly on 27 October 1997, 92 *American Journal of International Law*, pp. 612–17 at p. 614.

This study aims at bringing to the fore the way negotiations play a multifunctional role in the Court's jurisprudence, and this in order to provide us with more insight into the way the complementarity between the two mechanisms operates in their daily functioning. The time has come now to pay a first preliminary visit to this functional interaction.

This chapter will not be devoted to an in-depth analysis of the interaction in its various manifestations and forms; that will the object and purpose of subsequent chapters. At this stage we present a first and rather general picture.

2.1 Some Common and Distinctive Features of the two Mechanisms

Before looking into the political-legal context of the functional interaction between the two mechanisms it is appropriate to identify some of their traditionally well-known common and distinctive features which influence the whole process of interaction. Moreover, disputes are likely to involve *consultations* at some stage; one of their main functions is to establish a kind of classification of the dispute so that States can decide on the best way to handle it, without a predetermined idea of the parties to reach an agreement on matters of substance.[8]

Some Common Features

Both mechanisms for dispute settlement share, although perhaps to slightly different degrees, the unpredictability as far as the ultimate outcome of the process is concerned.

Negotiation and adjudication have in common that they are both taking place in the form of a process unfolding itself over a certain period of time, although the Court, while recognizing this 'process' aspect, may consider, in the appropriate circumstance of a particular case' the judicial proceedings to be the culmination of the overall process.[9] The Court takes care to maintain and safeguard the close link in the judicial process between the interlocutory decisions on provisional measures, preliminary objections, counterclaims and application for intervention and the principal stage on the merits.[10]

Although for different reasons and to a diverging extent uncertainty is marking both processes – and parties 'systematically overestimate the probability that the judge would rule in their favour'[11] – it has to be noted that both negotiations and litigation 'occur in the context of strategic interaction, the probability of any particular outcome as well as its potential costs or benefits depends on the counterpart's actions (and reactions) no less than one's own' and as far as litigation is concerned, of course and ultimately on the Court's handling of the case.[12]

When both parties 'are prepared to go to Court' this 'presupposes that both parties consider that their arguments have legal merit so absolute predictability is not possible'.[13] A case before the Court 'could always have certain unexpected and surprising elements, which had not been perceived at the beginning',[14] and this may be a manifestation of the functional interaction between the two mechanisms for peaceful settlement once the dispute has been brought before the Court.

Scholars within the discipline of international relations and also that of international law have rightfully recognized and underlined cultural diversity as an important factor for a proper understanding of the day-to-day functioning of international relations and international law. This cultural diversity has an impact on the willingness of States to start the process of negotiations and/or judicial proceedings, the unfolding of

8 F. Pazartzis, *Les engagements internationaux en matière de règlement pacifique des différends entre Etats* (Paris, 1992), p. 71.

9 *Maritime Delimitation in the Black Sea (Romania v. Ukraine), I.C.J. Reports 2009*, p. 61, at p. 87, para. 70.

10 B. Metou, *Le rôle du juge dans le contentieux international* (Brussels, 2012), p. 150. See also at pp. 114, 156, 286–7.

11 G. Blum and R. Mnookin, 'When *Not* to Negotiate', p. 108.

12 G. Blum and R. Mnookin, 'When *Not* to Negotiate', p. 102.

13 D. Bowett, 'Developments', 182.

14 L. Prott, 'The Role of the Judge', 503.

and the ultimate (degree of) failure or success of both processes, as this diversity has also a role to play in judicial procedures.[15]

'It has generally been established that negotiations to end a past conflict will have been ineffective unless they have also been able to build regimes and relationships for handling conflict in the future.'[16] The potential contradictory nature of these two demands[17] may in turn exacerbate the inherent difficulties each process of negotiations has already to face.

Negotiation is not really 'the search for a solution' when 'parties base their positions on a repetition of their past grievances, their past legalities, and their demands for reparations and punishment'.[18]

In spite of potentially maintaining such a backward and only partially forward-looking approach, bringing a dispute before the Court drastically and irreversibly changes the overall political and above all legal context in which the respective claims of the parties will be addressed and handled. The 'general context, as well political as legal, in which the deliberation of the Court takes place' is liable to influence the Court's *judicial policy*.[19]

The forward- and backward-looking approach presents itself in the exercise of the judicial function,[20] depending on the subject-matter of the dispute and the *petita* – e.g. determination of state responsibility and remedies or delimitation of territorial and maritime areas and particular regimes for future cooperation. The time factor reflects itself in the Court taking duly into account *the history of the dispute*, for instance through the prism of prior negotiations, while the operative paragraphs of the Court's judgment may require post-adjudicative negotiations.[21]

With regard to both methods of settlement it has to be recognized that 'a dispute is *really* settled only when each of the parties ceases to have a continuing sense of grievance, or at least ceases to continue actively to assert its claim'.[22] Both processes also have in common that normal diligence entails certain requirements when a State is participating in either of them, for instance a duty to inform itself.[23]

Some Distinctive Features

Traditional distinctive features include: the formal (adjudication) or informal nature of the process (negotiation); third party involvement (adjudication) or just bilateral encounters (negotiations); an outcome freely entered into by the parties (negotiations) or imposed by the Court and binding upon the parties (adjudication).[24]

---

15 J.-M. Thouvenin, 'Cultures juridiques et procédures judiciaires' in *International Law and Diversity of Legal Cultures* (Paris, 2008), pp. 387–98 and G. Guillaume, 'Cultures juridiques et délibére judiciaire' in *International Law and Diversity of Legal Cultures*, pp. 399–404.

16 W. Zartman, 'Negotiating Forward', p. 1.

17 W. Zartman, 'Negotiating Forward', p. 1.

18 W. Zartman, 'Looking Forward and Looking Backward on Negotiation Theory' in W. Zartman and V. Kremenyuk (eds), *Peace versus Justice: Negotiating Forward and Backward-Looking Outcomes* (Lanham, MD, 2005), p. 291.

19 P.-M. Dupuy, 'The Judicial Policy', p. 70.

20 See generally C. Baudenbacher and E. Busek (eds), *The Role of International Courts* ([Munich], 2008). On the men and women who decide the world's cases see *inter alia* D. Terris, C. Romano and L. Swigart, *The International Judge* and on a even more general level Lord Hope of Craighead, 'The Judges' Dilemma' (2009) 58 *International and Comparative Law Quarterly*, 4, 753–65.

21 On the role of the time factor see more generally R. Higgins, 'Time and International Law: International Perspective on an Old Problem' (1991) 3 *International and Comparative Law Quarterly*, 505-20. See also *Le droit international et le temps* (Paris, 2001) and more in particular J.-M. Thouvenin, 'Le délai raisonnable', pp. 109–30 and M. Kohen, 'L'influence du temps sur les règlements territoriaux', pp. 131–60, in particular pp. 155ff; and S. Rosenne, *The Time Factor in the Jurisdiction of the International Court of Justice* (Leyden, 1960).

22 R. Bilder, 'An Overview', 28.

23 *Application for Revision and Interpretation of the Judgment of 24 February 1982 in the Case concerning the* Continental Shelf (Tunisia/Libyan Arab Jamahiriya*) (Tunisia v. Libyan Arab Jamahiriya), Judgment, I.C.J. Reports 1985*, p. 192, at p. 206, para. 27.

24 In this last respect the question arises whether in the post-adjudicative phase in most cases parties are free to (re) start negotiations in order to find a settlement which is departing from the operative clauses of the judgment rendered.

Both the PCIJ and the ICJ fully recognized that the judicial settlement of international disputes 'is simply an alternative to the direct and friendly settlement of such disputes between the Parties'.[25]

In contrast to the process of negotiations, which is largely informal by nature, the exercise of the Court's judicial function is characterized by 'a certain degree of formalism which however is neither an objective in its own right nor systematic; it is rather "un instrument de la politique judiciaire"'.[26]

The main advantage of judicial settlement of disputes is that it '*produces* a settlement, rather than merely smoothing the way to a possible settlement which the parties may, or may not, choose to adopt'.[27] Adjudication by the Court could be *instrumental* in a longer process of peaceful settlement of the dispute, for instance through rendering a declaratory judgment providing the parties the necessary guidance of legal norms and principles which should guide them to restart their failed prior negotiations.

As adjudication is not synonymous with *effective settlement* of disputes it can be safely stated that adjudication and post-adjudicative negotiations are almost necessarily complementary to each other, as Part III of this study will demonstrate.

The interests of judicial settlement of disputes 'are best served by the recognition of the limits to international adjudication as it simply cannot *settle* all international disputes'.[28] Moreover, one should duly acknowledge that negotiations are not only concerned with *settling* international disputes as indeed their 'function in "*managing*" disputes, i.e. containing them in order to preserve other aspects of the parties' relationship, may be equally significant'.[29]

However, on a general level the respective functions of negotiations and adjudication do correspond, to a large extent, to a well-known fundamental distinction in law. Inter-state negotiations are a clear manifestation of *le droit transactionnel*, whereas adjudication as a matter of principle belongs to *le droit dispositif.*

However a recent study on the question '*dans quelle mesure le règlement juridictionnel des différends territoriaux a-t-il glissé vers un règlement politique*'[30] has used the expression *justice transactionnelle* in order to explain 'la façon dont le juge s'efforce de consacrer un équilibre entre les intérêts des parties en leur "imposant" des concessions mutuelles sur leurs revendications respectives, par le biais des décisions juridictionnelles'.[31]

One should duly note that as far as the process of adjudication is concerned we witness 'l'exercice hautement diplomatique que représente pour le juge le règlement d'un différend territorial'.[32]

In the political process of negotiating over a boundary dispute it may become natural for parties to make concessions, because 'the two States tried to find a *political solution* to their boundary dispute, and it was

---

25 *North Sea Continental Shelf case, I.C.J. Reports 1969*, at p. 47, para. 87 citing P.C.I.J., Series A, No. 22, at p. 13. Abi-Saab has recently observed the bad translation into English of this passage – 'le règlement judiciaire … *n'est qu'un succédané*' – which means 'a replacement to make up or fill in for something that does not exist or is unattainable: not merely an equivalent alternative, but a second best or an imperfect substitute': G. Abi-Saab, 'Negotiation and Adjudication: Complementarity and Dissonance' in L. Boisson de Chazournes, M. Kohen and J. Vinuales (eds) *Diplomatic and Judicial Means of Dispute Settlement* (Leiden, Boston, 2013), pp. 327–33, at p. 327. This observation had already been made by L. Marion, 'La saisine de la C.I.J. par voie de compromis' (1995) 99 *Revue Générale de Droit International Public*, 258–300, at 290: 'Le règlement judiciaire est choisi pour remplacer l'impossible règlement direct.'

26 R.-J. Dupuy, 'Formalisme juridique et Cour Internationale de Justice' in J. Makarczyk (ed.), *Theory of International Law at the Threshold of the 21st Century* (The Hague, 1996), pp. 392–401, at p. 401.

27 H. Thirlway, 'The International Court of Justice 1989–2009: At the Heart of the Dispute Settlement System?' (2010) 57 *Netherlands International Law Review* 347–95 at 355.

28 K. Oellers-Frahm, 'Nowhere to Go?', 449.

29 J. Merrills, 'The Means of Dispute Settlement', p. 561 (emphasis added).

30 .G. Giraudeau, *Les différends territoriaux*, p. 23.

31 G. Giraudeau, *Les différends territoriaux*, pp. 15–16. The 'transactional' concerns both the principal *revendications* (claims) of the parties (pp. 147–83) as secondary questions (pp. 183–223). Sometimes judges qualify the solution adopted as 'intermediate' (*Request for the Interpretation of the Judgment of 15 June 1962 in the Case concerning* the Temple of Preah Vihear (Cambodia v. Thailand) *(Cambodia v. Thailand), Judgment, I.C.J. Reports 2013*, p.281, Declaration by Judge *ad hoc* Guillaume, at p.347, para. 7). Sometimes they did expect a decision 'a little *less "transactional"* in a matter in which the Court could have afforded to speak out': *Interim Accord case, I.C.J. Reports 2011*, Separate opinion by Judge Simma, at p. 697, para. 6 (emphasis added).

32 G. Giraudeau, *Les différends territoriaux*, p. 1.

natural, indeed, necessary, in the circumstances in which the negotiations took place, to make concessions by waiving rights at the *political level* that they could have asserted at the *judicial level*'.[33]

In case the process of negotiations turns out to be ultimately unsuccessful, and the dispute is brought before the Court, the functional interaction starts to operate, one of its perhaps surprising aspects being the non-invocation of positions taken during the negotiations.[34]

While negotiations 'aim to end conflict' which may take the form of 'total settlement of the issues (conflict resolution)',[35] the objective of calling upon the Court is that it should exercise its *direct* judicial function which is to *decide* in accordance with international law such disputes as are submitted to it (Article 38, para. 1) (emphasis added). Its *consequential function* for society consists in the Court doing so.

Whereas in its Article 94, para. 2 the Charter 'recognizes that a judgment of the International Court of Justice might fail to bring about a settlement of even a legal issue',[36] in case of failed settlements a combination of power politics and the reluctance to address the root causes of the dispute is probably explanatory.[37]

Settlements 'that do not rest on some normative foundation that is separate from the power political considerations are unlikely to prove durable'.[38] It is basically these two aspects which clearly distinguish adjudication from negotiations as a method for PSD.

Of course, neither the instituting of proceedings before the Court nor the fact that negotiations are taking place make the dispute disappear.[39] The result of negotiations may be an 'agreed understanding of a situation and therefore a more healthy preservation of the status quo, or there may be an amelioration of the situation or the dispute among those concerned; there may be agreed adjustments, or, at the optimum, an agreed solution or settlement',[40] while adjudication will inevitably entail a change in the factual and legal relationship between the parties.

Also because of this *process* nature negotiation may have made that '[w]hat had been absolutely and empathically non-negotiable had become negotiable and had been satisfactorily settled',[41] while failed prior negotiations may have convinced (one of) the parties that the only way to settle their dispute is to resort to the other, judicial means of peaceful settlement of disputes.

In contrast to negotiations the entering of which 'may affect a party's *reputation*', the willingness to settle may trigger the perception that 'there must be something to the claims against them';[42] entering the Great Hall of Justice may create the opposite perception, that the claims must be firmly grounded for a party to risk losing the case.

On the other hand there is 'another type of spill over costs': 'if negotiating a resolution of this single dispute may make sense in light of the immediate cost savings, the *precedent* of a negotiated settlement here may bring a flood of similar claims later'.[43]

Parties tend to overlook the fact 'that in the future, precedents can always be distinguished',[44] as reflected in the Court's case law on Article 59 of the Statute, which in principle precludes such precedential effect.

The functional interaction does not merely, although, mainly situate itself on the level of what we may call secondary rules on their performance and related duties by both parties and the Court, but it may also be found as a result of the applicability of primary rules – for instance in cases of maritime delimitation, as the Court itself acknowledged with regard to 'the normative character of equitable principles as applied as part

33 *Application for Revision of the Judgment of 11 September 1992 in the Case concerning the* Land, Island and Maritime Frontier Dispute (El Salvador/Honduras: Nicaragua intervening) (*El Salvador v. Honduras), Judgment, I.C.J. Reports 2003*, p. 392, Dissenting opinion by Judge *ad hoc* Paolillo, at p. 419, para. 2 (emphasis added).

34 See Chapter 7.

35 W. Zartman, 'Negotiating Forward', p. 1.

36 A. Lall, *Modern International Negotiation*, p. 6.

37 A. Guelke, 'Negotiations and Peace Processes', p. 67.

38 A. Guelke, 'Negotiations and Peace Processes', p. 67.

39 The Court rejected the last part of this argument in the *Aegean Continental Shelf case, I.C.J. Reports 1978*, at p. 12, para. 30.

40 A. Lall, *Modern International Negotiation*, p. 8.

41 A. Lall, *Modern International Negotiation*, p. 129.

42 G. Blum and R. Mnookin, 'When *Not* to Negotiate', p. 105.

43 G. Blum and R. Mnookin, 'When *Not* to Negotiate', p. 105.

44 G. Blum and R. Mnookin, 'When *Not* to Negotiate', p. 109.

of general international law': they govern 'not only delimitation by adjudication or arbitration' but also 'and indeed, primarily, the duty of States to seek first a delimitation by agreement'.[45]

More efficiency is attributed to negotiations than to any other method of peaceful settlement of disputes because they can be 'tailored to the dispute in question, the specific issues that arise in its resolution and the likely solution'.[46] This may be true, but it has to be recognized that a similar tailoring to the dispute occurs through the conclusion of a Special Agreement. In case of unilateral seisin there is potentially a larger *tailoring role* for the Court in this respect.[47]

The mere existence of Article 60 of the Statute almost implies that in most post-adjudicative phases negotiations are needed and are in fact taking place in order to bring about compliance with the operative clauses of the judgment. Hence parties may have to go through various stages in order to reach an agreement on the ways and modalities to perform the obligations incumbent upon them under a judgment. Some of these bilateral means may still be in progress but proven to have been unsuccessful on the day an Application is being filed for interpretation of the judgment as parties have been unable to reach a joint interpretation.[48]

The party requesting the interpretation may have come to the conclusion that a persistent divergence of views on the interpretation remaining unsolved does not provide the parties with 'any prospect of achieving a mutually agreed solution within the framework of bilateral negotiations'.[49] As a result the functional link between the modes of settlement which may have existed prior to the institution of the proceedings which have led to the judgment in the first place is getting a new lease of life; we turn to this issue in Chapter 9.

2.2 Recognition of their Respective Functions

A Doctrinal Approach

For a 'large proportion of disputes or situations between States the most productive form of negotiation is direct discussion among the parties concerned'.[50]

With regard to the various means of PSD one has to recognize that each of them have to be seen 'in the context of other techniques and procedures'.[51] However, one should not disregard that recourse to the Court has 'the effect of legitimising a result which would have been difficult, if not impossible, to arrive at in direct negotiations'.[52]

45 *Continental Shelf case between Libya and Malta, Judgment, I.C.J. Reports 1985*, p. 13, at p. 39, para. 46.

46 M. Waibel, 'The Diplomatic Channel', p. 1090.

47 M. Waibel, 'The Diplomatic Channel', p. 1090.

48 *Request for the Interpretation of the 1962 Temple of Preah Vihear Judgment, I.C.J. Reports 2011*, Application by Cambodia, para. 13.

49 *Ibid.*, para. 17.

50 A. Lall, *Modern International Negotiation*, p. 17.

51 J. Merrills, *International Dispute Settlement*, p. 114.

52 J. Merrills, *International Dispute Settlement*, p. 228. For a comparative doctrinal list of the respective limits and advantages of adjudication and negotiations see *inter alia* R. Bilder, 'An Overview', 22–3, note 36 and pp. 29–30, note 53. For an overview of the advantages and disadvantages of adjudication see further also R. Bilder, 'International Dispute Settlement and the Role of International Adjudication' in L. Damrosh (ed.), *The International Court of Justice at a Crossroads* (New York, 1987), pp. 156–80, at pp. 162–72; and R. Bilder, 'International Dispute Settlement and the Role of International Adjudication' (1986–87) 1 *Emory Journal of International Dispute Resolution*, 131–73, at 144–61. See also of course the classic study by R. Anand, *Studies in International Adjudication* (Delhi, New York, 1969).

On characteristics limiting the effectiveness of the process of negotiations see *inter alia* J. Irvin, 'The Role of Law in the Negotiated Settlement of International Disputes' (1969) 3 *Vanderbilt International Law Journal* 58–73 at 61. On the advantages and disadvantages of negotiations see also M. Waibel, 'The Diplomatic Channel', pp. 1090–91. On some of the basic causes of State reluctance to resort to *dispute settlement procedures* see *inter alia* Roy S. Lee, 'A Case for Facilitation in the Settlement of Disputes' (1991) 34 *German Yearbook of International Law* 138–74, at 140–56. For a recent analysis of why States resort to *international adjudication* to resolve international law disputes see N. Klein (ed.), *Litigating International Law Disputes* (Cambridge, 2013).

The UN General Assembly and Security Council have 'become engaged in negotiations', while the ICJ 'does not and cannot function as a negotiating body'.[53] Although 'the jurisdiction of the Court is consensual, its proceedings are judicial and do not represent a delegated negotiation or a negotiation by proxy'.[54] We will later demonstrate how its intervention can have an impact on, for instance, the resumption of the process during the proceedings and of course on the post-adjudicative negotiations.

When parties 'maintain their just rights in their relationship' during a process of negotiations, no settlement is possible,[55] while settlement of the dispute is possible through a decision of the Court on precisely the status of the respective rights claimed by the parties.

Although for instance 'a judicial delimitation is a substitute for a delimitation by agreement',[56] parties should be fully aware that the Court 'will apply criteria other than the terms of the agreement which might have been reached'.[57] Conversely, the Court could, if so requested, *take note* of a pre-existing delimitation agreement between the parties before the start of the proceedings, but it cannot 'appropriate' its content 'in order to make it the substance of' its decision.[58]

Stalemate or deadlock, 'typically characterizes a situation that is ripe for negotiation and can be viewed as a signal to implement new strategies'.[59]

A *functional deadlock* can be a producer of 'a *de-escalation* process',[60] inducing for instance (one of) the parties to start proceedings before the Court. This step will require the parties 'to reframe the problem in such a way that a solution can be devised',[61] as reflected in Article 38, paras. 1 and 2 of the Rules of Court.

While in case of deadlock 'adding issues to the negotiation' may enable 'everyone to look for "packages" that integrate trade-offs that will help reach a jointly balanced solution',[62] the latter objective is not part of the judicial function, while even introducing a counterclaim cannot change the subject-matter of the dispute as initially submitted to the Court.

Whereas the parties' willingness to reciprocate concessions 'is the basis of the negotiation process'[63] – and which may continue or be resumed during proceedings before the Court[64] – the handling of a dispute by both the parties and the Court during the proceedings is of a completely different nature, although the (partial) result of negotiations may find its way into the judicial reasoning and may even form part of the basis of the Court's decision.[65]

The Attitude of States

The functional interaction may be firmly established in general international law, but States' attitude towards the two mechanisms may be impregnated with ambiguity as far as their respective roles and their functional interaction are concerned.

As part of their *negotiation strategy* States may decide *not* to bring a dispute before the Court in order to give negotiations another chance, for instance by imposing on themselves a time limit of two years for their attempt to negotiate a settlement first before recourse to the Court becomes possible;[66] or they may threaten to actually bring the dispute before the Court in order to create an impact on the presumed unwillingness of

53 A. Lall, *Modern International Negotiation*, p. 21.

54 *Jan Mayen case, I.C.J. Reports 1993*, Separate opinion by Judge Shahabuddeen, at p. 200.

55 W. Zartman, 'Looking Forward and Looking Backward', p. 290.

56 H. Thirlway, 'The Law and Procedure of the International Court of Justice 1960–1989.Supplement, 2007: Parts Four, Five and Six' (2007) 78 *British Yearbook of International Law* 17–175, at 136.

57 H. Thirlway, 'The Law and Procedure of the International Court of Justice 1960–1989: Part Four' (1992) 63 *British Yearbook of International Law*, 1–96 at 7.

58 *Frontier Dispute (Burkina Faso/Niger), Judgement, I.C.J. Reports 2013*, p. 44, at p. 69, para. 43.

59 G. Faure, 'Deadlocks', p. 27.

60 G. Faure, 'Deadlocks', p. 25 (emphasis added).

61 G. Faure, 'Deadlocks', p. 38.

62 G. Faure, 'Deadlocks', p. 45.

63 W. Zartman, 'Process and Stages', p. 96.

64 See Chapter 6 .

65 See Chapter 7.

66 *Maritime Delimitation in the Black Sea, I.C.J. Reports 2009*, at pp. 70–71, paras. 20–21.

the other party to enter into the process of negotiations;[67] or to overcome an impasse in the negotiations or to express discontent with the lack of progress.

Litigation, or rather the threat of litigation, can be used by parties 'to improve their bargaining positions; to resolve deadlocks and influence negotiations; and to change the rules of the broader institutional regimes themselves'.[68] Even requests for advisory opinions such as the *Namibia case* and the *Nuclear Weapons case* 'can also be seen as attempts to advance UN negotiations from an impasse'.[69]

In doing so they not only put additional pressure on the process of negotiations – which, in case of deadlock, may be kept going *inter alia* by 'the concession-making mechanism[70] – but they also keep the two processes separate and distinct for the time being.

That seisin of the Court has been in certain cases 'no more than a means of pressure exercised by one party upon another in a bid to lead it to a political settlement' has been duly acknowledged by the Court's President.[71]

In case the threat to initiate proceedings has not produced the intended effect of overcoming a deadlock and the case has been brought before the Court, it is rather unlikely that the Court, when exercising the *'facilitative'* aspect of its function, would address an encouragement to take the necessary steps to put the process back on track exclusively to one of the parties. Also, as part of their *litigation strategy* parties may rely on the argument that the two mechanisms should be sharply distinguished.

The question of judicial propriety of drawing a delimitation line is an illustration of the complexity of the functional interaction between the two modes of settlement and of the relevance of the subject-matter for that interaction.

A Respondent may argue that negotiation is 'prescribed as the proper and primary way of achieving an equitable maritime delimitation and the Court is not a forum for negotiations'.[72] If the competence to determine the boundary 'is confined by international law exclusively to the process of agreement by the parties' then the 'Court cannot determine it except on their joint request'. In the absence of such a request, the Court 'can at most only provide guidelines to enable the parties to determine the boundary by an agreement to *be negotiated* on the basis of such guidelines'.[73]

From the functional interaction perspective it should be duly noted that the Organization of African Unity/ African Union (OAU/AU) 'declined to lay down, as part of the public law of Africa, a specific peaceful method applicable to the settlement of all potential boundary disputes among all African States, or to the determination of the course of such boundaries'.[74]

---

67 As did Paraguay in the *Breard case* where the US was advised of 'of its intention to bring proceedings before the Court if the United States Government did not take steps to initiate consultations': *Vienna Convention on Consular Relations (Paraguay v. United States of America), Provisional Measures, Order of 9 April 1998, I.C.J. Reports 1998*, p. 248, at p. 254, para. 19.

68 M. Gehring, 'Strategic Use of Litigation to Influence Negotiations: The WTO, the EU and the UN' in H. Ruiz Fabri, R. Wolfrum and J. Gogolin (eds), *Select Proceedings of the European Society of International Law* (Oxford, Portland, 2010), pp. 356–77, at pp. 357–8.

69 M. Gehring, 'Strategic Use', at p. 361.

70 G. Faure, 'Deadlocks', p. 26.

71 Judge Bedjaoui, President of the ICJ before the UN General Assembly, 12 October 1995, *ICJ Yearbook 1995–96*, at p. 266.

72 *Land and Maritime Boundary case, I.C.J. Reports 2002*, at p. 422, para. 240. On the transactional nature of the judicial solutions in this category of disputes see further G. Giraudeau, *Les différends territoriaux*. Hence, when the Court appears to give satisfaction to both parties' main approaches to a dispute this is not really an '*unprecedented* solution' as argued by Judge *ad hoc* Orrego Vicuña: *Case concerning Maritime Dispute (Peru v. Chile), I.C.J. Reports 2014*, para. 27 (emphasis added).

73 *Jan Mayen case, I.C.J. Reports 1993*, Separate opinion by Judge Shahabuddeen, at p. 202. Judge Oda considered this to be 'a matter of principle': Separate opinion, at p. 91, para. 2.

74 *Frontier Dispute between Burkina Faso and Niger, I.C.J. Reports 2013*, Separate opinion by Judge Yusuf, at p. 142, para. 26. One should respectfully add that the AU did create a special frontier programme encouraging African States to negotiate on a bilateral basis their territorial and maritime frontiers in order to prevent conflicts: G. Giraudeau, *Les différends territoriaux*, p. 43, note 76. For a general overview of the Court's jurisprudence in this area of international law see *inter alia* Alvarez-Jimenez, 'Boundary Agreements in the International Court of Justice's Case Law, 2000–2010' (2012) 23 *European Journal of International Law*, 495–515.

With regard to the precise role of the Court – 'a descriptive statement or actually drawing the line' – , that is where the parties but also judges may disagree: should the Court's role be limited '*as a judicial tribunal applying international law*' to declare that the lines of delimitation must be drawn by the parties as provided for in UNCLOS[75] or should the Court, given the failure of prior negotiations, actually say what the boundary is.[76]

Bilateral treaties may have endowed the Court with a dual role; an example of an atypical function can be found in the 1975 Statute at the centre of the *Pulp Mills case*. Apart from its traditionally mainly *retrospective* dispute settlement function, the States Parties provided for the *prospective* adjudicative function on technical and scientific matters to assist the parties from an early stage in the process of realizing a project:[77] this way States are ensuring a more direct functional interaction between the negotiations which have failed and judicial intervention in order to bring the process back on track in order to achieve the object and purpose of the treaty.[78]

A State may face some difficulty in formulating its Application in such a way – given the unpredictability of the outcome of the judicial proceedings – referring 'to the element of chance which, no doubt, plays a role in many instances in the Court's decision, considering the choice to be made between different interpretations of the same rule of law or between the application of concurrent principles applicable to the same case, or simply in the argumentation of the case'[79] such 'as to leave room for continued negotiations between the two parties',[80] as to enable the Court to push forward the parties but while still retaining the final form of the result in the parties' hands. This could be based on the assumption that two friendly neighbours would comply with the judgment.[81]

The Court's Approach

Judicial awareness and recognition of the respective functions of both mechanisms for settlement of disputes is necessary in order to ascertain and assess the various manifestations of their functional interaction, which will be the subject-matter of the subsequent chapters of this study.

The respective roles of both functions – the judicial one by the Court and the political one through negotiations by the parties – has been described by the Court in the following terms, which also reflects its constant awareness of their respective limitations.

Negotiations and Calling in the Court

For the Court the functional link between negotiations and judicial settlement is firm and well established, as can be seen from this simple and concise but valid description of it when it affirmed that a dispute over asserted rights 'might be the subject of negotiation, leading either to its settlement … or to the conclusion of a special agreement for its resolution by a judicial body' as one of the methods of seisin.[82]

The Court has recognized that parties always have the possibility 'to have recourse to a conjunction of judicial determination and settlement by agreement'.[83]

75 *Jan Mayen case, I.C.J. Reports 1993*, Separate opinion by Judge Oda, at p. 111, para. 79.

76 *Ibid.*, Separate opinion by Judge Shahabuddeen, at pp. 202–3.

77 *Pulp Mills case, I.C.J. Reports 2010*, Joint dissenting opinion by Judges Al-Khasawneh and Simma, at pp. 117–18, paras. 19–21.

78 For a detailed description of the functional interaction prior, during and after the proceedings in the *Pulp Mills case* see, P. Sandonato de Leon, 'Diplomatic and Judicial Means of Dispute Settlement and How They Got Along in the *Pulp Mills* Case' in L. Boisson de Chazournes, M. Kohen and J. Vinuales (eds), *Diplomatic and Judicial Means of Dispute Settlement* (Leiden, Boston, 2013), pp. 71–86.

79 P.-M. Dupuy, 'Judicial Policy', at p. 70.

80 M. Koskenniemi, 'Debate' in C. Peck and R. Lee (eds), *Increasing the Effectiveness of the International Court of Justice: Proceedings of the ICJ/UNITAR Colloquium to Celebrate the 50th Anniversary of the Court* (The Hague, 1997), at p. 367.

81 M. Koskenniemi, 'Debate', p. 367.

82 *Continental Shelf case between Libya and Malta, I.C.J. Reports 1984*, at pp. 23–4, para. 37.

83 *Application for Revision and Interpretation of the Judgment of 24 February 1982 in the Case concerning* the Continental Shelf (Tunisia v. Libya), *I.C.J. Reports 1985*, p. 218, para. 47.

While recognizing that the '[m]ost appropriate method for the solution of the dispute is clearly that of negotiation',[84] the Court is fully aware of the limitations of negotiations to settle a dispute when, for instance, diplomatic correspondence reveals the objectives the parties were attempting to achieve: if the difference consists of a claim by one party that the other party would terminate a particular action which it refuses to halt, there is not much of a subject-matter to have negotiations in a proper sense about.[85]

'There is nothing strange in the abandonment of administrative negotiations when the nature of the dispute makes the intervention of a tribunal preferable';[86] neither can the recourse to the ICJ be considered an unfriendly act between States.[87]

One of the functions of negotiations consists in identifying the contours, the limits and the precise content of the judicial task. It is then not surprising that certainly in case of an Application a disagreement between the parties on the 'nature and extent of the role' of the Court 'will probably manifest itself' at various stages of the proceedings. It may happen that 'while the positions of the Parties' have 'undergone a significant change and have clearly become closer in the course of the proceedings, they still appear unable to agree on what the Court's precise task should be in this regard'.[88]

Parties' positions could and indeed do change as a result of the respective arguments used until the final submissions. This change, and thus the evolvement of parties' *petitum*, could also be the result of ongoing or resumed negotiations.[89]

The desirable outcome of negotiations leading up to the conclusion of a Special Agreement should also be that the States 'have indeed agreed to refer their dispute to the Court and that they were likewise in agreement as to the subject of the dispute and the method of seisin of the Court'.[90]

Functional interaction operates in a particular way when a Draft Special Agreement prepared by both parties respectively covers entirely different matters the parties want the Court to decide.[91] Parties could then 'have continued negotiations to work out a draft of a *special agreement*'.[92]

Although parties may deny themselves recourse to the Court during a period of good offices, even once proceedings are underway the good offices could have continued towards the achievement of a substantive settlement,[93] as provided between the parties;[94] this is an example of the double-track strategy to be discussed shortly.

Referring to its previous jurisprudence in the *Hostages* and *the Aegean Continental Shelf case*, the Court reaffirmed that 'even the existence of active negotiations in which both parties might be involved should not prevent both the Security Council and the Court from exercising their respective functions'.[95]

Questions raised during prior negotiations are almost inevitably bound to come up again and extensively in the pleadings and hearings on the merits.[96]

---

84 *Fisheries Jurisdiction (United Kingdom v. Iceland), I.C.J. Reports 1974*, at p. 31, para. 73.

85 *Nuclear Tests (Australia v. France), I.C.J. Reports 1973*, at p. 104, para. 25.

86 *South West Africa cases, I.C.J. Reports 1962*, Separate opinion by Judge Bustamente, at pp. 385–6.

87 General Assembly Resolution 3232 (XXIX), para. 6.

88 *Land and Maritime Boundary case, I.C.J. Reports 2002*, at p. 359, para. 83. This is not only an illustration that the recognition of the respective functions, and especially that of the judicial task, is not always to be taken for granted; it is also a reminder that judicial proceedings, just like negotiations, are certainly not static but develop and unfold as a dynamic process.

89 R. Kolb, *The ICJ*, pp. 926 and 1160. We will address the role and function of negotiations during the course of proceedings in Chapter 6.

90 *Maritime Delimitation and Territorial Questions between Qatar and Bahrain, Jurisdiction and Admissibility, Judgment, I.C.J. Reports 1994*, p. 112, Separate opinion by Judge *ad hoc* Valticos, at p. 132.

91 *Case between Qatar and Bahrain, I.C.J. Reports* 1994, Dissenting opinion by Judge Oda, at p. 144, para. 26.

92 *Ibid.*, at p. 149, para. 34.

93 *Maritime Delimitation and Territorial Questions between Qatar and Bahrain, Jurisdiction and Admissibility, Judgment, I.C.J. Reports 1995*, p. 6, Dissenting opinion by Judge Schwebel, at p. 38.

94 *Case between Qatar and Bahrain, I.C.J. Reports 1994*, at p. 121, para. 24.

95 *Military and Paramilitary Activities in and against Nicaragua (Nicaragua v. United States of America), Jurisdiction and Admissibility, Judgment, I.C.J. Reports 1984*, p. 392, at p. 439, para. 105 and at p. 440, para. 106.

96 *Fisheries Jurisdiction (United Kingdom v. Iceland), I.C.J. Reports 1974*, at p. 20, para. 43. See further on this aspect Chapter 7.

The Court's Contribution to the Settlement of Disputes: Its Primary Function and its Facilitative Role

It was first of all appropriate for the Court to recall that its resolution of legal questions 'may be an important, and *sometimes* decisive, factor in *promoting* peaceful settlement of a dispute';[97] that 'judicial settlement of international disputes, with a view to which the Court has been established, is simply an *alternative* to the direct and friendly settlement of such disputes between the Parties';[98] and that 'pending a decision of the Court on the merits, any negotiation between the Parties with a view to achieving a direct and friendly settlement is to be welcomed'.[99]

Hence, declining 'jurisdiction while a dispute persists does not represent a positive contribution to the settlement of international disputes, which is the central function of the Court',[100] and when parties fail to agree at the end of a particular procedure provided for in a bilateral treaty the 'Court cannot ignore its responsibility to resolve the dispute'.[101]

Neither does a judge fulfil his judicial duty (*judex decidere debet*) if he fails to give a decision on one of the *causae petendi* of the Application (*non est judex minus petita partium*).[102]

'Judicial settlement may hasten the final resolution of the dispute as a whole, as may simply having the matter before the Court.'[103] This 'latter point does indeed raise the issue as to whether the Court should itself seek to become more active in achieving a final settlement between the litigants'.[104] The way the Court has been trying to perform this 'facilitative' role in its case law will be looked at in various subsequent chapters of this study.

The question whether such a proactive approach 'might unnecessarily complicate any negotiations that are taking place either bilaterally or through the United Nations at the same time'[105] did not really prevent the Court from assisting the parties in several ways.

'The view that the sole function of a court of law is to decide the disputes brought before it through a judicial process is not a general principle of law recognized by the nations of the world, or a characteristic of all the principal legal systems of the world.'[106]

Writing in an extrajudicial capacity, Eli Lauterpacht draws attention 'to an important question that should not be overlooked' – namely to 'what extent may or should the judge assist the parties to reach an agreed settlement of the case?' Parties are reluctant 'to reveal to the judge before he reaches a decision on the disputed point of law or fact the extent to which that party is prepared to adjust its position' (taken for instance during prior negotiations) 'in order to reach a settlement'. That is the reason why it is 'undesirable that the judge charged with the decision in a case should be involved in such a process'. In particular circumstances 'a suggestion by the judge may help the parties to overcome the differences between them' as they became manifest during prior negotiations; in 'relation to a boundary dispute the judge may perceive that at a certain location the dispute could be resolved by a suggestion of an open border or a degree of free passage'. But in doing so the judge 'must be careful not to make the suggestion in a way that might undermine the binding quality of his final decision. He must always recall that he is not a politician or diplomat, though in his

97 *Hostages case, I.C.J. Reports 1980*, at p. 22, para. 40 (emphasis added).

98 *Free Zones of Upper Savoy and the District of Gex, P.C.I.J. Series A, No. 22*, at p. 13 as cited in *North Sea Continental Shelf case, I.C.J. Reports 1969*, at p. 47, para. 87 (emphasis added).

99 *Passage through the Great Belt (Finland v. Denmark), Provisional Measures, Order of 29 July 1991, I.C.J. Reports 1991*, p. 12, at p. 20, para. 35.

100 *Certain Property (Lichtenstein v; Germany), Preliminary Objections, Judgment, I.C.J. Reports 2005*, Dissenting opinion by Judge Elaraby, at p. 45, para. 17.

101 *Pulp Mills case, I.C.J. Reports 2010*, Dissenting opinion by Judge *ad hoc* Vinueasa, at p. 272, para. 23.

102 *Application for Review of Judgment No. 158 of the United Nations Administrative Tribunal, Advisory Opinion, I.C.J. Reports 1973*, p. 166, Dissenting opinion by Judge De Castro, at p. 291.

103 M. Shaw, 'The International Court of Justice: A Practical Perspective' (1997) 46 *International and Comparative Law Quarterly* 4, 831–65 at 837.

104 M. Shaw, 'The International Court of Justice', 837. The way the Court has been performing this 'facilitative' role in its case law will be looked at in various subsequent chapters of this study.

105 M. Shaw, 'The International Court of Justice', 837–8.

106 S. Rosenne, 'The Qatar/Bahrain Case: What is a Treaty? A Framework Agreement and the Seising of the Court' (1995) 8 *Leiden Journal of International Law* 1, 161–82, at 179.

relations with the parties he must display diplomatic qualities. Fundamentally, though, his task is to apply the law, not to bend it.'[107]

The collegiate nature of the Court's functioning will make it rather difficult and delicate to perform its facilitative task in such a particular way, but we will find examples of individual judges providing such guidance to the parties.

The Court's judicial function is not limited 'to the settlement of disputes and the development of law'[108] because part of its function is *to facilitate* a direct and friendly settlement between the Parties, provided the exercise of this particular task is compatible with its Statute.[109] When otherwise than by adjudication the Court 'assists, facilitates or contributes to the peaceful settlement of disputes between States if offered at any stage of the proceedings' it does not arrogate 'any powers excluded by its Statute[110] as the Court has the *inherent power* to assist the parties towards peaceful settlement'.[111]

In recent times the Court has shown a willingness 'to adapt itself to the requirements of diplomacy and to encourage out-of-court settlements of pending cases when it finds it appropriate'.[112]

General statements 'at large' made by the Court in an Order for provisional measures about the legal position, tendering 'some advice to each party, which assisted them in reaching an agreed solution of the dispute', are 'not *obiter dicta* in the strict common law sense, but are what have been called "judicial dicta" not part of the *ratio* but relevant to the collateral matter'. Leading to an out-of-court settlement would mean that the Court has achieved its primary function under Article 38 of its Statute.[113]

It would be unwise and rather counterproductive for any observer to neglect or even underestimate these judicial pronouncements which are 'a collegial production of the majority of the members of the court or tribunal making the pronouncement', in contrast to *obiter dicta*, a concept 'unknown to international law' and about which 'there is no clear conception' of what the term 'means or can mean in international law'.[114]

The judicial pronouncements mentioned here quite aptly captivate the respective roles and the very essence of the functional interaction. Any assessment of the effectiveness of the performance by the two modes of settlement in actually settling a dispute between States should adequately reflect their respective advantages and inherent limitations.[115]

The Court's 'gentle persuasion' can be referred to as 'disputes management' or as a 'judicial peace-making process'.[116]

---

107 E. Lauterpacht, 'The Role of the International Judge' in *Liber Amicorum Jean-Pierre Cot* (Brussels, 2009), pp. 185–92 at pp. 191–2. For an illuminating commentary on another authoritative view expressed in a different era of international law and international relations see S. Rosenne, 'Sir Hersch Lauterpacht's Concept of the Task of the International Judge' (1961) 55 *American Journal of International Law* 4, 825–62.

108 *Pulp Mills on the River Uruguay (Argentina v. Uruguay), Provisional Measures, Order of 23 January 2007, I.C.J. Reports*, p. 3, Declaration by Judge Koroma, at p. 20, para. 5.

109 *Free Zones case, P.C.I.J., Series A, No. 22*, at p. 13.

110 *Aegean Sea Continental Shelf case, I.C.J. Reports 1976*, Separate opinion by Judge Lachs, at p. 20. Rejecting preliminary objections to its jurisdiction the Court 'assuming a quasi-conciliatory posture has viewed its role as that of conciliator to the peaceful settlement of disputes'. C. Murphy, 'The World Court and the Peaceful Settlement of Disputes' (1977) 7 *Georgia Journal of International and Comparative Law*, 551–78 at 552 questioning whether the Court in doing so 'may also have compromised some of its authority as a judicial organ'. In case parties have been absolutely unwilling to participate in the selection procedure for the creation of a Commission and the 'relevant treaties have not made provision for such default' the Court would exceed its judicial function if it attempted to remedy the practical impossibility of creating that commission: *Interpretation of Peace Treaties (second phase), Advisory Opinion: I.C.J. Reports 1950*, p. 221, at pp. 229–30. See also more generally S. Rosenne, 'The International Court of Justice and International Arbitration', 297–322.

111 *Legality of Use of Force (Yugoslavia v. Belgium), Provisional Measures, Order of 2 June 1999, I.C.J. Reports 1999*, p. 124, Dissenting opinion by Judge Weeramantry, at p. 197 (emphasis added).

112 S. Rosenne, 'The Qatar/Bahrain Case', 180.

113 S. Rosenne, *Provisional Measures*, p. 213.

114 S. Rosenne, *Provisional Measures*, p. 213, note 63.

115 See generally also A. Pellet, 'Remarques sur l' (in)efficacité', pp. 193–213.

116 B. Ajibola, 'Compliance with Judgments of the International Court of Justice' in M. Bulterman and M. Kuijer (eds), *Compliance with Judgments of International Courts* (The Hague, 1996), pp. 9–42, at p. 36.

The case law substantiates 'the principle that the Court can lend its good offices and encouragement towards the settlement of a dispute by the Parties themselves'[117] and the good offices of the Court 'would continue to be available to facilitate this process' of working towards a settlement within the legal guidelines indicated.[118] Thus the Court 'should encourage parties in dispute to find a solution to their dispute on the basis of law rather than otherwise'.[119]

As to the Court's role in 'preventive diplomacy' and comprehensive conflict resolution, and although it is a 'matter of juridical and political judgment' whether it would be 'wise or useful to seek an advisory opinion', having 'this option more constantly in mind would have great advantages for the whole process of preventive diplomacy'.[120]

The Court's 'procedure is beginning to be seen as a resort to be employed in a closer relationship with normal diplomatic negotiations; no longer is resort to the International Court of Justice seen, to use the traditional phrase, as a 'last resort' when all negotiations have failed. Rather, it is sometimes now to be seen as a recourse that might usefully be employed at an earlier stage of the dispute',[121] and then this 'can well have repercussions on its procedure and the interpretation of its procedural rules, especially in regard to intervention'.[122]

Providing the parties – in the dispositif of a judgment – with an opportunity to submit to the Court the whole of a case 'may have been conceived of as an act of constructive diplomacy'.[123]

The facilitative role of the Court may consist of what Vaughan Lowe aptly called 'hidden contributions' made to the settlement of international disputes.[124] Whether this role might be consciously developed is a difficult question altogether 'because it touches on the delicate balance between the role of a tribunal as an impartial arbiter between the parties to a dispute, and its role as one among many elements in a broader system of dispute settlement, in which the parties may concurrently be engaged in litigation, negotiations, and perhaps conciliation'.[125]

However, it has been rightly pointed out that once the decision has been made to seise the Court, and depending on the way of seisin and the actual submissions of the parties, the Court 'must be acutely sensitive to the risk that any initiative it might take to facilitate a dispute may be seen as an attempt to lead the parties down a road towards a settlement that the tribunal has prejudged'.[126]

In case the submissions of (one of) the parties consist of more than pure and proper *petita*, the remaining *propositions* may not be addressed by the Court in its operative paragraphs.[127] However, the Court may in the exercise of its facilitative role, for instance, recommend the parties to negotiate on those issues either during or after the proceedings.

---

117 *Legality of Use of Force (Yugoslavia v. Belgium), Provisional Measures, Order of 2 June 1999, I.C.J. Reports 1999*, p. 124, Dissenting opinion by Judge Weeramantry, at p. 197.

118 *Ibid.*, at p. 202.

119 *Pulp Mills case, I.C.J. Reports 2007*, Declaration by Judge Koroma, at p. 20, para. 5.

120 Judge Jennings, President of the ICJ speech before the UN General on 8 November 1991, *ICJ Yearbook 1991–92*, at p. 207. President Bedjaoui spoke of the potential role of advisory opinions as 'an effective tool of *preventive diplomacy*' or an even substantial contribution 'to the settlement of a dispute that had already arisen': speech before the UN General Assembly on 13 October 1994, *ICJ Yearbook 1994–95*, pp. 207–15, at p. 213.

121 Judge Jennings, President of the ICJ before the UN General Assembly on 8 November 1991, *ICJ Yearbook 1993–94*, p. 218 at p. 220.

122 *Sovereignty over Pulau Ligitan and Pulau Sipadan (Indonesia/Malaysia), Application for Permission to Intervene, Judgement, I.C.J. Reports 2001*, Separate opinion by Judge *ad hoc* Weeramantry, at p. 643, para. 22. We will deal with the impact of negotiations on intervention in Chapters 6 and 8.

123 E. Lauterpacht, 'Partial Judgments and the Inherent Jurisdiction of the International Court of Justice' in V. Lowe and M. Fitzmaurice (eds), *Fifty Years of the International Court of Justice: Essays in Honour of Sir Robert Jennings* (Cambridge, 1996), pp. 465–86 at p. 473.

124 V. Lowe, 'The Interplay', p. 244.

125 V. Lowe, 'The Interplay', p. 245.

126 V. Lowe, 'The Interplay', p. 246.

127 B. Metou, *Le rôle du juge*, p. 287.

On the other hand 'principled pragmatism' may at times 'imply that the Court should decline jurisdiction lest in the long term parties would be less likely to resort to its procedures without any short-term benefit in resolving the immediate dispute'.[128]

The 'founders of the Court created a *Court* and not merely an agency for dispute resolution. As such the Court must be concerned with the wide import of its judgments even if to the detriment of the immediate case before it.'[129]

Reframing the conflict between the parties in new terms – while respecting *the non ultra petita* rule the significance of which 'is that there should be a precise correspondence between what the Court is asked to decide, and what it does in fact decide', although it 'may not always be a simple matter to ascertain what precisely are the *petita*'[130] – may enable the parties 'to achieve a large portion of their interests without it being at the expense of the other',[131] and may also be part of the *facilitating part of the Court's function*, e.g. through the indication of provisional measures which 'concern the extra-processuel conduct of the parties',[132] resulting in or even ordering the resumption of negotiations or through a jurisdictional judgment clarifying the exact nature and subject-matter of the dispute.

Non-Appearance of the Respondent

In case of non-appearance of the Respondent – a manifestation of 'considerable disrespect for the court and *international adjudication as a forum of dispute resolution between states*'[133] and 'un défi au principle de l'égalité des parties'[134] – the Court, in exercising this particular task as *facilitator*, may not have knowledge of that State's views on a particular matter and as a result should 'refrain from any unnecessary act which might prove an obstacle to an negotiated settlement' (on a request for damages).[135] The Court's awareness of both the respective roles and functional interaction between the two modes of settlement has brought the Court to this cautious and reluctant position.

It is also true that 'the extent to which the claimant State has knowledge of the possible arguments of the non-appearing defendant may vary considerably'.[136] The process of prior negotiations may play an important role here.

If the purpose of non-appearance would be forcing the Applicant back to the negotiating table it is probably not going to work, except maybe in a situation where the preponderant reason for the non-appearance is the alleged non-exhaustion of the diplomatic channel in the pre-adjudicatory phase. Also, in advisory proceedings States may boycott written and oral phases invoking the political nature of the matter to be 'negotiated'.[137]

No more should be said here about non-appearance except for mentioning that doctrine is divided on whether there is a duty to appear.[138]

128 B. Szewecyk, 'International Decisions' (2011) 105 *American Journal of International Law* 4, 747–54.

129 G. McGinley, 'Intervention in the International Court: The Libya/Malta Continental Shelf Case' (1985) 34 *International and Comparative Law Quarterly*, 4, 671–94 at 694.

130 H. Thirlway, 'The Law and Procedure of the International Court of Justice 1960–1989: Part Four' (1999) 70 *British Yearbook of International Law*, 1–63 at 22.

131 W. Zartman, ' Process and Stages', p. 97.

132 K. Oellers-Frahm, 'Article 41', pp. 923–66, at p. 930, MN 19.

133 J. Fry, 'Non-Participation in the International Court of Justice Revisited: Change or Plus ça Change?' (2010) 49 *Columbia Journal of Transnational Law*, 35–74, at 37 (emphasis added).

134 M. Bedjaoui, 'L'Egalité des etats dans le procès international, un mythe ?' in *Liber Amicorum Jean-Pierre Cot* (Brussels, 2009), pp. 1–27 at p. 21.

135 *Nicaragua case, I.C.J. Reports 1986*, at p. 143, para. 285.

136 D. Bowett, 'Developments', 209.

137 J. Fry, 'Non-Participation', 52.

138 See and compare *inter alia* H. Thirlway, *Non-Appearance before the International Court of Justice* (Cambridge, 1985); J. Elkind, *Non-Appearance before the International Court of Justice: A Functional and Comparative Analysis* (Lancaster, 1984); and J. Elkind, 'The Duty to Appear before the International Court of Justice' (1988) 37 *International and Comparative Law Quarterly* 674–81.

2.3 Mutual Impact of the Two Mechanisms When the Court Exercises its Contentious Jurisdiction

The mutual impact of the two mechanisms of peaceful settlement of disputes will be illustrated in more detail later in Chapter 6, when we discuss the potential role of the Court with regard to negotiations during the course of the proceedings; in Chapter 7, where we address the role of negotiations in the judicial settlement by the Court; and, in a changed political and legal context, in the post-adjudicative phase (Chapters 8 and 9). But should one, for instance, be able to detect an impact in more general terms of the Court's jurisprudence on States' general attitude towards the various means of peaceful settlement of disputes?

Are States, as a result of case law, resorting more to negotiations than bringing a dispute before the Court? Or is there nothing more than the traditional preference for negotiations?

As to the traditional preference of States for a negotiated settlement, one certainly has to notice that sometimes States may decide, however, to consider the judicial procedure before the ICJ as the 'principal procedure for the peaceful settlement of disputes'.[139]

States may exclude in their optional clauses disputes regarding subject-matters over which they just happened to conclude a Special Agreement with one State, subject to successful negotiations on a *modus vivendi* or over which they were still negotiating with neighbouring states or within the context of conference diplomacy.[140]

May the 'existence of effective international courts and tribunals' actually 'improve diplomatic negotiations as a means of dispute settlement' and make 'States use diplomacy with renewed vigour and patience'?[141] Conversely, is it possible to speak about such a more general impact of inter-state negotiations on the exercise by the Court of its judicial function? These questions will be reviewed in the concluding observations of our study.

This study will demonstrate that, apart from the real functional interaction, negotiations both prior and during the course of the proceedings have a certain impact on the performance of the judicial function and that, conversely, there is also a distinct impact of the performance of the judicial function on negotiations by States prior to and during the course of the proceedings, and in the post-adjudicative phase.

As litigation 'is never an end in itself' and 'needs to be complemented by other processes' there is a need 'to step outside the narrow focus of litigation and view the position from a broader perspective – a perspective that is as much concerned with questions of policy, practicability and expediency as with law'. This broader view must be negotiated not only by the parties to a dispute, but also by third States, for instance through their intervention.[142]

Parties, when conscious of the fact that a dispute could be settled by the Court at a relatively early date, might take this as an incentive to conclude the dispute by other means.[143]

It has been rightly pointed out that 'when negotiations are conducted against the background of compulsory third party' resolution 'States have an added incentive to agree'.[144] Indeed, the 'very presence of legal means of dispute settlement may well encourage parties to a dispute to settle by means of negotiation'.[145]

Sometimes, opening the doors of the Great Hall of Justice 'may bring about a solution to a dispute'.[146] Bringing a case to the Court has indeed 'been used in the past to urge a negotiated solution as the *Passage*

139 *Border and Transborder Armed Actions (Nicaragua v. Honduras), I.C.J. Reports 1988*, at p. 89, para. 46 (sub-committee's position during the *travaux préparatoires* of the Pact of Bogota; this position did not reach the final text of Article XXXI).

140 See the examples given by Judge Oda in the *Nicaragua case, I.C.J. Reports 1984*, Separate opinion by Judge Oda, at pp. 493–4.

141 L. Reed, 'Observations on the Relationship', p. 296.

142 V. Lowe, 'The Function of Litigation', 221.

143 *Fisheries Jurisdiction (United Kingdom v. Iceland), Interim Measures, Order of 12 July 1973, I.C.J. Reports 1973*, p. 302, Dissenting opinion by Judge Gros, at p. 308.

144 J. Merrills, 'New Horizons for International Adjudication' (2006) 1 *The Global Community Yearbook of International Law and Jurisprudence* 47–74 at 57.

145 D. French, M. Saul and N. White, 'Introduction' in D. French, M. Saul and N. White (eds), *International Law and Dispute Settlement: New Problems and Techniques* (Oxford and Portland, 2010), xix–xxviii at xix.

146 *Border and Transborder Armed Actions (Nicaragua v. Honduras), Jurisdiction and Admissibility, Judgment, I.C.J. Reports 1988*, p. 69, Declaration by Judge Lachs, at p. 108.

through the Great Belt and the *Status vis-à-vis the Host State of a Diplomatic Envoy to the United Nations* cases show'.[147] This raises indeed the general question of the relationship between 'the two modes of peaceful settlement of disputes'.[148]

It is clear that 'the elucidation of principles in one case before the Court may prove helpful in bilateral or multilateral negotiations in other situations',[149] for instance during negotiations about those disputes between the same parties or between the parties to a case and a third State.

It is one thing to ascertain and to assess the functional interaction proper between the two modes of settlement, but this may not fully capture the entire picture. The complexity and time-consuming aspect of the two processes also involves perhaps less detectable aspects such as their *potential mutual impact*, and this to a very limited extent almost irrespective of the applicability of certain substantive principles and rules of international law to both processes.[150]

The process of negotiations itself is a fact the conformity of which with international law the Court is competent to examine;[151] for instance, the mere negotiating of a treaty may constitute a violation of the duty to abstain from any action which is incompatible, for instance, with the right of self-determination.[152]

Negotiations taking place prior to and during the proceedings serve as indications – subsidiary of course to the *petita* of the parties – to the Court, while guarding the integrity of its judicial function in order to better orient its decision and the direction in which the parties wish to resolve their dispute. At the same time the court has to be conscious of the possibility that the Applicant has been using seisin as a means to put pressure on the Respondent for the post-adjudicative resumption of negotiations rather than to obtain a judicial settlement of the dispute dividing the parties.[153]

The Impact of the Time Factor

Negotiations scholars have suggested that 'increased duration is more amenable to settlement', although it has to be acknowledged that 'conflicts that continue too long tend to be less likely to lead to settlement'.[154] On the other hand, it is almost a truism that the 'timing of dispute settlement efforts may' be crucial as indeed 'the use of a particular technique, may be helpful at one stage of a dispute but not at another'.[155] Moreover, parties' perceptions of the dispute might 'be transformed during the period of negotiations'[156] or during the proceedings before the Court.[157]

As the 'past surely cast a long shadow over present and future relations between the Parties ... a proper evaluation of the Parties' present rights can only be arrived at taking the full spectrum of the parties' history',[158] in particular when, for instance, close relations of friendship have allowed 'an issue of sovereignty' to 'go virtually unnoticed' for a long period of time.[159]

---

147 M. Kohen, 'Interaction', p. 23 (internal citations omitted).

148 G. Abi-Saab, 'Negotiation and Adjudication', p. 327.

149 M. Shaw, 'The International Court of Justice', 833.

150 *Continental Shelf (Tunisia/Libyan Arab Jamahiriya), Application by Malta for Permission to Intervene, Judgment, I.C.J. Reports 1981*, p. 3, Dissenting opinion by Judge Oda, at p. 190, para. 55.

151 *East Timor case, I.C.J. Reports 1995*, Dissenting opinion by Judge Skubizewski, at p. 254, paras. 94–5 and Dissenting opinion by Judge Weeramantry, at p. 178.

152 *Ibid.*, Dissenting opinion by Judge Weeramantry, at p. 204.

153 B. Metou, *Le rôle du juge*, pp. 359 and 361.

154 D. Frazier and W. Dixon, 'Third-Party Intermediaries', p. 56.

155 R. Bilder, 'An Overview', 7.

156 R. Bilder, 'An Overview', 18.

157 See on these aspects separated by the time factor respectively Chapter 1 and Chapter 6.

158 *Case between Qatar and Bahrain, I.C.J. Reports 2001*, Separate opinion by Judge Kooijmans, at p. 226, paras. 2 and 4.

159 *Sovereignty case between Malaysia and Singapore, I.C.J. Reports 2008*, Dissenting opinion by Judge *ad hoc* Dugard, at p. 143, para. 25; *Case between Botswana and Namibia, I.C.J. Reports 1999*, Declaration by Judge Higgins, at p. 1115, para. 7 that she did agree with all the judgment had to say 'regarding the legal significance of the diplomatic history of the matter'.

The history of a dispute with endless negotiations is almost bound to have an impact on the performance of the Court's function, and this perhaps in such a way as there is an 'extra duty' for the Court 'to seek out, from among the possible solutions, that which appeared to be the most pacifying and likely to cause the least dissatisfaction on either side', deciding 'solely in accordance with international law'.[160]

On the other hand, needless continuation of litigation is an obstacle to 'international harmony' in circumstances of conflict,[161] and could thus turn out to be counterproductive as to the resumption of the negotiating process. Hence, 'the aim of the Court must be to discourage endless litigation'.[162] Such a situation can be considered as an example of an inversed, dysfunctional interaction. Conversely, a State may apply 'to the Court to start *de novo* what was close to an agreement between the Parties'.[163]

When the Court does not indicate provisional measures but welcomes negotiations, the question could be raised: where 'is the incentive for the Parties to negotiate *now*, when each must believe that the strength of its position depends upon the judicial determination of its right'?[164] Hence, 'neither Party can blame the other for reluctance to negotiate at [that] stage' and it is clear that 'neither side will be willing to risk prejudicing the case by making concessions'. The chance of deadlock is therefore great until 'the Court has resolved some central legal issues'.[165]

In such a situation it could be argued that the Court pointing the parties to the negotiating table 'may be of little avail'.[166] The 'readiness of the Parties to negotiate on the basis of law' makes it imperative for the Court to render a judgment as speedily as possible.[167]

Although the 'need for an expeditious resolution of the jurisdictional question is imperative',[168] deferring such a decision might not only provide a 'non-appearing State with further opportunity to reverse its own decision and participate in the proceedings',[169] but moreover also a further opportunity for both parties to resume negotiations.

Some Examples of (Potential) Mutual Impact

The potential impact of the two mechanisms is the object and purpose of Article 36, para. 4 of the Court's Statute: i.e. to prevent that the 'declarant can regulate its conduct and direct its negotiations from the vantage point of its certain knowledge that the matter is now justiciable before the Court, while its opponent negotiates in ignorance of this vital item of information regarding its rights' and perhaps 'has made some vital concession, in the belief that the matter is still under negotiation'.[170] Such inequality 'can have practical repercussions on the course of the informal negotiations between parties, that precede the formal institution of an action'.[171]

Moreover, it is important for international peace and security 'that the processes of negotiation between parties are given full scope, without the fear of a sudden and unexpected termination, followed by the dragging of a reluctant respondent to the Court'.[172]

---

160 *Case between Qatar and Bahrain, I.C.J. Reports 2001*, Joint Dissenting opinion by Judges Bedjaoui, Ranjeva and Koroma, at p. 150, para. 8.

161 *Legality of Use of Force (Serbia and Montenegro v. Belgium), Preliminary Objections, Judgment, I.C.J. Reports 2004*, p. 279, Separate opinion by Judge Higgins, at p. 338, para. 7 citing the 1974 *Nuclear Tests* judgment.

162 *Land and Maritime Boundary case, I.C.J. Reports 1998*, Dissenting opinion by Judge *ad hoc* Ajibola, at p. 595, para. 179.

163 *Ibid.*, at p. 550, para. 34.

164 *Great Belt case, I.C.J. Reports 1991*, Separate opinion by Judge Oda, at p. 26.

165 *Ibid.*

166 *Ibid.*, at pp. 26–7.

167 *Ibid.*, at p. 27. Judge Oda's observations are *mutatis mutandis* applicable to the situation of the Court rejecting provisional measures but inviting the parties to negotiate.

168 C. Murphy, 'The World Court', 556.

169 C. Murphy, 'The World Court', 559.

170 *Land and Maritime Boundary case, I.C.J. Reports 1998*, Dissenting opinion by Judge Weeramantry, at pp. 362–3 and 367.

171 *Ibid.*, at p. 375.

172 *Ibid.*

Judicial settlement of a dispute 'is only a substitute for a diplomatic one' and has to provide the parties 'with a full, balanced and clear response to all' of their arguments and claims[173] instead of embarking upon an exercise of providing the parties with an advisory opinion 'rather than examining in a fair and balanced way the arguments and conduct of the parties'.[174]

The dissenting opinions in *the Interim Accord case* provide us with a fine example of the delicate balance the Court should try to achieve in the context of the functional interaction, and which required that an interpretation of the provisions of the Interim Accord should give due account not only to its interim nature but also to the ongoing negotiations between the States Parties aimed at the settlement of the initial dispute.[175]

Precisely because the Court is aware of the *potential effect* of its judgment on the negotiation process, it may refrain from granting additional remedies requested by the Applicant. But on the other hand its decision is likely 'to be used by the Parties to harden their positions in the negotiations'.[176] Direct or even indirect involvement of the Court in this initial dispute could be considered 'undesirable'.[177]

The proper functional interaction may in certain circumstances even give rise to the perception that *exercising jurisdiction* might 'not be rendering a service conducive to a speedy settlement of the initial dispute'.[178]

In declining jurisdiction the Court would have helped to ensure that the negotiations were 'meaningful' and 'resulted in the adoption' of a name 'by common consent'. The position assumed by the Court is *capable* of 'being interpreted as contributing' to 'renewed deterioration of the negotiations'.[179] Because of the potential impact of the Court's jurisdictional decision on the effective resumption of the negotiations, the Court should have limited itself to emphasizing the duty for the parties to negotiate in good faith.[180]

In the particular circumstance of the case, the Court should operate in order to promote the realization of the object and purpose of the Interim Accord by putting emphasis on effective negotiations in good faith and, on the other hand, being careful not to prejudice, directly or indirectly, those negotiations.

In reaching its decision, the Court takes into account not only the submissions of the parties – which, as already indicated obliges, the parties 'to transform their occasionally overstated political assertions into factual and legal claims',[181] – an eventual request for the indication of provisional measures, but also diplomatic exchanges prior to and during proceedings, as the case law illustrates.

Although in a maritime delimitation dispute the parties may through their Special Agreement set out in a binding way the 'framework of the task assigned to the Court, from which the Court could not derogate', a similar result may flow from the Respondent not only not contesting the Application as to 'the existence and content' of the dispute but also from positively acting upon it 'as defining the framework and the scope of the dispute': such conduct during the proceedings 'should be regarded as constituting the agreed basis of the framework of the case before the Court'[182] without negotiations during the course of the proceedings.

In a maritime delimitation dispute negotiations with regard to more in-shore areas may have been unsuccessful, thus rendering more difficult the Court's task to 'determine [the] boundary in more remote zones in the absence of a difference of views between the parties on the legal *criteria* for the delimitation in these more remote zones as well'.[183]

173 *Belgium v. Senegal case, Judgment, I.C.J. Reports 2012*, Dissenting opinion by Judge *ad hoc* Sur, at p. 605, para. 3.

174 *Ibid.*, at p. 605, para. 2.

175 *Interim Accord case, I.C.J. Reports 2011*, Dissenting opinion by Judge Xue, at p. 712.

176 *Ibid.*, at p. 718.

177 *Ibid.*

178 *Ibid.*, at p. 719.

179 *Ibid.*, Dissenting opinion by Judge *ad hoc* Roucounas, at pp. 727–8, para. 18.

180 *Ibid.*, at p. 729, para. 23.

181 D. Prager, 'Procedural Developments at the International Court of Justice' (2002) 1 *Law and Practice of International Courts and Tribunals*, 189–215, at 197.

182 *Territorial and Maritime Dispute (Nicaragua v. Colombia), Judgment, I.C.J. Reports 2012*, p. 624, Dissenting opinion by Judge Owada, at p. 726, para. 17.

183 *Land and Maritime Boundary case, I.C.J. Reports 1998*, Separate opinion by Judge Kooijmans, at p. 359, para. 14.

2.4 Mutual Impact of the Two Mechanisms When the Court Exercises Its Advisory Function

The Wider Political Context

It first should be noted that the existence in the background of a dispute the parties to which may be affected as a consequence of the Court's decision does not change the advisory nature of the Court's task 'when it is requested to exercise this part of its judicial functions although the advisory procedure has also been misused for purposes of confrontational diplomacy'.[184]

The Court may be requested to pronounce itself directly upon the rights and obligations of States, but it may also be asked questions of law which 'may have their place within a wider problem the solution of which could involve such matters'.[185] This wider political context[186] may thus also contain a legal dispute between States over which they have been negotiating or towards the solution of which they would be willing to do so.

During a debate within the General Assembly parties may have put forward conflicting claims introducing a 'substantial difference, going beyond a mere broadening in the scope of the questions posed'.[187] As a result 'the legal questions which the Court has been seised with are located in a broader frame of reference than the settlement of a particular dispute',[188] thereby bringing to the fore a certain mutual impact but rendering the functional link itself more remote.

A Pending Legal Question

The functional interaction will of course be much less remote when the General Assembly would 'bring before the Court, by way of a request for an advisory opinion, a dispute or legal controversy, in order that it may later, on the basis of the Court's opinion, exercise its powers and functions for the peaceful settlement of that dispute or controversy'.[189]

In such a situation the Court would perform the function of assisting the General Assembly in conducting or monitoring negotiations in the post-adjudicative phase to settle a pre-existing dispute, the existence of which did not bring the Court to consider this as a compelling reason to decline the request. Identity of the subject-matter, involvement of States as parties and the question actually pending are the conditions to be fulfilled in order for the Court to consider the request before it as relating to a legal question pending between States.[190]

In the different context of a dispute between the UN and a Member State where 'efforts to resolve the dispute did not materialize in a negotiated settlement', one view is that the request should not have been submitted to the Court but that it should have been resolved on the basis of a relevant dispute settlement clause.[191]

One 'can hardly argue that a request for an advisory opinion should be denied since such dispute was to be dealt within a contentious case'.[192]

A distinction should be drawn between a dispute actually pending between two States and a legal question raised by one of them before the General Assembly.[193] Bilateral diplomatic conversations or discussions in principle in the UN may have taken place without, however, 'a single trace of a negotiation which might appear to be a *preliminary to the crystallization of a bilateral dispute*'.[194]

184 S. Rosenne, *The Law and Practice of the International Court, 1920–2005 Volume I: The Court and the United Nations* (Leiden, Boston, 2006), pp. 168–9. On the advantages and disadvantages of advisory opinions see *inter alia* R. Wolfrum, 'Advisory Opinions: Are They a Suitable Alternative for the Settlement of International Disputes?' in R. Wolfrum (ed.), *International Dispute Settlement: Room for Innovations?* (Heidelberg, 2013), pp. 35–67 and P.-M. Dupuy, 'Comment', pp. 69–77.

185 *Western Sahara Advisory Opinion, I.C.J. Reports 1975*, at p. 20, para. 19.

186 *Wall Advisory Opinion, I.C.J. Reports 2004*, Separate opinion by Judge Kooijmans, at p. 223, para. 12.

187 *Western Sahara Advisory Opinion, I.C.J. Reports 1975*, at p. 26, para. 38.

188 *Ibid.*

189 *Ibid.*, at pp. 26–7, para. 39.

190 *Namibia Advisory Opinion, I.C.J. Reports 1971*, Separate opinion by Judge De Castro, at p. 175.

191 *Difference Relating to Immunity from Legal Process of a Special Rapporteur of the Commission on Human Rights, Advisory Opinion, I.C.J. Reports 1999*, p. 62, Dissenting opinion by Judge Koroma, at p. 113, para. 8 and at p. 116, para. 15.

192 R. Wolfrum, 'Advisory Opinions', p. 42.

193 *Western Sahara Advisory Opinion, I.C.J. Reports 1975*, Declaration by Judge Gros, at p. 70, para. 1.

194 *Ibid.*, at p. 72, para. 3 (emphasis added).

The requirement of reasonable specificity 'for a question to constitute a "legal question" for the purpose' of Article 96, para. 1 of the Charter and Article 65, para. 1 of the Statute – because 'otherwise it would not be amenable to a response by the Court'[195] and to 'be asked in neutral terms rather than assuming conclusions of law that are in dispute'[196] – situates itself well beyond the mutual impact level as to some extent it mirrors one of the functions of negotiations, namely that they should act as a forum *inter alia* to determine the legal issues in dispute between parties to a contentious case.

Even the fact that one of the parties concerned made a proposal 'to submit for adjudication by the Court a dispute raising issues *related* to those contained in the request', a proposal that was rejected by the other party, cannot affect or prejudice the 'legitimate interest of the General Assembly in obtaining an opinion from the Court in respect of its own future action'.[197]

Although as far as the potential impact between the two mechanisms is concerned it is important to note that the Court reassured the State which did not give its consent to the advisory proceedings that the answers the Court may give do not compromise that State's legal position in subsequent negotiations,[198] it cannot be denied that 'an opinion cannot fail to exercise very great influence on the respective legal positions of the States, all the more so because the opinion may be used as a means of psychological pressure upon the governments of the States concerned'.[199]

Although some advisory opinions 'are not unlike indirect settlements of unspoken or implicit disputes' and 'the Court's advisory role is as much part of its judicial mission as its role in contentious cases',[200] the view that 'in practice, an advisory opinion given by the Court in regard to a dispute between States is nothing else than an unenforceable judgment' appears to be far-fetched.[201]

Potential Impact of an Advisory Opinion on Negotiations

It is also well known that the political implications such as a potential impact on current or future negotiations that an advisory opinion 'might have are of no relevance in the establishment of' the Court's jurisdiction.[202]

The attempt to have the allegedly adverse impact on negotiations considered as a compelling reason for the Court not to exercise its advisory function and to decline the request failed.[203]

Addressing the argument that a reply from the Court might have an *adverse* effect on disarmament negotiations, the Court was resolute in stating that its conclusions, quite to the contrary, 'have relevance for the continuing debate' and would 'present an additional element in the negotiations on the matter'.[204] From the perspective of the potential mutual impact, the opinion would certainly be an additional element in the negotiations, but nothing more. The Court, fully aware of this, rightly added that beyond that 'the effect of the opinion is a matter of speculation'.[205]

---

195 *Wall Advisory Opinion, I.C.J. Reports 2004*, at p. 152, para. 36 (contention during the proceedings).

196 *ILOAT Judgment Advisory Opinion, I.C.J. Reports 2012*, at p. 136, para. 62.

197 *Western Sahara Advisory Opinion, I.C.J. Reports 1971*, at p. 27, para. 41 (emphasis added).

198 *Ibid.*, at p. 27, para. 42.

199 *Interpretation of Peace Treaties, Advisory Opinion: I.C.J. Reports 1950*, p. 65, Dissenting opinion by Judge Zoricic, at p. 102.

200 *Belgium v. Senegal case, I.C.J. Reports 2012*, Dissenting opinion by Judge *ad hoc* Sur, at p. 605, para. 3.

201 *Interpretation of Peace Treaties, I.C.J. Reports 1950*, Dissenting opinion by Judge Zorici, at p. 101. One of the considerations cited by the Informal Inter-Allied Committee on the Future of the Permanent Court of Justice as 'advantages of opening' the Court's advisory function to States was 'that it would make it possible … (3) to facilitate negotiations by clarifying certain disputed points (certain rights and obligations, the correct interpretation of instruments, and so on) which might otherwise negotiations to founder': R. Kolb, *The ICJ*, p. 1051, note 96. The same objective can be reached by (one of) the parties opting for a declaratory judgment.

202 *Legality of the Use by a State of Nuclear Weapons in Armed Conflict, Advisory Opinion, I.C.J. Reports 1996*, p. 66, at p. 74, para. 17 and *Nuclear Weapons Advisory Opinion, I.C.J. Reports 1996*, at p. 234, para. 13. The Court reiterated this requirement in its *Wall Advisory Opinion, I.C.J. Reports 2004*, at pp. 155–6, para. 41.

203 For a brief history of the 1962–63 Test Ban Treaty negotiations see *inter alia* T. Hopmann, *The Negotiation Process*, pp. 7–23.

204 *Nuclear Weapons Advisory Opinion, I.C.J. Reports 1996*, at p. 237, para. 17.

205 *Ibid.*

However, the request could perhaps also be seen as another modality of (dys?)functional interaction and referred to earlier if one follows Judge Oda's argument that the Conference on Disarmament in Geneva never being able nor attempting to negotiate an agreement 'prohibiting the use or threat of nuclear weapons under any circumstances', the request was an attempt 'to secure the Court's endorsement of an alleged legal axiom ... in order to produce a breakthrough'.[206]

Also in the *Wall Advisory Opinion* proceedings the argument was put before the Court that it should 'exercise its discretion and decline to reply to the question put' because rendering an opinion 'could impede a political, negotiated solution to the Israeli-Palestinian conflict'; in particular it 'could complicate the negotiations envisaged in the "Roadmap"', although 'differing views' had been expressed with regard to 'what influence the Court's opinion might have on those negotiations'.[207] The Court did not 'regard this factor as a compelling reason to decline to exercise its jurisdiction'.[208]

The question whether the delivery of an advisory opinion might have *adverse political consequences* was raised again in the *Kosovo case*, but this time without any explicit reference to the potential impact on negotiations. Dealing with this objection, the Court referred to its relevant case law on that matter, quoting that 'there are no evident criteria by which it can prefer one assessment to another'[209] – an addition that was not included in its *Wall Advisory Opinion*.

If the only possible interpretation of the Court's opinion amounted to finding that a non-consenting State's 'contention' in relation to the 'legal question actually pending' was utterly unfounded in law, the position of that State would be seriously compromised at least in political terms, meaning that its negotiating position would be 'seriously compromised' indeed. However, 'its *rights* would be unaffected, and there would be no finding having the status of *res judicata*, that its contentions were legally unsound'.[210]

> The *legitimate interests* of a State in the outcome of an advisory opinion proceeding are adequately protected, however, by the opportunity accorded (to) it under the rules of procedure of the Court to participate fully in those proceedings and to make known to the Court its views regarding the legal norms to be interpreted and any jurisdictional objections it might have (Art. 52 of the Rules of Procedure).[211]

Conversely, it has to be recognized as a matter of fact that in contrast to the Court's 1971 *Namibia* Opinion, its Opinions on *Western Sahara*, the *Wall* and *Kosovo* did not 'have any concrete impact on the outcome of the crisis in question'.[212]

In doctrine it has been rather persuasively argued that the Court 'should exercise its discretion and refuse a request for an advisory opinion when the underlying problem can be resolved only by lengthy and difficult negotiations'. Such advisory opinions 'can in fact exacerbate the problem by giving the impression that the last word on the legal aspects has been said'.[213]

Alternatively, functional interaction could benefit from the Court not refraining 'from giving an advisory opinion *in toto*' but refraining 'from answering certain questions or parts thereof' – e.g. with regard to some aspects of the *dispute* better left for negotiations between the parties.[214]

---

206 *Ibid.*, Dissenting opinion by Judge Oda, at p. 348, para. 21 and at p. 350, para. 25.

207 *Wall Advisory Opinion, I.C.J. Reports 2004*, at p. 159, para. 51 and at p. 160, para. 53. In both the *Nuclear Weapons* and *Wall Advisory Opinions* this 'was clearly an argument as to appropriateness or expediency, turned into a question of admissibility': R. Kolb, *The ICJ*, p. 1082, note 252.

208 *Wall Advisory Opinion, I.C.J. Reports 2004*, at p. 160, para. 53.

209 *Kosovo Advisory Opinion, I.C.J. Reports 2010*, at p. 418, para. 35.

210 H. Thirlway, 'The Law and Procedure of the International Court of Justice 1960–1989: Part Eleven' (2000) 71 *British Yearbook of International Law*, 71–180 at 123 (emphasis added).

211 R. Wolfrum, 'Advisory Opinions', p. 66 (emphasis added).

212 P.-M. Dupuy, 'Recourse to the International Court of Justice for the Purpose of Settling a Dispute' in L. Boisson de Chazournes, M. Kohen and J. Vinuales (eds), *Diplomatic and Judicial Means of Dispute Settlement* (Leiden, Boston, 2013), pp. 61–9 at p. 68.

213 A. Aust, 'Advisory Opinions' (2010) 1 *Journal of International Dispute Settlement*, 123–51 at 123 and 148.

214 R. Wolfrum, 'Advisory Opinions', p. 46.

Finally, because it 'has been generally maintained, including by the ICJ itself, that advisory opinions cannot be formally viewed as a means of international settlement',[215] it follows that 'the Court is not necessarily to be blamed for the absence of *actual impacts* of its opinions related to the settlement of disputes'.[216]

However, they 'do have a significant impact on the settlement of existing international disputes and the prevention of prospective ones' because they can establish breaches of international law, ascertain the existence of rights and obligations of States, determine the limits of legal behaviour and contribute to the development of international law.[217]

Potential Impact of Negotiations on the Functioning of the Court

An example of a more direct impact between the two means of settlement could be found in the potential application of Article 17, para. 2 of the Statute.

Should involvement in previous negotiations by a Member of the Court on a subject-matter or question which is before it automatically and in all circumstances lead to its application – for instance when a Member of the Court has been exercising good offices to bring parties to a negotiating table?

According to Israel, in its written document transmitted to the Court on the occasion of the General Assembly's request on the Wall, participation would be inappropriate for a member 'who has previously played an active, official and public role as an advocate for a cause that is in contention in this case'.[218]

The Court, referring to the position it took in its 1971 *Namibia Advisory Opinion*, ruled that the activities challenged by Israel were performed by the member of the Court 'in his capacity of a diplomatic representative of his country, most of them many years before the construction of the wall ... arose'.[219] It is relevant to note that in this particular case the Court also took into account the time factor with regard to the potential application of Article 17, para. 2.

Participation as a government representative in UN organs, not even as an active one in the formulation of a Security Council resolution, did not justify a different conclusion.[220]

Another issue concerns the right of a State to appoint an *ad hoc* judge when an advisory opinion has been requested on a legal question pending between that State and other States. In this context regard should be had to the course of the discussion in the UN and the direct exchange between the governments concerned.[221]

The question was raised what would happen if the dispute had ceased to exists 'at the time when the Court takes its decision on the request for the appointment of a judge *ad hoc*'[222] for instance as the result of negotiations during the proceedings.

2.5 The Political-Legal Dimension of the Functional Interaction

The success of resorting to the Court depends 'on a certain amount of goodwill between the parties in drawing up the compromis' as well as 'actually enforcing' the judgment 'subsequently made'.[223]

215 A. Douhan, 'Advisory Opinions of the Economic Court of the Commonwealth of Independent States: A New Means of Settlement of International Disputes in the Region?' in R. Wolfrum (ed.), *International Dispute Settlement: Room for Innovations?*, pp. 76–108 at p. 104.

216 P.-M. Dupuy, 'Comment', p. 75 (emphasis added).

217 A. Douhan, 'Advisory Opinions', p. 105.

218 *Legal Consequences of the Construction of a Wall in the Occupied Palestinian Territory, Order of 30 January 2004, I.C.J. Reports 2004*, p. 3, at p. 4, para. 2.

219 *Wall Advisory Opinion, I.C.J. Reports 2004*, at p. 5, para. 8.

220 *Namibia Advisory Opinion, I.C.J. Reports 1971*, at p. 19, para. 9.

221 *Ibid.*, Separate opinion by Judge Petren, at p. 129. See on this question more generally S. Rosenne, *The Law and Practice of the International Court, 1920–2005 Volume 3*, pp. 1662–3.

222 *Western Sahara Advisory Opinion, I.C.J. Reports 1975*, Separate opinion by Judge Petren, at p. 106.

223 M. Shaw, 'Settling Territorial Disputes', p. 268, referring to arbitration.

In an ideal world, full compliance with the obligations of Article 2, para. 3 and Article 2, para. 4 of the UN Charter would render '*all* disputes and situations' either 'negotiable or justiciable'.[224] It has recently been recalled that there 'obviously are cases more suited to negotiation than others, and there are cases in which the only means to settle the dispute is through a third party adjudication'.[225]

It has also been observed that in 'times of high international tension, States avoid judicial recourse, (while) in times of low international tension, States are more inclined to settle their disputes judicially'.[226]

However, the observation made by the late Ian Brownlie 30 years ago that more research is needed to discover why certain types of disputes are more readily susceptible to adjudication than others is still valid today.[227]

Ian Brownlie's successor at Oxford took up this question and identified 'categories of disputes that it may be unwise to pursue through litigation':[228] 'litigation in areas where the law is in the process of rapid and fundamental change';[229] 'disputes that require decisions on systemic problems';[230] 'disputes where the practical consequences of implementing the rights that are found to exist' and where 'the perception of the utter impracticability of the implications of declaring the correct legal answer operates as a constraint upon the tribunal';[231] and disputes over 'honour and vital interest', 'where a judicial decision on the legal issues' may make a contribution towards the settlement of the overall conflict' but 'alone cannot settle it' as negotiation for instance can 'complement the litigation, for satisfactory progress to be made', which brings us back to the functional interaction.

In those four categories 'resort to litigation may be particularly imprudent'.[232]

On the other hand, as the system is 'crucially dependant [*sic*] on compromissory clauses', this favours a 'piecemeal approach' to dispute settlement whereby other areas of international relations are reserved to 'other typically less formalistic forms of dispute settlement'[233] such as negotiations. As a result 'only small parts of the real dispute come before the Court' as parties present 'their case in terms of a given treaty'.[234]

However, ultimately the selection of the dispute settlement method 'depends on the will of the parties and is not necessarily defined by the category of dispute'.[235] Moreover, the will of the parties 'allows addition of functions of other dispute settlement method to the ones that the parties chose themselves'.[236] The 'settlement method of each dispute itself enriches its contents' as a result 'while diversifying functions'.[237]

When States choose to negotiate meaningfully they 'should equally be prepared to seek the settlement of their disputes by other means'.[238]

A good starting point for any analysis of the functional link between negotiations as a diplomatic method to settle disputes in a friendly way and adjudication by the Court is the Court's acknowledgement that because of their very nature legal disputes between States 'are likely to occur in political contexts' and 'often form only one element in a wider and longstanding dispute between the States concerned',[239] but that in the exercise of its function

---

224 A. Lall, *Modern International Negotiation*, p. 124.

225 M. Kohen, 'Interaction', p. 24.

226 Judge Schwebel, President of the ICJ, speech before the UN General Assembly on 27 October 1998, *ICJ Yearbook 1998–1999*, pp. 316–23, at p. 317.

227 Observation made during the Conference at Nijmegen, 40 Years UN, on file with the author. See also I. Brownlie, 'Why Do States Take Disputes to the International Court', in N. Ando, E. McWhinney and R. Wolfrum (eds), *Liber Amicorum Judge Shigeru Oda* (2 vols, The Hague, 2002) vol. 2, 829–34.

228 V. Lowe, 'The Function of Litigation', 214.

229 V. Lowe, 'The Function of Litigation', 215.

230 V. Lowe, 'The Function of Litigation', 216.

231 V. Lowe, 'The Function of Litigation', 219.

232 V. Lowe, 'The Function of Litigation', 220.

233 C. Tams, 'The Continued Relevance', p. 489.

234 C. Tams, 'The Continued Relevance', p. 490. The case between Georgia and the Russian Federation illustrates attempts to present Russia's use of force as a violation of CERD.

235 S. Sakamoto, 'Revaluation', 2.

236 S. Sakamoto, 'Revaluation', 2.

237 S. Sakamoto, 'Revaluation', 2.

238 Manila Declaration, Part 1, Article 10.

239 *Hostages case, I.C.J. Reports 1980*, at p. 20, para. 37.

the Court 'cannot weigh the niceties of political advantages';[240] neither is it concerned 'with political motivation which may lead a State at a particular time, or in particular circumstances, to choose judicial settlement'.[241]

It is clear that every 'dispute about which an action is brought before the Court is as a rule "political" in as much as it raises important issues and is the consummation of *lengthy and abortive diplomatic negotiations*'.[242]

The functional interaction works both ways, although in different dimensions and to a varying extent, depending on factors of time, political relations between the parties concerned, particular circumstances: for instance, it will become difficult to conduct proceedings 'in a secure and peaceful manner while parts of the country continue to be occupied' and when the 'threat of armed conflict will overshadow the proceedings before the Court'[243] – a context to which we return later – and a variety of events, both domestic and abroad, the quality, content and sensitivity of the rights and obligations which form the subject-matter of the dispute, and, for instance, the absence or involvement of third States.

The 'state of international relations among the parties to a dispute' may determine whether conditions are 'ripe to open negotiations, for negotiations to break out of stalemate' or 'for negotiations to be broken off',[244] and to submit the justiciable part of the dispute to the Court. By 'restricting the scope of the legal issues which they submit to the Court' parties 'enjoy a certain amount of influence over the settlement of the dispute' while still preserving 'the binding effect of judicial decisions'.[245]

The *process nature* of negotiations implies that attitudes of parties may change underway as 'irreducible objectives and vital interests shift' and 'power relationships fluctuate' as well as 'the understanding of states of their duties under international treaties and agreements',[246] while also the 'handling of each case in the course of international adjudication has a dynamic of its own'.[247]

Functional interaction is beyond doubt because bringing a case before the Court 'generally already has a deescalating "cooling off" effect' and it may 'enhance readiness to find a mutually agreeable solution'[248] during or after the proceedings. In this regard the exchange of written pleadings is 'one of the most effective ways of disclosing the strengths and weaknesses in a case, and revealing the cases in which a settlement might be a prudent step'.[249]

The 'reply and rejoinder, if authorised by the Court', should 'be directed at bringing out the issues still dividing' the parties.[250] Hence, the precise issues for potential further negotiations during the proceedings are also being further delineated. Moreover, written pleadings 'may have an importance going beyond the immediate case before the Court'. They may indeed 'constitute, and be designed to constitute, a national statement for the record, an exposition of a particular position that will' not only 'stand as an authoritative commentary for historical purposes',[251] but also for future negotiations with the same or other parties.

In this respect it is important to note that adjudication 'is not just about final rulings, but may also involve preliminary decisions, the importance of which in practice should not be underestimated' as 'a catalyst for the parties to reach agreement when previous discussions had proved fruitless'.[252]

240 *Certain Norwegian Loans case, I.C.J. Reports 1957*, Separate opinion by Judge Lauterpacht, at p. 65.

241 *Territorial Dispute (Libyan Arab Jamahiriya/Chad), Judgment, I.C.J. Reports 1994*, at p. 91, para. 52.

242 H. Lauterpacht, 'The British Reservations to the Optional Clause' (1930) 29 *Economica.* 137–72, at 157 (emphasis added).

243 *Certain Activities carried out by Nicaragua in the Border Area (Costa Rica v. Nicaragua), Provisional Measures, Order of 8 March 2011, I.C.J. Reports 2011*, p. 6, Request by Costa Rica, para. 16.

244 T. Hopmann, 'The Negotiation Process', p. 195.

245 H. Mosler, 'Problems and Tasks of International Judicial and Arbitral Settlement of Disputes Fifty Years after the Founding of the World Court' in H. Mosler and R. Bernhardt (eds), *Judicial Settlement of International Disputes. The International Court of Justice, Other Courts and Tribunals, Arbitration and Consultation: An International Symposium*, (Berlin, 1974), pp. 3–15 at p. 14.

246 A. Lall, *Modern International Negotiation*, p. 123.

247 *Ahmadou Sadio Diallo (Republic of Guinea v. Democratic Republic of the Congo), Judgment, I.C.J. Reports 2010*, p. 639, Separate opinion by Judge Cançado Trindade, at p .802, para. 214.

248 K. Oellers-Frahm, 'Nowhere to Go?', 449.

249 V. Lowe, 'The Interplay', p. 241.

250 M. Shaw, 'The International Court of Justice', 855.

251 M. Shaw, 'The International Court of Justice', 856.

252 J. Merrills, 'New Horizons', 56.

The proceedings before the Court offer a forum to the parties in which unilateral statements containing an offer if accepted by the Respondent 'may be seen as a form of negotiation *in foro*'[253] which the Court then may adopt in its reasoning or operative paragraphs.

States, the Court and observers should be aware of one particular political-legal aspect of the functional interaction: pre-existing inequality between States during negotiations is, at least in legal and procedural terms, being wiped out during the proceedings, the Court acting as the ultimate *equalizer*. The Court itself may have hinted at this aspect when it affirmed that the procedural right to apply to the Court is by no means 'insubstantial' because, whatever the outcome, 'all aspects of the matter can be discussed in the objective atmosphere of a court of justice'.[254]

Another important aspect of the political-legal dimension of the functional interaction has been aptly described as follows: a claimant may be 'playing for the rules rather than for a decision'. The 'primary importance of the case is to elicit a clear and favourable statement of the law on a particular point, which can serve for future conduct, rather than to win a technical victory on what may be unsatisfactory grounds'. Indeed, 'in such cases the judgment will again often be primarily useful not as a decision on – a resolution of – the particular case in which it was rendered, but rather as a legal instrument which can be used to strengthen negotiations in subsequent cases'.[255] On the basis of a test case, 'it is very much easier to negotiate settlement in similar cases'.[256]

A public rejection of a claim may close the door to any possible negotiations prior to the institution of proceedings, and this may sharply contrast with the record of negotiations in the past between the two States over a series of disputes which were ultimately settled by negotiations eventually leading to the functional interaction being curtailed as the result of the withdrawal of an Application.[257]

Negotiations may turn out to be an inappropriate method for settlement 'where one party holding an entirely reasonable and just position is faced with unreasonable or even aggressive demands'.[258] Adjudication would then become a viable and optional alternative, certainly when one of the parties 'uses negotiation as a way to indefinitely postpone the settlement of the dispute'.[259] Although international courts and tribunals are to be considered capable of overcoming the difficulties which have caused a deadlock in the process of negotiations between the parties, it is still possible for the parties to resume negotiations during the proceedings, as we will find out, in Chapter 6.

In another configuration an effective basis for the Court's jurisdiction may be lacking, leaving 'a State desiring to litigate' with 'only diplomatic means of dispute settlement'.[260]

Although unsuccessful attempts to successively use various modes of settlement over several decades may have rendered a dispute a 'bitter one',[261] the Court may be blamed for giving only a 'brief and cursory attention to the *factual background*', while judges may rightly point out that the 'history of each case is not limited to the successive attempts of its peaceful settlement; [as] it also comprises its *causes* and *epiphenomena*, which have likewise to be taken carefully into account'.[262] It is particularly important that friendly settlement efforts cannot 'be approached in a "technical", isolated way, detached from the *causes* of the conflict'.[263]

Hence, inadequate handling by the parties of the real issues and problems between them may result in the whole procedure for bringing their dispute before the Court being ill-started,[264] while inappropriate drafting of

253 V. Lowe, 'The Interplay', p. 242.

254 *The Northern Cameroons case, I.C.J. Reports 1963*, p. 15, at p. 29.

255 V. Lowe, 'The Interplay', p. 239.

256 V. Lowe, 'The Interplay', p. 240.

257 *Aerial Incident of 10 August 1999 (Pakistan v. India), Jurisdiction of the Court, Judgment, I.C.J. Reports 2000*, p. 12, Dissenting opinion by Judge *ad hoc* Pirzada, at p. 62, para. 1; at p. 74, paras. 16 and 19; at pp. 75–6, paras. 21–2.

258 H. Darwin, 'Negotiation', p. 77.

259 M. Kohen, 'Interaction', p. 23.

260 L. Reed, 'Observations on the Relationship', p. 295.

261 *Case between Qatar and Bahrain, I.C.J. Reports 2001*, Joint Dissenting opinion, at p. 150, para. 8.

262 *Kosovo Advisory Opinion, I.C.J. Reports 2010*, Separate opinion by Judge Cançado Trindade, at p. 543, para. 46.

263 *Ibid.*, at p. 545, para. 51.

264 *Arbitral Award of 31 July 1989, Judgment, I.C.J. Reports 1991*, p. 53, Separate opinion by Judge Oda, at pp. 85–6, para. 11 (*mutatis mutandis)*.

a Special Agreement may prevent judicial settlement of the real issue,[265] the 'germ of the problem' lying less in the judgment than in the agreement concluded by the parties.[266]

During negotiations leading up to a Special Agreement counsel may caution that when going along with the other party's approach 'the Court may be tempted to take a middle way, if it is available'.[267]

A number of considerations 'might drive the Court to reach an equitable solution to the extent it is firmly grounded in law, appear legitimate'. Among such considerations we find 'the desire to avoid creating additional grounds of contention between the parties' and 'lay the ground for future negotiations between the parties'.[268] As our study will demonstrate, these considerations are claiming a growing role in the settlement of contentious cases.

A call for an enquiry 'into the various maritime and other boundary delimitations on which the Court has ruled and the ascertainment as 'to what extent the ultimate boundary followed the Court's indications, and to what extent the parties choose by agreement to diverge from these' has been partly heard.[269]

The result of a Respondent's actions taken at the domestic and international level after the Application was filed could indicate not only that in the pre-adjudicative phase diplomatic negotiations had not even begun but also, more importantly from our perspective, that the dispute could have been solved if such negotiations had actually taken place.[270]

Although settlements 'that do not rest on some normative foundation that is separate from the power political considerations are unlikely to prove durable',[271] Judge Alvarez referred to the modifying and creative function of the Court especially in cases where a strict application of existing law might lead to 'settlements which might be found unacceptable'.[272]

2.6 The Functional Interaction is Charter-Based

In modern times the functional interaction between the two mechanisms has found its first expression in one of the Purposes of the United Nations: namely 'to bring about by peaceful means, and in conformity with the principles of justice and international law, adjustment or settlement of international disputes or situations which might lead to a breach of the peace' (Article 1, para. 1). This general objective has to be achieved through compliance by all Members with their obligation to 'settle their international disputes by peaceful means in such a manner that international peace and security, and justice, are not endangered' (Article 2, para. 3). The overall purpose of the maintenance of international peace and security thus provides the ultimate frontier and limit for the use by States of all means of peaceful settlement of disputes. Whether in this regard the option of not submitting a dispute to the ICJ may become more of a prescriptive rule in case seising the Court

265 *Ibid.*, at pp. 86–7, paras. 13–15 (*mutatis mutandis*).

266 *Ibid.*, Separate opinion by Judge Lachs, at p. 94 (*mutatis mutandis*).

267 S. Yayakumar, *Pedra Branca*, p. 41. The recent study by G. Giraudeau, *Les différends territoriaux*, has demonstrated the degree of 'transactional' in international case law dealing with territorial and maritime delimitation disputes. On settling territorial disputes see also *inter alia* M. Shaw, 'Boundary Treaties and their Interpretation' in E. Rieter and H. de Waele (eds), *Evolving Principles of International Law: Studies in Honour of Karel C. Wellens* (Leiden, Boston, 2012), pp. 239–63. See further also J. Merrills, 'The International Court of Justice and the Adjudication of Territorial and Boundary Disputes' (2000) 13 *Leiden Journal of International Law*, 4, 873–901. For a wealth of rich contributions see finally Part IX; Land and Maritime Boundaries, International Watercourses and Other Waters in *Liber Amicorum Judge Shigeru Oda*, pp. 1011–203.

As far as lessons are concerned to be drawn from border dispute settlements see J. Dahlitz (ed), *Peaceful Resolution of Major International Disputes* (New York and Geneva, 1999), pp. 93–177.

268 D. Richemond-Barak, 'The International Court of Justice on Kosovo: Missed Opportunity or Dispute "Settlement"?' 23 *Hague Yearbook of International Law*, 3–16, at 13.

269 H. Thirlway, 'The International Court of Justice 1989–2009', 351 and G.Giraudeau, *Les différends territoriaux*, pp. 88–97.

270 *Fisheries Jurisdiction (Spain v. Canada), I.C.J. Reports 1998*, Separate opinion by Judge Oda, at p. 484, para. 19.

271 A. Guelke, 'Negotiations and Peace Processes', p. 67.

272 *Corfu Channel case, Judgment of 9 April 1949, I.C.J. Reports 1949*, p. 4, Individual opinion by Judge Alvarez, at p. 41.

would or could carry the risk of further endangering the maintenance of (regional) peace and security is an open question.

A further, more detailed regulation of the functional interaction is to be found in a combination of Article 33, para. 1 and Article 37, para. 1 and Article 36, para. 3 of the Charter. From our perspective the intention of the founding fathers of the UN was rather clear: parties to a 'dispute, the continuance of which is likely to endanger the maintenance of international peace and security shall, first of all, seek a solution by', for instance, negotiation. If they fail to settle it this way, 'they shall refer it to the Security Council', which already possesses, at any stage of such a dispute, the power to 'recommend appropriate procedures or methods of adjustment'. In making such a recommendation the SC 'should also take into consideration that legal disputes should as a general rule be referred by the parties to the International Court of Justice in accordance with the provisions of the Statute of the Court'.

Chapter VI of the UN Charter in its relevant articles establishes the constitutional foundation for the functional interaction between negotiations and adjudication by the Court. The Court has taken care to remind parties that whether they accepted the Court's jurisdiction or not, they remained 'in all cases responsible for acts attributable to them that violate the rights of other States' and that any resulting disputes should be resolved by peaceful means the parties are free to choose under Article 33 of the UN Charter,[273] but that they are 'nevertheless under an obligation to seek such a settlement, and to do so in good faith in accordance with Article 2, paragraph 2 of the Charter'.[274]

2.7 The Multifunctionality of Negotiations

Well before the Court's landmark judgment in the *CERD case*, a mere comparison of the main roles negotiations are playing from both the perspective of the parties and that of the Court already illustrated their functional interaction with adjudication: negotiations as one of the mechanisms for the crystallization and determining the very existence and the subject-matter of a dispute; for clarifying the legal positions of the parties; for identifying the contours, limits and precise content of the judicial task; and for eventually solving (part of the) the dispute, eventually also during the course of the proceedings and as an instrument to implement the Court's judgment on the merits.

It will not always be easy to more or less sharply distinguish these various functions of negotiations as in the practice of States they tend to manifest themselves simultaneously or in some sort of combination.

In some situations the various functions of negotiations do converge, for instance when the aim is to conclude a compromis in order to submit to the Court a dispute over an issue of State responsibility and prior to which (no) countermeasures had been taken by the injured State because the offer to negotiate with the responsible State had been accepted or alternatively such an offer had been rejected.

Compromissory clauses, which may be 'no mere severable clauses of minor significance but an essential element of the entire agreement',[275] do frequently contain a reference to first resort to negotiations. According to the Court, such a 'resort fulfils three distinct functions',[276] the Court thereby confirming the multifunctionality of negotiations as a mechanism for the peaceful settlement of disputes.

First of all, such a resort 'gives notice to the respondent State that a dispute exists and delimits the scope of the dispute and its subject-matter', in line with the *Mavrommatis* pronouncement.[277] Furthermore, by the inclusion of such a resort parties are encouraged 'to attempt to settle their dispute by mutual agreement, thus avoiding recourse to binding third-party adjudication'.[278] Finally it 'performs an important function in indicating the limit of consent given by States'.[279]

273 *Fisheries Jurisdiction (Spain v. Canada), I.C.J. Reports 1998*, at p. 456, para. 56.

274 *Aerial Incident between Pakistan and India, I.C.J. Reports 2000*, at p. 33, para. 53.

275 *Fisheries Jurisdiction (United Kingdom v. Iceland), I.C.J. Reports 1974*, Separate opinion by Judge Dillard, at pp. 54–5 and Separate opinion by Judge Waldock, at p. 114, para. 22.

276 *CERD case, I.C.J. Reports 2011*, at p. 124, para. 131.

277 *Ibid.*

278 *Ibid.*

279 *Ibid.*, at p. 125, para. 131.

At this stage it is suffcient to note that for instance the second function is in fact double-edged in the sense that a more thorough functional interaction between the two means of settlement is likely to occur in case of failed negotiations.

A general provision in an agreement that the parties are 'resolved to settle their difference by peaceful means through bilateral negotiations or by *any other peaceful means mutually agreed upon between them*' does not modify 'in any way' the 'specific rules governing recourse to any such means, including judicial settlement'.[280] Such a provision 'does not entail as such any obligation' to submit the dispute to the Court.[281]

The effect of reservations in optional clauses to exclude the Court's jurisdiction for disputes for which some other means of peaceful settlement has been agreed 'is to discourage another state from taking a case to the Court in violation of an agreement to use negotiation or some other means of peaceful settlement'.[282]

On the other hand, once a State has made a commitment to enter into negotiations this step is not a gratuitous one, as 'it is not the Court's function to contemplate that it will not comply with it'.[283] This applies to all kinds of adjudication-related negotiations, such as those taking place during the course of the proceedings, either on the initiative of one of the parties or as a result of the indication of binding provisional measures and also to the post-adjudicative negotiations once again initiated either on the initiative of the parties or as a result of the judgment of the Court obligating them to negotiate.

2.8 Potential Impact of *Una Via Selecta* and Wrongful Expectations

Given the rising tension between them over a particular situation, fact or action, States may be brought to embark upon a process of negotiations toward a mutually acceptable solution, a process during which the principle of good faith 'operates in protecting the legitimate expectations which a legal-factual relationship' between the parties 'has generated'.[284]

A problem though may arise when for a long period of time prior to the filing of an Application parties have in their regular dealings, for instance, accepted 'a duty to settle all boundary questions through the existing bilateral machinery' and this course of 'joint conduct' is considered by the Respondent to constitute 'an implied agreement to resort exclusively "to that machinery" and not to invoke the jurisdiction of the Court'.[285] Might such a pre-adjudicatory joint conduct of the parties lead to such an 'implied agreement' or alternatively does it bring into operation an estoppel for the Applicant?[286]

It was regretted that the Court did not determine 'whether the bilateral negotiations on boundary problems which both states have been conducting created an expressed or implied representation on which one or the other had come to rely as a means of resolving their boundary problems'.[287]

Applying the conditions for estoppel to the facts and circumstances of the case would, according to the Court, have required that the Applicant would have 'consistently' made 'it fully clear' that it agreed to settle the boundary dispute 'by bilateral avenues alone'[288] and that the Respondent had been prejudiced by the instituting of the proceedings 'instead of pursuing negotiations, which, moreover, were deadlocked when the Application was filed'.[289]

So, apart from the conditions for estoppel there should have been an unambiguous mutual understanding to use the existing bilateral mechanism to the exclusion of judicial settlement. However, at the very early stage when the prospective Applicant is about to take the decision to institute proceedings, 'the prospective

280 *Aerial Incident between Pakistan and India, I.C.J. Reports 2000*, at p. 31, para. 45 (emphasis added).

281 *Ibid.*, at p. 33, para. 49.

282 J. Merrills, 'The Mosaic', 370.

283 *Nuclear Tests (New Zealand v. France), I.C.J. Reports 1974*, at p. 477, para. 63.

284 R. Kolb, 'Principles as Sources of International Law (with Special Reference to Good Faith)' (2006) 53 *Netherlands International Law Review*, 1–36, at 20.

285 *Land and Maritime Boundary case, I.C.J. Reports 1998*, at p. 285, second preliminary objection Nigeria.

286 *Ibid.*

287 *Ibid.*, Dissenting opinion by Judge Koroma, at p. 386.

288 *Ibid.*, at p. 303, para. 57 (emphasis added).

289 *Ibid.*, at p. 304, para. 58.

respondent State will usually be unaware of what the prospective applicant State is doing by way of readying itself to initiate, or to propose the joint initiation of, litigation before an international tribunal'. Even 'if the two states are each separately considering the possibility of initiating litigation, each will still in principle be keeping its consideration of this issue as confidential as it can'.[290]

The fact that most compromissory clauses contain a number of preconditions for the submission of a dispute to the ICJ, and to which we shall turn in the next chapter, has brought States to argue that such a clause did not make the Court 'the primary forum for the resolution of disputes to which it applies, but rather assigned to the Court 'the role of guarantor' in the event of for instance failed negotiations.[291] Conversely, a compromissory clause providing for the exclusive jurisdiction of the Court may prevent the facultative clause to operate as between States Parties to the treaty.[292]

During negotiations parties may of course, more or less explicitly, agree, even on a temporary basis, to exclude any recourse to the Court 'on account of, and for the duration of, the ongoing negotiations'.[293] But in order to enable the Court to determine whether this has actually happened, parties should provide the Court with 'details of those negotiations, in particular with regard to the way they have been carried out, or to their duration, *scope or state of progress* at the time of the filing' of the Application.[294]

The generally relevant aspects of negotiations such as the way in which they are being or have been conducted, their duration, scope and state of progress acquire a particular importance when the matter of the Court's jurisdiction is disputed. This is clearly illustrated by the Court's assessment that a Respondent had not explained 'the precise consequences which it considered the holding of those negotiations, *or the holding of negotiations generally*, would have regard to the Court's jurisdiction'.[295]

This pronouncement by the Court not only demonstrates the inherent nature of the functional interaction between the two mechanisms, but it is almost an invitation in general to States, when in similar circumstances negotiations are going on, to explicitly deal with this potential impact on the question of the Court's jurisdiction.

One of the reasons why parties may also agree to preclude the possibility of using a number of procedures, 'and in particular judicial remedies', is not to reopen 'such matters as were settled between them because they had been the object of an international judicial decision or treaty'.[296]

Finally, a Respondent may blame the Applicant for a démarche such as seising the Court for a problem which could be solved through negotiations.[297]

2.9 Double-Track Strategy Prior to the Start of the Judicial Proceedings

The freedom of choice guaranteed by Article 33 of the Charter and the absence of any hierarchy between the various means to settle a dispute also implies that parties have at their disposal the option to follow a double-track strategy. Given the complexity of international disputes, 'the chances of a peaceful settlement are enhanced if different avenues can be explored simultaneously'.[298]

Indeed, negotiations 'should be thought of not so much as a first stage in the conduct of virtually all disputes, but rather as an option available to the parties at any time, for use either alongside, or as part of,

290 A. Watts, 'Preparation for International Litigation' in N. Malick and R. Wolfrum (eds), *Law of the Sea, Environmental Law and Settlement of Disputes Liber Amicorum Judge T. Mensah* (Leiden, 2007), pp. 327–40, at pp. 327–8.

291 *DRC v. Rwanda case, I.C.J. Reports 2002*, at p. 236, para. 43 (Rwanda).

292 *Territorial and Maritime Dispute (Nicaragua v. Colombia), Preliminary Objections, Judgment, I.C.J. Reports 2007*, p. 832, Separate opinion by Judge Abraham, at p. 918, para. 56.

293 *Arrest Warrant case, I.C.J. Reports 2000*, at p. 200, para. 66.

294 *Ibid.* (emphasis added).

295 *Ibid.* (emphasis added).

296 *Territorial and Maritime Dispute (Nicaragua v. Colombia), I.C.J. Reports 2007*, at p. 858, para. 77.

297 *Land and Maritime Boundary case, I.C.J. Reports 2002*, Separate opinion by Judge *ad hoc* Mbaye, at p. 508, para. 10. (Nigeria).

298 J. Merrills, 'The Mosaic', 368.

other processes'.[299] It should also be noted though that complaints presented to the Security Council may not produce a solution, but could be conducive to the conclusion of a Special Agreement.[300]

Such a 'parallel reliance on *whatever* other methods – be it informal – of the pacific settlement of a dispute' is 'litispendence in a broad sense'.[301]

Some disputes can because of the subject-matter involved and the measures envisaged only be resolved by negotiations, but there 'are many disputes in which a combination of methods would facilitate their resolution'[302] several methods being used simultaneously or successively.

When for instance an optional clause provides for resort to the Court unless other means of pacific settlement are agreed upon by the parties,[303] this does imply negotiations in order to initiate these other means, a clear and modest example of the functional interaction prior to the start of the proceedings, as the next chapter will demonstrate.

Moreover, the Court's pronouncement that a dispute does not simply disappear because negotiations are taking place is corroborated by state practice when the parties decide to follow such a double-track strategy: to start, with priority, negotiations on the delimitation of a disputed area, while also having talks on the conclusions of a Special Agreement to refer the dispute to the Court.[304]

Indeed, after initial consideration of a text of a Special Agreement by Ministers for Foreign Affairs, Prime Ministers may then shortly afterwards finalize the text. At the same time they may 'define the general lines on the basis of which subsequent meetings' on the substantive issues would take place.[305]

Once the decision has been made to employ such a double-track strategy it may easily happen that one party may consider itself not yet ready to discuss a draft text of a compromis submitted by the other party. It may consider that the other party has agreed to seek a negotiated settlement of the differences and to try to prepare, if necessary, a draft Special Agreement for the joint submission of those aspects which, they might agree, were the points of genuine disagreement between the two sides.[306]

So for a useful functional interaction to occur within the context of a double-track strategy prior to the start of judicial proceedings it is absolutely necessary that both parties agree on which points they might still find themselves in disagreement over after a successful round of negotiations on the substantive issues that already divided them. When provision has been made for further meetings on the substantive issues, this makes it unlikely that one party should have undertaken 'an immediate and unqualified commitment to accept the submission of the dispute to the Court unilaterally by Application'.[307]

A particular and, according to the other party concerned, controversial modality of such a double-track strategy may consist in the future Applicant continuing 'to maintain bilateral contacts with (the other party) on boundary questions while preparing itself to address the Court'.[308]

Would such conduct not infringe upon the principle of good faith in negotiations as argued by the Respondent?[309] Or was the principle 'not all disregarded' as contended by the Applicant[310] because the Respondent 'knew perfectly well' what the intentions were several weeks before the filing of the Application?[311]

---

299 J. Merrills, 'The Means of Dispute Settlement', p. 561. We will not consider the simultaneous resort to the SC and the filing of an Application, and/or of a request for the indication of provisional measures as examples of the double-track strategy for our purposes; examples here include the *Aegean Sea Continental Shelf case.*

300 *Territorial Dispute (Libyan Arab Jamahiriya/Chad), I.C.J. Reports 1994*, p. 6, Dissenting opinion by Judge *ad hoc* Sette-Camara, at pp. 100–101.

301 J. Sztucki, 'Case Concerning Land and Maritime Boundary (Cameroon v. Nigeria): Provisional Measures, Order of 15 March 1996' (1997) 10 *Leiden Journal of International Law*, 2, 341–58, at 347.

302 *Aegean Sea Continental Shelf case, I.C.J. Reports 1978*, Separate opinion by Judge Lachs, at p. 52.

303 *Case concerning the Temple of Preah Vihear (Cambodia v. Thailand), Preliminary Objections, Judgment of 26 May 1961: I.C.J. Reports 1961*, p. 17 at p. 23.

304 *Aegean Sea Continental Shelf case, I.C.J. Reports 1978*, at p. 12, para. 30 and at p. 9, para. 18.

305 *Ibid.*, at p. 9, para. 19.

306 *Ibid.*, at p. 42, para. 103.

307 *Ibid.*, at p. 43, para. 105.

308 *Land and Maritime Boundary case, I.C.J. Reports 1998*, at p. 296, para. 36 (Nigeria).

309 *Ibid.*, at p. 296, para. 36 (Nigeria).

310 *Ibid.*, at p. 296, para. 37 (Cameroon).

311 *Ibid.*

Is there room to argue that there is a certain duty for States during a final round of negotiations to inform the other party that, in case of failure, the dispute would be taken to the Court?

The Court, referring to the *Right of Passage case*, reaffirmed that a 'State accepting the jurisdiction of the Court must expect that an Application may be filed against it before the Court by a new declarant State on the same day on which that State deposits' its declaration of acceptance, and ruled that 'there is no specific obligation in international law for States to inform other States parties to the Statute that they intend to subscribe or have subscribed to the optional Clause'.[312] Neither was the Applicant 'bound to inform' the prospective respondent 'of its intention to bring proceedings before the Court'.[313] Hence there is no justification for the Respondent to 'rely upon the principle of good faith in support of its submissions'.[314] Furthermore, the Court added that the Respondent 'was not unaware' of the Applicant's intentions.[315]

But how then to assess the fact that the information available to the Court may indicate that during the prior negotiations no mention was made of an international agreement on settlement of disputes?[316] According to the Court it would certainly go too far to infer that there would be an obligation for States during prior negotiations to mention the possible submission of the dispute to the ICJ. The principle of good faith does not seem to require that kind of openness. It does not prevent, however, the Respondent using this fact during the proceedings as an argument amongst others about the Applicant's conduct during those prior negotiations which would then be for the Court to examine and assess.

The fact remains that the Respondent only has occasion to consider its position with regard to the applicability and invocability of such an agreement once the Application had been filed.[317]

It may happen that the diplomatic exchanges leave a party hardly in doubt 'as to the proposal regarding the Court' which the other party would understand to be the subject of discussions to come: 'namely, a *joint* submission of the dispute to the Court *by agreement*'.[318]

It may also happen that after the breaking down of a series of bilateral negotiations, the parties involved decide to have tripartite talks for a relatively short period of time before submitting the matter to the Court[319] and then confirming before the Court that the possibilities of negotiations have been exhausted and that no negotiated agreement would be possible 'for so long as the Court has not decided what principles and rules are applicable'.[320]

2.10 Double-Track Strategy after the Start of the Judicial Proceedings

A combination of negotiations and judicial settlement, in parallel and not necessarily with regard to the whole of the dispute, may, in appropriate circumstances, present itself as rather desirable, as indeed it 'is always up to the parties to a dispute to have recourse to a conjunction of judicial determination and settlement by agreement'.[321]

Parties are perfectly entitled to continue negotiations during the course of the proceedings. It was on such an occasion that the Court had the opportunity to affirm first of all that the obligation to negotiate is not exhausted when parties after a series of negotiations finally were able to conclude an interim agreement.[322] The absence of a provision in such an interim agreement, as a result of the deletion of a sentence to that effect, that parties would reconsider the position before the expiration of that interim agreement, does not

312 *Ibid.*, at p. 297, para. 39.
313 *Ibid.*
314 *Ibid.*
315 *Ibid.*, at p. 297, para. 40.
316 *Aegean Sea Continental Shelf case, I.C.J. Reports 1978*, at p. 18, para. 43.
317 *Ibid.*
318 *Ibid.* at p. 42, para. 102.
319 *North Sea Continental Shelf case, I.C.J. Reports 1969*, at p. 18, para. 9.
320 *Ibid.*, Dissenting opinion by Judge *ad hoc* Sorensen, at p. 254.
321 *Revision and Interpretation 1982 Continental Shelf judgment, I.C.J. Reports 1985*, at p. 218, para. 47.
322 *Fisheries Jurisdiction (United Kingdom v. Iceland), I.C.J. Reports 1974*, p. 32, para. 76.

release them from this obligation to negotiate in respect of the basic dispute.[323] In the circumstances of the case, such an intention would not correspond to the Applicant's submission that the Court should declare that the parties are under a duty to negotiate; neither would it be consistent with the Respondent's intention to continue negotiations.[324]

The Court added that given the *continuous nature* of the general obligation for parties to negotiate, it could not have been their intention to wait for the expiration date and 'for the reactivation of the dispute, with all the possible friction it might engender before one of them might require the other to attempt a peaceful settlement through negotiations'.[325]

In order to 'ensure a good administration of justice, it is necessary not to delay the settlement of any dispute'.[326] This primary objective entails specific duties for both the Court and the parties before it.

As the parties have to conduct themselves during the proceedings in such a way as not to frustrate this objective, while using all the procedural steps and arguments available to them under the Statute and the Rules of Court, the question may be raised whether they are also under an obligation to continue negotiations which may eventually lead to the discontinuance of the proceedings or which may assist the Court in bringing forward the judicial settlement of the dispute.

As to the Court, the indication of a provisional measure directing the parties back to the negotiating table on matters of substance when it had already become clear to it that, given the history of the prior negotiations, any resumption would reasonably be futile would not ensure a good administration of justice. These and other aspects of the functional interaction will be addressed in more detail in Chapter 6.

2.11 Negotiations and Determining the Existence and Subject-Matter of the Dispute for Jurisdictional Purposes[327]

An Applicant may persuasively assert that the Respondent's 'denial of the obligation to enter into negotiations' regarding a particular subject-matter 'evidences a fundamental difference in points of view'[328] and thus 'constitutes a legal dispute'. Moreover, the Respondent's attitude 'closes any possibility of negotiating a solution to this difference'.[329] This particular and important function of negotiations to determine the existence and the subject-matter of the dispute for jurisdictional purposes will be more fully addressed in Chapter 5.

From a functional interaction perspective a distinction has to be maintained between prior negotiations on the substance of the dispute and prior negotiations aiming at the conclusion of a compromis. The latter process must result in a clear and workable instrument in the hands of the Court in order to properly and efficiently perform its function.

Individual judges may regret a lack of clarity in the compromis, and they may also identify a change in the position of both parties towards the whole issue and regret that the compromis had not been drafted in a proper manner. To enable the functional interaction to operate in a manner conducive to the peaceful settlement of

323 *Ibid.*, at pp. 32–3, para. 77.

324 *Ibid.*, at p. 33, para. 77. Contra on this point Dissenting opinion by Judge Petren, at p. 159.

325 *Ibid.*, at p. 33, para. 77.

326 *Asylum case, Order of 17 December 1949, I.C.J. Reports 1949*, at p. 267. Good administration of justice may have 'flourished as a maxim' but it 'clearly gave expression to a principle': *Certain Activities carried out by Nicaragua in the Border Area (Costa Rica v. Nicaragua), Joinder of proceedings, Order of 17 April 2013, I.C.J. Reports 2013*, p.166, Separate opinion by Judge Cançado Trindade,at p.177, para. 13. One should note that 'joinder is a procedural step which does not have the effect of rendering applicable *ipso facto*' the 'measures prescribed with regard to a specific and separate situation' applicable to the facts underlying the other case: *Certain Activities carried out, in the Border Area (Costa Rica v; Nicaragua)* ; *Construction of a Road in Costa Rica (Nicaragua v. Costa Rica), Order of 16 July 2013, Provisional Measures, I.C.J. Reports 2013*, p. 230, at p. 237 para. 28. For a recent and incisive analysis on good administration of justice see H. Sakai, '*La Bonne Administration de la Justice*', 110–33.

327 This formulation is taken from the Separate opinion by Judge Owada in the *CERD case, I.C.J. Reports 2011*, at p. 173, para. 10.

328 Application by Bolivia instituting proceedings before the International Court of Justice against the Republic of Chile, I, para. 4.

329 *Ibid.*

the substance of the dispute, it may then have been a wise approach to ask the parties to clarify their positions after the start of the proceedings in the jointly submitted case.[330] When the parties duly do so, this 'may be regarded as a diplomatic success rather than a judicial one'.[331]

The Determination of the Existence of a Dispute and of the Moment it Did 'Arise'

Doctrinal views

A prior negotiation condition formulated in a jurisdictional clause 'est intimement liée à celle de l'existence d'un différend'.[332] The functional link should be noted between earlier exchanges, which do not necessarily have to take the form of proper negotiations but which might take place *within the context* of proper negotiations or pre-negotiations and the primary condition of the existence of a real legal dispute that can be brought before the Court.

It is possible for the Court 'to examine its jurisdiction on the assumption that there is, as asserted by the applicant State, a legal dispute between the parties' and 'having established that it has jurisdiction on that basis, to turn, in the exercise of the jurisdiction so established, to the question whether that dispute really exists'.[333]

Intimately related to the question of its existence is the question of the moment it presented itself as such to (one of) the parties: 'When does a dispute *arise*? Does the verb refer to the time at which the injurious event occurs? Or to the time when the claim is first put forward through appropriate channels? Or when the claim has been rejected and the parties have finally disagreed?'[334]

Whereas one of the main functions of the pre-negotiations phase is to provide parties an opportunity to 'determine if there really is a conflict of [legal] interest[s], or if the conflict is primarily illusory and the result of misunderstandings and misperceptions',[335] a deadlock of the process may be caused by 'a simple divergence or differing visions of the problem to be solved'.[336] It is thus up to the parties to openly and clearly state their respective objectives from the start of the negotiations.[337]

One of the 'primary prerequisites for negotiation' is 'that there must be something to negotiate about', in our context 'an identifiable dispute', the existence of which parties must readily admit[338] because the 'non-recognition of the existence of a dispute, for whatever reason, can frustrate possibilities of negotiation'.[339]

A dispute 'can be defined in several ways, some of them more susceptible of resolution than others', and finding common ground on 'resolvable definitions of the problem' should be part of 'successful prenegotiation works'.[340]

Judicial view(s)

Negotiations conducted by the parties in a recent or rather distant past do form part of the sequence of events leading to a situation that gave rise to the dispute the Court would like to retrace before entering into the legal arguments;[341] in doing so the Court may establish facts from the records of proceedings as disclosed in the minutes of, for instance, a Mixed Boundary Commission.[342]

---

330 *Case between Botswana and Namibia, I.C.J. Reports 1999*, Separate opinion by Judge Oda, at p. 1123, para. 14; at pp. 1125–26, paras. 18–19; at p. 1126, para. 21; at p. 1142, para. 60.

331 H. Thirlway, 'The International Court of Justice 1989–2009', 371.

332 G. Abi-Saab, *Les Exceptions Préliminaires dans la Procédure de la Cour Internationale de Justice. Etude des notions fondamentales de procédure et des moyens de leur mise en œuvre* (Paris, 1967), p. 116. On the jurisprudential evolution with regard to such a condition see pp. 118–23; on the doctrinal evolution with regard to such a condition see pp. 124–5.

333 H. Thirlway, 'The Law and Procedure of the International Court of Justice 1960–1989 (Part Eleven)', at p. 77.

334 H. Lauterpacht, 'The British Reservations', 143.

335 T. Hopmann, 'The Negotiation Process', p. 191.

336 G. Faure, 'Deadlocks', p. 28.

337 G. Faure, 'Deadlocks', p. 31.

338 A. Lall, *Modern International Negotiation*, p. 33.

339 A. Lall, *Modern International Negotiation*, p. 34.

340 W. Zartman, *Negotiation and Conflict Management*, p. 123.

341 *Temple of Preah Vihear case, I.C.J. Reports 1962*, at p. 19.

342 *Case concerning Sovereignty over certain Frontier Land, Judgment of 20 June 1959: I.C.J. Reports 1959*, p. 209 at p. 220.

When a party relies on records of negotiations in support of a particular argument or hypothesis it needs to establish it just like any other kind of material before the Court.[343]

Minutes are the 'agreed record of the discussion that had taken place',[344] but in case of lack of clarity they should be analysed with the assistance of the *travaux préparatoires*, provided it is complete: 'not composed of partial, self-serving statements by one side or another in a complex multilateral negotiation', but rather 'a terse but comprehensive preparatory document which comprises all that the two Parties directly concerned had to say on the matter on that juncture of their relationship'.[345]

Minutes 'are not a simple record of a meeting … they do not merely give an account of discussions and summarize points of agreement and disagreement'.[346] Perusal of incomplete minutes may 'reveal the adamant positions of the parties' but they may not 'explain how and with what arguments' a particular provision of a treaty was approved.[347]

Some documentary evidence may 'appear on their face to have envisaged a process of negotiations' on a particular subject-matter.[348] Hence, bilateral exchanges of letters between the parties may have the legal significance of establishing the existence of a dispute.[349]

In other situations the negotiations will function as the catalyst for the coming into being of a fully fledged dispute.

An Application should show the Court that 'both Parties had attempted to identify the *legal disputes* between them and to resolve those disputes by negotiation'.[350]

Given the absence of prior negotiations the view could be held therefore that there was no dispute prior to the filing of an Application,[351] or alternatively that, even if such a dispute did exist, it 'had not been the subject of any diplomatic negotiations between them'.[352]

Boundary negotiations may have failed, but this 'does not *in itself* mean that a legal dispute has arisen' Moreover, that parties have not started negotiations on a related legal question may be easily explained when the sovereignty over a particular territorial area was still uncertain.[353]

In cases where a particular claim had not been made the subject of diplomatic negotiations, prior to the filing of the Application, a Respondent may argue that the subject-matter of that claim could not have been determined and as a result there cannot be a legal and justiciable dispute.[354]

Whereas Judge Oda pointed to the absence of negotiations, of a legal dispute and of a Special Agreement,[355] Judge Higgins stressed that the 'real relevance of the issue of negotiation lies rather in providing an *indication*

343 *Certain Frontier Land case, I.C.J. Reports 1959*, at p. 224.

344 *Case between Qatar and Bahrain, I.C.J. Reports 1994*, Dissenting opinion by Judge Oda, at p. 138, para. 16.

345 *Case between Qatar and Bahrain, I.C.J. Reports 1995*, Dissenting opinion by Judge Schwebel, at pp. 38–9.

346 *Case between Qatar and Bahrain, I.C.J. Reports 1994*, at p. 121, para. 25.

347 *Territorial Dispute (Libyan Arab Jamahiriya/Chad), I.C.J. Reports 1994*, Dissenting opinion by Judge *ad hoc* Sette-Camara, at p. 97.

348 *CERD case, I.C.J. Reports 2011*, Separate opinion by Judge Simma, at p. 195, para. 14.

349 *Ibid.*, at p. 199, para. 25.

350 *Armed Activities on the Territory of the Congo (Democratic Republic of the Congo v. Uganda), Provisional measures, Order of 1 July 2000, I.C.J. Reports 2000*, p. 111, Declaration by Judge Oda, at p. 131, para. 4. Whether this requirement is necessary in all cases brought before the Court or just in the particular case of an alleged armed aggression which then cannot be 'declared suitable for judicial settlement by the Court' (Declaration by Judge Oda, at p. 131, para. 4) is rather unclear. The position taken by Judge Oda during his time of office as a Member of the Court is well known. In his view, which he expressed on many occasions, prior negotiations are a *conditio sine qua non* for bringing into existence a dispute and thus for bringing a case: see for instance *Oil Platforms case, I.C.J. Reports 1996*, Dissenting opinion by Judge Oda, at pp. 890–91, para. 3.

351 *Oil Platforms case, I.C.J. Reports 1996*, Dissenting opinion by Judge Oda, at pp. 890–91, para. 3.

352 *LaGrand (Germany v. United States of America), Judgment, I.C.J. Reports 2001*, p. 466, Dissenting opinion by Judge Oda, at p. 525, para. 3 and at p. 528, para. 8.

353 *Land and Maritime Boundary case, I.C.J. Reports 1998*, Declaration by Judge Oda, at p. 467, para. 28 and at p. 468, para. 30.

354 *Right of Passage case, I.C.J. Reports 1957*, p. 125, at pp. 132–3.

355 *Land and Maritime Boundary case, I.C.J. Reports 1998*, Declaration by Judge Oda, at p. 336, para. 20, at pp. 336–7, para. 21 and at p. 338, para. 26.

as to whether a dispute exists at all over this matter' rather 'than whether negotiation is a "free-standing" pre-condition for bringing a claim'.[356] We will return to this aspect later.

Although the question who is responsible for the failure (one of the parties or both of them) has a 'certain importance if the key issue is whether there is a duty to negotiate before bringing a maritime delimitation claim (and if so, whether this is a preliminary or substantive matter), it becomes less pertinent if the real preliminary issue is whether a dispute exists' between the parties.[357]

The functional interaction also seems to entail preclusion coming into play when, on reflection of objective facts, considerations of good faith prevent a State from raising before the Court an objection of 'no dispute' when in formal bilateral contacts it had recognized the existence of a dispute 'which might have to be settled by judicial means'.[358]

Government officials may participate in discussions taking place within a larger and pre-existing framework of collaboration. It would be wrong to consider these discussions as evidence of a dispute between governments which had already arisen because 'states taking part in discussions in the General Assembly to express divergent views on the questions under discussion cannot be regarded as constituting legal disputes between them'.[359]

The Determination of the Existence of a Dispute: Positive Opposition of Claims

Doctrinal views

Practice 'demonstrates that the threshold required in terms of communication between the parties for the existence of a dispute is fairly low. In certain situations a dispute may exist even in the absence of active opposition by one party to the claim of the other party', and the 'exchanges between the parties do not require a high degree of intensity or acrimony. The formulation of opposing positions by the parties is sufficient.'[360]

Absence of opposition does not 'negate the existence of a dispute', neither does the failure to respond 'to the demands of the other party' as the 'decisive criterion for the existence of a dispute is not an explicit denial of the other party's position but a failure to accede to its demands'.[361]

Another doctrinal view has also to be noted. Indeed, it has been pointed out that the definition of dispute as it is widely accepted both in case law and in doctrine connotes 'an adversarial process culminating in adjudication'. However, when 'disputes do arise, there is no inherent reason why they should be treated by states in an adversarial or contentious manner' instead of a much more needed cooperative approach.[362]

The fact that a dispute arises does not 'qualitatively alter the interaction from cooperation' to 'adversarial dispute settlement'.[363] In a number of situations this may actually be the case and will be reflected when parties decide to turn to the Court by mutual agreement.

Judicial view(s)

As to the condition of positive opposition of two claims as reflected in the case law of the PCIJ and the ICJ,[364] it may be observed that the emergence of opposing claims is frequently the reason for the parties to initiate

---

356 *Ibid.*, Separate opinion by Judge Higgins, at p. 346 (emphasis added).

357 *Ibid.*

358 *Certain Property case, I.C.J. Reports 2005*, Dissenting opinion by Judge *ad hoc* Berman, at p. 72, para. 5.

359 *Western Sahara Advisory Opinion, I.C.J. Reports 1971*, Separate opinion by Judge Petren, at p. 109.

360 C. Schreuer, 'What is a Legal Dispute ?' in I. Buffard, J. Crawford, A. Pellet and S. Wittich (eds), *International Law between Universalism and Fragmentation: Festschrift in Honour of Gerhard Hafner* (Leiden and Boston 2008), pp. 959–80, at p. 961 and pp. 962–3.

361 C. Schreuer, 'What is a Legal Dispute?', pp. 963–5.

362 C. Hutchinson, 'Coming in from the Shadow of the Law', 117.

363 C. Hutchinson, 'The Duty to Negotiate', 138.

364 And to which Judge *ad hoc* Mampuya referred to in the *Diallo case: Ahmadou Sadio Diallo (Republic of Guinea v. Democratic Republic of the Congo), Preliminary Objections, Judgment, I.C.J. Reports 2007*, p. 582, Separate opinion by Judge *ad hoc* Mampuya, at pp. 637–41.

the process of negotiations in the first place, and it may take parties quite some time before they realize that they have a dispute on their hands.[365]

The Court's approach in the *CERD case*, and to which we return in detail later, 'amounts to suggest' that the Applicant 'is required to *establish a positive act of manifestation of opposition* from the Respondent – a new stringent requirement'.[366]

Indeed, it has to be acknowledged that prior notice of a claim and explicit rejection by the Respondent has never been a requirement for the Court's 'objective determination as to whether a dispute exists'. The Court has always been flexible by 'drawing inferences from the parties' conduct and taking account of their positions as stated before the Court'.[367]

The Court has refused to take into account declarations and propositions with regard to a particular territorial limit made during prior negotiations in case the process has not borne fruit, although it 'is entitled to take account of the shared view' of the parties 'as to the basis and extent of their dispute'.[368] On the other hand, diplomatic correspodence 'joue alternativement comme preuve médiate et immédiate, propre à révêler ou infirmer l'existence soit du fait qu'il sagit d'établir, soit d'une admission'.[369]

Other judges in the *CERD case* either took the view that the Court has even 'further lowered the standard' as compared with the *Liechtenstein case*[370] as there was no specific CERD claim or negotiations[371] or limited themselves to observing that 'there must be a bona fide dispute between the parties about the *interpretation or application*' of the applicable convention.[372]

The question whether there is a dispute has to be approached in a realistic and concrete way and the opposed views may reveal themselves in whatever manner, although formal exchanges which have taken place have never been 'an absolute requirement in the eyes of the Court' for the existence of a dispute.[373] Indeed, formulating a protest 'may be the first step in a process to settle a dispute diplomatically; it is not a *sine qua non* for the existence itself of a dispute'.[374]

In our conclusions we will consider the potential impact of this *new requirement* on the functional interaction. It is sufficient at this stage to observe that this is 'a litmus test of sorts that the Court will have to apply to the facts of future cases in which the existence of a dispute is contested'.[375]

365 *Sovereignty case between Malaysia and Singapore, I.C.J. Reports 2008*, Dissenting opinion by Judge *ad hoc* Dugard, at p. 145, para. 29. See also *case between Botswana and Namibia, I.C.J. Reports 1999*, Separate opinion by Judge Oda, at p. 1123, para. 14.

366 *CERD case, I.C.J. Reports 2011*, Separate opinion by Judge Owada, at p. 174, para. 11 and at p. 175, para. 13.

367 *Ibid.*, Joint dissenting opinion by Judges Owada, Simma, Abraham and Donoghue and Judge *ad hoc* Gaja, at p. 143, para. 3.

368 R. Rivier, 'La preuve devant les juridictions interétatiques à vocation universelle (CIJ et TIDM)', in H. Ruiz Fabri and J.-M. Sorel (eds), *La preuve devant les juridictions internationales* (Paris, 2007), pp. 9–54, at p. 34, note 66; and, for instance, Land, *Island and Maritime Frontier Dispute, I.C.J. Reports 1992*, at p. 406, para. 73 and *Case between Qatar and Bahrain I.C.J. Reports 1994*, at pp. 125–6, para. 40 as referred to by R .Rivier.

369 R. Rivier, 'La preuve', pp. 40–41. On the question of evidence (before the Court) see *inter alia* G. Niyungeko, *La prevue devant les juridictions internationales* (Brussels, 2005), On presumptions and inferences in international litigation see for instance C. Amerasinghe, 'presumptions and inferences in evidence in International Litigation' (2004), 3 *Law and Practice of International Courts and Tribunals*, 3, 395–410. The author draws a clear distinction between 'legal presumptions' which are 'prescribed by law requiring conclusions of facts from established facts' and 'judicial presumptions' where 'courts draw inferences from established facts', at 395.

370 In the *Certain Property case*, Judge *ad hoc* Fleischhauer expressed his concern that a lower standard might 'have negative effects on the readiness of States to engage in an attempt at peaceful settlement of disputes': *Certain Property case, I.C.J. Reports 2005*, Declaration at p. 69; *CERD case, I.C.J. Reports 2011*, Declaration by Judge Tomka, at p. 182.

371 *CERD case, I.C.J. Reports 2011*, Declaration by Judge Tomka, at p. 182.

372 *Ibid.*, Separate opinion by Judge Koroma, at p. 185, para. 7.

373 *Ibid.*, Separate opinion by Judge Abraham, at p. 228, para. 14 and at p. 231, para. 24.

374 *Ibid.*, at p. 231, para. 24.

375 'Procedural Developments at the International Court of Justice' (2011), 10 *Law and Practice of International Courts and Tribunals*, 3, pp. 506–96 at p. 545.

The Determination of the Subject-Matter of a Dispute

Doctrinal views

When the parties are unable 'to define the subject of the dispute and possibly also the method of seising the Court', a so-called framework agreement may provide a solution as it allows 'either or both of the parties to bring the dispute before the Court, each in its own way, and even by unilateral application'. Each party will 'present to the Court its own definition of the dispute', enabling the Court to 'determine the legal position of each party and to settle the dispute or open the road to an agreed settlement within the concept of partial judicial settlement'.[376]

The role of negotiations in order to determine and clarify the legal issues to be decided by the Court and the corresponding obligation for the parties, pursuant to Article 40 of the Statute and Article 49, para. 4 of the Rules of Court, to indicate the subject of the dispute and to set out their submissions at the relevant stage of the case are prerequisites for a proper application by the Court of the principle of judicial economy, described as a 'fundamental canon of adjudication' and which 'requires the judge to obtain the best result in the management of a controversy with the most rational and efficient use possible of his or her powers'[377] – although the principle 'has to be applied keeping in mind the aim of the dispute settlement system'. This aim is to resolve the matter at issue and 'to secure a positive solution to a dispute'.[378]

Conversely it may be assumed that there is an impact of the application by the Court of judicial economy on the need for and the chances of success for post-adjudicative negotiation.

Prior negotiations will be part of the material before the Court to allow it to base its own appreciation 'of what it was it had to decide',[379] once more indicating the functional role of prior negotiations as a mechanism instrumental in contributing to the proper functioning of the Court.

On the other hand, the indication of the nature of the dispute in an Application also has a potential impact, for instance on the feasibility and chances of success of negotiations during the course of the proceedings, once the pleadings have allowed the parties 'to agree what are the real issues for decision to bring the dispute to an end',[380] and on the Court's assessment of the continuous existence of the dispute in light of such diplomatic talks.

Judicial view(s)

The *Djibouti case* has demonstrated that under particular circumstances the determination of the subject-matter of the dispute may cause some difficulties and controversy.

In order for negotiations to constitute suitable material for the Court to examine and assess, the discussions have to relate to legal rights and obligations, for instance when a perfectly lawful action has nevertheless caused injustice or hardship to another party.[381] Negotiations about claims for compensation for the damage caused would then come within the realm of justiciable questions.

Although the absence during exchanges of any reference to a particular treaty will not necessarily bar the other party from invoking the compromissory clause of that instrument,[382] those exchanges 'must refer to the subject-matter of the treaty with sufficient clarity to enable that States against which the claim is made to identify that there is, or may be, a dispute with regard to that subject-matter'.[383]

376 S. Rosenne, 'The Framework Agreement as the Basis for the Jurisdiction of the International Court of Justice and Some Problems of Language' in S. Rosenne (ed.), *Essays on International Law and Practice* (Leyden, 2007), p. 162.

377 F. Palombino, 'Judicial Economy and Limitation of the Scope of the Decision in International Adjudication' (2010) 23 *Leiden Journal of International Law*, 909–32, at 910 and 909.

378 F. Palombino, 'Judicial Economy', 920, note 60.

379 S. Rosenne, 'Unilateral Applications to the International Court of Justice: History Revisited' in S. Rosenne (ed.), *Essays on International Law and Practice*, pp. 171–95 at p. 194.

380 S. Rosenne, 'Unilateral Applications', p. 195.

381 *Appeal Relating to the Jurisdiction of the ICAO Council*, Judgment, *I.C.J. Reports* 1972, p. 46 at p. 58, para. 20.

382 *Nicaragua case, I.C.J. Reports 1984*, at pp. 428–9, para. 83.

383 *CERD case, I.C.J. Reports 2011*, at p. 85, para. 30.

Although 'previous negotiations and diplomatic exchanges may provide considerable information about the opposing legal positions of the Parties'[384] it is also true that the proceedings of a meeting to which one party may have referred may *assist* the Court in identifying the positions of the parties at the relevant time.[385]

The functional role of prior negotiations in establishing the legal positions of the parties is a subordinated one compared with the positions the parties will defend in their written and oral pleadings. The Court stressed this point when making it clear that although one of the aims of prior negotiations is to make precise the nature and the scope of the dispute between the parties are willing to bring before the Court, the dispute will be further and clearly defined by the parties in their pleadings and oral arguments,[386] although in particular circumstances parties still have to reach during the proceedings 'a common understanding of what constitutes " the whole of the dispute"'.[387]

A different scenario may unfold in case a Respondent argues that it did not have 'the opportunity to consider, in the context of diplomatic negotiations, any proposal' for a particular aspect of the dispute which was only put forward in the Memorial.[388]

Although a proposal to start negotiations could be seen by the Court as 'to mark the inception of the dispute over' part of the whole dispute as submitted,[389] this does of course not apply as a general rule to all kind of negotiations over a subject-matter which later may end up before the Court, as it may fairly be taken for granted that negotiations will always start with the parties taking rather opposing positions with regard to the issues at hand. In a number of situations the dispute will exist long before that particular moment in time, but it will then be sharpened, deepened perhaps and more precisely determined through the process of negotiations.

In the *Belgium Senegal case* the Court considered that 'in the light of the diplomatic exchanges between the parties' a dispute regarding obligations for the Respondent under *customary international law* did not exist on the date when the Application was filed.[390]

When the Court warns that 'the facts and the situations which have led to a dispute must not be confused with the dispute itself',[391] it reduces to its proper proportions the functional role of prior negotiations as a catalyst in the process of the crystallization of a dispute.

Accusations of violations of norms of international law may constitute the 'source of the alleged rights', but they are not the source or 'real cause' of the dispute – not 'the facts or situations to which the dispute in question relates'.[392]

The potential or real role non-governmental organizations (NGOs) could play or have actually played in order to identify the subject-matter and the legal issues of a dispute or a request for an advisory opinion became clear in both the *Pulp Mills case* – NGOs having expressed concern is 'the real origin' of the case which only became inter-state years later when States stepped in – and in the *Nuclear Weapons case*.[393]

Prior negotiations are instrumental in establishing the date of the facts underlying the dispute and in determining the moment of crystallization of the dispute,[394] both aspects being important for determining the Court's jurisdiction *ratione temporis*.

384 *Barcelona Traction case, I.C.J. Reports 1964*, at p. 25.

385 *Aegean Sea Continental Shelf case, I.C.J. Reports 1978*, at p. 42, para. 103.

386 *Case concerning the Application of the Convention of 1902 governing the Guardianship of Infants (Netherlands v. Sweden), Judgment of 28 November 1958: I.C.J. Reports 1958*, p. 55 at p. 62.

387 *Case between Qatar and Bahrain, I.C.J. Reports 1995*, Dissenting opinion by Judge Oda, at p. 50, para. 25.

388 *Land and Maritime Boundary case, I.C.J. Reports 1998*, Separate opinion by Judge Kooijmans, at p. 358, para. 11.

389 *Land, Island and Maritime Frontier Dispute, I.C.J. Reports 1992*, at p. 381, para. 31.

390 *Belgium v. Senegal case, I.C.J. Reports 2012*, at p. 444, para. 54.

391 *Interhandel Case, I.C.J. Reports 1959*, p. 6 at p. 22.

392 *Germany v. Italy case, I.C.J. Reports 2010*, at p. 320, para. 26.

393 *Pulp Mills case, I.C.J. Reports 2010*, Separate opinion by Judge Cançado Trindade, at pp. 198–9, paras. 167–70. As in the case of the St Lawrence Waterway 'pressures of private interests, and regional interests on both sides of the border' played an important role in the coming into being and course of the dispute: A. Lall, *Modern International Negotiation*, pp. 65 and 66. See also for instance *Nuclear Weapons Advisory Opinion, I.C.J. Reports 1996*, Separate opinion by Judge Guillaume, at pp. 287–8.

394 J. Soubeyrol, 'La négociation diplomatique', 345–6.

The absence from a Counter-Memorial of any diplomatic correspondence identifying (a) particular dispute(s) after the critical date, inevitably results in the exclusion of jurisdiction *ratione temporis* because the source or real cause of the dispute before the Court have to be situated prior to the critical date.[395]

In order to improve the operation of the functional interaction an oral hearing 'might have helped the Court to identify the date when the dispute arose and the facts and situations to which the dispute related. It may have allowed the Court to establish which claims had been the object of "repeated attempts to reach an agreement" before the 1961 agreements.[396]

2.12 Negotiations and Determining or (De)Freezing the Legal Positions of the Parties

A dispute 'may be seen as the outward manifestation of deeper underlying conflicts' which arguably should be resolved 'before meaningful negotiations can take place'.[397]

In the period prior to the start of the pre-negotiation process relaxation 'of international tensions and increased international cooperation' in many cases 'facilitates the negotiation process and enhances the ripeness of international disputes for negotiated settlement'[398] once the process itself has started in earnest.

Negotiations are not only functional in determining the existence and the subject-matter of a dispute; their role is also to determine and to clarify the legal positions of the parties, perhaps to the extent of (de) freezing them, that is at least up to the start of judicial proceedings. In this regard it is worth recalling the need to distinguish between the 'subject-matter of the dispute', the 'dispute' and 'the claim'. Indeed, negotiations may give rise to (one of) the parties putting forward a number of new claims without changing the dispute.[399]

When countries embark upon a diplomatic correspondence these may result 'in a very clear legal dispute'.[400]

The Applicant may change the legal basis for its original claim and the solution being sought rather than the subject-matter of the dispute.[401] Such a new claim may be the result of negotiations going on during the proceedings either between the parties themselves or between the Respondent and a third State.

If the dispute would become different in character, this would not only prejudice the interest of third States given their right to request intervention and affect the Court's jurisdiction, but also the fair administration of justice applicable to both parties and 'the consideration of legal stability and predictability'.[402]

Raising a Question with Regard to a Particular Claim or Situation

Although 'international law does not prescribe any set form for the filing of complaints by States'[403] raising a question with regard to a particular claim or situation during prior negotiations is of crucial importance from a dual functional perspective.

1. It will enable the parties to substantiate their legal position afterwards and to determine whether that issue has really become the subject-matter of the dispute.
2. It will enable the Court to determine the moment in time when the dispute actually arose and what the real subject-matter of the dispute is as submitted by the parties.

---

395 *Germany v. Italy case,Counter-claim, Order of 6 July 2010, I.C.J. Reports 2010*, p. 310, Joint Declaration by Judges Keith and Greenwood, at p. 325, para. 6.

396 *Germany v. Italy case, I.C.J. Reports 2010*, Declaration by Judge *ad hoc* Gaja, at p. 398.

397 T. Hopmann, *The Negotiation Process*, p. 201.

398 T. Hopmann, *The Negotiation Process*, p. 207.

399 *Interhandel Case, I.C.J. Reports 1959*, Separate opinion by Judge Spender, at p. 61.

400 *Asylum case, I.C.J. Reports 1950*, Dissenting opinion by Judge Azevedo, at p. 349.

401 *Territorial and Maritime Dispute (Nicaragua v. Colombia), Judgment, I.C.J. Reports 2012*, p. 624, at p. 665, para. 111.

402 *Ibid.*, Dissenting opinion by Judge Owada, at p. 721, para. 8 and at p. 728, para. 23.

403 *DRC v. Rwanda case, I.C.J. Reports 2006*, at p. 38, para. 86 (DRC).

These opportunities for the parties may have been presenting themselves more or less frequently, but the Court considers it 'natural' for a party to raise the matter at any of these opportunities and the party concerned 'should have done so'.[404] Although it does not necessarily have to be at the earliest possible opportunity, the Court may have to observe that there may have been 'an outstanding opportunity' to do so.[405]

'Evidence of the change' which may have been introduced by a counterclaim could be found in the fact that a question amply discussed during the proceedings 'had not even been mentioned during the diplomatic discussions',[406] without any explanation being given as to why that decisive argument had 'not been invoked at the very outset in the diplomatic correspondence'.[407]

At the same time 'removed from the environment in which it arose, was understood and defined' a case may begin to 'undergo the effects of a process of change, at first discreet' but 'which may finally' result in 'completely transforming the dispute'.[408]

From the perspective of functional interaction the principle of estoppel, which is substantive in character, is 'also rooted in the necessity of avoiding controversies as a matter of public policy (*interests rei publicae ut sit finis litium*)'.[409] Hence, a State 'must be held barred from claiming before the Court the rights it failed to assert or to preserve when they were openly challenged by word or deed'.[410]

The failure of a party to invoke a particular argument throughout a whole period of negotiations lends support to a particular presumption.[411] On the other hand, 'it is not conceivable that' while a party recognized 'that it did not have any claim to sovereignty' over a particular cay, had it really possessed such a claim 'it would have refrained from at least mentioning it during the negotiations'.[412]

In a case of maritime delimitation the Court may consider that an exchange of letters 'did not mark the point at which the dispute crystallized' according to the *Mavrommatis* criteria, because 'no claims or counter-claims were articulated by the two parties at the time and the suggested negotiations came to nought'.[413]

As an exchange of letters may have taken place between former colonial powers,[414] negotiations do not always have to have taken place between the actual parties to the case, but the exchange of letters should if it claims to constitute a legally binding international agreement.[415]

'A dispute may arise long before it crystallizes into its component parts or reveals all its different facets. No special formality is necessary. It need not arise in the course of diplomatic negotiations. It may do so independently thereof and may precede negotiations.'[416]

It is in the context of negotiations that the *crystallization* of a dispute actually takes place[417] and which then becomes 'more clearly articulated';[418] then the 'issues are sufficiently specified in terms of law or legally relevant facts to constitute a legal or justiciable dispute'.[419]

Although the dispute must have 'crystallized' at the same moment for each of the parties to it, they 'may nevertheless not agree on the identification of that moment'.[420] As long as claims have not been formulated,

404 *Temple of Preah Vihear case, I.C.J. Reports 1962*, at pp. 27 and 28.

405 *Ibid.*, at p. 28.

406 *Asylum case, I.C.J. Reports 1950*, Dissenting opinion by Judge *ad hoc* Caicedo Castilla, at p. 381.

407 *Ibid.*, Dissenting opinion by Judge Badawi Pasha, at p. 314.

408 *Ibid.*, Dissenting opinion by Judge Azevedo, at p. 350.

409 *Temple of Preah Vihear case, I.C.J. Reports 1962*, Separate opinion by Judge Alfaro, at pp. 41–2.

410 *Ibid.*, at p. 40.

411 *Sovereignty case between Malaysia and Singapore, I.C.J. Reports 2008*, at p. 79, para. 219.

412 *Territorial and Maritime Dispute (Nicaragua v. Colombia), I.C.J. Reports 2007*, at p. 864, para. 100 (Colombia).

413 *Territorial and Maritime Dispute between Nicaragua and Honduras, I.C.J. Reports 2007*, at p. 700, para. 130.

414 *Territorial Dispute (Libyan Arab Jamahiriya/Chad), I.C.J. Reports 1994*, at p. 18, para. 29.

415 *Case between Qatar and Bahrain, I.C.J. Reports 1994*, Dissenting opinion by Judge Oda, at p. 137, para. 10.

416 *Interhandel Case, I.C.J. Reports 1959*, Separate opinion by Judge Spender, at p. 60.

417 *Sovereignty over Pulau Ligitan and Pulau Sipadan (Indonesia/ Malaysia), Judgment, I.C.J. Reports 2002*, p. 265, at p. 642, para. 31 (emphasis added).

418 *CERD case, I.C.J. Reports 2011*, Separate opinion by Judge Owada, at p. 176, para. 17.

419 G. Abi-Saab, 'Negotiation and Adjudication', p. 329.

420 H. Thirlway, 'The Law and Procedure of the International Court of Justice 1960–1989. Supplement, 2009: Parts Seven and Eight' 80 *British Yearbook of International Law*, 10–216, at 80. See for instance *Territorial and Maritime Dispute (Nicaragua v. Colombia), I.C.J. Reports 2012*, p. 624, at pp. 652–3, paras. 69 and 70.

negotiations are not capable of having this 'legal effect' with regard to the functional interaction between the two mechanisms.

One of the discernible limits of the functional interaction noted by the Court is that the 'political climate between States does not alter their legal rights'.[421]

But just as one of the functions of negotiations is to clarify the legal positions of the parties, could it then not be argued that close collaboration between the parties may have 'justifiably led' one of them to believe that the other party 'had no intention of resurrecting [by way of a counterclaim] certain allegations from the period concerned and of seeking to engage' its state responsibility?[422]

There is no need to dwell on this aspect, as ongoing negotiations do not take away the right of the other party to raise issues of state responsibility for a particular period dating from prior to those negotiations: the principle of good faith does not seem to stretch that far. The Court had this to say about such an inference: 'waivers or renunciations of claims or rights must either be expressed or unequivocally implied from the conduct of the State alleged to have waived or renounced its right'.[423]

Fully aware of the daily reality of inter-state relations, the Court added, on a more general level, that a 'period of good or friendly relations between States should not, without more, be deemed to prevent one of the States from raising a pre-existing claim against the other, either when the relations have again deteriorated or even while the good relations continue'.[424]

Indeed, as a conventional duty to cooperate implies a duty to negotiate, States may have done that for years 'without feeling the need to resort to judicial settlement provided for' until a case had been brought before the Court.[425]

(De)freezing the Legal Positions

The functional interaction takes a particular form when for instance an Application makes it clear that the two governments had maintained their respective positions during the prior diplomatic negotiations.[426] The situation is different when a Special Agreement amounts to 'novation of the application, resulting from negotiations' and therefore implies 'mutual concessions on the positions originally adopted'.[427]

While maintaining your positions during negotiations is hardly in conformity with the content of the obligation to negotiate as indicated by the Court – namely not to keep inflexibly your position – the Court is not saying anything about this aspect, although the parties' attitude during the negotiations had caused the deadlock and ultimately the filing of the Application. On the other hand it has to be admitted that, in general terms, when territorial and maritime claims are at stake there probably is not that large a margin for real flexibility during the negotiations; for instance the question of the applicability of the equidistance line may have given rise to disagreement from the beginning of the negotiations.[428]

It is then difficult to accept the view that 'the absence of agreement despite genuine negotiations must be proved by the party wanting to rely on the equidistance principle' which arguably would 'terminate the possibly endless repetition of detailed negotiations'.[429]

While in the *Jan Mayen case* the Court acknowledged that the positions of the two parties became clear from 'earlier diplomatic exchanges',[430] the Court in the *Corfu Channel case* poignantly observed that the

421 *Case between the DRC and Uganda, I.C.J. Reports 2005*, p. 168, at p. 267, para. 294.

422 *Ibid.*, at p. 263, para. 281.

423 *Ibid.*, at p. 266, paras. 292–3.

424 *Ibid.*, at pp. 266–7, para. 294.

425 *Pulp Mills case, I.C.J. Reports 2010*, at pp. 105–6, para. 281.

426 *Aegean Sea Continental Shelf case, I.C.J. Reports 1978*, at pp. 36–37, para. 87. In this case the Application was nicely divided into two sets of subparagraphs containing the respective positions of the parties: at pp. 6–7, para. 12.

427 *Corfu Channel case, I.C.J. Reports 1949*, Dissenting opinion by Judge Badawi Pasha, at p. 67.

428 *North Sea Continental Shelf case, I.C.J. Reports 1969*, Separate opinion by Judge Padilla Nervo, at p. 86.

429 *Ibid., I.C.J. Reports 1969*, Dissenting opinion by Judge Tanaka, at pp. 185 and 196.

430 *Jan Mayen case, I.C.J. Reports 1993*, at p. 55, para. 36.

'exchanges of diplomatic notes did not lead to any clarification' of the legal position during the coming into existence of the dispute.[431]

But even after the eruption of a dispute in full force subsequent negotiations may be needed in order to bring about further clarification of the opposing legal claims aiming at the subsequent formulation of the *petita*.

The *Qatar Bahrain case* has demonstrated, if need be, the importance for parties to a dispute to negotiate carefully if they do not want the whole of an existing dispute to be decided by the Court.[432]

The Court may find it appropriate, in retrospect, to infer from the attitude of parties during negotiations at a later time that during a much earlier period of the evolving controversy they must have shared the same desire of finality with regard to territorial questions pending between them.[433]

The fact that in a dispute over maritime delimitation a particular point may have been the last point on which there was agreement does not mean 'that it was the last point on which there were negotiations'.[434] During partially successful negotiations it is indeed important to distinguish points of agreement and outstanding issues which prevent a successful outcome.[435]

The negotiations which ultimately turn out to be unsuccessful may have been intense and focused from the very beginning on the entire maritime boundary.[436] The scope of negotiations does not change when only a partial result has been achieved. The impossibility of a negotiated agreement concerning the entire maritime boundary may then convince one of the parties to bring the matter to the Court,[437] thereby bringing the functional interaction into operation.

2.13 Some Examples of a Dysfunctional Interaction

Functional interaction between negotiations and adjudication may have achieved a Charter-based importance, but this obviously does not mean that its actual operation has become standard practice in all circumstances. Indeed, state practice and thus case law in this regard provides us with some examples where the interaction intentionally has become dysfunctional as part of the litigation strategy of one of the parties to a case. In such a scenario we find ourselves well beyond the potential mutual impact perspective mentioned earlier. The approach taken here by some parties basically finds its foundation on the attempts to sharply distinguish the two modes of settlement also referred to earlier.

A remarkable example of a *dysfunctional* link between negotiations and judicial settlement may be found when a party is referring to an earlier Exchange of Notes with another State in an attempt to exclude from current negotiations and from a forthcoming agreement any provision for judicial settlement given the Exchange of Notes with that other State: any unilateral act for instance to extend the State's maritime limits would entail the other government certainly referring that matter to the Court on its own initiative.[438]

Another illustration of a potentially dysfunctional interaction is the so-called *1984 notification* by the US during the course of the proceedings in the *Nicaragua case*. This notification contained mainly a provision to exclude from its 1946 declaration 'disputes with any Central American State or arising out of or related to events in Central America, any of which disputes shall be settled in such manner as the parties to them may agree'.[439]

431 *Corfu Channel case, I.C.J. Reports 1949*, at p. 30.

432 *Case between Qatar and Bahrain, I.C.J. Reports 2001*, at p. 77, para. 116.

433 *Temple of Preah Vihear case, I.C.J. Reports 1962*, at p. 35.

434 *Land and Maritime Boundary case, I.C.J. Reports 2002*, at p. 423, para. 243 (Cameroon).

435 At some point in the process 'enough points of agreement have been reached and enough alternatives eliminated so that remaining differences no longer involve interests, substantive criteria, and various forms of power' but instead 'initial offers' or 'previous agreements': W. Zartman, *Negotiation and Conflict Management*, p. 19 referring to Ickle.

436 *Land and Maritime Boundary case, I.C.J. Reports 2002*, at p. 423, para. 243 (Cameroon).

437 *Ibid.*

438 *Fisheries Jurisdiction (Federal Republic of Germany v. Iceland), I.C.J. Reports 1973*, at p. 58, para. 22 (Iceland).

439 *Military and Paramilitary Activities in and against Nicaragua (Nicaragua v. United States of America), Provisional Measures, Order of 10 May 1984, I.C.J. Reports 1984*, p. 169, at p. 174, para. 11.

The proviso taking effect immediately was aimed 'to foster the continuing regional dispute settlement process which seeks a negotiated solution to the interrelated political, economic and security problems of Central America'.[440] The US concern was 'that bilateral judicial proceedings initiated by Nicaragua would impede this ongoing multilateral diplomatic process'.[441] The exhaustion of such a regional process is a Charter-based precondition, the US argument continues, for referring a dispute to the Security Council because of its primary responsibility for the maintenance of international peace and security. Since the Court has no specific responsibility in this respect, the precondition imposes itself *a fortiori*. Raising certain issues involved in the regional process in the Application would inevitably render them 'largely immune to further adjustment in the course of the negotiations, thus disrupting the balance of the negotiations'. The US went as far as to contend that the Application was 'incompatible with the Contadora process'.[442]

Nicaragua argued that they would continue to be involved in the Contadora process, but first of all that this process was unable to resolve or even address 'our legal claims' and that, moreover, the judicial proceedings cannot 'prejudice the legitimate rights of any other States, or disrupt the Contadora process'.[443]

In the same case it became clear that the dysfunctional interaction between the two mechanisms may form part of the diplomatic and litigation strategy of one of the parties. Indeed, the 'entire premise of United States diplomatic efforts was that Nicaragua was not a party to the optional Clause'.[444] The diplomatic efforts of a party may thus be based on the serial assumptions that the other party has not made such a declaration, is thus not bound by the optional clause system and that, at least on that basis, the Court would lack jurisdiction to settle a dispute which forms the subject of the diplomatic efforts to solve it.

Certainly a State is entirely free in negotiations not to refer to a particular treaty as having been violated by conduct of the other State, but the Court ruled that 'it does not necessarily follow' that such a State 'is debarred from invoking the compromissory clause in that treaty'.[445]

This statement illustrates that the functional interaction has been *institutionalized* by the drafting of compromissory clauses, the conclusion of a compromis and by the making of a facultative declaration containing such a prior negotiation clause.

In the *Cameroon Nigeria case* the Court rejected an argument put forward by the Respondent and which would have rendered the interaction dysfunctional. A party cannot refer to a process of boundary demarcation which is underway in order to call for judicial restraint on grounds of judicial propriety. The Court held that the Respondent cannot have it both ways: arguing that the demarcation procedure was not yet completed while it would at the same time render the Application moot.[446] Judge Ajibola's position that the Application was intended for the Court 'to start *de novo* what was close to an agreement between the Parties' reflects the resulting dysfunctional interaction.[447]

Negotiations may have been partially successful so that in a case submitted by compromis the 'Court's judgment will thus substitute for the non-existing agreement … and shall resolve all such matters which have not been settled by the Parties',[448] a textbook example it seems of the functional interaction and complementarity between the two mechanisms, although Parties may strongly disagree about further implications of the interaction: are the principles recognized in an Agreement 'applicable both to the diplomatic negotiations between the States and for the eventual settlement of the dispute by the Court'[449] or is the Court obliged to decide according to Article 38 of the Statute?[450]

440 *Nicaragua case, I.C.J. Reports 1984*, at p. 174, para. 11.

441 *Ibid.*, at p. 183, para. 33. Such an alleged impact would constitute a compelling reason for the Court to deny the request for provisional measures: at pp. 184–5, paras. 35 and 36 (US).

442 *Ibid.*, at p. 438, para. 102 (US).

443 *Ibid.*, at pp. 185–86, para. 38. See more on the (dys)functional interaction in this case *infra*.

444 *Ibid.*, at p. 414, para. 50.

445 *Ibid.*, at p. 428, para. 83.

446 *Land and Maritime Boundary case, I.C.J. Reports 1998*, at pp. 308–9, para. 72.

447 *Land and Maritime Boundary case, I.C.J. Reports 2002*, Dissenting opinion by Judge *ad hoc* Ajibola, at p. 550, para. 34.

448 *Maritime Delimitation in the Black Sea, I.C.J. Reports 2009*, at p. 74, para. 29.

449 *Ibid.*, at pp. 75–76, paras. 33–34, no distinction being made (Romania).

450 *Ibid.*, at p. 77, para. 37 (Ukraine).

The argument continues that some of these principles may be relevant to the Court as part of established rules, 'but not as part of any bilateral agreement'.[451] Not surprisingly, by referring to the *chapeau* of these principles the Court considered them '*to be taken into account*' during the negotiations but that they '*do not constitute the law to be applied by the Court*'.[452]

The argument that failed is another example of (an attempt at) dysfunctional interaction. Dysfunctional interaction may not only occur as a result of the litigation or negotiation strategy of (one of) the parties; it may also underlie the position taken by dissenting judges when they consider the Court's decision on its *prima facie* jurisdiction to be wrong because 'it has neither succeeded in establishing the existence of a dispute' over the *CERD*'s interpretation or application 'nor demonstrated that the precondition for the seisin of the Court has been satisfied'.[453]

Individual judges may also be signalling the pendulum of functional interaction swinging back from adjudication to negotiation on the occasion of disagreeing with a decision on a request for intervention. The alleged existence of a more expansive trend to grant such requests may be put back by 'a reversion to the more restrictive jurisprudence of the admissibility of requests for intervention at least in the field of maritime delimitation'.[454]

The qualification that a disputed decision may signal such reversion 'at least in the field of maritime delimitation' corresponds to a view held by some of the most senior judges at the relevant period: that this is a subject-matter which almost by nature does not lend itself to adjudication as a process of negotiations is the appropriate mechanisms to deal with it.

The functional interaction necessarily also contains an element of time. As in international law there is no specific time limit for the filing of an Application, a party considering taking this step may be 'engaged in a variety of activities at the diplomatic and consular level'.[455] Although these various activities are not negotiations proper, the related question is whether this aspect of delay is also applicable when negotiations have failed or whether in such a situation there is room for at least a presumption that the State would not wait too long before filing its Application. That question will be addressed in the next chapter.

A final example of dysfunctional interaction presents itself when parties have 'not even started negotiations to agree upon' the delimitation of for instance the continental shelf because the status of the starting land area was still uncertain. In such a context the Court cannot 'initiate compulsory procedures entailing a binding decision'.[456]

451 *Ibid.*, at p. 77, para. 37 (Ukraine).

452 *Ibid.*, at p. 78, para. 41 (emphasis added).

453 *CERD case, I.C.J. Reports 2008*, Joint dissenting opinion, at pp. 404–5, para. 19.

454 *Territorial and Maritime Dispute (Nicaragua v. Colombia), Application for Permission to Intervene, Judgment, I.C.J. Reports 2011*, p. 348, Dissenting opinion by Judge Al-Khasawneh, at p. 375, para. 6.

455 *LaGrand case, I.C.J. Reports 2001*, at p. 487, para. 56 (Germany).

456 *Land and Maritime Boundary case, I.C.J. Reports 2002*, Declaration by Judge Oda, at p. 468, para. 30.

Chapter 3
Negotiations as a Precondition for the Submission of a Dispute to the Court

Introduction

Because the Court's first duty is to ascertain the 'true subject of the dispute, the object and purpose of the claim' a dispute cannot be separated 'from the situation in which it has arisen, and from further developments which may have affected it'.[1] These two extra-judicial factors include both prior negotiations, the subject of this chapter, and subsequent negotiations during the course of the proceedings which we will discuss in Chapter 6.

The functional interaction may be summarily described as having its origin in a legal claim or a fact causing a dispute to erupt between two States and then giving rise to negotiations and diplomatic correspondence between them in an attempt to arrive at a friendly solution; if these do not produce a satisfactory solution to (one or both) of the parties, either or both of them may decide to submit the dispute to the Court.[2]

The first role negotiations are presumed to play, chronologically speaking, is to function as an alleged or desirable or necessary precondition for the submission of a dispute to the Court.[3]

A duty for the parties first to try to settle the dispute by diplomatic negotiations may find its legal basis in general international law and/or in particular provisions contained in compromissory clauses, facultative declarations or in a compromis.[4]

Is there a rule of customary international law according to which prior negotiations are a necessary precondition for the seisin of the Court and can it not, because of its importance, be considered to have 'tacitly been dispensed with, in the absence of any words making clear an intention to do so'?[5]

If there is such a rule does it really impose *a legal obligation* upon the parties to a dispute or is it *merely a matter of fact* later to be *objectively* assessed by the Court?

Or is there no such rule and does seisin of the Court only require prior negotiations if such a condition has been explicitly provided for?

A brief survey of compromissory clauses,'which have not always been a model of clarity'[6] will provide us with the manner in which the precondition of prior negotiations has found its way to be followed by a similar exercise with regard to optional clauses. It should not necessarily be assumed that its appearance in these instruments is a clear indication that also general international law requires parties first to go through a process of negotiations before turning to the Court.

---

1 *Nuclear Tests (New Zealand v. France), I.C.J. Reports 1974*, at p. 467, para. 31.

2 See for instance *Case concerning the Aerial Incident of 27 July 1955 (Israel v. Bulgaria), Preliminary Objections, Judgment of 26 May 1959: I.C.J. Reports 1959*, p. 127 at p. 135.

3 For an overview of the prior negotiation clause and its application in traditional arbitral practice see *inter alia* N.-E. Ghozali, 'La négociation diplomatique', 325–9. For an overview of the same practice under the PCIJ see pp. 331–3 and in more detail N. Kaasik, 'La clause de négociations diplomatiques dans le droit international positif et dans la jurisprudence de la Cour Permanente de Justice Internationale' (1933) XIV *Revue de Droit International et de Législation Comparée*, 62–95.

4 On the more general impact of these three modes of acceptance of the Court's jurisdiction see *inter alia* C. Romano, 'The Shift from the Consensual to the Compulsory Paradigm in International Adjudication: Elements for a Theory of Consent' (2006–07) 39 *New York University Journal of International Law and Politics*, 791–872.

5 *Elettronica Sicula S.p.A. (ELSI), Judgment, I.C.J. Reports 1989*, p. 15, at p. 42, para. 50, the Chamber dealing with the local remedies rule.

6 M. Kohen, 'Interaction', p. 19.

We will not address issues and questions related to the adequateness or appropriateness as such of the various formulations, exclusions and exceptions in these clauses. Our focus will be on the functional interaction as it manifests itself in these instruments by which States have accepted the compulsory jurisdiction of the Court.

From our perspective what significance has to be attributed to expressions such as a *dispute which has not been settled, which is not settled* and *which cannot be settled*? What is the extent – *ratione temporis* and *ratione materiae* – of the obligation to negotiate prior to the seisin of the Court?

In the event of an impasse in the negotiations, States, according to the General Assembly, 'should use their best endeavours to continue to work towards a mutually acceptable and just solution',[7] raising the question whether the obligation to negotiate is unlimited and how deadlock should be approached by parties and by the Court, the latter aspect to be discussed in Chapter 5.

- Does the obligation to negotiate apply also in times of armed conflict?
- When primary rules of a *ius cogens* nature are part of the subject-matter of the dispute, does this characteristic automatically rule out 'negotiations' over the alleged violation as a precondition, or would such a consequence be too far-fetched at this stage of the development of international law?
- How does this particular aspect of the mutual functional interaction – prior negotiations as a precondition for the submission of a dispute to the Court – operate in the case-law of the Court?
- Are negotiations a necessary but sufficient precondition for establishing the jurisdiction of the Court?
- Must parties to a dispute have fulfilled their duty to at least attempt to solve the dispute by negotiations in order to render a seisin of the Court admissible?
- Is the functional role of negotiations as a precondition limited to disputes and cases which will find their judicial resolution by way of a declaratory judgment only?

These questions which concern us here – whether prior negotiations have actually taken place as required or whether at least an attempt has been made by (one of) the parties to initiate them – have to be distinguished from the subsequent questions (to be addressed in Chapter 5) whether the negotiations have fulfilled their functional role of clarifying the legal claims and of establishing the existence of a dispute and whether or not the process has reached a deadlock, has ultimately failed or has, perhaps as a result of a deadlock, resulted in a partial solution of the dispute.

3.1 Prior Negotiations Perform a Substantive and/ or a Rather More Procedural Function

International relations experts find 'interesting situations where an institution is designed to, *encourage* or even *require* negotiation as a prerequisite to some other method of dispute resolution'.[8] The Court is of course no such institution, but the instruments governing the acceptance of its jurisdiction do contain in many cases either such an encouragement or requirement. Such prior negotiations clauses may make operational the rebuttable presumption in favour of negotiation.[9] Prior negotiation clauses may be considered to be *ratione materiae, ratione pre-adjudicatory conduct* or, in many cases, a combination of both.

A Different Function, Object, Purpose and Context

An important distinction imposes itself between prior negotiations which are being conducted as a mechanism to find a solution to the substantive issues of a dispute and negotiations aiming at the conclusion of a compromis in order to submit a dispute to the Court. Although in both situations negotiations are predating the seisin of the Court, their respective functions are different. In the latter context the focus of the negotiations is to find common ground between the parties to a dispute with regard to its joint submission. Determining the

7 General Assembly Resolution 53/101, para. 2 (g).
8 G. Blum and R. Mnookin, ' When *Not* to Negotiate', p. 111.
9 G. Blum and R. Mnookin, ' When *Not* to Negotiate', p. 111.

subject-matter of the dispute and the precise requests to the Court is at the heart of these discussions which may follow previous negotiations performing a different function, namely to actually settle (the) various aspects and issues of the dispute.

Although in a situation of a double-track strategy both categories of negotiations may take place almost simultaneously or in a slightly subsequent order and of course between the same parties, their function, focus, object and purpose and context are different and are characterized by a different internal logic and dynamic.[10]

Negotiations towards a settlement of the substantive issues are of course larger in scope; they are multifaceted, much more complex, perhaps also even more intense and very time-consuming, whereas negotiations towards a compromis are of a more, albeit not exclusively, procedural nature, rather limited in scope, sometimes less complex but perhaps even intense and sometimes also being carried out under prefixed pressures of time.

The quality of a Special Agreement may be affected by the failure of the negotiation process on the merits of the dispute; for instance the disagreeement between the parties on the precise subject-matter of the dispute and what they will request from the Court[11] is then being transferred from the pre-adjudicative to the adjudicative phase of the functional interaction.

The Court's pronouncement that in general 'jurisdictional clauses are adjectival not substantive in their nature and effect'[12] may help to explain the argument that a disagreement which cannot be settled by negotiations 'would normally be confined to the substantive merits of the issue involved' since 'disagreements about jurisdiction' are 'not usually in the negotiable category'.[13] Obviously this last remark does not apply to the negotiation process towards the conclusion of compromissory clauses or of a compromis, preceding any subsequent preliminary objection on the Court's jurisdiction.

The view that talks in order to draft a Special Agreement should be held only 'following suitable preparation'[14] *a fortiori* applies to the more substantive negotiations.

The wording of a compromissory clause is frequently the result of a cut and paste exercise 'from previous treaties without much thought about what would happen if the procedures were actually needed. Most dispute settlement clauses are coarse in many regards and could be greatly improved.'[15]

Of course the overall context within which the negotiations take place is completely different. By the nature of things the functional interaction is in most cases still or rather more remote when the discussions centre on the substantive issues of the dispute – perhaps even without any prospect of adjudication being considered – whereas the aim of negotiating a compromis is definitely to actually bring the functional interaction into operation.

The information available to the Court may indicate that during prior negotiations on substantive issues no mention was made of an international agreement on settlement of disputes,[16] thereby largely reducing the potential of functional interaction. As already indicated, it is not possible to infer that there would be an obligation for States during negotiations to mention the possible submission of the dispute to the Court.

It has been pointed out that the purpose of the insertion of prior negotiations clauses is 'to protect the parties, so far as possible, from international litigation that is unnecessary, premature, inadequately motivated, or merely specious',[17] thereby reducing the potentially negative effects of undesirable functional interaction.

10 Although parties may differ on the legal status of a joint communiqué signed after an 'exchange of views' between the Prime Ministers (*Aegean Sea Continental Shelf case, I.C.J. Reports 1978*, at p. 5, para. 1), such a communiqué as an additional ground for jurisdiction (at p. 38, para. 95) could provide that some problems should be resolved by negotiations whereas other issues would be resolved by the Court (at pp. 39–40, para. 97), thereby illustrating once again the functional interaction.

11 L. Marion, 'La saisine', 282.

12 *South West Africa, I.C.J. Reports 1966*, at p. 39, § 64.

13 *Appeal Relating to the Jurisdiction of the ICAO Council, I.C.J. Reports 1972*, at p. 55, para. 17 and Separate opinion by Judge Petren, at p. 77. Intra-organizational jurisdiction issues though may become an obstacle to negotiations on the merits: Separate opinion by Judge Jimenez de Arechaga, at p. 145.

14 *Aegean Sea Continental Shelf case, I.C.J. Reports 1978*, at p. 41, para. 101 (Greece).

15 C. Romano, 'The Shift', 868.

16 *Aegean Sea Continental Shelf case, I.C.J. Reports 1978*, at p. 18, para. 43.

17 *South West Africa cases, I.C.J. Reports 1962*, Joint Dissenting opinion by Judges Spender and Fitzmaurice, at p. 563.

The Special Agreement 'énonce un *Pactum de agendo*, l'engagement de réaliser ce qui sera décidé par le juge' during the post-adjudicative phase, at least when the Court's mission limits the powers of the parties to a strict implementation of the judgment,[18] but the obligatory force of the judgment flows from the nature itself of the judicial function.[19]

Functional Interaction and Freedom of the Parties

In matters of maritime delimitation the priority of negotiation and agreement is a principle of a procedural nature.[20]

The 1975 Statute in the *Pulp Mills case*, which did contain a dual obligation to negotiate[21] through a *pactum de negotiando* explicitly brought about a link between its procedural obligations and the substantive ones 'through the instituting of proceedings before the Court' following a failure to agree 'during the third stage of the procedure'.[22]

This functional link may be implicit; but it may also be articulated, formulated, explicitly in a formal way through a provision such as the 'compromissory arrangement' in Article 12 which, as a *lex specialis*, institutionalizes the functional interaction.[23] 'In that sense the obligation to negotiate is linked to the obligation to refer the dispute to the International Court of Justice to form a non-severable course of action.'[24]

When the obligation to negotiate is 'exhausted' it is 'replaced by the obligation to settle the dispute at the International Court of Justice'.[25]

Judges in that case held opposing views as to the freedom of the parties to the 1975 Statute to jointly depart from the procedures as laid down in the treaty. According to one view the mandatory, not permissive language of the relevant provisions of the 1975 Statute makes it compulsory for the parties to follow the procedures provided for.[26]

Although 'parties can agree to depart from all or part of the procedures laid down in a treaty', *unilaterally* bypassing them 'is a serious matter'.[27] Such *a common decision* of parties may be triggered by the treaty framework no longer being viable as a result, for instance, of an impasse in the negotiations. The non-application of the treaty time limits should in such circumstances not be considered a wrongful act.[28]

If indeed no evolutive interpretation is justified with regard to the procedural obligations of the parties and, because of their lack of *ius cogens* character they can jointly depart therefrom,[29] and it could be argued that this applies to all obligations of a procedural nature, the question arises whether this should apply in general to the duty to negotiate, provided it is of a (merely) or rather procedural nature and not of a more fundamental nature than for instance a reporting duty.

In the *CERD case* Judge Greenwood held the view that the question whether Article 22 of the CERD contains a requirement of prior negotiations and 'if so, whether it had been satisfied at the time' the Application was lodged, is an issue 'of substance, not of form',[30] a view to which we return later.

18 L. Marion, 'La saisine', 287.

19 L. Marion, 'La saisine', 288.

20 *North Sea Continental Shelf case, I.C.J. Reports 1969*, Dissenting opinion by Judge Tanaka, at p. 195.

21 *Pulp Mills case, I.C.J. Reports 2010*, Declaration by Judge Skotnikov, at pp. 132–4, paras. 3, 5 and 9.

22 *Ibid.*, Separate opinion by Judge Greenwood, at p. 223, para. 5.

23 *Ibid.*, Dissenting opinion by Judge *ad hoc* Vinuesa, at p. 269, para. 13 and at p. 270, para. 16.

24 *Ibid.*, at p. 270, para. 16 and at p. 268, para. 10.

25 *Ibid.*, at pp. 271–72, para. 19.

26 *Ibid.*, Separate opinion by Judge Cançado Trindade, at pp. 206–7, paras. 187–90.

27 *Ibid.*, Separate opinion by Judge Greenwood, at p. 224, para. 9.

28 *Ibid.*, Separate opinion by Judge *ad hoc* Torres Bernardez, at p. 245, paras. 42–3; at p. 247, para. 48; at p. 248, para. 51; and at p. 260, para. 87. However, when the Applicant includes in its Application a controversy between the parties which situates itself beyond the matter governed by such common accord, and this without having followed the original treaty procedure, the inadmissibility of that part of the Application seems appropriate: at p. 264, para. 101. It is only reasonable that this consequence applies to all kinds of joint arrangements departing from previous agreements with regard to the duty to negotiate, for instance, within a particular deadline: at p. 260, para. 86.

29 *Ibid.*, Separate opinion by Judge *ad hoc* Torres Bernardez, at p. 236, para. 13 and at p. 239, para. 24.

30 *CERD case, I.C.J. Reports 2011*, Separate opinion by Judge Greenwood, at p. 325, paras. 6 and 7.

3.2 Does General International Law Require Prior Negotiations?

The Court first reaffirmed the absence both in the Charter and in general international law of 'any general rule' to the effect 'that the exhaustion of diplomatic negotiations' – an essentially relative notion 'qu'on ne peut enfermer *a priori* dans des limites précises'[31] – 'constitutes a precondition for a matter to be referred to the Court'.[32]

In fact, 'contrary to a proposal by the Advisory Committee of Jurists in 1920', such a precondition 'was not embodied in the Statute'.[33]

The Committee's intention was not 'to enable a party to avoid the jurisdiction of the Court by alleging that there was still some hope of settlement by diplomatic means'.[34] The purpose was thus to prevent dysfunctional interaction. Indeed, the 'Court, after satisfying itself *in limine litis* that an attempt has been made to settle the case by diplomatic means', should then deliver judgment under certain conditions.[35]

Negotiations 'may be helpful' in 'clarifying the terms of the dispute and delimiting its subject-matter', but they are '*as a general rule* not a mandatory precondition to be satisfied in order for the Court to be able to exercise jurisdiction'.[36] Only an express provision to that effect can bring about a departure from this general rule of long-standing.[37]

This may be true as a matter of law, although it could also be questioned whether 'in the light of the increasing number of unilateral applications' the 'offhand or casual unilateral referral of cases by some states … without the government of the state concerned first exhausting diplomatic channels, is really consistent with the purpose of the International Court of Justice as the principal judicial organ of the United Nations'[38] even to the extent that it might be 'termed an abuse of the right to institute proceedings before the Court'.[39]

Although prior negotiations do not function anymore as a condition for the admissibility of a claim – considered, more than half a century ago, to be 'une survivance de la période au cours de laquelle les gouvernements étaient hésitants à soumettre leurs différends à la Cour'[40] (that is in the absence of a contrary conventional provision) – they certainly and will always play an important role with regard to the definition of the dispute.

Reviewing the multiple instruments conferring jurisdiction upon the Court in light of the only slightly decreased reluctance towards adjudication, it is difficult to regard Jessup's assessment as overtaken by developments over the last five decades.

In case the parties, as they often do, insert such a precondition of prior negotiations in jurisdictional clauses or in a Special Agreement the right of seising the Court is then suspended until prior negotiations have failed and/or after a certain lapse of time or unless 'in any case it is agreed by the parties to have recourse to another mode of settlement'.[41]

---

31 M. Bourquin, 'Dans quelle mesure', p. 47.

32 *Land and Maritime Boundary case, I.C.J. Reports 1998*, at p. 303, para. 56. The absence of such a requirement also covers the existence and the utilization of regional negotiation processes: at p. 307, para. 68.

33 *Ibid.*, at p. 303, para. 56.

34 As cited by Judge Cançado Trindade in his dissenting opinion in the *CERD case, I.C.J. Reports 2011*, at p. 243, para. 12.

35 *Ibid.*, at p. 244, para. 12.

36 *CERD case, I.C.J. Reports 2011*, Joint dissenting opinion, at p. 149, para. 24 (emphasis added).

37 *Ibid.*, at p. 149, para. 25.

38 S. Oda, 'The Compulsory Jurisdiction of the International Court of Justice: A Myth? A Statistical Analysis of Contentious Cases' (2000) 49 *International and Comparative Law Quarterly* 2, 251–77 at 265.

39 S. Oda, 'Compulsory Jurisdiction', at 265.

40 Jessup as cited by J. Soubeyrol, 'La négociation diplomatique', 330. For a clear and succinct overview of doctrinal developments in this regard, 'un net revirement de la doctrine, qui a pris acte d'une jurisprudence absolument claire' (at p. 328); see *inter alia* pp. 323–8, and G. Geamanu, 'Théorie et pratique', pp. 422–4.

41 *Land and Maritime Boundary case, I.C.J. Reports 1998*, at p. 303, para. 56. See for instance Section 30 of the General Convention on the Privileges and Immunities of the United Nations. The UN Secretary-General. considering that no prior negotiations are required for the submission of a request for a binding advisory opinion, may anyhow have made an attempt 'to reach an agreement' with the government concerned 'on a joint submission to the International Court of Justice': *Cumaraswamy Advisory Opinion, I.C.J. Reports 1998*, at p. 70, paras. 13 and 14.

In the *CERD case* the Court ruled that a qualification by a temporal element is not necessary for conditions – at least to 'the extent that the procedural requirements of Article 22 may be conditions' – to be 'conditions precedent to the seisin of the Court'.[42]

Also in the optional clause system States are free to insert a reservation 'excluding from the latter those disputes for which the parties involved have agreed or subsequently agree to resort to alternative methods of peaceful settlement' such as negotiations.[43] Such reservations are 'open to criticism on the ground that the criteria, although objectives, are so broadly stated as to leave doubts as to their true scope'.[44]

In its Application in the *Border and Transborder case* Nicaragua relied on Article XXXI of the Pact of Bogota and the respective optional clauses of the two parties[45] as foundations for the Court's jurisdiction. As to the jurisdiction, Honduras relied on the reservation in its optional clause which applies irrespective of the basis of jurisdiction invoked by the Applicant. In the alternative, the invocation of Article XXXI carries with it the application of Article XXXII of the Pact of Bogota which excluded unilateral application except in particular circumstances which did not occur here.[46] Hence the compromissory clause could not be invoked.[47]

Nicaragua denied that the dispute was the subject of an agreement 'by the Parties to resort to other means for the pacific settlement of the dispute' as contained in the reservation in the Honduran optional clause,[48] and 'neither the Contadora process nor the provisions of the Pact of Bogota constitute the "other means" to which the pertinent reservation refer'. Furthermore, Article XXXI provides an 'independent basis of jurisdiction' under Article 36, para. 1 of the Statute and thus the reservations invoked by Honduras are not applicable. Accordingly the argument goes that the Court's jurisdiction is based upon the respective optional clauses and/or Article XXXI of the Pact of Bogota.[49]

In all other circumstances prior negotiations and seisin of the Court cannot, in law, be considered as mutually exclusive.[50]

The view was also held that a prior negotiation condition is 'a condition of principle on which the Court' should pronounce itself even in the absence of a relevant preliminary objection to that end.[51]

The fact that general international law does not impose prior negotiations as a precondition for seisin does not diminish both the *factual and legal functional* importance of prior negotiations, even if they failed, be it only in order to enable the Applicant to succinctly present the facts and its claims and to fulfil for instance the requirements established in Article 38, para. 2 of the Rules of Court, and by doing so to render the Application admissible.[52] In this perspective the condition of prior negotiations is a matter of common sense and of comity as a State 'is normally reluctant to drag another State before the Court without first making a serious attempt to arrange the matters in dispute by diplomatic negotiations'.[53]

A clause in a friendship, commerce and navigation (FCN) treaty may provide that if one party 'does choose to make representations affecting the operation of the Treaty the other party is obliged to "accord sympathetic consideration" and "opportunity for consultation"; this does not however mean that negotiations on the matter affecting the operation of the Treaty must take place before proceeding to the Court': *Nicaragua case, I.C.J. Reports 1984*, Separate opinion by Judge Singh, at p. 445.

42 *CERD case, I.C.J. Reports 2011*, at p. 124, para. 130.

43 *Land and Maritime Boundary case, I.C.J. Reports 1998*, at p. 303, para. 56. Such a proviso has been included in approximately 53 per cent of the optional clauses: R. Kolb, *The ICJ*, p. 465.

44 H. Waldock, 'Decline of the Optional Clause', XXXII *British Yearbook of International Law* (1955–1956), 244–87, at 271.

45 *Border and Transborder Armed Actions case, I.C.J. Reports 1988*, at p. 71, para. 1.

46 *Ibid.*, at p. 73, para. 13.

47 *Ibid.*, at p. 74, para. 13.

48 *Ibid.*, at p. 80, para. 24. This is relevant for the general question concerning optional clauses under the peaceful settlement of disputes: see *infra.*

49 *Border and Transborder Armed Actions case, I.C.J. Reports 1988*, at pp. 74–5, para. 13.

50 *Land and Maritime Boundary case, I.C.J. Reports 1998*, at p. 303, para. 56.

51 *Diallo case, I.C.J. Reports 2010*, Separate opinion by Judge *ad hoc* Mampuya, at pp. 833–4, para. 4., referring to the joint dissenting opinion in the *CERD case*.

52 See on this aspect the *Land and Maritime Boundary case, I.C.J. Reports 1998*, at pp. 317–19, paras. 96–101 and *Territorial and Maritime Dispute between Nicaragua and Honduras, I.C.J. Reports 2007*, at p. 695, para. 108. On these aspects see further Chapter 5.

53 H. Waldock, 'Decline', 266.

From a functional interaction perspective a Special Agreement in which the parties have established their inability to have settled the dispute by negotiations has in fact a dual nature: '*as a diplomatic act*' it is 'an element *introducing new factors into the negotiations* between the Parties; but, *as a legal act*, it determines the elements structuring the object of the dispute'.[54]

Negotiating in good faith does not imply or entail a renunciation of the right to bring the dispute before the Court. The functional interaction between the two mechanisms does not prevent or render inadmissible conduct by one of the parties consisting in following the double-track strategy. A jointly undertaken double-track strategy clearly reinforces that functional interaction.

3.3. Parties at the Crossroads of the Functional Interaction between Negotiations and Adjudication

From the moment a dispute arises parties could hold different opinions as to what is the most appropriate method for its settlement, and in case of a double-track strategy whether the two modes could or should be followed in a particular chronological order, thereby putting the potential of functional interaction under (unnecessary) pressure.

Negotiate while Preparing for Court: A Good Faith Course of Action?

As already indicated, a double-track strategy does not necessarily have to be followed by both parties; prior negotiations to find a solution of the dispute do not bar a State from preparing to bring the dispute before the Court in the not too distant future.

A different question altogether is whether it would be possible to use the fact that the Applicant did not mention the invocability of a compromissory clause against that party during the proceedings.

When in the running up to the filing of an Application a prospective Applicant, as part of this strategy, continues 'to maintain bilateral contacts with (the future Respondent) on boundary questions while preparing itself to address the Court', this could lead to the accusation that such conduct 'infringes upon the principle of good faith' which nowadays 'plays a larger role in the case-law of the Court'.[55] A straightforward response to such an accusation could consist in arguing that the other party 'knew perfectly well' what 'our intentions were several weeks before the filing of the Application'. Hence, 'the principle of good faith was not at all disregarded'.[56] This argument seems to imply that if the other party was not fully aware of the future Respondent's intentions of a unilateral submission of the dispute, the principle of good faith might have suffered indeed.

The decision 'implies that it is no breach of good faith for a State to seise the Court of a dispute with another State without first affording that State an opportunity to settle it by negotiation'.[57] Hence a party to a dispute is 'free to make direct recourse to jurisdictional means'.[58]

In examining its jurisdiction the Court must exercise the greatest caution in attributing to a sovereign State bad faith,[59] for instance with regard to prior negotiations. This whole question has to be placed within the more general context of the functional interaction. On the one hand, parties have to respect and comply with the requirement to negotiate in good faith and not to give up after a first deadlock. On the other hand,

54 *Arbitral Award case, I.C.J. Reports 1991*, Joint dissenting opinion by Judges Mawdsley and Ranjeva, at p. 124, para. 14 (emphasis added).

55 *Land and Maritime Boundary case, I.C.J. Reports 1998*, at p. 296, para. 36 (Nigeria).

56 *Ibid.*, at p. 296, para. 37 (Cameroon).

57 H. Thirlway, 'The Law and Procedure of the International Court of Justice 1960–1989, Supplement 2005: Parts One and Two', at 10.

58 P. Sandonato de Leon, 'Diplomatic and Judicial Means', p. 76. There is no condition for a dispute to arise 'that one State must indicate that it intends to resort to international judicial or arbitral procedure or action unless its claim is satisfied': *Interhandel, Case, I.C.J. Reports 1959*, Separate opinion by Judge Spender, at p. 60.

59 *Interhandel, Case, I.C.J. Reports 1959*, Dissenting opinion by Judge Lauterpacht, at p. 111.

'delay on the part of the Claimant State may render an application inadmissible'.[60] Although 'international law does not lay down any specific time-limit in that regard', it will ultimately be for the Court 'to determine in the light of the circumstances of each case whether the passage of time renders an application inadmissible',[61] circumstances which include pre-existing relations between the parties and attempts made by the Applicant before instituting the proceedings.[62]

Negotiate on Matters of Substance and/or towards the Conclusion of a Special Agreement?

The double-track strategy may cause additional difficulties in case it has been the view of just one of the parties to start, with priority, negotiations on the delimitation of a disputed area, but also having talks on the conclusion of a Special Agreement to refer the dispute to the Court[63] while the other party maintains that the issue would first be submitted to the Court and that 'talks with a view of an eventual agreed solution were not to be excluded to follow'.[64]

Even during those initial stages of the unfolding of the dispute parties may disagree about the need to have prior negotiations before submitting the dispute to the Court. Both parties may have agreed that only those issues 'which could not be resolved by negotiations, would be jointly submitted to the Court'.[65]

The functional interaction becomes rather more explicit when in the course of the negotiations necessary to draft a Special Agreement proposals would be made for the elimination of points of disagreement concerning the maritime delimitation and 'those proposals would be given appropriate consideration'.[66] When parties have then provided for further meetings on substantive issues, it is then unlikely that one of them should have undertaken 'an immediate and unqualified commitment to accept the submission of the dispute to the Court unilaterally by Application'.[67]

A joint communiqué may according to one party contain an obligation to negotiate and an ensuing commitment to conclude an implementing agreement needed for the performance of that obligation.[68] If under such circumstances then the other party refuses to conclude that agreement, the way of a unilateral seisin is open[69] because, according to this line of reasoning, if such 'a complementary agreement is a legal prerequisite' for seisin then 'the two parties are under an obligation to negotiate in good faith the conclusion of such an agreement'.[70]

The Respondent may deny the existence of a commitment 'to submit to the Court without a special agreement'.[71] Arguably, priority was given to negotiations on the substance of the question and nothing was said in that connection 'even about the negotiation of a special agreement'.[72]

In assessing this contention, the Court turned to the context in which the meeting took place and the communiqué was drawn up.[73] One party may see 'considerable advantage in *reaching jointly*' a Special Agreement,[74] while the other party refers 'to meaningful negotiations' as the best method.[75] As those

60 *Certain Phosphate Lands in Nauru (Nauru v. Australia), Preliminary Objections, Judgment, I.C.J. Reports 1992*, p. 240, at p. 253, para. 32.

61 *Nauru case, I.C.J. Reports 1992*, at pp. 253–4, para. 32.

62 *Ibid.*, at p. 254, para. 36.

63 *Aegean Sae Continental Shelf case, I.C.J. Reports 1971*, at p. 9, para. 18 and para. 20 (Turkey).

64 *Ibid.*, at p. 9, para. 20 (Greece).

65 *Ibid.*, at p. 9, para. 20 (Turkey).

66 *Ibid.*, at p. 10, para. 21 (Greece).

67 *Ibid.*, at p. 43, para. 105.

68 *Ibid.*, at p. 40, para. 98 (Greece).

69 *Ibid.*, at p. 40, para. 98 (Greece).

70 *Ibid.*, at p. 40, para. 98 (Greece).

71 *Ibid.*, at p. 40, para. 99 (Turkey).

72 *Ibid.*, at p. 40, para. 99 (Turkey).

73 *Ibid.*, at p. 40, para. 100.

74 *Ibid.*, at p. 40, para. 100 (Greece).

75 *Ibid.*, at p. 41, para. 101 (Turkey).

negotiations have not taken place, one of the functional roles of prior negotiations had not been fulfilled: 'the issues relating to the disputes have neither been fully identified nor elucidated'.[76]

Although two parties may disagree on the preconditions for the submission of (part) of their dispute to the Court – prior meaningful negotiations on the substance matter or immediate submission[77] – they still may both consider it necessary to conclude a Special Agreement.[78] In such a situation the functional interaction between the two mechanisms of peaceful settlement is rather limited.

During bilateral negotiations parties may differ on the appropriate forum to settle disputes in the future. Acceptance of a proposal for reference to the ICJ of future disputes does not necessarily bring to an end discussions between the parties as they may disagree on 'the precise formulation of a compromissory clause, including, in particular, the method whereby the agreement to have recourse to the Court would be effected'.[79]

The discussions about whether submission would be made jointly by the parties or by Application may for instance continue for several weeks before the parties finally agree on one of these alternatives.[80]

In an interim arrangement containing a compromissory clause parties may commit themselves to continue negotiations towards an agreement on a particular difference, related to and even underlying the dispute before the Court on alleged violations of that interim agreement. The Respondent may argue that such a Court ruling would not only 'interfere with ongoing negotiations mandated by the Security Council' and as such 'would be incompatible with the Court's judicial function', but moreover that judicial intervention would effectively decide on the underlying difference between the parties, thereby taking away 'any incentive the applicant might have had to negotiate' towards a solution on that matter.[81]

The argument rests on a perceived risk of future dysfunctional interaction. The Court rejected part of this argument by drawing a distinction between that difference and the alleged violations. On the possible interference of its judgment with those ongoing negotiations, the Court succinctly observed that if that would have been the case the parties would not have agreed to refer to it disputes over the interpretation and application of the Interim Accord.[82]

3.4 Do Prior Negotiations Function as a Precondition to the Court's Jurisdiction?

'Admissibility and jurisdiction are distinct notions, even though there is often in practice some overlap.'[83]

While jurisdiction is linked to the requirement of consent of the parties, admissibility covers situations where 'the Court has been validly seised of, and has jurisdiction over, the merits but cannot exercise that jurisdiction in the concrete circumstances'.[84] Differently phrased and in 'extremely simplified terms, the rules on jurisdiction concern defaults as to the propriety of the organ seized, whereas rules on admissibility concern defaults as to the propriety of the particular request'.[85]

The examination of conditions attached to such consent relates to the Court's jurisdiction and such conclusion 'applies *mutatis mutandis*' to all other similarly worded compromissory clauses.[86]

---

76 *Ibid.*

77 *Ibid.*, at pp. 43–4, para. 106.

78 *Ibid.* Indeed, a communiqué may clearly commit both parties to the negotiation of a compromis (Separate opinion by Judge Lachs, at p. 51).

79 *Fisheries Jurisdiction (United Kingdom v. Iceland) I.C.J. Reports 1973*, at p. 11, para. 19.

80 *Ibid.*

81 *Interim Accord case, I.C.J. Reports 2011*, at p. 654, para. 20; at p. 655, para. 24; at p. 656, para. 26; and at p. 657, para. 32.

82 *Ibid.*, at p. 658, para. 35; at p. 659, para. 37; at p. 665, para. 59. As Judge Torres Bernardez observed in a different case, even when in common accord parties depart from a treaty procedure, they may maintain the negotiations and judicial recourse regime provided for in the treaty: *Pulp Mills case, I.C.J. Reports 2010*, Dissenting opinion by Judge *ad hoc* Torres Bernardez, at pp. 257–8, paras. 77–8.

83 R. Jennings, 'The LaGrand Case' (2002) 1 *Law and Practice of International Courts and Tribunals*, 1, 13–54, at 22.

84 S. Rosenne, *The Law and Practice of the International Court of Justice* (1st edn, Leyden, 1965), vol. 1, p. 442.

85 R. Kolb, 'General Principles of Procedural Law' in A. Zimmermann, C. Tomuschat, C. Tams and K. Oellers-Frahm (eds), *The Statute of the International Court of Justice: A Commentary* (Oxford, 2012), pp. 871–908, at p. 874, MN 4.

86 *DRC v. Rwanda case, I.C.J. Reports 2006*, at pp. 39–40, para. 88.

It can be argued 'that all the cases we tend to group under the admissibility really involve jurisdiction *sensu lato*'.[87]

The 'question of the *nature* of the distinction between the two categories – if indeed such a distinction exists or can be usefully employed – is a disputed one'.[88] While 'categorization of objections as relating to jurisdiction or admissibility is a practical issue for purely procedural purposes, the underlying distinction is linked with considerations of principle going to the nature of jurisdiction'.[89]

Whether prior negotiations are considered 'a separate admissibility condition' or 'a constitutive part of the condition of the existence of a dispute', it seems that 'some kind of exchange or negotiation' between the parties 'is a necessary prelude to adjudication'.[90]

The Court itself has declared that 'objections to admissibility (*recevabilité*) normally take the form of an assertion that, even if the Court has jurisdiction and the facts stated by the applicant State are assumed to be correct, nonetheless there are reasons why the Court should not proceed to an examination of the merits'.[91]

The Court cannot adjudicate on the admissibility of an Application until it has established its jurisdiction and previous negotiations 'cannot be laid down as a general condition to the jurisdiction of the Court',[92] as the case law has demonstrated.

When examining questions of jurisdiction and admissibility the Court is entitled 'to go into other questions which may not be strictly capable of classification of matters of jurisdiction or admissibility but are of such a nature as to require examination before those matters'.[93]

The Court is in fact not attaching 'much importance to questions of classification'[94] and did not see the need 'to determine whether all of them are objections to jurisdiction or to admissibility or based on other grounds',[95] a position still unchanged until the present day.

It is by the nature of things within the context of the examination of preliminary objections that the question whether prior negotiations are a precondition for the seisin of the Court poses itself prominently.

It is sufficient to recall that the Court should *ex officio* examine the question of its jurisdiction, whereas invoking inadmissibility is up to the parties themselves.[96]

Precondition to the Court's Jurisdiction

Although it 'is hardly ever the case that an optional clause case does not require separate hearings on jurisdiction' also the invocation of a compromissory clause may bring to the fore the question about the fulfilment of 'certain preconditions' claimed 'to be required under the treaty', and also in Special Agreement cases 'there is potential for controversy as to the meaning and scope of the agreement'.[97]

'The faculty of invoking a jurisdictional clause depends upon what tests or conditions of the right to do so are laid down by the clause itself'.[98]

---

87 J. Crawford and A. Pellet, 'Anglo-Saxon and Continental Approaches to Pleading before the ICJ' in I. Buffard, J. Crawford, A. Pellet and S. Wittich (eds), *International Law between Universalism and Fragmentation: Festschrift in Honour of Gerhard Hafner* (Leiden, 2008), pp. 831–68 at 834.

88 H. Thirlway, 'The Law and Procedure of the International Court of Justice 1960–1989: Part Eleven', 73.

89 H. Thirlway, 'The Law and Procedure of the International Court of Justice 1960–1989: Part Eleven', 73 note 2.

90 G. Abi-Saab, 'Adjudication and Negotiation', p. 329.

91 *Oil Platforms (Islamic Republic of Iran v. United States of America), Judgment, I.C.J. Reports 2003*, p. 161, at p. 177, para. 29.

92 M. Hudson, *The Permanent Court of International Justice 1920–1942: A Treatise* (New York, 1943), p. 413 relating to relevant PCIJ cases at pp. 413–16.

93 *Territorial and Maritime Dispute (Nicaragua v. Colombia), I.C.J. Reports 2007*, at p. 851, para. 49.

94 J. Crawford and A. Pellet, 'Anglo-Saxon and Continental Approaches', at p. 835.

95 *The Northern Cameroons case, I.C.J. Reports 1963*, at p. 27.

96 J. Crawford and A. Pellet, 'Anglo-Saxon and Continental Approaches', pp. 839–40.

97 Judge R.Higgins, President of the International Court of Justice before the Sixth Committee of the UN General Assembly on 31 October 2008 (text on the Court's website).

98 *South West Africa, I.C.J. Reports 1966*, at p. 37, para. 60.

The basic premise for any examination of prior negotiations as preconditions for bringing a case to the Court is that parties 'are free to make their consent to the seisin of the Court and hence the Court's jurisdiction, subject to whatever pre-conditions, consistent with the Statute'.[99]

It is important for parties to know that they are free to invoke a jurisdictional clause on its own independent and purely jurisdictional foundation without running the risk of destroying their case on the merits by that process.[100]

In a compromissory clause, in a compromis and in the optional clause declarations consent is given by States to the compulsory jurisdiction: 'any conditions to which such consent is subject must be regarded as constituting the limits thereon. The Court accordingly considers that the examination of such conditions relates to its jurisdiction and not the admissibility of the application.'[101]

The alleged non-exhaustion of avenues of negotiation and arbitration should be considered an objection pertaining to the Court's jurisdiction.[102] The conditions for seisin of the Court 'must be examined in the context of the issue of the Court's jurisdiction'.[103]

Although diplomatic correspondence may show the Applicant's attempt to resolve the dispute by negotiations, this process may not have resolved the dispute. The Court may then conclude that the requirement that the dispute was one which 'cannot be resolved through negotiation' must be considered to have been fulfilled, at least *prima facie*.[104]

The Court may conclude that it has jurisdiction 'from the text of the compromissory clause, read in the context' of an earlier exchange of notes and 'in light of the history of the negotiations'.[105] Prior negotiations thus play an important but subordinated function as part *of the context* for the interpretation of the compromissory clause endowing the Court with jurisdiction to decide the case.

It is a different matter altogether when a compromissory clause explicitly formulates prior negotiations as a precondition for the seisin of the Court, as the *CERD case* has amply demonstrated. Whether a compromissory clause, such as Article 22 of the CERD, 'establish[es] preconditions to be fulfilled before the seisin of the Court'[106] as a matter of legal obligation or as a matter of fact will be reviewed shortly.

As part of its preliminary objections, Nigeria in the *Land and Maritime Boundary case* argued with regard to the Court's jurisdiction that Cameroon's Application violated 'its obligations to act in good faith', that it was an 'abuse of the system' of Article 36, para. 2 of the Statute and that it was disregarding the terms of Nigeria's optional clause.[107]

---

99 *Revision and Interpretation of the 1982 Continental Shelf Judgment, I.C.J. Reports 1985*, at p. 216, para. 43.

100 *Appeal Relating to the Jurisdiction of the ICAO Council, I.C.J. Reports 1972*, at p. 54, para. 16 (d).

101 *DRC v. Rwanda case, I.C.J. Reports 2006*, at p. 39, para. 88. Hence the correct doctrinal position has been formulated by H. Thirlway: 'anything which is a condition of the consent given to the jurisdiction of the Court has to be treated as a jurisdictional matter, whether or not it would have been otherwise characterized had it not been mentioned in the title of jurisdiction'. The Law and Procedure of the International Court of Justice 1960–1989: Part Eleven', 81–2. Moreover, 'the Court's jurisprudence is not consistent as far as the determination is concerned of the legal nature of admissibility conditions included in a jurisdictional clause': G. Abi-Saab, *Les exceptions préliminaires*, p. 177.

102 *Belgium v. Senegal case, I.C.J. Reports 2012*, Separate opinion by Judge Sebutinde, at p. 592, paras. 5–6. It will as a matter of course be the Applicant claiming that the States gave exhaustive diplomatic means to resolve their dispute: see for instance *Dispute regarding Maritime Delimitation in the Caribbean Sea and Pacific Ocean between Costa Rica and Nicaragua*, Application of Costa Rica, 25 February 2014, Press Release No. 2014/11 of 26 February 2014 (text available on the Court's website).

103 *Belgium v. Senegal case, I.C.J. Reports 2012*, Separate opinion by Judge Sebutinde, at p. 592, para. 6. As this conclusion applies *mutatis mutandis* to all compromissory clauses invoked by an Applicant, it is then not surprising that the Court may repeatedly conclude that an Applicant has not proven that it had attempted to settle the dispute by negotiations: *Armed Activities on the Territory of the Congo, I.C.J. Reports 2006*; see for instance at p. 43, para. 100 and at pp. 45–6, para. 108.

104 *Belgium v. Senegal case, I.C.J. Reports 2009*, at p. 150, para. 50.

105 *Fisheries Jurisdiction (Federal Republic of Germany v. Iceland), I.C.J. Reports 1973*, at p. 51, para. 23.

106 *CERD case, I.C.J. Reports 2011*, Joint dissenting opinion, at p. 145, para. 12 responding to the Court's position at pp. 126–8, paras. 136–41.

107 *Land and Maritime Boundary case, I.C.J. Reports 1998*, at pp. 284–5, para. 18 (1) (Nigeria). The Court's interpretation (at p. 297, para. 39) of its 1988 *dictum* in the *Border and Transborder Armed Actions* case, 'as to good

Furthermore, part of the dispute has to do with the Lake Chad region, which is of the exclusive competence of the Lake Chad Basin Commission; as those procedures of settlement are obligatory for the parties, the necessary implication is that 'jurisdiction under Article 36, paragraph 2, would not be invoked'.[108]

Although Articles 74 and 83 provide for prior negotiations as a precondition before parties can resort to the procedures of Part IV of UNCLOS for instance seising the Court, in this case it had been seised not on the basis of Article 36, para. 1 but on the basis of Article 36, para. 2 of the Statute: as neither of the optional clause contains a similar requirement of prior negotiations to be conducted within a reasonable period of time, the objection could not be upheld.[109]

The circumstances of the case did thus not allow the Court to examine and assess, from an admissibility point of view that is, how those prior negotiations have in fact been conducted by both parties.

3.5 Do Prior Negotiations Function as a Precondition to the Admissibility of the Claim?

The multifunctionality of prior negotiations as referred to in Chapter 1 re-enters the stage at this point because, apart from trying to achieve an amicable settlement of the controversy, negotiations do also perform this important and preliminary function to establish, between the parties and for the Court to evaluate, the very existence of a legal dispute; and they are instrumental in clarifying the respective legal claims of the parties the opposition of which is necessary for the objective judicial determination of the existence of a dispute, aspects which we will discuss in Chapter 5.

> Objections to admissibility normally take the form of an assertion that, even if the Court has jurisdiction and the facts stated by the applicant State are assumed to be correct, nonetheless there are reasons why the Court should not proceed to an examination of the merits.[110]

Could the non-fulfilment of a conventional requirement of prior negotiations be one of those reasons? Parties may indeed disagree on the preliminary question whether the claim is admissible for adjudication without further or prior diplomatic negotiations 'such as would disclose the existence of a dispute'.[111]

When it is impossible for the parties to reach an understanding during prior negotiations, 'one of the parties may claim' that the condition of prior negotiations has been fulfilled, while 'the other may in turn raise a preliminary objection to admissibility'.[112] Does this then inevitably always mean that recourse 'to a judicial settlement of the dispute can only be made to the extent that the earlier phase of negotiations has failed'?[113]

A State may also submit that an Application is premature: perhaps because negotiations are still going on, or because no negotiations have taken place at all.[114] In case prior negotiations have been foreseen in a compromissory clause, the Respondent may submit that the Application is premature.[115]

---

faith not being a source of obligation' was considered 'too sweeping' by H. Thirlway, 'The Law and Procedure of the International Court of Justice 1960–1989 Supplement, 2005: Parts One and Two', at 11.

108 *Land and Maritime Boundary case, I.C.J. Reports 1998*, at p. 285, third preliminary objection (Nigeria).

109 *Ibid.*, at pp. 321–2, paras. 108–9.

110 *Oil Platforms case, I.C.J. Reports 2003*, at p. 177, para. 29.

111 *Nottebohm case, I.C.J. Reports 1955*, at pp. 7–11 and at p. 11 (Guatemala).

112 P.-M. Dupuy, 'Recourse to the International Court of Justice', p. 61.

113 P-M. Dupuy, 'Recourse to the International Court of Justice', p. 61.

114 Non-compliance with a conventional precondition of prior negotiations raised by a Respondent against a first Application does not necessarily result in a new Application containing even a suggestion or *prima facie* indication that any such attempt had been made on its part prior to or after the withdrawing of that first Application. The rejection of proposals by the Applicant for the settlement of 'certain specified armed conflicts' at a number of conferences manifests what the real dispute between the parties is about: *DRC v. Rwanda case, I.C.J. Reports 2002*, Separate opinion by Judge *ad hoc* Dugard, at pp. 269–70, paras. 10 and 11.

115 *Aegean Sea Continental Shelf case, I.C.J. Reports 1976*, at p. 5, para. 8 (Turkey).

But does the warning expressed by the Court that a State filing an Application 'should normally be expected to demonstrate sufficient care to avoid doing so prematurely'[116] actually also mean that the filing should not be done before the required prior negotiations have actually failed?[117]

Functional Interaction Operating to Cure a Procedural Defect?

Would it be reasonable and sensible to apply realism and flexibility, traditionally called in when questions of form are at hand, also to prior negotiations as a condition of admissibility of a claim? The answer depends on the reply to the following question.

Is a conventional precondition of prior negotiations to be considered as a merely procedural act the defect of which can actually be cured after the start of the proceedings or is it of a more substantive nature,[118] which would make it harder or even impermissible to cure during the proceedings?

In other words, is the absence of prior negotiations not a defect which is similar to the one in a procedural act which can easily be remedied by a willing Applicant under the principle enunciated by the PCIJ in the *Mavrommatis case*?[119] At first glance one would be tempted to follow this path of reasoning, but the clarification added to the principle by the PCIJ in the *Polish Upper Silesia case* makes it rather less likely; indeed, 'if the existence of a definite dispute were necessary'[120] prior negotiations would then function as a prime precondition. However, the *subsequent* fulfilment of this condition would in fact not depend 'solely on the Party concerned'.[121]

Does suspension of the prior negotiations by the Applicant and eventually resulting in a failure of that process in all cases automatically justify the conclusion that the precondition of prior negotiations had not been fulfilled? As deficiencies by either of the parties may be overcome in the course of the proceedings, prior to the Court's decision on its jurisdiction,[122] it seems then that *only joint action* consisting in resuming the negotiations during the course of the proceedings would be able to bring about the fulfilment of this precondition, as for the Court it is 'of no importance which condition was unmet at the date the proceedings were instituted'.[123]

The other but related question whether a particular procedure of negotiations has been 'concluded' – either for instance because a partial arrangement has been agreed upon over some aspects of the dispute or as a result of the lapse of a certain period of time as provided beforehand in a compromissory, optional clause or compromis – situates itself on the borderline with the other question whether or not prior negotiations have actually failed, to be discussed in Chapter 5.

Although in the past individual judges may have refrained from entering into the discussion whether a *legal* dispute 'may be submitted unilaterally to the Court only after diplomatic negotiations have been

116 *Application of the Convention on the Prevention and Punishment of the Crime of Genocide (Croatia v. Serbia), Preliminary Objections, Judgment, I.C.J. Reports 2008*, p. 412, at p. 443, para. 90.

117 On the other hand, negotiations do not always have to be mentioned explicitly in a prior negotiations clause, for instance when the parties refer to all political means including conciliation providing for timing and a one-year deadline. However, this may be subject to an alternative decision by the Heads of State, for instance when they would depart from this requirement of prior political means. A political settlement not forthcoming, the parties may already decide to submit the dispute to the Court: *Territorial Dispute (Libyan Arab Jamahiriya/Chad), Order of 26 October 1990, I.C.J. Reports 1990*, p. 149, at p. 150. According to the late Ian Brownlie, compulsory conciliation is not a bad alternative for States afraid for what we call adjudication (remark made during the Nijmegen Conference 40 Years UN; on file with the author).

118 As Nigeria argued with regard to Articles 74 and 83 of the UNCLOS Convention: *Land and Maritime Boundary case, I.C.J. Reports 2002*, at p. 422, para. 240.

119 *P.C.I.J. Series A, No. 2*, p. 34.

120 *P.C.I.J. Series A, No. 6*, p. 14.

121 *Application of the Convention on the Prevention and Punishment of the Crime of Genocide, Preliminary Objections, Judgment, I.C.J. Reports 1996*, p. 595, at p. 613, para. 26.

122 *Croatian Genocide Case, I.C.J. Reports 2008*, at p. 441, para. 85.

123 *Ibid.*, at p. 442, para. 87. The conduct of negotiations during the proceedings will be dealt with in Chapter 6.

exhausted, or at least initiated',[124] the *CERD case* has completely changed this picture, as we will find out in the next section.

The exhaustion of and failure of prior negotiations may *in fact* have been the necessary conditions before initial proceedings could be brought. In assessing whether the available possibilities have been *exhausted* the Court, referring to the *dictum* of its predecessor in the *Mavrommatis Palestine Concessions case*, will obviously take into account the attitude of both parties. Indeed:

> Negotiations do not of necessity always presuppose a more or less lengthy series of notes and dispatches; it may suffice that a discussion should have been commenced, and this discussion may have been very short; this will be the case if a deadlock is reached, or finally a point is reached at which one of the Parties definitely declares himself unable, *or* refuses, to give way, and there can therefore be no doubt that the *dispute cannot be settled by diplomatic negotiation*.[125]

Not giving way may be the result of not being able *or* being unwilling to do so.

Prior negotiations becoming 'stalled owing to the diametrically opposed positions' of the parties, may ultimately bring one of them to unilaterally submit the dispute to the ICJ and then lead afterwards through mediation to joint submission.[126]

Two Case Law Examples Prior to the CERD Case

Both the *Nicaragua case* and the *Border and Transborder Actions case* provide good examples of prior negotiations functioning as a precondition for the admissibility of the claim, having in common the interpretation and application of Article XXXI of the Pact of Bogota.

In challenging the admissibility of Nicaragua's claim, the US argued that the Applicant 'has failed to exhaust the established process for the resolution' of the conflicts, namely the Contadora process recognized by the Security Council and the Organization of American States (OAS) as 'the appropriate method', the aim of those negotiations being to 'go to the heart of the claims and issues raised by the Application'.[127]

Nicaragua argued that the US could not 'shelter behind negotiations between third States in a forum in which it is not participating'. Moreover neither the UN Charter nor the Charter of the OAS requires 'the exhaustion of prior regional negotiations'.[128] The Court dismissed the objection as there is no requirement 'of prior exhaustion of regional negotiating processes as a precondition for the seisin of the Court'. Moreover, the existence of the Contadora process in this case 'is (not) an obstacle to the examination by the Court' of the Application.[129]

In the *Border and Transborder Actions case* as to the admissibility of the Application Honduras submitted *inter alia* that 'an essential precondition' to the use of the procedures of the Pact of Bogota, including a reference to the ICJ had not been fulfilled, namely that 'the dispute cannot be settled by direct negotiations'. Nicaragua had 'failed to show that' this was 'the opinion of the Parties'.[130] According to Honduras both parties must share the opinion that the dispute could not be settled by direct negotiations.

The other relevant Honduran objection to the admissibility was that the Contadora process has been accepted as a 'special procedure' within the meaning of the Pact of Bogota (Article II); hence Nicaragua was precluded from 'commencing any other procedure' for pacific settlement 'until such time as the Contadora process has been concluded': this preclusion being based upon Article IV of the Pact and one should not fail to note this additional foundation for the exclusion – 'elementary considerations of good faith'.[131]

---

124 *Fisheries Jurisdiction case (Spain v. Canada), I.C.J. Reports 1998*, Separate opinion by Judge Oda, at p. 484, para. 20.

125 *PLO case Advisory Opinion, I.C.J. Reports 1988*, at pp. 33–34, para. 55 and *P.C.I.J. Series A, No. 2*, p. 13.

126 *Gabcikovo case, I.C.J. Reports 1997*, at p. 53, para. 73.

127 *Nicaragua case, I.C.J. Reports 1984*, at p. 438, para. 102.

128 *Ibid.*, at p. 438, para. 103.

129 *Ibid.*, at p. 440, para. 108.

130 *Border and Transborder Armed Actions case, I.C.J. Reports 1988*, at p. 73, para. 13.

131 *Ibid.*

According to Nicaragua the grounds of inadmissibility 'alleged to derive' from Articles II and IV of the Pact of Bogota 'have no legal basis'.[132] Article II of the Pact of Bogota contains 'the precondition to recourse to the procedures established by the Pact'.

According to Honduras it is not sufficient 'that both parties should share the opinion that the dispute cannot be settled by negotiations', but moreover 'that they should have "manifested" that opinion'.[133]

All possibility of settlement by direct negotiation not having been exhausted, the dispute could still be settled through the normal diplomatic channels, as 'confirmed by the intense diplomatic activity which is in progress in Central America'.[134] The negotiations in the context of the Contadora process were 'direct negotiations' involving 'proposals and counter-proposals'. The Court's jurisprudence justifies to 'discount any distinction between the direct bilateral negotiations' which took place prior to 1983 and the negotiations in the context of the Contadora process.[135]

According to Nicaragua the circumstance of recourse to pacific procedures envisaged in Article II is not an exclusive one.[136]

The Court accepted that the provision of Article II constitutes a 'condition precedent to recourse to the pacific procedures of the Pact in all cases'. It then remained for the Court to examine how that condition applied in this particular case.[137]

As part of its description of the Contadora process and its aftermath, to which we will return in Chapters 5 and 7, the Court observed that on the date of the filing of the Nicaraguan Application 'no other negotiation which would meet the conditions' of Article II was '*contemplated*'.[138]

In this context one should not only note that even the mere contemplation of resumed or new negotiations would suffice to fulfil that precondition, but that the Court's approach once again illustrates the identifiable continuum, in a number of cases that is, between negotiations and judicial settlement.

The Court then did not accept as plausible Honduras's argument that at the date of the filing of the Application 'the dispute' was still 'capable of being settled by direct negotiation through the usual diplomatic channels'.[139]

Prior Negotiations and the Special Nature of the Rights involved

As to the admissibility of a claim, a Respondent may object that no legal dispute concerning the maritime delimitation was at present 'appropriate for resolution by the Court': in order to render those issues admissible there should be first 'sufficient action by the Parties, on a footing of equality, to effect a delimitation by agreement on the basis of international law'.[140]

Articles 74 and 83 of UNCLOS require States first to attempt to reach an agreement on the delimitation of the Exclusive Economic Zone and of the Continental Shelf.[141]

The Applicant denying 'that the conduct of negotiations is a precondition for instituting proceedings before the Court in case of delimitation' may furthermore take the position that 'it had sufficiently negotiated' before seising the Court, and that 'it seised the Court only when it became clear that any new negotiation would be doomed to failure'. In fact, the actual occupation of a particular territorial area by the Respondent has made impossible 'any negotiation on the delimitation of the maritime boundary'.[142]

---

132 *Ibid.*, at pp. 74–5, para. 13.
133 *Ibid.*, at p. 93, para. 60 (original emphasis).
134 *Ibid.* (Honduras).
135 *Ibid.*, at pp. 93–4, para. 60 (Honduras).
136 *Ibid.*, at p. 94, para. 61.
137 *Ibid.*, at p. 94, para. 62.
138 *Ibid.*, at p. 99, para. 75 (emphasis added).
139 *Ibid.*
140 *Land and Maritime Boundary case, I.C.J. Reports 1998*, at p. 286, Seventh preliminary objection (Nigeria).
141 *Ibid.*, at p. 320, para. 104 (Nigeria).
142 *Ibid.*, at p. 320, para. 105 (Cameroon).

The Court accepted that 'it will be difficult if not impossible to determine the delimitation of the maritime boundary between the Parties as long as the title' over the disputed territorial area 'has not been determined'.[143]

The Court recalled the fact that there were 'extensive negotiations' on part of the maritime boundary between 1970 and 1975.[144] The Court had to decide 'whether the alleged absence of sufficient effort at negotiation constitutes an impediment for the Court to accept the Applicant's claim as admissible or not'.[145]

3.6 Prior Negotiations as a Precondition in Compromissory Clauses: A Legal Obligation or Just a Matter of Fact?

Given the purpose and scope of our study, we will briefly look into the practice of compromissory clauses[146] exclusively from the functional interaction perspective, irrespective of the subject-matter of the convention concerned and of the bilateral or multilateral nature of the agreement.

Except for the limited number of clauses where the parties agreed to refer their future dispute directly to the Court without mentioning any recourse to prior diplomatic negotiations – and where the functional interaction is in fact limited to the negotiation of the actual compromissory clause itself – in the majority of the clauses States Parties express their determination that in case of a dispute arising between them they will first of all and initially endeavour to settle it by negotiations.

That commitment to embark upon a process of negotiations aims at finding a solution expeditiously, as soon as possible, within a reasonable period of time or sometime within a fixed time-limit.

143 *Ibid.*, at p. 320, para. 106. Judge Kooijmans added that prior negotiation 'cannot be seen as a necessary precondition' even if a governing multilateral treaty 'were to be interpreted as making such negotiations indispensable', that is 'if negotiations on a particular part of a boundary cannot lead to results because of surrounding disputes': Separate opinion by Judge Kooijmans, at p. 355, para. 4.

144 *Ibid.*, at p. 321, para. 107.

145 *Ibid.* The Respondent had argued that the prior negotiations provisions of UNCLOS 'lay down a substantive rule, not a procedural prerequisite' (*Land and Maritime Boundary dispute between Cameroon and Nigeria, I.C.J. Reports 2002*, at p. 422, para. 240) and that hence part of the Applicant's claim was inadmissible since negotiations which had been held were 'not even remotely concerned with the line now claimed' (at p. 422, para. 241). In his dissenting opinion Judge *ad hoc* Ajibola also considered the UNCLOS prior negotiations condition to be 'a requirement of substance and not just merely procedural one' (*Land and Maritime Boundary case, I.C.J. Reports 1998*, Dissenting opinion by Judge *ad hoc* Ajibola, at p. 415).

146 Recent analysis covering the period 1920–2002 has shown that 'civil law states are more likely to accept the jurisdiction of the ICJ than common law or Islamic states', while 'common law states place the greatest number of restrictions on their ICJ commitments' and 'Islamic law states have the most durable commitment': E. Powell and S. McLaughlin Michell, 'The International Court of Justice', 397. Other research has shown that common law states 'place the highest number of reservations on their optional clause declarations, with the majority of those reservations relating to specific areas of international law. Civil law states typically embed compromissory clauses in multilateral treaties, while common law states prefer recognition of the ICJ's jurisdiction through bilateral treaties': S. McLauglin Mitchell and E. Powell, 'Legal Systems and Variance in the Design of Commitments to the International Court of Justice' (2009) 26 *Conflict Management and Peace Science*, 164–90 at 164. Their research has also shown that for the period 1922–2002 36 per cent (civil law) 82 per cent (common law) and 76 per cent (Islamic law) of states accepting the Court's jurisdiction reservations are relating to recourse to other method of peaceful settlement: at p. 168.

See also E. Powell and S. Mclaughlin Mitchell, *Domestic Law Goes Global: Domestic Traditions and International Courts* (Cambridge, 2011). See also Judge Oda writing in his scholarly capacity in 2000 for a statistical analysis of contentious cases, 'Compulsory Jurisdiction'

As far as compromissory clauses are concerned, the object and purpose of Article 37 of the Statute is 'to create a special regime which, as between the Parties to the Statute, would automatically transform references to the Permanent Court in these jurisdictional clauses, into references to the present Court': *Barcelona Traction case, I.C.J. Reports 1964*, at p. 31. This automatic transformation includes that part of jurisdictional clauses which contain a precondition of prior negotiations. Hence, any decision of the Court in this respect 'must affect a considerable number of surviving treaties and conventions' and 'would thus be liable to have far-reaching effects': *Ibid.*, at p. 29.

A Compromissory Clause May Provide for a Procedure Consisting of Various Stages

A Treaty may contain a general obligation to submit a dispute to compulsory jurisdiction in case '*it may not have been possible to settle amicably by the normal methods of diplomacy*' between the parties[147] to be followed by a more detailed jurisdictional clause which may include a *pactum de contrahendo* in case, for instance, methods of conciliation fail or have not been utilized; then the parties are under an obligation to draw up a compromis.[148]

The functional interaction properly enters the scene with the inclusion of a prior negotiation condition, the expression of which may be found in the well-known variety of formulations: a dispute *which is not settled*; a dispute *which cannot be settled* or *has not been satisfactorily settled or adjusted by usual diplomatic means*.

When that condition is fulfilled and States Parties cannot reach agreement, within a reasonable period of time, on another mode of procedure, the road to the Peace Palace is open to (one of) the parties, bringing into operation the functional interaction.

The question whether prior negotiations function as a precondition in compromissory clause is an objective one, in both a factual and legal sense.

Either party may plausibly argue that under a bilateral treaty failure of negotiations is not a prerequisite to recourse to the Court.[149]

Parties' commitment to bring the dispute before the Court by appropriate means does not mean that the dispute has yet been brought before the Court by such reciprocal promises.[150]

The Court's case law provides us with this classical judicial description of the very essence of a compromissory clause:

> an agreement to submit to the Court, at the unilateral request of either party, a particular type of dispute which was envisaged and anticipated by the parties. The right to invoke the jurisdiction of the Court was deferred until the occurrence of well-defined future events and was therefore subject to a suspensive condition.[151]

A good starting point on a rather general level and fully in line with this judicial description of a compromissory clause is the awareness that it 'is precisely when difficulties arise' that a Treaty of Amity assumes its greatest importance: the whole object of a compromissory clause is 'to establish the means for arriving at a friendly settlement of such difficulties by the Court or by other peaceful means'.[152]

A compromissory clause may contain a number of preconditions which must be satisfied before the jurisdiction of the Court could be founded, and thereby does not make the Court 'the *primary forum* for the resolution of the disputes to which it applies'. The Court is thereby being given the role of '*guarantor* in the event' of failure of the negotiations.[153] These preconditions may be 'cumulative'.[154]

Prior negotiations culminating in their insertion as a (pre)condition in a compromissory clause, or in the conclusion of a compromis for that matter, have to take place within the limiting framework of their compatibility with the Statute and the Rules of Court.[155]

---

147 *Barcelona Traction case, I.C.J. Reports 1964*, at p. 37 (emphasis added).

148 *Ibid.*, at p. 27. The 1927 Hispano-Belgian Treaty of Conciliation, Judicial Settlement and Arbitration further provided that in case the parties were unable through negotiations to reach an agreement on the terms of such a compromis within a certain period of time, each of them might, on the expiry of one month's notice, bring the question before the Court by way of Application: *ibid.*

149 On the way the Court is dealing with compromissory clauses see generally J. Charney, 'Compromissory Clauses and the Jurisdiction of the International Court of Justice' (1987) 81 *American Journal of International Law* 855–87.

150 *Corfu Channel case, Judgment on Preliminary Objection: I.C.J. Reports 1948*, p. 15, Dissenting opinion by Judge *ad hoc* Daxner, at p. 37.

151 *Fisheries Jurisdiction (Republic of Germany v. Iceland), I.C.J. Reports 1973*, at p. 60, para. 28.

152 *Hostages case, I.C.J. Reports 1980*, at p. 28, para. 54.

153 *DRC v. Rwanda case, I.C.J. Reports 2002*, at p. 236, para. 43 (Rwanda) (emphasis added).

154 *DRC v. Rwanda case, I.C.J. Reports 2006*, at p. 39, para. 87.

155 *Delimitation of the Maritime Boundary in the Gulf of Maine Area, Constitution of Chamber, Order of 20 January 1982, I.C.J. Reports 1982*, p. 3, at p. 4, para. 7.

If a party considers that there have been no negotiations, or that there have been negotiations but that they have failed, the invocation of the governing self-judging prior negotiations clause may 'affect the standard of review that' the Court would 'apply in relation to the state invoking the operation of such a clause'.[156]

Although great care is called for when 'the meaning of the *compromissory clause* in a bilateral treaty' is considered,[157] in light of the Court's case law 'there is no rule that requires a restrictive interpretation of compromissory clauses' and there is 'no judicial policy of being either liberal or strict in deciding the scope of compromissory clauses'.[158]

Overall the fact remains that, exception made for the *Pulp Mills case*, there is 'not a single case in which the typical form of the *compromissory clause* included in a bilateral treaty has been invoked as a main basis of jurisdiction'.[159]

The issue before us here – whether prior negotiations as a precondition in compromissory clauses do impose *a legal obligation* upon the parties or are *just a matter of fact* to be established by the parties and then to be verified and accepted by the Court – has given rise to the argument that even if a disagreement constitutes a dispute in the sense of a particular compromissory clause, it is one which cannot be settled by negotiations; and even if this were not the case anyhow no such negotiations have taken place with a view to its settlement.[160] Hence the Court may find itself compelled to consider the question what the chances are 'of success of further negotiations between the Parties' for reaching a settlement.[161]

In the *CERD case* the Court 'appears to treat as synonymous the various forms or wording found in compromissory clauses making reference' to negotiate a dispute 'which is not settled' or 'which has not been settled', and others 'referring to a dispute "which cannot be settled by negotiation"'.[162] The divergent interpretations of Article 22 CERD have been at the heart of the debate between the parties and within the Court.

A Dispute which Cannot be Settled

This is the case for instance when 'finally a point is reached at which one Party definitely declares himself *unable, or refuses* to give way'.[163]

This formula appears to cover two different types of situation. Indeed, the subject-matter of a dispute may be of such a nature that it seems *impossible* that it can *ever* be settled by negotiation. Here we face a situation which is the exact opposite of the one we reviewed in Chapter 1 on the inherent link between the subject-matter of a dispute and the process of negotiations. There the subject-matter made it (almost) inevitable and (almost) compulsory for the parties to embark upon such an endeavour.

Here the situation entails consequences for the prior negotiations requirement if contained in a jurisdictional clause of any kind. Indeed, if a dispute is inherently incapable of settlement by negotiations and therefore

156 S. Schill and R. Briese, 'If the State Considers', 62.

157 *Oil Platforms case, I.C.J. Reports 1996*, Dissenting opinion by Judge Oda, at p. 896, para. 16.

158 *Ibid.*, Separate opinion by Judge Higgins, at p. 857, para. 35.

159 *Ibid.*, Dissenting opinion by Judge Oda, at pp. 897–8, para. 19 and at p. 891, para. 4. See however also C. Tams, 'The Continued Relevance', 483, and note 107.

On the other methods of accepting the Court's jurisdiction see for instance J. Merrills, 'Does the Optional Clause Still Matter?' in K. Kaikoboad and M. Bohlander (eds), *International Law and Power: Perspectives on Legal Order and Justice. Essays in Honour of Colin Warbrick* (Leiden, Boston, 2009) pp. 431–54 at p. 453: 'the commitment is likely to lie as much in the incentive it provide to avoid the Court, as in the number of cases actually litigated'. See also J. Merrills, 'The Optional Clause at Eighty' in N. Ando, E. McWhinney and R. Wolfrum (eds), Liber Amicorum Judge Shigeru Oda (2 vols, The Hague, 2002), vol. 1, pp. 435–50. On Special Agreements see *inter alia* L. Marion, 'La saisine', 258–300. States may prefer a Special Agreement even though the conditions for instituting proceedings by application are fulfilled: 261, note 6.

160 *South West Africa cases, I.C.J. Reports 1962*, at p. 344 (South Africa). President Winiarski disagreed with the latter part of this argument: the 'issue is not whether there have been really negotiations and whether they have reached a deadlock' (Dissenting opinion, at p. 457).

161 *South West Africa cases, I.C.J. Reports 1962*, at p. 344.

162 *CERD case, I.C.J. Reports 2011*, Joint dissenting opinion, at p. 148, para. 23.

163 *The Mavrommatis Palestine Concessions, P.I.C.J. Series A, No. 2*, at p. 13 (emphasis added).

could not be settled, 'then clearly a requirement that the dispute be one that "cannot" be settled by negotiation would be meaningless'. Starting from this premise dissenting judges further argued that the absence of 'direct diplomatic interchanges' between the parties did constitute 'a formal bar to the present proceedings'.[164]

The premise of both judges has been persuasively rejected by Judge Tanaka when he rightly observed that a 'dispute in which the interest incorporated is of a humanitarian character' 'does not appear to be compatible with the possibility of settlement by negotiation',[165] precursing the position put forward decades later by Judge Koojmans and in a more elaborated way by Judge Trindade in various recent cases.

Whether it then follows that the condition cannot be fulfilled or that it is a dispute not covered by the compromissory clause at all, and thus *in fact and in law* preventing a functional interaction, still is another matter.

Compromissory clauses do play an essential part in the protection of the object and purpose of a treaty, especially when a particular system or regime has been established, for instance for the protection of a sacred trust like the Mandates; they form one of the securities 'for the observance of the obligations by the Mandatory'.[166] For instance, also the object of Article 66 of the Vienna Convention on the Law of Treaties (VCLT) 'is not to allow for the substitution of the judicial settlement' under the VCLT 'for the settlement machinery for disputes relating to the interpretation or application of specific treaties'.[167]

The inherent incapability of a subject-matter such as sacred trust to be settled by negotiation, however, 'does not exclude the possibility of compromise concerning detailed policies and measures in order to implement the fundamental principles of the Mandate'.[168] As such 'the nature of a dispute which is concerned with the sacred trust is incompatible with settlement by negotiation'.[169] For that reason the dispute must be considered to fall altogether outside the scope of the applicable compromissory clause invoked.[170]

The General Assembly allegedly took the same position with regard to the question whether the administration of the Northern Cameroons was in accordance with the Trusteeship Agreement: it 'could be settled only by the Court who had been entrusted with judicial protection'.[171]

However, it has rightly been pointed out that a 'situation which is of legitimate concern to the organized international community and a bilateral dispute with regard to the same situation may exist simultaneously'.[172]

The object and purpose of the Genocide Convention did play an important role in the *DRC Rwanda case* as far as the jurisdiction of the Court was concerned.[173]

The comparison between the two situations or cases is the more striking as in both cases the (Security) Council was unable or unwilling to impose its view on the party concerned with regard to upholding a fundamental value of the international community. In both cases the *only effective recourse* has been the submission for adjudication, although with a different jurisdictional outcome.

The question whether a State's reservation 'is contrary to the object and purpose of the treaty is not a matter to be left exclusively to the States making that reservation' as the Court 'has a role to play' in this regard.[174]

---

164 *South West Africa cases, I.C.J. Reports 1962*, Joint Dissenting opinion by Judges Spender and Fitzmaurice, at p. 551 and p. 562.

165 *South West Africa, I.C.J. Reports 1966*, Dissenting opinion by Judge Tanaka, at p. 257.

166 *South West Africa cases, I.C.J. Reports 1962*, at p. 337.

167 *DRC v. Rwanda case, I.C.J. Reports 2002*, at p. 246, para. 75. See further also J. Verhoeven, 'Jus cogens and reservations or "counterreservations" to the jurisdiction of the International Court of Justice' in K. Wellens (ed.), *International Law: Theory and Practice: Essays in Honour of Eric Suy* (The Hague, 1998), pp. 195–208; and H. Ruiz-Fabri, 'Article 66: Procedures for Judicial Settlement, Arbitration and Conciliation' in P. Klein and O. Corten (eds), *The Vienna Convention on the Law of Treaties: A Commentary* (2 vols, Oxford, 2011),, vol. 2, pp. 1513–36.

168 *South West Africa, I.C.J. Reports 1966*, Dissenting opinion by Judge Tanaka, at p. 257.

169 *Ibid.* See also in the same sense the *Northern Cameroons case, I.C.J. Reports 1963*, Separate opinion by Judge Spender, at pp. 89–90 and Separate opinion by Judge Fitzmaurice, at p. 125.

170 *The Northern Cameroons case, I.C.J. Reports 1963*, Separate opinion by Judge Fitzmaurice, at p. 125.

171 *Ibid.*, Dissenting opinion by Judge *ad hoc* Beb a Don, at p. 192.

172 *Wall Advisory Opinion, I.C.J. Reports 2004*, Separate opinion by Judge Kooijmans, at p. 227, para. 27.

173 *DRC v. Rwanda case, I.C.J. Reports 2006*, at pp. 22, para. 29 and at pp. 30–33, paras. 61–8.

174 Judge Owada, President of the International Court of Justice, introductory remarks in his personal capacity at the Seminar on the Contentious Jurisdiction of the International Court of Justice on 26 October 2010.

The other situation consists of the impossibility to settle the dispute not because of its subject-matter but as result of failed attempts to achieve that objective through a process of prior negotiations. 'There is certainly no absolute litmus test which would enable a court to assert in all situations at just what moment settlement by negotiation becomes impossible.'[175] In fact, as observed by the PCIJ, the States concerned 'are in the best position to judge as *to political reasons* which may prevent the settlement of a given dispute by diplomatic negotiation'.[176]

Article 30 of the Convention Against Torture (CAT) refers to a dispute which 'cannot be settled through negotiation'. The expression which '"is not settled by negotiation" implies a factual finding, and not an assessment of whether a deadlock or a refusal by one of the parties has occurred'.[177] This is 'a question of factual verification and requires no inquiry into the exhaustion of the possibilities of settling the dispute through negotiations'.[178]

A formula '"cannot be settled through negotiations" requires such an enquiry and a determination by the Court that further negotiations became futile and showed no *reasonable probability* that they could result in a settlement of the dispute'.[179]

A Respondent may not have 'initiated or sought to prolong the negotiations', thereby, according to the Applicant, rendering the dispute 'not capable of being settled through negotiation'. Hence the negotiations which started only eight months ago had proven futile.[180]

The Respondent may disagree and argue that no negotiations have ever taken place as there 'has never been an offer' to do so and that the Applicant 'failed in its duty to negotiate in as far as its diplomatic exchanges consisted of general questions'.[181]s

The case law is invoked to support the view that the 'which cannot be settled through negotiations' condition is 'met only where genuine attempts at negotiations, aimed at resolving the dispute, have actually taken place between the Parties and have failed or become futile or deadlocked'.[182]

The times that a dispute between States 'was, or could be considered the private affairs of the states concerned' are gone as inter-state disputes 'have become a matter of concern to the whole world community'[183] and this may trigger multiparty involvement[184] which may structurally be limited 'to playing an auxiliary role' and whose contribution is difficult to quantify.[185] In the concluding part of this study we will return to the possible or likely impact of this view on the functional interaction.

A Dispute Which Has Not Been Settled

A compromissory clause may also provide that resort to the Court would only become available when the dispute had '*not satisfactorily (been) adjusted by diplomacy*'.[186] '[T]he words "which is not settled by negotiation" have the same importance' and are equivalent to 'the words "not satisfactorily adjusted by diplomacy"'[187] – a formulation according to the Court to be found especially in older compromissory clauses.[188]

175 *South West Africa cases, I.C.J. Reports 1962*, Separate opinion by Judge Jessup, at p. 435.

176 *Mavrommatis Palestine Concessions, Judgment, Series A, No. 2*, 1924, at p. 15 as cited by Judge Jessup, at p. 435, (emphasis added).

177 *Belgium v. Senegal case, I.C.J. Reports 2012*, Separate opinion by Judge Yusuf, at p. 560, para. 4.

178 *Ibid.*, at p. 561, para. 6.

179 *Ibid.* (emphasis added).

180 *Ibid.*, Separate opinion by Judge Sebutinde, at p. 594, para. 11 referring to Belgium's contention.

181 *Ibid.*, at p. 594, para. 12 referring to Senegal's contention.

182 *Ibid.*, Separate opinion by Judge Sebutinde, at p. 594, para. 13.

183 A. Lall, *Modern International Negotiation*, p. 1.

184 A. Lall, *Modern International Negotiation*, p. 19.

185 T. Whitfield, 'New Arrangements for Peace Negotiation' in B. Jones, S. Forman and R. Gowan (eds), *Cooperating for Peace and Security: Evolving Institutions and Arrangements in a Context of Changing U.S. Security Policy* (Cambridge, 2010), pp. 227–46 at p. 242.

186 *Hostages case, I.C.J. Reports 1980*, at p. 27, para. 51 (emphasis added).

187 *Nicaragua case, I.C.J. Reports 1984*, Separate opinion by Judge Singh, at p. 446.

188 *CERD case, I.C.J. Reports 2011*, at p. 126, para. 136.

The formulation has to be considered *neutral* as to the political or legal nature of the dispute, although it is most probably on the way to becoming a legal one, ripe for adjudication.

In contrast, one should note that the other applicable provision – Article 1 of the Optional Protocol concerning the Compulsory Settlement of Disputes accompanying the 1961 Vienna Convention of Diplomatic Relations – does not require the parties first to attempt to resolve the dispute through negotiations.[189] This is a 'precise and categorical provision'.[190]

The fact that Articles 2 and 3 of the Protocol provide for a two-month period, after the notification of the existence of a dispute, during which the parties 'may agree to resort not to the International Court of Justice but to an arbitration tribunal or alternatively first to conciliation'[191] should not be read as 'laying down a precondition of the applicability' of Article 1.[192]

Although parties may not contest that 'it has not been possible to adjust that dispute by diplomacy', they may not have agreed 'to settlement by some other pacific means' and they may differ as to whether the dispute was one about the interpretation and application of a bilateral Treaty of Amity, Economic Relations and Consular Rights between them.[193]

Submitting a counterclaim, the Respondent may argue that 'it was clear that diplomatic measures were not a viable means of deterring' the Applicant from further attack,[194] while the counter-claim may then be considered as inadmissible because the Respondent did not satisfy the requirements of that Treaty 'with respect to the satisfactory diplomatic adjustment of the claim'.[195] The Court could not uphold such an objection because it had to take judicial notice of the fact 'that the dispute has not been satisfactorily adjusted by diplomacy'.[196]

For the purposes of assessing the admissibility of the counterclaim the Court may consider it irrelevant whether 'the fact that diplomatic negotiations have not been pursued is to be regarded as attributable to the conduct of one Party or to the other'.[197]

Would it be possible to extend the application of this rather general formulation chosen by the Court, although qualified by the phrase *for present purposes* towards the assessment of the admissibility of main claims in case of such a prior negotiation requirement?

This is corroborated by the subsequent additional reference to the *Hostages and Nicaragua cases* 'involving virtually identical treaty provisions'; it is in such cases 'sufficient for the Court to satisfy itself that the dispute was not satisfactorily adjusted by diplomacy before being submitted to the Court'.[198] Expressed in a purely negative form, the clause does not contain 'an exigent requirement'.[199]

According to a different view the requirement of prior negotiations is 'rather an obligation of conduct than of result' – post-adjudicative negotiations would belong to the latter category – and it is 'for the Court to rule *proprio motu* on compliance or non-compliance with that obligation'.[200] Already in its assessment at the stage of the indication of povisional measures the 'attitude of each Party during the prior negotiations is crucial in order to assess whether or not this requirement has been met'.[201]

The majority view in the *DRC Rwanda case* with regard to this condition that no attempt to settle the dispute had been made 'merely by virtue of the fact' that the Applicant 'failed to refer explicitly' to one of the conventions invoked has been qualified by individual judges as 'unrealistic' and 'unduly restrictive' and not

189 *Hostages case, I.C.J. Reports 1980*, at p. 24, para. 46.

190 *Ibid.*, at p. 25, para. 48.

191 *Breard case, I.C.J. Reports 1998*, at p. 25, para. 26.

192 *Ibid.* In 1996 negotiations took place between the parties concerning the consular function: *ibid.*, Declaration by Judge Oda, at p. 261, para. 3.

193 *Oil Platforms case, I.C.J. Reports 1996*, at pp. 809–10, para. 16.

194 *Oil Platforms case, I.C.J. Reports 2003*, at p. 186, para. 49.

195 *Ibid.*, at p. 171, para. 19 and at p. 209, para. 103 (a).

196 *Ibid.*, at p. 210, para. 107.

197 *Ibid.*

198 *Ibid.*

199 *Nicaragua case, I.C.J. Reports 1984*, Separate opinion by Judge Jennings, at p. 556.

200 *DRC v. Rwanda case, I.C.J. Reports 2002*, Separate opinion by Judge *ad hoc* Mavungu, at p. 280, para. 30.

201 *Ibid.*, at p. 281, para. 31.

'in line with its previous case-law, which reflects a certain flexibility with regard to the requirement of prior negotiations', particularly when 'the attempts to negotiate' in 'a more general, multilateral context did not lead to any positive response by the other party'.[202]

The humanitarian nature of a relevant treaty makes it even more regrettable that the Court is setting a rather high threshold 'by the requirement that a number of preconditions must be met', in particular when the Convention 'does not contain a (parallel) procedure for state complaints to a body established under that treaty'.[203] This latter element will be an important feature in the *CERD case.*

When drafting compromissory clauses parties may have abstained from setting out specific criteria for the element of *not settled by negotiation*, except perhaps for a fixed time limit for that process. That is then, from the functional interaction perspective, not necessarily a disadvantage as it 'leaves sufficient room to allow full consideration to be given to the context of' (attempted) negotiations.[204]

The CERD Case

The *CERD case* is the first one 'in which the Court has found that it lacks jurisdiction *solely* on the basis that a condition of prior negotiations has not been fulfilled' and this was not justified in the circumstances of the case.[205]

The Russian Federation's position was related *inter alia* to the non-fulfilment of the procedural requirements of the compromissory clause contained in Article 22, that is if CERD would be applicable:[206] the Applicant has failed to produce or could not produce evidence that it had proposed to negotiate or to employ the mechanisms of the CERD Committee.[207]

Georgia maintained that the present dispute had not been settled by negotiations and, moreover, that the procedures provided in CERD were 'not designed to be exclusive or compulsory' in respect of disputes concerning the subject-matter of the Convention.[208]

Whether this interpretation goes for all similarly worded compromissory clauses during the same period of time may be doubted as 'any assessment has to proceed from the specific formulation of the relevant compromissory clause. This is, in particular, because States have often introduced very subtle distinctions concerning preconditions of court proceedings (such as prior negotiations or lapse of time).'[209]

The disagreement between the parties went far beyond the preliminary but important question on the legal or factual nature of the formula *which cannot be settled through negotiation* as it also related to 'what constitutes negotiations, including the extent to which they must be pursued before it can be concluded that the precondition' had been fulfilled. Moreover, the parties also held different views as to the format of the negotiations and the extent to which they should refer to the substantive obligations under the CERD.[210]

In its Order on the request for the indication of provisional measures the Court interpreted Article 22 'on its plain meaning' as not suggesting 'that formal negotiations in the framework of the Convention or recourse to the procedure referred to in Article 22 thereof constitute preconditions to be fulfilled before the seisin of the Court'.[211]

Article 22 does however 'suggest that some attempt should have been made by the claimant party to initiate with the respondent party, discussions on issues that would fall under the CERD'.[212] In the Court's view

---

202 *DRC v. Rwanda case, I.C.J. Reports 2006*, Declaration by Judge Kooijmans, at p. 74, paras. 6 and 7 and at p. 75, para. 11.

203 *DRC v. Rwanda case, I.C.J. Reports 2006*, Declaration by Judge Kooijmans, at p. 76, para. 15.

204 *Ibid.*

205 *CERD case, I.C.J. Reports 2011*, Joint dissenting opinion, at p. 161, para. 63 (emphasis added).

206 *Application of the International Convention on the Elimination of all Forms of Racial Discrimination (Georgia v. Russian Federation), Provisional Measures, Order of 15 October 2008, I.C.J. Reports 2008*, p. 353, at p. 376, para. 83.

207 *CERD case, I.C.J. Reports 2008*, at p. 376, para. 83.

208 *Ibid.*, at p. 380, para. 94.

209 C. Tams, 'The Continued Relevance' p. 465.

210 *CERD case, I.C.J. Reports 2011*, at p. 121, para. 120.

211 *CERD case, I.C.J. Reports 2008*, at p. 388, para. 114.

212 *Ibid.*

because of its structure and its wording the compromissory clause of Article 22 is merely suggestive and not compulsory, while some attempt is sufficient to bring the claimant party's conduct in line with that suggestion.

In a joint dissent to the Court's 2008 Order, judges argued that the Court 'cannot ignore' an explicit prior negotiation clause 'without explanation'; neither can it 'dispose of this condition merely by observing that the question has not been resolved by negotiation'.[213]

Whether the precondition of prior negotiations as formulated in a compromissory clause such as *which has not been settled* should be considered to reflect and express a legal obligation or as nothing more than a statement of fact was just one of the crucial issues. The Court in a clear and succinct way presented the extent of the disagreement between the parties on the formula 'which is not settled by negotiation *or* by the procedures expressly provided for'.[214]

According to the Russian interpretation, Article 22 of CERD contains two cumulative preconditions: an attempt must have been made to resolve the dispute by those means; and those attempts must have failed before the dispute could be referred to the Court.

Georgia on the other hand contended that the preconditions are alternative ones and that accordingly there was no such affirmative obligation: 'all that is required is that' the dispute 'has not been resolved' as a matter of fact.[215]

There is nothing in the compromissory clause of Article 22 'expressly or implicitly – about any general duty to attempt to settle the dispute before seising the Court':[216] the expression *which is not settled* is 'merely a statement of fact'; 'otherwise the drafters would have used *cannot be settled* as in many other conventions, which is more than *is not settled*. As this was a deliberate choice of the drafters no preconditions were imposed.[217]

According to the Court the nature of the precondition of prior negotiations, namely suggestive and not compulsory, involves 'a series of issues': namely 'assessing what constitutes negotiations; considering their adequate form and substance; and determining to what extent they should be pursued before it can be said that the precondition has been met'.[218] These issues will be addressed in detail in Chapters 5 and 7, and in the conclusions of this study.

As the Court after having considered these issues came to the conclusion that both parties did not 'engage in negotiations with respect to' the Respondent's compliance 'with its substantive obligations under CERD'[219] based on a reasoning to be analysed later, there was no need for the Court to examine whether the conditions of Article 22 were cumulative or alternative.[220]

The view shared by several judges that the conditions were alternative[221] reinforces the autonomous character of negotiations within the context of the invocation of a compromissory clause and of seising the Court.

The Principle of Effectiveness Requires that a Previous and Genuine Attempt to Settle the Dispute Has Been Made

That negotiations are a precondition for seisin underlies the argument that an Application has been filed 'although the two Governments had not yet begun negotiations on the substantive issue'.[222] In this case, 'diplomatic exchanges and talks' had already taken place, 'but no settlement of that dispute had been achieved'.[223]

213 *Ibid.*, Joint dissenting opinion by Judges Al-Khasawneh, Ranjeva, Shi, Koroma, Tomka, Bennouna and Skotnikov, at p. 403, para. 13.

214 *CERD case, I.C.J. Reports 2011*, at p. 121, para. 118 (emphasis added).

215 *Ibid.*, at p. 121, para. 119.

216 *Ibid.*, at p. 123, para. 126 (Georgia).

217 *Ibid.*, at p. 123, para. 128 (Georgia).

218 *Ibid.*, at p. 132, para. 156.

219 *Ibid.*, at p. 140, para. 182.

220 *Ibid.*, at p. 140, para. 183.

221 See for instance dissenting opinion by Judge Cançado Trindade, *CERD case, I.C.J. Reports 2011*, at p. 290, para. 116.

222 *Aegean Sea Continental Shelf case, I.C.J. Reports 1978*, at p. 11, para. 27 (Turkey).

223 *Aegean Sea Continental Shelf case, I.C.J. Reports 1976*, at p. 7, para. 16 (Greece).

Invoking the principle of effectiveness with regard to the interpretation of the compromissory clause and referring to the French version of it – 'qui n'aura pas été règlé' – the Russian Federation argued that the phrase *which is not settled* requires 'that a previous attempt to settle has been made bona fide'.[224]

According to the Court, Georgia's interpretation of the words 'which is not settled' would render a key phrase of the provision without any effect, and this would run counter to the Court's established jurisprudence.[225]

The express choices of two modes of dispute settlement 'suggest an affirmative duty to resort to them prior to the seisin of the Court',[226] this interpretation being reinforced by the French version of the compromissory clause.[227]

The crucial question is: is it a real precondition? What is the extent and scope of the obligation: merely making such an attempt or having made such serious attempts and that in spite of them the negotiations have unfortunately failed? Does 'the right to have recourse to the Court, and reciprocally the competence of the Court to entertain the claim, depend on the attempts to satisfy this condition and can [it] not arise unless and until such attempts have been made and have failed'.[228]

The Travaux Préparatoires of CERD

The Russian Federation relied on the *travaux préparatoires* of CERD to confirm that the drafters 'considered the seisin of the Court as a last resort, after the settlement procedures referred to in Article 22, including negotiations had been attempted and exhausted'.[229]

Georgia did not find 'during the final discussion' any statement to that effect, or that the two modes (CERD conciliation machinery and negotiation) were cumulative. The intention of the drafters when including negotiations in Article 22 was 'merely to point out the existence of non-mandatory opportunity to resort' to alternative settlement procedures before seising the Court, and 'not to establish preconditions to such seisin'.[230]

According to the Court a reasonable assumption could be made that in addition to the possibility of making reservations to the compulsory dispute settlement provisions of the Convention further limitations 'to resort to judicial settlement in the form of prior negotiations and other settlement procedures without fixed time-limits were provided for with a view to facilitating wider acceptance of CERD by States'.[231]

Although CERD's drafting history did not allow to draw 'firm inferences' as to whether negotiations were meant as preconditions for the seisin of the Court', the *travaux préparatoires* 'do not suggest a different conclusion from that at which the Court has already arrived through the main method of ordinary treaty interpretation'.[232]

Judge Trindade took a different reading of the *travaux*: 'Resort to negotiations was generally referred to as a factual *effort or attempt* only, rather than as a resolutory obligation'.[233]

(In)Consistency with Previous Case Law

Form our perspective the Court's general approach to prior negotiations as a legal precondition for seising the Court appears, at first glance, to contribute to potentially maximizing the functional interaction. This seems also to be the direction of the position of some individual judges.[234] However, the manner in which the Court

224 *CERD case, I.C.J. Reports 2011*, at p. 122, paras. 123–4.

225 *Ibid.*, at pp. 125–6, para. 133.

226 *CERD case, I.C.J. Reports 2011*, at p. 126, para. 134.

227 *Ibid.*, at p. 126, para. 135.

228 *Ibid.*, at p. 122, para. 124 (Russian Federation).

229 *Ibid.*, at pp. 128–9, paras. 143–4.

230 *Ibid.*, at p. 129, para. 145.

231 *Ibid.*, at p. 129, para. 147. In this last respect one could note that the fixing of time limits would constitute a further indication of States' reluctance to submit to the compulsory jurisdiction of the Court being eroded.

232 *CERD case, I.C.J. Reports 2011*, at p. 130, para. 147.

233 *Ibid.*, Dissenting opinion by Judge Cançado Trindade, at p. 286, para. 101.

234 Under Article 22 the power of States to refer disputes to the Court is subject to their duty first to attempt to settle their dispute by negotiations. Otherwise, 'a respondent could be forced to appear before the Court without having had a

has elaborated and applied the various elements of this precondition in the *CERD case* tends to significantly reduce this potential functional interaction.

The Court, first of all and 'as a preliminary matter', noted that compromissory clauses containing a reference to negotiation 'though similar in character' are 'not always uniform', as our review has demonstrated.[235] States may have included in a clause a time-element for negotiations, 'the expiry of which would trigger a duty to arbitrate or to have recourse to the Court'.[236]

As to the language used, variations such as *is not settled by* or *cannot be settled*, the Court noted that the compromissory clauses in those cases 'were comparable to that included in CERD' and in 'each of' those cases the Court has 'interpreted the reference to negotiations as constituting a precondition to seisin'.[237]

The Court has indeed consistently interpreted such compromsisory clauses 'as meaning that the Court cannot exercise jurisdiction unless an attempt at negotiations has been made and had led to deadlock that is to say that there is no reasonable hope – or no longer any – for a settlement by diplomatic means'.[238]

However, the precondition *which is not settled* is 'a factual condition which the Court must assess in all cases and on the fulfilment of which its jurisdiction is dependent',[239] but it must be 'understood and applied realistically and substantively, not in the *unrealistic and formalistic manner* applied' by the majority.[240] Moreover, the jurisprudence of the Court 'would appear to fluctuate much more than the present judgment suggests'.[241]

Reviewing the Court's case law, including the Court's 2008 Order in this case, the dissenting judges came to the conclusion that the present judgment was 'at variance with the position it took on a *prima facie* basis three years ago in the same case'.[242] The majority's reasoning has not only been considered to be unsound and unfounded[243] but, moreover, there was 'no reason to depart' from the 'Court's long-standing practice' as that 'would create juridical uncertainty, in the understanding of States, as to the circumstances in which the Court would exercise jurisdiction'.[244]

The *jurisprudence constante* of the PCIJ as reflected in the *Mavrommatis case* did approach prior attempts to solve a dispute as a factual element,[245] whereas in doctrine attempts of friendly settlement by diplomatic means were considered to be a 'matter of *courtoisie internationale*'.[246]

From the case law of both Courts no inclination can be inferred 'to set up an excessive prerequisite of prior negotiations for the exercise of jurisdiction … an *attempt* of negotiations is sufficient, there being no mandatory "precondition" at all of *resolutory* negotiations'.[247]

The majority's requirement 'is a particularly strict and rigorous one'. It purports to establish rigid "preconditions" rendering access to the Court particularly difficult.'[248]

Although one can hardly make abstraction of the nature and substance of a treaty when considering an optional clause, or else the compromissory clause enshrined therein,[249] including the prior negotiations requirement, the Court's approach results in 'newly proposed – if not imposed – obstacles to the fulfilment

---

chance to resolve the dispute amicably': *CERD case, I.C.J. Reports 2011*, Separate opinion by Judge Koroma, at p. 186, para. 8, note 1.

235 *Ibid.*, at p. 126, para. 136.

236 *Ibid.*, referring for instance to the *DRC Rwanda case* and to the *PLO case Advisory Opinion, I.C.J. Reports 1988*, at p. 14, para. 7 and at p. 27, para. 34.

237 *Ibid.*, at pp. 127–8, paras. 137–9, and at p. 139, para. 140.

238 *CERD case, I.C.J. Reports 2011*, Joint dissenting opinion, at p. 150, para. 28.

239 *Ibid.*, Joint dissenting opinion, at pp. 145–6, para. 15.

240 *Ibid.*, Joint dissenting opinion, at p. 145, para. 12.

241 *Ibid.*, Joint dissenting opinion, at p. 151, para. 29.

242 *Ibid.*, Joint dissenting opinion, at pp. 150–52, paras. 28–31; at pp. 152–4, paras. 33–7; and at p. 153, para. 34.

243 *Ibid.*, Dissenting opinion by Judge Cançado Trindade, at p. 288, para. 109.

244 *Ibid.*, at p. 289, para. 111.

245 *Ibid.*, at p. 291, para. 119.

246 *Ibid.*, at p. 292, para. 123.

247 *Ibid.*, at pp. 296–7, para. 135.

248 *CERD case, I.C.J. Reports 2011*, Dissenting opinion by Judge Cançado Trindade, at p. 282, para. 89.

249 *Ibid.*, at p. 268, para. 70.

of the object and purpose of the convention'.[250] Such an approach should also affect the negotiation strategy of states.[251]

The setting forth of 'such preconditions' 'amounts to erecting an undue and groundless obstacle to access to justice under a human rights treaty' not only running counter to the Court's jurisprudence constante but also to its 2008 Order in the case.[252]

When States raise legal concerns they first seek to resolve them 'through some form of diplomacy' and less commonly 'choose instead to proceed directly to the Court'.[253]

An Attempt Has (To Be) or Has Been Made to Settle the Dispute

For a precondition such as that contained in Article 22 of CERD to be fulfilled it 'is not enough that a dispute *has not been settled* … an attempt must have been made to settle',[254] but it is almost self- evident that a State cannot 'be expected to attempt to negotiate a dispute if no steps have been taken to make it aware that it might be a party to a dispute'.[255]

A claimant State may wish to submit certain clarifications within the framework of a negotiation procedure provided for in a compromissory clause. The Court then may take it as a demonstration of that State's attempt to resolve the dispute by negotiations; at the same time such a demarche would prevent the conclusion 'that the negotiations thus proposed had the effect of resolving the dispute'.[256]

The condition for this judicial acceptance seems to be that the diplomatic note explicitly makes reference to the negotiation procedure contained in the compromissory clause.

The precondition that a dispute has not been settled only requires evidence 'that an attempt has been made and not that such negotiations have reached deadlock'.[257] The evidence before the Court may clearly show 'that neither a deadlock nor an impasse was ever reached in the negotiaitons between the parties, and that those negotiations continue for a long time even after the filing' of the Application.[258] There may be no indication 'that the dispute could not be settled through negotiations *and* that the parties fully and defintively gave up hope of reaching a settlement through negotiations'.[259]

The fact 'that the negotiations between the Parties were *never permanenetly interrupted*, but were *resumed* on many occasions, even after the filing of the application' indeed 'demonstrates that the possibility of a settlement through negotiations never disappeared'.[260]

A permanent interruption of the process would mean that all attempts to settle the dispute have been exhausted and that there is no real prospect of any resumption, and this in contrast to a temporary suspension by (one of) the parties. The attitude of the parties as it can can be inferred from, for instance, public statements should be the decisive factor in this regard.

The question of prior debates between the parties and thus of any attempt to solve the dispute is only pertinent if the prior negotiations condition has been expressly provided for; otherwise 'it is merely a matter of ascertaining whether a dispute exists'.[261]

With regard to compromissory clauses similar to the relevant one of Article 30 CAT in the *Belgian Senegal case* the Court in the past 'has set a standard of compliance'.[262] Referring to its judgment in the *CERD case*

250 *Ibid.*, at p. 288, para. 108.
251 *Ibid.*, at p 298, para. 138.
252 *Ibid.*, at p. 315, paras. 192 and 193.
253 *Ibid.*, Separate opinion by Judge Donoghue, at p. 339, para. 24.
254 *Ibid.*, Separate opinion by Judge Greenwood, at p. 327, para. 11.
255 *Ibid.*, at p. 326, para. 9.
256 *Ibid.*, at p. 94, para. 50.
257 *Ibid.*, at p. 132, para. 155 (Georgia).
258 *Belgium v. Senegal case, I.C.J. Reports 2012*, Separate opinion by Judge Yusuf, at p. 561, para. 5.
259 *Ibid.* (emphasis added).
260 *Ibid.* (emphasis added).
261 *CERD case, I.C.J Reports 2011*, Separate opinion by Judge Abraham, at pp. 231–2, paras. 24–5.
262 *Belgium v. Senegal case, I.C.J. Reports 2012*, Separate opinion by Judge Sebutinde, at p. 592, para. 3.

and to the *SWA cases*, the Court examined whether a *genuine attempt* was made and whether there was *no reasonable probability* that further negotiations would lead to a settlement.[263]

A Respondent may not have disputed the Applicant's qualification that in the exchange of correspondence it was acting within the framework of the negotiating porcess as provided in the compromissory clause.[264]

To confirm its conclusion that 'negotiations did not and could not lead to the settlement of the dispute' the Court may refer to the fact that, owing to the Respondent's position the process did not make any progress towards a solution, that there was no change in the respective positions and that these positions did not 'subsequently evolve' during the pleadings,[265] another example of the close functional interaction between prior negotiations and judicial proceedings.

It is worth noting that in contrast to its previous case law the Court explicitly blamed the Respondent for the lack of progress in the process of negotiations which did not and could not lead to a settlement.

The Court's judgment in the *Belgium v. Senegal case* – delivered just over a year after the judgment in the *CERD case* and explicitly citing the precondition approach taken in that case – does not contribute to alleviate the concerns expressed by the joint dissent and by doctrine regarding the potential impact of that judgment on prospective parties and the Court alike regarding the further development of the relevant case law from the perspective of the functional interaction.

What Exactly Does the Condition Requiring an Attempt to Settle the Dispute by Negotiations Consist of?[266]

The Court, by taking the position that prior to 9 August there had been no dispute relating to matters falling under CERD, had no difficulty in ruling that those prior negotiations 'cannot be said to have covered such matters'.[267]

The Court did not consider statements made after 9 August 'as genuine attempts by Georgia to negotiate matters falling under CERD', although they 'attest to the existence of a dispute on a subject-matter capable of falling under CERD'.[268]

This position is a clear departure from the position it took almost three years earlier in its Order on provisional measures[269] and in a joint dissent on which judges argued that the very subject-matter of CERD was never debated prior to the start of the proceedings.[270]

As each case has its own circumstances, how to prove that negotiations were 'sufficiently utilized' as this notion is 'imprecise and relative'?[271]

'There is no general criterion – nor can there be one – which makes it possible to determine at which point a State is regarded as having complied with the obligation to attempt to negotiate … and to pursue those attempts as far as possible … Everything depends on the circumstances' and 'the level of the Court's requirements is bound to vary, according to the nature of the questions which form the subject-mater of the dispute, and the conduct of the State that is being implicated'. In fact 'some questions, by their nature, lend themselves more than others to negotiation, the reconciling of opinions and the search for a compromis'; the States concerned 'may have a range of' options 'from complete receptiveness to the most strenuous or indeed point blank rejection'.[272]

---

263 *Ibid.*, at pp. 445–6, para. 57.

264 *Ibid.*, at p. 446, para. 58.

265 *Ibid.*, at p. 446, para. 59.

266 Formulation taken from the Joint dissenting opinion in the *CERD Case, I.C.J. Reports 2011*, at p. 158.

267 *CERD case, I.C.J. Reports 2011*, at p. 136, para. 170.

268 *Ibid.*, at p. 139, para. 181. The legal significance to be attached to bilateral exchange of letters could very well consist of considering them as attempts at a negotiated settlement, prior to the critical date adopted by the majority: Separate opinion by Judge Simma, at p. 190, para. 5; at pp. 198–9, para. 22; and at p. 199, para. 25.

269 *CERD case, I.C.J. Reports 2008*, at p. 388, paras. 114–15.

270 *Ibid.*, Joint dissenting opinion, at p. 402, para. 12.

271 *CERD case, I.C.J. Reports 2011*, Dissenting opinion by Judge Cançado Trindade, at p. 293, para. 124 referring to Bourquin.

272 *Ibid.*, Joint dissenting opinion, at p. 159, para. 56.

As the Court was of the opinion that no genuine attempt at negotiation had been made, there was no need for it to assess whether the Applicant had pursued these negotiations as far as possible and to determine whether the process 'failed, became futile or reached a deadlock' prior to the filing of the Application.[273]

With regard to a 'kind of dispute which rarely gives rise to a reconciliation of positions', an Applicant 'should not be expected to make a formal offer to negotiate, or to suggest ways to a compromise'. It must suffice for that State 'to make known the existence and tenor of its claims' so as to enable the other party 'to express its position' and to make known 'that it categorically rejects the essence of the asserted claims'.[274] This argument is in line with our earlier observation that some subject-matters are by the nature of the rights and obligations involved not negotiable.

The functional interaction comes under pressure because as a result of the Court's 'questionable' interpretation – that 'all possibility of negotiated settlement must have been exhausted because "there has been a failure of negotiations, or ... negotiations have become futile or deadlocked"'[275] – in case of prior negotiations coming to an end after the start of the proceedings 'by virtue of the *acknowledged impossibility* of reaching agreement, the Court should decline jurisdiction and thereby require the applicant to bring fresh proceedings'.[276]

In contrast, the functional interaction could be maximized when 'if it seems *reasonably possible* by recourse to means enabling the parties to reach agreement' the Applicant 'must have made the necessary efforts to attempt to settle the dispute', thereby 'leaving the Court to act as the last resort' – thus reserving 'judicial settlement for those disputes which cannot be settled by an out-of-court settlement based on agreement between the parties'.[277]

Such a *reasonable possibility* did not exist on the date of the filing of the Application and it would have been *unreasonable* to require the Applicant 'to attempt to resolve' the dispute after that date because a sufficient attempt to settle it had already been made and it was 'unrealistic to believe that on that date there remained even the slightest chance' of a negotiated settlement.[278] On the date of instituting the proceedings there was no more *reasonable possibility* of that happening.[279]

Although of course 'a favourable outcome depends on the readiness of the parties to come to an agreement, in other words, on their willingness to negotiate', the functional interaction is reaching its limits because it would be 'senseless to require' a future Applicant 'to follow a special procedure' after an attempt of direct negotiations has been unsuccessful', and it would make even less sense after an unsuccessful 'intricate procedure' as provided in a compromissory clause to require the Parties 'to undertake direct negotiation *destined to fail* before seising the Court'.[280]

In case a party claims that certain activities are violations of both treaty *and* customary law it would, according to the Court, 'be excessively formalistic to require' first the exhaustion of the procedure provided for in a compromissory clause 'before bringing the matter to the Court'.[281]

In case the compromissory clause has been inserted in a bilateral treaty, each of the parties is entitled to invoke the Court's jurisdiction.[282] Once a dispute has been brought before the Court, it may turn out to be 'exactly of the character anticipated in the compromissory clause',[283] and this brings us to the next aspect of prior negotiations.

---

273 *Ibid.*, at p. 134, para. 162.

274 *Ibid.*, Joint dissenting opinion, at p. 163, para. 72.

275 *Ibid.*, at p. 133, para. 159 and Joint dissenting opinion, at p. 146, para. 16.

276 *Ibid.*, at p. 134, para. 162 and Joint dissenting opinion, at p. 154, para. 36 (emphasis added).

277 *Ibid.*, Joint dissenting opinion, at p. 156, para. 43 (emphasis added).

278 *CERD case, I.C.J. Reports 2011*, Joint dissenting opinion, at p; 168, para. 84 (emphasis added) and at p. 162, para. 66.

279 *Ibid.*, Joint dissenting opinion, at p. 162, para. 67.

280 *Ibid.*, Joint dissenting opinion, at p. 156, para. 43 (emphasis added).

281 *Nicaragua case, I.C.J. Reports 1986*, at p. 137, para. 274.

282 *Fisheries Jurisdiction (Federal Republic of Germany v. Iceland), I.C.J. Reports 1973*, at p. 61, para. 31.

283 *Ibid.*, at p. 65, para. 43.

When to Decide Whether It Has Been Settled?

When on the date of the start of the proceedings, or alternatively on the date of its jurisdictional decision, the Court finds that there is no longer a reasonable prospect of 'the dispute as presented to the Court, being settled by negotiations', then 'it must find jurisdiction without entering into a convoluted examination of every single action taken by the Applicant, or those that it could have taken'.[284]

Although the 'very fact that proceedings were instiututed before the ICJ militates strongly against the assumption or conclusion that the dispute could have been resolved by *prior* negotiations between the contending parties',[285] a reasoning aptly reflecting the proper functional interaction – the Court's pronouncement that the deficiency in fullfing the conditions for the Court's jurisdiction may also be overcome in the course of the proceedings by the Respondent – [286] is 'general in scope', hence 'terms precluding all doubt as to the fact that its reasoning applies to any intially unmet condition for jurisdiction or admissibility that is fulfilled between the date on which the proceedings were initiated and the date on which the Court decides on its jurisdiction'.[287]

This brings to the fore the functional interaction operating through the resumption of negotiations during the proceedings and which we will address in Chapter 6.

A Provisional Assessment of the Court's Handling of the Case

From our perspective the Court's general approach to prior negotiations as a legal precondition for seising the Court appears, at first glance, to contribute to potentially maximizing the functional interaction. However, the manner in which the Court has elaborated and applied the various elements of this precondition in the *CERD case* tends to significantly reduce this potential. Moreover, the judgment 'can have an adverse impact on the future acceptance of the Court's compulsory jurisdiction under international treaties'.[288]

The majority's requirement 'is a particularly strict and rigorous one'. It purports to establish rigid 'preconditions', thereby 'rendering access to the Court particularly difficult'.[289]

For a State 'with limited resources' and 'lack of experience' before the Court such a 'State's access to this Court could', as result of the Court's decision, 'be barred unless it follows new procedural requirements that it will not find in the text of the treaty, the Statute or the Rules of Court', even if it 'considers that it is the victim of a clear violation by another State, and even if the "precondition" in a compromissory clause is hidden, as in the CERD'.[290]

3.7 Prior Negotiations as a Precondition in the Optional Clause System

With regard to the rise and decline of the optional clause, it is worth recalling the Court's pronouncement that each optional clause 'does constitute a certain progress towards extending to the world in general the system of compulsory judicial settlement of international disputes'.[291]

As far as its interpretation is concerned, there is no reason for the Court to deal with a declaration accepting its compulsory jurisdiction in a different way than any other text emanating from a government as it should 'in principle, be interpreted as producing and as intended to produce effects in accordance with existing law and not in violation of it'.[292]

284 *CERD case, I.C.J. Reports 2011*, Joint dissenting opinion, at p. 159, para. 57.
285 *Ibid.*, Dissenting opinion by Judge Cançado Trindade, at p. 286, para. 102 (emphasis added).
286 *Croatian Genocide case, I.C.J. Reports 2008*, at p. 441, para. 85.
287 *CERD case, I.C.J. Reports 2011*, Joint dissenting opinion, at p. 154, para. 37.
288 *Ibid.*, Dissenting opinion by Judge Cançado Trindade, at p. 298, para. 138.
289 *Ibid.*, at p. 282, para. 89.
290 *Ibid.*, Separate opinion by Judge Donoghue, at p. 339, para. 25.
291 *Nicaragua Case, I.C.J. Reports 1984*, at p. 407, para. 34.
292 *Right of Passage case, I.C.J. Reports 1957*, at p. 142.

An optional clause may not only contain the conduct of negotiations as a precondition to the institution of proceedings; it may also imply, based on a proposal made earlier, the readiness to negotiate an agreement to submit the dispute to the Court, provided the case were decided *ex aequo et bono*.[293]

In some compromissory clauses States Parties do bind themselves by a mutual obligation to accept the jurisdiction of the Court pursuant to Article 36, para. 2 of the Statute.

A Closer Look at the Practice of Optional Clauses

Given the scope and purpose of our study there is no need to review the declarations made in a detailed and tentatively exhaustive way. We will look into the practice of acceptance of the Court's jurisdiction from the functional interaction perspective, irrespective of the identity of the State having deposited the declaration or of the date and successive versions of a particular declaration, also given the fact that many States are looking for inspiration in existing declarations, in some cases even explicitly bearing in mind the text of similar declarations made by other States Members of the United Nations.

First of all, one may safely assume that the formulations chosen by States and the way reference is made to other peaceful methods of settlement are based on States' firm conviction that in general and most preferably disputes should be settled by negotiations, and that in general terms there is no need to make that preference explicit.[294]

If this is correct, then formulations such as *have agreed or shall agree to have recourse to some other method of peaceful settlement* would be referring to the mechanisms listed in Article 33 of the Charter, such as arbitration, mediation or other methods of conciliation or accommodation. We obviously are not concerned here with those declarations which have been made *pure and simple* and unconditionally.

Those qualified formulations however do imply a process of past or future negotiations of a procedural nature with regard to those other modes of settlement, such as *disputes the solution of which Parties shall entrust to other tribunals by virtue of agreements already in existence or which may be concluded in the future*.

Sometimes litispendence is excluded for *disputes in respect of which arbitral or judicial proceedings are taking or have taken place*, thereby conferring the *una via selecta* approach referred to in Chapter 2.

From a functional interaction perspective it should be noted that the exclusion of disputes *in respect of which any other Party to a dispute has accepted the compulsory jurisdiction of the International Court of Justice for or in relation to the purpose of such dispute* seems to aim at preventing sudden acceptance of the Court's jurisdiction prompted by a final failure of prior negotiations.

A slightly different and increasingly becoming more frequent exclusion with regard to declarations deposited or ratified less than 12 or six months prior to the filing of an Application substantially reduces the potential for parties to opt for a double-track strategy, at least within that specific time frame, almost immediately preceding the filing of an Application. Whether such an exclusion *ratione temporis* could on the other hand have a positive impact on the progress and outcome of the process of prior negotiations is an open question.

Clauses preserving the right of a State to suspend judicial proceedings under certain conditions in the case of a dispute under consideration by the Security Council manifest not only a functional interaction between two principal organs of the UN as far as peaceful settlement is concerned, but more importantly also create at least an opportunity for parties to start or continue negotiations during the course of the proceedings, *a fortiori* when the suspension does not contain a time limit.

The functional interaction becomes more operational when the exclusion clause does not apply *to a dispute in relation to which the Parties have agreed upon a modus vivendi pending the final decision of the Court in the dispute*, a clear manifestation of the State concerned maintaining its willingness to negotiate prior to the start of the proceedings.

---

293 *Nottebohm case (Preliminary Objection), I.C.J. Reports 1953*, p. 111 at p. 113: declaration of Guatemala of January 1947.

294 The intent 'underlying' a particular reservation excluding particular categories of disputes may be to 'give effect to its belief that its overlapping maritime claims are best resolved by negotiations': *Whaling in the Antarctic case, Judgment, I.C.J. Reports 2014*, para. 34 (emphasis added).

With regard to the important factor of the state of the relations between parties to a dispute, the exclusion of disputes in the absence of diplomatic relations between the parties – an exception clause which *will not ordinarily be invoked in cases where relations have been broken off after or as a result of the dispute* (an expression of a more nuanced and more realistic approach to the prospect of avenues of settlement apart from bilateral avenues) – rules out recourse to the Court but inevitably increases the need to look for other modes of dispute settlement, most likely with the assistance of a third party, for instance in a role of mediator.

As far as the process of prior negotiations of a substantial nature is concerned, one should mention the few declarations where a dispute is excluded from the Court's jurisdiction which *has been settled* by some other method of peaceful settlement.

The inclusion of disputes which *are not settled* by other means of peaceful settlement does not apply to disputes to which the parties have agreed or shall agree to refer for final and binding decision to arbitration or judicial settlement and is clearly based on the premise that prior negotiations have been unsuccessful.

Apart from the more traditional exclusion clauses such as *parties have or will agree*, sometimes there is a further margin of appreciation for the State with regard to disputes for which it would be *appropriate* to apply, directly or indirectly, agreements and conventions concluded and providing for a different method of settling disputes. Prior negotiations may have led to the State's view that, given for instance the nature of the dispute, and perhaps also the outcome of previous proceedings before the Court in which the State had been involved, it would be more *appropriate* to prefer another mechanism than recourse to the Court.

Functional interaction is also very much present when the acceptance concerns a dispute as to which no other means of pacific settlement *is* agreed upon between the parties – i.e. after the dispute has come into existence, for instance during a process of prior negotiations and for the solution of which further negotiations of a procedural nature have been in vain.

How to interpret the reservation contained in an optional clause that prior negotiations have to take place before a dispute can be submitted to the Court?

Because jurisdiction 'only exists within the limits within which it has been accepted',[295] reservations 'operate to define the parameters of the State's acceptance of the compulsory jurisdiction of the Court. Thus there is no reason to interpret them restrictively.'[296] Moreover, the declarations and the reservations 'are to be read as a whole'.[297] Accordingly, a reservation expressing the precondition of prior negotiations has to be interpreted 'in a natural and reasonable way' and 'having due regard to the intention of the declarant'.[298]

A variety of reasons may bring States to insert a reservation. From the perspective of the functional interaction, the prior negotiation reservation *may partly but not necessarily* be linked to the fact that States 'feel vulnerable about the legality of their position or policy'[299] but also and rather to their preoccupation to give this normally bilateral mechanism of peaceful settlement of disputes a final chance before bringing the dispute before the Court.

An optional clause providing for resort to the Court unless other means of pacific settlement are agreed upon by the parties[300]does imply negotiations in order to start these other means, or at least the political will to enter into such a process of negotiations.

With regard to the readiness to start negotiations, acceptance or rejection of proposals, or the decision to break off negotiations or to resume them, parties and ultimately the Court do enjoy a large margin of interpretation because international law 'which places the principal emphasis on the intention of the parties' does not prescribe any 'particular form' and as a result 'parties are free to choose what form they please provided their intention clearly results from it'.[301] This applies more generally to negotiations whether they take place prior, during or after the judicial proceedings.

---

295 *Phosphates in Morocco case, P.C.I.J. Series A/B, No. 74*, p. 23. For an overview of the declarations accepting the PCIJ's compulsory jurisdiction see *inter alia* M. Hudson, *The Permanent Court*, pp. 681–703.

296 *Fisheries Jurisdiction (Spain v. Canada), I.C.J. Reports 1998*, at pp. 452–3, para. 44.

297 *Ibid.*, at p. 454, para. 47.

298 *Ibid.*, at pp. 463–4, para. 76.

299 *Ibid.*, at p. 455, para. 54.

300 *Temple of Preah Vihear case, I.C.J. Reports 1961*, at p. 23.

301 *Ibid.*, at p. 31.

What course of action should the Court take when negotiations at the highest level were in fact in progress when it was seised? Could in such a situation the Respondent successfully invoke the reservation in its declaration that 'parties have agreed or may agree to have recourse to another method of pacific settlement'?[302]

It is for the Court to determine whether 'the Parties had agreed temporarily to exclude any recourse to the Court on account of, and for the duration of, the ongoing negotiations'.[303] But then in order to enable the Court to make that determination it should be provided with further details 'in particular with regard to the way in which they have been carried out, or to their duration, scope or *state of progress* at the time of the filing' of the Application.[304]

These are in general relevant aspects for any judicial assessment of prior or ongoing negotiations, but they take on a particular importance in the process of establishing the Court's jurisdiction and considering the admissibility of any claim.

3.8 Prior Negotiations as a Precondition in a Special Agreement

A Special Agreement may not only provide that proceedings may be instituted on the Application of either of the parties, but moreover that such a formal step would not be regarded as an unfriendly act toward the other or as affecting the good relations between the two countries.[305]

A party to a dispute may propose to enter into a Special Agreement to submit it to the Court without making any reference to an existing compromissory clause.[306]

The object and purpose of prior negotiations may be to make a final attempt to reach a solution on the substantive issues in dispute, but also to reach an agreement to refer the (remaining issues in controversy of the) dispute to the ICJ for decision,[307] a distinction we made earlier.

Even when these negotiations have been conducted in a spirit of understanding, the parties may have been unable to reach an agreement on the terms in which they might jointly refer the dispute. In this respect negotiations may have failed, but providing in the agreement for the right of each party to institute proceedings unilaterally, with a reasonable advance notice, should not necessarily be considered an undesirable outcome of those negotiations.

With regard to the question whether and how the functional interaction has (not) found its way into Special Agreements, it is sufficient to note that only in a few of them do parties explicitly refer to the fact that they have been unable to resolve by (detailed) negotiations the dispute between them. In most Special Agreements there is no mention at all of the (partial) failure of the process of prior negotiations.

In case of a Special Agreement the question of invoking the absence or insufficiency of prior negotiations as an exception of admissibility does not normally arise[308] as joint submission of the dispute constitutes proof either that the prior negotiations have failed or that both parties share the opinion that further negotiations are useless and unnecessary.[309]

A negative reply to an invitation to negotiate towards the conclusion of a Special Agreement – this proposal being considered to be totally unfounded – coupled with the absence of a declaration of acceptance of the compulsory jurisdiction of the Court leaves the Court with no other option than to order the removal of a case from the List.[310]

302 *Arrest Warrant case, I.C.J. Reports 2000*, at p. 200, para. 65 and at p. 195, para. 46 (Belgium).

303 *Ibid.*, at p. 200, para. 66.

304 *Ibid.* (emphasis added).

305 *Columbian–Peruvian asylum case, Order of 20 October 1949: I.C.J. Reports 1949*, p. 225, at p. 225 and *Asylum Case, I.C.J. Reports 1950*, at p. 268.

306 *The Northern Cameroons case, I.C.J. Reports 1963*, at p. 25.

307 *Asylum Case, I.C.J. Reports 1950*, at pp. 267–8.

308 M. Bourquin, 'Dans quelle mesure', p. 43.

309 G. Salvioli, 'Problèmes de procédure dans la jurisprudence internationale' (1957) 91 *Recueil des Cours de L'Académie de Droit International*, 553–617 at 566.

310 *Aerial incident of 7 October 1952, Order of 14 March 1956: I.C.J. Reports 1956*, p. 9 at pp. 10–11.

3.9 Prior Negotiations and an Obligation to Arbitrate

Parties to an interstate dispute may have decided beforehand, or when the dispute perhaps unexpectedly presents itself, to go for a successive or alternative path to resolve it in a peaceful manner. Prior negotiations may then for instance precede recourse to arbitration and/or ultimately adjudication by the ICJ.[311]

The presumption that *travaux préparatoires* would not normally indicate that they even 'contemplated the eventuality of all disputes remaining without a solution' is almost untenable.[312] Moreover, a party to an agreement providing for arbitration in case prior negotiations have failed cannot 'legally avoid that obligation by denying the existence of a dispute or by maintaining that arbitration of it would not serve a useful purpose',[313] a pronouncement that equally applies to an obligation to negotiate.

States have a variety of different options and modalities at their disposal. A compromissory clause may, for instance, provide for a two-stage process to settle a dispute concerning the interpretation or application of the Convention: prior negotiations or another agreed mode of settlement operate as a precondition for submission to arbitration at the request of either party. If these means turn out to be unsuccessful, this new situation would bring into operation an obligation to arbitrate. Failing negotiations on the organization of the arbitration within a six-month period could then make it possible for either of the parties to submit the dispute to the ICJ, as the *Lockerbie cases* have demonstrated.[314]

The argument as to whether 'the dispute that' in the opinion of the Applicant exists 'could be settled by negotiation'[315] was rejected by the Court, which reminded the Respondent that it had always maintained that there 'was nothing to be settled by negotiation' because there was no dispute.[316] Furthermore, as the proposal for arbitration 'met with no answer' and the Respondent 'clearly expressed its intention not to accept arbitration' the Court concluded that consequently 'the alleged dispute between the Parties could not be settled by negotiation or submitted to arbitration under the Montreal Convention'.[317] And finally, the refusal to enter into arbitration absolved the Applicant from the obligation to observe the six-month period before seising the Court.[318]

In case of a similarly worded compromissory clause providing for prior negotiations on the merits of a dispute as a precondition for seising the Court, a mere refusal would have the same effect of absolving the Applicant from the observation of any period of delay.

A diplomatic note without any response could very well indicate a dispute when it is has been worded in such a way that the silence of the other party can only be interpreted as a refusal.[319]

This exchange of arguments reflects the parties' preliminary disagreement about the applicability and invocability of a particular convention and its compromissory clause to the events and facts at the origin of the dispute.[320]

---

311 Representations by a government may include a proposal to submit the dispute to arbitration. A new unsuccessful proposal for a Special Agreement, after a compromissory clause has been rendered operative again, may lead to one party's decision to refer the dispute unilaterally to the Court: *Barcelona Traction case, I.C.J. Reports 1970*, at p. 3, at p. 11, para. 24.

312 *Interpretation of Peace Treaties (second phase), Advisory Opinion: I.C.J. Reports 1950*, p. 221, Dissenting opinion by Judge Azevedo, at p. 249, para. 4.

313 *PLO case Advisory Opinion, I.C.J. Reports 1988*, Separate opinion by Judge Schwebel, at p. 42.

314 *Questions of Interpretation and Application of the 1971 Montreal Convention arising from the Aerial Incident at Lockerbie (Libyan Arab Jamahiriya v. United States of America), Preliminary Objections, Judgment, I.C.J. Reports 1998*, p. 115, at p. 121, para. 17.

315 *Lockerbie case, I.C.J. Reports 1998*, at p. 122, para. 19 (US).

316 *Ibid.*, at p. 122, para. 20.

317 *Ibid.*

318 *Ibid.*

319 *Belgium Senegal case, I.C.J. Reports 2012*, at p. 448, para. 61 and Separate opinion by Judge Setubinde, at p. 600, para. 29. We will return to refusal to enter into the process in Chapter 5.

320 In the parallel case against the UK, the Applicant had argued that the UK 'had clearly shown that it was not interested in proceeding within the framework of the Montreal Convention'; that it had not been possible to settle the dispute by negotiation; and that the request for arbitration had been rejected: *Questions of Interpretation and Application of the 1971 Montreal Convention arising from the Aerial Incident at Lockerbie (Libyan Arab Jamahiriya v. United Kingdom), Provisional Measures, Order of 14 April 1992, I.C.J. Reports*, p. 3, at p. 6, para. 6 and at p. 10, para. 22.

The Court's jurisdiction to decide whether a party is under an obligation to accept arbitration under a compromissory clause to that effect in case the means of settling the dispute directly by negotiations as provided by the applicable agreement are exhausted necessarily implies a decision on the (non)-fulfilment of that particular condition.[321]

In order to enable the Court to determine that a Respondent is under such an obligation to arbitrate, the claimant State, or international organization as the case may be, has to show that it 'has made a good faith attempt to resolve the dispute through negotiations or some other agreed mode of settlement and that such negotiations have not resolved the dispute'.[322]

Referring to the *Hostages case*, the Court in the *PLO case* regarded it 'as similarly beyond any doubt' that the dispute is one 'not settled by negotiation' within the meaning of the relevant compromissory clause.[323] As a result the Respondent was 'bound to respect the obligation to have recourse to arbitration'.[324]

Parties have to prove that they have made attempts to start the negotiations either on the solution of the merits of the dispute or subsequently on the organization of the arbitration as provided in the compromissory clause.[325] In the process of demonstrating that such attempt have been made, accusations that no progress could be made owing to the other party's bad faith are not unusual;[326] but, as we have noted, the Court in most cases considers it irrelevant for the purposes of assessing the admissibility of the (counter)claim whether 'the fact that diplomatic negotiations have not been pursued is to be regarded as attributable to the conduct of one Party or to the other'.[327]

However, prior negotiations do not always in fact function as a precondition for adjudication. During a multilateral conference a State may take the position that in case a unilateral act of a State causes a disagreement, the dispute over such an act may be subject to arbitration, thereby probably cutting off the negotiations stage.[328]

In a Note Verbale a State may consider that the attempted negotiation has not succeeded, and may accordingly ask the other State 'to submit the dispute to arbitration' under 'conditions to be agreed mutually' in accordance with the applicable compromissory clause;[329] and it may subsequently express its wish 'to constitute an arbitral tribunal' to that effect.[330]

Such a Note Verbale containing an explicit offer to have recourse to arbitration may receive no response from the other party;[331] the fact that the Applicant 'did not make any detailed proposal for determining the issues to be submitted to arbitration and the organization of the arbitration proceedings' does not mean that the condition that 'the Parties are unable to agree on the organization of the arbitration' has not been fulfilled.[332]

Although the aim of such a Note Verbale was to alert 'the other party to the prospect' that the Applicant 'reserved its right, at some future date, to refer the dispute, if unresolved, to arbitration' – and although arguably the response cannot be regarded as 'non-responsive' or 'a rejection of an arbitration request'[333] – the absence

321 In the *Ambatielos case* the Court did not go into this aspect, as it considered its task to be completed when it decided whether the difference between the parties was one of the validity of a claim on behalf of a private person based on the provisions of the 1886 Treaty: *Ambatielos case (merits: obligation to arbitrate), Judgment of 19 May 1953: I.C.J. Reports 1953*, p. 10 at p. 16.

322 *PLO case Advisory Opinion, I.C.J. Reports 1988*, at pp. 32–3, para. 52 (UN Secretary-General).

323 *Ibid.*, at p. 34, para. 55.

324 *Ibid.*, at p. 34, para. 57 and at p. 35, para. 58.

325 *DRC v. Rwanda case, I.C.J. Reports 2006*, at p. 41, para. 92.

326 *Ibid.*, at p. 38, para. 86 and at p. 43, para. 98.

327 *Oil Platforms case, I.C.J. Reports 2003*, at p. 210, para. 107. In this regard one should not forget that 'no activity of a State is subject to international judicial scrutiny unless and so far as accepted by the State concerned': H. Thirlway, 'The Law and Procedure of the International Court of Justice 1960–1989. Supplement, 2007: Parts Four, Five and Six' (2007) 78 *British Yearbook of International Law*, 17–175, at 59.

328 *Fisheries Jurisdiction (Federal Republic of Germany v. Iceland), I.C.J. Reports 1973*, at p. 57, para. 20.

329 *Belgium v. Senegal case, I.C.J. Reports 2012*, at pp. 434–5, para. 26.

330 *Ibid.*, at p. 436, para. 30.

331 *Ibid.*, at p. 447, para. 60.

332 *Ibid.*, at p. 447, para. 61.

333 *Ibid.*, Separate opinion by Judge Sebutinde, at pp. 599–600, para. 28.

of any response to a later request could lead to the conclusion that the preconditions of the compromissory clause had not been fulfilled.[334]

The Court's conclusion in the case did not convince Judge Yusuf, who held that the inability to agree implies 'an attempt to initiate the organization of the arbitration, or a suggestion of modalities by one or both Parties regarding such organisation'. Neither of the parties has made such a proposal or has attempted to organize the arbitration.[335]

A request for arbitration must be followed by an effort or proposal: 'it is only failure to agree on the organization … in the sense that an attempt had been made to organize or propose modalities without however reaching agreement, which triggers the possibility to refer the dispute to the Court'.[336]

A State 'may defer proposals concerning these aspects to the time when a positive response is given *in principle* to its request to settle the dispute by arbitration'. [337]

In case such proposals on the subject-matter and on procedural issues are not forthcoming but a request for arbitration is accompanied by other demarches on judicial cooperation *or the continuation of negotiation* it may cause the Respondent 'in good faith to question whether the request for arbitration was still valid or whether it has been superseded by proposals of a return' for instance to negotiations.[338]

From our perspective Judge Sur was right in pointing out that the Court should have clarified that such 'a request for arbitration should be put to the other party in an autonomous, distinct and separate way, with no other communications extraneous to the request, and should clearly set out the dispute in question and the essential organizational arrangements of the said arbitration'.[339]

3.10 Prior Negotiations and the (Dys)Functional Interaction between the Compromissory and the Optional Clause System

Parties may hold diverging views on the existence, scope and interpretation of a compromissory clause which has been invoked by one of them in order to bring a dispute before the Court, and this in relation to an optional clause excluding from the Court's jurisdiction *inter alia* 'disputes in respect of which the parties have agreed or may agree to resort to other means for the pacific settlement of disputes'.[340]

One of the essential purposes of the OAS is 'to ensure the pacific settlement of disputes that may arise among the Member States'. Article 20 of the OAS Charter reads: 'All international disputes that may arise between American States shall be submitted to the peaceful procedures set forth in this Charter, before being referred to the Security Council of the United Nations.' Under Article 22, in case such a dispute in the opinion of one of the Parties 'cannot be settled through the usual diplomatic channels, the parties shall agree on some other peaceful procedure that will enable them to reach a solution'. Pursuant to Article 23 a special treaty would 'establish adequate procedures for the pacific settlement of disputes and will determine the appropriate means for their application'.[341]

Article XXXI of this 'special treaty', the Pact of Bogota, is the relevant compromissory clause which, except for some small changes, is identical to Article 36, para. 2 of the Statute: providing for the recognition of the compulsory jurisdiction of the Court 'without the necessity of any special agreement as long as the present Treaty is in force'.[342]

In the *Border and Transborder Armed case* the parties maintained different views on the existence, scope and interpretation of the compromissory clause.

334 *Ibid.*, at p. 600, para. 29.
335 *Ibid.*, Separate opinion by Judge Yusuf, at p. 563, para. 11.
336 *Ibid.*, at p. 564, para. 12.
337 *Ibid.*, at p. 447, para. 61 (emphasis added).
338 *Ibid.*, Dissenting opinion by Judge *ad hoc* Sur, at p. 609, para. 15.
339 *Ibid.*, at p. 609, para. 16.
340 *Border and Transborder Armed Actions case, I.C.J. Reports 1988*, at p. 80, para. 24.
341 *Ibid.*, at p. 77, para. 18.
342 *Ibid.*, at p. 78, paras. 19–20.

According to Honduras, because of the almost identical wording with that of Article 36, para. 2 of the Statute, Article XXXI of the Pact of Bogota 'contains a jurisdiction which can be more precisely defined by means of a unilateral declaration'; hence 'an additional subscription' of an optional clause is necessary, inclusive any exceptions such declaration might contain.[343] Article XXXI 'is an incorporation' of 'the system of recognition of the Court's jurisdiction under the regime of the "optional clause", i.e., Article 36, paragraph 2 of the Statute'.[344]

States Parties to the Pact of Bogota dispose of two options: to take no further action, and then Article XXXI 'operates as a joint acceptance of jurisdiction under Article 36, paragraph 2, free of reservations and conditions other than the basic condition of reciprocity'; alternatively, they can make a declaration under Article 36, para. 2 inclusive reservations which then will apply to the other States Parties to the Pact of Bogota.[345]

According to Nicaragua the 'Court could entertain the case both on the basis of Article XXXI of the Pact of Bogota and on the basis of the declarations of acceptance of compulsory jurisdiction made by Nicaragua and Honduras under Article 36 of the Statute'[346] since 'Article XXXI falls under Article 36, paragraph 1, and therefore confers jurisdiction on the Court on a conventional basis'.[347]

The question was thus whether Article XXXI has to be considered to exist as a compromissory clause under Article 36, para. 1 (Nicaragua) or as joint declaration pursuant to Article 36, para. 2 of the Statute (Honduras).[348]

The Court, however, saw no need to pursue this argument. Even the adoption of the Honduran reading would not take away the fact that such a collective declaration 'was incorporated in the Pact of Bogota as Article XXXI' and that consequently all modifications had to follow the rules contained in the Pact.[349]

Taking into account also other provisions of the Pact, the Court came to the conclusion that Article XXXI 'is an autonomous commitment independent of any other which the Parties may have undertaken or may undertake' pursuant to Article 36, para. 2 of the Statute.[350]

In its search for confirmation of this interpretation the Court resorted to the *travaux préparatoires*, but 'with caution, as not all stages of the drafting of the texts at the Bogota Conference were the subject of detailed records'.[351]

3.11 Prior Negotiations and the Invocation of an Additional Ground for Jurisdiction

If in case of a dispute brought before the Court under a Special Agreement another ground of jurisdiction is added by one of the parties, containing a prior negotiation clause, the Court may not find the need to consider the question of such an additional ground.[352]

The situation is different in case a compromissory clause is put forward as the primary ground for jurisdiction and an optional clause or a separate joint agreement is invoked as an additional ground.

343 *Ibid.*, at p. 82, para. 29 (Honduras).

344 *Ibid.*, at p. 83, para. 30 (Honduras).

345 *Ibid.*

346 *Ibid.*, at p. 82, para. 26.

347 *Ibid.*, at p. 84, para. 33. As Honduras has given two successive interpretations of Article XXXI – first claiming that it must be supplemented by an optional clause, then that such a supplementary action was not necessary – the Court concluded that the first interpretation was 'incompatible with the actual terms of the Article': at p. 83, para. 31 and p. 84, para. 32.

348 *Border and Transborder Armed Actions case, I.C.J. Reports 1988*, at p. 84, para. 33.

349 *Ibid.*, at p. 84, para. 34.

350 *Ibid.*, at p. 85, para. 36. In taking this position the Court did not fail to notice that in contrast to its position in the 1980s Nicaragua case, where it contended that Article XXXI is a collective acceptance under Article 36, para. 2 of the Statute, in this case Nicaragua considered Article XXXI to be a compromissory clause under Article 36, para. 1 (at p. 84, para. 33). In case such a declaration is made, which Article XXXI does not require, 'it has no effect on the commitment resulting from that Article' (at p. 85, para. 36).

351 *Ibid.*, at p. 85, para. 37. This cautious approach is more generally applicable to all similar situations where the availability of records of negotiations turns out to be rather more limited.

352 *Territorial Dispute (Libyan Arab Jamahiriya/Chad), I.C.J. Reports 1994*, at p. 15, para. 22.

The Relationship between Two Grounds of Jurisdiction

It is important first of all to determine with more precision the relationship between such two grounds of jurisdiction in more general terms before entering into the particular scenario of prior negotiations (not) having been included as a precondition for the seisin of the Court.

In the *Territorial and Maritime Dispute* between Nicaragua and Colombia, in raising preliminary objections to the jurisdiction of the Court the Respondent recalled the Court's ruling in its 1988 judgment in the *Border and Transborder Armed Actions case* that the commitment in Article XXXI is an 'autonomous commitment, independent of any other which the Parties may have undertaken or may undertake' by 'a declaration of acceptance of compulsory jurisdiction under Article 36, paragraphs 2 and 4 of the Statute',[353] thereby laying down 'the principle of the primacy of the title of jurisdiction under the Pact of Bogota'. The conclusion put forward would then be 'that when an Applicant invokes both the Pact of Bogota and optional clause declarations, it is the Pact of Bogota, as *lex specialis*, which governs or, in other words is determinative and conclusive'.[354]

Nicaragua, on the contrary, contended that the Court's pronouncement on the Pact of Bogota cannot 'destroy the value of the Optional Clause declarations as an independent basis of jurisdiction' because they 'have an intrinsic value in and of themselves, and their operation is not predetermined by other titles of jurisdiction'. Primacy does not signify exclusiveness.[355]

The two bases of jurisdiction are 'complementary' and 'it is for the Court to decide whether to rely upon only one of them or to combine them'.[356]

The Court, having already concluded that it has jurisdiction on the basis of Article XXXI of the Pact of Bogota to deal with particular aspects of the dispute, found that 'no purpose (was) served by examining, whether, in relation to those aspects, the declarations of the Parties under the optional clause could also provide a basis for the Court's jurisdiction'.[357]

Faced with two titles of jurisdiction, the Court cannot deal with them simultaneously and may decide 'to proceed from the particular to the more general', as it did in the *Armed Actions case*.[358] This does not imply prevalence or exclusion of the second title of jurisdiction.

Recalling the PCIJ's pronouncement in the *Electricity Company case* – that the multiplicity of agreements accepting the compulsory jurisdiction of the Court express the intention of the States 'to open new ways of access to the Court rather than to close old ways or to allow them to cancel each other out with the ultimate result that no jurisdiction would remain'[359] – the Court considers that the two bases of jurisdiction are 'distinct' and 'not mutually exclusive'.[360]

Absence or Inclusion of a Prior Negotiations Condition

Pursuant to the Court's further reasoning, it may be held that in case the optional clause declarations of the parties do not contain the prior negotiation reservation, such a precondition contained in a compromissory clause 'would not be applicable to jurisdiction under the optional clause'.[361] It would also mean that if the Court would have come to the conclusion that it would lack jurisdiction owing to the non-fulfilment of the precondition of prior negotiations as provided for in a compromissory clause, it would then be impossible for the Court to hold otherwise under a similar reservation in an optional clause declaration.[362]

353 *Territorial and Maritime Dispute (Nicaragua v. Colombia), I.C.J. Reports 2007*, at p. 870, para. 123.
354 *Ibid.*, at p. 870, para. 124.
355 *Ibid.*, at p. 871, para. 128.
356 *Ibid.*, at p. 872, para. 130.
357 *Ibid.*, at p. 872, para. 132.
358 *Ibid.*, at p. 873, para. 133.
359 *Ibid.*, at p. 873, para. 132.
360 *Ibid.*, at p. 873, para. 136.
361 *Ibid.*, at p. 873, para. 137.
362 *Ibid.*, at p. 874, para. 138.

After having filed an Application based upon a compromissory clause, a State may invoke as an additional ground of jurisdiction a joint letter sent by two Respondents to the Chairman of an Arbitration Commission challenging its competence. According to this letter 'all questions involved in the overall settlement' of a pending crisis 'should be resolved in an agreement' and 'all legal disputes which cannot be settled by agreement' should then 'be taken to the ICJ'. The Respondent may have proposed that since all the issues raised in a letter from the Commission's Chairman are of 'a legal nature' they should be 'adjudicated by the ICJ, in accordance with its Statute' in 'the event that an agreement is not reached'.[363]

This letter apparently implies that the parties concerned should first attempt to solve the legal questions by negotiations before resort could be had to adjudication, but could it be considered as an unequivocal and firm offer to bring the dispute before the ICJ?

That was in fact the position taken by the Applicant who, relying on that offer, submitted 'all of the legal disputes' between it and that Respondent to the ICJ. The letter was a 'formal expression of intention to submit' these disputes to the Court and 'provides an additional jurisdiction'.[364]

Although the focus here obviously was on the value of the letter as to the existence and scope of the commitment, what is interesting for our purpose is the inclusion in the letter of prior negotiations as a precondition for any submission to the Court.

We have seen other examples of instruments expressing a commitment after negotiations during a Summit for instance, but there as well the exact intention and scope of the commitment was not always clear, except when the instrument was the culmination of sometimes a long series of attempts to settle by negotiations a *particular dispute*.

But what solution should then prevail in case an Applicant has invoked an additional ground of jurisdiction which requires the exhaustion of preliminary procedures as a necessary precondition for the seisin of the Court – thereby rendering recourse to the Court a subsidiary remedy – and which allegedly the Applicant had failed to fulfil.[365]

As the invocation of a new basis for jurisdiction 'in the second round of oral arguments on a request for the indication of provisional measures' was 'unprecedented' and was not accepted by the other party, the Court did not take it into consideration at that stage of the proceedings for reasons of 'procedural fairness and the sound of administration of justice'.[366] Hence the answer to the question remains for the time being speculative.

An Applicant may maintain that exceptions contained in declarations of acceptance of the Court's jurisdiction do not affect the Court's jurisdiction on the basis of a compromissory clause referring to negotiations as one of the procedural preconditions 'to be fulfilled prior to the seisin of the Court, rather than as "alternatives" modes of dispute settlement'. Allegedly the Court's jurisdiction under the compromissory clause is additional to the one under the optional clause.[367]

The Court's case law provides examples of its jurisdiction being wider than under the compromissory clause, while optional clause reservations could not be incorporated into the compromissory clause.[368]

The question is whether the Court 'may entertain a convention-related dispute on the basis of Article 36 declarations where these preconditions have not been met'.[369] Failure to fulfil the Convention's preconditions should have no bearing on the Court's jurisdiction under the optional clause, not even in relation to a dispute concerning the Respondent's obligations under the Convention.[370]

363 *Bosnian Genocide Case, I.C.J. Reports 1993*, at p. 17, para. 29.

364 *Ibid.*, at p. 18, para. 30.

365 *Legality of Use of Force (Yugoslavia v. Belgium), I.C.J. Reports 1999*, p. 124, at p. 138, paras. 42–3 (Belgium).

366 *Ibid.*, at p. 199, para. 44.

367 *Belgium v. Senegal case, I.C.J. Reports 2012*, Separate opinion by Judge Sebutinde, at p. 602, para. 35 referring to Belgium's arguments.

368 *Ibid.*, at pp. 602–3, paras. 36–8.

369 *Ibid.*, at p. 603, para. 39.

370 *Ibid.*, at pp. 603–4, paras. 39–40.

3.12 The Obligation of Prior Negotiations *Ratione Temporis*

The Impact of the Time Factor on the Process of Negotiations

What have negotiation scholars to teach us lawyers about the impact of the time factor on the process of negotiations?

They have pointed out that 'surrounding factors largely determine the speed of negotiation. If certain negotiations are extremely protracted, generally the main reason is that an awareness of impending crisis has either not developed or has not been operative long enough to produce a sense of urgency'.[371]

The nature of the process is undergoing changes, separated by the turning points mentioned earlier,[372] but parties may underestimate the possible transformative nature of the process as their positions and interests can change and evolve over time.[373]

In case parties have allowed themselves only a limited period of time to reach an agreement, this 'may also have a significant impact on negotiations', but even without a pre-existing agreed time-frame parties may find themselves 'under considerable pressure to reach agreement before the "point of no return" is reached, at an uncertain but nonetheless definite point in the near future'.[374]

Although deadlines 'are more likely to be suboptimal than agreements arrived at without', the possibilities of exploring 'innovative and mutually beneficial outcomes' are reduced by pressures of time.[375] On the other hand there is 'a tendency to seize whatever agreement may be available at the last moment' while then there probably 'is a significant decrease in demands and increase in concessions'.[376]

Individual judges are fully aware that the 'passage of time changes perceptions'[377] and also the Court has to deal with the time factor in its case law.

The Time Factor in the Court's Case Law

Prior negotiations as a precondition to the seisin of the Court do not necessarily and in all cases require parties during a long period of time to make attempts to solve the dispute.

The Court has rightly pointed out 'what periods of time may be involved in the observance of duties to consult and negotiate' are 'matters which necessarily vary according to the requirements of the particular case'.[378]

Parties may agree upon the duty for one of them to give six months' notice with regard to a unilateral act which may give rise to a disagreement: in such a case the Court may then assume 'that they considered such a period would allow sufficient time to settle the question through negotiations or, if no settlement were reached, to submit the whole issue' to the Court.[379]

According to the PCIJ's classic pronouncement in the *Mavrommatis case*:

> Negotiations do not … always presuppose a more or less lengthy series of notes and dispatches; it may suffice that a discussion should have been commenced, and that this discussion may have been very short; this will be the case if a deadlock is reached, or if finally a point is reached at which one of the Parties definitely declares

371 A. Lall, *Modern International Negotiation*, p. 3.

372 W. Zartman, 'Negotiations: Theory and Reality', 74 and Preliminary Chapter.

373 G. Blum and R. Mnookin, 'When *Not* to Negotiate', p. 108.

374 T. Hopmann, *The Negotiation Process*, p. 215.

375 T. Hopmann, *The Negotiation Process*, p. 216.

376 T. Hopmann, *The Negotiation Process*, p. 216.

377 *Arrest Warrant case, I.C.J. Reports 2002*, Joint Separate opinion by Judges Higgins, Kooijmans and Buergenthal, at p. 74, para. 39.

378 *Interpretation of the Agreement of 25 March 1951 between the WHO and Egypt, Advisory Opinion, I.C.J. Reports 1980*, p. 73, Separate opinion by Judge El-Erian, at p. 176. There is an obvious link between the obligation of prior negotiations *ratione temporis* and the question whether the obligation of prior negotiations is (un)limited, an issue to be addressed later.

379 *Fisheries Jurisdiction (United Kingdom v. Iceland), I.C.J. Reports 1973*, at p. 13, para. 22.

> himself unable, or refuses, to give way, and there can be therefore no doubt that the dispute cannot be settled by diplomatic negotiations.[380]

Compromissory and optional clauses provide for the compulsory jurisdiction of the Court to adjudicate interstate disputes which might arise in the future, without affecting in any way States' freedom not to invoke them although the conditions and situations anticipated do present themselves at a particular moment in time.

Parties may commit themselves in a bilateral agreement to a three-year moratorium respectively not to invoke (a)/(the) reservation in an optional clause or to initiate proceedings on 'any matter mentioned in treaties or agreements currently in force between the two countries'. Once the three-year period has passed without any resolution of the problem then Application may follow.[381]

This extraordinary mutual understanding is (rather) unprecedented and demonstrates once again the functional interaction as the aim of the three-year period was in fact to provide the parties an opportunity to settle their differences. It was only when they seemed to be unable to find a solution that, immediately after the lapse of that period, the Applicant filed its Application.[382]

The precondition of prior negotiations may take a particular shape and dimension if for instance 'diplomatic negotiations between the Governments commence at a point where the previous discussions left off' and 'the nature of' those previous discussions 'is such as to render superfluous renewed discussions of the opposing contentions in which the dispute originated'.[383] This has brought the PCIJ and its successor to the inevitable conclusion that it is impossible to lay down a 'general and absolute rule' as it 'is a matter for consideration in each case'. Essentially the 'question of the importance and chances of success of diplomatic negotiations is' a 'relative one'.[384]

It remains to be seen whether the analysis in this study will allow us in the concluding part to qualify, refine or amend this traditional judicial approach.

Diplomatic correspondence between two parties over a long period of time may reveal the objectives they were attempting to achieve. It then may happen that one month of negotiations just prior to the instituting of the proceedings by Application held after such a long period of correspondence may not bear fruit and not lead to an agreement.[385]

A General Treaty of Peace may contain a provision on the settlement of disputes with regard to the determination for instance of islands and maritime spaces whereby parties are given five years to negotiate concerning the areas subject to controversy; in the absence of a total agreement they will then, within the following six months, negotiate and sign a Special Agreement to jointly submit the existing controversies to the ICJ.[386] The relevant article was brought into practice according to its detailed time frame.[387]

Given the history of failed negotiations and the complexity of the dispute, five years is not surprising and this is complemented by a *pactum de contrahendo* on the compromis under a six-month time pressure.

A bilateral agreement providing for the sustainable development of the resources of an international river may contain a dual and rather detailed mechanism for settlement of disputes and referral to the Court. Parties may disagree on which of the procedures on prior negotiations allegedly had not been followed, thereby also disagreeing on the basis for submission of the matter to the Court.[388]

The Court may be of the opinion that there was no need to make a distinction because the purpose of the first basis for referral actually comes to an end 'when negotiations fail to produce an agreement within the

---

380 *Mavrommatis Palestine Concessions, P.C.I.J. Series A, No. 2*, p. 13 as cited for instance in the *South West Africa cases, I.C.J. Reports 1962*, at p. 345–6.

381 *Dispute regarding Navigational and Related Rights, I.C.J. Reports 2009*, at p. 231, para. 27: the 2002 Tova Calde Agreement between Nicaragua and Costa Rica.

382 *Ibid.*, at p. 231, para. 28.

383 *Mavrommatis Palestine Concessions, P.C.I.J. Series A, No. 2*, p. 13 as cited for instance in the *South West Africa cases, I.C.J. Reports 1962*, at p. 345–6.

384 *Ibid.*

385 *Nuclear Tests (New Zealand v. France), I.C.J. Reports 1974*, at p. 464, para. 26.

386 *Land, Island and Maritime Frontier Dispute, I.C.J. Reports 1992*, at p. 384, para. 37 (Article 31).

387 *Ibid.*, at p. 385, para. 38.

388 *Pulp Mills case, I.C.J. Reports 2010*, at pp. 64–5, para. 135.

180-day period' and the second basis then takes over with regard to any dispute which cannot be settled by direct negotiations, including those over the interpretation and application of the Article forming the first basis.[389]

Time may play a different functional role when for instance a time exclusion clause in a unilateral declaration accepting the compulsory jurisdiction of the Court would enable States 'to withdraw their acceptance of the compulsory jurisdiction of the Court if faced with an application that they considered lacking in bona fide'.[390]

The mere insertion of the clause may have an impact on the willingness to negotiate and on the scope and progress of that process.

As it is always possible for parties to reach an impasse within a fixed time limit, good administration of justice does not seem to 'oblige the Parties to wait for the official time-limit has elapsed before they are freed of the obligation'.[391]

3.13 The Obligation of Prior Negotiations *Ratione Materiae*

Failure to Refer Explicitly to Particular Treaty (Provisions)

Such a failure was sufficient for the Court not to consider a complaint to a regional human rights commission 'as attempts to settle the dispute by negotiation'. This approach was labelled 'unrealistic', given the 'multifaceted conflict' and making it 'virtually impossible to characterize protests in a multilateral context as attempts to negotiate as required by' applicable compromissory clauses.[392]

Judge Dugard observed that the Applicant had failed to 'indicate with precision the nature of its complaint' and did not show that it had 'clearly identified the Convention in question' during a 'conference or parliamentary diplomacy'.[393] However, as rightly pointed out by Judge Al-Khaswaneh, complaints before the Security Council 'are not usually compartmentalized on a treaty-by-treaty basis'.[394]

The Court's case law reflects 'a certain flexibility with regard to the requirement of prior negotiations'. Hence particularly when such attempts to negotiate in a multilateral context were not met by a positive response by the other party, the Court should not take an 'unduly restrictive' position[395] especially in the absence of a '(parallel) procedure for state complaints to a body established under that treaty'.[396] There should however always be a link 'between the substantive provisions of the treaty in question and the dispute'.[397]

Because of the seriousness of the violation of a *ius cogens* norm of international law, Article IX of the Genocide Convention does not require States to first attempt to settle a dispute relating 'to the interpretation, application or fulfilment of the present Convention, *including those relating to the responsibility of a State* for genocide' by prior negotiations. Article IX is crucial 'to fulfilling the object and purpose of the Convention since it is the *only* avenue for adjudicating the responsibilities of States'.[398]

It appears almost self-evident that one can 'hardly make abstraction of the nature and substance of a treaty when considering the optional clause, or else the compromissory clause enshrined therein'.[399] However, parties may hold diverging views on that impact. For the Applicant the human rights nature of the relevant treaty is a 'reason for the broad interpretation of compromissory clauses, and not for their narrow or restrictive

389 *Ibid.*, at p. 65, para. 137.

390 *Legality of Use of Force case, I.C.J. Reports 1999*, Separate opinion by Judge Oda, at p. 150, para. 12.

391 *Pulp Mills case, I.C.J. Reports 2010*, Separate opinion by Judge *ad hoc* Torres Bernardez, at pp. 261–2, para. 93.

392 *DRC v. Rwanda case, I.C.J. Reports 2006*, Declaration by Judge Kooijmans, at p. 74, para. 6 and Separate opinion by Judge Al-Khasawneh, at p. 78, para. 7 and at p. 80, para. 12.

393 *Ibid.*, Separate opinion by Judge *ad hoc* Dugard, at pp. 92–4, paras. 17–19.

394 *Ibid.*, Separate opinion by Judge Al-Khasawneh, at p. 79, para. 7 and at p. 81, para. 13.

395 *Ibid.*, Declaration by Judge Kooijmans, at p. 75, para. 11.

396 *Ibid.*, at p. 75, para. 12 and at p. 76, para. 15. This last feature distinguishes the *DRC Rwanda case* from the *CERD case*.

397 *Ibid.*, Separate opinion by Judge Al-Khasawneh, at p. 80, para. 12.

398 *Ibid.*, Dissenting opinion by Judge Koroma, at p. 58, para. 13.

399 *CERD case, I.C.J. Reports 2011*, Dissenting opinion by Judge Cançado Trindade, at p. 268, para. 70.

interpretation',[400] while the Respondent limited itself to observe that the *erga omnes* nature must have 'a bearing on interpretation and application of' the compromissory clause.[401]

Judge Trindade persuasively argued that in its reasoning the Court did not take into account the nature of the Convention.[402]

Within the functional interaction what judicial weight or consequence should be attached to the failure of the Applicant during a process of prior negotiations to refer explicitly to (a) particular treaty (provision)?

Is it necessary in an interstate exchange to expressly refer to a specific treaty in order to be able later to invoke that instrument before the Court?[403] What is necessary is that the exchanges 'must refer to the subject-matter of the treaty with sufficient clarity to enable' the other party 'against which the claim is made to identify that there is, or may be, a dispute with regard to that subject-matter'.[404]

While the parties may 'agree that that express specification does not appear in this case' the Court may not find in one party's record of talks that any claims were made related to the subject-matter of the convention.[405]

Once again we encounter the functional link between earlier exchanges which do not necessarily have to take place *in the form* of proper negotiations but which may situate themselves within *the context* of proper negotiations or pre-negotiations and the primary condition of the existence of a dispute that has been brought or could be brought before the Court, a question to be addressed in Chapter 5.

At the provisional measure stage of the proceedings in the *CERD case* the joint dissent took the view that prior contacts must have been regarding the subject of the dispute and that 'the very substance of CERD was never debated between the Parties before the filing of a claim before the Court'.[406]

At the jurisdictional stage the Court pointed out that according to the case law 'absence of an express reference to the treaty in question does not bar the invocation of the compromissory clause to establish jurisdiction', but that 'negotiations must relate to the subject-matter of the treaty' and 'to the subject-matter of the dispute, which, in turn, must concern the substantive obligations contained in the treaty in question'.[407]

While Judge Greenwood succinctly observed that although 'the judgment states that an express reference to the convention would remove any doubt and place the other state on notice, it does not make that a requirement',[408] Judge Owada rightly observed that an 'express specification' of the subject-matter of the treaty 'is not a legal requirement for the *existence of the dispute*'.[409]

Judge Trindade noted that there 'is no *requirement* that the negotiations include an *express reference' to* the relevant Convention as it 'is sufficient that the subject-matter of the dispute to have been discussed, brought to the attention of each other'.[410]

Parties disagreed on this particular issue.[411] Georgia contended that the negotiations did not need 'expressly refer to CERD or its substantive provisions', the only requirement being that the 'subject-matter of the dispute under CERD – i.e. racial discrimination – must have been discussed'.[412]

The Court, by taking the position that prior to 9 August there had been no dispute relating to matters falling under CERD, had no difficulty in ruling that those prior negotiations 'cannot be said to have covered such matters'.[413]

---

400 *Ibid.*, at p. 272, para. 74.

401 *Ibid.*, at p. 274, para. 75.

402 *Ibid.*, at p. 307, para. 167.

403 *Ibid.*, at p. 84, para. 30.

404 *Ibid.*

405 *Ibid.* and at p. 104, para. 75.

406 *CERD case, I.C.J. Reports 2008*, at p. 388, paras. 114–15 and Joint dissenting opinion at p. 402, para. 1é and at p. 404, para. 15.

407 *CERD case, I.C.J. Reports 2011*, at p. 133, para. 161.

408 *Ibid.*, Separate opinion by Judge Greenwood, at p. 326, para. 9, note 1.

409 *Ibid.*, Separate opinion by Judge Owada, at p. 177, para. 20 (emphasis added).

410 *Ibid.*, Dissenting opinion by Judge Cançado Trindade, at p. 290, para. 115.

411 *Ibid.*, at pp. 134–5, paras. 164–6.

412 *Ibid.*, at p. 132, para. 154.

413 *Ibid.*, at p. 136, para. 170.

The Court did not consider statements made after 9 August 'as genuine attempts by Georgia to negotiate matters falling under CERD, although they attest to the existence of a dispute on that subject-matter'.[414]

3.14 Is the Obligation of Prior Negotiations (Un)limited?

The mere fact that parties to a dispute may after their respective cost-benefit analysis decide not to enter into a process of negotiations is already an indication that the obligation of prior negotiations is not unlimited.

Once a process has been started it is not surprising that one or both parties may resort to tactics 'that involve claims that one will negotiate no further'.[415]

The point made by negotiation scholars that it makes 'no sense to *initiate* negotiations' if a party 'believes that a deal could never be made' or if made 'implemented, due to a lack of will or of capacity on the part of the adversary'[416] equally applies to a party's perception that for the same reason there is no point in *continuing* the process. Past experiences with their counterpart could play an important role in this regard.[417]

In the event of an impasse in the negotiations States, according to the General Assembly, 'should use their best endeavours to continue to work towards a mutually acceptable and just solution',[418] raising the question to be dealt with in Chapter 5 whether the obligation to negotiate is unlimited and how deadlock should be approached by parties and by the Court.

Although one can only agree that the 'obligation to negotiate is an obligation of *tracto continuo*; it never ends and is potentially present in all relations and dealings between States',[419] it seems appropriate to address now the question whether if the obligation of prior negotiations is (un)limited. This is bound to have an impact on the distinct but related issue of whether prior negotiations have actually failed, to be determined by the Court.

Is there, as argued by a Respondent, a rule of customary international law requiring States to undertake diplomatic negotiations and to continue them to a point where it is no longer possible to pursue?[420] The Court did not take a position 'on the existence of this challenged customary rule'.[421]

The filing of an Application immediately after having made a declaration accepting the compulsory jurisdiction of the Court necessarily brings about a functional change in the legal relations between the parties. Does this change entail, as argued by a Respondent, an obligation for the parties to make an attempt to pursue negotiations that had been going on previously?[422]

Or does general international law not contain such a requirement of prior negotiations, and is the institution of proceeding only dependent on the prior *exhaustion* of diplomatic negotiations in case the parties can invoke an explicit treaty-making provision to that end, as the Applicant argued? Only such an explicit provision could require the parties to pursue diplomatic negotiations up to the point at which they 'become *futile*'.[423]

This question is albeit not exclusively and certainly not predominantly linked to the time factor mentioned earlier. Indeed, when an assessment has to be made whether an Applicant has pursued negotiations as far as possible, a genuine attempt at negotiating may have been made, but doubt may be raised whether the pursuance as far as possible actually took place when only a short period of time elapsed since the first

414 *Ibid.*, at p. 139, para. 181. As indicated earlier, this position is a clear departure from the position it took three years earlier in its Order on provisional measures.

415 G. Blum and R. Mnookin, 'When *Not* to Negotiate', p. 102.

416 G. Blum and R. Mnookin, 'When *Not* to Negotiate', p. 104 (emphasis added).

417 G. Blum and R. Mnookin, 'When *Not* to Negotiate', p. 109.

418 General Assembly Resolution 53/101, para. 2 (g).

419 *North Sea Continental Shelf case, I.C.J. Reports 1969*, Separate opinion by Judge Padilla Nervo, at p. 92.

420 *Right of Passage case, I.C.J. Reports 1957*, at p. 130.

421 M. Kohen, 'Interaction', p. 21.

422 *Right of Passage case, I.C.J. Reports 1957*, at p. 130.

423 *Ibid.*, at p. 135 (emphasis added).

reference to negotiations had been made,[424] although such a short period of time does 'not per se preclude the failure or deadlock of negotiations' for instance as a result of a complete refusal to enter into the process.[425]

In a Note Verbale a State may clarify its legal position on its alleged non-compliance with certain conventional obligations – thus attesting the existence of a dispute – but this does not necessarily mean 'a failure or collapse of negotiation on the matter'.[426]

Does prior resort to diplomatic negotiations not constitute an absolute requirement 'to be satisfied even when the hopelessness of expecting any negotiations to succeed is clear from the state of relations between the parties'?[427]

When direct negotiations between two States through various traditional channels have failed,[428] does the duty of pursuance imply that a meeting between the Heads of States has to be arranged?

There is in our view room to distinguish between the formulation of the precondition in terms of a dispute *not having been capable to be settled* and not *being capable now to be settled*: from the perspective of the functional interaction this last aspect is also linked to the function of negotiations going on during the course of the proceedings, and to which we will turn in Chapter 6.

The case law provided us with a further distinction which could be made between the question whether a dispute has proven *not having been capable to be settled* through prior negotiations and the issue whether a particular pacific procedure had been *concluded* as a precondition for the recourse to the Court.

The Dispute 'Not Having Been Capable to Be Settled'

Whereas on the one hand diplomatic negotiations are only one of the methods in which the existence of a dispute may manifest itself in a formal way and which moreover is not required as such, it would, however:

> be desirable that a State should not proceed to take as serious a step as summoning another State to appear before the Court without having previously, *within reasonable limits, endeavoured* to make it quite clear that a difference of views is in question *which has not been capable of being otherwise overcome*.[429]

It is not quite clear whether what the Court is saying in connection with an Application under Article 60 of the Statute does apply more generally to any unilateral seisin of the Court. In case one considers prior negotiations to be no precondition, then this reasoning only applies to this particular situation.

A further question is whether the qualification that *an endeavour* has to be made *within reasonable limits* also applies to prior negotiations as a precondition contained in a compromissory clause or an optional clause.

Apart from denying that here was a dispute, a Respondent may argue that the 'procedural conditions' laid down in a compromissory clause had not been fulfilled[430] while the Applicant contends that it had unsuccessfully attempted to resolve the dispute by negotiations.[431]

At the stage 'of considering *prima facie* jurisdiction, 'it was sufficient for the Court 'to note that an attempt has been made' by the Applicant to negotiate and thus that the procedural conditions of the compromissory clause had been fulfilled *prima facie*.[432]

The assessment of whether the point has been reached where pursuance of negotiations has become futile is, at first instance, within the political discretion of each party, but the overall, objective and judicial appreciation of this state of affairs – to which we will return in Chapter 5 – is bound to take into account

---

424 *Belgium v. Senegal case, I.C.J. Reports 2012*, Separate opinion by Judge Sebutinde, at p. 595, para. 15.

425 *Ibid.*, at pp. 596–7, paras. 19 and 20.

426 *Ibid.*, at p. 597, para. 21.

427 *Nicaragua Case, I.C.J. Reports 1984*, Separate opinion by Judge Ago, at p. 516, para. 4.

428 *Pulp Mills case, I.C.J. Reports 2006*, at p. 115, para. 9 (Argentina).

429 *Revision and Interpretation of the 1982 Continental Shelf Judgment, I.C.J. Reports 1985*, at p. 218, para. 46 (emphasis added).

430 *Belgium v. Senegal case, I.C.J. Reports 2009*, at p. 145, para. 28.

431 *Ibid.*, at p. 150, para. 49.

432 *Ibid.*, at p. 150, para. 50.

various factors such as the complexity of the subject-matter, the pre-existing and traditional relations between the parties, the controversy being part of a larger conflict and so on.

It is sufficient here to refer to the argument raised by the Applicant in the *CERD case* that even if such an obligation of prior negotiations does exist, 'it does not require the parties to continue with negotiations which show every sign of being *unproductive*'.[433]

The case law indeed makes it clear that 'it is sufficient for an attempt to have been made *and* for it to have become clear at some point that there was no chance of success'.[434]

Raising the Issues within a Multilateral Framework

In the process of dealing with a particular question parties may have agreed to establish a group of technical experts to assist them in carrying out several aspects of what perhaps has been agreed before on delimitation. It then may occur that such a group turns 'into a body for *diplomatic negotiation* between the two States ... to discussing the more general legal dispute on territorial issues'.[435]

The *Pulp Mills case* is a fine example of the way the parties have in their bilateral treaty provided for a particular framework for the bilateral negotiations as their envisaged cooperation will necessarily require for a long period of time to come. Judges held divergent opinions on the scope of the obligation for parties to the 1975 Statute to utilize the Administrative Commission of the River Uruguay (CARU) and the option if need be to establish an *ad hoc* substitute framework.[436]

Furthermore, one should in general acknowledge that 'no settlement could realistically be expected through a procedure at a much lower level when all the attempts to reach a settlement at the highest possible intergovernmental level had failed'.[437]

Is a party entitled to claim that it is offering to enter into direct bilateral negotiations through the usual diplomatic channels 'where it is in fact insisting on a multilateral framework as the only acceptable basis for negotiating'? The imposition of such an indispensable condition is not acceptable.[438]

The Court may consider it not necessary to determine whether the subject-matter within the multilateral framework is identical to that of the case before it, thus leaving that question open although its judgment logically assumes an answer in favour of the Respondent.[439]

The failure of a party to have recourse to and exhaust multilateral means of peaceful settlement could be mitigated by factors such as the maintenance of diplomatic relations and the expressed readiness to negotiate on a bilateral basis and the taking part in a substantial multilateral effort at peaceful settlement rebuffed by the other party and the alleged support given to a regional peace process and taking part in the SC handling of the matter brought before it by the Applicant.[440]

As far as *parliamentary diplomacy* is concerned, the Court has recognized 'the negotiation of solutions of international problems within the framework and through procedures of an organized body acting under established rules of procedure, such as the General Assembly of the United Nations'[441] as 'one of the established modes of international negotiation'.[442] Moreover, if 'the question in issue is one of mutual interest to many States, there is no reason why each of them should go through the formality and pretence of direct

433 *CERD case, I.C.J. Reports 2008*, Joint dissenting opinion, at p. 402, para. 13 (emphasis added).

434 *Ibid.*, at p. 403, para. 13. (emphasis added). As we have already seen, parties may disagree about whether or not there has been even an attempt to negotiate: *DRC v. Rwanda case, I.C.J. Reports 2002*, at p. 236, para. 44 (Rwanda).

435 *Case between Botswana and Namibia, I.C.J. Reports 1999*, Separate opinion by Judge Oda, at p. 1125, para. 17.

436 Compare in this regard *Pulp Mills case, I.C.J. Reports 2010*, Separate opinion by Judge Greenwood, at pp. 223–4, para. 7 and Separate opinion by Judge *ad hoc* Torres Bernardez, at p. 260, para. 88.

437 *Gabcikovo case, I.C.J. Reports 1997*, Dissenting opinion by Judge Vereshchetin, at p. 221.

438 *Border and Transborder Armed Actions (Nicaragua v. Honduras), I.C.J. Reports 1988*, Separate opinion by Judge Shahabuddeen, at p. 151.

439 *Ibid.*, at p. 153.

440 *Nicaragua case, I.C.J. Reports 1986*, Dissenting opinion by Judge Schwebel, at pp. 364–5, para. 205.

441 *South West Africa cases, I.C.J. Reports 1962*, Separate opinion by Judge Jessup, at p. 434.

442 *South West Africa cases, I.C.J. Reports 1966*, Dissenting opinion by Judge Padilla Nervo, at p. 452.

negotiation with the common adversary State, after they had participated in the collective negotiation with the same State in opposition'.[443]

The *SWA and Northern Cameroons cases* did provide a unique opportunity for judges to elaborate on this new form of diplomacy and negotiations. Judges Sir Percy Spender and Sir Gerald Fitzmaurice considered the exchange of arguments across the floor of an international assembly as *disputation* and not as *negotiation*, and argued that even if those exchanges could be considered to have failed there was still the need for direct discussions between the parties.[444]

Whether the use of parliamentary diplomacy, prior to or after a failure of direct negotiations between the parties, was able to and in fact settled the dispute was one of the main questions dividing the judges in the N*orthern Cameroons case* depending on whether the subject matter of the two processes was identical.

In order to fulfil the requirement those negotiations should deal with the substantive issues of the dispute and not merely with the question of the method of adjudicating the dispute,[445] although of course also those talks can end in deadlock.[446]

For Judge Wellington Koo the question whether the exchange of notes between the parties just before the termination of the Trusteeship by the General Assembly 'can be properly considered as another step of negotiation or merely as relating to the proposal to refer the dispute to the court for adjudication (was) immaterial'.[447]

On other occasions as well the Court has found that 'talks within international bodies can be regarded as negotiations'.[448]

This case-law can thus be relied by both parties to argue that '*intense discussions and negotiations before the competent organs*' of the UN and OAU had taken place, although they still may differ on what has really been the subject-matter of that process.[449]

The General Assembly 'where States discuss political matters of general interest (open diplomacy)' is 'in a good position to reconcile Law and Politics'.[450]

At the stage of dealing with a request for the indication of provisional measures in the *CERD case*, the case file made it apparent to the Court 'that such issues have been raised in bilateral contacts between the Parties, and that these issues have manifestly not been resolved by negotiation prior to the filing of the Application'; the same issues were raised by the claimant and commented upon by the respondent before the Security Council.[451]

We could note that the Respondent, in arguing that it had made every effort to 'resolve this crisis by diplomatic means', referred to its immediate request for a meeting of the SC.[452]

It may seem that also in the Court's preliminary evaluation of the sequence of events, conference diplomacy plays a role, albeit a subordinated one, in its assessment whether negotiations on the subject-matter had actually taken place. The alternative reading of the Court's position could be that the conference diplomacy as it takes place within the context of and within the SC is nothing more than a forum so that the

443 *Ibid.*, at p. 452.

444 *The Northern Cameroons case, I.C.J. Reports 1963*, Separate opinion by Judge Fitzmaurice, at p. 123 and *South West Africa cases, I.C.J. Reports 1962*, Joint dissenting opinion, at p. 562.

445 *The Northern Cameroons case, I.C.J. Reports 1963*, Separate opinion by Judge Fitzmaurice, at p. 124.

446 *Ibid.*, Dissenting opinion by Judge Bustamente, at p. 166.

447 *Ibid.*, Separate opinion by Judge Wellington Koo, at p. 50, para. 27. It has been pointed out in doctrine that for assimilation or even substitute of such a collective process to direct contacts and negotiations not only should there be substantial identity *ratione materiae* of the issues raised, 'such as to render further direct negotiations superfluous', but the Court 'should also be satisfied that there is no reasonable chance that further direct negotiations between the parties would lead to a settlement or substantially narrow down the issues raised': C. Fombad, 'Consultation and Negotiation in the Pacific Settlement of International Disputes' (1989) 1 *African Journal of International and Comparative Law*, 707–24 at 720.

448 *DRC v. Rwanda, I.C.J. Reports 2006*, Dissenting opinion by Judge *ad hoc* Mavungu, at p. 105, para. 44.

449 *Ibid.*, Dissenting opinion by Judge *ad hoc* Mavungu, at p. 101, paras. 23–4 referring to statements by Rwanda and confirmation by the DRC.

450 *Reservations Genocide Convention, I.C.J. Reports 1951*, Dissenting opinion by Judge Alvarez, at p. 52.

451 *CERD case, I.C.J. Reports 2008*, at p. 388, para. 115.

452 *Ibid.*, at pp. 370–71, para. 66.

Respondent is made aware of the claimant party's position, and that no real and proper negotiations have taken place as the Respondent had argued.

The question whether a particular (multilateral) procedure of negotiations has been concluded – either for instance because a partial arrangement has been agreed upon over some aspects of the dispute or as a result of the lapse of a certain period of time as provided beforehand in a compromissory, optional clause or compromis – situates itself on the borderline with the other question whether or not prior negotiations have actually failed, to be discussed in Chapter 5.

A Previous Procedure Has to be Concluded

The leading case for present purposes is the *Border and Transborder Armed Actions case between Nicaragua and Honduras*.

An objection to the admissibility of a claim may consist in contending that a regional process such as the Contadora process has been accepted as a *special procedure* within the meaning of the Pact of Bogota (Article II): hence the Applicant was allegedly precluded from 'commencing any other procedure' for pacific settlement 'until such time as the Contadora process has been *concluded*', this preclusion being based upon Article IV of the Pact 'and elementary considerations of good faith'.[453] One should particularly note this latter foundation for the exclusion.

The Court may find it to be 'common ground between the Parties' that the proceedings before it were 'a "pacific procedure" as contemplated by the Pact of Bogota, and that therefore if any other "pacific procedure" under the Pact has been initiated and not concluded, the proceedings were instituted contrary to Article IV and must therefore be found inadmissible'.[454]

Whether the Contadora process was such *a special procedure* may be disputed between the parties because '*inter alia*, its subject-matter is distinct from the dispute before the Court'.[455] Parties and Court may hold different though both plausible views as to the question whether a particular procedure had been concluded or not[456] by the date of the filing of the Application and on how that should be determined.

Is a formal act necessary in order to establish that a pacific procedure can be said to be 'concluded'?[457] For the purposes of Article IV of the Pact that was not necessary. In the Court's view this procedure 'does not have to have failed *definitively* before a new procedure can be commenced'.[458] Whether this applies *a contrario* and in principle for all prior negotiations except in case of an explicit condition is another question.

The judicial assessment whether prior negotiations have failed *inter alia* to establish the existence of a dispute or to determine the critical date will be dealt with in Chapter 5.

For the purpose of evaluating the admissibility conditions contained in a compromissory clause, it is sufficient 'if, at the date on which a new procedure is commenced, the initial procedure has come to a standstill in such circumstances that there appears to be no prospect of it being continued or resumed'.[459]

It is of course first of all for the parties to make this assessment before deciding to start judicial proceedings, but it is ultimately up to the Court either to accept or reject the approach taken by both or either of the parties.

In order to decide this particular question, the Court resumed its survey of the Contadora process.[460]

In spite of some aspect remaining outstanding, the five Central American governments were willing and prepared to formally adopt the Contadora Act and thus thereby to formally declare the Contadora process

453 *Border and Transborder Armed Actions case, I.C.J. Reports 1988*, at p. 73, para. 13 and pp. 99–100, para. 72 (Honduras) (emphasis added).

454 *Ibid.* at p. 100, para. 78.

455 *Ibid.* In Chapter 5 we will find out how the Court has dealt with the question whether and to what extent the subject-matter of prior negotiations has to be identical to the subject-matter of the dispute before the Court in order to fulfil the precondionality.

456 *Border and Transborder Armed Actions case, I.C.J. Reports 1988*, Separate opinion by Judge Schwebel, at pp. 126–7.

457 *Ibid.*, at p. 100, para. 80.

458 *Ibid.* (emphasis added).

459 *Ibid.*

460 *Ibid.*, at p. 101, para. 81.

concluded.[461] However, as the differences could not be solved in time, the signature of the Contadora Act became impossible, although the governments concerned were determined 'to continue to *promote* the diplomatic negotiation process',[462] considering thus 'another phase of the negotiations' on matters of an operational character.[463] The governments' determination was thus limited to the *promotion* of further negotiations.

For reasons of security Honduras rejected the last project of the instrument, while noting that the Contadora Group would be available for collaboration in further negotiations to which Honduras remained willing to collaborate as well.[464] Nicaragua, on the other hand, considered the Final Act to be the only instrument 'capable of producing a quick and efficient conclusion of the negotiating process'.[465]

Under those circumstances the Court could only ascertain that the 'Act, and the proposal for negotiation, were not accepted, and the Contadora process was thus at a standstill',[466] just seven to eight weeks prior to the filing of the Application, and this for almost eight months.

The functional interaction took a particular turn and modality in this case because negotiations which took place *during the proceedings* had a decisive impact on the Court's decision with regard to the preliminary admissibility objection that the prior negotiations had not been *concluded*.

Indeed, the question whether for the purposes of Article IV of the Pact of Bogota the Contadora-Esquipulas II process 'should be regarded as having ensured the continuation of the initial procedure without interruption, or whether on 28 July 1986 that initial procedure should be regarded as having "concluded", and a procedure of a different nature as having got under way thereafter' was of 'crucial importance'.[467]

Replying to a question put by a Member of the Court, the parties surprisingly took the same position. Could it be argued that it would not be necessary for the Court to look for the opinion of the parties in the absence of a similar formulation in the compromissory clause? According to both parties the Contadora process had not been abandoned, suspended or interrupted.[468]

Although the Court 'fully' appreciated this concordance of views on the subject of regional initiatives, it could not detect a concordance of views as 'to the interpretation of the term "concluded" in Article IV of the Pact of Bogota, in relation to the position of the Contadora process at the moment of the filing of the Nicaraguan Application', as for that purpose both action of the Contadora Group, prior to June 1986 and during the proceedings cannot be regarded as on the same footing.[469]

In the Court's view both processes differ in object and nature. The Contadora Group played a fundamentally different role in both processes: a decisive one prior to the filing of the Application and a much more limited one afterwards.[470]

Indeed, the Contadora Group considered 'its mission as completed, at least as far as the negotiation of any substantive accord is concerned' when it presented the final and definitive Act of Contadora to the Central American States.[471] There was also a time gap between the end of the initial Contadora process and the start of the Contadora-Esquipulas II process; the filing of the Application took place 'during this gap'.[472]

The Court finally concluded that the Contadora procedures 'had been "concluded" within the meaning of Article IV' at the date of the filing of the Application. Accordingly the Court dismissed the Honduran objection in this respect and found no need to determine whether the Contadora process was a *special procedure* for the

461 *Ibid.*
462 *Ibid.*, at p. 101, para. 82 (emphasis added).
463 *Ibid.*, at p. 102, para. 82 (emphasis added).
464 *Ibid.*, at p. 102, para. 83.
465 *Ibid.*, at p. 102, para. 84.
466 *Ibid.*, at p. 103, para. 85.
467 *Ibid.*, at p. 104, para. 89.
468 *Ibid.*, at p. 104, para. 90.
469 *Ibid.*, at p. 104, para. 91.
470 *Border and Transborder Armed Actions case, I.C.J. Reports 1988*, at p. 105, para. 91.
471 *Ibid.*, at p. 105, para. 92.
472 *Ibid.*

purposes of Articles II and IV of the Pact of Bogota,[473] 'and whether that procedure had the same object as that now in progress before the Court'.[474]

With regard to the other preclusion ground invoked by Honduras – elementary considerations of good faith – the Court reaffirmed its position that the principle of good faith is 'one of the basic principles governing the creation and performance of legal obligations' and that it is not 'in itself a source of obligation where none would otherwise exist'.[475]

Whether Nicaragua's conduct consisting in successive acts and the Esquipulas declaration of 25 May 1986 created a commitment to the Contadora process rendering the subsequent Application incompatible as Honduras had argued was irrelevant as the events of June/July 1986 constituted a 'conclusion' of the initial procedure 'both for the purposes of Article IV of the Pact and in reality to any other obligation to exhaust that procedure which might have existed independently of the Pact'.[476]

3.15 Prior Negotiations in Times of Armed Conflict

Negotation Scholars' Findings

Leaving 'a dispute between nations unnegotiated for a long period of time may provoke armed conflict between the parties'[477] and although 'blatant threats to resort to force normally remove an issue from the sphere of negotiation to that of conflict'[478] it does not require further elaboration to accept that the 'unwillingness of both parties to the conflict to enter into negotiations in the early stages of a conflict may be explained by the belief of both parties in their ability to achieve their aims through other means, typically physical coercion'.[479]

In an atmosphere of 'high level of tensions, negotiators tend to be cautious, unwilling to explore novel options or risk being taken advantage of if they initiate new proposals or make concessions' and more likely to adopt 'a confrontational bargaining style in the negotiations'.[480]

As a result the process may encounter stalemates,[481] certainly when the international environment reaches the point of crisis entailing 'a set of environmental conditions that are usually qualitatively different from the normal ebb and flow of tensions between nation-states',[482] making it 'very unlikely that negotiators will be able to adopt a problem-solving orientation'.[483]

Because parties are then compelled 'to rethink their policies' mediation 'is likely to be particularly relevant'.[484]

Once an armed conflict has come to an end, it is important that negotiators ensure that 'forward-looking provisions to deal with the underlying causes' of the dispute 'formed the basis of the agreement'.[485]

Since 'the end of the Cold War the landscape in which peace negotiations are conducted was transformed quite comprehensively',[486] characterized mainly by the emergence of new peacemakers and peacemaking arrangements, rendering the peace negotiation processes 'unparalleled' complex.[487]

473 *Ibid.*, at p. 100, para. 79.
474 *Ibid.*, at p. 105, para. 93.
475 *Ibid.*, at p. 105, para. 94.
476 *Ibid.*, at p. 106, para. 94.
477 A. Lall, *Modern International Negotiation*, p. 131.
478 A. Lall, *Modern International Negotiation*, p. 233.
479 A. Guelke, 'Negotiations and Peace Processes', p. 68.
480 T. Hopmann, *The Negotiation Process*, p. 203.
481 T. Hopmann, *The Negotiation Process*, p. 205.
482 T. Hopmann, *The Negotiation Process*, pp. 210–11.
483 T. Hopmann, *The Negotiation Process*, p. 213.
484 J. Merrills, *International Dispute Settlement*, p. 31.
485 W. Zartman, 'Looking Forward and Looking Backward', p. 293.
486 T. Whitfield, ' New Arrangements', p. 227.
487 T. Whitfield, 'New Arrangements', p. 235.

Armed Conflict and Prior Negotiations in the Court's Case Law

Notwithstanding the fact that the absence of a compromissory clause in the 1949 Geneva Conventions and the 1977 Protocols 'represents an almost insurmountable jurisdictional barrier to the Court's involvement in disputes arising in an armed conflict situation',[488] the question of the potential or real impact of the ongoing of an armed conflict on the fulfilment of the precondition of prior negotiations came up in a number of recent cases before the Court.[489]

Although the absence of diplomatic relations is not a sufficient argument to justify a refusal to enter into negotiations, it is beside the point.[490] In general the intervention of war may bring to an end all processes of negotiations between parties whether in the fulfilment of a conditional precondition or not,[491] although even in a situation of hostilities parties may express, at the highest level, their willingness to negotiate.[492]

In this regard it should be noted that '[c]easefire agreements are designed to provide a "breathing space for the negotiation of more lasting agreements"'.[493] Moreover, signing an agreement may be the only way for a State to prevent a threat of imminent military defeat at the time of the negotiations.[494]

How should a conventional precondition of prior negotiations operate and be judicially assessed in case refusal by one party to enter into the negotiation process is based on the contention that the conditions required by the governing convention were not met and thereby making it impossible for the other party to faithfully fulfil that requirement for seisin of the Court? How could an Applicant first exhaust the negotiation process when the other party 'does not even accept the minimum conditions for peace permitting recourse to the machinery peculiar to the' conventions.[495]

The argument was put forward that the question of the alleged violation of a convention had not been raised during any of numerous meetings between the parties involving '*general negotiations to settle the armed conflict*'.[496]

In a previous Order the Court may have decided that the Applicant has made no attempts to enter into negotiations. Is it arguable that war between two parties renders negotiations impossible over a specific dispute under a particular convention or would an Applicant anyway 'certainly have been capable of entering into' such negotiations?[497]

Although a state of armed conflict is not conducive to direct negotiations in order to settle 'the totality of the dispute' between the parties,[498] the question whether parties should not use every single opportunity to discuss a pending or impending dispute within the context of a more general framework such as a regional peace process[499] seems appropriate.

When diplomatic means are closed to one party while military action is underway, '[a]pplications and the concomitant request for provisional measures appeared as the only peaceful means to try to stop the military operation or, at least, as a way to demonstrate the illegality of the use of force by' a regional defence organization 'and its member states participating in the operation'.[500]

It has been rightly questioned whether in situations of armed conflict 'strict compliance with the requirement' of prior negotiations 'should be a conditon *sine qua non* for the Court to indicate provisional

488 G. Zyberi, 'Provisional Measures of the International Court of Justice in Armed Conflict Situations' (2010), 23 *Leiden Journal of International Law*, 571–84 at 578.

489 In a different perspective one could note the way the Court has dealt with, for instance, a ceasefire agreement in cases before it: A. Lang, 'Modus Operandi'.

490 *DRC v. Rwanda, I.C.J. Reports 2002*, at p. 236, para. 44 (Rwanda) and *I.C.J. Reports 2006*, at p. 37, para. 84 (Rwanda).

491 *Fisheries Case, I.C.J. Reports 1951*, Dissenting Opinion by Judge Read, at p. 203.

492 A. Lall, *Modern International Negotiation*, p. 125; A. Guelke, 'Negotiations and Peace Processes', p. 64.

493 A. Lang, ' Modus Operandi', 115.

494 A. Lang, 'Modus Operandi', 127.

495 *DRC v. Rwanda, I.C.J. Reports 2002*, at p. 231, para. 30 (DRC).

496 *DRC v. Rwanda case, I.C.J. Reports 2006*, at p. 37, para. 83 (Rwanda) (emphasis added).

497 *Ibid.* (Rwanda).

498 *Ibid.*, Dissenting opinion by Judge *ad hoc* Mavungu, at p. 100, para. 22.

499 See for instance *mutatis mutandis DRC v. Rwanda case, I.C.J. Reports 2006*, at p. 37, para. 84 (Rwanda).

500 M. Kohen, 'Interaction', p. 16.

measures'. Indeed, 'depending on the magnitude and the intensity of the conflict, the threat it poses to peace and security, and the imminent risk of irreparable prejudice to the life and property of a considerable part of the population' the Court should be 'entitled to issue provisional measures whether or not these requirements are met'.[501]

3.16 Did Prior Negotiations Actually Take Place?

Parties to a case such as the *CERD case* may not only fundamentally disagree over the nature of the relevant provisions (descriptive in nature/compulsory precondition) but also whether the subject-matter of the interpretation and/or application of the Convention has ever been discussed in bilateral contacts between them.

A compromissory clause may explicitly provide for prior negations as a precondition for recourse to the Court, but what is the legal position in the absence of such an explicit requirement?

Georgia's position was clear: even if Article 22 were considered to lay down such a precondition there 'have been extensive bilateral contacts between the Parties' thereby fulfilling this precondition for seisin.[502]

The Russian Federation argued that Article 22 lays down 'procedural preconditions for the seisin of the Court, namely that only if the dispute in question "is not settled by negotiation or by the procedures expressly provided for in this Convention" can it be referred to the Court'. The *travaux préparatoires* confirm the interpretation that the Court cannot be seised of a dispute "failing negotiation and/or recourse to the procedures laid down in the convention'.[503] The seisin of the Court *functions* as 'a last resort when all other possibilities have proved to be ineffective'.[504] While the Russian Federation vehemently denied that there had been 'the slightest negotiations between the Parties' on the interpretation or application of the Convention,[505] Georgia maintained that 'bilateral discussions and negotiations relating to the issues which form the subject-matter of the Convention' had been held.[506]

The assessment whether prior negotiations did actually take place, and if so if they have failed, is ultimately for the Court to decide, and we will address this aspect in more detail in Chapter 5. It is sufficient at this stage to recall that the joint dissent made it clear that the very 'least that the Court should have done was to ask itself whether negotiations had been opened and whether they were likely to lead to a certain result, but it did not do so'.[507]

3.17 Prior Negotiations and a Request to Intervene

Negotiation scholars drew attention to the fact that in the same way 'as all aspects of the conflict are not likely to be solved, so it may not be possible to include all parties in an agreement' or in the process of negotiations leading to that result for that matter.[508] Indeed, parties to a dispute have to take care in choosing an exclusive or inclusive approach to the process, as leaving out a major contender 'may produce an agreement but not a solution' to the dispute.[509]

'Maritime boundary delimitation is a bilateral operation' and 'the fundamental rule is that States are free to adopt any boundary they wish by agreement'. And 'although, the practical consequences for third States with an interest in the area or a neighbouring boundary are well understood, it is clear that it is for the parties themselves to decide whether to include other states in their negotiating or dispute settlement process'.

---

501 G. Zyberi, 'Provisional Measures', 578–9.
502 *CERD case, I.C.J. Reports 2008*, at p. 380, para. 94.
503 *Ibid.*, at pp. 382–3, para. 101.
504 *Ibid.*, at p. 383, para. 101.
505 *Ibid.*, at p. 383, para. 102.
506 *Ibid.*, at p. 387, para. 113.
507 *Ibid.*, Joint dissenting opinion, at p. 404, para. 16. In order to make that assessment records of negotiations are important, an issue we will address in Chapter 7.
508 W. Zartman, *Negotiation and Conflict Management*, p. 124.
509 W. Zartman, *Negotiation and Conflict Management*, p. 124.

Indeed, it 'is not for a tribunal seised of the matter by the parties to do so'.[510] We will later ascertain whether and in which particular way the Court in such cases, and in the absence of intervention, *includes* third States in its reasoning and perhaps even in its operative part, namely to such an extent that it employs judicial restraint with regard to any area beyond a particular tripoint.[511]

Is there room for the functional interaction in case of a State submitting a request to the Court to be permitted to intervene in the sense that bringing an issue before the Court without prior discussion between the would-be intervener and either of the parties would be premature and, moreover, contrary to an established rule 'that before proceedings are brought in the Court, there must be a defined dispute' which has matured through the process of negotiations between the parties?[512]

The Court denied the existence of such a requirement 'for the definition of a dispute in prior negotiations before an application can be made for permission to intervene'[513] because the 'function' of intervention is 'wholly different from the determination of a further dispute between the State seeking to intervene and one or both of the parties'. Requiring 'the existence of such a dispute, defined by prior negotiations' as a condition of intervention would be 'inappropriate'.[514]

An assertion of a claim to a maritime area under international law can be made during prior (failed) negotiations and can 'easily be understood as an assertion of an interest' of a legal nature.[515]

However, much prior to proceedings between two parties and a request to intervene States may in a tripartite accord take note of the claim by the now would-be intervener and agree 'to exert their best endeavours to bring the claim to a just and expeditious resolution by peaceful means'.[516]

Finally, 'States must not be allowed to negotiate bilateral agreements for the commencement of proceedings in total disregard of the interests of third parties'. Therefore, intervention 'should not be perceived as an unfriendly act'.[517]

---

510 M. Evans, 'Intervention, the International Court of Justice and the Law of the Sea' (1995) 48 *Revue Hellénique de Droit International* 73–94 at 90–91.

511 See generally A. Pellet, 'Land and Maritime Tripoints in International Adjudication' in H. Hestermeyer (ed.), *Coexistence, Cooperation and Solidarity: Liber Amicorum Rüdiger Wolfrum* (2 vols, Leiden, 2012), vol. 1, pp. 245–63.

512 *Land, Island and Maritime Frontier Dispute (El Salvador/Honduras), Application to Intervene, Judgment, I.C.J. Reports 1990*, p. 92, at p. 113, para. 50 (Honduras).

513 *Land, Island and Maritime Frontier Dispute, I.C.J. Reports 1992*, at p. 113, para. 51.

514 *Ibid.*, at p. 114, para. 51.

515 *Territorial and Maritime Dispute (Nicaragua v. Colombia), Application by Honduras to intervene, I.C.J. Reports 2011*, Dissenting opinion by Judge Donoghue, at p. 474, para. 11.

516 *Sovereignty over Pulau Ligitan and Pulau Sipadan (Indonesia/Malaysia), Application for Permission to Intervene, Judgment, I.C.J. Reports 2001*, p. 575, Declaration by Judge Kooijmans, at p. 627, para. 5.

517 C. Chinkin, *Third Parties*, p. 184.

PART II
Negotiations and the Adjudicative Phase

Introduction

In Part I of this study we have demonstrated to what extent and how prior negotiations perform multiple functions during the pre-adjudicative phase, i.e. when parties to a dispute have deliberately embarked upon a process of substantive discussions in order to peacefully settle their dispute. We have underlined the importance of that process for the adjudicative phase which then may follow but which in situations, for instance of alleged violations of fundamental obligations of public international law, could also be started by the Applicant without prior negotiations altogether.

Under both scenarios entering the Peace Palace basically means that the functional interaction between negotiations and adjudication becomes active and operational. Seising the Court means that the focus is shifting from what the parties have (in vain) attempted to achieve between themselves to what they can expect from the Court's performance of its judicial function.

The following illustrate that the functional effectiveness of prior negotiations has not to be exclusively or rather not predominantly measured in terms of the actual settlement of the dispute.

When (one of) the parties decides to take the road to the Court, that decision will irreversibly change the factual and legal relations between the parties to the dispute from the moment the case is entered in the Court's General List.

The role of seisin in the functional interaction deserves to be analysed as well as the functional role of meetings with the Court's President as a necessary and primordial prerequisite for an orderly course of the proceedings. We will address these issues in Chapter 4.

Together with the existence of a dispute and the indication of its subject-matter, failed negotiations are the keys to the Great Hall of Justice.

In case prior negotiations on the subject-matter had been successful that situation would not have brought into play the functional interaction at all, except perhaps for the impact of a prospective adjudication upon such an outcome of the process.

The unifying thread between the pre-adjudicative and the adjudicative phase from a functional interaction perspective is that the prior negotiations actually come to an end but continue to exercise their influence and impact on the proceedings which have just started; it is indeed once the step towards adjudication has been taken that the full potential of their functional interaction is becoming clear for the parties, for the Court and for all observers, including of course third States.

At first glance the existence and the subject-matter of the dispute are now beyond doubt, at least for (one of) the parties, subject to the Court's assessment in light of their pleadings and submissions. Hopefully prior negotiations have clarified the respective claims of the parties and are a useful instrument for the Court to determine the critical date.

Recourse to the Court necessarily implies that the process had not been (wholly) satisfactory to (one of) the parties. In this sense failed negotiations are in most cases the factual and perhaps also the legal prerequisite for the Court's exercise of its functions. Hence it is relevant to explore, in Chapter 5, both from the parties' perspective and that of the Court, the functional role of a refusal to enter into the process, what value could be attached to a deadlock situation and of course whose decision it is ultimately that the negotiations have failed, to eventually blame (one of) the parties for that failure, and also for the Court to be presented with only part of the dispute.

It would be wrong to assume that from the moment a case has been brought before the Court there is no room anymore to discuss and analyse the functional interaction because it would be exclusively a matter of adjudication as allegedly the only remaining method of peaceful settlement. Prior negotiations may have failed for a variety of reasons, but the changed factual and legal context of the new situation created by entering the adjudicative phase together with the subject-matter and complexity of the dispute may, in addition to the continuous nature of their obligation to negotiate, convince the parties that, subject to some general principles as to the judicial process, they can start or in most cases resume the negotiations during the proceedings. That will be the focus in Chapter 6.

The functional interaction between the parties and the Court achieves particular significance as result of the parties' choice for such a double-track strategy.

Parties' willingness to give negotiations another chance may bring them to ask the Court for extensions of particular time-limits, while on the other hand the resumed process should not result in aggravating or extending the dispute as it had been brought before the Court.

The functional interaction between the two modes of peaceful settlement thus acquires once more both a procedural and a substantive aspect, a combination which also finds its expression in a request for and the indication of provisional measures as a result of prior or resumed negotiations.

Just as it was the case in the pre-adjudicative phase with the process of prior negotiations, negotiations during the course of the proceedings may perhaps unexpectedly lead to a (partial) settlement of the dispute, leading to discontinuance of those proceedings and bringing to an end the functional interaction as well.

However, perhaps the distance between the parties' views as already reflected in the failure of the prior negotiations may have continued once the Court had been seised – sharpened even as a result of their pleadings and submissions; but this may not have prevented them from agreeing on interim arrangements which would govern particular (practical) aspects of their dispute at least until the delivery of the Court's judgment.

Does the functional interaction stretch its operational impact merely to both parties to a dispute or should parties to a dispute when negotiating either prior to or during the course of the proceedings – and as well as during the post-adjudicative phase, as Chapter 8 will illustrate – both legally and in fact have to take due account of the legal interests of third States?

Whereas Chapter 6 is mainly looking at the functional interaction of negotiations *during the proceedings*, it is true that such a review does not teach us much about the functional role of negotiations *in the judicial settlement by the Court* (Chapter 7). Indeed, parties may have their own and in many cases diverging perception or recollection of the process of negotiations during which they have attempted to solve the dispute, but this is entirely different from for instance the judicial significance the Court is going to attach to records of negotiations and to the parties' (lack of) readiness to negotiate. It is for the Court to come forward with a judicial qualification of the negotiations and for instance to assess the progress or lack of it and the deadlock situation which brought the parties before it.

Does the functional interaction operate in this way that there should be consistency between the positions taken during negotiations and the arguments advanced before the Court?

Does the functional interaction operate in this way that positions taken during the negotiations should (not) or could (not) be invoked during the proceedings?

In *elaborating the reasoning* which will ultimately and convincingly lead to the operative paragraphs, what kind of influence could the Court draw from positions during negotiations?

In taking its decision on the merits of the case, would functional interaction allow the Court to take (un) successful negotiations as part *of the basis* for that judicial decision?

The bilateral nature of the dispute as it had been submitted to the Court does not rule out of course that (one of) the parties are engaged or will engage in negotiation with third States, which may or may not have requested intervention: is there room for a (dys)functional role for those negotiations in the judicial settlement of the pending dispute?

The Court may in the operative paragraphs of its judgment on the merits oblige the parties to (re-)enter into a process of negotiations leading them from the adjudicative into the post-adjudicative phase, another and particular mode of functional interaction which then forms the focus of Part III of this study.

Chapter 4
Entering the Peace Palace: Seisin of the Court and Meetings with the President

Introduction

The seisin of the Court – by way of filing an Application or through a joint submission of the dispute – constitutes the decisive transition between the pre-adjudicative and the adjudicative phase, from negotiations to judicial settlement. Until that very moment prior negotiations either in their substantive or in their rather procedural mode have been functioning as paving the way to the Peace Palace. Parties have been unable or unwilling to finally settle (all aspects of) a dispute which has been dividing them perhaps for a long period of time, or which may have suddenly arisen out of certain events, actions, omissions or facts. To some extent irrespective of prior negotiations clauses either or both of the parties may have come to the conclusion that the negotiations have been unsuccessful or just futile, and that the time has come to submit the legal aspects of the dispute to the Court for adjudication.

Seisin 'signifies that the Court, as a dispute-settlement machine, has been "switched on", and can begin to operate, even though the machinery may, for lack of subject-jurisdiction, not complete its cycle, but (as it were) switch itself off again'.[1]

A good starting point for this particular question is the recognition that the 'joint referral of any case to the Court, as a result of the consent of the parties thereto, is undoubtedly the closest to the ideal in terms of the application of international legal justice'.[2] Hence, the Court 'always leans in favour of allowing a subsequent special agreement' – resulting from resumed or ongoing negotiations – 'to replace a unilateral application'.[3]

Although the conduct of the Applicant can be taken into account by the Court 'in reaching its judgment on the merits', one could add in passing that the conduct of both parties may be relevant for the Court; as to their (un)willingness during the proceedings to negotiate, it would be quite a different matter altogether for the Court to assess the intentions underlying the seisin in order to conclude that there could have been an abuse of the procedure.[4]

Seisin brings into operation new factual and legal relations not only between the Court and the parties[5] but also between the parties themselves as new cooperational duties impose themselves upon them[6] both *in foro* and outside the court room.[7] Indeed, dispute resolution 'is not just a matter of seising the Court; it also requires an appropriate state of mind'.[8]

The 'mutual duty of loyalty' which 'they also owe to the Court' is 'modulated in light of the particular circumstances between them in a given case'.[9] Even in case of a Special Agreement parties have to agree during their prior negotiations on one of the possible methods of seisin, namely joint notification of the Special Agreement, successive notification or unilateral notification.[10]

---

1 H. Thirlway, 'The Law and Procedure of the International Court of Justice 1960–1989 Supplement, 2010: Parts Nine and Ten' 82 *British Yearbook of International Law*, 13–170, at 39.

2 *Oil Platforms case, I.C.J. Reports 1996*, Dissenting opinion by Judge Oda, at p. 892, para. 6.

3 R. Kolb, *The ICJ*, p. 162.

4 R. Higgins as cited by M. Forteau, 'La saisine des juridictions internationales à vocation universelle (CIJ et TIDM)', in H.Ruiz-Fabri and J.M.Sorel (eds.), *La saisine des juridictions internationales,* (Paris, 2006), pp. 9–87, at p. 35, note 94.

5 M. Forteau, 'La saisine', p. 11.

6 A. Peters, 'International Dispute Settlement'.

7 M. Forteau, 'La saisine', p. 72.

8 R. Kolb, *The ICJ*, p. 863.

9 R. Kolb, *The ICJ*, p. 946.

10 M. Forteau, 'La saisine', pp. 45 and 47.

4.1 The Role of Seisin in the Functional Interaction

Prior Negotiations in the Applications: A Brief Review

A 'State may consider that it has a good and valid legal claim against another State', but it may 'nevertheless choose not to press it as far as litigation, in order not to jeopardise relations in another, and more important sphere'.[11]

By its Application one of the parties institutes the proceedings, thereby bringing to an (abrupt) end the pre-adjudicative phase but not necessarily the functional interaction, as a brief review may illustrate, without going into more details such as the particular case or the requests to the Court as formulated. To the contrary, seising the Court means bringing into full operation the *comprehensive potential* of the functional interaction.

In a number of Applications there is no mention of any process of prior negotiations, especially in cases involving state responsibility resulting from (alleged) serious violations of fundamental norms of international law or because the (alleged) wrongful act has taken the Applicant so completely by surprise that there was no time to negotiate.

In a number of Applications explicit reference is made to the process of prior negotiations. The variation of formulations used to convey to the Court, the other party and third States why this important step towards adjudication has been taken is almost unlimited, but the message is always identical.

In general terms the situation leading to the exercise of the procedural right to apply to the Court has been described and depicted along the following lines. Repeated, sustained and sometimes protracted attempts to reach a friendly and satisfactory solution of the opposing claims through the diplomatic channel have proven to be fruitless, in vain or unsuccessful, achieving no reconciliation of views and have systematically failed, and this in spite of the Applicant always having taken a constructive attitude and having made every effort.

Indications as to the causes of this situation may be found when the Applicant refers to the lack of interest by the other party in arriving at a negotiated settlement, the Respondent having denied that the question could be the subject of negotiations: in such a scenario the Applicant has reached the conclusion that the dispute was incapable of being settled by diplomatic means.

The blame for the failure is clear when it is said that the Respondent has been acting in bad faith because for instance it had not been possible to reach an agreement on even holding discussions on the issues involved, or when the other party has declared itself unable or refuses to give way.

Sometimes external events such as a period of armed conflict, characterized by the breaking off of diplomatic relations, will not allow the parties to settle the dispute by peaceful means such as a process of negotiations that would be vain and illusory.

Obviously, the Applicant or sometimes negotiators of both sides has (have) come to conclusion that the efforts to resolve the dispute through diplomatic means have been exhausted – and by the same token the obligation to settle the dispute by negotiations – and that there was no prospect anymore of success and all possibilities of reaching an agreement have disappeared.

As the UN Charter does not require parties to a dispute to seek a solution by negotiation rather than through a judicial settlement, the assessment that no other diplomatic options are available leaves the Applicant with no other alternative but to submit the case to the Court, although the bonds of friendship which link both countries have required that whatever could be done to avoid legal proceedings should have been done as perhaps they were both anxious not to have to litigate. In the end, recourse to judicial settlement may constitute the necessary measure for the peaceful settlement of the dispute (PSD), and this also in order to avoid indefinite prolongation of discussions that obviously cannot lead to any outcome, and while no other efforts toward settlement are pending.

---

11 H. Thirlway, 'Some Observations', 5.

The Functional Interaction Continues

Continued attempts to negotiate during the pre-adjudicative phase may have been unsuccessful in themselves, but they may result in both parties exercising considerable restraint in a particular disputed area, an attitude which may turn out to be rather helpful during the course of the proceedings.

Seisin of the Court does not prevent either of the parties amending their *petita* until the end of the oral proceedings, for instance as a result of (partial) success of negotiations they have conducted during the proceedings and/or in order to evacuate, in light of the pleadings, some issues from The Hague to the negotiating table either prior to or after the Court's decision on the merits of the case. This would amount to some kind of partial discontinuance.[12]

It is perfectly possible that prior to the proceedings there was no dispute between the parties regarding some particular features and no diplomatic efforts to negotiate the matter have been undertaken.[13] Efforts to reach an agreement on the subject-matter of a dispute 'are independent of the act of seising the Court' and may continue during the proceedings.[14]

Negotiations immediately following the filing of an Application after two separate notifications of a Framework Agreement may result in an agreement between the parties that the proceedings in the case have been instituted by two successive notifications relating to one single case[15] or to the conclusion of a proper Special Agreement.[16]

Although the *Upper Silesia ruling* on defects which can be cured by a subsequent act or event does not 'justify the application of the principle in a generalized form in which it is claimed to have an extended application to any and all flaws in procedure',[17] the absence of consent can always be repaired subsequent to the instituting of the proceedings.[18]

Any 'government qualified to appear before' the Court 'may file its Application without prior special agreement', that is 'well settled'.[19] In its Application the Applicant may invite the other party to take the necessary steps to confirm the Court's jurisdiction.

Functional interaction is not completely absent in case of *forum prorogatum* as 'diplomatic soundings (may) have been taken and given the green light for the applicant to go ahead and seise the Court in this way'.[20]

In any situation of *forum prorogatum* the invited State has to 'meticulously' draft 'its positive response if it wishes to avoid any surprises on the part of the Court'. Hence it is preferable to propose to the inviting State to conclude a Special Agreement 'clearly specifying the legal matters' which the parties would wish the Court to decide.[21] The invited State can agree to negotiate a compromis, albeit only to achieve a clear and consensual determination of the subject-matter of the dispute.[22]

When in case of *forum prorogatum* the prior negotiations condition was not fulfilled the functionality of negotiations operates in a particular, exceptional mode. Although conduct of the parties could provide the basis for the Court's jurisdiction, such conduct should be *in foro*.

Out-of-court conduct such as negotiations may very well render moot the object of the Application, but they can only provide a basis for the Court's jurisdiction if the resulting agreement clearly provides so.

Deadlock can ultimately result in instituting the proceedings on the basis of *forum prorogatum*.

---

12 R. Abraham, 'Commentaire' in *La Saisine des Juridictions Internationales* (Paris, 2006) at p. 90.

13 *Case between Qatar and Bahrain, I.C.J. Reports 2001*, Separate opinion by Judge Oda, at p. 123, para. 5.

14 *Case between Qatar and Bahrain, I.C.J. Reports 1995*, Dissenting opinion by Judge Koroma, at p. 69. This particular mode of functional inter action will be addressed in Chapter 6.

15 *Territorial Dispute (Libyan Arab Jamahiriya/Chad), I.C.J. Reports 1990*, at p. 151.

16 *Corfu Channel case, I.C.J. Reports 1949*, at p. 6.

17 *Croatian Genocide case, I.C.J. Reports 2008*, Dissenting opinion by Judge Owada, at p. 505, para. 16 and at p. 511, para. 24 (b).

18 *Ibid.*, at p. 512, para. 25.

19 *Case concerning the Aerial Incident of 4 September 1954 (United States of America v. Union of Soviet Socialist Republic), Order of 9 December 1958: I.C.J. Reports 1958*, p. 158 at p. 160 (USA).

20 R. Kolb, *The ICJ*, p. 549.

21 *Case between Djibouti and France, I.C.J. Reports 2008*, Separate opinion by Judge Tomka, at p. 277, para. 31.

22 *Case between Qatar and Bahrain, I.C.J. Reports 1995*, Dissenting opinion by Judge Shahbuddeen, at p. 62.

The *Gabcikovo case* is interesting as an example of seisin by an Application with no basis for jurisdiction, no reaction by the prospective respondent State, then to be followed by the signing of a Special Agreement as a result of mediation by the Commission of the EC.[23]

It cannot have been easy to draw up the agreement as the text 'appears to have been *inspired* by the desire to reconcile elements which remain contradictory'.[24]

(Pre-)Conditions for Seisin

The procedural right to apply to the Court is by no means 'insubstantial' whatever the outcome of adjudication; one of the main differences with negotiations is that 'all aspects of the matter can be discussed in the objective atmosphere of a court of justice'.[25]

It is the Statute of the Court which governs and imposes limitations on the functional interaction between negotiations and adjudication. Parties are free to make their consent to the seisin of the Court subject to whatever pre-conditions they want, but they are to be consistent with the Statute.[26]

The seisin of the Court is a 'procedural step independent of the basis of jurisdiction invoked',[27] but the 'use of the correct method of seisin is a condition – precedent to the exercise of jurisdiction'.[28] The condition(s) for seisin as contained in a compromissory clause must be met and 'must be examined in the context of the issue of the Court's jurisdiction'.[29]

On the other hand the Court can never ignore the 'inherent limitations on the exercise of (its) judicial function';[30] neither is the suggestion to enjoin parties to come to the Court by way of Special Agreement after a case has been instituted by Application[31] consistent with the Statute of the Court.

Although parties are free in their Special Agreement to define the limits of the Court's jurisdiction '*stricto sensu*, which they intend to confer upon the Court', they are not allowed 'to alter the limits of the Court's judicial function' which 'because they are defined by the Statute, are not at the disposal of the parties, even by agreement between them, and are mandatory for the parties just as for the Court itself'.[32]

The Court inviting the parties to negotiate towards such a Special Agreement in order then to jointly submit the (whole of) the dispute, like it did in the *Qatar Bahrain case*, would be in conformity with the Statute. If no reply is forthcoming to a proposal to submit a question dividing the parties jointly to the Court, this may later result in, for instance, the General Assembly requesting an advisory opinion on one of the legal aspects of the question.[33]

A framework agreement on the peaceful settlement of a dispute usually contains a commitment by the parties to submit the dispute to the Court in the absence of a settlement through a process of negotiations within a specified period of time.[34]

In a framework agreement parties to a dispute do recognize its existence but they are unable 'to define it with the necessary precision'.[35] They 'agree that the dispute may be submitted to the Court, also specifying how the Court is to be seised, while leaving the definition of the dispute to be established through the actions

23 *Gabcikovo case, I.C.J. Reports 1997*, at p. 27, para. 24.

24 *Ibid.*, Separate opinion by Judge Bedjaoui, at p. 126, para. 24.

25 *The Northern Cameroons case, I.C.J. Reports 1963*, at p. 29.

26 *Revision and Interpretation of the 1982 Continental Shelf Judgment, I.C.J. Reports 1985*, at p. 216, para. 43.

27 *Case between Qatar and Bahrain, I.C.J. Reports 1995*, at p. 23, para. 43.

28 *Ibid.*, Dissenting opinion by Judge *ad hoc* Shahabuddeen, at p. 60.

29 *DRC v. Rwanda case, I.C.J. Reports 2006*, at p. 39, para. 88.

30 *The Northern Cameroons case, I.C.J. Reports 1963*, at p. 29.

31 *Land and Maritime Boundary case, I.C.J. Reports 1998*, Dissenting opinion by Judge *ad hoc* Ajibola, at p. 417: a series of facts particular to a case instituted by Application could provide 'cogent reasons why the Parties should be enjoined to come to the Court by way of Special Agreement'.

32 *Frontier Dispute between Burkina Faso and Niger, I.C.J. Reports 2013*, p. 44, at p. 70, para. 46.

33 *Western Sahara Advisory Opinion, I.C.J. Reports 1975*, Separate opinion by Judge De Castro, at pp. 129–30.

34 See generally S. Rosenne, 'The Framework Agreement' and 'The Qatar/Bahrain Case'.

35 S. Rosenne, 'The Qatar/ Bahrain Case', 172.

of the parties'.[36] A framework agreement 'frequently contains a statement to the effect that unilateral recourse to the Court will not be regarded as an unfriendly act by the respondent state'.[37]

The question whether bringing a matter before the Court while other means of settlement are still ongoing is not a manifestation of bad faith was answered positively by Judge Ajibola.[38]

4.2 Meetings with the President

The functional interaction between the two modes of peaceful settlement of disputes is based on their almost inherent complementarity.

Even if negotiations leading up to a Special Agreement have been conducted in a good way, there is a risk of parties disagreeing on the scope of the task entrusted to the Court, as the *Land, Island and Maritime Dispute case* has demonstrated: pre-adjudicative negotiations have to spell out very clearly what the parties are asking the Court to do.[39] It is thus not surprising that when prior negotiations are failing in this particular respect, parties have to take care of this during the adjudicative phase using all the procedural means at their disposal.

As we have indicated in the introduction to this study, the conceptual, legal and factual distinction between two methods of PSD should not obscure the continuum which exists between them, as the previous chapters have shown and as Chapters 6, 7 and Part III will further demonstrate.

Parties will have plenty of opportunity to resume their negotiations on matters of substance during the proceedings, if they wish to do so, but the good administration of justice will also require them to cooperate with the Court throughout the adjudicative phase on various matters and issues of a procedural nature as regulated by the Statute and the Rules of Court, depending on the methods of seisin employed.[40] Moreover, the general duty of good faith between the parties 'when engaging in judicial proceedings' and the principle of loyalty between them entail for instance the prohibition of abuse of procedure, and the application of estoppel.[41]

The fundamental structural relationship between the Court and the parties involves judicial endeavours to cooperate with the litigants through discussions aiming at the development of appropriate procedures to fit best the parties' priorities and the circumstances of the case at hand.[42]

Article 31 of the Rules of Court 'is an important expression of the requirements of cooperation and good faith that link together *all actors* in legal proceedings'.[43]

This will require regular contact between the parties and the Court through the office of the Registrar as the regular channel of communication, and this in order to enable the Court to ensure the orderly conduct of the case. The matters to be dealt with are wide-ranging from the title or name under which the case will be entered into the General List over the number and the order of the written pleadings – although the Court, according to Practice Direction I, expects them to regulate this order either in their Special Agreement or as result of later agreements between themselves – the opening of oral proceedings, and even the removal of the case in case of discontinuance.

In pre-trial meetings with the President parties ordinarily agree on, for instance, the distribution of speaking time and the order of the written pleadings.[44] Shortly after the filing of an Application parties may

---

36 S. Rosenne, 'The Qatar/ Bahrain Case', 172–3.

37 S. Rosenne, 'The Qatar/ Bahrain Case', 173.

38 *Land and Maritime Boundary case, I.C.J. Reports 1998*, Dissenting opinion by Judge *ad hoc* Ajibola, at p. 399 and at p. 403.

39 *Land, Island and Maritime Frontier Dispute, I.C.J. Reports 1992*, at p. 582, para. 372 and at p. 586, para. 380.

40 *Case between Qatar and Bahrain, I.C.J. Reports 1995*, at pp. 23–4, para. 43.

41 R. Kolb, 'General Principles', p. 877, MN 8. For a list of cases where the prohibition of abuse of procedure has been invoked see pp. 904–5, MN 50.

42 A. Riddell and B. Plant, *Evidence*, p. 21.

43 R. Kolb, *The ICJ*, p. 965 (emphasis added).

44 R. Kolb, 'General Principles', pp. 878–9, MN 13.

during a meeting with the President agree that 'no measure should be taken in the case' until the decision in the separate arbitral award case before the Court.[45]

Meetings with the President of the Court taking place at various intervals throughout the proceedings to discuss the orderly conduct of the case will by the nature of things involve an exchange of views between the parties before the President.

Questions of procedure are approached through a consultative process, often producing a consensus during the President's consultations.[46] Pre-existing legal and diplomatic relations between the parties might affect the nature of these consultations.[47]

Partially successful or failed prior negotiations could play an important role in the Court's 'procedural negotiations with the parties'.[48]

In case of establishment of a Chamber, what 'happens in practice even if not in law is that, prior to any meeting with the President, the litigating Parties first negotiate, on an individual basis, a list of names of judges they wish to present to him'.[49]

In Chapter 6 we will review a number of Orders of the Court: for instance fixing time-limits, identifying aspects the parties have to address first; postponing the opening of the oral proceedings *taking into account the agreement reached between the Parties*, an agreement that has been reached *either before the President*, in which case there certainly is room for a kind of *mediation* by the President or *outside the President's office* as a result of direct contacts and consultations between the parties.

Our present focus is on the initial stages of the adjudicative phase. Indeed, after the filing of an Application an exchange of views may take place, prior to the meeting with the President, on the preparation of the written pleadings and the time required for that purpose.[50]

At a meeting with the President both parties may refer to the need for further elaboration of certain points which were still in dispute after the first round of written pleadings and request authorization for a Reply and Rejoinder.[51] A similar request can be made unilaterally by the Applicant.[52]

At a more advanced stage of the proceedings the parties in the *Qatar Bahrain case*, after a meeting with the President, agreed that the Counter-Memorials would not cover the question of the authenticity of certain documents. This agreement was the result of mediation by the President as the parties reiterated their respective positions.[53]

Although this is a clear and unambiguous but rather exceptional explicit reference to the active role of the President in securing an agreement between the parties on matters of a procedural nature,[54] the Order of March 2001 in the *Qatar Bahrain case* has made it abundantly clear that such negotiations before the President are not always successful.

Article 4 of the Special Agreement between Benin and Niger provided that the parties would negotiate to find an agreement on the order for the oral proceedings, this agreement being subject to the approval of the Chamber. If the negotiations failed then the Chamber would prescribe the order.[55]

---

45 *Maritime Delimitation between Guinea-Bissau and Senegal, Order of 8 November 1995, I.C.J. Reports 1995*, p. 423, at p. 424.

46 A. Riddell and B. Plant, *Evidence*', p. 22.

47 A. Riddell and B. Plant, *Evidence*, p. 23.

48 A. Riddell and B. Plant, *Evidence*, p. 25.

49 P.-M. Dupuy, 'The Judicial Policy', p. 74.

50 *Maritime Dispute (Peru v. Chile), Order of 31 March 2008, I.C.J. Reports 2008*, p. 6, at p. 7.

51 *Dispute regarding Navigational and Related Rights (Costa Rica v. Nicaragua), Order of 9 October 2007, I.C.J. Reports 2007*, p. 829, at pp. 829–30.

52 *Maritime Dispute (Peru v. Chile), Order of 27 April 2010, I.C.J. Reports 2010*, p. 295, at p. 296.

53 *Maritime Delimitation and Territorial Questions between Qatar and Bahrain, Order of 30 March 1998, I.C.J. Reports 1998*, p. 243, at p. 244.

54 Compare with the rather succinct formulation on the agreement of the parties on time limits expressed at the meeting with the President: *Bosnian Genocide case, Order of 16 April 1993, I.C.J. Reports 1993*, p. 29, at p. 29.

55 *Frontier Dispute (Benin/Niger), Judgment, I.C.J. Reports 2005*, p. 90, at p. 95, para. 2.

The *Gabcikovo case* is interesting, for the formula used is more vague as the joint notification of a Protocol of Agreement between the parties 'with a view to proposing to the ICJ the arrangements for a visit *in situ'* followed 'certain exchanges between the President of the Court and the Agents of the Parties'.[56]

4.3 The Complexity of the Functional Interaction: The *Qatar v. Bahrain Case*

That the functional interaction between negotiations and adjudication may result in complex problems from the very start of the proceedings is amply illustrated by the *Qatar/Bahrain case*. As is well known, initially each of the parties would present a draft Special Agreement; then came the Bahraini formula permitting presentation 'of distinct claims by each of the Parties' but presupposing that 'the whole of the dispute would be submitted to the Court'.

The Court concluded that both States had committed themselves to submit the whole of the dispute to the Court whatever the mode of seisin,[57] although Qatar's Application only concerned part of the dispute.[58] The Court provided the parties with an opportunity to submit the whole of the dispute.

As far as the mode of seisin was concerned, a time limit was fixed for the parties either to act jointly or unilaterally.[59] As the parties could not agree on joint notification, Qatar unilaterally seised the Court with the whole of the dispute.[60] Bahrain argued that, given the absence of joint action, the Court was without jurisdiction.[61] The Court, having analysed the negotiations between the parties, did come to the conclusion that unilateral seisin was allowed pursuant to paragraph 2 of the Doha Minutes.[62]

Then Qatar proposed to amend it and to have two annexes to the Special Agreement, each one defining 'the subjects of dispute it wants to refer to the Court'.[63] Once Qatar declared itself ready to accept the Bahraini formula, further consultations were held between the parties in the presence of a mediator. The minutes of that meeting provided that good offices would continue for another five months before the dispute could be submitted to the Court by the (two) parties.[64] The different interpretations to this particular formulation substantially complicated the transition between the pre-adjudicative negotiations and the very start of the adjudicative phase, initiated by Qatar's Application.

The one and only explanation for the 1994 judgment is that in the absence of complete agreement on the subject-matter of the dispute, further negotiations are still 'required before the Court (could) consider itself to have jurisdiction and to have been validly seised'.[65]

In its 1995 judgment the Court duly acknowledged that 'the long negotiations which preceded the conclusion of the 1990 Minutes showed the difficulties the Parties had constantly met in their attempts to define the entire dispute, because for each of them there were sensitivities about the express mention of certain aspects of that dispute'.[66] However the parties 'continue[d] to differ on the question of the method of seisin'.[67]

The Court, interpreting the verb 'may' in its ordinary meaning, came to the conclusion that it 'does not require a seisin by both Parties acting in concert, but, on the contrary, allows a unilateral seisin'.[68] The object

56 *Case concerning the Gabcikovo-Nagymaros Project (Hungary/Slovakia), Order of 5 February 1997, I.C.J. Reports 1997*, p. 3, at p. 4.

57 *Case between Qatar and Bahrain, I.C.J. Reports 1994*, at p. 123, para. 33.

58 *Ibid.*, at p. 124, para. 36.

59 *Ibid.*, at p. 125, para. 38.

60 *Ibid.*, at pp. 9–10, para. 12.

61 *Ibid.*, at p. 10, para. 13.

62 *Ibid.*, at p. 21, para. 40.

63 *Ibid.*, at pp. 117–18, para. 18.

64 *Ibid.*, at pp. 119–20, para. 20.

65 *Case between Qatar and Bahrain, I.C.J. Reports, 1995*, Dissenting opinion by Judge *ad hoc* Valticos, at p. 77, para. 19.

66 *Ibid.*, at p. 17, para. 31.

67 *Ibid.*, at p. 17, para. 32.

68 *Ibid.*, at pp. 18–19, para. 35.

and purpose of the 1990 Minutes were to advance the settlement of the dispute, hence its aim must have been opening the way to 'a possible unilateral seisin' in the event the mediation would fail (by May 1991).[69]

From the perspective of the functional interaction we first have to note that this judicial emphasis on the 'purpose of accelerating the dispute settlement process'[70] is fully in line with the Court's earlier pronouncement that there is a reasonable limit to the pre-adjudicative negotiation process in case a particular avenue has already proven to be ineffective.

The functional interaction would certainly not be suspended by the seisin of the Court as the good offices were meant to continue during the proceedings.[71] But would there then still be a suspension in the period between the expiry of the May 1991 time limit and the seisin of the Court?

The Court in considering the various modalities and challenges the parties would be facing after the good offices would not yield a positive result by May 1991 was fully aware of the functional interaction. According to one interpretation, negotiations towards the conclusion of a Special Agreement could well take a long time, during which 'any mediation would have been ruled out during the course of that negotiation'.[72] Mediation would not only have been temporarily ruled out, but also 'would have become impossible' altogether 'if no agreement was reached between the Parties and if as a result the Court was never seised'.[73]

As the aim of the Minutes could not have been 'to delay the resolution of the dispute or to make it more difficult', the 'right of unilateral seisin was the necessary complement to the suspension of the mediation';[74] the functional interaction between the two means of settlement could hardly be more intense and pronounced.

After having reviewed the developments subsequent to the Bahraini formula and Qatar's acceptance of it[75] the Court took the view, in light of the failure to negotiate a Special Agreement, 'that the only procedural implication of the Bahraini formula on which the Parties could have reached agreement in Doha was the possibility that each of them might submit distinct claims to the Court',[76] thus allowing unilateral seisin.[77]

The recourse by the Court to the *travaux préparatoires* of the Doha Minutes, in order to confirm its interpretation of the text, left no doubt about the disagreement between the parties as to the method of seising the Court. Bahrain maintained its approach 'excluding any possibility of referring the dispute to the Court by means of a unilateral application', whereas Qatar contended that 'there was no plan to hold other negotiations in order to induce the Parties to agree to submit the dispute jointly to the Court'.[78]

Because of their fragmentary nature the *travaux préparatoires* of the Doha Minutes had to be 'used with caution' given the 'absence of any document relating to the progress of the negotiations';[79] they did not provide the Court 'with conclusive supplementary elements for the interpretation' of the text.[80]

As to the context in which the Minutes were signed, the Court observed that the fact that the principal concern of that meeting of the Co-operation Council of the Arab States of the Gulf was the conflict between Iraq and Kuwait 'could explain why the Parties were not able to reach agreement on a more explicit text'.[81]

In its judgment of 1 July 1994 the Court decided to 'afford the Parties the opportunity to ensure the submission of the entire dispute … by a joint act by both Parties with, if need be, appropriate annexes, or by separate acts',[82] these negotiations thus taking place during the proceedings.

69 *Ibid.*, at p. 19, para. 35.
70 *Ibid.*
71 *Ibid.*, at p. 19, para. 36.
72 *Ibid.*
73 *Ibid.*
74 *Ibid.*
75 *Ibid.*, at pp. 20–21, paras. 37–8.
76 *Ibid.*, at p. 21, para. 39.
77 *Ibid.*, at p. 21, para. 40.
78 *Ibid.*, at p. 22, para. 41.
79 *Ibid.*, at p. 21, para. 41.
80 *Ibid.*, at p. 22, para. 41.
81 *Ibid.*, at p. 23, para. 42.
82 *Case between Qatar and Bahrain, I.C.J. Reports 1994*, at p. 123, para. 38.

In its judgment of 15 February 1995 the Court, 'while regretting that no agreement could be reached between the Parties as to how it should be presented', concluded that it was seised of the whole of the dispute and it declared the Application of Qatar admissible.[83]

83 *Case between Qatar and Bahrain, I.C.J. Reports, 1995*, at p. 25, para. 48.

Chapter 5
The Existence and Nature of a Dispute and Failed Negotiations are the Keys to the Great Hall of Justice, But Who is the Key Holder?

Introduction

Once an Application has been filed or the Court has been seised by a joint action and the transition between the pre-adjudicatory and the adjudicatory stages actually happens, both the parties and the Court are facing a triple question: does there really exist a dispute between the parties? What is the nature of the dispute? And did prior negotiations really fail so that the road to the Peace Palace was properly open to (one of) the parties?

The answers to these questions will not only determine the Court's jurisdiction and the admissibility of the claim, but they will also co-determine, in conjunction with the submissions of the parties, the Court's actual and precise role in the adjudication of the merits as, for instance, the resolution of the question about the very existence of a dispute has potentially a decisive impact on the continuation of the proceedings.[1]

As indicated in Chapters 1 and 2, negotiations between States do perform multiple functions. The fact that States have engaged themselves in a process of negotiations is not in itself a necessary or sufficient proof that a dispute is dividing them. The existence of a dispute does not solely or necessarily depend on the fact that two States are actually conducting negotiations. We will examine how the functional interaction operates with regard to the role of negotiations in the ascertainment of the existence of a dispute.

Parties may not only disagree whether the *controversy* or *difference* between them really amounts to a dispute; they may also hold different opinions as to the nature of the alleged dispute. Here again negotiations will be used by both the parties and by the Court to ascertain the existence of a dispute at the critical date, and to identify and delineate the nature, the subject-matter, of the dispute.

Negotiations may have been going for a long period of time without having produced a definite and satisfactory result, i.e. the solution of the pre-existing dispute, and this in spite of all the efforts (one of) the parties have undertaken in good faith. The failing of negotiations is the ultimate vehicle to transport a dispute from the round table of discreet inter-party discussions to the solemnity of the Great Hall of Justice.

In this chapter we will examine more closely the way parties and the Court are involved in the search for answers to the above-mentioned triple question. Do parties and Court have a similar and perhaps complementary role to play here? Or is the opinion of the parties as to the existence and the nature of a dispute, and the assessment whether their negotiations have failed, of rather minor and subordinated importance because the Court is the ultimate key holder?

The assessment that a dispute cannot be settled by negotiations can be left to one of the parties (such as in the Pact of Bogota) and/or it can be left to an objective assessment by the Court.[2]

The Court's view that a dispute cannot be separated 'from the situation in which it has arisen'[3] reflects judicial awareness of the functional link between the two modes of settlement, as prior negotiations are in many case part and parcel of that situation.

We will first have a closer look at some features of the functional interaction at work before embarking upon a review of the questions just mentioned.

---

1 *Nuclear Tests (New Zealand v. France), I.C.J. Reports 1974*, at p. 463, para. 24.

2 *Belgium v. Senegal case, I.C.J. Reports 2012*, Separate opinion by Judge Yusuf, at p. 561, para. 6 and *Border and Transborder Armed Actions case, I.C.J. Reports 1988*, at p. 94, para. 63 (Nicaragua).

3 *Nuclear Tests (New Zealand v. France), I.C.J. Reports 1974*, at p. 467, para. 31.

5.1 The Functional Interaction at Work

The functional interaction between negotiations and adjudication is particularly visible when for instance the mere refusal, for compelling reasons, by one party to enter into the process of negotiations plays an important role in the determination of the critical date on which, according to the Court, the dispute was brought into existence.

By the very nature of things failed negotiations have not solved the dispute ; this state of affairs may have been partly due to disagreement between the parties about the nature of the dispute, a disagreement that will then almost inevitably resurface once the road of adjudication has been chosen by (one of) the parties.

Negotiations may also not have been completely unsuccessful and parties may have been able to reach an understanding on parts of the dispute; this in turn will influence and determine the precise contours and content of the Court's exercise of its judicial function.

One of the common features between negotiations and adjudication is that they are aiming at achieving the same objective: both the process of negotiations and a judgment 'must have some practical consequences in the sense that it can affect existing rights and or obligations of the parties, thus removing uncertainty from their legal relations'.[4] By demonstrating the existence of an actual and real dispute, prior negotiations on the subject-matter of a dispute will enable the Court to exercise its function.

According to the history of facts presented by the Court, several attempts at settlement by direct negotiations may turn out to be unfruitful, one indication – perhaps the decisive one – being the non-ratification of a protocol that had been reached.[5] The process of negotiation itself may have been successful, although the overall exercise did not ultimately bear fruit as the final step was missing.

Although an unratified Convention does not – except for the application of Article 18 of the VCLT – create legal rights and obligations between the parties, it may show the existence of a legal claim by one of the parties and the awareness of such a claim by the other party.[6]

The process may have 'enabled both parties to indicate the nature of their claims'.[7] Hence, raising a question with regard to a particular claim or situation during prior negotiations is of great importance from the perspective of the functional interaction. It will enable the parties to substantiate their legal position afterwards and to determine whether that issue has really become the subject-matter of the dispute. It will enable the Court to determine the moment in time when the dispute actually arose – the critical date – and the real subject-matter of the dispute as submitted by the parties.

These opportunities may have presented themselves more or less frequently during the negotiations but the Court considers it 'natural' for a party to raise the matter at any of these opportunities, and the party concerned 'should have done so';[8] and although it does not necessarily have to be at the earliest possible occasion,[9] there may have been 'an outstanding opportunity' to do so.[10] This *dictum* illustrates the Court's determination to actually examine and asses the format, scope and extent of prior negotiations between the parties in order to determine the existence and subject-matter of a dispute as the absolute precondition for the exercise of its judicial function.

As to the format, it should be recalled that any 'negotiation is adequate if not in conflict with international custom'.[11]

Provided the claimant State has raised the questions on two occasions with the other parties also 'given the nature of the relations' between the parties, a letter confirming a government's position which 'did not elicit any immediate reaction' and with which the claimant State 'took issue with' only 15 years later does

4 *The Northern Cameroons case, I.C.J. Reports 1963*, at p. 34.
5 *Arbitral Award case King of Spain, I.C.J. Reports 1960*, at p. 203.
6 *Certain Frontier Land case, I.C.J. Reports 1959*, at p. 229.
7 *Land, Island and Maritime Frontier Dispute, I.C.J. Reports 1992*, at p. 381, para. 32.
8 *Temple of Preah Vihear case, I.C.J. Reports 1962*, at p. 28.
9 *Ibid.*, at p. 27.
10 *Ibid.*, at p. 28.
11 *South West Africa cases, I.C.J. Reports 1962*, Separate opinion by Judge Bustamente, at p. 384.

not necessarily render an application inadmissible. However, such a delay may 'cause prejudice' to the other party 'with regard to the establishment of the facts and the determination of the content of the applicable law'.[12]

A fine example of the functional interaction can be found in a case where the dispute on the conventional obligations of the Respondent 'was revealed by the exchanges between the Parties even before the Application was introduced', whereas the dispute over the compliance with its customary obligations 'only became apparent during their exchanges before the Court'.[13]

5.2 The Existence of a Dispute[14]

The Court 'cannot exercise its function in contentious proceedings, by giving a decision on the merits, unless a dispute genuinely exists between the parties. The absence thereof would require to be found by the Court even *proprio motu*'; in case no dispute exists, the Court must 'confine itself to a finding that the claim is inadmissible'.[15]

Objections to the admissibility of a claim, if accepted, would constitute for the Court a compelling reason 'not [to] proceed to an examination of the merits':[16]

> Such a [legal] reason is often of such a nature that the matter should be resolved in *limine litis*, for example where without examination of the merits it may be seen that there has been … the agreement of the parties to use another method of pacific settlement …[17]

Parties may thus after the start of the proceedings still decide to use another method, for instance resuming negotiations (Chapter 6). The Court's pronouncement is also a good illustration of the continuum between the two modes of settlement.

The admissibility of a claim may also be challenged on the ground that there had been no prior diplomatic negotiations 'such as would disclose the existence of a dispute'.[18]

Within the functional interaction negotiations, apart from trying to achieve an amicable settlement of the controversy, also perform this important and preliminary function to establish – first between the parties and then afterwards also to the outside world, including the Court – the very existence of a legal dispute.

On the other hand the Court might not accept the argument that 'there is no dispute between the parties while negotiations continue'.[19] The Court is thus not willing to rally itself with a party's dysfunctional use of the link between the two modes of peaceful settlement on the question of the (continued) existence of a dispute. Furthermore it is clear that a dispute may *persist* in spite of the fact that negotiations took place.[20] This view reflects the realistic approach towards negotiations as the most preferred method to settle a dispute and it is in line with the question of the limits to the obligation to negotiate we discussed earlier in Chapter 3).

---

12 *Nauru case, I.C.J. Reports 1992*, at pp. 254–5, para. 36 and at p. 254, para. 34.

13 *Belgium v. Senegal case, I.C.J. Reports 2012*, Separate opinion by Judge Abraham, at p. 474, para. 12.

14 In a small number of cases, such as the case concerning the maritime dispute between Peru and Chile, the term dispute' has made its way into the title of the case because parties did not object to it. It implies that they do not disagree about the mere existence of the dispute. The Applicant considered the exchanges between the parties as having revealed 'totally dissenting and opposed juridical positions' as evidence of the existence of the dispute: *Maritime Dispute between Peru and Chile, I.C.J. Reports 2014*, para. 162.

15 *South West Africa Cases, I.C.J. Reports 1962*, Dissenting opinion by Judge Morelli, at p. 565.

16 *Oil Platforms case, I.C.J. Reports 2003*, at p. 177, para. 29.

17 *Croatian Genocide case, I.C.J. Reports 2008*, at p. 456, para. 120.

18 *Nottebohm case, I.C.J. Reports 1955*, at p. 11 (I). See Judge Klaestad on the relevance of this argument in his dissenting opinion, at p. 33.

19 *Aegean Sea Continental Shelf case, I.C.J. Reports 1978*, at p. 12, para. 30.

20 *Fisheries Jurisdiction (Federal Republic of Germany v. Iceland), I.C.J. Reports 1973*, at p. 56, para. 17.

The Court's Position

The Court's position is well established and long-standing: a mere assertion or denial by either of the parties is not sufficient to establish the existence of a dispute; neither is a conflict of interests. What has to be shown is that 'the claim of one party is positively opposed by the other'.[21] A complaint by one party before an organ of an international organization (IO) provides an opportunity to the other party to 'set out its claim with sufficient particularity' for the first State to be able to oppose it.[22] This is important for the existence of a dispute: not only must a claim be made, but it has to be made, also during negotiations, in such a way as to enable the other party to oppose it in order to fulfil the *Mavrommatis* criterion.

One also has to bear in mind the PCIJ's well-known *dictum* that 'the manifestation of the existence of a dispute in a specific manner, and for instance by diplomatic negotiations, is not required'.[23] Diplomatic negotiations are *only one* of the manifestations in a formal way of the existence of a dispute. Moreover, even if one assumes 'that there is substance in the contention that Article 36 (2) of the Statute, by referring to legal disputes, establishes as a condition of the jurisdiction of the Court a requisite definition of the dispute through negotiations', the Court may find that 'the condition was complied with *to the extent permitted by the circumstances of the case*'.[24]

From the perspective of the functional interaction it is important to note the Court's pronouncement that while 'the existence of a dispute and the undertaking of negotiations are distinct *as a matter of principle*, the negotiations may *help to demonstrate* the existence of a dispute and delineate its subject-matter'.[25]

Do diplomatic exchanges between various parties concerning the implementation of particular provisions of various conventions (*necessarily)* disclose the existence of a dispute which in turn is subject to the dispute settlement provisions of that Convention?

Directly focusing on one of the functions of diplomatic exchanges, namely did they disclose disputes, this was one of the questions submitted by the General Assembly to the ICJ in 1949.[26]

In its Advisory Opinion the Court reaffirmed that whether 'there exists an international dispute is a matter for objective determination'.[27] This is a firm and unequivocal pronouncement that ultimately it is for the Court to determine whether there is a real dispute between the parties before it. Consequently, the 'mere denial of the existence of a dispute does not prove its non-existence'.[28] The opposite is also true: the mere claim that it does exist does not prove its existence either.

Diplomatic exchanges between a number of States and the three States concerned demonstrate the existence of a situation 'in which the two sides hold clearly opposite views concerning the performance or non-performance of certain treaty obligations'; hence 'international disputes have arisen'[29] and the relevant documents presented to the Court show that the parties 'have not succeeded in settling their disputes by direct negotiations'.[30] Hence the Court's reply to the question asked that 'the diplomatic exchanges' indeed 'disclose disputes subject to the provisions for the settlement of disputes'.[31]

Establishing the existence of a dispute is one of the multiple functions prior negotiations have to perform, but they are thus only performing a *subsidiary, supporting, secondary and contributing function* in that respect: and the same goes for the delineation of the subject-matter. Indeed, other important factors here are, as established by the Court in its caselaw, the submissions of the parties and the conduct of the parties

---

21 *South West Africa cases, I.C.J. Reports 1962*, at p. 328.

22 *DRC v. Rwanda case, I.C.J. Reports 2006*, at p. 47, para. 112 (Rwanda).

23 *The Chorzow Factory case* as cited in *Revision and Interpretation of the 1982 Continental Shelf Judgment, I.C.J. Reports 1985*, at p. 216, para. 43.

24 *Right of Passage case, I.C.J. Reports 1957*, at p. 149 (emphasis added).

25 *CERD case, I.C.J. Reports 2011*, at p. 84, para. 30 (emphasis added).

26 *Interpretation of Peace Treaties, Order of 7 November 1949: I.C.J. Reports 1949*, p. 229, at p. 229.

27 *Interpretation of Peace Treaties, Advisory Opinion: I.C.J. Reports 1950*, p. 65, at p. 74.

28 *Ibid.*

29 *Ibid.*

30 *Ibid.*, at p. 76.

31 *Ibid.*, at p. 77.

during the course of the proceedings.[32] This conduct may include negotiations during the proceedings, and to which we will turn in the next chapter, but it may also consist of 'preparing for the settlement of the dispute by the use of armed force',[33] an operation 'calculated to undermine respect for the judicial process in international relations'.[34]

Interpreting Parties' Positions during Negotiations

Exchange of diplomatic notes can afford 'at least *prima facie* evidence' of the existence of a dispute,[35] although in the process of examining such notes it is important to differentiate 'conciliatory language designed to secure' if possible the abandonment of a proposal and 'the language employed when claims or rights are made',[36] in the absence of which there is only a 'quarrel' between the parties.[37]

However, in most cases it will manifest itself in such a way that 'a disagreement on a point of law or fact, a conflict of legal views or interests, or the positive opposition of the claim of one party by the other need not *necessarily* be expressed *expressis verbis*'.[38] The fact that it does not need to be expressed *expressis verbis* may have an impact not only on the conduct of the parties during the negotiations but certainly also on the Court's assessment of the conduct of the parties during those negotiations in order to assess (whether or not) there has been a deadlock and to establish the existence of a dispute, although no 'so-called *final* deadlock is necessary to establish a dispute'.[39]

'In the determination of the existence of a dispute, as in other matters, the position or the attitude of a party can be established by inference, whatever the professed view of that party.'[40]

Inferences may thus also flow from positions taken by the parties during the negotiations, but the 'fact that a particular proposal is not adopted by an international organ does not necessarily carry with it the inference that a collective pronouncement is made in a sense opposite to that proposed. There can be many reasons determining rejection or non-approval'.[41] The putting forward during negotiations of a proposal 'is not sufficient for them to survive rejection'.[42]

We will return to the question whether and to what extent the Court's judgment in the *CERD case* could mark a turning point in the Court's jurisprudence on this particular aspect of the functional interaction. It is sufficient at this stage to refer to one dissenting view holding that there is no requirement that a Respondent must have the opportunity to 'oppose' a claim prior to the filing of an Application[43] and that the disagreement does not need 'necessarily [to] be stated *expressis verbis*'.[44]

However, interpreting parties' positions during the negotiations is never an easy task to perform. For instance it would be impossible to rely upon a few words taken from a single note – sent in reply to a request

---

32 In order to affirm the existence of a dispute an Applicant may refer not only to prior negotiations where parties were unable for instance to reach an agreement on the starting point of the maritime boundary but also to views and positions expressed by both States during the Applicant's request to intervene in proceedings between the Respondent and another State: *Dispute on the Maritime Delimitation in the Carribean Sea and the Pacific Ocean*, Application of Costa Rica, dated 25 Feburary 2014, Press Release No. 2014/11 of 26 February 2014 (text available on the Court's website).

33 *Hostages case, I.C.J. Reports 1980*, Dissenting opinion by Judge Morozov, at p. 56.

34 *Ibid.*, at p. 43, para. 93.

35 *Nuclear Tests (Australia v. France), I.C.J. Reports 1973*, Declaration by Judge *ad hoc* Barwick, at p. 110 (emphasis added).

36 *Nuclear Tests (Australia v. France), I.C.J. Reports 1974*, Dissenting opinion by Judge *ad hoc* Barwick, at pp. 424–5. In contrast, the exchanges between New Zealand and France did result in the 'emergence of a dispute between them a to their respective legal rights': *Nuclear Tests (New Zealand v. France), I.C.J. Reports 1974*, Dissenting opinion by Judge *ad hoc* Barwick, at p. 525.

37 *Nuclear Tests (Australia v. France), I.C.J. Reports 1974*, Separate opinion by Judge Gros, at p. 288.

38 *Land and Maritime Boundary case, I.C.J. Reports 1998*, at p. 315, para. 89 (first emphasis added).

39 *Interhandel Case, I.C.J. Reports 1959*, Separate opinion by Judge Spencer, at p. 71.

40 *Land and Maritime Boundary case, I.C.J. Reports 1998*, at p. 315, para. 89.

41 *Namibia Advisory Opinion, I.C.J. Reports 1971*, at p. 36, para. 69.

42 *Fisheries Jurisdiction (United Kingdom v. Iceland), I.C.J. Reports 1974*, Dissenting opinion by Judge Gros, at pp. 127–8, para. 3.

43 *CERD case, I.C.J. Reports 2011*, Separate opinion by Judge Donoghue at p. 331, para. 7 and note 2.

44 *Ibid.*, at p. 332, para. 8.

for information – to draw the conclusion that a government had abandoned a position indicated earlier in official documents.

Although a large degree of consistency should be a real value in a government's position during negotiations – in due respect of course to the prohibition of complete inflexibility – not too much importance should be attached to a few uncertainties or contradictions.[45]

Isolated expressions found in diplomatic correspondence might be regarded as acknowledgements of the claim by a party, if considered without regard to their context. But the 'general tenor' of the correspondence cannot be ignored. Both parties could be looking for a solution, based upon mutual agreement, but without the intention to concede their legal position.[46]

Compromissory Clauses Governing the Coming into Being of a Dispute

Although the general perception is that compromissory clauses are aiming at solving in a peaceful way disputes which may arise between States Parties over the interpretation and application of the substantive provisions of a particular Convention, the coming into being of a dispute may also be governed by the compromissory clause when it lays down a series of sequential steps of procedure to be taken before that point can be reached.

Once the proceedings have been instituted and thus the Rubicon between negotiations and adjudication has been crossed, a Respondent may first of all deny the existence of a dispute; divergent views between parties may hence relate to the question whether there really exists a dispute between them in accordance with the settlement provisions contained in a compromissory clause.

One party may argue that the clause provides for a five-stage process before a 'matter' has crystallized into a 'dispute' involving procedures established under the Convention[47] relying also on the different formula used in the convention: 'matter', 'complaints' and 'dispute'. This five-stage process includes 'communication and adjustment of a non-crystallized matter' through bilateral negotiations or any other procedure prior to its submission to a Committee established under the Convention to monitor the Convention's application; it is only after escalation of the matter through that procedure, 'and only then', that it could be 'properly characterized as a dispute'.[48] For the 'matter' to be recognized as a 'dispute' a 'specific degree of crystallization is required',[49] demonstrating the issue of threshold to be dealt with in the next subparagraph.

The other party may hold that the intention of the drafters of the Convention was not to attach a special meaning to the various formulas as 'matter', 'issue' and 'dispute' are used interchangeably.[50]

For the Court the word 'dispute' appears in exactly the same way 'as it appears in several other compromissory clauses adopted' around the same time.[51] Because of the consistency of usage 'there is no reason to depart from the generally understood meaning of "dispute" in' this particular compromissory clause.[52]

The general meaning of the word 'dispute' when used in relation to the Court's jurisdiction as demonstrated by the 'established case law on the matter' is 'a disagreement on a point of law or fact, a conflict of legal views or interests', to be objectively determined by the Court, meaning that it must be shown 'that the claim of one party is positively opposed by the other'. Failure to respond to a claim in circumstances where a response is called for 'may lead the Court to infer the existence of a dispute'.[53]

45 *Fisheries case, I.C.J. Reports 1951*, at p. 138.

46 *Case concerning rights of nationals of the United States of America in Morocco, Judgment of 27 August 1952: I.C.J. Reports 1952*, p. 176 at p. 200.

47 *CERD case, I.C.J. Reports 2011*, at p. 82, para. 26 (Russian Federation).

48 *Ibid.*, at p. 83, para. 27.

49 *Ibid.*

50 *Ibid.*, at p. 83, para. 28 (Georgia).

51 *Ibid.*, at p. 84, para. 29.

52 *Ibid.*

53 *Ibid.*, at p. 84, paras. 29 and 30.

The Question of Threshold

A Respondent may raise the question whether the nature and content of a conflict or a disagreement between governments are reasons for not considering it to be a dispute as envisaged in an international agreement[54] and subsequently argue that if there was a dispute it was not one falling within the terms of a particular compromissory clause,[55] and moreover that if there has been a dispute it was arguably one between the Applicant and the UN.[56]

The Court did consider the alleged existence of such a latter dispute even in relation to the same subject-matter as of no concern to it.[57] Moreover, *the state of development* of such a conflict or disagreement may be such that it is not a dispute which cannot be settled by negotiation.[58]

It is also for the Court to identify the very essence of a dispute.[59] The Applicant may argue that the Respondent may have recognized the existence of the Applicant's claims and a divergence of legal opinions over these claims 'both in the course of bilateral consultations' and in a letter.[60]

In the Respondent's view 'a discussion of divergent legal opinions should not be considered as evidence of the existence of a dispute in the sense of the Court's Statute' before 'it reaches a certain *threshold*'.[61]

An Applicant referring to the *Right of Passage case* might argue that 'it is only when the parties "adopt clearly-defined legal positions" that the dispute arises, and it arises *in relation* to the triggering event, not the whole legal and factual matrix against the background of which the event is to be understood';[62] and that is exactly what negotiations do.

In the Court's view there is a legal dispute because of the denial of fact and law by the Respondent.[63] The Court added that in this regard the position taken by the Respondent 'in the course of bilateral consultations' provides 'evidentiary value in support of the proposition' that the Applicants's 'claims were positively opposed by' the Respondent.[64]

Should indeed 'a discussion of divergent legal opinions' reach *a certain threshold* before the existence of a dispute could be acknowledged? Do the judicial requirements for the recognition of such an existence include *a built-in de minimis rule*? Has the Court been using a 'sufficiently' criterion?

There is no doubt that the threshold for the existence of a dispute is being determined by the Court in light of the circumstance of the case before it, although the case law provides us with only a few indications in this regard.

The existence of a dispute 'does presuppose a claim arising out of the behaviour or a decision by one of the parties'; it does not require that a contested decision 'must already have carried into effect'.[65] 'What is more, a dispute may arise even if the party in question gives an assurance that no measure of execution will be taken until ordered by decision of the domestic courts'.[66]

The 'mere fact' that the party accused of behaviour that allegedly constitutes a breach of a treaty 'does not advance any argument to justify its conduct under international law[;] does not prevent the opposing attitudes of the parties from giving rise to a dispute concerning the interpretation or application of the treaty'.[67] Hence,

---

54 *South West Africa cases, I.C.J. Reports 1962*, at p. 327 (South Africa).
55 *The Northern Cameroons case, I.C.J. Reports 1963*, at p. 20 (UK).
56 *Ibid.*, at p. 27 (UK).
57 *Ibid.*
58 *South West Africa cases, I.C.J. Reports 1962*, at p. 327 (South Africa) (emphasis added).
59 *Aegean Sea Continental Shelf case, I.C.J. Reports 1978*, at p. 35, para. 83.
60 *Certain Property case, I.C.J. Reports 2005*, at p. 18, para. 23 (Liechtenstein).
61 *Ibid.* (Germany) (emphasis added).
62 *Ibid.*, at p. 21, para. 34 (Liechtenstein).
63 *Ibid.*, at pp. 18–19, para. 25.
64 *Ibid.*, at p. 19, para. 25.
65 *PLO case Advisory Opinion, I.C.J. Reports 1988*, at p. 30, para. 42.
66 *Ibid.*
67 *Ibid.*, at p. 28, para. 38.

the Court may then be obliged to find 'that the opposing attitudes' of two parties 'show the existence of a dispute' between them.[68]

A claim by one party about wrongful conduct and the non-invocation of a circumstance precluding wrongfulness by the other State is thus sufficient to bring about a dispute.

A dispute may arise during talks between officials representing their governments and in charge of the subject-matter; the fact that 'the dispute had not been formalized in diplomatic exchanges from the higher channels' does not cause a problem as this is not a criterion.[69]

A Dispute May Consist of Several Phases and It May Take Various Forms

Although 'a dispute may presuppose the existence of some prior situation or fact' it does not necessarily follow 'that the dispute arises in regard to that situation or fact'.[70]

Does this mean that a dispute may arise almost on its own, independently, during the course of negotiations? That seems to depend on whether the negotiations are dealing with 'situations or facts which constitute the *source of the rights claimed* by one of the Parties' or with 'the situations or facts which are *the source of the dispute*'.[71]

As 'one situation may contain disputes which relate to more than one body of law and which are subject to different settlement procedures',[72] it is then first of all for the parties to decide during the pre-adjudicative stages which are those disputes and to embark upon perhaps various settlement of disputes procedures required, not all of them demanding parties to negotiate beforehand. This may then during the adjudicative stage result in the invocation of additional grounds of jurisdiction.

Parties may have been and may still be engaged in direct negotiations over their larger disputes, but they may disagree over the existence of a dispute relating to the interpretation or application of the treaty containing the compromissory clause in point.[73]

A State may have made numerous protests 'both at the bilateral level through direct contact' and at the 'multilateral level within the framework of international institutions'. The Court noted that 'whatever may be the legal qualification of such protests as regards the requirement of the existence of a dispute', the compromissory clause also required such a dispute to be the subject of negotiations.[74]

There may in fact, as already indicated, be two distinct but related disputes between the parties: one on *matters of substance* which finally has been submitted to the Court; and one of a *more procedural nature* regarding the method by which that substantive dispute will have to be resolved: either by negotiation alone or, under the double-track strategy, in parallel with judicial proceedings. This latter choice can be made irrespective of whether previous negotiations have already taken place.[75]

Negotiations on the matters of substance of a dispute may have failed at one point in time, bringing the parties to initiate the more procedural negotiations on the method of seisin of the Court. In spite of having

---

68 *Ibid.*, at p. 30, para. 43. See most recently on this question H. Thirlway, 'Quelques observations sur le concept de *dispute* (différend, contestation) dans la jurisprudence de la C.I.J' in M. Kamga and M. Mbengue (eds), *Liber Amicorum Raymond Ranjeva. L'Afrique et le Droit International: Variations sur l'Organisation Internationale* (Paris, 2013), pp. 611–22.

69 *Interhandel Case, I.C.J. Reports 1959*, Separate opinion by Judge Hackworth, at p. 37. Officials representing their respective governments may exchange correspondence in order to make 'technical arrangements': 'while acting within the limits of [their] technical responsibilities' they may seem not to be 'aware that the question of principle which the subject of the correspondence might imply had not been settled, and that the technical arrangements … should not prejudge' their country's 'position in *subsequent negotiations* between governments': *Gulf of Maine case, I.C.J. Reports 1984*, at p. 307, para. 139 (emphasis added).

70 *Case concerning Right of Passage over Indian Territory (Merits), Judgment of 12 April 1960: I.C.J. Reports 1960*, p. 6 at p. 35, the Court referring to its predecessor.

71 *Right of Passage case, I.C.J. Reports 1960*, at p. 35 (emphasis added).

72 *CERD case, I.C.J. Reports 2011*, at pp. 85–6, para. 32, on the events between June 1992 and August 2008.

73 *Nicaragua case, I.C.J. Reports 1984*, Dissenting opinion by Judge Schwebel, at p. 629, para. 119.

74 *DRC Rwanda case, I.C.J. Reports 2006*, at p. 40, para. 91.

75 *Aegean Sea Continental Shelf case, I.C.J. Reports 1978*, at pp. 12–13, para. 30. The Court supported the Greek view as to the existence of these two distinct disputes.

conducted successful negotiations in this regard and of having concluded a Special Agreement the parties may still find themselves in disagreement about what exactly they are asking the Court to do.[76]

5.3 A Dispute in the Sense of Article 60 of the Statute

What negotiation scholars have observed with regard to the outcome of negotiations arguably also applies *mutatis mutandis* to adjudication by the Court: the less detailed the terms of operative paragraphs, 'the greater the difficulties are likely to be at the stage of implementation'.[77]

Post-adjudicative negotiations 'to put flesh on the bare bones' of the judgment are needed and it is 'at this stage that disputes over the interpretation are likely to arise'[78] and that shifts in the balance of power between the parties may be important and may even undermine 'the normative rationale' of the judgment so that the implementation 'falls short' of what one of the parties and the international community see as legitimate.[79]

Although requests for interpretation of a judgment of the Court of course belong to the post-adjudicative phase – to be dealt with in Part III – it is appropriate here to look briefly at the requirement for the existence of a dispute in the sense of Article 60 of the Statute of the Court.

The point of reference in this regard is the so-called *Avena II case* where the Court took the opportunity to provide some clarifications in this regard. Comparing Articles 60 and 36, para. 2 of the Statute, the Court held that:

> although in their ordinary meaning, both terms in a general sense denote opposing views, the term 'contestation' is wider in scope than the term 'différend' and does not require the same degree of opposition; whereas, compared to the term 'différend' the concept underlying the term 'contestation' is more flexible in its application to a particular situation; whereas … the term 'dispute' in English also may have a more flexible meaning than that generally accorded to it in Article 36, § 2 Statute.[80]

In its judgment the Court reaffirmed its position that the existence of a dispute/contestation under Article 60 of the Statute was not subject to the same criteria as that of 'dispute' referred to in Article 36, para. 2.[81] Contestation expressed during negotiations may though be *the start* of the coming into being of a dispute in the sense of Article 36, para. 2.

In the circumstances of the case the Court weighed on the one hand that a 'variety of factors suggest that there is a difference of perception that would constitute a dispute' under Article 60.[82] These elements 'could suggest a dispute between the Parties within the sense of 60'.

On the other hand, the Court found 'factors that suggest, on the contrary, that there is no dispute between the Parties'.[83] Thus the Court actively searched for factors indicating both ways. Pursuant to Article 98, para. 2 of the Rules of Court a party has to indicate 'the precise point or points in dispute as to the meaning or scope of the judgment'.[84]

---

76 *Continental Shelf case between Tunisia and Libya, I.C.J. Reports 1982*, at p. 39, para. 26.

77 A. Guelke, 'Negotiations and Peace Processes', p. 73.

78 A. Guelke, 'Negotiations and Peace Processes', p. 73.

79 A. Guelke, 'Negotiations and Peace Processes', p. 74.

80 *Request for Interpretation of the Avena judgment, I.C.J. Reports 2008*, at p. 325, para. 53.

81 *Request for Interpretation of the Judgment of 31 March 2004 in the Case concerning* Avena and Other Mexican Nationals (Mexico v. United States of America) *(Mexico v. United States of America), Judgment, I.C.J. Reports 2009*, p. 3, at p. 9, para. 17.

82 *Request for Interpretation of the Avena judgment, I.C.J. Reports 2009*, at p. 13, para. 31.

83 *Ibid.*, at p. 14, para. 35 and at pp. 14–15, para. 36.

84 *Ibid.*, at p. 15, para. 38.

5.4 A Different Key Holder in Advisory Proceedings?

When in contentious cases the existence of the dispute may be the subject of disagreement between the parties, the question arises whether a similar situation may present itself on the occasion of advisory proceedings given the absence, in most cases that is, of 'parties' before the Court.

Obviously the starting point for looking into this question is that when the Court has to pronounce itself 'on legal issues upon which radically divergent views exist' between a State and the UN, and this in order to answer the question submitted to it, this 'does not convert the (present) case into a dispute nor bring it within the compass of Article 82 and 83 of the Rules of Court'.[85] As in daily life of international relations 'differences of views among States on legal issues have existed in practically every advisory proceeding; if all were agreed, the need to resort to the Court for advice would not arise'.[86]

However, material submitted to the Court may 'indicate that' when a particular resolution was adopted by the General Assembly, 'there appeared to be a legal dispute between' two Member States, but not between one of them and a third State,[87] the requesting resolution referring to a 'legal controversy'.[88] Hence there is no difficulty in acknowledging that statements made within the framework of an organ of an IO may give rise to a *legal controversy*.

It is then not surprising that in advisory proceedings it is normally the organ requesting the opinion (or in appropriate cases the IO's Secretary-General) which has come to the conclusion that a difference or controversy or dispute has actually arisen and which requires the Court's assistance in solving it, either more directly by answering the question the organ's majority had decided to submit or indirectly by providing an answer to the more procedural question whether for instance there is an obligation for the State involved to enter into a process of arbitration.[89,90]

In the *Wall case* the Court ruled that 'the subject-matter of the General Assembly request can(not) be regarded as only a bilateral matter between Israel and Palestine' as the GA considers to have 'permanent responsibility towards the question of Palestine until the question is resolved in all its aspects in a satisfactory manner in accordance with international legitimacy'.[91]

There is thus not that much of a difference with regard to the entity which first claims that there exists a dispute which is in need of being solved. In contentious cases one of the parties will normally have taken this position at a certain moment in time, whereas in the pre-advisory stage it will normally be the organ dealing with a particular matter under a Privileges and Immunities Convention or otherwise which reaches a similar conclusion, provisional in nature because depending on the Court's ultimate assessment about the existence or not of a dispute.

5.5 Negotiations as a Mechanism to Clarify the Respective Legal Claims

After the eruption in full force of a dispute negotiations may become necessary in order to bring about further clarification of the opposing claims of the parties in order afterwards to determine the *petitum* in case of adjudication.

The Court has regularly and clearly emphasized that in its function of determining and crystallizing a dispute, negotiations must lead the parties to adopt 'clearly-defined legal positions as against each other'.[92] Whereas such opposition is essential to bring about the existence of a dispute, an exchange of diplomatic

85 *Namibia Advisory Opinion, I.C.J. Reports 1971*, at p. 24, para. 34.

86 *Ibid.*, at p. 24, para. 34.

87 *Western Sahara, Order of 22 May 1975, I.C.J. Reports 1975*, p. 6, at pp. 7and 8.

88 *Western Sahara Advisory Opinion, I.C.J. Reports 1975*, at p. 14, para. 2.

89 *Applicability of Article VI, Section 22, of the Convention on the Privileges and Immunities of the United Nations, Order of 14 June 1989*, p. 9, at pp. 9–10.

90 *Cumaraswamy Advisory Opinion, I.C.J. Reports 1999*, at p. 69, para. 9 (UN Legal Counsel).

91 *Wall Advisory Opinion, I.C.J. Reports 2004*, at p. 159, para. 49.

92 *Right of Passage case, I.C.J. Reports 1960*, at p. 34.

notes may not have led to any clarification of the legal positions,[93] perhaps as a result of incidents occurring in a disputed area.[94]

It is paramount for the parties to reckon with the classic ruling of the Court about the very essence of its judicial function, namely to 'pronounce judgment only in connection with concrete cases where there exist at the time of the adjudication an actual controversy involving a conflict of legal interests between the parties'.[95]

Hence during the course of negotiations in order to conclude a Special Agreement parties have to take care not to submit to the Court questions which situate themselves 'outside the sphere in which a Court of Justice, concerned with the application of rules of law, can help in the solution of disputes between two States'[96] as 'it is always a matter for the determination of the Court whether its judicial functions are involved'.[97]

In some cases the Court will delineate the *petitum* by indicating what it is *not* called upon to declare or to do.[98]

An Applicant may argue that its constant protest against the violation of claimed rights, coupled with raising the state responsibility of the other party, makes it impossible to consider the negotiations *not* to be situated on the legal plane. Hence, negotiations may make clear beyond doubt, in the eyes of (one of) the parties, the existence of a dispute between them.[99] Parties may hold diverging views on the very nature, let alone the scope of talks between them.

A Respondent contending that the Court is without jurisdiction may ask the Court to declare that the controversy has actually ended.[100]

Meetings took place between officials of both foreign ministries 'concerning contentious issues between the two States' but 'the Parties do not agree on the content and significance of those discussions'.[101]

The Court may for instance also find that the Respondent did not provide it 'with any further details of these negotiations, *in particular with regard to the way in which they have been carried out, or their duration, scope or state of progress* at the time' an Application was filed.[102] Negotiations may be held the content of which remains unclear. Discussions during 'consultations' may focus on the applicability of the compromissory clause itself.[103]

5.6 Negotiations and the Determination of the Critical Date

The opinion has been voiced that the case law supports the view 'that it has never been the concern of the Court' to 'ascertain the exact date on which a dispute came into being'. In general it has no importance whether it arose long ago or just prior to the start of the proceedings. Only 'in the context of territorial disputes' does the Court 'concern itself with determining the exact date on which the dispute between the parties crystallized' because of reasons related to their specific nature. But in 'all other situations' the notion of 'crystallization of the dispute' is inoperative'.[104]

93 *Corfu Channel case, I.C.J. Reports 1949*, at p. 30.

94 *Right of Passage case, I.C.J. Reports 1960*, at p. 34.

95 *The Northern Cameroons case, I.C.J. Reports 1963*, at p. 33–4.

96 *Free Zones case, P.C.I.J., Series A/B, No. 46*, p. 162 as cited in the *Northern Cameroons case, I.C.J. Reports 1963*, at p. 30.

97 *The Northern Cameroons case, I.C.J. Reports 1963*, at p. 30.

98 For an example see *Northern Cameroons case, I.C.J. Reports 1963*, at p. 32.

99 *Right of Passage case, I.C.J. Reports 1957*, at p. 135.

100 *Territorial and Maritime Dispute (Nicaragua v. Colombia), I.C.J. Reports 2007*, at p. 839, para. 12.

101 *Ibid.*, at p. 847, para. 32.

102 *Arrest Warrant case, I.C.J. Reports 2000*, at p. 200, para. 66.

103 *PLO case Advisory Opinion, I.C.J. Reports 1988*, Separate opinion by Judge Oda, at p. 40, para. 8.

104 *CERD case, I.C.J. Reports 2011*, Separate opinion by Judge Abraham, at p. 229, paras. 16 and 17. On the importance of the critical date see *inter alia* the *Croatian Genocide case, I.C.J. Reports 2008*, at p. 438, para. 80.

In territorial disputes the critical date is 'not the date at which the situation concerning the disputed territory is claimed to have become established, but the date at which it became evident that there was a dispute in existence over the territory'.[105]

However, also in different types of cases, the determination of the exact time when the dispute arose, the critical date, obviously plays an important role, for instance, in determining the Court's jurisdiction and the admissibility of the claim – because of the Court's assessment whether (one of) the parties have failed to (have attempted to) negotiate – and once more illustrates the functional interaction between the two modes of peaceful settlement.

Negotiations could be part of a sequence of acts and events situating themselves prior to or after that critical date. In the latter case they can be taken into consideration by the Court provided they 'are a normal continuation of prior acts and are not undertaken for the purpose of improving the legal position of the Party which relies on them'.[106] On the other hand, negotiations preceding the siesin of the Court contribute to postponing the submission of the dispute to the Court and make the determination of the critical date more complex.[107]

The particular circumstances of each case make it rather hazardous if not impossible to formulate any general rule or principle with regard to fixing the critical date. The critical date may be determined by the Court as the moment, for instance, a proposal to start negotiations was made, when the other party had accepted an offer to hold negotiations; when a protest was voiced; when a final and negative reply was given by one party; or when a deadlock was reached.

Object and critical date are linked to the extent that the dispute results from a claim and the rejection of it. These claims may evolve, hence the dispute may become evolutive, partly solved, partly persisted, altered on some points; hence the Court determines as well as its subject-matter 'all of the critical dates which may exist across the various stages of a dispute which is still evolving'.[108]

The Court 'cannot take into consideration acts having taken place after the date on which the dispute between the Parties crystallized unless such acts are a normal continuation of prior acts and are not undertaken for the purpose of improving the legal position of the Party which relies on them'.[109]

When we leave out of consideration for the moment the related issue of the judicial requirement about how parties should conduct themselves during the process of negotiations, the process of influencing by such acts can be twofold: such acts by nature do have an impact on ongoing negotiations and eventually lead to their failure; on the other hand also by nature participation in negotiations would include in most cases as one of the aims the recognition if not the improvement of a party's legal position, which could be part of the overall objective of the process, namely the peaceful *settlement* of the dispute.

Merely a *proposal to start negotiations* was seen by the Court as 'to mark the inception of the dispute over the land boundary'.[110]

In other situations the dispute will exist long before that time, but it will be sharpened, deepened and more precisely determined through the process of negotiations.

In bilateral relations there may occur 'growing crystallization' of the dispute which then later become 'more clearly articulated'.[111]

While negotiations may thus have marked 'the inception of the dispute over the land boundary', in contrast, the 'maritime dispute was slower to come to light'.[112]

105 H. Thirlway, 'The Law and Procedure of the International Court of Justice 1960–1989. Supplement, 2009: Parts Seven and Eight', 79.

106 *Indonesia/Malaysia case, I.C.J. Reports 2002*, at p. 682, para. 135 as cited by the Court in the *Territorial and Maritime Dispute (Nicaragua v. Colombia), I.C.J. Reports 2012*, at p. 652, para. 68.

107 B. Metou, *Le rôle du juge*, p. 295, note 33.

108 *Belgium v. Senegal case, I.C.J. Reports 2012*, Dissenting opinion by Judge *ad hoc* Sur, at p. 606, para. 7. That a dispute which is both a political and legal one takes various forms and passes through various stages had already been observed by Vice-President Badawi in the *Right of Passage case, I.C.J. Reports 1960*, Dissenting opinion, at p. 160.

109 *Indonesia/Malaysia case, I.C.J. Reports 2002*, at p. 682, para. 135.

110 *Land, Island and Maritime Frontier Dispute, I.C.J. Reports 1992*, at p. 381, para. 31.

111 *CERD case, I.C.J. Reports 2011*, Separate opinion by Judge Owada, at p. 176, para. 17.

112 *Land, Island and Maritime Frontier Dispute, I.C.J. Reports 1992*, at p. 381, para. 32.

In other cases negotiations will give rise to the actual coming into being of the dispute or to its (re) discovery: a 'claim, not having been settled by diplomatic means, has given rise to a legal dispute of an international character between the two States'.[113]

In case of *interrelated* disputes there is not necessarily one critical date. It might then be necessary for the Court to distinguish here between two critical dates: one for the islands claims – when the Memorial was submitted to the Court; and one of delimitation of the disputed maritime area with regard to which the exchange of letters 'did not mark the point at which the dispute crystallized' as 'no claims or counter-claims were articulated by the two parties at the time and the suggested process of negotiations came to nought' but the occurrence of two incidents when the parties disagreed about the existence of a 'traditionally accepted line'.[114]

Does *the acceptance of an offer to hold negotiations* mark the 'critical date'?[115]

Because the dispute over maritime delimitation may encompass by implication the dispute over some islands, does the critical date for both disputes coincide?[116] Or is it at the earliest the day when the Applicant filed its Memorial asserting for the first time 'a particular claim as the diplomatic correspondence exchanges between the two countries makes no mention of those maritime features'?[117]

Acceptance of the invitation 'to initiate conversations leading to a definitive marine and sub-marine delimitation' allegedly 'did not mark the crystallization of any dispute as no conflicting claims were raised at the time'.[118] This question underlines the importance of the start of or the acceptance of an offer to negotiate on the determination of the critical date in the context of assessing the *effectivités*.

The (dys)functional link between the two means of settlement is also apparent here because for the first time a claim is being asserted in the Memorial while allegedly that claim was not or was made prior to the Memorial during the pre-adjudicative negotiations. The real subject-matter of the negotiations and eventual claims raised during the process were thus crucially important in this respect in order to determine the critical date.

Conversely, the timing of a dispute arising has an important legal significance for the question of negotiations as well: when was an attempt made and what was the subject-matter, as amply demonstrated by the second preliminary objections in the *CERD case*.

Negotiations aiming at for instance delimitation can take place outside the context of the crystallization process of a dispute in case no opposing claims are or have been made, thus there being no dispute (yet).

This is in line with the multiple roles of negotiations mentioned earlier: to find for instance an agreement on delimitation without there being a dispute at all; the other settlement of dispute orientation and function in case of a pre-existing dispute; providing the parties an opportunity to formulate their respective and opposing claims in a clear manner giving rise to the crystallization of a dispute. Hence the importance for parties to formulate their claims from the start or during the negotiations on the subject-matters of those talks in order to bring about the crystallization of the dispute: because as long as that has not happened, the negotiations do not have that *legal effect* in the subsequent link with the judicial proceedings dealing with the dispute.

The critical date is the moment in time when the dispute crystallized, for instance *as result of protest voiced*,[119] or when the parties have 'clearly recognized in writing the existence of a dispute' and 'have set the framework for future negotiations' regarding maritime delimitation, that agreement's 'provisions regarding the existence of the dispute' being 'a mere confirmation of a factual situation that had already existed for a long time'.[120]

---

113 *Certain Norwegian Loans Case, I.C.J. Reports 1957*, at p. 15 and at p. 17 (France).

114 *Territorial and Maritime Dispute between Nicaragua and Honduras, I.C.J. Reports 2007*, at p. 700, para. 129, at p. 699, para. 123, and at pp. 700–701, para. 130.

115 As Nicaragua argued in the *Territorial and Maritime Dispute between Nicaragua and Honduras, I.C.J. Reports 2007*, at p. 687, para. 76.

116 *Ibid.*, at p. 698, para. 121 (Nicaragua).

117 *Ibid.*, at p. 688, para. 81 and at pp. 698–9, para. 122 (Honduras).

118 *Ibid.*, at p. 699, para. 122 (Honduras).

119 *Sovereignty case between Malaysia and Singapore, I.C.J. Reports 2008*, at p. 28, para. 34.

120 *Maritime Delimitation in the Black Sea, I.C.J. Reports 2009*, at pp. 125–6, para. 194 (Romania).

It has been rightly pointed out that 'the dispute must have 'crystallized' at the same moment for each of the parties to it; but they may nevertheless not agree on the identification of that moment'.[121] For instance, although the Respondent may consider the start of negotiations between itself and a third party over particular maritime features, which were excluded from the scope of an earlier treaty, as the critical date, it may ultimately limit itself to taking note of the critical date proposed by the Applicant – namely an exchange of notes containing opposing claims and protests.[122] The Applicant becoming aware of these negotiations between the Respondent and a third State may then be well advised to reserve its rights over the relevant maritime features.[123]

In another situation where an exchange of divergent opinions on a clearly defined legal question is followed by negotiations that quite rapidly reach a *deadlock*,[124] it is important to determine when the negotiations actually took place in order to determine the critical date. *A negative reply containing the final and considered view* of one party has then been taken by the Court as the start of the dispute as submitted to it.[125] Discussions may also be held without reaching any conclusion accepted by the two parties.[126]

Under a phased and elaborated compromissory clause it can be important to determine through the diplomatic exchanges when there was an impasse.[127] Following a deadlock over a particular aspect of a dispute parties may agree to suspend the negotiation and choose that breakdown as the *critical date* in respect of their larger dispute concerning sovereignty, an issue which 'arose only as a result of the Parties' manoeuvring for better bargaining positions' in the delimitation part.[128]

Compromissory clauses may themselves govern in general terms the determination of the critical date by providing that the treaty shall not apply to disputes relating to facts or situations prior to the entry into force of the convention. The 'critical issue is not the date when the dispute arose, but the date of the facts or situations in relation to which the dispute arose'.[129]

Oral hearings might help the Court to identify when the dispute arose and the date of the facts and situation to which the dispute related. The Court may then be able to establish which claims had been the object of 'repeated attempts to reach an agreement'.[130]

That differences of opinion and complaints about the 'way and method of settlement do not count with regard to determining the applicability of the relevant time clause'[131] seems also to apply to negotiations as a mechanism of peaceful settlement.

In the exercise of its advisory function in a quasi-contentious fashion the Court might feel no need for the purposes of an advisory opinion 'to seek to determine the date at which the dispute came into existence, once the Court has reached the conclusion that there is such a dispute at the date on which its opinion is given'.[132]

Although with regard to the existence and the nature of a dispute the Court's point of reference is the Application[133] – existence which could *inter alia* also be demonstrated for instance through the exchanges between two permanent representatives in the Security Council and the claim and the rejection of it[134] – it is also well established that a dispute must not only exist at the time of the start of the proceedings but must continue 'to exist at the time the Court makes its decision'.[135] This may be considered to be a clear judicial reference to the functional interaction as it may operate after the start of the proceedings, and to the operational aspects of which we will turn in Chapter 6.

---

121 H. Thirlway, 'The Law and Procedure of the International Court of Justice 1960–1989. Supplement, 2009: Parts Seven and Eight', 80.

122 *Territorial and Maritime Dispute (Nicaragua v. Colombia), I.C.J. Reports 2012*, at pp. 652–3, paras. 69 and 70.

123 *Ibid.*, at p. 658, para. 87.

124 *Interhandel Case, I.C.J. Reports 1959*, at p. 21.

125 *Ibid.*

126 *Ibid.*

127 *Pulp Mills case, I.C.J. Reports 2010*, Separate opinion by Judge *ad hoc* Torres Bernardez, at p. 262, para. 94.

128 *Indonesia/Malaysia case, I.C.J. Reports 2002*, Declaration by Judge Oda, at pp. 688 and 689.

129 *Germany v. Italy case, I.C.J. Reports 2010*, at p. 317, para. 18.

130 *Ibid.*, Declaration by Judge *ad hoc* Gaja, at p. 398.

131 *Ibid.*, Dissenting opinion by Judge Cançado Trindade, at p. 353, para. 58 (referring to Germany's argument).

132 *PLO case Advisory Opinion, I.C.J. Reports 1988*, at p. 30, para. 44.

133 *Nuclear Tests (New Zealand v. France), I.C.J. Reports 1974*, at p. 463, para. 24.

134 *CERD case, I.C.J. Reports 2011*, at p. 120, para. 113.

135 *Nuclear Tests (New Zealand v. France), I.C.J. Reports 1974*, at p. 476, para. 58.

5.7 A Refusal to Enter into the Process

A Word from Negotiation Scholars

While 'in practice, the circumstances on which parties are willing to enter into negotiations vary widely',[136] what can negotiation scholars tells us about the refusal to enter into the process?

Admitting the existence of a dispute does not necessarily mean that the parties are willing to take part in negotiations[137] unless sometimes pressured into it by third parties through some preliminary work 'embracing more states than those directly concerned'.[138]

It may be within the context of or as a result of *pourparlers* that a party decides not to enter into the process of negotiations. Pourparlers 'are informal discussions, generally preliminary to substantive negotiations and having the objective of promoting peaceful settlement'.[139]

Sometimes 'what appears to be a refusal to negotiate is the rejection rather of a particular form or method of negotiation'.[140] Difference in power levels especially 'when the vital interests of the more powerful country are involved'[141] is 'one of the factors of prime importance which' may bring a party to refuse to enter into negotiation, although such refusal may also result from 'reason of a deep moral aversion' towards the party's counterpart.[142]

A potential cost-benefit analysis may bring a party to refuse to negotiate and instead to pursue a unilateral alternative provided this is 'clearly superior in terms of its expected value to any possible negotiated agreement',[143] for instance unilateral seisin of the Court. Conversely, attempts by one party to negotiate may reach a deadlock owing to the other party's refusal 'to enter into any discussion into the matter' and which may bring a State to file its Application.[144]

Although 'systematic empirical evidence' may be lacking, or perhaps even difficult to get access to, negotiation scholars believe 'that on average parties too often refuse to enter into negotiations where it would make sense'. Hence, parties 'should begin their decision-making process from a presumption – rebuttable to be sure – in favour of entering into negotiations'.[145]

A Judicial Word

A public rejection of a claim may (temporarily) close the door to any possible negotiations.[146]

A flat refusal by the potential Respondent to accept an appropriate resort to a procedure of conciliation or recourse to the UN could not be assumed in advance when that country 'subsequently had to accept an invitation with much graver consequences, e.g. that of entrusting the settlement of the whole dispute to the Security Council, although it later raised an objection to a reference to the Court'.[147]

In case parties disagree over the existence of a dispute, one party may take the view that entering into the PSD procedure provided for in a compromissory clause is not 'timely' or 'appropriate' as it is willing to enter into consultations over the matter on a purely informal basis, as there is no dispute,[148] while the other party is convinced that there does exist a dispute given its claim with regard to the other party's behaviour or

136 A. Guelke, 'Negotiations and Peace Processes', p. 63.
137 A. Lall, *Modern International Negotiation*, p. 27.
138 A. Lall, *Modern International Negotiation*, p. 56.
139 A. Lall, *Modern International Negotiation*, p. 18.
140 A. Lall, *Modern International Negotiation*, p. 130.
141 A. Lall, *Modern International Negotiation*, p. 132.
142 G. Blum and R. Mnookin, 'When *Not* to Negotiate', p. 107.
143 G. Blum and R. Mnookin, 'When *Not* to Negotiate', pp. 101 and 103.
144 *Hostages case, I.C.J. Reports 1980*, at p. 27, para. 51.
145 G. Blum and R. Mnookin, 'When *Not* to Negotiate', p. 110.
146 *Aerial Incident between Pakistan and India, I.C.J. Reports 2000*, Dissenting opinion by Judge *ad hoc* Pirzada, at p. 62, para. 1.
147 *Corfu Channel case, I.C.J. Reports 1949*, Dissenting opinion by Judge Azevedo, at p. 111.
148 *PLO case Advisory Opinion, I.C.J. Reports 1988*, at p. 25, para. 29 and at p. 20, para. 18.

decision, and that both parties are under an obligation to enter into the PSD procedure, the first part of which are negotiations.[149] The Court may then conclude that the obligations deriving from a compromissory clause prevail over the question of the 'appropriateness' of arbitration.[150]

Unless the party changes its attitude afterwards, the refusal to even enter into the process of negotiations inevitably carries with it the assessment – first by the party that had taken the initiative for negotiations and later by the Court – that 'in consequence, there existed at that date not only a dispute, but, beyond doubt, a "dispute" ... not satisfactorily adjusted by diplomacy' within the meaning of the relevant compromissory clause.[151]

The tone of certain remarks by one party may not have been quite appropriate; the Court may still consider that 'overall' that party 'did not dismiss the possibility of future negotiations on the armed activities in which it was engaged at the time'. However, in the circumstances of the case, the Court may consider the Respondent's (un)willingness towards negotiations on that matter to be of no relevance.[152]

Is that really so, or should the Court take into account the position of one party towards negotiations on a different but related dispute when ascertaining that party's attitude towards the subject-matter that did reach the Court?

Remarks by both sides regarding the prospects of talks not pertaining to matters which are the subject of an Application do not terminate the possibility of negotiations relating to the subject-matter before the Court in case such negotiations were 'never genuinely or specifically attempted' according to the Court.[153]

The Court may 'be unable to consider' statements by the Applicant as genuine attempts to negotiate relevant matters, although they attest 'to the existence of a dispute on a subject-matter capable of falling' under the relevant Convention.[154]

Does this mean that in the Court's view States should be unambiguous and straightforward when it comes to their position as to whether or not to be willing to engage in negotiations on the subject-matter of a particular dispute? If that is the case, this condition should be added to the Court requirements on good faith, which starts with the clear intention to enter into (pre)negotiations.

A Respondent's refusal to negotiate two days prior to the filing of an Application is insufficient to vest the Court with jurisdiction under the applicable compromissory clause.[155]

As the facts of the record may show no attempt by the Applicant to negotiate relevant matters, the Court may conclude that the parties 'did not engage in negotiations with respect' to compliance with the substantive obligations as required by the compromissory clause.[156]

Could one infer from this that it is only the Applicant that should have made an attempt? The last part of the Court's *dictum* does not provide us with a clear answer as 'accusations and replies ... on the issue of " extermination" and " ethnic cleansing" attest to the existence of a dispute between them on a subject-matter capable of falling under CERD. However, they fail to demonstrate an attempt at negotiating these matters.'[157]

In the case law a distinction can be drawn between *a mere refusal to enter into negotiations* resulting in the deadlock of attempts to negotiate and *failed negotiations* once they have been embarked upon. In the latter case the ICJ considers the attribution of the responsibility for the failure as irrelevant, whereas in the former situation the identification of and the attribution to the refusing party is a given.

Admittedly, a Respondent might be 'right in dismissing' wholesale 'completely unfounded' allegations and hence refuse 'to enter into negotiations over artificial claims which, in its opinion, do not warrant negotiation'.[158]

149 *Ibid.*, at p. 19, para. 16.
150 *Ibid.*, at p. 29, para. 40.
151 *Hostages case, I.C.J. Reports 1980*, at p. 27, para. 51.
152 *CERD case, I.C.J. Reports 2011*, at p. 139, para. 180.
153 *Ibid.*
154 *Ibid.*, at p. 139, para. 181.
155 *Ibid.*, at p. 139, para. 182.
156 *Ibid.*, at p. 140, para. 182.
157 *Ibid.*, at p. 139, para. 181.
158 *Ibid.*, Joint dissenting opinion, at p. 168, para. 85.

At the same time there should be no room for intentional dysfunctional interaction in case of preconditional prior negotiations by a putative respondent artificially prolonging negotiations 'while declining to negotiate in good faith' in order to 'prevent the exercise of jurisdiction by the Court'.[159]

5.8 Deadlock in the Negotiations

A Word from Negotiation Scholars

'The breaking-off of a negotiation is a fait accompli', whereas 'deadlock is an event one stage before break-off', a situation in which each 'side issues a tacit message' to the other side 'concerning the possible interruption of the process or, if it is already viewed as a stalemate, the restarting of the discussions'.[160]

A 'basic concept in negotiation analysis',[161] a '*deadlock* is an impasse in terms of position, a situation in which no concessions or constructive action takes place', although the 'absence of concessions does not necessarily mean that both parties are caught in a deadlock'.[162]

Realism dictates to acknowledge that it 'seldom happens that long and complex negotiations reach completion without any period of deadlock'.[163]

Deadlock may be seen as 'an omen of a failed negotiation' but also 'as the sign of a well-conducted process in which everyone has explored the possibilities to their limits'.[164]

Deadlock may be caused by the parties waiting 'to open negotiations until conditions in the external environment are perfect'. Negotiations 'on some of the preliminary or surface issues may help to create an atmosphere more conducive to tackling the deeper issues in dispute at a later stage'.[165]

A situation of deadlock occurs 'when both parties behave conflictually and reciprocate this non-cooperation in a seemingly endless spiral',[166] for instance through the use of redundant arguments, and parties sticking to their initially stated positions which are incompatible: then a deadlock is reached.[167]

Causes of deadlock have been diagnosed as comprising cognitive and perceptual aspects (different views about the final purpose are not being acknowledged by the other party); personal and relational causes of prestige and reputation; contextual causes (settings of a social, political or legal nature); and structural causes (nothing more can be given).[168]

In a situation of deadlock unilateral initiatives, signalling a clear desire to de-escalate the conflict, may be taken by one party as a 'cooperative response to the other's noncooperative behaviour' with the aim 'to encourage a positive, cooperative response from the other party, usually reciprocity'.[169]

A so-called 'hurting stalemate' may 'be *functional* for making breakthroughs in negotiation' when 'parties locked in a dispute' do 'realize that neither can benefit from continuation' and that 'both have no choice but to reach a negotiated accommodation'[170] and thus to restore the process.[171]

A forward-looking strategy (future development-oriented) initiated by one of the parties, to substitute backward looking approach (positions based on legalities of past titles) which may have caused a deadlock may render a solution possible.[172]

---

159 *Ibid.*, Separate opinion by Judge Greenwood, at p. 328, para. 12.
160 G. Faure, 'Deadlocks', p. 26.
161 G. Faure, 'Deadlocks', p. 49.
162 G. Faure, 'Deadlocks', p. 25.
163 G. Faure, 'Deadlocks', p. 27.
164 G. Faure, 'Deadlocks', p. 27.
165 T. Hopmann, *The Negotiation Process*, p. 202.
166 T. Hopmann, *The Negotiation Process*, p. 183.
167 G. Faure, 'Deadlocks', p. 24.
168 G. Faure, 'Deadlocks', pp. 31–4.
169 T. Hopmann, *The Negotiation Process*, pp. 184–5.
170 T. Hopmann, *The Negotiation Process*, p. 206, referring to Touval and Zartman (emphasis added).
171 G. Faure, 'Deadlocks', pp. 23–4.
172 W. Zartman, 'Looking Forward and Looking Backward', pp. 291 and 295.

Differing views of the problem to be solved may give rise to a type of deadlock which 'do[es] not elicit a conflictual spiral' and is not 'an indication of a negotiation failure, but rather the sign of a motionless process, so paralysis rather than death'.[173]

Pursuant to relevant General Assembly Resolutions, the view has been put forward that in case of deadlock States 'should seek out another dispute settlement mechanism to move the process forward'.[174] It should be noted that doing justice to (past) legal claims and the construction of future peaceful relations are not mutually exclusive as negotiations scholars seem to believe. In this sense deadlock may provide an opportunity 'to move into a de-escalation process',[175] e.g. by starting proceedings before the ICJ.

A Judicial Approach to Deadlock

As indicated earlier, prior negotiations are not the only points of reference for the Court to assess *the stage of development of the dispute* between parties. Equally important is their conduct during the proceedings.

In his seminal article on prior negotiations Santiago Torres Bernardez rightly pointed to the role of the pleadings in the Court's assessment of negotiations. He identified four different scenarios: the deadlock may still be there; there is no chance for resumed negotiations; there is no deadlock; and there is a chance of resumed negotiations.[176] Our concern here is with the first two scenarios; the latter ones will be dealt with in the next chapter.

One should be aware that a legal controversy may remain 'in a latent state' for a period of years,[177] for instance during a period when no negotiations are taking place or any form of exchange of views. This situation does not automatically and in all cases qualify as a 'deadlock' in the negotiations, and it applies to all kinds of negotiations and all disputes between States, whether within or without the framework of an organ of an IO.

In its presentation of the facts, the Court may feel obliged to describe in some detail 'the nature' of the prior negotiations[178] to interpret and to give some *qualifications* to those prior negotiations. For instance, negotiations may reach an 'early deadlock'[179] also in order to bring to light what was the main reason they have broken down.[180]

Negotiations may break down as a result of the refusal by one party to discuss the legal aspects of a particular matter within the framework of a broader conference to discuss various territorial matters in dispute.[181]

The diplomatic exchanges may not only disclose the existence of a dispute but also that negotiations have reached a deadlock.[182] It is up to the State claiming that the negotiations should have been pursued to prove their insufficiency. This proof may be hard to adduce in case the available documents contain certain contrary indications.[183]

A party may invoke the (new) terms of reference of an organ of the UN within the framework of which negotiations were held before, in order to argue that, in its view, it is 'doubtful whether there is any hope that new negotiations within the scope' of those terms of reference will lead to any positive results.[184]

A deadlock reached in such collective negotiations may indeed, as Torres Bernardez observed, be confirmed later on by the arguments put before the Court.

Even 'cursory examination of the views, propositions and arguments consistently maintained by the two sides' may convince the Court that an impasse was reached prior to the institution of the proceedings and that

173 G. Faure, 'Deadlocks', p. 28.
174 C. Hutchinson, 'The Duty to Negotiate', 146, commenting on 2625, § 1 and Manila § 7.
175 G. Faure, 'Deadlocks', p. 25.
176 Torres Bernardez, 'Are Prior Negotiations?', p. 515, para. 30.
177 *Western Sahara Advisory Opinion, I.C.J. Reports 1975*, at p. 26, para. 36.
178 *North Sea Continental Shelf case, I.C.J. Reports 1969*, at p. 16, para. 5.
179 *Fisheries Jurisdiction cases, I.C.J. Reports 1974*, at p. 201, para. 68 and at p. 32, para. 76.
180 *North Sea Continental Shelf case, I.C.J. Reports 1969*, at p. 17, para. 7.
181 *Temple of Preah Vihear case, I.C.J. Reports 1962*, at p. 32.
182 *Right of Passage case, I.C.J. Reports 1957*, at p. 149.
183 *Ibid.*, at p. 135 (Portugal).
184 *South West Africa cases, I.C.J. Reports 1962*, at p. 345 (South Africa).

it continued to exist.[185] Adding to this the new terms of reference, it was possible for the Court to conclude that there is no real possibility that further negotiations would lead to a settlement.[186] In such a situation the chances that the Court would invite or even order the parties to resume negotiations during the course of the proceedings are almost nonexistent.

A compromissory clause may provide that the dispute must 'not have been satisfactorily adjusted by diplomacy'. Resort 'to a diplomatic move to settle the dispute would appear to be a condition essential before submitting the case' to the ICJ, although 'negotiations have not been specifically prescribed as a *sine qua non*'.[187] Under these terms it 'is not always necessarily the case' that 'diplomatic negotiations must be ascertained to have been first begun and then pursued, and finally to have broken down'.[188]

In the *CERD case* the Applicant argued that 'the ordinary meaning of the phrase "*is not* settled" as opposed to "*cannot* be settled by negotiation" only requires evidence that (it) has made an attempt at negotiations and not that such negotiations have reached a deadlock'.[189]

According to the Respondent the Court's jurisprudence has shown that the Court takes into account several factors when it is 'evaluating whether or not negotiations have been attempted and have reached deadlock, such as the duration of the negotiations and the authenticity of the efforts to reach a negotiated conclusion'.[190] Review of the case law then can lead to the conclusion 'that whatever form they may take, substantially, negotiations are an exchange of points of view and facts, of mutual compromises in order to reach an agreement'.[191]

Past efforts to reach an agreement may have 'failed for a variety of reasons, many of them' deriving from 'the lack of direct communication, and the situation being dominated by factors unrelated to the specific nature of the dispute'.[192]

Failure of negotiations may ensue when during protracted diplomatic correspondence both parties maintain their points of view. This will happen when one party extending its original claim finds the other party not being prepared to agree to proposals tabled by the other side.[193]

A series of intergovernmental talks may not 'bring a solution to the matter' and given 'the *lack of progress* in the bilateral negotiations' parties may then decide to submit the dispute to the Court.[194] Perhaps only a thin line separates lack *of progress* from *failure*?

5.9 Failed Negotiations

The question whether prior negotiations did take place and whether or not they have failed is an objective one, in both a factual and legal sense. The initial assessment by (one of) the parties is subject to a monitoring assessment by the Court.

Multiple factors may lead to an assessment by either the parties or by the Court that negotiations have actually failed: there may have been a straightforward refusal by one of the parties to enter into the process altogether; parties may have been in good faith engaged for quite some time in proper negotiations on the subject-matter of the dispute or on the most appropriate method to solve the dispute when a point is reached where no further progress appears to be possible and deadlock is a reality; parties may also have continued negotiations after having overcome an impasse but then towards the very end of the talks a stalemate makes it impossible for them to bring the whole process to a successful conclusion and the failure of the whole process becomes a reality.

185 *Ibid.*, at p. 345.
186 *Ibid.*
187 *Nicaragua case, I.C.J. Reports 1984*, Separate opinion by Judge Singh, at pp. 444–6.
188 *Ibid.*, Separate opinion by Judge Ago, at p. 515, para. 4.
189 *CERD case, I.C.J. Reports 2011*, at p. 132, para. 155 (Georgia).
190 *Ibid.*, at p. 130, para. 150 (Russian Federation).
191 *Ibid.*, at pp. 130–31, para. 150 (Russian Federation).
192 *Hostages case, I.C.J. Reports 1980*, Separate opinion by Judge Lachs, at pp. 49–50.
193 *Certain Norwegian Loans Case, I.C.J. Reports 1957*, at pp. 19–20.
194 *Sovereignty case between Malaysia and Singpaore, I.C.J. Reports 2008*, at p. 27, para. 31 (emphasis added).

A Word from Negotiation Scholars

Interaction of tactics 'and modifications of positions not their unilateral pursuit'[195] determines the outcome of negotiations, and thus also their eventual failure.

Negotiations 'need to be judged for what they are and what they produce, and not be assigned a single pass-fail grade', as it would be inaccurate 'to ignore the distinction between conflict management' or 'minimal settlement' and 'full forward-looking transformation'.[196]

Backward-looking refusals of 'no recognition'[197] may result in either a concomitant refusal to enter into the process in the first place or to cause an almost immediate deadlock.

Case-studies have shown that '*forward-looking* outcomes are clearly closely related to success in negotiating conflict settlements and that *backward-looking* efforts bring failure'.[198]

Failure of negotiations does not necessarily flow from inappropriate conduct by (one of) the parties during the process; it may just simply result from the fact that they have been unable to agree;[199] a negotiated settlement 'may prove beyond' the capabilities of the parties which may have 'miscalculate[d] what they can achieve through negotiations'.[200]

In case any perspective of a successful resumption has definitively to be excluded, then it is only reasonable to admit that 'l'obligation de négocier est caduque faute d'objet',[201] thus paving the way for the functional interaction to come into play and for (one of) the parties to resort to adjudication.

> International negotiations should not be expected to succeed in one, two, or three rounds of discussion. Most issues require years of consideration, during which time a variety of procedures have to be tried. The outcome might then be some amelioration of the situation, with increased hope for a future settlement.[202]

Parties may disagree about the nature of the discussions they had

Before any assessment can be made of the alleged failure of negotiations, parties may disagree about the nature of the discussions they had before. Indeed, an Applicant may argue that it has unsuccessfully attempted to resolve the dispute by negotiations, while the Respondent contends that the 'diplomatic correspondence' relied on 'cannot be regarded as amounting to negotiations; that correspondence does not justify the conclusion that the supposed negotiations have failed'.[203]

A party may in its regular assessment of the process of negotiations within a pre-existing institutional bilateral framework come to the conclusion that the lack of agreement may require a different approach and propose direct negotiations; direct negotiations may then be held, bypassing the original institutional structure. This subsequent process may then ultimately be considered by the Applicant as having failed as well.[204]

A party may note another State's acknowledgement that the exchanges which have been taking place were 'within the framework of negotiations' as provided under a compromissory clause and recall its wish to open negotiations, and then conclude that 'the attempted negotiation' has not succeeded.[205]

---

195 T. Hopmann, *The Negotiation Process*, p. 180.

196 W. Zartman, 'Looking Forward and Looking Backward', p. 290.

197 W. Zartman, 'Looking Forward and Looking Backward', p. 291.

198 W. Zartman, 'Looking Forward and Looking Backward', p. 289 (emphasis added).

199 P. Reuter, 'De l'obligation de négocier', 729.

200 A. Guelke, 'Negotiations and Peace Processes', p. 71.

201 P. Reuter, 'De l'obligation de négocier', 729.

202 A. Lall, *Modern International Negotiation*, p. 3.

203 *Belgium v. Senegal case, I.C.J. Reports 2009*, at p. 150, para. 49.

204 *Pulp Mills case, I.C.J. Reports 2010*, Separate opinion by Judge *ad hoc* Torres Bernardez, at p. 254, paras. 66 and 68 and at p. 256, para. 72.

205 *Belgium v. Senegal case, I.C.J. Reports 2012*, Separate opinion by Judge Sebutinde, at p. 596, para. 18, referring to Belgium's arguments.

The response by the other party does not necessarily have to be interpreted as a refusal to enter into the process or as a demonstration of a failure or collapse of negotiations on the matter raised, but rather as a statement attesting the existence of a dispute.[206]

A declaration by one party that the negotiations have been 'unsuccessful' does not prevent further diplomatic exchanges indicating that the Applicant 'nonetheless continued *de facto* to negotiate'.[207] Prior negotiations in fact can continue, without failing, almost right up to the filing of an Application.[208]

A Word from the Court

If one assumes for the sake of argument that Article 36, para. 2 of the Court's Statute does require the definition of the dispute through prior negotiations as a condition for the exercise of the Court's jurisdiction, the Court may then consider that condition to be fulfilled 'to the extent permitted by the circumstances of the case'.[209]

A failure of prior negotiations conducted in good faith constitutes one of the scenarios for the Court to conclude that the prior negotiations condition has been fulfilled, the other situations being the process having become futile or deadlocked.[210]

The *CERD case* is once more a major point of reference as its case file demonstrates that issues have been raised in bilateral contacts between the parties, 'and that these issues have manifestly not been resolved by negotiation prior to the filing of the Application'.[211]

As the Court already made clear later in its judgment in the case the 'concept of "negotiations" differs from the concept of "dispute" and requires – at the very least – a genuine attempt by one of the disputing parties to engage in discussion with the other disputing party, with a view to resolving the dispute'.[212]

It is clear that a genuine attempt by (one of) the parties is the very minimum but sufficient requirement for discussions to qualify as negotiations; but it is equally clear that 'evidence of such an attempt to negotiate – or of the conduct of negotiations – does not require the reaching of an actual agreement between the disputing parties'.[213] In this respect the distinction between a *pactum de negotiando* and a *pactum de contrahendo* still stands firm.[214]

Who Decides Whether the Process Has Failed?

(One of) the parties

The ascertainment not only of whether negotiations have taken place but also, and more importantly for present purposes, 'whether they have failed, or become futile or deadlocked, are essentially questions of fact "for consideration in each case"'.[215]

In the *Pulp Mills case* referral to the Court took place on the basis of an Article 'which allows either Party to apply to the Court in the event of the negotiations failing to produce an agreement within the period of 180 days'.[216] After 12 meetings in a period of six months both parties may have determined 'that the negotiations undertaken within GTAN (a high level technical group)' have failed.[217]

---

206 *Ibid.*, Separate opinion by Judge Sebutinde, at p. 597, para. 21.

207 *Ibid.*, at p. 597, para. 22.

208 *Ibid.*, at p. 597, para. 23.

209 *Right of Passage case, I.C.J. Reports 1957*, at p. 149.

210 *CERD case, I.C.J. Reports 2011*, at p. 133, para. 159.

211 *CERD case, I.C.J. Reports 2008*, at p. 388, para. 115.

212 *CERD case, I.C.J. Reports 2011*, at p. 84, para. 30 and at p. 132, para. 157.

213 *Ibid.*, at p 132, para. 158; *Pulp Mills case, I.C.J. Reports 2010*, at p. 68, para. 150.

214 For instance 'Article 74 and 83 of UNCLOS do not require that delimitation negotiations should be successful; like other similar obligations in international law, the negotiations have to be conducted in good faith': *Land and Maritime Boundary case, I.C.J. Reports 2002*, at p. 424, para. 244.

215 *CERD case, I.C.J. Reports 2011*, at p. 133, para. 160.

216 *Pulp Mills case, I.C.J. Reports 2010*, at p. 64, para. 133 (Uruguay).

217 *Ibid.*, at p. 38, para. 40.

By authorizing the construction of a mill 'before the expiration of the negotiation' the Respondent failed to comply with the obligation to negotiate 'as it was laid down in the 1975 Statute'.[218] In this case it was for the parties to determine at a particular date that the negotiations have failed,[219] that is to say to determine prior to the instituting of the proceedings whether they have failed: determining whether there is a dispute and whether and when the negotiations have failed as a condition of jurisdiction/admissibility.

The Court concluded that the Respondent had breached its procedural obligations 'to inform, notify and negotiate to the extent and for the reasons given above'.[220]

Recognition that negotiations have actually failed may be the conclusion of an assessment carried out by either of the parties;[221] it may also be a joint decision.

A Party may notify the Court and thus also the other party that the negotiations have failed, and that no decision had been taken by the Heads of State 'to vary the procedures established by the Accord'; hence it may find itself *bound* to submit the dispute to the ICJ.[222]

In an arbitration agreement both parties may recognize that 'they have been unable to settle by means of diplomatic negotiations the dispute'.[223]

The Court's Assessment

In addition to a treaty provision, which explicitly confers the power to either of the parties to decide whether the period of negotiations is over, it will ultimately be for the Court to decide with hindsight, an exercise which may prove to be not without difficulty.[224]

Whether one or both of the parties must think that the dispute '*cannot be settled* by negotiations' is not really the question, but whether it '*can in fact* be settled by such means', and this issue has to be resolved by 'an objective evaluation by the Court of the possibilities for settlement of the dispute by direct negotiations'.[225]

However, the Court observed that as Article II of the Pact of Bogota refers to the opinion of the parties as to such possibility, consequently the Court 'does not have to make an objective assessment of such possibility, but to consider what is the *opinion of the Parties* thereon'.[226]

The Court must be free, 'in the exercise of its judicial function', to 'make its own determination' of the question 'whether the "opinion" of both Parties was that it was not possible to settle the dispute by negotiations'.[227]

Would it be possible then to infer that in other cases, where this assessment has not been explicitly reserved to the parties, the Court has to make such a judicial assessment?

The Court is assessing not only whether the Applicant 'genuinely attempted to engage in negotiations' but also if that should have been the case whether it 'pursued these negotiations as far as possible with a view to settling the dispute'.[228]

218 *Ibid.*, at pp. 67–8, para. 149.

219 *Ibid.*, at p. 38, para. 40 and at p. 70, para. 157.

220 *Ibid.*, at p. 70, para. 158.

221 See for instance *Dispute on the Maritime Delimitation in the Caribbean Sea and the Pacific Ocean*, Application by Costa Rica, dated 25 February 2014, Press Release No. 2014/11 of 26 February 2014 (text available on the Court's website).

222 *Territorial Dispute (Libyan Arab Jamahiriya/Chad), I.C.J. Reports 1994*, at p. 10, para. 3 (Libya).

223 *Arbitral Award case, I.C.J. Reports 1991*, at p. 58, para. 14.

224 A diplomatic note may refer to instructions given to a State representative to negotiate, followed by a publication giving 'some substance to the suggestion that as a result of those negotiations a protocol had been concluded in that connection': *Western Sahara Advisory Opinion, I.C.J. Reports 1975*, at p. 54, para. 121 (Morocco). Examination of the archives by the other party may not bring to light the existence of such a protocol; press publications on the subject at the time were erroneous: at pp. 54–5, para. 122 (Spain). Anyway, the material before the Court did not dispel the doubt raised as to the alleged protocol: at p. 55, para. 123.

225 *Border and Transborder Armed Actions case, I.C.J. Reports 1988*, at p. 94, para. 63 (Nicaragua) (emphasis added).

226 *Ibid.*, at p. 94, para. 63 (emphasis added).

227 *Ibid.*, at p. 95, para. 65.

228 *CERD case, I.C.J. Reports 2011*, at p. 134, para. 162.

We find a close connection here, it could not have been otherwise, between the (un)limited nature of the obligation to negotiate, discussed in Chapter 3, and the Court's assessment whether the parties have done their utmost to bring the dispute to a successful, peaceful and final solution.

Obviously the requirement is pursuing *as far as possible*, but what does this mean in practical terms?

The precondition of a dispute not having been settled through prior negotiations is not met 'in the absence of a genuine attempt to negotiate'; however, 'where negotiations are attempted or have commenced, the jurisprudence of this Court and of the PCIJ clearly reveals that the precondition is met only when there has been a failure of negotiations, or when negotiations have become futile or have reached deadlock'.[229]

Failure, futile or deadlock are thus the three situations one of which has to present itself for the precondition to be fulfilled. Relevant evidence can be the Applicant's 'factual narrative of the alleged failed negotiations which it contends took place' during a short period of time immediately prior to the filing of its Application and its submission that a Respondent's public statement made further contacts impossible.[230]

Still another option is of course when prior negotiations have been partially successful.

As the alleged *impossibility* of settling the dispute by negotiations can only refer to the time when an Application was filed,[231] it is possible to infer that there is an obligation for parties to continue to attempt to settle it by negotiation until just prior to the filing of an Application.

Although diplomatic correspondence between two parties over a period of ten years may reveal the objectives they were attempting to achieve, one month of negotiations just prior to the instituting of the proceedings by Application may not bear fruit and not lead to an agreement.[232]

Such diplomatic correspondence may still continue after the start of the proceedings[233] and they may even produce developments in the controversy, but not of such a nature as to resolve the dispute to the satisfaction of the Applicant.[234]

It is worth noting the potential impact of such subsequent diplomatic correspondence on the continued existence and scope of the dispute as it was submitted to the Court in the first place; this will be discussed in the next chapter.

Did the Court also outline general criteria against which to ascertain whether the negotiations 'have failed, became futile, or reached deadlock'?[235] Did the Court reach this assessment in this particular case, or did the Court limit itself to assess whether 'there had been negotiations' and 'these negotiations had been unsuccessful'?[236] And how much proof would be needed to demonstrate that negotiations on these matters would be futile?

In the circumstances of the case the period between the critical date and the Application led the Court to consider that negotiations on the subject-matter of the dispute could only have taken place between 9 and 12 August, a 'period during which the Court found that a dispute capable of falling under CERD had arisen between the parties'.[237] Apparently the scenario of the negotiations being futile or becoming deadlocked did not come into the assessment of the Court.

When two governments are unable during the post-adjudicative phase to come to an agreement on how to give effect to a previous judgment[238] it is within the discretion of each party to come to that conclusion and to return to the Court which will finally decide this particular issue.

229 *Ibid.*, at p. 133, para. 159.

230 *Ibid.*, at p. 136, para. 171. That parties are making instrumental and selective use of history is inevitable and requires a cautious approach by the Court in its assessment of the facts. It may also happen that 'extensive attempts' to resolve through negotiations the dispute failed and that the process 'ended just days' after the filing of the Application: *Whaling in the Antarctic case, Judgment of 31 March, I.C.J.Reports 2014*, Declaration by Judge Keith, para. 6.

231 South West Africa cases, I.C.J. Reports 1962, at p. 344.

232 *Nuclear Tests (New Zealand v. France), I.C.J. Reports 1974*, at p. 464, para. 26.

233 *Ibid.*, at p. 465, para. 27.

234 *Ibid.*

235 *CERD case, I.C.J. Reports 2011*, at p. 134, para. 162.

236 *Ibid.*, at p. 134, para. 163.

237 *Ibid.*, at p. 135, para. 168.

238 *Haya de la Torre case, Order of 3 January 1951: I.C.J. Reports 1951*, p. 4, at p. 4.

Who is to Blame for the Failure?

A party may state the view that an impasse reached in negotiations was only '*in large measure*' due to the other side's 'rigid position'.[239]

With regard to the *breakdown* of the negotiations towards the Contadora Act, at the stage of considering its jurisdiction and the admissibility of the claim, the Court was '*not called to pronounce on the legal consequences*' of a breakdown in the negotiations, but merely to determine whether the negotiations in the Contadora process were 'direct negotiations through the usual diplomatic channels'.[240]

Determining the exact chronology of unilateral decisions having been taken by (one of) the parties during the course of negotiations is only relevant 'in the event it has to be decided whether the parties negotiated in good faith' and not when the Court 'has not been called upon to pronounce on the Parties' responsibility for the failure of the negotiations',[241] an argument clearly based on the view that good administration of justice does not allow a dysfunctional use of the link between the two modes of settlement.

Whether such a determination of the attribution for the breakdown and its legal consequences could be part of the Court's judicial function entirely depends on the arguments of the parties before it, as the *Land and Maritime Boundary case* illustrates. In that case the parties first of all held diverging views as to the state of the discussions, whether these were real negotiations becoming unsuccessful or part of a still ongoing process.[242]

According to Cameroon, 'if the two parties were unable to go further in the negotiations, it was because the bad faith displayed by Nigeria either ruined any hope of reaching a new agreement or removed in advance the value of any agreement which might have arrived at'.[243] The Court did not feel any need to address this particular issue.

A party that is responsible for the impasse in the negotiations cannot take advantage of its own wrongful behaviour 'to prevent' the other party 'from achieving full and final settlement of the dispute between the two states by bringing the matter before this Court'.[244]

What consequences should the Court attach to the fact that an Applicant, *prima facie* having negotiated in good faith, has *suspended* the negotiations, as result of the inflexible attitude taken by the other party, and this has led to a failure of the negotiations? Is then the condition of prior negotiations fulfilled? Is it then for the Applicant to determine that the negotiations have failed, and thus that such condition for seisin had been fulfilled? Furthermore, negotiations may also '*appear*' to have been suspended.[245]

Failed Negotiations and a Party Changing its Claim

A clear and firm judicial backing of the functional link – and a rejection of dysfunctional use of this link – but also of the distinct and separate functional role of the two mechanisms – exception made for renewed negotiations during the proceedings producing an agreement and leading to discontinuance – may be found in the *Land and Maritime Boundary case* where the Court first reaffirmed that 'negotiations have indeed taken place'.[246]

239 CERD case, I.C.J. Reports 2011, Separate opinion by Judge Simma, at p. 218, para. 52, citing a Georgian statement.

240 *Border and Transborder Armed Actions case, I.C.J. Reports 1988*, at p. 99, para. 75 (emphasis added).

241 *Gabcikovo case, I.C.J. Reports 1997*, Dissenting opinion by Judge Herczegh, at p. 192.

242 According to Cameroon during several years 'a number of unsuccessful attempts to reach agreement on the delimitation of further parts of the maritime boundary were made' (*Land and Maritime Boundary case, I.C.J. Reports 2002*, at p. 426, para. 252), whereas Nigeria maintained that the Yaounde II declaration was 'not a binding agreement' but that it 'represented the record of a meeting which formed part of an ongoing programme of meetings relating to the maritime boundary' and that the matter ' was subject to further discussion at subsequent meetings': at p. 427, para. 257.

243 *Land and Maritime Boundary case, I.C.J. Reports 2002*, at p. 423, para. 243.

244 *Ibid.*, at p. 423, para. 243 (Cameroon).

245 *Fisheries Jurisdiction case (FRG v. Iceland), I.C.J. Reports 1973*, p. 57, para. 20 (emphasis added).

246 *Land and Maritime Boundary case, I.C.J. Reports 2002*, at p. 424, para. 244.

But the Court immediately and poignantly added that 'if following unsuccessful negotiations, judicial proceedings are instituted and one of the parties alters its claim, Article 74 and 83 of UNCLOS would not require that the proceedings be suspended while new negotiations were conducted'.[247]

'In such a situation, however, the new claim would have to be dealt exclusively by judicial means', otherwise 'delays and complications' might result in the process of maritime delimitation. UNCLOS does not require suspension of the proceedings. Moreover, 'the Court is not a negotiating forum'.[248]

This study is about the functional interaction between negotiations and adjudication, but this does not take away that there is also a functional interaction between negotiations and further political action the accordance with international law of which may be for the Court to determine in the course of an advisory proceeding.[249]

5.10 The Nature and the Real Subject-Matter of the Dispute

The general principle which found its expression in Article 40, para. 1 of the Statute is that an Applicant must present its view of the 'subject of the dispute', while Article 38 of the Rules of Court requires the Applicant to 'specify the precise nature of the claim'; but it is for the Court to determine 'the subject-matter of the dispute before it, taking into account the submissions of the Parties'.[250]

While 'giving particular attention to the formulation of the dispute chosen by the Applicant' it is for the Court to determine 'on an objective basis the dispute dividing the parties, by examining the positions of both Parties', and it is its duty 'to isolate the real issue in the case and to identify the object of the claim'.[251] The Court will determine 'the real dispute that has been submitted to it'.[252]

The functional link can be found here in the sense that prior negotiations will have enabled the parties to formulate their respective claims; based *inter alia* on this aspect of the functional role of negotiations they will be able to formulate their submissions during the written and oral proceedings.

'It has never been contested that the Court is entitled to interpret the submissions of the parties, and in fact is bound to do so; this is one of the attributes of the judicial function',[253] and this 'even when it is seised on the basis of a special agreement concluded between the two States that appear before it'.[254]

The important role of prior negotiations in assisting the Court in its clarification of the real subject of the dispute is beyond doubt, as in doing so the Court will base itself 'not only on the Application and final submissions' but also 'on diplomatic exchanges'.[255]

It is important of course that the Court provides a 'sufficient reflection' of negotiations which may have been going on for several decades.[256] The history of the negotiations may justify a presumption that when two powerful States 'negotiate a convention settling a long boundary in a distant theatre of their colonial

247 *Ibid.*

248 *Ibid.*

249 The Kosovo case illustrates if need be that a UDI may reflect 'the awareness of its authors that the final status negotiations had failed': *Kosovo Advisory Opinion, I.C.J. Reports 2010*, at p. 445, para. 105. In this case of internationally sponsored negotiations the assessment of failure by one of the main parties to the dispute is in line with that of an international group that was actively involved in the process. The UDI was indeed 'expressly put' in the 'context of the failure of the final status negotiations': at p. 445, para. 105.

250 *Fisheries Jurisdiction (Spain v. Canada), I.C.J. Reports 1998*, at pp. 447–9, paras. 29–31 and *Territorial and Maritime Dispute (Nicaragua v. Colombia), I.C.J. Reports 2007*, at p. 848, para. 38.

251 *Nuclear Tests (New Zealand v. France), I.C.J. Reports 1974*, at p. 466, para. 30 and *Fisheries Jurisdiction (Spain v. Canada), I.C.J. Reports 1998*, at p. 448, para. 30.

252 *Case between Qatar and Bahrain, I.C.J. Reports 1995*, at pp. 24–5 and *Fisheries Jurisdiction (Spain v. Canada), I.C.J. Reports 1998*, at p. 449, para. 31.

253 *Territorial and Maritime Dispute (Nicaragua v. Colombia), I.C.J. Reports 2007*, at p. 848, para. 38.

254 *Frontier Dispute between Burkina Faso and Niger, I.C.J. Reports 2013*, p. 44, at p. 70, para. 41.

255 *Fisheries Jurisdiction (Spain v. Canada), I.C.J. Reports 1998*, at p. 449, para. 31.

256 *Case between Qatar and Bahrain, I.C.J.Reports1994*, Dissenting opinion by Judge Oda, at p. 139, para. 18.

interaction' the Court should presume 'that the boundary was meant to cover all the area's potential points of conflict'.[257]

In a number of cases prior negotiations may have been partially successful in reaching an agreement to submit *a dispute* or *the* dispute but without resolving the (pre-)existing disagreement about its nature: prior negotiations in such cases are falling short of determining with the necessary degree of precision even the subject-matter or more generally the qualification of the dispute, another example of an incomplete functional link.

Negotiations are not only relevant to determine the subject-matter of a dispute but also, in appropriate cases, to disclose whether the present dispute is not merely an extension of a prior one that has already been dividing the parties.[258]

Disagreement between the Parties about the Nature of the Dispute

Within the functional interaction it is up to the Court to examine to what extent during prior negotiations the parties have been dealing with the subject-matter of the dispute. It is sufficient that a substantial part of the diplomatic exchanges has been devoted, even indirectly, to the question at hand.[259]

Between the parties 'uncertainties or disagreements (may) arise with regard to the real subject of the dispute with which the Court has been seised, or to the exact nature of the claims submitted to it'.[260]

Parties may also disagree as *to the nature of the dispute*.[261]

In examining what is the subject-matter of the dispute referred to in an Application the Court may find that the subject-matter 'corresponds to only part of the dispute contemplated' in an earlier formula[262] which 'sufficiently clearly comprehend the entire dispute' and the acceptance of which by the other party 'put an end to the persistent disagreement of the Parties as to the subject of the dispute to be submitted to the Court'.[263]

Although disagreement about the nature of a dispute is most likely to present itself in cases introduced by way of Application, 'even in proceedings instituted by Special Agreement' the Court has to determine for itself 'having examined all relevant instruments, what was the subject of the dispute before it, in circumstances where the parties could not agree on how it should be characterized'.[264]

A textbook example of how the Court sees a particular dispute before it can be found, for instance, in the way the Court summarized the dispute between the parties in regard to a particular sector of the boundary.[265]

The way the Court interpreted Canada's optional clause perfectly illustrates the fundamental principle that the 'establishment or otherwise of jurisdiction is not a matter for the parties but for the Court itself'.[266]

In other cases parties simply disagree about the nature of the dispute even without embarking upon a process of negotiations. A Respondent may, for instance, deny the existence of a dispute, arguing that a particular convention is not relevant because 'it was not a question of "bilateral differences" but one of "threat to international peace and security resulting from State-sponsored terrorism"'[267] or of the international

257 *Indonesia/Malaysia case, I.C.J. Reports 2002*, Dissenting opinion by Judge *ad hoc* Franck, at p. 692, para. 5; at p. 699, para. 27; and at pp. 705–6, para. 45.

258 *Right of Passage case, I.C.J. Reports 1957*, at p. 151.

259 *Ibid.*, at p. 148.

260 *Fisheries Jurisdiction (Spain v. Canada), I.C.J. Reports 1998*, at p. 448, para. 29.

261 *Territorial Dispute (Libyan Arab Jamahiriya/Chad), I.C.J. Reports 1994*, at pp. 14–15, paras. 18–19.

262 *Case between Qatar and Bahrain, I.C.J. Reports 1994*, at p. 124, paras. 35 and 36.

263 *Case between Qatar and Bahrain, I.C.J.Reports 1995*, at p. 17, para. 31.

264 *Fisheries Jurisdiction (Spain v. Canada), I.C.J. Reports 1998*, at p. 448, para. 29.

265 *Frontier Dispute (Benin/Niger), I.C.J. Reports 2005*, at pp. 142–3, para. 126.

266 *Fisheries Jurisdiction (Spain v. Canada), I.C.J. Reports 1998*, at p. 450, para. 37. A reservation in an optional clause excluding 'disputes arising out of or concerning' does, given the 'broad and comprehensive character of the formula employed' not only exclude 'disputes whose immediate "subject-matter" is the measures in question and their enforcement, but also those "concerning" such measures and, more generally, those having their "origin" in those measures "arising out of" that is to say, those disputes which, in the absence of such measures, would not have come into being': at p. 458, para. 62.

267 *Lockerbie case, I.C.J. Reports 1998*, at p. 123, para. 23 (US).

community's reaction to the Applicant's failure to respond to 'the most serious accusations of State involvement in acts of terrorism'.[268]

The Court in such a case may then conclude that as the parties differ on the governance by the Convention a dispute 'thus exists between the parties as to the legal regime applicable to the event'.[269] And this 'dispute of a general nature' is not the only one to exist as there is, moreover, 'also a specific dispute which concerns the interpretation and application' of a particular Article of the relevant Convention,[270] and still another one concerning the interpretation and application of another Article.[271]

An agreement between a regional integration organization and the Respondent settles as between them 'certain aspects of a dispute provoked by the unilateral actions' of the Respondent State, but the Application filed may be based on 'a right exclusive to [the Applicant] and concerns a dispute whose subject-matter differs from that covered by the agreement'.[272]

Having been involved in negotiations leading to a Convention with third parties covering a dispute between an IO of which the Applicant State is a member and a third party does not take away that Member State's separate and exclusive right to submit an Application on a dispute with a different subject-matter, although the fact leading to it, causing it, at the origin of it has a link with the subject-matter of the dispute covered by that agreement.

The Respondent may argue that 'a dispute consists of an indivisible whole comprising facts and rules of law' and that consequently the Court cannot 'have jurisdiction with regard to one of these elements and not have jurisdiction with regard to the other'.[273]

The 'primary dispute between Georgia and the Russian Federation was about the allegedly unlawful use of force by the Russian Federation after 7 August 2008',[274] whereas Georgia contended that its dispute with the Russian Federation 'over ethnic cleansing [was] long-standing'.[275] The Court did not find 'any basis for a finding that there was' a dispute over ethnic cleansing by July 1999.[276]

The methodology used by the Court to appreciate 'the nature of' a dispute and to 'define its subject-matter' may give rise to divergent views of individual judges[277] and may be qualified as 'too formalistic and somewhat artificial'.[278] As the Court engaged 'in an exercise of dismembering the organic whole' of a conventional framework and of 'assessing whether there was a dispute relating to each of the' provisions,[279] this resulted in distorting the subject-matter of the dispute.[280] In line with the object and purpose of the Convention, the Court should have interpreted the subject-matter of the dispute as 'comprising in its scope the whole of the process' of implementation by the Respondent.[281]

There is a dispute 'even if the scope of that dispute may have changed since the Application was filed',[282] for instance as a result of negotiations during the proceedings, as we will see in Chapter 6.

---

268 *Questions of Interpretation and Application of the 1971 Montreal Convention arising from the aerial Incident at Lockerbie (Libyan Arab Jamahiriya v. United Kingdom), Preliminary Objections, Judgment, I.C.J. Reports 1998*, p. 9, at p. 18, para. 24 (UK).

269 *Lockerbie case, I.C.J. Reports 1998*, at p. 123, para. 24.

270 *Ibid.*, at p. 127, para. 28.

271 *Ibid.*, at p. 128, para. 32.

272 *Fisheries Jurisdiction (Spain v. Canada), I.C.J. Reports 1998*, at pp. 446–7, para. 25 (Spain).

273 *Ibid.*, at p. 447, para. 26 (Canada). Looking at the notes of protests by the EC and Spain, Canada contended that there was 'no trace of distinction between a dispute with the European Community and a dispute with Spain': at p. 447, para. 27.

274 *CERD case, I.C.J. Reports 2011*, at p. 88, para. 38 (Russian Federation).

275 *Ibid.*, at p. 94, para. 50 and at p. 86, para. 34.

276 *Ibid.*, at p. 100, para. 63.

277 *Belgium v. Senegal case, I.C.J. Reports 2012*, Declaration by Judge Owada, at p. 464, para. 1.

278 *Ibid.*, Declaration by Judge Owada, at p. 466, para. 11.

279 *Ibid.*, at pp. 466–7, para. 11.

280 *Ibid.*, at p. 467, para. 12.

281 *Ibid.*, at p. 467, para. 13.

282 *Belgium v. Senegal case, I.C.J. Reports 2009*, at p. 149, para. 48.

5.11 Part of a Dispute being Submitted to the Court

The functional interaction does not always take the form of the submission of the entire dispute which had been the subject of prior negotiations. Proceedings could be instituted 'solely to resolve a question of law or fact which will affect the settlement of the dispute'.[283]

In case prior negotiations have been partially successful, the parties' intention may indeed have been to submit only 'certain differences' concerning a delimitation to the Court, with the exception of those areas for instance where agreements had already been concluded.[284]

Within the context of a double-track strategy chosen by both parties, a communiqué at the end of a round of negotiations may provide that some problems should be resolved by negotiations whereas other issues would be resolved by the Court.[285]

In a negotiation strategy acceptance of a proposal to negotiate and the refusal to accept a proposed moratorium of activities in the disputed area are not mutually exclusive; they may constitute the stage at which the existence of a dispute, even a limited one, becomes established, the refusal to accept the proposed moratorium bringing the dispute into being despite the acceptance of negotiations on a particular delimitation.[286]

A maritime boundary delimitation may have remained a partial one and 'despite many attempts to complete it, the two parties have been unable to do so',[287] the Respondent denying that there is dispute 'concerning the whole of the frontier'.[288] When a negotiated agreement concerning the entire boundary had proved impossible one of the parties may decide to submit the matter to the Court.[289]

Partial failure of negotiations may thus lead to the submission of the whole boundary dispute to the Court even on those parts where an agreement had been reached. This could be regarded as a good example of a parties' originated dysfunctional interaction.

When parties had not even started negotiations upon the delimitation of the continental shelf, the 'Court could not initiate compulsory procedures entailing a binding decision'.[290]

Parties' intention when drafting a Special Agreement should not be interpreted as reflecting their will only to submit part of the dispute to the Court if that would run counter to a reasonable interpretation of the actual wording of the agreement and its coherence.

The Court being fully aware of its judgments opening the way to the post-adjudicative stage held that giving effect to such an assumed intention of the parties would not only result in the dispute not being finally decided, but it also 'would leave open the possibility of further dispute'.[291]

Political and legal factors may have been involved in the decision of a party not to raise a particular question 'either in the diplomatic correspondence, in the pleadings or in the oral proceedings' while reserving the right to raise it in the post-adjudicative phase. Both parties may have been in tacit agreement to preserve the matter in *status quo* both during the period of diplomatic negotiations and while the case was pending before the Court.[292]

A multifaceted situation may in fact cover a variety of disputes[293] of which, at a particular moment in time, only one may have been brought before the Court.

283 *South West Africa Cases, I.C.J. Reports 1962*, Dissenting opinion by Judge Morelli, at p. 568.

284 *North Sea Continental Shelf case, I.C.J. Reports 1969*, at pp. 12–13, paras. 1 and 2. The same did happen in the *Territorial and Maritime Dispute (Nicaragua v. Colombia), I.C.J. Reports 2012*, p. 624, Separate opinion by Judge Abraham, at p. 731, para. 5.

285 *Aegean Sea Continental Shelf case, I.C.J. Reports 1978*, at pp. 39–40, para. 97.

286 *Gulf of Maine case, I.C.J. Reports 1984*, at pp. 280–81, para. 64.

287 *Land and Maritime Boundary between Cameroon and Nigeria, Provisional Measures, Order of 15 March 1996, I.C.J. Reports 1996*, p. 13, at p. 14, para. 4 (Cameroon).

288 *Land and Maritime Boundary case, I.C.J. Reports 1996*, at p. 21, para. 32 (Nigeria).

289 *Land and Maritime Boundary case, I.C.J. Reports 2002*, at p. 243, para. 243 (Cameroon).

290 *Ibid.*, Declaration by Judge Oda, at p. 468, para. 30.

291 *Corfu Channel case, I.C.J. Reports 1949*, at p. 26.

292 *Asylum case, I.C.J. Reports 1950*, Dissenting opinion by Judge Read, at p. 331.

293 *CERD case, I.C.J. Reports 2011*, at pp. 84–5, para. 32.

In other situations, such as the Central American cases in particular, a State may be involved in a number of serial proceedings, each one dealing with a particular aspect involving the same parties either as Applicant or Respondent.

Such a strategy to divide a more general conflict when bringing a case before the Court could potentially distort the functional link between adjudication and prior negotiations. It may be qualified as artificial by the Respondent who allegedly may suffer negative consequences because certain facts will be absent from the proceedings while other facts have already been in issue in another case. Moreover, *the splitting-up* of an overall conflict into separate disputes would arguably be contrary to good faith requirements and contrary to the proper functioning of international justice.[294]

According to the Court certain issues may be 'regarded as part of a wider regional problem'.[295]

The Court was aware of difficulties 'where particular aspects of a complex general situation are brought before the Court for separate decision'[296] but as in the *Hostages case*[297] the Court did not find this a reason for declining jurisdiction.

A *partial* settlement of a dispute may occur either as result of the way (one of) the parties brought the case before the Court or as result of the way the Court has decided a particular case in light of the submissions of the parties. Whatever the mode of peaceful settlement followed, an 'incomplete settlement of the dispute is tantamount to an absence of settlement'.[298]

Although the Court may express its awareness that the conduct the identification of the legal consequences of which the Court is requested to determine 'is part of a greater whole' and that it would 'take this circumstance fully into account in any opinion'[299] or that a UDI 'must be seen in its larger context',[300] both advisory opinions do not adequately reflect this awareness.

This aspect of adjudication does not present itself in the same way in contentious cases, as illustrated by the *DRC Uganda case* where the alleged involvement of third parties was not fully taken into account in the Court's 2005 judgment.

Finally, it should be noted that the decision to reject a counterclaim may deprive the Court 'of the examination and settlement of the dispute in its entirety'.[301]

---

294 *Border and Transborder Armed Actions case, I.C.J. Reports 1988*, at p. 91, para. 53 (Honduras).

295 *Ibid.*, at p. 92, para. 54.

296 *Ibid.*

297 *Hostages case, I.C.J. Reports 1980*, at p. 19, para. 36.

298 *Arbitral Award case, I.C.J. Reports 1991*, p. 53, Dissenting opinion by Judge *ad hoc* Thierry, at p. 179.

299 *Wall Advisory Opinion, I.C.J. Reports 2004*, at p. 160, para. 54.

300 *Kosovo Advisory Opinion, I.C.J. Reports 2010*, at p. 444, para. 104.

301 *Germany v. Italy case, I.C.J. Reports 2010*, Dissenting opinion by Judge Cançado Trindade, at p. 368, para. 100.

Chapter 6
Negotiations during the Course of the Proceedings

Introduction

A dispute has been submitted to the Court, perhaps following a long period of intense negotiations which ultimately did not bear fruit. In the Court's assessment of the state of prior negotiations between the parties their views as expressed in their pleadings play an important role: either the deadlock is still there and there is no chance of resumed negotiations or there is no deadlock and there is a chance that the process could be resumed.[1]

In any case, once a dispute has been moved from the process of unsuccessful negotiations to the Great Hall of Justice the parties are subject to some fundamental general principles of the judicial process – the dispute must continue to exist and the facts on which the judgment is based are to be those occurring up to the close of the oral hearings on the merits of the case – giving rise to a negative duty – to abstain from any action which might prejudice the Court's exercise of its judicial function – and a positive one – to undertake every possible action to facilitate the Court's task.[2]

Does this positive duty entail that the parties should endeavour to restart the process of negotiations?

Does the entry into the adjudicative phase put an abrupt end to the functional interaction between the two means of pacific settlement? Have the parties, or at least one of them, decided to leave for good the process of negotiations in the state of failure and to exclusively rely on recourse to the Court in a comprehensive and irreversible way?

Does the adversarial nature of the proceedings before the Court exclude or render impossible – or at least less likely – (resumed) negotiations between the parties parallel to and during the course of those proceedings?

It can be reasonably assumed that in general and in most cases, depending on a number of variable factors, the decision to move from the process of negotiations to that of adjudication – whether it has been taken jointly or on a unilateral basis – does not need to be by the nature of things irreversible.

Prior negotiations may have (almost) failed but there is indeed no compelling reason why they may not still continue after one of the parties has filed an Application. In case 'negotiations stalled owing to the diametrically opposed positions'[3] this may lead to the filing of an Application, sometimes later substituted by a joint submission as a result of the conclusion of a Special Agreement reached through mediation.

Whether the instituting of proceedings may be considered an act of bad faith while negotiations were still in progress is another question which we dealt with earlier. Negotiations may have failed actually just prior to the filing of an Application. The Court may qualify the prior negotiations as 'deadlocked' when an Application was filed, and it does not rule out as such that a Respondent might be prejudiced as a result of the institution of proceedings instead of the pursuance of those negotiations.[4]

A party cannot modify, by a mere manifestation of will, during the course of the proceedings and to the detriment of the other party the conditions in which the dispute presents itself;[5] neither can any action '*pendente lite* by a State engaged in a dispute before the Court with another State' have 'any effect whatever as regards the legal situation which the Court is called upon to define'.[6]

---

1 Torres Bernardez, 'Are Prior Negotiations?', at p. 515, para. 30.

2 E. Zoller, *La bonne foi*, p. 147, § 155.

3 *Gabcikovo case, I.C.J. Reports 1997*, at p. 53, para. 73.

4 The Court was not persuaded that this was the case for Nigeria: *Land and Maritime Boundary case, I.C.J. Reports 1998*, at p. 304, para. 58.

5 *Right of Passage case, I.C.J. Reports 1960*, at p. 18 (India).

6 *Great Belt case, I.C.J. Reports 1991*, at p. 19, para. 32.

Neither of these Court pronouncements can be taken to apply to an invitation by one party to start or resume negotiations or to positions taken by (one of) the parties during negotiations pending the proceedings or to their options to modify their positions through such a process. This is not surprising as the Court in general terms welcomes 'any negotiation between the Parties with a view to achieving a direct and friendly settlement' pending a decision of the Court on the merits.[7]

We will shortly look into the question whether and to what extent the freedom of the parties to change their (legal) position, and which they enjoy under both modes of peaceful settlement of disputes – either until the end of the oral proceedings when the final submissions have to be formulated or until the final and decisive round of negotiations when a draft agreement has been tabled by (one of) the parties – may nevertheless be limited.[8]

The Court will take into account the breaking off of negotiations which were already underway prior to the start of the proceedings, while also taking into account pledges and commitments made by (one of) the parties during the proceedings to resume that process, as did happen for instance in the *Belgium Senegal case*.

The legal positions of the parties becoming more refined through their pleadings and submissions, events outside the courtroom – occurring abroad or on the home front – are among the various factors which may bring about a change of heart with one of the parties and/or a common desire of parties to initiate, even after the first steps in the proceedings have been taken, a resumption of the negotiations on the substantive issues in a genuine attempt to reach a (partial) settlement of the dispute.

As a result of such resumed negotiations the subject-matter of the dispute might undergo some (minor) changes, either because some pre-existing controversial issues have in the meantime been resolved or removed, or in other cases because as a result of the broadening of the dispute the Court is called upon to address additional matters.

Following a successful outcome of such resumed negotiations one of the parties might request the discontinuance, resulting in the removal of the case from the Court's General List.

Under the original 1922 Rules of Court at the time of the PCIJ the Court 'should record agreements that either settled the dispute *or* discontinued proceedings',[9] a distinction which was abolished by the current Article 88, para.1, while Article 88, para. 2 refers to an out-of-court settlement of the dispute as such, a fact which the Court 'may record' in the exercise of its ministerial function.[10]

Alternatively, whereas the Court's jurisdiction continues 'regardless of subsequent events', for instance, resumed negotiations which turn out to be overall and with respect to every legal issue of the dispute successful 'might lead to a finding that an application has subsequently become moot and to a decision not to proceed to a judgment on the merits'.[11] The important condition which has to be fulfilled is that those negotiations must 'in fact put an end to the dispute between the Parties' and must 'have deprived the Application of its object'.[12]

The Court's 'duty to safeguard the judicial function' implies that it has to examine whether the dispute has become devoid of purpose since the filing of the Application or the compromis as a result of resumed negotiations during the course of the proceedings.[13]

We have already noted in the previous chapter the evident need for the parties to consult and negotiate on matters of procedure in order to enable the Court to ensure an orderly conduct of the case.

7 *Ibid.*, at p. 20, para. 35. Judge Tarassov would have preferred a 'more straightforward and somewhat stronger' position of the Court by indicating the aim of such negotiations: Declaration by Judge Tarassov, at p. 23.

8 A unilateral act which 'could be interpreted as an intention to modify the essence of the situation presented before the Court' is a different matter because as result of the (joint) submission of the dispute 'a judicial situation arose that obligates both countries not to modify their positions': *Land, Island and Maritime Frontier Dispute, I.C.J. Reports 1992*, at p. 576, para. 362 (Honduras). The Court agreed that 'States may and do draft definitions of disputes to be submitted to a settlement procedure in terms which will avoid any clear surrender of the legal position of either of them': at p. 585, para. 378.

9 G. Wegen, 'Discontinuance of International Proceedings: The Hostages Case' (1982) 76 *American Journal of International Law* 4, 717–36, at 721 (emphasis added).

10 On the subsequent changes of the relevant Articles see also G. Wegen, 'Discontinuance', 722–3 and S. Rosenne, *The Law and Practice*, vol. 3, pp. 1424–38.

11 *Arrest Warrant case, I.C.J. Reports 2002* at, pp. 12–13, para. 26.

12 *Ibid.*, at pp. 14–15, para. 32.

13 *The Northern Cameroons case, I.C.J. Reports 1963*, at p. 38.

The functional interaction operating both ways, our focus here will be on the impact of ongoing substantive negotiations on the manner in which the Court is (obliged) to handle the dispute, including some procedural matters, and on the way the Court's performance of its judicial function potentially influences the readiness of parties to start a renewed process of negotiations and the progress of such a process. We will first look at the general legal and some factual parameters for such negotiations before addressing more particular aspects of this mode of the functional interaction.

6.1 General Legal and Some Factual Parameters for Negotiations during the Course of the Proceedings

General Legal Parameters

The continuous nature of the obligation to negotiate

In Chapter 3 we discussed the (un)limited nature of the obligation for States to negotiate towards a peaceful settlement of the dispute during the pre-adjudicative phase. The questions then arise whether the start of proceedings brings this pre-adjudicatory obligation to an abrupt and irreversible end; whether that obligation would at least be suspended until the end of the proceedings;[14] or whether the initiation of the proceedings merely brings about a change of scenery and of the overall legal and institutional framework without affecting that obligation because of its continuous character under general international law, under the Charter or pursuant to a compromis or compromissory clause.

Although the Court has made it perfectly clear 'that the Court is not a negotiating forum',[15] it is worth recalling the observations made before the General Assembly in 1993 by President Jennings with regard to the functional interaction between the two means of settlement. The role of the ICJ has been changing; it is no longer considered to be the forum of last resort. After the seisin of the ICJ 'the intervention of some parts of the procedures before the Court', when completed, made further negotiations possible and 'made it possible for them to succeed'. Recourse to the Court is nowadays sometimes seen as a useful mechanism to be employed at an early stage of a dispute, as part of preventive diplomacy.[16]

This observation is in line with the view expressed earlier that a sharp and clear-cut distinction and separation between the two mechanisms is no longer fully justified in all circumstances. The question about the continuous character of the obligation to negotiate has to be placed in that context.

Various indicators may be found pointing to such a continuous character surviving the start of proceedings. Whether, to what extent and in what way this obligation continues to impose itself even in the post-adjudicative phase will be dealt with in Part III.

Negotiations may have continued 'up to, and beyond the date of the submission' of an Application, and this evidence may show 'that the positions of the parties continued to evolve'[17] and the emergence of new factors, 'indicating a clear evolution of the negotiations and of the positions of the Parties'.[18]

It is then perhaps not very persuasive for the Court to conclude that the 'dispute could not be settled through negotiation or that negotiations had been exhausted and offered no further prospect for the settlement' already three years prior to the start of the proceedings.[19]

The continuous nature as perhaps reflected in two general duties

The first general duty for parties is to conduct themselves in such a way as not to render the performance of the Court's function more difficult or impossible.

---

14 U. Beyerlin, 'Pactum de contrahendo', 438 and note 126.

15 *Land and Maritime Boundary case, I.C.J. Reports 2002*, at p. 424, para. 244.

16 Judge R.Jennings, President of the ICJ before the UN General Assembly on 15 October 1993, *Vol. 48, Yearbook 1993–1994 International Court of Justice*, pp. 219–23.

17 *Belgium Senegal case, I.C.J. Reports 2012*, Separate opinion by Judge Yusuf, at p. 561, para. 7.

18 *Ibid.*, at p. 562, para. 8.

19 *Ibid.*, at p. 563, para. 10.

Should this litigation-linked obligation be interpreted in such a way as to almost imply a continuous character of the obligation to negotiate? And/or could this litigation-linked obligation be interpreted in such a way as also to imply that parties must make every effort to *facilitate* the Court's task, in the sense that they have to attempt to reach (at least a partial) settlement of the dispute through (resumed) negotiations?

The Court has pointed out that it is precisely because 'judicial settlement may provide a path to international harmony in circumstances of conflict' that 'needless continuance of litigation is an obstacle to such harmony'.[20] Does this require parties to resume negotiations only in those particular circumstances where continuance of the litigation has become needless? Or should parties at regular intervals (re)consider the possibility to suspend or postpone particular phases of the proceedings and to return to the negotiating table?

Although negotiations during the course of the proceedings 'might interfere with the subject-matter of a dispute while judicial proceedings are pending',[21] they cannot be considered to constitute an action with negative consequences, except of course when as a result of bad faith they fail and render the judicial settlement even more difficult.

The legal basis for the parties' second duty – not to aggravate the dispute pending the delivery of the judgment, and which is closely linked to the first one – could be found under general international law in the principle of good faith; in some cases it may originate in conventional provisions or it may be the result of judicial law through the indication of provisional measures. In the latter case, the Court merely recalls the parties in a more solemn way a pre-existing obligation.[22]

Does this negative duty also entail, perhaps *in statu nascendi*, a corollary positive duty to continue negotiations and to resume the process which has previously failed?

Such a change in the parties' strategy is not without risk as the resumed process of negotiations may in turn fail and then contribute to or provoke an aggravation of the pending dispute.

Given also that, because in order to 'ensure a good administration of justice, it is necessary not to delay the settlement of' any dispute[23] and parties have to conduct themselves in such a way as not to frustrate this primary objective, is there room to argue that in particular circumstances parties may find themselves even under *a duty to abstain* from resumed negotiations?

The decision to resume negotiations after the start of the proceedings may be taken by (one of) the parties or it may be the result of (more or less subtle) judicial encouragements or be contained in an Order indicating provisional measures of protection, the binding nature of which does not prevent the Court from carefully wording it 'in such a way as to make it, if not a mere exhortation, at any rate not one intended to be in all respects legally binding'.[24]

Either of these litigation scenarios may very well stem from the conviction, perhaps even shared by both the parties and by the Court, that the obligation to negotiate has a continuous character indeed.

The continuous nature as reflected in Court pronouncements

Once a state has made a commitment to enter into negotiations, 'it is not the Court's function to contemplate that it will not comply with it'.[25]

This general judicial attitude applies to negotiations during the course of proceedings, either on the initiative of one of the parties or as a result of the indication of provisional measures, and also for the post-adjudicative negotiations either on the initiative of the parties or as result of the judgment delivered by the Court obliging the party to negotiate as it did in the *Gabcikovo case*.

20 *Nuclear Tests (New Zealand v. France), I.C.J. Reports 1974*, at p. 477, para. 61.

21 *LaGrand case, I.C.J. Reports 2001*, at p. 498, para. 93 (Germany).

22 P.-M. Eisemann, 'Quelques observations sur les mesures conservatoires indiquées par la Cour de La Haye' in N. Boschiero et al. (eds), *International Courts and the Development of International Law: Essays in Honour of Tullio Treves* (The Hague, 2013), pp. 121–36, at p. 127.

23 *Columbian-Peruvian Asylum case, Order of 17 December 1949: I.C.J. Reports 1949*, p. 267.

24 R. Jennings, 'The *LaGrand* Case', at 35.

25 *Nuclear Tests (New Zealand v. France), I.C.J. Reports 1974*, at p. 477, para. 63.

The Functional Role of Temporary Arrangements

A temporary arrangement may be one of the means to overcome a deadlock in the negotiations 'by which to save face with a move that will not be viewed as a sign of weakness'.[26]

Temporary arrangements may have been set up during the pre-negotiation phase or during the negotiation process proper, removing 'the danger of misinterpretation of intentions' and 'the possibility of unilateral acts either to effect or affect a solution'.[27]

From a functional perspective the question has also been raised why lengthy negotiations are needed when 'the Parties have already agreed', pending the solution of the actual dispute, that they would be free to conduct themselves in the matter at hand as they wish.[28]

Evidently even in case interim arrangements have been concluded to maintain peace and good neighbourly relations in the region and between the parties, they will always require 'a good deal of good faith and mutual trust' for their implementation.[29]

Although for instance under the 1982 UNCLOS provisional arrangements 'cannot be used at a later stage by a State as a legal argument justifying a specific boundary line', it has been submitted that:

> in practice the nature of provisional arrangements may exert a considerable influence on negotiations on the delimitation of maritime boundaries by influencing the political context on which the negotiations will be taking place, the nature of a provisional arrangement may influence the willingness of States to make concessions in the negotiations on the delimitation of a maritime boundary.[30]

It is important to recall the Court's ruling that the obligation to negotiate is not exhausted when parties after a series of negotiations finally were able to conclude an interim agreement as the interim arrangement reached during the course of the proceedings may not have been a 'settlement' of the dispute as an earlier agreement.[31]

The absence of a provision in such an interim agreement, as result of the deletion of a sentence to that effect that parties would reconsider the position before the expiration of that interim agreement, does not release the parties from their obligation to negotiate in respect of the basic dispute between them.[32] Such an intention would not correspond to the Applicant's submission that the Court should declare that the parties are under a duty to negotiate; neither would it be consistent with the Respondent's intention to continue negotiations.[33]

Given the continuous nature of the general obligation for parties to negotiate, it cannot have been their intention to wait for the expiration date and 'for the reactivation of the dispute, with all the possible friction it might engender'[34] 'before one of them might require the other to attempt a peaceful settlement through negotiations'.[35]

26 G. Faure, 'Deadlocks', p. 37.

27 W. Zartman, *Negotiation and Conflict Management*, p. 125.

28 *Interim Accord case, I.C.J. Reports 2011*, Dissenting opinion by Judge *ad hoc* Roucounas, at p. 725, para. 9.

29 *Ibid.*, Dissenting opinion by Judge Xue, at p. 714.

30 A. Oude Elferink, 'The Influence of Provisional Arrangements on Negotiations on the Delimitation of Maritime Boundaries' (1993) 1 *Boundary and Security Bulletin*, 92–4 at 92.

31 *Fisheries Jurisdiction, (United Kingdom v. Iceland), I.C.J. Reports 1974*, at p. 32, para. 76. We will deal with the particular functional role of such interim arrangements later in this chapter.

32 *Fisheries Jurisdiction, (United Kingdom v. Iceland), I.C.J. Reports 1974*, at pp. 32–3, para. 77.

33 *Ibid.*, at p. 33, para. 77.

34 *Ibid.*

35 *Ibid.* Judge De Castro held a different position when he considered the agreement to reflect the parties' belief that the Court would be unable to settle their dispute by a judgment the effect of which the parties decided to suspend for two years and which by not taking into account 'the indicative value of the agreement, could be an insurmountable obstacle to a negotiated settlement of the dispute': Dissenting opinion, at pp. 77–8.

The Freedom of the Parties is Limited by General Principles as to the Judicial Process

The Dispute Must Continue to Exist

An agreement covering the delimitation of the frontier in two particular sectors, and having resulted from negotiations prior to the start of the proceedings, cannot be considered still to be the subject-matter of a dispute existing when the Court is seised with a dispute concerning the remaining unsolved sectors of that frontier.[36]

In a remarkable way the functional interaction also limits the freedom of the parties as the dispute must not only exist at the time of the start of the proceedings, but it must also *continue* 'to exist at the time the Court makes its decision'.[37]

The duty for the Court 'to satisfy itself, whether at the instance of a party or *proprio motu*, that a dispute has not become devoid of purpose since the filing of the Application and [that] there remains reason to adjudicate that dispute'[38] is of a continuous nature and thus also concerns the circumstance that negotiations have been resumed between the parties. This also seems to imply a duty for the Court to assess *proprio motu* the (partial) success of those negotiations, either by putting questions to the parties during the hearings or afterwards during its deliberations by its own examination of their conduct.

Both parties may exercise their right to amend their submissions until the end of the oral proceedings.[39] This may also be the result of partially successful negotiations, the amended submissions to cover then the remaining part of the claims upon which no agreement had been reached. The limit to be respected in this regard has been clearly set by the Court in its settled jurisprudence: we 'cannot, in principle, allow a dispute brought before it by Application to be transformed by amendments in the submissions into another dispute which is different in character'.[40]

Although resumed negotiations after the start of the proceedings may contribute further to clarifying the precise subject-matter of the dispute and the opposing legal claims of the parties, pursuant to Article 40, para. 1 of the Statute and Article 38, para. 2 of the Rules of Court, the Court has held inadmissible 'certain new claims, formulated during the course of the proceedings, which, if they had been entertained, would have transformed the subject of the dispute originally brought before it under the terms of the Application'.[41]

Also in the exercise of its advisory jurisdiction, if there is a dispute the Court has to satisfy itself that it is one 'not settled by negotiations or other agreed mode of settlement'.[42]

Negotiations taking place and becoming (partially) successful after the close of the hearings cannot result in changing the submissions but only in a request for discontinuance of the proceedings.

The Facts on Which the Judgment is Based Should Not be Changed

The freedom of parties is further limited because 'general principles as to the judicial process' do 'require that the facts on which the Judgment is based should be those occurring up to the close of the oral proceedings on the merits of the case',[43] and these facts could very well include ongoing negotiations and their possible results.

As to later facts 'apparently of such a nature as materially to affect its decision', for instance failure of resumed negotiations, parties may be afforded an opportunity to comment 'had it considered that the interests of justice so required'.[44]

Resumed negotiations would only qualify as 'facts subsequent to the filing of the Application' on condition that they 'directly (arise) out of the question which is the subject-matter of that Application': this requirement

36 *Frontier Dispute between Burkina Faso and Niger, I.C.J. Reports 2013*, at p. 71, para. 50.

37 *Nuclear Tests (New Zealand v. France), I.C.J. Reports 1974*, at p. 476, para. 58 (emphasis added).

38 *The Northern Cameroons case, I.C.J. Reports 1963*, at p. 38. *Nuclear Tests (New Zealand v. France), I.C.J. Reports 1974*, at p. 476, para. 58 and *Fisheries Jurisdiction (Spain v. Canada), I.C.J. Reports 1998*, at p. 468, para. 88.

39 *Arrest Warrant case, I.C.J. Reports 2002*, at p. 16, para. 35 (DRC).

40 *Ibid.*, at p. 16, para. 36.

41 *Territorial and Maritime Dispute between Nicaragua and Honduras, I.C.J. Reports 2007*, at p. 695, para. 108.

42 *PLO case Advisory Opinion, I.C.J. Reports 1988*, at p. 27, para. 34.

43 *Nicaragua case, I.C.J. Reports 1986*, at p. 39, para. 58.

44 *Nuclear Tests (Australia v. France), I.C.J. Reports 1974*, at p. 264, para. 33 and *Nuclear Tests (New Zealand v. France), I.C.J. Reports 1974*, at p. 468, para. 34.

limits the potential impact of resumed negotiations as they have to deal with the subject-matter of the dispute as it has been brought before the Court. The Court may deal with a submission based on that process in order to consider the dispute in all its aspects.[45]

It is the Court's duty to examine whether an Application did sufficiently indicate 'the dispute as it has developed in the course' of the proceedings and as formulated in the final submissions.[46]

In the exercise of its advisory jurisdiction the Court may have been informed of subsequent events since a request was made[47] and such events may include negotiations both on a bilateral basis and within a multilateral framework.

The Court is not requested to close 'its eyes to subsequent events of possible relevance ... hence the Court will therefore set out here the developments in the affair subsequent to the General Assembly resolution' regarding a dispute between the UN and a host State.[48]

Mediation and Good Offices during the Proceedings

'Contacts' between parties after an armed incident in order to 'ensure that peace prevail[ed]' in the region pending the judgment[49] may lead to mediation rendering the request for provisional measures 'moot'.[50] When 'discussions' under mediation have led to a cease-fire 'this does not deprive the Court of the rights and duties pertaining to the case'.[51]

It is thus clear that from a functional interaction perspective, and in view of the object and purpose of adjudication, that negotiations during the course of the proceedings have to deal with the subject-matter of the dispute at hand and not with some *collateral* aspects. How this condition influences the negotiations leading to an interim arrangement will be dealt with shortly.

Although we can already observe that successful negotiations leading to a partial interim result would never entail such a deprivation of judicial powers, only an *overall* settlement out of court as a result of those resumed negotiations could render the dispute without purpose and lead to discontinuance of the proceedings, which 'must necessarily be unconditional'.[52]

The Court may confirm the binding nature of commitments entered into by the parties prior to the institution of the proceedings and which did provide for good offices to continue afterwards.[53] Because they 'thus create rights and obligations in international law for the parties'[54] this includes their undertaking to submit the whole of the dispute to the Court.[55] Hence, the Court may decide to afford the parties the opportunity to comply with this undertaking through further negotiations[56] within a time limit fixed by the Court.[57]

The question was raised what would be the follow-up if the parties were not willing to take action. Would that be a case of non-compliance with the judgment? Would the Court decide to discontinue the case?[58] For Judge Oda the Court was 'simply making a gesture of issuing an invitation in the guise of a judgment, to the Parties to proceed to the submission of a new case [following a new round of negotiations] independently of the present Application',[59] playing a 'role of conciliator rather than acting as a judicial institution'.[60]

---

45 *Nuclear Tests (Australia v. France), I.C.J. Reports 1974*, at p. 263, para. 30; *Fisheries Jurisdiction (Federal Republic of Germany v. Iceland), Merits, Judgment, I.C.J. Reports 1974*, p. 175, at p. 203, para. 72.

46 *Certain Norwegian Loans case, I.C.J. Reports 1957*, Dissenting opinion by Judge Read, at p. 81.

47 *Mazilu case Advisory Opinion, I.C.J. Reports 1989*, at p. 186, para. 26.

48 *PLO case Advisory Opinion, I.C.J. Reports 1988*, at p. 22, para. 23.

49 *Land and Maritime Boundary case, I.C.J. Reports 1996*, at p. 17, para. 16.

50 *Ibid.*, at p. 22, para. 36 (Nigeria).

51 *Ibid.*, at p. 22, para. 37.

52 R. Kolb, *The ICJ*, p. 193.

53 *Case between Qatar and Bahrain, I.C.J. Reports 1994*, at p. 121, para. 24.

54 *Ibid.*, at p. 121, para. 25.

55 *Ibid.*, at p. 126, para. 41 (2).

56 *Ibid.*, at p. 127, para. 41 (3).

57 *Ibid.*, at p. 127, para. 41 (4) and *I.C.J. Reports 2001*, at p. 45, para. 8.

58 *Ibid.*, Dissenting opinion by Judge Oda, at p. 135, para. 4.

59 *Ibid.*

60 *Ibid.* at p. 135, para. 5.

The fact that in the *Pulp Mills case* a mediation by Spain, officially called a 'facilitation', did not bear fruit was a further indication that the dispute was a complex one.[61]

Changing the Task of the Court as a Result of Resumed Negotiations?

Following prior negotiations and given the dynamic nature of the proceedings and under the influence of the pleadings, submissions, the hearings and the overall progress of the proceedings and in spite of resumed negotiations parties may still hold different views as to the 'nature of the task which the Court should undertake'.[62]

The change in the respective positions of the parties on this point in the course of the proceedings[63] may be the result of resumed or ongoing negotiations, and although their positions may 'have undergone a significant change and have become closer in the course of the proceedings, Parties (may) still appear unable to agree with regard to (part of) the Court's task'.[64]

More likely to happen in cases of joint submission, also in case of an Application, it would be possible for the parties, in light of the results of negotiations, to jointly (slightly) amend the nature of the task of the Court, provided submissions are being presented on those points.[65]

Oral procedure 'enables the parties to interact directly, and perhaps to limit the scope of the dispute by making concessions'.[66] Also more generally it will up to the Court to critically assess the potential impact of negotiations conducted during the proceedings upon their further course from the perspective of the proper administration of justice.

The Court's Jurisdiction

Given the importance of the peaceful settlement of disputes in the relations between States and the expansion of bilateral and multilateral treaties establishing methods in that regard, the problem of the co-existence of such different instruments does arise. In such a situation the Court may in order to establish or not its *jurisdiction* have to examine the relation between the obligations of the parties under those respective instruments.[67]

With regard to the Court's *jurisdiction* it is for the State bringing proceedings to ascertain that all conditions have been met. 'If this is not done and regardless of whether these conditions later come to be fulfilled, the Court must in principle decide the question of its jurisdiction on the basis of the conditions that existed at the time of the institution of the proceedings', and as the PCIJ we have 'shown realism and flexibility in certain situations where … conditions were not fully satisfied but were subsequently satisfied, before the Court ruled on its jurisdiction'.[68]

This judicial policy does not rule out the possibility, in the absence of prior negotiations, for parties to start such a process even if they eventually fail prior to the Court's jurisdictional decision. An attempt by the Applicant to make such negotiations fail for that particular reason would run counter to the principle of good faith applicable to both mechanisms of peaceful settlement, *a fortiori* in case of a double-track strategy.

But it is also important to recall that if 'at the date of the filing of an Application all the conditions necessary for the Court to have jurisdiction were fulfilled, it would be unacceptable for that jurisdiction to cease to exist as the result of a subsequent event'.[69]

So the unwillingness of the Respondent, which allegedly may be responsible for the breaking off of prior negotiations, to resume the process is incapable of depriving the Court of its jurisdiction and comes too late. That is the reason why the consent of both parties is required to discontinue a case.

61 Pablo Sandonato, 'Diplomatic and Judicial Means', p. 80.

62 *Land and Maritime Boundary case, I.C.J. Reports 2002*, at p. 357, para. 77.

63 *Ibid.*, at p. 357, para. 77.

64 *Ibid.*, at p. 359, para. 83 (on the land boundary).

65 *Ibid.*, at p. 399, para. 191.

66 R. Kolb, *The ICJ*, p. 911.

67 See for instance *Aegean Sea Continental Shelf case, I.C.J. Reports 1978*, at p. 38, paras. 92–3.

68 *Croatian Genocide case, I.C.J. Reports 2008*, at p. 438, paras. 80 and 81.

69 *Ibid.*, at p. 438, para. 80.

The alleged (un)willingness of one party to resume failed negotiations in order to work towards an out-of-court settlement may belong to 'events already examined, so far as was necessary to the Court, in the context of another case'[70] and there may be no reasons for the Court to decline to entertain a particular case because its judgment may have implications in the other case.[71]

A Respondent asserting that the subject-matter of the dispute is being discussed between the parties has to provide the Court with further details of such negotiations in order to allow the Court to determine whether the parties' intention has been to exclude for the time being recourse to the Court because of that process going on. The Respondent should explain the 'precise consequences which it considered the holding of those negotiations, *or the holding of negotiations generally*, would have in regard to the Court's jurisdiction'.[72]

Prima facie jurisdiction cannot be excluded 'solely by reason of the negotiations' referred to by a Respondent.[73] A Respondent introducing a preliminary objection in order 'to slow the proceedings down'[74] may do so to explore the Applicant's willingness to resume negotiations to the 'partial' success of which the Respondent has no longer contributed as a result of the Applicant having brought the dispute before the Court.

The Admissibility of a Claim

The *admissibility* of a claim may be contested on the ground that there had been no prior diplomatic negotiations 'such as would disclose the existence of a dispute' between the parties,[75] the process thus having been unable to perform one of its important and preliminary functions.

The principle 'according to which it should not penalize a defect in a procedural act which the application could easily remedy' is well established:[76] even if the existence of a definite dispute were necessary, this condition could at any time be fulfilled by means of a unilateral action on the part of the Applicant. 'The Court cannot allow itself to be hampered by a mere defect of forms, the removal of which depends solely on the Party concerned.'[77]

Would this mean that such a defect cannot be remedied by the parties *jointly* embarking upon a resumed process of negotiations after the start of the proceedings? Are realism and flexibility also applicable on the prior negotiations condition to such an extent that this defect not only could but perhaps should be cured during the proceedings as an Applicant could easily remedy this situation?[78]

Although such a situation could be easily remedied by the Applicant, that State is unlikely to be willing to (re)negotiate during the course of the proceedings, unless for instance ordered by the Court to do so by way of a provisional measure. However, it may also happen that as part of the functional interaction the Applicant has started proceedings also as a means to put more pressure on the Respondent during renewed parallel negotiations.

Since the Court has the power 'to take into consideration all relevant elements in administering justice between the parties'[79] these elements do include negotiations conducted during the course of the proceedings and their eventual outcome; we will deal in more detail with this aspect of the functional interaction in the next chapter.

---

70 *Legality of Use of Force (Serbia and Montenegro v. Belgium), I.C.J. Reports 2004*, p. 279, at p. 301, para. 54.

71 *Ibid.*, at p. 296, para. 40 and at p. 301, para. 54.

72 *Arrest Warrant case, I.C.J. Reports 2000*, at p. 200, para. 66 (emphasis added).

73 *Ibid.*, at p. 200, para. 66.

74 R. Kolb, *The ICJ*, p. 229.

75 *Nottebohm case, I.C.J. Reports 1955*, at p. 11 (I).

76 *Mavrommatis Palestine Concessions, P.C.I.J. Series A, No. 2,* p. 34 and *Polish Upper Silesia, P.C.I.J. Series A, No. 6*, p. 14.

77 *Application of the Convention on the Prevention and Punishment of the Crime of Genocide, Preliminary Objections, Judgment, I.C.J. Reports 1996*, p. 595, at p. 613, para. 26.

78 *Croatian Genocide case, I.C.J. Reports 2008*, Dissenting opinion by Judge Owada, at p. 506, para. 18; at p. 507, para. 19; at p. 511, para. 24 (b) and (d) and (e); and at p. 512, para. 25.

79 *Fisheries Jurisdiction, (United Kingdom v. Iceland), I.C.J. Reports 1974*, at p. 22, para. 48.

Legal Parameters Once the Decision to Resume Negotiations Has Been Taken

The two general duties for parties and the Court's pronouncements – both indicators of the continuous nature of the obligation to negotiate as mentioned earlier – also function as legal parameters once the decision to resume the negotiations has been taken.

Even in a jointly submitted case 'the substance of the dispute and the basis on which the Court is asked to rule' may seem to be rather unclear. Judicial wisdom may then require the Court to hand the case back to the parties with the request 'to clarify their common position on the subject of the dispute'.[80]

Could such negotiations during the course of the proceedings be considered to run counter to the rule that *pendente lite* 'the Court's judgment should not be anticipated by reason of any initiative regarding the matters in issue before the Court'.[81] A negative answer appears to be self-evident, even if the outcome of the process does not lead to discontinuance.

On the other hand parties clearly consider both the risk of an armed conflict to hang as a shadow over the proceedings[82] and the actual occurrence of armed conflict during which an attempt is made 'to secure by force what constitutes the actual subject-matter of the dispute' as 'wholly destructive of the peaceful settlement procedure represented by the seisin of the Court'.[83]

6.2 Some Factual Parameters

The initial attitude taken by each of the parties from the moment a dispute between them is coming into existence, especially if for a long period of time no agreement has been reached during prior negotiations,[84] probably is the first factual and rather influential parameter for their eventual resumption during the course of the proceedings. For instance, a protracted deadlock may have as one of the main consequences 'the tacit message the situation conveys that there is no opportunity to restart the process'.[85]

Various factual parameters may surround resumption in addition to the usual determining or surrounding factors such as, for instance, 'the diplomatic skills of the parties'[86] or the resignation of the leader of the government.[87] Mention could also be made of divergent positions taken by a government during negotiations and a President's lack of reaction.[88]

Bilateral and multilateral negotiations aimed at stopping an armed conflict require the guaranteed participation by the Foreign Secretary, whose freedom to travel worldwide may be restricted by a course of State action forming the source of a dispute before the Court.[89]

---

80 *Case between Botswana and Namibia, I.C.J. Reports 1999*, Separate opinion by Judge Oda, at p. 1128, para. 26 and at p. 1142, para. 60.

81 *Pulp Mills case, I.C.J. Reports 2007*, at p. 14, para. 46 (Uruguay).

82 *Border Area Activities case (Costa Rica v. Nicaragua), I.C.J. Reports 2011*, Request by Costa Rica for the indication of provisional measures, para. 16.

83 *Frontier Dispute, Provisional Measures, Order of 10 January 1986, I.C.J. Reports 1986*, p. 3, at p. 7, para. 6 (6) (Mali).

84 *Fisheries case, I.C.J. Reports 1951*, at p. 124, the Applicant making urgent representations 'in the course of which the question of referring the dispute to the Permanent Court of International Justice was raised', while the Respondent would adopt a lenient approach pending 'the result of the negotiations', lenience which was then abandoned since 'no agreement had been reached' for a period of 13 years.

85 G. Faure, 'Deadlocks', p. 28.

86 *Case between Qatar and Bahrain, I.C.J. Reports 2001*, Dissenting opinion by Judge Oda, at p. 140, para. 37.

87 *Case between Botswana and Namibia, I.C.J. Reports 1999*, Dissenting opinion by Judge Parra-Aranguren, at p. 1208, para. 2. Also the 'personal characteristics and qualities of a negotiator are of importance, provided it is assumed that he is in close contact with the sources of power and authority in his government': A. Lall, *Modern International Negotiation*, p. 323.

88 *Case between Botswana and Namibia, I.C.J. Reports 1999*, Dissenting opinion by Judge Weeramantry, at p. 1168, para. 44 and at p. 1169, para. 48.

89 *Arrest Warrant case, I.C.J. Reports 2000*, Dissenting opinion by Judge *ad hoc* Bula-Bula, at p. 234, para. 22 and *I.C.J. Reports 2002*, Dissenting opinion by Judge *ad hoc* Bula-Bula, at p. 129, para. 88.

The fact of the dispute being *sub judice* does of course not prevent incidents from occurring even during those resumed negotiations, as several cases have demonstrated.[90]

When diplomatic discussions following protests against a particular action by one of the parties may have led to the signing of a Special Agreement to bring the matter before the Court, the expected calming effect of the start of the proceedings might not have prevented further actions afterwards and which in turn may lead to protests.[91]

When litigation 'is in progress an Applicant may address requests to a Respondent to give an assurance that it will not pursue the contested activity',[92] such a request eventually resulting in a resumption of prior negotiations.

Obviously, differences of opinion between parties about the extent or even the existence of a particular power claimed by one of them might disappear as a result of resumed negotiations, but this may also be the result of the progressive exchange of views during the oral proceedings.[93]

Occasionally judges may observe that in their view 'facts intervening during the diplomatic negotiations or pending the proceedings before this Court have been treated as irrelevant'.[94]

6.3 Pursuance of Negotiations and Adjudication *Pari Passu*: The Double-Track Strategy

The Choice for a Double-Track Strategy

Once a dispute has arisen between parties its complexity, its sensitive nature at home, external pressure from the international community to work towards a peaceful settlement may contribute to their view that perhaps a double track strategy could very well turn out to be the most viable option in a medium- and long-term perspective of their mutual relations. A joint effort to embark on a double-track strategy will not only testify to both parties embracing the principle of good faith, but it may also help to mitigate the perception of irreversibility adjudication could carry with it.

The functional interaction is likely to reach its full potential in the course of a double-track strategy: at the negotiating table parties are of course fully aware of every progress, or lack of it as the case may be, in the proceedings before the Court, while at the same time they will be able to amend their legal positions in The Hague until the close of the oral proceedings, and even beyond that moment if and when they decide in favour of discontinuance.

The Court itself on several occasions has reminded parties and in fact States at large that it 'is always open to the parties to a dispute to have recourse to a conjunction of judicial determination and settlement by agreement',[95] although such a combination does not necessarily have to cover the whole of the dispute.

As part of a double-track strategy parties may decide to start, with priority, negotiations on the delimitation of a disputed area while also having talks on the conclusion of a Special Agreement to refer the dispute jointly to the Court.[96] Once the text of the compromis has been finalized, parties may then 'define the general lines on the basis of which subsequent meetings' on the substantive issues would take place.[97]

Resumed negotiations may not only be the part of a chosen double-track strategy but they may also take place, as a special kind of double-track strategy – a State having referred the matter simultaneously to the Security Council and the ICJ – following a call by the SC while the case was already pending before the Court. The SC may then invite both parties to 'continue to take into account the contribution that appropriate judicial

90 *Territorial and Maritime Dispute between Nicaragua and Honduras, I.C.J. Reports 2007*, at p. 681, para. 58.

91 *Continental Shelf between Tunisia and Libya, I.C.J. Reports 1982*, at p. 37, para. 21.

92 *Nuclear Tests (Australia v. France), I.C.J. Reports 1974*, Joint dissenting opinion by Judges Oneyama, Dillard, Jimenez de Arechaga, Waldock, at p. 317.

93 *Dispute regarding Navigational and Related Rights, I.C.J. Reports 2009*, at p. 248, para. 86. See also *East Timor case, I.C.J. Reports 1995*, Separate opinion by Judge Ranjeva, at p. 132.

94 *Asylum case, I.C.J. Reports 1950*, Dissenting opinion by Judge Read, at p. 329.

95 *Revision and Interpretation of the 1982 Continental Shelf Judgment, I.C.J. Reports 1985*, at p. 218, para. 47.

96 *Aegean Sea Continental Shelf case, I.C.J. Reports 1978*, at p. 9, para. 18.

97 *Ibid.*, at p. 9, para. 19.

means, in particular the International Court of Justice, are qualified to make to the settlement of any remaining legal differences that they may identify in connection with the present dispute'.[98]

Parties may then resume their negotiations while the case was pending and agree that these negotiations would be confidential.[99] One of the parties may then express its expectation of the resolution 'to clear away the obstacles to a resumption of the dialogue'.[100]

The fact that both parties have expressed their willingness to seek a peaceful solution through negotiations does not rule out resorting to the Court in order to have a point of law, for instance the extent of a particular right, 'as a preliminary to negotiations over the modalities of' the exercise of that right.[101]

Various Modes of (Dys)Functional Interaction

While pre-adjudicatory negotiations are part and parcel of the *causa petendi* consisting of a set of originating facts and circumstances, and may also intend to render more precise the *petitum*, negotiations during the course of the proceedings may result in the *petitum* being subject to a modification of the submissions 'without exceeding the scope of the subject of the dispute as reflected in the Application'.[102] This way negotiations may bring about not only a fundamental change in the factual circumstances but also in the legal ones since the Court has been seised.[103]

Conversely, since the final submissions of the parties should normally clearly put forward the points of disagreement between them, this may have an impact on their willingness eventually to resume the negotiations and on the chances of that process becoming successful prior to the Court's final decision on the merits of the case.

The Court is unable to share the view that 'the existence of active negotiations in progress constitutes an impediment' to the exercise of its jurisdiction,[104] neither could the establishment of a fact-finding mission by the UN Secretary-General with the agreement of the two States concerned be 'considered in itself as in any way incompatible with the continuance of parallel proceedings before the Court';[105] although the Court refers to the fact that both negotiations and judicial settlement are 'enumerated together in Article 33 of the UN Charter' and that there are various examples of cases in which they have both 'been pursued *pari passu*'[106] it does not pronounce itself on the alleged negative impact of the continuation of the proceedings at the negotiating table.

An initial agreement on the procedure to be followed may provide that the talks 'shall be frank, thorough going and pursued in good faith with a view to reaching an agreement based on their mutual consent'.[107]

Dysfunctional interaction may arise when, after negotiations have been going in parallel with the proceedings before the Court, the party which was not very much in favour of this strategy (or really opposed, or saying that there was no common ground for this strategy) takes the position that the continuation of the proceedings is not reconcilable with the necessary conditions for the conduct of such frank and serious negotiations and the spirit in which they should be conducted. It may hold the view that discontinuance and removal of the case from the list would 'be more conducive to the creation of a favourable climate for an agreed settlement'.[108]

98 *Ibid.*, at p. 10, para. 23: Security Council Resolution 395 (1976), para. 4.

99 *Ibid.*, at p. 10, para. 24.

100 *Aegean Sea Continental Shelf case, I.C.J.Reports 1976,* at p. 12, para. 40 (Greece).

101 H. Thirlway, 'The Recommendations Made by the International Court of Justice: A Sceptical View' (2009) 58 *International and Comparative Law Quarterly*, 1, 151–63 at 155.

102 *Fisheries Jurisdiction (Spain v. Canada), I.C.J. Reports 1998*, Dissenting opinion by Judge *ad hoc* Torres Bernardez, at pp. 602–3, para. 56 and at p. 625, para. 109.

103 *Questions of Interpretation and Application of the 1971 Montreal Convention arising from the Aerial Incident at Lockerbie (Libyan Arab Jamahiriya v. United Kingdom), Provisional Measures, Order of 14 April 1992, I.C.J. Reports 1992*, p. 3, Dissenting opinion by Judge Ranjeva, at p. 74 (*mutatis mutandis).*

104 *Aegean Sea Continental Shelf case, I.C.J. Reports 1978*, at p. 12, para. 29.

105 *Hostages case, I.C.J. Reports 1980*, at p. 23, para. 43.

106 *Aegean Sea Continental Shelf case, I.C.J. Reports 1978*, at p. 12, para. 29.

107 *Ibid.*, at p. 12, para. 27.

108 *Ibid.*, at p. 12, para. 28 (letter Turkey).

Diplomatic correspondence exchanged as part of the parallel negotiating process after the start of the proceedings may be brought to the attention of the Court.[109] In these circumstances the Court 'is bound to take note of further developments both prior and subsequent to the close of the oral proceedings'[110] because it is its duty to ascertain the 'true subject of the dispute, the object and purpose of the claim' and a dispute cannot be separated 'from the situation in which it has arisen, and from further developments which may have affected it'.[111]

The Court may become aware of subsequent negotiations and their outcome if they have entered the public domain without one of the parties having drawn its attention to them. The question arises whether it is possible for the Court to reopen the oral proceedings to provide the parties with an opportunity to address comments on those further developments.[112]

This possibility, as part of the previously mentioned duty of ascertainment resting upon the Court, is subject to strict conditions. Not only must the matter be completely new, and not have been raised during the proceedings; moreover those developments must not merely supplement and reinforce matters already discussed in the course of the proceedings.[113]

This may be precisely what happens in case the process of parallel negotiations has led to significant progress. A successful outcome does not have to be comprehensive; indeed, a first agreement may be signed without taking away the need for further negotiations on other aspects of the dispute or to determine further details and modalities with regard to its implementation. Indeed, a first agreement signed between the parties just three months after the instituting of the proceedings may be limited for instance to the procedure to be followed during the negotiations.[114]

Alternatively, in spite of diplomatic correspondence continuing during the proceedings before the Court, developments in the controversy may not be of such a nature as to resolve the dispute to the satisfaction of the Applicant.[115]

A Jurisdictional Decision

The expiry, after the institution of proceedings by Application, of the Respondent's declaration of acceptance of the compulsory jurisdiction of the ICJ may result in that government denying the Court's jurisdiction and in its inability/unwillingness, *for the moment*, to appear before the Court. However, the Respondent may express its readiness to begin negotiations with the Applicant to arrive at an amicable solution. This could be either a direct settlement out of court, resort to arbitration or a preference for judicial settlement by the ICJ.[116]

Another mode of functional interaction would consist in the Court 'introducing an intermediate procedure prior to making its final decision' on its jurisdiction, by giving 'indications' of its reaction and then allowing 'the parties a period of time to come to a consensual solution of the problem' of interpretation of the initial act of seisin.[117]

Once the parties or at least one of them has during bilateral consultations recognized that settlement of a dispute by judicial decision could be necessary, 'it would have been an entirely civilized way to handle the matter' if the disputants would have been able to reach, prior to or even during the proceedings before objections being made, 'some form of *ad hoc* understanding not to contest jurisdiction'.[118]

On the other hand, it has to be recognized that the chances of a Respondent having raised preliminary objections to the Court's jurisdiction being willing to withdraw that objection as a result of negotiations are

---

109 *Nuclear Tests (New Zealand v. France), IC.J. Reports 1974*, at pp. 467–8, para. 32.

110 *Ibid.*, at p. 468, para. 32.

111 *Ibid.*, at p. 467, para. 31.

112 *Ibid.*, at p. 468, para. 34.

113 *Ibid.*, at p; 469, para. 34.

114 *Aegean Continental Shelf, Order of 18 April 1977, I.C.J. Reports 1977*, p. 3, at p. 4.

115 *Nuclear Tests (New Zealand v. France), I.C.J. Reports 1974*, at pp. 464–5, para. 27.

116 *Nottebohm case, Order of 21 March 1953: I.C.J. Reports 1953*, p. 7 at pp. 7–8.

117 *Case between Qatar and Bahrain, I.C.J. Reports 1995*, Dissenting opinion by Judge Sahabuddeen, at p. 51, referring to the 1994 judgment in the case.

118 *Certain Property case, I.C.J. Reports 2005*, Dissenting opinion by Judge *ad hoc* Berman, at p. 81, para. 28.

rather remote, taking into account the fact that in case of unilateral seisin the willingness of either party to resume prior negotiations must be considered rather slim, although not necessarily completely non-existent.

With regard to a negative jurisdictional decision by the Court upholding a preliminary objection, it may seem clear that it 'does not create legal obligations *stricto sensu* which the parties … are required to comply with',[119] although '[s]ome elements of *res judicata* attaches to' the findings of the Court that the parties are in a legal dispute the subject-matter of which it has objectively determined,[120] and this in turn may very well influence the post-adjudicative resumption of negotiations.

Impact on the Court's Final Decision

Failure of a resumed process of negotiations as result of one party having broken off the talks abruptly may bring the most willing party to submit a request for the indication of a provisional measure aiming at the resumption of those talks. It will then be for the Court to decide about the appropriateness of using its powers under Article 41 of the Statute. We will return to this scenario later on.

In case negotiations have been ordered by the Court as a provisional measure shortly after the start of the proceedings, a failure of the talks after the close of the oral hearings may constitute a new development which the Court may be called upon to examine and to take into account in its final deliberation on the merits.

With regard to the exercise of its advisory jurisdiction, one should note that the fact that 'important recent and current activities relating' for instance to nuclear disarmament 'are being pursued in other fora' than the requesting organ is immaterial.[121]

Various cases remind us that a double track strategy does not offer guarantees for an obstacle-free journey. Indeed, as already indicated, in case of (partial) failure of resumed or continued negotiations during the course of the proceedings parties take the risk that the dispute aggravates and/or that the ultimate and unsuccessful attempt to find a negotiated solution renders it more difficult or even impossible for the Court to perform the task it was called upon to perform in the first place. It will then be for the Court to consider how to integrate the conduct and the outcome of these negotiations in its deliberations and judgment. We will deal with this aspect in the next chapter.

6.4 Resumed Substantive Negotiations and the Court's Decisions on Questions of Procedure

In adjudicatory proceedings an important functional role is assigned to questions of procedure[122] to which parties scrupulously pay attention in designing their litigation strategy which moreover by nature is characterized by the interlinkage between matters of substance and questions of procedure. Conversely, States may find the conduct of their negotiations rendered more difficult by judicial procedural decisions.[123]

It is then not surprising that even minor changes in parties' positions on the merits of a case might affect the procedural aspects of the proceedings. Such changes may result from the dynamic evolvement of the written and oral pleadings, but they may also be the product of parallel negotiations. We now turn to this particular functional feature of a double track strategy.

119 *Application of the Convention on the Prevention and Punishment of the Crime of Genocide (Bosnia and Herzegovina v. Serbia and Montenegro), Judgment, I.C.J. Reports 2007*, p. 43, Dissenting opinion by Judge *ad hoc* Kreca, at pp. 468–9, para. 17.

120 *Certain Property case, I.C.J. Reports 2005*, Dissenting opinion by Judge *ad hoc* Berman, at p. 81, para. 28.

121 *Nuclear Weapons Advisory Opinion, I.C.J. Reports 1996*, at p. 233, para. 12.

122 See generally E. Lauterpacht, 'Principles of Procedure in International litigation' (2009) 345 *Recueil des Cours de L'Académie de Droit International*, 387–530 and A. Nolkaemper, 'International Adjudication of Global Public Goods: The Intersection of Substance and Procedure' (2012) 23 *European Journal of International Law*, 769–91.

123 *Fisheries Jurisdiction (United Kingdom v. Iceland), Interim Measures, Order of 12 July 1973, I.C.J. Reports 1973*, p. 302, Dissenting opinion by Judge Gros, at p. 309.

In practice many 'decisions on minor procedural issues, such as fixing time-limits for pleadings, may indeed 'be based on practical considerations of convenience' – such as for instance a feasible progress in a resumed process of negotiations – 'rather than rules of law'.[124]

It goes without saying that 'States engaged in proceedings before the Court' are 'under a duty to conform with all decisions as to procedure'.[125] It 'is of course a matter of propriety' that the parties 'should not attempt to manipulate the machinery and the authority of the Court back and forth, depending on changing diplomatic contingencies'.[126]

It is not always easy to identify and distinguish between those negotiations which were directly dealing with questions of procedure[127] and those addressing matters of substance as part of the double track strategy.

In the performance of its duty under Article 48 of the Statute to secure an orderly conduct of the case the Court will have to fix and frequently extend time limits for the filing of the written pleadings, the date for the opening of the oral proceedings and so on. In doing so the Court takes into account 'agreement concerning the procedure expressed by the Parties, consulted under Article 31 of the Rules' and thus expressed before the President [128] or 'outside the President's office'.[129]

In the first scenario the President's role may entail more than just ascertaining the views of the parties, as it may involve a kind of *mediation* – although as the same case has clearly illustrated, such *negotiations* before the President are not always successful.[130]

In the alternative scenario such agreements are the result of direct contacts and consultations.[131]

Parties may request Court decisions on a variety of rather traditional procedural matters, such as extension of time limits, but as far as the functional interaction is concerned States may reserve for themselves the right to require the *suspension* of the proceedings in case a dispute before the Court has been submitted to the Security Council and is under examination by that body,[132] or even postponement of a particular phase in the proceedings.

Changing the subject-matter of the dispute does not always have to occur, although this may have been the intention of (one of) the parties; their consultations or negotiations may also deal with important matters which, however, are not exclusively of a procedural nature without, however, addressing the merits as such of the dispute.

Indeed, the main intention of the parties, after the instituting of the proceedings by unilateral Application, may have been such as through negotiations 'to establish a complete equality between them by replacing the original procedure based on a unilateral Application by a procedure based on a Special Agreement'. But, as the Court pointed out, such a change as to the procedure does not necessarily reflect an intention to involve any change with regard to the merits[133] or for an objection taken by the Respondent in its Counter-Memorial to

124 H. Thirlway, 'The Law and Procedure of the International Court of Justice 1960–1989 Supplement, 2011: Parts Eleven, Twelve and Thirteen' 82 *British Yearbook of International Law*, 1–177, at 6.

125 *Land, Island and Maritime Frontier Dispute, I.C.J. Reports 1992*, at p. 581, para. 371.

126 J. Sztucki, *Interim Measures in the Hague Court: An Attempt at a Scrutiny* (Deventer, 1983), p. 200.

127 Such as for instance on the subject of the expert opinion and the name of the experts in the *Corfu Channel case, Order of 9 April 1949: I.C.J. Reports 1949,* at p. 172.

128 *Border and Transborder Armed Actions (Nicaragua v. Honduras), Order of 22 October 1986: I.C.J. Reports 1986*, p. 551, at p. 552.

129 *Case between Qatar and Bahrain, I.C.J. Reports 2001*, at p. 48, para. 26: communication to the Court by separate letters of 'joint statement embodying the results of their consultations concerning the organization of the oral proceedings'. *Pulp Mills case, I.C.J. Reports 2010,* at p. 26, para. 15: agreement between the Parties without the assistance of the President on producing new documents, pending of course the authorization of the Court. See also *Obligation to Negotiate Access to the Pacific Ocean (Bolivia v. Chile), Order of 18 June 2013, I.C.J. Reports 2013*, p. 223, at p. 224.

130 *Case between Qatar and Bahrain, I.C.J. Reports 1999*, pp. 3–7 and *I.C.J. Reports 2001*, at p. 48, para. 25.

131 *Fisheries Jurisdiction (Spain v. Canada), I.C.J. Reports 1998*, at p. 435, para. 4.

132 *Anglo-Iranian Oil Co. case (jurisdiction), Judgment of 22 July 1952, I.C.J. Reports 1952*, p. 93, at p. 99: that was indeed in the Persian declaration, penultimate paragraph, exception (c).

133 *Corfu Channel case, I.C.J. Reports 1949*, at p. 25. Another example belonging to the same category presents itself when negotiations may also lead to a Special Agreement, for instance asking the Court to join two cases (*North Sea Continental Shelf (Denmark/Federal Republic of Germany; Federal Republic Germany/Netherlands) Order of 26 April 1968, I.C.J. Reports 1968*, p. 9 at p. 10).

the admissibility of the Application to 'be heard and determined within the framework of the merits pursuant to Article 79, paragraph 8, of the Rules of Court'.[134]

Requests for the Extension of Time Limits for the Submission of Memorials

An Applicant may, for instance almost two years after having filed its Application, ask for a stay of the proceedings or to extend the time limit by 12 months referring *inter alia* 'to certain diplomatic initiatives'.[135] In doing so the party concerned is resorting to the *fonction dilatoire* in order to 'différer le moment d'entrer en vigueur d'une altération de la situation juridique préexistante'.[136]

During a meeting with the President parties may agree, relatively soon after the filing of an Application, that 'no measure should be taken in the case until a decision in another pending case'.[137]

When in that judgment the Court did consider it 'highly desirable that the elements of the dispute that were not settled by the Arbitral Award of 31 July 1989 be resolved as soon as possible, as both Parties desire',[138] parties shortly afterwards (February 1992) requested no time limit be fixed for the initial pleadings 'pending the outcome of negotiations on the question of maritime delimitation, which were to continue for six months in the first instance'.[139]

Parties themselves are best placed to assess the time they would probably need to reach an agreement, when more than six months later they reported 'some progress'and jointly requested a further period of three months with a possible extension of another three months 'for continuation of the negotiations'.[140]

A first agreement signed between the parties just three months after the instituting of the proceedings may be limited for instance to the procedure to be followed during further negotiations on matters of substance. The state of the relations between the parties may require certain efforts to implement even this first agreement and then to start 'meaningful negotiations'.[141]

The Respondent may have no objection to the request 'that the time-limit for the Memorial be extended by three months in order to facilitate to the fullest extent possible the negotiations in progress' on the subject of the merits of the dispute without this implying 'any undertaking on the part of his Government'.[142] Having regard to these negotiations, the Court may then extend the time limit.[143]

Although the Court, acting upon the notification by each of the parties that certain agreements had been reached on a regional level containing *inter alia* the Applicant's commitment to request postponement of the time limit for submission of its Memorial on the merits, granted this extension, it was also cautious by reserving a decision with regard to the Counter-Memorial.[144]

A few months later an agreement reached at another Regional Summit recorded the agreement between the parties to the case 'in the context of arrangements aimed at achieving an extra-judicial settlement of the dispute which is the subject of the present proceedings' to 'request postponement of the date for the fixing of time-limit for the presentation of the counter memorial' until 11 June 1990. It further provided that if no 'extra-judicial settlement' had been reached by that date, either party may request that the Respondent be

134 *Elettronica Sicula S.p.A. (ELSI), Order of 17 November 1987, I.C.J. Reports 1987*, p. 185, at p. 185.

135 *Legality of Use of Force case, I.C.J. Reports 2004*, at p. 285, para. 12 (Yugoslavia).

136 J.-M. Thouvenin, 'Le délai raisonnable', p. 114.

137 *Maritime Delimitation between Guinea-Bissau and Senegal, I.C.J. Reports 1995*, at pp. 423 and 424.

138 *Arbitral Award case, I.C.J. Reports 1991*, at p. 75, para. 68.

139 *Maritime Delimitation between Guinea-Bissau and Senegal, I.C.J. Reports 1995*, at p. 425.

140 *Ibid.*. In fact further extensions were granted in the course of 1993, and in early 1994 agreement was reached and notified to the Court. The President expressed his satisfaction and informed the parties about the removal from the General List as soon as they notified him of their decision to discontinue. It took the parties another 18 months to make that notification: *Ibid.*

141 *Aegean Sea Continental Shelf case, I.C.J. Reports 1977*, at p. 4 (Turkey).

142 *Ibid.*, at pp. 3–4.

143 *Ibid.*, at p. 4.

144 *Border and Transborder Armed Actions (Nicaragua v. Honduras), Order of 31 August 1989, I.C.J. Reports 1989*, p. 123, at pp. 123–4.

granted six months for the filing.[145] The Court, taking into account the agreement of the parties in accordance with Article 44, para. 2 of its Rules, granted the extension of the time-limits.[146]

This case typifies a situation in which at various intervals during the proceedings the parties agree to request a postponement of further steps in the procedure because of and as a result of ongoing negotiations within a larger and multiparty framework and in light of certain agreements reached between the parties to the case within that context.

While being another example of parties attempting to find an extra-judicial settlement of the dispute, the functional interaction reflects the mutual caution as regards the chances of reaching such a settlement in the short term by fully preserving each party's procedural rights, when each of the parties informed the Court of an agreement reached by the Presidents of the Central American countries in San Isidro de Coronado.[147]

The fact that apparently some kind of negotiation is taking place does not automatically mean that both parties are willing to request and accept an extension of a time-limit. Indeed, an extension of the time limit for the filing of a Counter-Memorial may be granted by a senior judge as suggested by the Respondent in light of 'recent diplomatic initiatives' and in spite of refusal by the Applicant.[148]

When drafting a Special Agreement parties may take care to include rather detailed provisions on procedural matters for the proceedings to come. Once the adjudicative phase has really started they are free to modify those provisions and to inform the Court by a joint letter about those changes and to request a four-month extension for the filing of their Counter-Memorial.[149] It should be noted that in all other respects the Special Agreement remained unchanged.

After the instituting of the proceedings consultations could be held between the parties with a view to reaching an agreement regarding, for instance, the extension of a particular time-limit for the presentation of a written statement of observations and submissions in regard to preliminary objections.[150]

It goes almost without saying that when an extension of time-limits, although initially less than requested, can be granted by the Court for reasons of the number, importance and the complexity of the questions raised in preliminary objections, the same flexibility would be called for in case such an extension would enable the parties, ready to do so, at least to seize the opportunity for resumed negotiations during the course of the proceedings.[151]

Given *inter alia* new developments in the case since the filing of the Memorial and the number of points still in dispute between the parties after the first round of written pleadings, an Applicant may request a reply and rejoinder.[152] Such new developments and outstanding points of controversy could also be resumed negotiations and their rather unsuccessful outcome.

145 *Border and Transborder Armed Actions (Nicaragua v. Honduras), Order of 14 December 1989, I.C.J. Reports 1989*, p. 174, at p. 175.

146 *Ibid.*, at p. 175. As two and a half years later neither party had made such a request, the Court was informed on 11 May 1992 that the parties 'had reached an out-of-court agreement aimed at enhancing their good neighbourly relations'; hence their decision to renounce all further right of action based on the case: *Border and Transborder Armed Actions (Nicaragua v. Honduras), Order of 27 May 1992, I.C.J. Reports 1992*, p. 222, at p. 223.

147 *Border and Transborder Armed Actions case, I.C.J. Reports 1989*, at p. 175.

148 *Questions of Interpretation and Application of the 1971 Montreal Convention arising from the Aerial Incident at Lockerbie (Libyan Arab Jamahiriya v. United States of America), Order of 17 December 1998, I.C.J. Reports 1998*, p. 749, at pp. 749–50.

149 *Sovereignty over Pulau Ligitan and Pulau Sipadan (Indonesia/Malaysia), Order of 14 September 1999, I.C.J. Reports 1999*, p. 1012, at p. 1013. In this case this happened three times in a period of one year: *Order of 11 May 2000, I.C.J. Reports 2000*, p. 9, at p. 9 and *Order of 19 October 2000, I.C.J. Reports 2000*, p. 173, at pp. 173–4.

150 *Interhandel Case, Order of 26 June 1958: I.C.J. Reports 1958*, p. 31, at p. 32.

151 *Case concerning the Barcelona Traction, Light and Power Company, Limited (Belgium v. Spain), Order of 20 June 1960: I.C.J. Reports 1960*, p. 183 at p. 184. Forthcoming consultations within an IO may also be the reason for a request to extend a time-limit for the submission of written comments: *Judgment No. 2867 of the Administrative tribunal of the International Labour Organization upon a Complaint Filed against the International Fund for Agricultural Development, Advisory Opinion, I.C.J. Reports 2012*, p. 10, at p. 17, para. 7.

152 *Pulp Mills on the River Uruguay (Argentina v. Uruguay), Order of 14 September 2007, I.C.J. Reports 2007*, p. 656, at pp. 656–7.

Particular Requests

With regard to extensions of time limits in general, one can only agree that 'unreasonable prolongation of time-limits for the performance of procedural acts is to be curtailed and avoided'.[153]

Proper administration of justice is the decisive criterion in these matters. In recent times Judge Trindade has poignantly observed that the procedural (and substantive) practice of the proper administration of international justice has to be kept in line with the fundamental structural changes contemporary international law has been undergoing to the effect that when an individual is the ultimate titulaire of a right or the beneficiary of a reparation due, the test of reasonableness should be applied accordingly.[154] Providing the parties another six months to first attempt to negotiate an agreement on reparation as requested by the Applicant and in case of failure to settle the question itself does not appear to survive this test when parties had already had 12 years since the proceedings started.[155]

The 'Rules of Court are silent on the suspension of proceedings, but it cannot be doubted that the Court has an inherent power to do so if it wishes. The Court has traditionally avoided formally suspending proceedings and has instead preferred, where necessary, to extend time-limits. These extensions often amount to *de facto* suspensions'.[156]

The Court may be requested to render an advisory opinion *on a priority basis*. For a new case to be heard 'in priority to other pending cases' urgency is required and the Court 'remains competent to adjudicate on urgency even where a case formally falls within a category of priority prescribed by the Rules of Court'.[157] Although expressed in relation to a request for an advisory opinion on a priority basis, this observation also applies to contentious proceedings.

From a functional perspective it does not *prima facie* seem that ongoing negotiations which eventually would enable parties to settle the whole of the dispute as it has been submitted to the Court would qualify as a factor of urgency, unless of course the parties themselves have requested the postponement of oral proceedings for that particular reason.

Requests for the Postponement of the Opening of the Oral Proceedings

The expiry, after the institution of proceedings by Application, of the Respondent's declaration of acceptance of the compulsory jurisdiction of the ICJ may result in that government denying the Court's jurisdiction and in its inability, *for the moment*, to appear before the Court.

However, the Respondent State may express its readiness to begin negotiations with the Applicant to arrive at an amicable solution. This could be either a direct settlement out of court, resort to arbitration or, as in this case, a preference for judicial settlement by the ICJ.[158]

As both parties informed the President of their common desire to settle their dispute by negotiation, the President abstained from ordering any further steps relating to the continuation of the proceedings.[159]

The Court waited six months for results, but when no information about the conclusion of any agreement reached the Court it could not refrain from using its powers under Article 48 of the Statute and fixed a time limit for the Applicant to present a written statement of its observations in response to the earlier communication by the Respondent.[160] Later on the Court, not having been informed that the negotiations had achieved any result, fixed the date for a hearing.[161]

153 *Diallo case, I.C.J. Reports 2010*, Separate opinion by Judge Cançado Trindade, at p. 798, para. 202.

154 *Ibid.*, at p. 798, para. 203; at p. 800, para. 209; and at p. 804, para. 220.

155 *Ibid.*, at p. 798, para. 202.

156 D. Prager, 'Procedural Developments at the International Court of Justice' (2002) 1 *The Law and Practice of International Courts and Tribunals* 1, 189–215 at 198.

157 *Applicability of Article VI, Section 22 of the Convention on the Privileges and Immunities of the United Nations, Advisory Opinion, I.C.J. Reports 1989*, p. 177, Separate opinion by Judge Shahabuddeen, at p. 212.

158 *Nottebohm case, Order of 21 March 1953: I.C.J. Reports 1953*, at pp. 7–8.

159 *Ibid.*, at p. 8.

160 *Ibid.*

161 *Nottebohm case (Preliminary Objection), I.C.J. Reports 1953*, at p. 117.

Could it then be inferred to be a normal duty for parties to inform the Court about the positive or negative outcome of their negotiations with regard to the dispute that one party had already submitted to the Court? Although the outcome of those negotiations should not be considered by the Court to constitute 'an extrinsic fact'[162] such a notification would allow the Court either to avail itself of its powers under the Statute with regard to the resumption of the proceedings or, upon request by both parties, to decide to remove the case from the General List. The Court rightly pointed out that seising the Court is one thing, but the administration of justice is quite another, governed by the Statute and the Rules of Court.[163]

Once more one should note the particular matter of the Court's jurisdiction. Indeed, the Court may decide not to accede to a request by the Applicant, made just over two years after it instituted the proceedings, to postpone the opening of the oral proceedings 'for a substantial period' as the hearings would be limited to the question of the Court's jurisdiction and thus would 'not affect the issues of substance dividing the parties, which were the subject of negotiations between them'.[164]

In taking this decision the Court took into account the fact as just mentioned that the parties had already been negotiating on issues of substance for a period up to almost two years after the signing of an initial agreement on the procedure to be followed during those negotiations. This is in line of course with both the priority and the autonomous nature of the question of the Court's jurisdiction.[165] The proper administration of justice would indeed not benefit from the postponement requested.

Parties may, instead of leaving the matter to be discussed during their first meeting with the President, include in their Special Agreement that they would negotiate to find an agreement on the order for the oral proceedings, such an agreement being subject to the approval of the Court. If those negotiations were to fail, then the Court would prescribe the order.[166]

The opening of the oral proceedings may be considered by (one of) the parties as not really being conducive to an atmosphere of calm for the process of negotiations they have been engaged in since the start of the proceedings.[167]

The opening or resumption of negotiations during the course of the proceedings does not necessarily and in all cases result in rapid discontinuance. Parties may inform the Court that they had 'entered into negotiations that may lead to a full and final settlement of [the] case' and request the Court to postpone *sine die* the opening of oral proceedings.[168]

From a functional interaction perspective it should be noted that a request for postponement of the opening of oral proceedings is likely to put additional pressure on negotiators to achieve a full and final settlement, probably less pressure resulting from a *sine die* postponement.

One and a half years later the parties requested discontinuance because of 'an agreement in full and final settlement of all disputes, differences, claims, counterclaims and matters directly or indirectly raised by or capable of arising out of, or directly or indirectly related to or connected with the case'.[169]

An Applicant may request the Court to defer the setting of a date for the opening of the oral proceedings – which in the circumstances of the case would immediately deal with the merits of the case due to the non-appearance of the Respondent – 'owing to the delicate stage of negotiations' on the substantive issues of the dispute.[170]

162 *Ibid.*, at p. 123.

163 *Ibid.*, at p. 122.

164 *Aegean Sea Continental Shelf case, I.C.J. Reports 1978*, at p. 6, para. 9.

165 *Ibid.*

166 *Frontier Dispute (Benin/Niger), I.C.J. Reports 2005*, at p. 96, para. 2, Article 4.

167 *Case between the DRC and Uganda, I.C.J. Reports 2005*, at p. 178, para. 17 (the DRC merely 'enquiring' about such a possibility).

168 *Aerial Incident of 3 July 1988 (Islamic Republic of Iran v. United States of America), I.C.J. Reports 1996*, p. 9, at p. 10.

169 *Ibid.*

170 *Hostages case, I.C.J. Reports 1980*, at p. 22, para. 41.

After having filed within the time limits fixed by the Court their written pleadings, parties may agree between themselves, with the approval of the Court, to adjourn the opening of the oral proceedings.[171]

After having requested the Court to indicate interim measures of protection, that State may subsequently decide to withdraw that request.[172]

Parties may request the Court to accept the adjournment for a period of three months of the opening of the oral proceedings on the question of jurisdiction. The agreement between the parties may provide that they would review the situation 150 days later and fix that as the critical date for the examination of that question. The Court would fix the date for the opening of the oral proceedings after consulting the Parties.[173]

Although 'the critical date for determining the admissibility of an Application is the date on which it is filed', to have certainty of 'what the situation was' on that date, the Court may need to examine the relations between the parties prior to that date, and indeed during the subsequent period.[174] This applies thus also for negotiations during the course of the proceedings and which, in spite of a revival of the process even leading to another Accord, may then reach another standstill.[175]

One should particularly note that by posing a question to the parties[176] the Court is thus looking for their view on the matter. The absence of a formulation such as in *the opinion of the parties* in the applicable clause would not oblige the Court to act in a similar way towards the parties, but it would still allow it to take such a step within the context of its firm conviction about the complementarity and functional interaction between the two modes of peaceful settlement.

A request for the postponement of the opening of the hearings in order to enable the parties to resume negotiations should, 'as a matter of respect to the Court, and in the interest of a sound and efficient administration of justice', not be made 'only a few days before the scheduled opening of the hearings'.[177] When discontinuance occurs very shortly before the planned opening of the oral proceedings this 'may of course have been the outcome of intensive negotiations between the parties'.[178]

In case a Treaty has not laid down a specific obligation for a party to abstain from a particular course of action between the end of a period of negotiation and the decision of the Court, that State regains its freedom of action 'at its own risk'.[179] This goes for all kind of state conduct in general during judicial proceedings, including the freedom to resume negotiations subject to the limitations mentioned earlier, for instance, the obligation not to aggravate or to extend the pending dispute.

6.5 The Obligation Not to Aggravate or Extend the Dispute

A Duty for the Parties

Although some negotiation scholars put forward that it 'is entirely rational – and indeed, may be a sign of seriousness of intent – for parties to resort to tactical violence during peace negotiations as they try to improve their position on the margins in moving toward a final agreement',[180] such conduct is hardly compatible with

171 *Border and Transborder Armed Actions (Nicaragua v. Honduras), Provisional Measures, Order of 31 March 1988, I.C.J. Reports 1988*, p. 9, at p. 9.

172 *Border and Transborder Armed Actions case, I.C.J. Reports 1988*, at p. 10.

173 *Ibid.*, at p. 72, para. 8.

174 *Ibid.*, at p. 95, para. 66.

175 *Ibid.*, at p. 103, paras. 87–8.

176 *Ibid.*, at p. 104, para. 90.

177 D. Prager, 'Procedural Developments at the International Court of Justice' (2004) 3 *The Law and Practice of International Courts and Tribunals* 1, 125–42 at 128. In the *Seizure and Detention of Certain Documents* case both Parties on 1 September 2014 requested the Court to postpone the hearings scheduled to open on 17 September 2014 and this in order to enable them to reach an amicable settlement. By its Order of 3 September 2014 the Court decided to grant the Parties'request (Press Release No.2014/28, text available on the Court's website).

178 H. Thirlway, 'The Law and Procedure of the International Court of Justice 1960–1989. Supplement, 2011: Parts Eleven, Twelve and Thirteen', 177.

179 *Pulp Mills case, I.C.J. Reports 2010*, at p. 69, para. 154. A recent example is the *Aerial Herbicides Spraying case.*

180 W. Zartman, 'Negotiating Forward', p. 297 referring to Darby.

the obligation to negotiate in good faith. Moreover, occurring during the proceedings, it would also violate the general or judicial obligation – through the indication of provisional measures[181] – for parties not to aggravate the dispute.

The principle of good faith, conventional instruments and judicial law provide the basis for the parties' duty not to aggravate the dispute pending the delivery of the judgment. This duty is also distinct but related to their general obligation to conduct themselves in such a way as not to render the performance of the Court's function more difficult or impossible. This duty – part of the Court's established jurisprudence – is perhaps the main general legal parameter governing the process of negotiations *pari passu*. The following examples may help to illustrate how this legal parameter actually works.

An Applicant may consider that the Respondent has violated 'the obligation to refrain from any action which might *interfere* with the subject-matter of a dispute while judicial proceedings are pending',[182] this obligation flowing 'from the very nature of the judicial process'.[183]

Negotiations during the course of the proceedings would not normally qualify as actions negatively interfering with the subject-matter of the dispute, except in those cases where as a result of bad faith by one of the parties they fail, thereby rendering the judicial settlement even more difficult, and aggravating the dispute.

Although parties may not have agreed in their Special Agreement to negotiate on the merits of the dispute during the forthcoming proceedings, they may have agreed to take concomitant measures pending the proceedings[184] and to proceed to the signature of a bilateral treaty.[185]

Such measures may also include their undertaking to preserve peace, security and quiet among the peoples of the two States, which will imply, pending the delivery of the judgment, intergovernmental negotiations, for instance with regard to carrying out certain works of socio-economic infrastructure.[186]

When a State has first requested the Court to postpone the opening of the oral proceedings because of the delicate stage of certain negotiations, a military operation for humanitarian considerations to save hostages, while the case is under deliberation by the Court, is 'of a kind calculated to undermine respect for the judicial process in international relations' especially also in the light of a provisional measure that no action should be taken which might 'aggravate the tension between the two countries'.[187]

The Court may also when indicating provisional measures in fact oblige the parties to follow a particular conduct, for instance to allow observers appointed by an International Organization to have access to a particular area in the immediate vicinity of the disputed area.[188]

Parallel negotiations may be potentially changing the nature of the dispute, but without aggravating or extending it.[189]

An additional Application filed in order to extend the dispute[190] can also be the result of failed resumed negotiations.

---

181 See for instance *Nuclear Tests (New Zealand v. France), Interim Protection, Order of 22 June 1973, I.C.J. Reports 1973*, p. 135, at p. 142, para. 36.

182 *LaGrand case, I.C.J. Reports 2001*, at p. 498, para. 93 (Germany) (emphasis added).

183 R. Jennings, 'The *LaGrand* Case', at 30.

184 *Territorial Dispute (Libyan Arab Jamahiriya/Chad), I.C.J. Reports 1994*, at p. 9, para. 2, Article 2 (b) and (d).

185 *Ibid.*, at p. 10, para. 2, Article 4 (d).

186 *Frontier Dispute (Benin/Niger), I.C.J. Reports 2005*, at p. 10, para. 2, Article 10. A similar commitment was taken by the parties in their Special Agreement between Burkina Faso and Niger: preliminary consultations would be held prior to the implementation of the judgment already during the course of the proceedings: *Frontier Dispute between Burkina Faso and Niger, I.C.J. Reports 2013*, at p; 52, para. 2, Article 10. The title of these Articles 10, 'Special undertaking', already indicates its special nature, additional to the normal and general obligations which apply during the course of the proceedings.

187 *Hostages case, I.C.J. Reports 1980*, at p. 43, para. 93.

188 *Request for Interpretation of the Judgment of 15 June 1962 in the Case concerning the* Temple of Preah Vihear (Cambodia v. Thailand*), (Cambodia v. Thailand), Provisional measures, Order of 18 July 2011, I.C.J. Reports 2011*, at p. 555, para. 69.

189 *Fisheries Jurisdiction (United Kingdom v. Iceland), I.C.J. Reports 1974*, at p. 21, para. 43.

190 *Land and Maritime Boundary between Cameroon and Nigeria, Order of 16 June 1994, I.C.J. Reports 1994*, p. 105, at p. 106.

Interesting from a functional interaction perspective is a provision in a bilateral treaty containing a duty to abstain from particular actions during a period between the end of negotiations and a decision of the Court.[191] Parties may, however, disagree whether the treaty actually provides for such a duty of abstention.

Once the process of negotiations then having been unsuccessfully completed, through the continued application of the principle of good faith, the duty not to aggravate the existing dispute even prior to entering the Great Hall of Justice provides a functional link between two modes of settlement of disputes.

An *extension* of a pending dispute does not in all circumstances produce also its aggravation. The obvious *legal* consequences of an attempted or actual extension situate themselves in the area of jurisdiction and/or admissibility. From our perspective *factual* consequences may be found in the sudden unwillingness of the other party to continue negotiations during the proceedings on (aspects of) the original dispute, and as far as an Applicant is concerned, to decide unilaterally to discontinue the proceedings at once and then to resume a process of negotiations towards an out-of-court settlement, or in a worst case scenario to turn to a settlement of the larger dispute by non-peaceful means.

A Respondent faced with an extension of the dispute may of course not only challenge this attempted transgression of the Court's jurisdiction, but it may also decide to suspend or to terminate its participation in the proceedings, thus bringing to an abrupt end its active role in the judicial part of the functional interaction.

Measures requiring parties to refrain from actions which might aggravate or extend a dispute 'are not limited to the protection of rights which might be adjudged to belong to either party but serve a wider purpose'.[192] Apparently 'aggravation of the dispute' is increasingly 'being regarded as a sort of *malum in se* against which a State is entitled to seek protection independently of the nature of the rights asserted in the dispute'.[193]

A Duty for the Court as Well?

The obligation not to aggravate or extend the dispute may at first glance apply *ratione personae* by the nature of things exclusively to the parties. However, it would be difficult to adduce a convincing reason why the Court itself should not be subject to the same obligation.

In recent times judicial voices have been heard in that direction.

The object and purpose of the rule of *non ultra petita*, which requires strict observance, is *inter alia* to prevent the Court from extending the dispute between the parties.

The *non liquet* principle does not allow the Court to abstain from delivering a judgment on the basis that such a judgment would endanger international peace and security.

Although the Court has constantly 'sought to avoid leaving inflammatory issues unresolved in the relations between the parties' in order to discharge 'its pacificatory role' to the 'fullest possible extent',[194] in case the delivery of a judgment would carry the risk of aggravating or actually aggravates the original dispute, it might be argued that Article 94 of the Charter could be turned to, although that is not that provision's prime object and purpose.

Examples of Court decisions which could be considered as not (fully) in conformity with that particular duty of the Court include provisional measures framed in non-self-executing terms, thus not containing 'all the legal elements required for its interpretation'[195] such as limiting the movement of troops without prescribing a 'clear physical benchmark';[196] the 'dispatch of civilian personnel charged with the protection of

191 See in this regard in particular *Pulp Mills case, I.C.J. Reports 2010*, Separate opinion by Judge *ad hoc* Torres Bernardez, at p. 260, para. 89 and at p. 261, para. 91.

192 *Certain Activities in the Border Area case (Costa Rica v. Nicargaua), Provisional Measures, Order of 8 March 2011, I.C.J. Reports 2011*, p. 6, Declaration by Judge Greenwood, at p. 48, para. 8.

193 H. Thirlway, 'The Law and Procedure of the International Court of Justice 1960–1989. Supplement, 2011: Parts Eleven, Twelve and Thirteen', 80.

194 R. Kolb, *The ICJ*, p. 429.

195 *Land and Maritime Boundary case, I.C.J. Reports 1996*, Declaration by Judge Shahabuddeen, at p. 28.

196 *Ibid.*

the environment to the disputed territory';[197] and the measure that parties 'shall immediately withdraw their military personnel currently present in the provisional demilitarized zone' defined by the Court itself.[198]

A counterclaim 'in a way *enlarged* the object of the contentious case at issue' and came to be regarded 'as a means of achieving more consistency in the Court's decisions' on both the original claim and the counter-claim.[199]

Such Court decisions or rulings sometimes carry the risk of exacerbating the dispute or providing the basis for a new one sharply in contrast, from a functional interaction perspective, with the Court calling upon parties to negotiate.

The 'almost tautological' nature of provisional measures not to aggravate the dispute has been pointed out by Judge Trindade because a dispute or a situation calling for such indication 'is already – *per definitionem* – endowed with gravity and urgency'. Hence, it would 'be more accurate' to describe their object and purpose as to 'prevent or avoid the "*further aggravation*" of the dispute or situation at issue'.[200] This does not exclude the possibility that a provisional measure 'might give rise to a further dispute'.[201]

6.6 Indication of Provisional Measures and Resumed Negotiations: A Two-Way Street of Functional Interaction

General Picture

Irrespective of the proposed need to construct 'an *autonomous legal regime* of provisional measures',[202] the fact remains that the Court 'as a body appears determined to make of the provisional measures system a powerful institution impelling States towards compliance with their international obligations – more powerful perhaps than was foreseen when the Statute and its predecessor the PCIJ Statute were drafted'.[203] Moreover, 'the indication of provisional measures itself would be regarded as an instrument for assuring *la bonne administration de la justice*'.[204]

The functional interaction between negotiations and adjudication operates in a particular way through the indication of provisional measures by the Court. Compliance with the measures indicated may be conducive to creating a climate favourable to the resumption of negotiations during the proceedings. Conversely, both non-indication of provisional measures by the Court[205] and non-compliance with measures ordered may negatively

197 *Certain Activities in the Border Area case (Costa Rica v. Nicargaua), I.C.J. Reports 2011*, Declaration by Judge Skotnikov, at p. 42, para. 4.

198 *Request for Interpretation of the 1962 Preah Vihear Judgment, I.C.I. Reports 2011*, at p. 555, para. 69 (1) and at pp. 552–3, paras. 61–2.

199 *Germany v. Italy case, I.C.J. Reports 2010*, Dissenting opinion by Judge Cançado Trindade, at p. 335, para. 15 and at pp. 337–8, para. 21.

200 *Request for Interpretation of the 1962 Preah Vihear Judgment, I.C.I. Reports 2011*, Separate opinion by Judge Cançado Trindade, at p. 588, para. 63.

201 H. Thirlway, 'The Law and Procedure of the International Court of Justice 1960–1989: Part Twelve' (2001) 72 *British Yearbook of International Law* 37–181, at 98, note 229.

202 *Certzain Activities Carried out by Nicaragua in the Border Area (Costa Rica v.Nicaragua) ; Construction of a Road in Costa Rica along the San Juazn River (Nicaragua v. Costa Rica), Order of 16 July 2013, Provisional Measures ,I.C.J. Reports 2013*, p. 230, Dissenting opinion by Judge Cançado Trindade, at p. 267, para. 69.

203 H. Thirlway, 'The Law and Procedure of the International Court of Justice 1960–1989. Supplement, 2011: Parts Eleven, Twelve and Thirteen', 93. On the function of provisional measures see generally S. Rosenne, *Provisional Measures* and K. Oellers-Frahm, 'Article 41', pp. 1026–77 MN 923–66. See furthermore Y. Lee-Iwamoto, 'The Repercussions of the *LaGrand* Judgment: Recent ICJ Jurisprudence of Provisional Measures' (2012) 5 *Japanese Yearbook of International Law*, 237–62.

204 H. Sakai, '*La Bonne Administration de la Justice*', 114.

205 *Costa Rica v. Nicaragua and Nicaragua v. Costa Rica, Joined Proceedings, I.C.J. Reports 2013*, Dissenting opinion by Judge Cançado Trindade, at p. 262, para. 53. A request for the indication of provisional measures which are outside the Court's jurisdiction must be considered 'in the context of efforts being invested' by a multilateral conference 'to seek out a political settlement' to an unfolding 'tragedy'. When the 'conclusion may be drawn that the purpose of the provisional measures is also to prevent the adoption' of a particular peace plan, then such a request 'should prompt the Court, bearing in mind the crucial importance of the peace negotiations as the only way' to end the civil war, 'to find a way to urge the Applicant to continue' those peace negotiations: *Bosnian Genocide case, I.C.J. Reports 1993*, Dissenting opinion

influence the parties' readiness to embark upon a resumption of negotiations during the proceedings and the potential lack of progress during that process.

The exercise of these powers 'of *general prevention*' reflects 'the modern approach to international disputes as objects of *management* rather than of *settlement* comprising 'an integrated role of the Court in this process of 'management'.[206] If there is a role for the Court in management of crises such as the one in Yugoslavia and the Congo 'it would be at most an auxiliary or supporting role'.[207]

Even a refusal to indicate measures can through 'general statements', if 'carefully worded', lay 'the basis for satisfactory negotiations to settle the dispute, or prevent it from growing more serious'.[208]

According to a different view the Court 'should refrain from orders with diplomatic or political content or matters concerning mediation or negotiation, since strictly speaking these issues are apparently outside the legal assignment of the Court'.[209] Moreover:

> in view of the fact that negotiations are continuing on a bilateral bass between the Parties, it may not be out of place to take this present situation into account, in order to ensure that nothing is done to jeopardize such an amicable solution to a border dispute between two neighbouring countries.[210]

The Court's jurisprudence has been recited 'in order to substantiate the principle that the Court can lend its good offices and encouragement towards the settlement of a dispute by the Parties themselves'. Hence, the good offices of the Court 'would continue to be available to facilitate this process' of working towards a settlement 'within the legal guidelines indicated'.[211]

In exercising its competences and powers with regard to the maintenance of international peace and security the Security Council frequently reaffirms the obligation for States to work towards a peaceful settlement of the dispute.

It may be recalled that the provisional measures the SC may have deemed necessary or desirable under Article 40 of the Charter are aimed at calming down a situation and creating the conditions to settle a dispute peacefully through negotiations. One should add here that SC involvement under Chapter VII is not per se an obstacle for the Court's consideration of a request under Article 41 of the Statute[212] which is characterized by some special features distinguishing the exercise of this power by the Court from other aspects of the proceedings.

For instance, after the unilateral instituting of the proceedings the Council may recall the need for the parties not only to respect each other's international rights and obligations, but also 'to avoid any incident which might lead to the aggravation of the situation and which, consequently, might compromise their efforts towards a peaceful solution'.[213]

---

by Judge *ad hoc* Kreca, at pp. 456–7. Moreover, when the Court has first ordered the parties, for instance to negotiate, it should be 'justified in refraining', – following 'similar requests to indicate provisional measures *ratione materiae* and *ratione personae*' – from 'issuing a second Order until the first set of measures has been implemented': *Bosnian Genocide case, I.C.J. Reports 1993*,Separate opinion by Judge Ajibola, at p. 394.

206 J. Sztucki, 'Case Concerning Land and Maritime Boundary', at 357. See also generally S. Rosenne, 'A Role for the International Court of Justice in Crisis Management?' in G. Kreijen (ed.), *State, Sovereignty and International Governance* (Oxford, 2002), pp. 195–219.

207 S. Rosenne, 'A Role for the International Court of Justice', pp. 216–17.

208 S. Rosenne, *Provisional Measures*, pp. 221 and 219.

209 *Land and Maritime Boundary case, I.C.J. Reports 1996*, Separate opinion by Judge *ad hoc* Ajibola, at p. 36, para. 3.

210 *Ibid.*, at p. 45.

211 *Legality of Use of Force case, I.C.J. Reports 1999*, Dissenting opinion by Judge Weeramantry, at pp. 196–7 and at p. 202.

212 J. Merrills, 'Interim Measures of Protection in the Recent Jurisprudence of the International Court of Justice '(1995) 44 *International and Comparative Law Quarterly*, 1, 90–146, at 130.

213 *Aegean Sea Continental Shelf case, I.C.J. Reports 1976*, at p. 12, para. 39. It can be noted that although the Council is referring to the *situation*, its appeal comes close to the Court's own classic approach that during the proceedings no action should be taken undertaken which might aggravate the *dispute*.

The question whether the exercise of its power under Article 41 may entail 'the fixation of the *status quo* pending its decision'[214] has to be answered positively. However, if the Court orders the parties to negotiate it does not necessarily imply that the objective has to be such a fixation as, for instance, working towards the putting into place of an interim arrangement already indicates.

Although the Court 'in deciding whether to indicate provisional measures is concerned not so much with the past as with the present and with the future',[215] the time factor has its own role to play and makes this mode of functional interaction a two-way street indeed.

The functional role of provisional measures clearly is a preventive one, the future conduct of the parties forming part and parcel of the 'circumstances' of Article 41.[216] As provisional measures are *inter alia* motivated by urgency, they call for prompt compliance,[217] meaning that a process of resumed negotiations has to start without delay.[218]

As far as the condition of irreparable prejudice is concerned, one should note that this could be remedied by negotiations to put in place an interim arrangement.

As to the timing of a request for provisional measures, it should be noted that as part of its managerial role for the proper conduct of the proceedings the Court has ruled that a request for the indication of provisional measures should be made 'in good time',[219] which may present itself once one party is convinced that the resumed negotiations have failed. On the other hand the timing of the request may have an impact on the timing of the decision of the parties to resume negotiations during the proceedings.

Although 'most cases accompanied by the requests for provisional measures have been referred to the Court unilaterally',[220] parties may not have resumed negotiations after the start of the proceedings while devoting their attention to the filing of their written pleadings. The exchange of Memorial and Counter-Memorial may have convinced one of the parties that in light of the submissions and the arguments developed to formulate them there might be a chance for perhaps a partial solution of the dispute if negotiations were resumed. That party may then request the Court to indicate provisional measures aiming at such resumption.

In other cases parties may have resumed negotiations on matters of substance in parallel with the proceedings. This process may evolve and in spite of all efforts on both sides reach a deadlock; one of the parties may then be of the opinion that indication of provisional measures by the Court ordering the parties to resume the process could overcome the impasse. Any progress made could subsequently bring a party to request the Court to postpone or suspend the application of such measures.

In case the negotiations have resulted in a *modus vivendi* for the period of further negotiations and which is 'very similar in substance' to the Court's Order, and the process may have settled substantive matters as well, this may result in a request for the revocation of the Order.[221] Furthermore, there is no legal obstacle for a State to apply, as a result of another round of (partial) successful negotiations, 'anew for interim protection following the revocation at its own request of an earlier grant'.[222]

---

214 Zan He, *The ICJ's Practice on Provisional Measures* (Frankfurt am Main, 2010), at p. 6.

215 *Bosnian Genocide case, I.CJ. Reports 1993*, at 16, para. 25.

216 *Costa Rica v. Nicaragua and Nicaragua v. Costa Rica, Joined Proceedings, I.C.J.Reports 2013*, Dissenting opinion by Judge Cançado Trindade, at p. 268, para. 71 and P.-M. Eisemann, 'Quelques observations', at p. 123.

217 Zan He, *The ICJ's Practice*, p. 37.

218 On the notion of urgency in international adjudication see *inter alia Le contentieux de l'urgence et l'urgence dans le contentieux devant les juridictions internationales: regards croisés* (Paris, 2001) and also E. Roucounas, 'L'urgence et le droit international' in *Le Droit international et le temps* (Paris, 2001), pp. 200–228.

219 *Avena and other Mexican nationals (Mexico v. United States of America), Provisional Measures, Order of 5 February 2003, I.C.J. Reports 2003*, p. 77, at p. 90, para. 54.

220 H. Sakai, 'New Developments of the Orders on Provisional Measures by the International Court of Justice' (2009) 52 *Japanese Yearbook of International Law*, 231–80 at 233, the exception being the *Frontier Dispute case* between Burkina Faso and Mali.

221 J. Sztucki, *Interim Measures*, pp. 143–4.

222 J. Sztucki, *Interim Measures*, p. 200.

A request by a State for the adjournment of proceedings on its request of provisional measures for instance 'to facilitate negotiations'[223] inevitably 'shows lack of urgency'.[224] The 'fact that parties are actively pursuing a solution' for instance through negotiations 'may also play [a] role' in the Court's assessment of urgency.[225]

Given the conditions for the application of Article 41 as they have been established by the case law at present, the particular circumstances of a case will co-determine whether a judicial assessment that there is any hope for another round of negotiations is appropriate.

'Parallel outside action', i.e. negotiations, 'could constitute a circumstance which can influence in the negative sense the assessment of the need for interim measures'.[226] Sztucki's observation that the case law has demonstrated 'that direct negotiations entered after the indication of provisional measures have not been regarded as a reason necessarily calling for their revocation or modification'[227] is still valid today.

Whether it could be desirable for the Court to consider the possibility of revocation of measures – aiming to preserve the respective rights of either party – before a specific date as a judicial means to put pressure on the parties to negotiate is rather doubtful.

In case of revocation upon request the Court may explicitly make it clear that interim protection 'does not depend, in principle, on the prospect or progress of direct negotiations',[228] but in deciding whether circumstances do require the indication of provisional measures the Court may 'reject a request' if 'it considers that the conciliatory spirit' of pending negotiations 'is sufficiently reassuring'.[229] The potential impact of the functional interaction between the indication of provisional measures and negotiations is thus easily discernable.

Given the binding nature of a Court Order indicating parties to start or resume negotiations – perhaps also fixing a time limit for them to reach an understanding – inevitably turns the parties' traditional freedom of action during the course of the proceedings whether or not to embark upon another process of negotiations into a full-fledged legal obligation. It has been argued 'that reaching' an agreement 'would be impeded rather by a legally binding order, which is given at the request of a party and creates legal obligations on the other'.[230]

In contrast also to their traditional freedom to choose which aspects and issues of the dispute would be eligible for another attempt towards a peaceful settlement, the Court may even provide the parties with more or less detailed instructions on the subject-matter of the negotiations.

Alternatively, the nature of the measures may require a process of bilateral negotiations to give them effect, a process which may not succeed.[231]

Also in contrast to a traditional process of negotiations on an strictly bilateral basis, when parties are negotiating pursuant to provisional measures the Court will monitor their compliance and any progress made – as the Court indeed has also jurisdiction to deal with a submission that an Order indicating provisional measures 'has not been complied with':[232] reducing the issues in dispute may, if reached before the end of the oral proceedings, bring the parties to amend their final submissions and hence perhaps facilitate the Court's task in deciding the outstanding issues.

From the perspective of the functional interaction this aspect of the Court's function has only gained in importance since *LaGrand*.

In case of non-compliance or when some progress is not forthcoming, the Court could decide to remedy the situation in a subsequent Order. Moreover, the Court's jurisdiction to determine an alleged non-compliance

223 J. Sztucki, *Interim Measures*, p. 53.

224 H. Thirlway, 'The Law and Procedure of the International Court of Justice 1960–1989: Part Twelve', at 95, note 204.

225 K. Oellers-Frahm, 'Article 41', p. 942, MN 47.

226 J. Sztucki, *Interim Measures*, p. 129.

227 J. Sztucki, *Interim Measures*, p. 131.

228 J. Sztucki, *Interim Measures*, p. 131, referring to the *Oscar Chinn case*.

229 J. Sztucki, *Interim Measures*, p. 132.

230 H. Sakai, 'New Developments', 239.

231 *Request for the Interpretation of the Judgment of 15 June 1962 in the Case concerning* the Temple of Preah Vihear (Cambodia v. Thailand*) (Cambodia v. Thailand), Judgment, I.C.J. Reports 2013*, p. 281, Separate opinion by Judge Cançado Trindade, at p. 335, para. 37 (Cambodia).

232 *LaGrand case, I.C.J. Reports 2001*, at pp. 483–4, para. 45.

with an Order of provisional measures is established 'irrespective of whether or not the respondent State raised that issue by way of counter-claim'.[233]

At the same time it should be recalled that the indication of measures cannot signify that the Court regards itself necessarily competent 'also to order such measures in its final judgment'.[234]

Finally it should not be forgotten that the Court may decide *motu proprio* that a new round of negotiations should take place, if circumstances so require. In this respect it should not be overlooked that circumstances may be such that after the occurrence of a serious incident implicating state authorities, a State may not only refuse to enter into negotiations as proposed by the injured State, but also even to have any direct contact whatsoever, and this in spite of calls to that end by the Security Council.[235]

In such circumstances a Court Order, although recommendatory in those days, that the parties should negotiate, would not be a decision conducive to an appeasement of the tension between the parties.

Although with regard to its power to indicate provisional measures the Court has ruled that its judgment on the merits 'should not be anticipated by reason of any initiative regarding the matters in issue before the Court',[236] this obviously does not include a successful outcome of negotiations resumed either on the initiative of the parties or as result of a Court Order. The functional interaction between such an outcome and discontinuance of the proceedings altogether will be dealt with in the final paragraph of this chapter.

Depending on the phase of the proceedings when the Order is made and in the absence of a fixed time-limit, this obligation to negotiate will remain in force during the whole adjudicative phase.[237]

When the Court is of the opinion that the circumstances do not require the indication of provisional measures but welcomes any negotiation between the parties to achieving a direct and friendly settlement, there is potential interaction even in case of failure of such a process: indeed, the results of such negotiations, in particular technical solutions that may be explored, could be helpful to the Court.[238]

Expressing their regret that the Court did not indicate provisional measures, judges may observe that the measures should 'have had as their object to bring the parties to the negotiating table' on the basis of the intention of the Respondent;[239] that would have been in conformity with the Court's mission and in 'perfect harmony with the spirit and letter' of Article 41 of the Statute.[240]

We will now look at some examples of resumed negotiations taking place prior to the indication of provisional measures.

Resumed Negotiations and (a Request for) the Indication of Provisional Measures

It should first be noted that the functional link between *prior negotiations* and the indication of provisional measures is quite natural given the requirement that there has to be a connection between the request for such measures and the original Application.[241]

233 *Certain Activities carried out by Nicaragua in the Border Area (Costa Rica v. Nicaragua)* ; *Construction of a Road in Costa Rica along the San Juan River (Nicaragua v. Costa Rica), Counter-claims, Order of 18 April 2013, I.C.J.Reports 2013*, p. 200, at p. 215, para. 40.

234 *Fisheries Jurisdiction (United Kingdom v. Iceland), I.C.J. Reports 1974*, Dissenting opinion by Judge Petren, at p. 152.

235 *Hostages case, I.C.J. Reports 1980*, at p. 15, para. 26 and at p. 16, para. 28.

236 *Aegean Sea Continental Shelf case, I.C.J. Reports 1976*, at p. 9, para. 25.

237 Whether parties are under a similar obligation in the post-adjudicative phase will depend mainly although not exclusively on the Court's final decision, as we will review in Part III of this study.

238 *Great Belt case, I.C.J. Reports 1991*, Separate opinion by Judge *ad hoc* Broms, at p. 39. We will deal with this aspect in Chapter 7.

239 *Arbitral Award of 31 July 1989, Provisional Measures, Order of 2 March 1990, I.C.J. Reports 1990*, Dissenting opinion by Judge Thierry, at p. 80.

240 *Arbitral Award case, I.C.J. Reports 1990*, Dissenting opinion by Judge Thierry, at p. 84.

241 *Request for Interpretation of Avena Judgment, I.C.J. Reports 2008*, at p. 327, para. 58; and *Costa Rica v. Nicaragua* ; *Nicaragua v. Costa Rica, Joined Proceedings, I.C.J. Reports 2013*, at p. 238, para. 30. See also *Case between Timor-Leste and Australia, I.C.J. Reports 2014*, para. 23.

On the other hand, although the Court 'in deciding whether to indicate provisional measures is concerned, not so much with the past as with the present and the future'[242] it may still take into account whether prior negotiations have taken place, the extent to which they may have been successful or not and in appropriate cases the conduct of both parties during that pre-adjudicative process.

The question here is whether and to what extent resumed negotiations conducted after the start of the proceedings on the initiative of (one of) the parties may have an impact on (the granting of) a request for the indication of provisional measures.

An Applicant may just two months after having instituted proceedings inform the Court that it expects 'that negotiations will take place' between the two parties 'in the near future in which the issues which are the subject of its Application will be under discussion'. Given this development the Applicant may not actually withdraw its request for the indication of provisional measures, but it may ask the Court to postpone its consideration in order to 'facilitate those negotiations'.[243]

It should be noted that there is no absolute certainty that the process will take place; the Applicant merely has the *expectation* that it will happen. There is neither a real commitment on both sides to enter into the process nor a decision on timing and place.

As the objective of the request for postponement is *to facilitate those negotiations* the functional interaction is conditional: in case the process, sooner or later, reaches a deadlock, the Applicant may then still request the Court to resume the consideration of its request for provisional measures. The postponement is thus not necessarily meant to last until a successful outcome of the process. Given this request for postponement, the Court may then consider that the condition of urgency has disappeared, and as a result it is 'not therefore called upon to pronounce upon the said request'.[244]

A Respondent may, in an attempt to prevent functional interaction, object to the indication of provisional measures on grounds that it 'would be particularly inappropriate at this time' and that the indication 'could [not only] irreparably prejudice the interests of a number of states', but moreover 'seriously interfere with the negotiations being conducted' 'pursuant to a regional peace process[245] especially since all parties including the Applicant have accepted this process which has been endorsed by the SC and the GA and which has already made substantial progress towards the achievement of a comprehensive and enforceable resolution' of the problems. Not only the indication of the provisional measures requested but also the mere 'taking cognizance' of the Application would have a detrimental effect on the process 'in unpredictable and irremediable ways'.[246]

According to the Respondent the impact of the indication on the negotiations is part of the compelling reasons which should bring the Court to deny the request.[247]

The Applicant may argue that it would continue to be involved in the process, which however cannot resolve or even address the 'legal claims',[248] and that moreover the judicial proceedings cannot 'disrupt' the regional process. Its endorsement by the international community 'does not constitute an obstacle to the exercise by the Court of its jurisdiction'.[249]

It is clear that parties may hold diverging views on the functional interaction: the resolving potential of a regional peace process and the impact of the judicial proceedings on that process.

In the view of one party, the degree of progress made during a process of negotiations – which it qualifies as *substantial* – appears to be important as to its impact on the appropriateness of procedural steps in the

242 *Bosnian Genocide case, I.C.J. Reports 1993*, at p. 16, para. 25.

243 *Trial of Pakistani Prisoners of War, Interim Protection, Order of 13 July 1973, I.C.J. Reports 1973*, p. 328 at p. 330, para. 10.

244 *Trial of Pakistani Prisoners of War, I.C.J. Reports 1973*, at p. 330, para. 14; *contra* but unconvincingly Separate opinion by Judge Spencer, at p. 336.

245 *Nicaragua case, I.C.J. Reports 1984*, at p. 183, para. 33.

246 *Ibid.*, at pp. 184–5, para. 36.

247 *Ibid.*, at p. 184, para. 35.

248 *Ibid.*, at pp. 185–6, para. 38.

249 *Ibid.*, at p. 438, para. 103 (Nicaragua). This related but more general question of the impact of endorsement by organs of the international community of a (regional) process of negotiations on the 'appropriateness' of judicial proceedings remains outside the scope of this study.

judicial proceedings, whereas the other party cannot see a *disrupting* effect of the judicial proceedings on the regional process as this is incapable of addressing its legal claims.

The Court recalled its earlier jurisprudence and ruled that 'even the existence of active negotiations in which both parties might be involved should not prevent both the Security Council and the Court from exercising their respective functions',[250] thereby confirming the functional interaction.

After the filing of the written pleadings and when the case becomes ready for the oral proceedings, parties may agree between themselves, with the approval of the Court, to adjourn the opening of the oral proceedings.[251]

The State having requested the indication of provisional measures may only ten days later decide to withdraw that request.[252]

The Court did not accept the argument that mediation by a third party would render a request for provisional measures 'moot';[253] moreover, even partially successful negotiations leading to a cease-fire in the disputed region are not capable of depriving the Court 'of the rights and duties pertaining to the case brought before it'.[254]

The Court reaffirmed this position in reply to the argument that it 'would be inappropriate for the Court to rule', following a request for the indication of provisional measures, 'upon an aspect of the conflict which is the subject of direct agreement between the Heads of State of the two Parties' within the framework of an IO (ANAD).[255]

By confirming that States have the liberty 'to negotiate or resolve particular aspects of a dispute brought before the Court' and that the actual exercise of this freedom is not 'incompatible with the Court's exercise of its own functions',[256] the Court once more stressed the functional link.

The Indication of Provisional Measures and Resumed Negotiations

If there is a general obligation for the parties not to aggravate the dispute, irrespective of the Court ordering this in a provisional measure, does this not imply an expectation/duty for the parties that they will attempt to negotiate during the course of the proceedings even if the failure of prior negotiations brought them to the Court in the first place?

If there is a positive good faith obligation for the Parties to take action to render the settlement of the dispute easier, should the Court not lend its judicial power to assist the parties in reaching that goal?[257]

Would it be possible for the Court to recommend and nowadays to oblige the parties to (re)negotiate on particular aspects of the dispute, e.g. to clarify certain issues of the original claims or to reach a partial solution? Would such a recommendation be in conformity with the Court's judicial function *to contribute* to the final settlement of the dispute?[258]

Or would such an approach run counter to the judicial function of the Court *to settle the dispute*? In case such an Order would not be forthcoming, would it then be perceived by the parties as the Court abandoning its constitutional duties under the Charter? Could perhaps the negative obligation for the parties not to aggravate the dispute have its counterpart in a positive judicial duty to alleviate the dispute by ordering the parties to (re)negotiate?

---

250 *Ibid.*, at pp. 439–40, para. 105 and at p. 440, para. 106.

251 *Border and Transborder Armed Actions case, I.C.J. Reports 1988*, at p. 9.

252 *Ibid.*, at p. 10.

253 *Land and Maritime Boundary case, I.C.J. Reports 1996*, at p. 22, paras. 36 (Nigeria).

254 *Ibid.*, at p. 22, para. 37.

255 *Frontier Dispute, I.C.J. Reports 1986*, at p. 7, para. 6 (8) (Mali).

256 *Ibid.*, at p. 10, para. 24.

257 One of the arguments used against any legally binding effects of the Orders indicating provisional measures was that reaching an agreement between the parties 'would be impeded rather by a legally binding order, which is given at the request of a party and creates legal obligations on the other': H. Sakai, 'New Developments', 239, referring to those doctrinal views.

258 *DRC Rwanda case, I.C.J. Reports 2002*, Declaration by Judge Koroma, at p. 255, para. 16, responding positively.

Could the 'promotion of the satisfactory conduct of the proceedings[259] as one of the circumstances the Court has to consider bring it to oblige the parties to negotiate? The Court 'usually urges the parties to negotiate when making an order granting (or indeed declining) provisional measures'.[260]

The 'greater emphasis on the prevention of aggravating the dispute or the facilitation of dispute settlement among the objects of provisional measures may lead the Court to serve the good offices or the conciliation between the parties'.[261]

Rejecting a request for the indication of provisional measures because of the lack of *prima facie* jurisdiction may be accompanied by such recommendations and 'which might bring out any legal judgment on the merits, can do severe damages to its contributions to the dispute settlement through the negotiations between the parties and even might bring about reverse results'.[262] However, if the 'recommendations enter the realm of legal evaluations of the concrete facts beyond providing the parties with legal frameworks for their negotiations or presenting legal principles, they might give legal advantages to one of the parties and direct bad influences to the negotiations between the parties'.[263]

As ruled by the PCIJ, the *applicability* of provisional measures cannot be dependent 'upon the position of negotiations that may be in progress between the Parties'. Hence their revocation of the Order can 'only be so finally and in its entirety'.[264]

A request for provisional measures may be withdrawn 'to facilitate negotiations between the parties'.[265] When the Court issues an Order indicating provisional measures this 'does not prevent the conclusion of an interim agreement designed to prevent further incidents'.[266]

States may abstain from letting their views be known with regard to an Order indicating provisional measures 'during the course of negotiations towards the conclusion of a new treaty' between the parties,[267] thereby demonstrating a particular feature of the functional interaction.

By way of a provisional measure the Court may indicate the obligation to ensure that no action is taken which might aggravate or extend the dispute.

Even in case no measures are indicated the Court may stress the necessity for the parties 'to implement in good faith the consultation and cooperation procedures provided for in' a bilateral treaty through the use of a joint mechanism established by that treaty.[268] Subsequent conduct in conformity with such a pronouncement may in turn influence not only the progress and outcome of such negotiations, but also, at least to some extent, of the judicial proceedings.

Clearly functional interaction is facilitated by the common features of the two modes of settlement as indicated in Chapter 2. Their distinct features and the recognition of and respect for their respective functions carry with it that the interaction operates within those limits. Indeed, as part of its inherent powers the Court may assist parties towards a peaceful settlement by indicating the substance of provisional measures without however setting out 'the details of an acceptable arrangement to be worked out by the Parties'.[269]

---

259 Zan He, *The ICJ's Practice*, p. 42.

260 M. Shaw, 'Settling Territorial Disputes', p. 260, note 16. In the *Aegean case*, President Arechaga argued that the 'Court's specific power' under Article 41 'does not consist in a police power over the maintenance of international peace nor in a general competence to make recommendations relating to peaceful settlement of disputes': *Aegean Sea Continental Shelf case, I.C.J. Reports 1976*, Declaration by President Arechaga, at p. 16.

261 Akira Takada as referred to by H. Sakai, 'New Developments', 251, note 72.

262 H. Sakai, 'New Developments', 275–6.

263 H. Sakai, 'New Developments', 278.

264 As cited by S. Rosenne, *Provisional Measures*, p. 206.

265 *Border and Transborder Armed Actions (Nicaragua v. Honduras), Provisional Measures, Order of 31 March 1988, I.C.J. Reports 1988*, p. 9, at p. 9 as referred to by S.Rosenne, *Provisional Measures*, p. 206.

266 *Fisheries Jurisdiction (United Kingdom v. Iceland, I.C.J. Reports 1974*, at p. 19, para. 38 as referred to by S. Rosenne, *Provisional Measures*, p. 154, note 17.

267 J. Sztucki, *Interim Measures*, p. 36 referring to the *Oscar Chinn case*.

268 *Pulp Mills case, I.C.J. Reports 2006*, at p. 134, para. 82.

269 *Legality of Use of Force case, I.C.J. Reports 1999*, Dissenting opinion by Judge Weeramantry, at p. 201.

Sometimes individual judges expressed the view that the circumstances of the case did require the Court to order the parties to negotiate in co-operation with a treaty-monitoring body, on a broader scope of matters than those actually formulated.[270]

An Applicant may request the Court to provide the parties with some guidance as to the principles which they should take into account in their negotiations.[271]

The fact that formal notice has been given that an Application would follow shortly does not rule out the readiness to continue discussions to find satisfactory practical arrangements for the period while the case is before the Court.

When these subsequent negotiations do not bring an agreement on such an interim regime, the Applicant may request the Court to indicate provisional measures containing the putting in place of what had been the objective of those interim regime negotiations.[272]

The fact that the Court in its provisional measures has gradually transcended the purely state nature of the rights that have to be preserved[273] has the potential of affecting the subject-matter, orientation and scope of negotiation parties might be willing or compelled, as the case may be, to undertake prior to the judgment on the merits.

A conventional requirement of consultation implies 'prior contact between the Parties'.[274] Consultation and co-operation procedures provided for in a treaty have to be implemented in good faith[275] as Article 26 VCLT applies 'to all obligations established by a treaty, including procedural obligations which are essential to co-operation between states'.[276]

A joint body established by a treaty may not merely constitute a transmission mechanism between the parties, as the Court may consider it as a 'framework for consultation between the parties'[277] which can 'at the proposal of either party' act 'as a conciliation body in any dispute which may arise between the parties (Article 58)'.[278]

In the following cases involving a request for the indication of provisional measures the functional interaction between negotiations and adjudication is rather pronounced.

Towards a Compatibility Test?

In its request for the indication of provisional measures submitted prior to the Court's judgment in *LaGrand*, a State could specify that through negotiations parties may not depart from one of the provisional measures requested 'unless with the consent of each other'.[279]

---

270 *Certain Activities in the Border Area case (Costa Rica v. Nicargaua), I.C.J. Reports 2011*, Separate opinion by Judge Sepulveda, at p. 36, para. 4 and at p. 41, para. 34; Declaration by Judge Skotnikov, at p. 44, para. 13; and Declaration by Judge Greenwood, at p. 51, para. 15.

271 *Fisheries Jurisdiction (Federal Republic of Germany v. Iceland), I.C.J. Reports 1974*, at pp. 201–2, para. 68 (FRG).

272 Whether proposals and counter-proposals related to those negotiations for an interim regime could be indicative of the nature of the original dispute can be a matter for debate: see *Fisheries Jurisdiction (United Kingdom v. Iceland), I.C.J. Reports 1974*, Dissenting opinion by Judge Oneyma, at p. 172.

273 *Belgium v. Senegal case, I.C.J. Reports 2009*, Dissenting opinion by Judge Cançado Trindade, at p. 175, para. 26.

274 *Dispute regarding Navigational and Related Rights, I.C.J. Reports 2009*, at p. 229, para. 19; at p. 234, para. 38; and at p. 251, para. 93. See also the *Certain Activities in the Border Area case (Costa Rica v. Nicaragua), I.C.J. Reports 2011*, at p. 25, para. 79. One should note that in its request to modify this part of the 2011 Order Nicaragua requested that 'both Parties shall consult in regard to these actions and use their best endeavours to find common solutions wioth the other Party in this respect': *Costa Rica v. Nicaragua ; Nicaragua v. Costa Rica, Joined Proceedings, I.C.J. Reports 2013*, at p. 234, para. 14. One should also note that in its request to modify the 2011 Order Costa Rica pointed out that in addition to formal protests against certain activities by Nicaragua it 'has exhausted all efforts to resolve the dispute by diplomatic means': Dissenting opinion by Judge Cançado Trindade, at p. 249, para. 17.

275 *Pulp Mills case, I.C.J. Reports 2006*, at p. 134, para. 82.

276 *Pulp Mills case, I.C.J. Reports 2010*, at p. 67, para. 145.

277 *Ibid.*, at p. 53, paras. 87 and 90.

278 *Ibid.*, at p. 54, para. 92.

279 *Aegean Sea Continental Shelf case, I.C.J. Reports 1976*, at p. 4, para. 2 (1) (Greece).

After the indication of provisional measures as requested the Applicant may make it clear that 'any settlement between the parties of an interim regime should be compatible with the Court's Order'.[280]

This *compatibility test – LaGrand avant la lettre* – is another aspect of the functional interaction; the Court 's Order then provides the legal framework within which these discussions have to be held and the legal benchmark against which the outcome of the negotiations will have to be assessed later on by the Court, parties and third States.

Negotiations on such an interim agreement may be held intermittently for a period of time and may ultimately lead to the conclusion of an interim agreement on the dispute[281] notwithstanding an increased frequency of incidents.

The legally binding nature of provisional measures should not prevent the Court from *recommending*, encouraging parties 'to make an effort to try to solve the present dispute' in accordance with a governing bilateral treaty 'pending the final decision on the merits', as in the *Great Belt case*.[282]

Circumstances may be such that a mere recommendation to the Applicant to negotiate, if need be, with the Respondent was considered insufficient, resulting in a negative vote as the judge took the view that it would have been better *to oblige* both parties to negotiate.[283]

In a situation of an armed conflict the Court may in its Order of provisional measures offer the parties an opportunity to negotiate within 20 days an agreement to determine the lines behind which withdrawal of troops has to take place and the terms of such withdrawal.[284] The functional interaction takes front stage because in case of unsuccessful negotiations on such an agreement 'the Chamber will indicate them by means of an Order'.[285] The Court may call upon the parties to notify the Registrar 'without delay' of such an agreement.[286]

As negotiations between one of the parties and a third State 'would be set in train'[287] with a view of determining the frontier, the question could be raised about a potential impact on the later decision.

The Court, underlying the difference with the *Libya Malta case*, emphasized the fundamental distinction between the two modes of settlement because from 'the mere fact that the same documents are used as a starting-point for the Chamber's reasoning' and 'for the negotiations between' one of the parties and a third State, 'it cannot be inferred that the practical conclusions reached in both operations ... would necessarily be the same'.[288]

A close functional interaction takes place when the measures are indicated in order to 'maintain the peace that is necessary to such negotiations as the Parties have contemplated or might be contemplating, and for the execution of the judgment that the Court might hand down in the case'.[289]

Rejection of a Request for Provisional Measures and Willingness of the Parties to Negotiate

One of the benefits of an unsuccessful request could very well consist in strengthening the negotiating position of the requesting State.[290] The rejection of a request for provisional measures could also have an impact on the willingness of the parties to reach an agreement 18 months later and to request discontinuance.[291]

---

280 *Fisheries Jurisdiction (United Kingdom v. Iceland), I.C.J. Reports 1974*, at p. 17, para. 33.

281 *Ibid.*, at p. 17, para. 35.

282 *Pulp Mills case, I.C.J. Reports 2006*, Dissenting opinion by Judge *Ad Hoc* Vinuesa, at p. 154.

283 *Certain Activities in the Border Area case (Costa Rica v. Nicaragua), I.C.J. Reports 2011*, Declaration by Judge *Ad Hoc* Guillaume, at pp. 57–8, paras. 18–19 and at p. 59, para. 21. This is another example of the impact situations or events on the ground, or in this case on the contested maritime area, can have on ongoing negotiations as an extra stimulus for the parties to reach agreement for practical problems connected with the dispute over the unilateral extension.

284 *Frontier Dispute, I.C.J. Reports 1986*, at p. 12, para. 1 (D) and para. 2. See also recently G. Zyberi, 'Provisional Measures'.

285 *Frontier Dispute, I.C.J. Reports 1986*, at p. 12, para. 1 (D).

286 Within eight days of the date of the Order the parties did reach an agreement which they notified to the Registrar, but not 'without delay': *Frontier Dispute, Judgment, I.C.J. Reports 1986*, p. 554, at p. 559, paras. 9–10.

287 *Ibid.*, at p. 563, para. 16.

288 *Ibid.*, at p. 577, para. 45; at p. 578, para. 47; and at p. 579, para. 48.

289 *Land and Maritime Boundary case, I.C.J. Reports 1996*, Declaration by Judge *Ad Hoc* Mbaye, at pp. 33–4.

290 J. Merrills, 'Interim Measures of Protection', at 141 and H. Sakai, 'New Developments', 260.

291 *Great Belt case, I.C.J. Reports 1991*, at p. 6 (d) (Finland) and *Passage through the Great Belt (Finland v. Denmark), Order of 10 September 1992, I.C.J. Reports 1992*, p. 348, at pp. 348–9.

In an unprecedented way a Respondent may indicate that it would not object to the Court indicating a provisional measure 'which called upon the Parties jointly, in good faith, to address the difficulties caused by the issuance of the arrest warrant with a view of achieving a resolution to the dispute in a manner that (was) consistent with their obligations under international law … including resolutions 1234 and 1291'.[292]

Such a measure would then come down to a judicially approved commitment to negotiate within the international legal parameters of public international law and the resolutions of the Security Council. The Applicant may then be asking the Court 'to decide the case, having regard to the readiness of both Parties to seek a friendly settlement by diplomatic means'.[293]

The case is unique in the sense that both parties explicitly expressed their willingness during the oral proceedings to seek an out-of-court settlement. Although the Court acknowledged this new situation, it also duly noted that the positions of the parties 'as set out before the Court regarding their respective rights are still a long way apart'.[294]

In a clear example of functional interaction the Court was assessing the chances of a friendly settlement being reached in resumed negotiations given the diverging positions of the parties 'as set out before the Court' and in a realistic approach observed that 'whereas, while any bilateral negotiations with a view to achieving a direct and friendly settlement will continue to be welcomed, the outcome of such negotiations cannot be foreseen'.[295]

The Court concluded that the 'issues before the Court should be determined as soon as possible'; therefore it is appropriate 'to ensure that a decision' be 'reached with all expedition'.[296]

As the chances of the negotiations becoming successful are rather remote, the Court goes for judicial settlement and rejects the removal from the General List as requested by the Respondent, but it did not indicate provisional measures either.

A request for provisional measures does not have to contain an explicit reference to desirable negotiations; a measure ordering the Respondent to co-operate in good faith to ensure a particular objective implies negotiations during the course of the proceedings.[297]

The Court may prefer to 'treat' the measures requested 'in the motivations only and not to indicate the measures requested'.[298] When in turn the Respondent later requests a different kind of measure it may indicate its 'strong preference that this matter be resolved diplomatically and amicably between the two Parties'.[299]

In case the Applicant were to commit itself to fulfil the agreement, the Respondent would accept it in good faith and there would be no longer 'a need for judicial intervention or for the provisional measures requested herein',[300] a position almost tantamount to an offer to discontinue the proceedings altogether.

In rejecting a request for lack of *prima facie* jurisdiction the Court 'prevents the parties from abusing the provisional measures procedure'; when it nevertheless includes in its Order a recommendation for the parties to resume negotiations it 'may get involved in the dispute settlement process between the parties in a different way from the indication of provisional measures'.[301]

6.7 Discontinuance of the Proceedings

Once the decision has been taken by (one of) the parties to cross the Rubicon into the adjudicative phase after in vain having tried to find a peaceful solution to the dispute through a process of negotiations, the expectation

292 *Arrest Warrant case, I.C.J. Reports 2000*, at p. 193, para. 39 (Belgium).
293 *Ibid.*, at p. 195, para. 44.
294 *Ibid.*, at p. 202, para. 76.
295 *Ibid.*
296 *Ibid.*
297 *Pulp Mills case, I.C.J. Reports 2006*, at p. 118, para. 20 (b) (Argentina).
298 D. Muller, 'Procedural Developments at the International Court of Justice' (2006) 5 *The Law and Practice of International Courts and Tribunals* 3, 529–46 at 541.
299 *Pulp Mills case, I.C.J. Reports 2007*, at p. 7, para. 14 (Uruguay).
300 *Ibid.*
301 H. Sakai, 'New Developments', 265.

is that the Court in fulfilling the precise task it has been entrusted with will provide the parties with the long-awaited realization of their ultimate objective – i.e. a final settlement of the dispute. To this end the parties will have to comply with their duty of co-operation with the Court and in a different way with each other, as governed by the Court's Statute, the Rules of Court and any Order the Court may deem to be appropriate for a speedy conduct of the proceedings.

As mentioned before, litigation should not continue endlessly or needlessly, a situation the Court should strive to discourage[302] because it would constitute an obstacle to international harmony in circumstances of conflict.[303]

The existence of an oral ceasefire may be the result of negotiations taking place on the very same day as the Application was filed; but even if the negotiations took place later it 'does not deprive' the Court 'of the rights and duties pertaining to it in the case brought before it'[304] unless in case of discontinuance.

Consensual discontinuance is a 'mere procedural facility' at the disposal of the parties and for which the Court is called upon to exercise 'a pure ministerial function'.[305] Hence, the 'Court has no power to examine the underlying amicable settlement since the motives of the parties are of no relevance for the discontinuance of the proceedings'.[306]

When parties turn to this procedural facility, 'it is not necessary to inform the Court about the cause of the consensus notified'. Furthermore, it 'is also not a prerequisite that the parties have reached a settlement of the underlying dispute (*argumentum a contrario* from Art. 88, para. 2 of the Rules)'.[307]

A distinction imposes itself between an amicable settlement leading to discontinuance and a procedural agreement to terminate the proceedings without the dispute between the parties having been basically solved.[308]

'A "discontinuance with prejudice" means a final disposition of the case, creating *res judicata* and preventing the parties from relitigating the same claims or facts'[309] and the Applicant's right to recommence the proceedings does not continue to exist.[310]

There is no distinction in the rules between discontinuance with and without prejudice, and the Court 'has traditionally just referred to the discontinuance' of the case, even in an instance where a party requested a 'discontinuance with prejudice'.[311]

The applicable Articles of the Court's Rules 'require formal procedural actions by agents, in writing' *inter alia* to 'protect the interests of each of the two parties'.[312]

Discontinuance, under Article 68 of the (old) Rules of Court, is '(in effect) an agreed one, taking the form of an agreed communication to the Court'. In such a situation the likelihood of the dispute having been settled as a result of successful negotiations is rather high, whereas the discontinuance under Article 69 always takes the form of a unilateral communication, even when there has been an agreed settlement of the dispute.[313]

---

302 *Land and Maritime Boundary case, I.C.J. Reports 2002*, Dissenting opinion by Judge *ad hoc* Ajibola, at p. 595, para. 179.

303 *Legality of Use of Force case, I.C.J. Reports 2004*, Separate opinion by Judge Higgins, at p. 338, para. 7 citing the 1974 *Nuclear Tests judgment.*

304 *Request for Interpretation of the Judgment of 15 June 1962 in the Case concerning the* Temple of Preah Vihear (Cambodia v. Thailand) *(Cambodia v. Thailand), Provisional measures, Order of 18 July 2011, I.C.J. Reports 2011*, at p. 551, para. 54.

305 G. Wegen, 'Discontinuance and Withdrawal 'in A. Zimmermann, C. Tomuschat and K. Oellers-Frahm (eds), *The Statute of the International Court of Justice: A Commentary* (Oxford, 2012), pp. 1447–68, at p. 1454, MN 3.

306 G. Wegen, 'Discontinuance and Withdrawal', at p. 1459, MN 35.

307 G. Wegen, 'Discontinuance and Withdrawal', at p. 1454, MN 3.

308 G. Wegen, 'Discontinuance and Withdrawal', at p. 1459, MN 35.

309 D. Prager, 'Procedural Developments at the International Court of Justice' (2003) *The Law and Practice of International Courts and Tribunals* 3, 551–7 at 557.

310 H. Thirlway, 'The Law and Procedure of the International Court of Justice 1960–1989: Part Thirteen' (2003) 73 *British Yearbook of International Law* 7–114, at 109.

311 D. Prager, 'Procedural Developments at the International Court of Justice' (2003), 557.

312 *Nuclear Tests (Australia v. France), I.C.J. Reports 1974*, Joint dissenting opinion by Judges Oneyama, Dillard, Jimenez de Arechaga, Waldock, at p. 324, para. 25.

313 *Barcelona Traction case, I.C.J. Reports 1964*, p. 6 at p. 20. A unilateral discontinuance may be unique because of the 'unclear circumstances' surrounding the filing of the Application: President Owada speech before the UN General Assembly on 28 October 2010, p. 6 referring to the Honduras Brazilian case and the Court's Order of 12 May 2010: *Certain*

Any understandings between the parties 'may certainly exist' in case of discontinuance under Article 69, but they 'must precede and be sought for outside' the act itself. The aim of both Articles 68 and 69 is 'to facilitate as much as possible the settlement of disputes'…'.[314]

This clearly illustrates the distinction between the case and the dispute because discontinuance of the case may not correspond completely to the end of the dispute out of which the case arose. There is indeed 'a presumption that a discontinuance is intended merely as a withdrawal of the proceedings before the Court, with no abandonment of the original claim'.[315]

Because discontinuance 'itself is a purely procedural act' the framework for establishing its real import can only be provided by the surrounding circumstances;[316] as a result, 'each case of discontinuance must be approached individually in order to determine its real character'.[317]

The willingness to negotiate may be one of these relevant circumstances.

In 'the construction of discontinuance on the basis of Article 89 of the Rules' of Court the Court performs a 'ministerial function'[318] and it 'prefers not to elaborate the parties' reasons for discontinuance, considering that they may wish the least publicity possible or the least "official" notice of their *diplomatic actions*'.[319] On the other hand, the Court 'may retain if not a control at least an interest in the final settlement of the dispute'.[320]

As negotiations may either precede or follow this unilateral act of discontinuance, a natural distinction presents itself between pre- and post-discontinuance negotiation.[321]

Although the notice of discontinuance may contain an undertaking of the parties, for instance, to resume the negotiations, such an undertaking may also be inferred from circumstances surrounding the notice of discontinuance.[322]

6.8 Successful Pre-discontinuance Negotiations and Discontinuance

At first glance discontinuance of the proceedings may be *perceived* as preventing the functional interaction from operating properly and from reaching its full potential through a judicial decision on the merits; but, as the Court has poignantly observed, the aim of both relevant Articles of its Rules is 'to facilitate as much as possible the settlement of disputes…'.[323]

This pronouncement clearly illustrates the close and even institutionalized aspect of the functional interaction at work: not only the underlying assumption but its very object and purpose is that the parties, after having turned to the Court, will return to the negotiating table to peacefully settle the dispute by non-judicial means.

Functional interaction takes a particular shape and colour when successful pre-discontinuance negotiations are followed by proper discontinuance of the proceedings.

Also in the case of Article 69 discontinuance may be the result of a settlement of the actual dispute having been concluded between the parties[324] and which does not necessarily need to be mentioned as the reason for the discontinuance.[325]

Questions concerning Diplomatic Relations (Honduras v. Brazil), Order of 12 May 2010, I.C.J. Reports 2010, p. 303. On this case see for more details *inter alia* L. Reed, 'Observations on the Relationship', pp. 302–3.

314 *Barcelona Traction case, I.C.J. Reports 1964*, p. 6 at p. 20.

315 H. Thirlway, 'The Law and Procedure of the International Court of Justice 1960–1989: Part Thirteen', 108.

316 *Barcelona Traction case, I.C.J. Reports 1964*, at pp. 17–18 (Spain).

317 *Ibid.*, at p. 19.

318 *Legality of Use of Force case, I.C.J. Reports 2004*, Dissenting opinion by Judge *ad hoc* Kreca, at p. 395, para. 35.

319 G. Wegen, 'Discontinuance', 734 (emphasis added).

320 R. Donner, 'Discontinuance of Proceedings in the International Court of Justice: Six Recent Cases' (1999) *Finnish Yearbook of International Law* 244–50 at 245. On the sequence of events and the role played by the President in the *Arbitral Award case* see *inter alia Ibid.*, at 247–8.

321 *Barcelona Traction case, I.C.J. Reports 1964*, at p. 19.

322 *Ibid.*, at p. 21.

323 *Ibid.*, at p. 20.

324 *Ibid.*, Dissenting opinion by Judge Morelli, at p. 102.

325 *Ibid.* at p. 103.

In case the parties have found common ground – within the framework of an initial double-track strategy or for instance as a result of developments of their respective positions as reflected in the written or oral proceedings – to resume the process of negotiations or when they are bound to restart the process because a Court Order has obliged them to do so even partially successful negotiations *may* ultimately bring about the discontinuance of the proceedings.

Indeed, 'judicial proceedings *may* be discontinued' when negotiations during the course of those proceedings 'result in the settlement of the dispute'.[326]

However, where negotiations on the core subject-matter of the dispute have been successful, discontinuance is not in all cases automatically to follow – for instance when questions of compensation still have to be resolved.

Moreover, 'the parties might agree to ask for an agreed declaratory judgment, for example'. Ultimately, discontinuance 'is a faculty open to the applicant party to a case, and its exercise depends solely on the appreciation by that party of its interests'.[327]

Unilateral Action

There is no need for either an Applicant or both parties as the case may be to motivate a notice of discontinuance – in fact 'there are a few limits to the motives that might inspire a discontinuance'[328] – or to give any indications as to future intentions.[329]

It is indeed only when the party or parties concerned explicitly refer to a successful outcome of another round of negotiations that it is possible to confirm that the functional interaction has been working satisfactorily.

Following an 'out of court agreement aimed at enhancing their good neighbourly relations' an Applicant may decide 'to renounce all further right of action based on the case' and express the wish '(not) to go on with the proceedings'.[330]

Discontinuance, for instance more than two and a half years after the filing of an Application, is not always the result of successful negotiations.[331] Discontinuance may also be the direct result of a decision by the Respondent to withdraw the contested measures, thereby *virtually* settling the dispute.[332]

Joint Action

Parties may jointly notify the Court of their agreement 'to discontinue with prejudice the proceedings'.[333] Sometimes the Court's Order does not indicate whether the discontinuance takes place with prejudice.[334] Discontinuance may follow the conclusion of two separate satisfactory arrangements as a result of 'conversations'.[335]

---

326 *Aegean Sea Continental Shelf case, I.C.J. Reports 1978*, at p. 12, para. 29.

327 H. Thirlway, 'The Law and Procedure of the International Court of Justice 1960–1989: Part Thirteen', 113.

328 *Barcelona Tract ion case, I.C.J. Reports 1964*, at p. 19.

329 *Ibid.*, at p. 17.

330 *Border and Transborder Armed Actions case, I.C.J. Reports 1992*, at p. 223. See also the *Aerial Herbicides Spraying case, Order, I.C.J. Reports 2013*, p. 278, at p. 279, the Order containing the essence of the agreement reached according to letters received from the parties.

331 *Case concerning the Aerial Incident of 27 July 1955 (United States of America v. Bulgaria), Order of 30 May 1960, I.C.J. Reports 1960*, p. 146 at p. 147.

332 *Protection of French Nationals in Egypt, Order of 29 March 1950, I.C.J. Reports 1950*, at p. 60.

333 *Questions of Interpretation and Application of the 1971 Montreal Convention arising from the Aerial Incident at Lockerbie (Libyan Arab Jamahiriya v. United States of America), Order of 10 September 2003, I.C.J. Reports 2003*, p. 152, at p. 153.

334 *Certain Phosphates Lands in Nauru (Nauru v. Australia), Order of 13 September 1993, I.C.J. Reports 1993*, p. 322, at pp. 322–3. Negotiations leading to discontinuance do not necessarily have been restricted to a purely bilateral process where an Applicant, in explaining its decision to discontinuance the proceedings, makes reference for instance to the Esquipulas II Agreement signed by the Presidents of the five States of Central America and discontinues the proceedings: *Border and Transborder armed Actions case, I.C.J. Reports 1987, Order of 19 August 1987*, p. 182, at p. 183.

335 *Case concerning the Compagnie du Port, des Quais et des Entrepôts de Beyrouth and the Société Radio-Orient (France v. Lebanon), Order of 31 August 1960, I.C.J. Reports 1960*, p. 186, at p. 187.

Part of an agreement reached may have been that once the settlement was made the Applicant would discontinue the proceedings which it has instituted just under a year ago.[336]

A joint notification from the parties mentioning that the discontinuance is the result of having reached a settlement may not be reflected in the Court's Order when it simply places on record that the discontinuance is by agreement of the parties.[337] In such a case discontinuance can 'in effect be exceptionally declared to be a *désistement d'action*' when the parties ask the Court to record the fact that they have reached a settlement of the dispute.[338]

In another similar case the parties may not have specifically asked that the Court should record that the discontinuance was the consequence of an agreement on the merits of the dispute.[339]

A Catch-22 Situation

The functional interaction could operate both ways, for instance when representatives of private interests approached their counterparts with a view to reopening negotiations, but a positive reply was made conditional on the discontinuance of the case before the Court and a mere suspension of the proceedings would not meet that demand.[340]

The Court made it clear that although various contacts at governmental level may take place, the real exchanges situate themselves at the level between the representatives of the private interests. The fact that the governments are being kept *informed* does not change this state of affairs.[341]

As to the functional interaction, the Court pointed out that real negotiations between the governments concerned could only be considered to actually take place if and to the extent that the positions taken by those representatives could engage their responsibility.[342] The Court recalled the general rule that it can only take into account acts and attitudes of governments in order to establish the existence of understanding between States Parties to a litigation before it.[343]

However, the Court did not fail to duly note that in this case both parties deliberately avoided a problem: the unwillingness on the part of the Respondent to negotiate with the proceedings continuing; and the unwillingness of the Applicant to relinquish its right to bring new proceedings in case the negotiations failed.[344] Respective unwillingness on the part of both parties may create a catch-22 situation, preventing any further operation of the functional interaction between negotiations and adjudication.

A Court Decision

Discontinuance may be the result of an initiative taken by (one of) the parties and approved by the Court; it may also result from a Court's decision.

When negotiations have been conducted successfully on the dispute, but the parties are not requesting discontinuance of the proceedings for reasons of national pride or otherwise, then the Court 'must not fail to take cognizance of a situation in which the dispute has disappeared because the final objective which the Applicant has maintained throughout has been achieved by other means'.[345] In such a situation the functional interaction must be deemed to have operated in a comprehensive and successful way.

---

336 *Electricité de Beyrouth Company case, Order of 29 July 1954, I.C.J. Reports 1954*, p. 107 at p. 108.

337 H. Thirlway, 'The Law and Procedure of the International Court of Justice 1960–1989: Part Thirteen', at 107, note 276.

338 H. Thirlway, 'The Law and Procedure of the International Court of Justice 1960–1989: Part Thirteen', 111.

339 H. Thirlway, 'The Law and Procedure of the International Court of Justice 1960–1989: Part Thirteen', 111.

340 *Barcelona Traction case, I.C.J. Reports 1964*, at p. 22 (Spain).

341 *Ibid.*, at p. 22.

342 *Ibid.*, at p. 23.

343 *Ibid.*

344 *Ibid.*, at p. 24.

345 *Nuclear Tests (New Zealand v. France), I.C.J. Reports 1974*, at p. 476, para. 58.

As a general rule an Applicant may request the Court to discontinue the proceedings if it has the conviction that the case has in effect been concluded, a decision normally welcomed by the Respondent.[346] The fact that the Applicant has not done so, for whatever reason, 'does not prevent the Court from making its own independent finding on the subject'.[347]

6.9 Post-Discontinuance Negotiations in the Absence of a Court Judgment on the Merits

Discontinuance means the termination of the then proceedings before the Court, and brings the parties into the post-adjudicative phase *sensu lato*, that is to say without a judgment on the merits being delivered by the Court.

As an Applicant may keep hidden the real motives for its decision to discontinue, it is under no obligation to do so or to give any indications as to its future intentions. These intentions can very well include a resumption of the negotiations aiming at the solution of the dispute through a new process of negotiations.

When after a round of negotiations which at the most lasted for just six weeks an agreement was reached, an Applicant may request discontinuance of the proceedings 'with a view to facilitate further negotiations',[348] thereby transferring the resumed negotiations process into the post-adjudicative phase *sensu lato* as an 'accomplishment' of the dispute had not yet been reached.

Although this situation situates itself at the crossroads of the adjudicative and the post-adjudicative phase, a clear intention expressed by (one of) the parties to resume the negotiations aiming at the solution of the dispute may really confirm that the functional interaction will operate beyond the removal of the case from the General List. This situation is different from the post-adjudicative phase *sensu stricto* when the Court has been able to deliver a judgment, and which we will deal with in Part III of this study.

It may later turn out that the discontinuance has in fact been made with a view of negotiations between representatives of private parties.[349] The breaking down of these negotiations may then lead to the institution of new proceedings with regard to the same matters of complaint.[350] Sometimes it is for that reason rather unclear whether discontinuance took place with the aim of and was followed by negotiations.[351]

The 'conclusion of a settlement is not the discontinuance of an action (as a) dispute may subsequently arise in connection with the implementation of this settlement giving rise (possibly) to new proceedings'.[352] In giving a decision in those subsequent proceedings the Court 'must take account of the settlement concluded between the parties'.[353]

Discontinuance even by mutual agreement 'is not necessarily a *pactum de non petendo*'.[354] Indeed, discontinuance does not necessarily mean that the dispute has been the subject of a settlement between the parties; it may very well persist until the institution of a new Application, which a previous discontinuance is not able to bar.[355]

Although the notice of discontinuance may contain an undertaking of the parties for instance to resume the negotiations, such an undertaking may also be derived from circumstances surrounding the notice of discontinuance.[356]

---

346 *Military and Paramilitary Activities in and against Nicaragua (Nicaragua v. United States of America), Order of 26 September 1991, I.C.J. Reports 1991*, p. 47, at p. 48.

347 *Nuclear Tests (Australia v. France), I.C.J. Reports 1974*, at p. 270, para. 54.

348 *Trial of Pakistani Prisoners of War, Order of 15 December 1973, I.C.J. Reports 1973*, p. 347, at p. 348.

349 *Barcelona Tract ion case, I.C.J. Reports 1964*, at p. 17.

350 *Ibid.*, at p. 17 (Belgium).

351 *Case concerning the Barcelona Traction, Light and Power Company, Limited (Belgium v. Spain), Order of 10 April 1961, I.C.J. Reports 1961*, p. 9 at p. 10.

352 *Barcelona Traction case, I.C.J. Reports 1964*, Declaration by Judge Koretsky, at p. 48.

353 *Ibid.*, Dissenting opinion by Judge Morelli, at p. 102. On the various acts which may accompany the discontinuance see Judge Morelli, at pp. 105–6.

354 *Ibid.*, Declaration by Judge Koretsky, at p. 49.

355 *Ibid.*, at p. 13 (Belgium).

356 *Ibid.*, at p. 21.

The exhaustion of and the failure of prior negotiations may have been the necessary condition before initial proceedings could be brought. However, in case of discontinuance there is no reason why in a situation where the original Applicant intends to bring new proceedings on the basis of the same jurisdictional clause the parties should be absolved from going through the same process of negotiations again in relation to the same claim and Court.[357]

There may be 'an element of artificiality involved in the repetition of the Treaty process in regard of the same matters of complaint',[358] but the right to bring new proceedings has to be upheld.

In case of discontinuance in order to resume negotiations, the functional link between judicial settlement and settlement by negotiations is rather close. Indeed, awareness of the risk of new proceedings being brought in case of failure of post-discontinuance negotiations might have affected the attitude of the Respondent *vis-à-vis* discontinuance of earlier proceedings in order to facilitate those negotiations.[359]

In case of refusal of discontinuance, proceedings would have continued, 'whereas negotiations offered a possibility of finally settling the dispute'.[360]

On the other hand there is also a functional link between proceedings and negotiations in this sense: successful preliminary objections and negotiations would have in common the prevention of any discussion of all the allegations made against the Respondent. In case of unsuccessful negotiations, the restart of the case would still offer the Respondent the possibility to raise preliminary objections.[361] In such circumstances it is difficult to envisage what a Respondent has to lose by agreeing to negotiate on the basis of a simple discontinuance, as the Court put it.[362]

Although the Court is making reference to the functional interaction between the two mechanisms, the formulation used seems to express the Court's expectation that a final settlement of the dispute is more likely to occur through a process of negotiations.

'It is in accordance with the true function of the Court that the dispute submitted to it should be determined by its own decision and not by the contingent operation of an attitude of accommodation on the part of the disputants.'[363]

A *pactum de non-contrahendo* not to 'make' agreements with States outside the region 'that could prejudice either Party' may be complemented by another commitment by one of the parties not to ratify a maritime delimitation treaty it had concluded with a third State; in exchange the Applicant may agree to discontinue the case it had pending before a regional Court of Justice.[364]

This is a rather particular example of functional interaction between attempts to create circumstances that would be conducive for future negotiations between the parties on a maritime boundary dispute and the discontinuance of judicial proceedings initiated by one of the parties before another Court of Justice.

6.10 Interim Arrangements Reached during the Course of the Proceedings

In most cases and by the nature of things, the dispute has been brought before the Court because the major legal issues could not be resolved through a process of prior negotiations. The subject-matter of the dispute, the state of relations between the parties, external events could have required the parties to reach some common understanding, on a temporary basis, with regard to for instance problems of a practical nature which they cannot afford to be left 'unsolved' pending the delivery by the Court of its judgment on the merits of the case.

A '*modus vivendi*' by nature 'implies something temporary or precarious'.[365]

---

357 *Ibid.*, at p. 26 (Spain).

358 *Ibid.*, at p. 26.

359 *Ibid.*, at p. 24.

360 *Ibid.*

361 *Ibid.*, at p. 25.

362 *Ibid.*

363 Hersch Lauterpacht as cited by Judge *Ad Hoc* Chagla in *Right of Passage case, I.C.J. Reports, 1960*, at p. 120.

364 *Territorial and Maritime Dispute between Nicaragua and Honduras, I.C.J. Reports 2007*, at pp. 680–81, para. 62.

365 H. Thirlway, 'The Law and Procedure of the International Court of Justice 1960–1989. Supplement, 2006: Part Three' 77 *British Yearbook of International Law*, 1–82 at 12.

The inherent incapability of settlement by negotiation of a dispute 'in which the interest incorporated is of a humanitarian character',[366] however, 'does not exclude the possibility of compromise concerning detailed policies and measures in order to implement the fundamental principles of the Mandate'.[367]

Interim arrangements have a somewhat ambiguous and indirect connection with the subject-matter of the pending dispute as their practical urgency and desirability is dictated by the outstanding issues between the parties. The question could be raised whether there is *a formal functional link* between negotiations and judicial settlement – they do not have to contain an express reference to the ongoing proceedings before the Court, but they may merely emphasize the interim nature pending a settlement on the substantive dispute and that it was of a without prejudice nature altogether[368] – or *only a factual one* because such an interim arrangement was concluded during the proceedings without prejudice to the matters of substance in dispute because as a result of these saving clauses there can be no doubt that the dispute still continues.[369]

The Court's General Attitude

What is the Court's general attitude towards attempts by the parties to conclude such interim arrangements?

The Court is anxious not 'to discourage the making of interim arrangements in future disputes with the object of reducing friction and avoiding risk to peace and security' provided such an interim agreement does not prevent it from 'from rendering a judgment' or compel it to dismiss the claim 'as one without object'. Such a result 'would run counter to the purpose enshrined' in the Charter on PSD.[370]

The conclusion of an interim arrangement may 'render moot the question of compliance with the provisional measures' indicated.[371]

The absence of a provision in such an interim agreement, as result of the deletion of a sentence to that effect, that parties would reconsider the position before the expiration of that interim agreement does not release the parties from this obligation to negotiate in respect of the basic dispute between them.[372] Such an intention would not correspond to the Applicant's submission that the Court should declare that the parties are under a duty to negotiate; neither would it be consistent with the Respondent's intention to continue negotiations.

Given the continuous nature of the general obligation for parties to negotiate, it cannot have been their intention to wait for the expiration date and 'for the reactivation of the dispute, with all the possible friction it might engender' before 'one of them might require the other to attempt a peaceful settlement through negotiations'.[373]

A special situation arises when the Court orders the parties to negotiate and conclude an interim arrangement to govern some practical problems in a disputed area pending the delivery of the judgment on the merits. We deal with this scenario in the penultimate paragraph of this chapter. Even prior to the start of the proceedings parties may have been unable or unwilling to conclude an interim arrangement.[374]

Reasons of Practical Urgency

An Applicant may inform the Court that negotiations are taking place with a view to reaching an interim arrangement pending final settlement of the dispute.[375]

---

366 *South West Africa, I.C.J. Reports 1966*, Dissenting opinion by Judge Tanaka, at p. 257.

367 *Ibid.*

368 *Fisheries Jurisdiction (United Kingdom v. Iceland), I.C.J. Reports 1974*, at p. 18, para. 37.

369 *Ibid.*

370 *Ibid.*, at p. 20, para. 41.

371 H. Thirlway, 'The Law and Procedure of the International Court of Justice 1960–1989: Part Twelve', 112.

372 *Fisheries Jurisdiction (United Kingdom v. Iceland), I.C.J. Reports 1974*, at pp. 32–3, para. 77.

373 *Ibid.*

374 *Gabcikovo Case, I.C.J. Reports 1997*, Dissenting opinion by Judge Oda, at p. 165, para. 24.

375 *Fisheries Jurisdiction (Federal Republic of Germany v. Iceland), Interim Measures, Order of 12 July 1973, I.C.J. Reports 1973*, p. 313, at p. 314, para. 6.

The legal issues may be of such a nature or complexity that pending the proceedings important practical problems flowing from the controversy, such as an increased frequent occurrence of incidents in the disputed area, require an urgent albeit temporary arrangement.[376]

In such a situation the parties may very well be successful in concluding an interim agreement pending a settlement of the substantive dispute 'without prejudice to the legal position or rights of either government in relation thereto' taken in the course of the written and oral proceedings.[377]

Negotiations may take place to settle practical problems arising *in connection* with a legal right but without raising, let alone solving, the question of the legal right underlying the dispute.[378] This paragraph deals with this kind of negotiation which may result in the conclusion of a Memorandum of Understanding or Interim Arrangement.

Interim Arrangements and the Indication of Provisional Measures

What is, from a functional interaction perspective, the potential relationship between such attempts by the parties to conclude an interim arrangement – discussions about which they have referred to in an Exchange of Notes[379] – and a request for the indication of provisional measures, or even the continuance of measures already indicated?

The Court made it clear that[380] continuance of interim measures of protection do not 'exclude an interim arrangement which may be agreed upon by the governments concerned': such an arrangement may be based on data different from those indicated by the Court in an earlier Order.[381]

It is important here to recall the Court's ruling that the obligation to negotiate is not exhausted when parties after a series of negotiations finally were able to conclude an interim agreement, as the interim arrangement reached during the course of the proceedings was not a 'settlement' of the dispute, as was an earlier agreement between the parties.[382]

The successful outcome of these negotiations on an interim regime does not affect the judicial function of the Court, as one of the objects of the arrangements may have been to prevent the continuation of incidents.[383] Indeed, the interim regime 'could never prevent the Court from pronouncing' on the Applicant's submissions. Otherwise this would mean 'imposing a penalty on those who negotiate an interim agreement to avoid friction as a preliminary to the settlement of a dispute'.[384] The Court has been constantly aware, as from the time of its indication of provisional measures, that those negotiations were taking place and were not excluded by its Order.[385]

The common feature between provisional measures ordered by the Court and an interim arrangement concluded between the parties pending the judgment is their temporary nature, as they both cease to operate on the delivery of the judgment of the merits (or on discontinuance, as the case may be). However, with regard to the functional interaction in the post-adjudicative phase, the Applicant may argue that the existence of an interim arrangement does not affect the duty of the parties 'to regulate their relations in accordance with the

376 *Fisheries Jurisdiction (United Kingdom v. Iceland), I.C.J. Reports 1974*, at p. 17, para. 35.

377 *Ibid.*, at p. 5, para. 4. Judge Petren rightly noted that given the chronology of events the Applicant's Memorial on the merits of the case could not have taken into account the effects of the interim agreement: Dissenting opinion by Judge Petren, at p. 158.

378 *Right of Passage case, I.C.J. Reports 1957*, at p. 151.

379 *Fisheries Jurisdiction (Federal Republic of Germany v. Iceland), I.C.J. Reports 1973*, at p. 55, para. 15.

380 *Fisheries Jurisdiction (Federal Republic of Germany v. Iceland), Interim Measures, Order of 12 July 1973, I.C.J. Reports 1973*, p. 313, at p. 314, para. 7; *Fisheries Jurisdiction (United Kingdom v. Iceland), Interim Measures, Order of 12 July 1973, I.C.J. Reports 1973*, p. 302, at p. 303, para. 7.

381 *Fisheries Jurisdiction (Federal Republic of Germany v. Iceland), Interim Measures, Order of 12 July 1973, I.C.J. Reports 1973*, p. 313, at p. 314, para. 7.

382 *Fisheries Jurisdiction (United Kingdom v. Iceland), I.C.J. Reports 1974*, at p. 32, para. 76.

383 *Ibid.*, at p. 19, para. 38.

384 *Ibid.*, Declaration by Judge Singh, at p. 42.

385 *Ibid.*, at p. 19, para. 38. Such compatibility requirement had been put forward by the UK in its exchanges with the Respondent (at p. 17, para. 33). In the *pre-LaGrand* period the Court did not go so far as to require and assess the compatibility of such an interim arrangement with its previous Order of provisional measures.

terms of the judgment' as soon as the interim regime ceases to be in force.[386] On the other hand, the judgment 'may provide a basis for the negotiation of arrangements to follow those contained in the Interim Agreement'.[387]

A ruling of the Court could constitute *a* but not *the* basis for post-adjudicatory negotiations replacing the interim agreement concluded during the course of the proceedings but after the indication of provisional measures.

It should be duly noted that in a related dispute negotiations were also held and carried on intermittently for a period of two years but without leading to any agreement,[388] in spite of the subject-matter being identical to the one that was the subject of the interim arrangement concluded with one of the parties in the other case with the UK. However, from a functional interaction perspective the fact that such an interim arrangement had not been concluded did, in the opinion of the Court, not fail to produce some consequences during and even beyond the proceedings.

First of all it does not mean that the parties are at liberty 'to conduct their fishing activities in the disputed waters without limitation' given *inter alia* a catch-limitation fixed by the Court in an Order indicating provisional measures.[389]

Secondly, the negotiations in good faith which the Court may order in its judgment could involve an obligation for the parties, pending the conclusion of such negotiations, to pay reasonable regard to each other's rights and to conservation requirements, a self-evident principle the Court found appropriate, in the circumstances of the case, to reaffirm.[390]

When ordering provisional measures the Court may oblige the parties to refrain from certain actions 'until such time as the Court has decided the dispute on the merits *or the Parties have come to an agreement on this subject*'.[391]

When directing the parties to 'co-operate with each other in a spirit of good neighbourliness'[392] with regard to criminal activity in the disputed area, this implies that the parties should consult and negotiate.

The origin and source of the obligation for the parties to negotiate towards a interim arrangement may not only stem from factors of practical urgency, from provisions in their Special Agreement, from a Court Order, as it may also be found in pre-existing obligations resting upon one of the parties.

In order for one of the parties to carry out its pre-existing obligations with regard to the disputed area, the Court could order that party not only to give the other party prior notice of actions to protect the environment in a disputed territory, but also to 'use its best endeavours to find common solutions',[393] and thus in fact obliging both parties to negotiate a temporary arrangement pending the delivery of the judgment on the merits.

As the Court imposed the obligation of conduct exclusively on the Applicant, it apparently reckoned with the possibility that, given the tense relations between the parties over the disputed territory, no such temporary arrangement might come into existence.

Special Agreement Provisions

In their Special Agreement parties may not only have acknowledged their inability to settle their dispute by negotiations; they may also have committed themselves to negotiate during the proceedings and apply a temporary (water management) regime.[394]

---

386 *Fisheries Jurisdiction (United Kingdom v. Iceland), I.C.J. Reports 1974*, at p. 19, para. 39.

387 *Ibid.*, (UK).

388 *Fisheries Jurisdiction (Federal Republic of Germany v. Iceland), I.C.J. Reports 1974,* at p. 188, para. 32.

389 *Ibid.*, at p. 202, para. 70.

390 *Ibid.*

391 *Certain Activities in the Border Area case (Costa Rica v. Nicaragua), I.C.J. Reports 2011*, at p. 25, para. 77 (emphasis added).

392 *Ibid.*, at p. 25, para. 78.

393 *Ibid.*, at p. 26, para. 80.

394 *Gabcikovo case, I.C.J. Reports 1997*, at p. 11.

They may further agree that when during those negotiations one party believes that its rights are being endangered by the conduct of the other, a request for immediate consultation will be made and no request for provisional measures will be addressed to the Court.[395]

This is a unique example of parties deliberately restricting the functional interaction between negotiations during the proceedings on an interim arrangement and a possible judicial intervention under Article 41 of the Statute by mutually renouncing well in advance the exercise of this procedural right. Such *a pactum de negotiando* and *de contrahendo* could find its way in other Special Agreements as well, but when this happens it is not very likely that the parties will also provide that such a commitment is 'fundamental to the conclusion and the continuing validity of the Special Agreement'.[396]

The conclusion of any such Special Agreement, perhaps following years of unsuccessful negotiations to solve a long-standing dispute, is impossible without both parties demonstrating the necessary political will. Any refusal to negotiate in good faith the interim arrangement as envisaged would constitute a material breach of the Special Agreement, the continued validity of which, and hence the Court's jurisdiction, would however not be affected unless both parties decide in favour of discontinuance. In case the Court would *proprio motu* have ordered the parties to negotiate such an interim arrangement, in a departure from the provisions in the Special Agreement, any refusal to comply would constitute an additional wrongful act. In fact the temporary (water) regime during the proceedings 'could not easily be settled' as the parties could not agree on recommendations issued by the EC. 'After lengthy negotiations, they finally concluded an agreement ... temporary one ... that would come to an end 14 days after the Judgment of the Court.'[397]

6.11 Negotiations during the Proceedings and the Position of Third States

Except in particular and presently rather rare cases, adjudication by the ICJ involves those two parties to the dispute which in the pre-adjudicatory phase have been actively participating in the process of negotiations towards an out-of-court settlement. It is this prior bilateral process which forms the substratum for the subsequent functional interaction with adjudication.

In Chapter 3 we have already indicated that during the pre-adjudicatory phase third States may have been involved in negotiations. Negotiations with third States may take place during the proceedings, after the delivery of the judgment or both. Only the first time frame is our concern now; the second one will reappear in Part III of this study.

The starting point for looking at the functional interaction when the position of third States is involved has to be the Court's ruling that it has no 'jurisdiction to rule upon the conformity with international law of any conduct of States not parties to the present dispute, or of conduct of the Parties unconnected with the dispute'.[398] This lack of jurisdiction covers *inter alia* negotiations between the parties and with third States, for instance on aspects of the dispute which have not been submitted to the Court.

Conversely, another mode of functional interaction arises when negotiations between one of the parties and a third State 'would be set in train' with a view to determining the frontier,[399] and when this process is likely to have an impact on the later decision of the Court in the case pending before it.

The involvement of third States in a regional peace process may have attracted the praise of the parties to the case, but what could the Court say about this? Such efforts merit the 'full respect' and consideration of the Court 'as a unique contribution to the solution of the difficult situation in the region'.[400]

By expressing its awareness 'that considerable progress has been achieved on the main objective of the process', namely a number of agreements on a variety of issues, the Court is assessing the progress made to be measured against the 'main objective' of a particular series of negotiations. As far as functional interaction

395 *Ibid.*, at p. 12, Article 4 (1) and (2).
396 *Ibid.*, at p. 12, Article 4 (3).
397 *Ibid.*, at pp. 27–8, para. 25.
398 *Nicaragua case, I.C.J. Reports 1986*, at p. 109, para. 207.
399 *Frontier Dispute, I.C.J. Reports 1986*, at p. 563, para. 16 and pp. 576–80, paras. 44–50.
400 *Nicaragua case, I.C.J. Reports 1986*, at p. 145, para. 291.

is concerned, the Court added that the work of the 'Contadora Group may facilitate the delicate and difficult negotiations' which 'are now required'.[401]

The fact that third States are involved in regional negotiations has been used by parties in order to object to the indication of provisional measures, as arguably those States have become 'indispensable parties' for the pending proceedings.[402]

The Court may not always feel the need to assess the progress of a regional peace process or of a series of bilateral meetings between the parties. However, it may address itself to third States and third parties when unequivocally expressing its opinion about the conduct it expects from all parties involved when stating that 'it is incumbent on *all those involved in the conflict* to support the peace process in the DRC and other peace processes in the Great Lakes area, in order to ensure respect for human rights in the region'.[403]

Access for Third States to the Pleadings of the Parties

Pursuant to Article 53 of its Rules, the Court may decide, after ascertaining the views of the parties, that third States, entitled to appear before it, upon request will be furnished with copies of the written pleadings and documents annexed. *Requests* by several States may, given objection raised by one of the parties 'for the present', be denied.[404]

Access to the pleadings will better enable the would-be intervener to comply with the requirements of Article 81 of the Rules.[405]

The *right* to be supplied with copies flows from the Court's admittance of the Application to intervene.[406] Pursuant to Article 53, para. 1 of its Rules, the Court 'may order the production of the pleadings even if one of the parties to the case object':[407]

> If, from the circumstances of the case and of the request, it is apparent to the Court that the purpose of the request is to enable the requesting State to ascertain whether it has a legal interest in the case, the Court would be well advised to grant the request and make the pleadings available so as not to impair the requesting State's 'statutory right to request intervention'.[408]

In the *Nicaragua Colombia case* no less than seven States asked to be furnished with copies of the pleadings and documents annexed in the case;[409] both Honduras and Costa Rica requested and obtained *anticipated access* to the written pleadings in the case. Later they both applied for permission to intervene.[410]

Practice shows that 'not all States which have received pleadings have gone on to claim intervention'. As already indicated, States 'may be interested in pleadings before publication for reasons other than considering intervention',[411] for instance in view of upcoming negotiations with one or both of the parties to the case before the Court.

---

401 *Ibid.*

402 *Nicaragua case, I.C.J. Reports 1984*, at p. 184, para. 35.

403 *Case between the DRC and Uganda, I.C.J. Reports 2005*, at p. 245, para. 221 (emphasis added).

404 *Continental Shelf case between Tunisia and Libya, I.C.J. Reports* 1981, at p. 5, para. 4.

405 C. Chinkin, 'Article 62' in A. Zimmermann, C. Tomuschat C. Tams and K. Oellers-Frahm (eds), *The Statute of the International Court of Justice: A Commentary* (Oxford, 2012), pp. 1529–72, at p. 1541, MN 30.

406 A suggestion also has been made in the past 'to the effect that a state which can establish *prima facie* that it has an interest in the case should be allowed to have access to the memorials and annexed documents in the case'. P. Palchetti, 'Opening the International Court of Justice to Third States: Intervention and Beyond' (2002) 6 *Max Planck Yearbook of United Nations Law,* 139–81 at 158, note 47 referring to the 2009 study by A. Riddell and B. Plant, *Evidence.*

407 D. Prager, 'Procedural Developments at the International Court of Justice' (2002), at 199.

408 *Ibid.*, at 200.

409 *Territorial and Maritime Dispute (Nicaragua v. Colombia), I.C.J. Reports 2012*, at pp. 631–2, para. 9.

410 *Territorial and Maritime Dispute (Nicaragua v. Colombia), I.C.J. Report 2007*, at p. 837, para. 7; *Territorial and Maritime Dispute (Nicaragua v. Colombia), Application for Permission to Intervene, Judgment, I.C.J. Reports 2011*, p. 420, at p. 426, paras. 6 and 12; *Territorial and Maritime Dispute (Nicaragua v. Colombia), Application by Costa Rica for Permission to Intervene, I.C.J. Reports 2011*, p. 348, at p. 354, paras. 10 and 12.

411 C. Chinkin, *Third Parties*, p. 188.

The fact that many governments have asked for copies of the pleadings may be evidence of a general view among States that the decision of the Court 'will be of the very greatest importance to the world generally as a precedent'.[412]

Furnishing third States with copies of the written pleadings may serve various purposes. First of all, it would enable them to assess whether it would be useful/necessary for them to make use of Article 62 or 63 of the Statute. Furthermore, once having access to the documents third States may use them for (future) disputes with one or both of the parties in a case before the Court or with third States absent from the ongoing proceedings altogether, or for future negotiations unconnected with any existing dispute.

The request made by a third State may also originate from its intention to open a process of negotiation with (one of) the parties regarding (one of) the legal issues at the heart or even at the margin of the pending dispute.

Protecting the Legal Rights of Third States: Article 59 and/or Article 62 of the Statute

One should not put aside the fact that the object and purpose of intervention under both Articles 62 and 63 of the Statute 'was to seek to overcome the bilateralisation of the controversy at stake, thus widening the dispute-settlement, when it could be of direct interest or concern to other states', and this would call 'for a more proactive attitude as to the institute of intervention in international judicial proceedings'.[413]

The most recent and most far-reaching judicial view on intervention consists of accepting that under Article 62 there is a right for States to intervene, subject to conditions the satisfaction of which the Court has to verify.[414]

Once those conditions have been fulfilled the Court 'is obliged to authorize the intervention'.[415] The mere possibility of the third State's legal interests to be affected is sufficient.[416] Moreover, 'the criteria in Article 62 do not preclude intervention simply because such a technique [of the Court to protect and not affect] is available even absent intervention'.[417]

Although in a dispositive judgment allocating rights and duties the protection offered by Article 59 is a purely technical one, such a protection is 'unlikely to be determinative' given the 'complexities of international negotiations and disputes'.[418]

Intervention 'does no more than provide a minimal defensive coating the need for which has become so evident in certain types of delimitation cases, and which may be anticipated for other multilateralised disputes'.[419]

Simply because the Court's technique to protect and not affect legal rights of third States is available even absent intervention, the criteria of Article 62 do not preclude intervention.[420] Article 62 of the Statute implies continuance of the proceedings in the absence of a State whose 'interests of a legal nature' might be 'affected' to be the normal course of action.[421]

Thus when negotiations with a third State are underway, because third States may decide to follow their own double track strategy when they combine their request with 'other activities pursued within the political or diplomatic arena'[422] or would become necessary after a judgment in a case between two other parties, that

412 The UK Attorney-General as cited in the *Anglo-Norwegian Fisheries case, I.C.J. Reports 1951*, Individual opinion by Judge Alvarez, at p. 145.

413 *Whaling in the Antarctic (Australia v. Japan), Declaration of Intervention by New Zealand, Order of 6 February 2013, I.C.J.Reports 2013,* p. 3, Separate opinion by Judge Cançado Trindade, at p. 27, para. 34, and at p. 32, para. 51.

414 *Territorial and Maritime Dispute (Nicaragua v. Colombia), Application by Honduras for Permission to Intervene, Judgment, I.C.J. Reports 2011*, p. 348, Dissenting opinion by Judge Abraham, at p. 448, para. 8 and at p. 450, para. 12.

415 *Ibid.*, Dissenting opinion by Judge Abraham, at p. 450, para. 12.

416 *Ibid.*, at p. 455, para. 30.

417 *Ibid.*, Dissenting opinion by Judge Donoghue, at p. 480, para. 21.

418 C. Chinkin, *Third Parties*, p. 158 referring to Judge Jennings dissenting in 1984.

419 S. Rosenne, *Intervention in the International Court of Justice* (Dordrecht, 1993), p. 158.

420 *Territorial and Maritime Dispute (Nicaragua v. Colombia), Application by Honduras for Permission to Intervene, I.C.J. Reports 2011*, Dissenting opinion by Judge Donoghue, at p. 480, para. 21.

421 *Land, Island and Maritime Frontier Dispute, I.C.J. Reports 1990*, at pp. 115–16, para. 55. On the legislative history of Article 62 see *inter alia* the *Indonesia/Malaysia case, I.C.J. Reports 2001*, Separate opinion by Judge *ad hoc* Weeramantry, at pp. 644–5, para. 26.

422 For some examples see *inter alia* C. Chinkin, *Third Parties*, p. 212.

is not a reason for the Court not to deal with a case. It is up to the third State to make its alleged rights being considered by the Court through intervention.

The Court has drawn a clear distinction between two fundamentally different situations as far as a third State is concerned. The interest of a third State may arise out of its 'involvement in the facts' of the case because of, for instance, its geographical location *vis-à-vis* the parties. But the Court's reasoning may also contain 'substantive elements that in content' must or may have invariably 'an impact upon subsequent relations' with the parties to the case.[423] The third State may then request the Court to be provided with the documents in the case without necessarily considering intervention.

The interest of a legal nature concerns 'rather the potential implications of reasons which the Court might give in its decision in the present case on matters in issue as' between the requesting State and one or both of the parties.[424] Here the functional interaction is becoming closer and institutionalized by the Statute.

The fear of the requesting State may indeed be that the reasoning of the Court 'may afterwards have a prejudicial effect on' the state's own legal interests 'in future settlement' with the parties (or with other states),[425] irrespective of whether this will take place by way of negotiations or by adjudication.

The State requesting intervention could argue that correspondence with one of the parties relating to respective claims and the existence of a Special Agreement with one of the parties concerning their claims being brought before the Court are further indications of its legal interest.[426]

At a time when the requirement of a jurisdictional link was almost at the heart of the debate about the proper use of Article 62, the question was raised whether a would-be intervener could 'negotiate a Special Agreement with' the parties, 'thereby gaining *locus standi* for intervention', and whether the third State could 'have such a special agreement negotiated, signed and ratified before the closing of the written proceedings in the principal case'. Such a course of action 'would obviously be unfeasible'.[427]

It may be 'useless to suggest a special agreement to the third State in the course of the procedure', especially if obtaining communication of the documents had not led to steps to intervene in the proceedings.[428]

The requesting State's argument that the possibility of a later appearance before the Court as a principal party in parallel proceedings against one or both of the parties should not affect the pertinence of a request for intervention as any decision in that case would come considerably later[429] applies *a fortiori* with regard to the potential impact of the decision in the case on subsequent negotiations. The Court's decision would in some measure prejudge the merits of those separate disputes.[430]

Prior Negotiations with (One of) the Parties

Article 62 does not require the 'would-be intervenor' to establish that intervention is the 'only means to protect'[431] its legal interests. Although an assertion of a claim by a State to a maritime area under international law is a prime and easy example of an assertion of an interest of a legal nature, the possibility should not be ruled out 'of a third State demonstrating an "interest of a legal nature" without framing it as a "claim" of a legal right'.[432] This may have taken place during bilateral negotiations with one or each of the parties to the case. Moreover, bilateral or trilateral negotiations prior to, during the proceedings or in the post-adjudicative phase could indeed also provide the protection the would-be intervener is looking for.

---

423 *Continental Shelf case between Tunisia and Libya, I.C.J. Reports 1981*, at p. 9, para. 13 (Malta).

424 *Ibid.*, at p. 12, para. 19.

425 *Ibid.*, at p. 17, para. 29.

426 *Ibid.*, at p. 18, para. 30 (Malta).

427 *Continental Shelf case between Libya and Malta, I.C.J. Reports 1984*, Dissenting opinion by Judge *ad hoc* Sette-Camara, at p. 89, para. 90.

428 *Corfu Channel case, I.C.J. Reports 1949*, Dissenting opinion by Judge Azevedo, at p. 90.

429 *Continental Shelf case between Tunisia and Libya, I.C.J. Reports 1981*, at p. 10, para. 40 (Malta).

430 *Ibid.*, at p. 18, para. 31.

431 *Territorial and Maritime Dispute (Nicaragua v. Colombia), Application by Honduras for Permission to Intervene, I.C.J. Reports 2011*, Dissenting opinion by Judge Donoghue, at p. 475, para. 14.

432 *Ibid.*, Dissenting opinion by Judge Donoghue, at p. 474, para. 11 and at p. 476, note 1.

In contrast, parties to a case may have concluded a *pactum de non-negotiando* through the adoption of a joint declaration in which they have committed themselves not to make agreements with third States outside the same region 'that could prejudice either Party'.[433]

It is within the power of the Court to recommend that parties should invite for their negotiations the experts of third countries or should conduct the negotiations under the aegis of an international organization.[434]

Intervention in the proceedings pursuant to Article 62 or 63 of the Statute is a complicating factor for the functional interaction, as it can be based not only on prior negotiations but also on negotiations still to be conducted with one or both of the parties before the Court or eventually with third States.

The Court has rejected the argument by one of the parties that, given one of the functional roles of negotiations, it is an established requirement that the requesting State and either of the parties should have conducted prior negotiations with regard to a particular maritime area as a mechanism towards the maturation of a dispute 'before an application can be made for permission to intervene'.[435]

The Court's view is in line with its position regarding such a requirement under general international law outside the situation of intervention. The reason for not accepting such a requirement stems from the fundamentally different functional role of intervention as compared with 'the determination of a further dispute between the State seeking to intervene and one or both of the parties'. Requiring 'the existence of such a dispute, defined by prior negotiations' as a condition of intervention would be 'inappropriate'.[436]

433 *Territorial and Maritime Dispute between Nicaragua and Honduras, I.C.J. Reports 2007*, at p. 681, para. 62.
434 *Great Belt case, I.C.J. Reports 1991*, Declaration by Judge Tarassov, at p. 24.
435 *Land, Island and Maritime Frontier Dispute, I.C.J. Reports 1990*, at pp. 113, paras. 50–51.
436 *Ibid.*, at p. 114, para. 51.

Chapter 7
Negotiations and their Role in the Judicial Settlement by the Court

Introduction

The functional interaction operates in various modes and under diverse appearances when we attempt to determine in general and in more precise terms the role (to be) played by the process of negotiations in the actual judicial settlement by the Court of the dispute before it.

The multifunctionality of negotiations (re)appears through the various roles the process is likely to perform in the actual settlement of the dispute by the Court. Prior or ongoing negotiations always play a role in the unfolding of the proceedings, as previous chapters have demonstrated.

The aim of this chapter is to contribute to the clarification of the functional role of (prior) negotiations in the actual judicial settlement of a dispute.

In a number of cases negotiations still to come in the post-adjudicative phase might also play a role in the Court's judgment. Although this will be the focus of Part III we will briefly touch upon the way the Court may lead the parties towards a process of negotiations in the post-adjudicative phase.

The *first question* in this chapter is related to the Court's exercise of its judicial function: to what extent and how does the pacificatory function of the Court influence the judicial weight the Court wishes to attribute in its judicial settlement of the dispute to (failed) prior and ongoing negotiations between the parties? An international judge is determined 'de ne pas attiser les tensions', and this in order to 'favoriser la continuité du processus diplomatique de règlement des différends'.[1]

On the other hand one should not 'résumer l'office de la Cour Internationale de Justice à sa mission pacificatrice, sous peine de présenter la fonction du droit international de façon erronée, en oubliant sa principale function au sein de la société des Etats: celle de régir les rapports entre ses sujects'.[2]

This question comprises several aspects.

Negotiations are, for instance, inherent to (disputes over) maritime delimitation and parties may have been steering this function of negotiations into the adjudicative phase. It may also be the Court that brings negotiations between the parties into the process of judicial settlement of the dispute by encouraging them to resume a process.

Negotiations between the parties may find their way in the judicial reasoning through *judicial inferences* from the views as expressed by the parties during the course of the negotiations; they may take place *on* the basis of a provisional measure indicated by the Court; they may be part *of* the basis for the Court's ruling, where the potential impact of the judicial decision on current or future negotiations may or should be taken into account; and ultimately they may appear in the judgment's or advisory opinion's operative paragraph where the Court may then, depending on the circumstances of the case, provide the parties with directions for post-adjudicative negotiations either to implement the judgment it will deliver or to settle outstanding issues.

Irrespective of whether parallel negotiations have actually taken place, the Court may – after having qualified the nature, scope and purpose of the negotiations – agree with the view held by (one of) the parties that the process of negotiations has reached a deadlock. Should such a judicial assessment lead the Court in its decision on the merits, having regard to the submission of the parties of course, not to include solutions which have already proven to be unacceptable to (one or both of) the parties?

1 G. Giraudeau, *Les différends territoriaux*, p .184.
2 G. Giraudeau, *Les différends territoriaux*, p. 240.

Conversely, should the Court incorporate in its decision those elements which in spite of the deadlock still have already turned out to be acceptable to (one or both of) the parties, for instance interim arrangements they have been able to conclude?

Are parties allowed to request the Court to include in the operative part of its judgment a line of their common frontier in sectors on which the parties have agreed 'so as to endow this line with the force of *res judicata*'?[3] This question is part of the broader issue whether the Court does 'favour the finding of transactional solutions given to concrete questions, aimed at the dissatisfaction of one or the other litigating Parties'.[4]

One authoritative commentator opines that with 'rare exceptions, the Court avoids the making of compromise solutions',[5] while the incisive study by Géraldine Giraudeau has persuasively demonstrated the transactional dynamic when territorial disputes are before an international judge.

Splitting the difference between conflicting claims 'is no part of the judicial function'; hence, 'that would not only be an abandonment of the duty of independent judgment, it would actively encourage extreme claims so as to extract from a court an acceptable compromise'[6] However, if the exercise of the judicial discretion to apply the law to the facts is done 'by reference to a principle, and in a logical persuasive manner, then this must be accepted as a valuable part of the judicial function, and it not to be castigated as mere compromises'.[7]

Would the Court, faced with a deadlock and having considered the written and oral pleadings, be ill-advised, while answering to the submissions, to exercise too much judicial caution, even at the risk of deciding *infra petita*, and to refer the parties back to the negotiating table?

In a case such as *Gabcikovo*, 'the Court is, in effect, transferring the burden of decision-making back to the parties. While the intention is to be constructive, the result is contradictory because the parties in the Special Agreement of 1993 had expected the *Court* to answer the questions formulated in Article 2'.[8]

In case of a declaratory judgment in which the Court finds not having jurisdiction by 'setting a higher standard of State consent for the exercise of its jurisdiction', the result is 'the remittance by the Court' of the dispute 'back to the contending parties'.[9]

The second main question which concerns us here has to do with the positions of the parties when the functional interaction may indeed come under pressure.

In the *Posphates in Morocco case* the Court wanted:

> to preclude the possibility of the submission to the Court by means of an Application of situations or facts dating from a period when the State whose action was impugned was not in a position to foresee the legal proceedings to which these facts and situations might give rise.[10]

Does this pronouncement also cover the process of pre-adjudicative negotiations? Should and could positions taken during the negotiations (not) be invoked during the adjudicative phase?[11] Or is reliance not allowed 'upon proposals made in the course of direct negotiations which do not lead to a complete agreement'?[12] Moreover, should there be consistency between the positions during the negotiations and the arguments invoked before the Court?

3 *Frontier Dispute between Burkina Faso and Niger, I.C.J. Reports 2013*, at p. 66, para. 37 (Burkina Faso's request).

4 P.-M. Dupuy, 'The Judicial Policy', p. 67.

5 I. Brownlie, ' The Peaceful Settlement of Disputes' (2008) 8 *Chinese Journal of International Law* 2, 267–83 at para. 44.

6 D. Bowett, 'Developments', 199.

7 D. Bowett, 'Developments', 200.

8 I. Brownlie, 'The Peaceful Settlement of Disputes', at para. 57.

9 *CERD case, I.C.J. Reports 2011*, Dissenting opinion by Judge Cançado Trindade, at p. 305, para. 162 and at p. 316, para. 197.

10 *Phosphates in Morocco case, P.C.I.J. Series A/B, No. 74*, p. 24.

11 The view was expressed that 'proposals made during negotiations cannot be taken into account when a decision based on law is to be made, and the same should hold good for provisional arrangements within the framework of negotiations'. *Land, Island and Maritime Frontier Dispute, I.C.J. Reports 1992*, Separate opinion by Judge *ad hoc* Valticos, at p. 626.

12 *Certain Frontier Land case, Order of 12 December 1957, I.C.J. Reports 1957*, Dissenting opinion by Judge Armand-Ugon, at p. 247 referring to the settled case law of the PCIJ and the ICJ.

Under the principle of preclusion a State 'should not be permitted to benefit by its own inconsistency to the prejudice of another State (nemo *potest mutare consilium suum in alterius injuriam*)'.[13] The act may take the form of a declaration or representation during negotiations when 'it implies consent to or agreement with a determined factual or juridical situation'.[14]

The condition of an ensuing 'change of position' must be understood as having 'brought about a change in the *relative* positions of the parties, worsening that of the one, or improving that of the other, or both',[15] which could easily occur during a process of negotiations. A general *caveat* applies here as 'there can be no equation between governmental statements made' before the Court and 'governmental statements made outside of it'.[16]

7.1 The Functional Role and Availability of Records of Negotiations

The Functional Role of Records

The Court drew a fine distinction between records of negotiations and minutes of a meeting which 'are not a simple record of a meeting ... (as) they do not merely give an account of discussions and summarize points of agreement and disagreement'; this is what records of negotiations should contain.[17] Perusal of incomplete minutes may 'reveal the adamant positions of the parties' but they may not 'explain how or with what arguments' a particular provision of a treaty was approved.[18]

Positions taken by States during negotiations may 'intentionally, or by implication or unwittingly, affect their legal position for the future'. On the other hand, the necessary freedom for parties to 'float ideas and make proposals' is vital to any process of negotiations and 'to that extent' they 'have to be treated as taking place under the protection of a general' without "prejudice" clause'.[19] The absence of such a clause – as it was formulated in Article 5 of the Special Agreement between the United States and Canada in the *Gulf of Maine case* – 'is likely to temper the parties' willingness to offer concessions in the preceding negotiations'.[20]

The possibility of estoppel, preclusion, admission or acquiescence cannot be excluded, but much will depend on the particular circumstances and the general context of the process.[21]

Official records of negotiations, draft texts prepared during the process and diplomatic exchanges constitute 'elements that are intrinsic to the negotiating process' and 'will generally be accepted as preparatory work',[22] although the influence of a declaration made by a State during the negotiations 'on the interpretation (of a treaty) could be limited'.[23]

How does the Court deal with such declarations made during an unsuccessful process of negotiations? As part of its judicial reasoning the Court might consider and take into account the views as expressed by the parties during the course of prior or parallel negotiations.

A distinction imposes itself between 'judicial findings' on the one hand and the Court 'recording the positions of one Party'.[24]

13 *Temple of Preah Vihear case, I.C.J. Reports 1962*, Separate opinion by Judge Alfaro, at p. 40.

14 *Ibid.*

15 *Ibid.*, Separate opinion by Judge Fitzmaurice, at p. 63.

16 *Nicaragua case, I.C.J. Reports 1986*, Dissenting opinion by Judge Schwebel, at p. 277, para. 27.

17 *Case between Qatar and Bahrain, I.C.J. Reports 1994*, at p. 121, para. 25; *Case concerning Maritime Dispute (Peru v. Chile), I.C.J.Reports 2014*, para. 65: Minutes of a Conference may 'summarize the discussions leading to the adoption' of a tripartite declaration 'rather than record[ing] an agreement of the negotiating States'.

18 *Territorial Dispute, (Libyan Arab Jamahiriya/Chad), I.C.J. Reports 1994*, Dissenting opinion by Judge *ad hoc* Sette-Camara, at p. 97.

19 A. Watts, 'Negociation and International Law', p. 535.

20 M. Waibel, 'The Diplomatic Channel', p. 1092.

21 A. Watts, 'Negociation and International Law', p. 535.

22 Y. Le Bouthillier, 'Article 32' in P. Klein and O. Corten (eds), *The Vienna Conventions on the Law of Treaties: A Commentary* (2 vols, Oxford, 2011), vol. 1, pp. 841–65, at p. 852, para. 23.

23 Y. Le Bouthillier, 'Article 32' at p. 855, § 27.

24 H. Thirlway, 'The Law and Procedure of the International Court of Justice 1960–1989: Part Twelve', at 75, note 139. In its judgment in the *Jan Mayen case*, the Court – although it raised the question 'whether a decision of the Court

The Availability of Records

In order to enable the Court to do this, the official records of such negotiations should either be available as part of the case file or belong to the public domain. When a document referred to by a particular service of one of the parties' administration is not 'among the case-file supplied by the parties' in such a situation the Court has 'no means of knowing how far this draft correspond with the text which was ultimately adopted'.[25]

Parties have a 'right to produce any evidence they deem appropriate to support their claims',[26] and this includes records of the process of negotiations. Whether parties are also under a duty to do so is a matter for debate.[27] A party's refusal to provide evidence 'for instance records of negotiations' is 'a sign that the document in question would in fact be prejudicial to the position of that party'.[28]

Direct negotiations on matters of substance between two countries do not necessarily have to be reported;[29] neither do parties have to reveal the content of lengthy negotiations which have resulted for instance in the conclusion of a Special Agreement.[30]

As a preliminary matter it has to be noted that the process of negotiations does not always have to be accompanied by the drafting of written minutes or records, as the revived *Temple of Preah Vihear case* illustrates where an oral ceasefire had been negotiated.[31]

In line with its established jurisprudence the Court 'will limit itself to official documents and statements',[32] although they may vary 'in their authors, their intended, likely and actual recipients and audience, the occasion of their delivery and their content'.[33]

Material before the Court may include statements by representatives of States, sometimes at the highest political level, 'before official organs for instance of' an IO and 'appear in the official records of those bodies'.[34]

Although it is true that material has not necessarily been drawn to the Court's attention by the parties,[35] for obvious reasons this does not seem to apply to records of negotiations.

The objection of one party – expressed on the occasion of the presentation during the oral proceedings of documents 'not previously produced' – that a document was 'not part of a publication readily available' within the meaning of Article 56, para. 4 of the Rules[36] is not likely to also apply to minutes of negotiations.

---

may be based on the positions expressed by a State at a diplomatic conference for the adoption of a multilateral convention' – nevertheless made an observation that a particular delimitation method was subscribed to 'in the context of the conference' by both parties: *I.C.J. Reports 1993*, at p. 56, para. 39. However, in his declaration Judge Ranjeva, noting that the Court in 1982 'was unable to remain indifferent to the positions stated by the parties in a bilateral negotiation', critized the Court for having taken into account a particular document at UNCLOS where 'proposals or draft provisions were regarded as unofficial and entirely non-committing', in particular since 'in the circumstances of this case the Court had no need to explore the legal scope of statements made by a State' at UNCLOS: *I.C.J. Reports 1993*, Declaration by Judge Ranjeva, at pp. 87–8. In different cicumstances statements made at UNCLOS may 'relate to the prospective maritime boundary agreements' and as a result may 'not shed light on the extent on the existing maritime boundary between' the parties: *Case Concerning Maritime Dispute (Peru v. Chile), I.C.J. Reports 2014*, para. 135.

25 *Frontier Dispute, I.C.J. Reports 1986*, at p. 609, para. 102.

26 A. Riddell and B. Plant, *Evidence*, p. 48.

27 A. Riddell and B. Plant, *Evidence*, p. 49. The confidentiality privilege does not seem to apply to records of negotiations since both parties have been involved in the process; but what about 'whether copies of confidential records not available to all parties to the proceedings should be admitted as evidence' (at p. 208)?

28 A. Riddell and B. Plant, *Evidence*, p. 116.

29 *Case between Botswana and Namibia, I.C.J. Reports 1999*, Separate opinion by Judge Oda, at p. 1122, para. 12.

30 *Gulf of Maine case, I.C.J. Reports 1984*, Dissenting opinion by Judge Gros, at p. 370, para. 16.

31 *Request for Interpretation of the 1962 Temple of Preah Vihear Judgment, I.C.J. Reports 2011*, at p. 549, para. 49. In the original case the minutes 'were manifestly prepared with considerable care and in great detail' and were 'a complete record of deliberations' held: *Temple of Preah Vihear case, I.C.J. Reports 1962*, Dissenting opinion by Judge Spender, at p. 104.

32 *CERD case, I.C.J. Reports 2011*, at p. 86, para. 33.

33 *Ibid.*, at p. 86, para. 35.

34 *Nicaragua case, I.C.J. Reports 1986*, at p. 41, para. 64.

35 *Ibid.*, at p. 44, para. 72.

36 *East Timor case, I.C.J. Reports 1995*, at p. 93, para. 9 (Portugal).

Records of the negotiations may have been 'drawn up by and have been brought to the Court's attention by the Applicant'[37] or by the Respondent.[38]

In case official records are not available, the Applicant may give the account of the negotiations to the Court without any prior request being made.[39] However, 'a report of a meeting' may be a unilateral one the accuracy of which cannot be assumed as against the other party.[40]

As adjudication of a dispute is, similar to negotiations, an unfolding process, *procès verbaux* of prior negotiations may eventually be produced by the Applicant in accordance with Article 56 of the Rules of Court if in light of arguments developed in the Respondent's Rejoinder they turn out to be more important than previously thought.[41] This may also happen when, for instance, during the course of the proceedings the other party has referred to those negotiations in spite of an understanding or an agreement that this would not be allowed or simply not be done.

Diplomatic correspondence exchanged prior to the conclusion of a Special Agreement and having being produced by the parties will in many cases manifest their opposing claims.[42]

In order to refute an allegation that a party did not agree 'to enter into negotiations in relation to the counter-claim' an Applicant may attach relevant correspondence to prove its willingness to enter into negotiations, admittedly on a broader range of subjects but still 'in relation to the period covered by the case'.[43]

The Applicant may maintain that despite its own agreement to negotiations the Respondent had 'effectively refused to seek to resolve these wider disputes by diplomatic negotiations'.[44]

The Court may also request (one of) the parties to submit to the Court correspondence that may throw light on the subject.[45]

7.2 Judicial Significance Accorded to (Records of) Negotiations

Diplomatic documents may consist of minutes of the meetings 'recording the state of progress of the negotiations, which possessed no legally binding force'.[46] A Respondent may argue that, hence, minutes 'did not rank as an international agreement and could not, therefore, serve as the basis for the jurisdiction of the Court'.[47]

Although normally minutes are a simple record of a meeting giving an account of discussions and summarizing points of agreement and disagreement[48] and of 'hesitations or second thoughts which had occurred' when a text was adopted,[49] the Court may consider in the particular circumstances of a case that they 'enumerate commitments to which the parties have consented and that they thus create rights and obligations in international law for the parties; they constitute an international agreement'.[50]

---

37 *Fisheries Jurisdiction (United Kingdom v. Iceland), I.C.J. Reports 1973*, at p. 10, para. 18.

38 *Case concerning Maritime Dispute (Peru v. Chile), I.C.J. Reports 2014*, para. 131.

39 *Fisheries Jurisdiction (Federal Republic of Germany v. Iceland), I.C.J. Reports 1973*, at p. 56, para. 19. Sometimes it is not quite clear which of the parties did bring diplomatic exchanges to the Court's attention: *Nuclear Tests (Australia v. France), I.C.J. Reports 1974*, at p. 263, para. 30.

40 *Nicaragua case, I.C.J. Reports 1986*, at p. 88, para. 166 and *Case concerning Maritime Dispute (Peru v. Chile), I.C.J. Reports 2014*, para. 132 (Peru).

41 *Land and Maritime Boundary case, I.C.J. Reports 2002*, at p. 315, para. 22.

42 *Land, Island and Maritime Frontier Dispute, I.C.J. Reports 1992*, at p. 555, para. 327.

43 *Oil platforms case, I.C.J. Reports 1998*, p. 190, at p. 194, para. 6 (Iran).

44 *Ibid.*, at p. 196, para. 12 (Iran).

45 *North Sea Continental Shelf case, I.C.J. Reports 1969*, at p. 35, para. 53.

46 *Case between Qatar and Bahrain, I.C.J. Reports 1995*, at p. 16, para. 29.

47 *Case between Qatar and Bahrain, I.C.J. Reports 1994*, at p. 121, para. 21 (Bahrain).

48 *Ibid.*, at p. 121, para. 25.

49 *Oil Platforms case, I.C.J. Reports 1996*, Separate opinion by Judge Ad Hoc Rigaux, at p. 865.

50 *Case between Qatar and Bahrain, I.C.J. Reports 1994*, at p. 121, para. 25.

In case the *travaux préparatoires* of such minutes are of a fragmentary nature, they must be used with caution, when they contain only references to successive drafts submitted by third States and the amendments made to them.[51]

Although one has no difficulty accepting the Court's general approach, Judge Shahabuddeen was right in adding that the 'fragmentary' nature does not mean that they are useless provided they 'show the state of the original draft; who presented it; who changed what; and in what sequence the changes were made. Those are the steps which normally occur in the drafting of a negotiated text.'[52]

The material presented by the parties about various rounds of negotiations extending over a long period of time may be considered by the Court as 'inconclusive' and not allowing the Court 'to evaluate the significance of the meetings held'.[53]

The Court may consider negotiations between the Parties dealing with related territorial issues as (not) 'significant for the extent of the maritime boundary between the Parties'.[54]

7.3 Judicial Significance Accorded to a Party's Readiness to Negotiate

As indicated in the first chapter, the 'obligation to be ready to negotiate with a view to concluding' an agreement represents 'the minimum of international co-operation'. In according judicial significance to a party's readiness to negotiate, the Court should never overlook 'the psychological value of the opening of negotiations' as it is 'often a decisive step toward the conclusion of an agreement'.[55]

In response to the Respondent's position that it would not object to the Court indicating provisional measures calling upon the parties to jointly address, in good faith, the difficulties dividing them, the Applicant may request the Court to decide the case 'having regard to the readiness of both Parties to seek a friendly settlement by diplomatic means'.[56]

This case is of course not unique in the sense that both parties to a case may during the course of the proceedings come to the conclusion that they are both willing to start or resume negotiations in order to reach an out-of-court settlement, as indicated in Chapter 6.

From a functional interaction perspective it should be noted that the Court found that the Respondent had not explained 'the precise consequences which it considered the holding of those negotiation *or the holding of negotiations generally*, would have in regard to the Court's jurisdiction, and in particular its jurisdiction to indicate provisional measures'.[57] This could be seen as a more or less implicit invitation to States generally when in similar circumstances negotiations are ongoing to explicitly deal with this potentially twofold impact on the Court's jurisdiction.

Although the Court was cautious to immediately add that the reference by the Respondent to such negotiations could not constitute a decisive reason to exclude, at that stage of the proceedings (request for indication of provisional measures), the Court's jurisdiction based on optional clauses of the parties,[58] it is rather unclear whether the Court's pronouncement would mean that if details would have been given on the scope, the way, duration etc. of those negotiations they could have been the sole reason for exclusion of the *prima facie* jurisdiction.

Individual judges may have preferred the parties' willingness to achieve a resolution of the dispute 'to have been embodied' within 'the confines of the Order'.[59]

---

51 *Case between Qatar and Bahrain, I.C.J. Reports 1995*, at p. 21, para. 41. For the various interpretations put forward by the parties see also para. 41.

52 *Ibid.*, Dissenting opinion by Judge Sahabuddeen, at p. 58.

53 *Territorial and Maritime Dispute (Nicaragua v. Colombia), I.C.J. Reports 2007*, at pp. 868–9, para. 119.

54 *Case concerning Maritime Dispute (Peru v. Chile), I.C.J. Reports 2014*, para. 133.

55 *International status of SWA, I.C.J. Reports 1950*, Dissenting opinion by Judge De Visscher, at p. 189 and at p. 188.

56 *Arrest Warrant case, I.C.J. Reports 2000*, at p. 193, para. 39; at p. 195, para. 44; at p. 201, para. 74; and at p. 202, para. 75.

57 *Ibid.*, at p. 200, para. 66 (emphasis added).

58 *Ibid.*, at p. 200, para. 68.

59 *Ibid.*, Separate opinion by Judge Koroma, at p. 210.

In assessing the chances of a friendly settlement being reached in resumed negotiations the Court, while taking due note of the parties' willingness to consider a friendly settlement of their dispute, clearly and inevitably in a way attaches greater importance to the positions 'as set out before the Court regarding their respective rights' as these 'are still a long way apart'.[60]

The Court's approach in this regard is the corollary of the other modality of the functional interaction to be discussed later: whether and to what extent positions taken during negotiations could be used in the arguments before the Court.

While the Court will continue to welcome bilateral efforts 'with a view to achieving a direct and friendly settlement' it is at the same time realistic in pointing out that 'the outcome of such negotiations cannot be foreseen'.[61]

In light of this judicial assessment of the situation the Court may resolutely decide in favour of the judicial part of the functional interaction as the 'issues before the Court should be determined as soon as possible' and hence its decision should 'be reached with all expedition'.[62] The Court did not remove the case from the General List as requested by the Respondent, but it did not indicate the provisional measure as requested by the Applicant either.

7.4 One of the Parties May Request the Court to Oblige them to Negotiate

In proceedings instituted by Application the legal situation is of course entirely different, but in their Special Agreement parties may provide that after the delivery of the judgment they will (have to) enter into a new or resumed process of negotiations, thereby imposing upon themselves a legally binding obligation.

In the absence of a contrary provision in a Special Agreement or a request in a submission by one of the parties, and prior to the *LaGrand* decision on the binding nature of an Order indicating provisional measures, the 'Court is [was] not entitled to oblige parties to enter into negotiations'. However, 'its judgment should where appropriate encourage them to do so, in consonance with its role as an institution devoted to the cause of peaceful settlement'.[63]

The nature of the legal rights in dispute may be such that unilateral action appears to be excluded; hence the Applicant may request the Court to declare that the parties have a duty to negotiate for the establishment of a particular regime (for the conservation of fishing stocks).[64]

The duty to negotiate may thus acquire a judicial basis, while at the same time the objective of the negotiations is being identified and for which the Court should provide the parties with a substantive legal framework within which such negotiations should take place:

> by arrangements agreed between those two countries, whether or not together with other interested countries and whether in the form of arrangements reached in accordance with the North-East Atlantic Fisheries Convention of 24 January 1959, or in the form of arrangements for collaboration in accordance with the Resolution on Special Situations relating to Coastal Fisheries of 26 April 1958, or otherwise in the form of arrangements agreed between them that give effect to the continuing rights and interests of both of them in the fisheries of the waters in question.[65]

Not only the objective of the negotiations but also the factors to be taken into account and the parameters of the talks may have to be granted judicial approval, such as the opposing interests of the parties and of other States.[66]

60 *Ibid.*, at p. 202, para. 76.
61 *Ibid.*
62 *Ibid.*
63 *Hostages case, I.C.J. Reports 1980*, Separate opinion by Judge Lachs, at p. 49.
64 *Fisheries Jurisdiction (United Kingdom v. Iceland), I.C.J. Reports 1974*, at p. 7, para. 11 (e).
65 *Ibid.*, at p. 6, para. 11 (b).
66 *Ibid.*, at p. 7, para. 11 (e).

As to the question whether the Court has jurisdiction to pronounce upon such matters,[67] the Court pointed out that the question of the extent and the scope of the respective rights of the parties in the fishery resources and the adequacy of measures to conserve them had been raised and discussed during several rounds of negotiations during different periods of time. The dispute before the Court includes these disagreements also in light of the proceedings taking place.[68]

The functional impact of the matters discussed during prior negotiations on the extent and scope of the Court's jurisdiction is of a supporting nature, but there is a clear and more direct impact on the scope and interpretation by the Court (and by the parties obviously) of the subject-matter of the dispute.[69]

The Court may finally rule that the 'most appropriate method for the solution of the dispute is clearly that of negotiation'.[70] In accordance with the particular subject nature of maritime international law, it may determine the objective of such negotiations, building on its pronouncements at the stage of the indication of provisional measures.[71]

In delimitation cases a compromis regularly provides agreed directives to the ICJ with regard to the substantive aspects of the decision it is requested to deliver.[72] Thus *res judicata* authority attaches to the framework for post-adjudicatory negotiations, for instance on compensation fixed in the operative paragraph(s) of a judgment.[73] What is stated there is thus *established.*

7.5 Judicial Qualification of Negotiations: Their Nature, Scope and Purpose

The Court may attach 'corroborative weight' to 'the conduct of the parties in negotiations during the 19th Century'.[74]

In the presentation of the facts of a case, there is some room for the Court to interpret and to give some qualifications to prior negotiations. In doing so the Court may feel obliged to describe in some detail the *nature* of the prior negotiations, and this also in order to bring to light what was the main reason they had broken down.[75]

The Court may undertake a brief review of the negotiations that led up to the exchange of notes in order 'to fully ascertain *the scope and purpose* of that exchange.[76]

A party may contest the Court's assessment on the scope of prior negotiations made during an earlier stage of the proceedings.[77]

Even in case of a negative jurisdictional decision, the Court may have found that there is a legal dispute between the parties and what its actual subject-matter is. 'Some elements of *res judicata* attaches to those findings.'[78]

7.6 Judicial Qualification of Negotiations: The Progress or Lack of it and the Deadlock Situation

We have already examined the not unlimited character of the obligation to negotiate. We have also established that it is up to the Court to determine whether and to what extent negotiations have been taking place on the subject-matter of the dispute.

---

67 *Ibid.*, at p. 20, para. 40.

68 *Ibid.*, at p. 21, para. 47.

69 *Ibid.*

70 *Ibid.*, at p. 31, para. 73.

71 *Ibid.*

72 See for instance J. Merrills, *International Dispute Settlement*, pp. 148–50.

73 See for instance *Gabcikovo Case, I.C.J. Reports 1997*, at p. 83, para. 155, 2 (D).

74 *Land, Island and Maritime Frontier Dispute, I.C.J. Reports 1992*, at pp. 550–51, para. 317.

75 *North Sea Continental Shelf, I.C.J. Reports 1969*, at p. 16, para. 5 and p. 17, para. 7.

76 *Fisheries Jurisdiction (Federal Republic of Germany v. Iceland), I.C.J. Reports 1973*, at p. 56, para. 18 (emphasis added); the Court obviously leaving aside the well-known fact that 'certain "Notes" delivered by a government of a strong power to the government of a small nation, may have the same purpose and the same effect as the use or threat of force': Dissenting opinion by Judge Padilla Nervo, at p. 91.

77 *Land and Maritime Boundary case, I.C.J. Reports 2002*, at pp. 422–3, para. 241.

78 *Certain Property case, I.C.J. Reports 2005*, Dissenting opinion by Judge *ad hoc* Berman, at p. 81, para. 28.

It is in the first place for the parties themselves to assess at regular intervals whether the process they both have been willing to go through is making (some) progress towards achieving its ultimate objective. Depending on a variety of factors – such as the state of their relations, the nature and the complexity of the dispute – the moment may come sooner or later for making a final assessment, i.e. acknowledging the lack of progress or even a complete deadlock, before they unilaterally or jointly decide to bring the dispute before the Court.

Once the proceedings have been instituted it will be for the Court to make its own judicial assessment of the situation resulting from that process, in light of the positions taken by the parties during the written or oral proceedings. The following overview of relevant case law may help to demonstrate how the Court has been performing this particular aspect of its judicial function.

When exercising its advisory jurisdiction the Court may lend its judicial support to Security Council Resolutions the implementation of which is the only way to bring a tragic situation to an end, while at the same time not failing to critically observe that the roadmap approved by the SC 'represents the most recent of efforts to *initiate* negotiations to this end'.[79]

At the jurisdiction and admissibility stage of contentious proceedings the Court may not be called to pronounce on the legal consequences of a breakdown in negotiations merely to determine whether the negotiations in the Contadora process were 'direct negotiations through the usual diplomatic channels', although it may note that the Respondent had taken 'a more guarded attitude' compared to the Applicant's positive approach *vis-à-vis* the Contadora Act.[80]

Perhaps a decisive indication, according to the Court, for the fact that several attempts at settlement by direct negotiations have turned out to be unfruitful could be the non-ratification of a Protocol that has been reached.[81]

Negotiations may have continued for quite some time 'though only slowly and with difficulty'.[82] In case of a region-wide process of negotiations thus involving third States as well 'substantial progress' may allegedly have been made as a Respondent's argument for the *inappropriateness* of the judicial proceedings.[83]

The Court, noting that the parties have praised that process, declares that the efforts made merit the 'full *respect*' of the Court, which 'is aware that *considerable progress* has been achieved on the main objective of the process', namely a number of agreements on a variety of issues and 'the work of the Contadora Group may facilitate the delicate and difficult negotiations' that 'are now required'.[84]

The progress made has to be measured against the *main objective* of a particular series of negotiations.

In spite of a large number of exchanges of letters and various meetings, the positions of the parties may have been not only 'comprehensively defined, and would scarcely develop any further' as they were 'diametrically opposed'.[85]

As to the attribution of the failure of finding an agreement, the record before the Court may make it impossible to blame solely one party[86] as the Court did not find sufficient evidence to conclude that one party 'has consistently refused to consult'.[87]

It may however observe that one party by its own suspension of a bilateral treaty has 'contributed to the creation of a situation which was not conducive to the conduct of fruitful negotiations'.[88] This implies a certain duty for States to conduct themselves in such a way as to contribute to a situation which is conducive to the conduct of fruitful negotiations

Finally the Court was blaming both parties for the failure.[89]

79 *Wall Advisory Opinion, I.C.J. Reports 2004*, at p. 201, para. 162 (emphasis added).
80 *Border and Transborder Armed Actions case, I.C.J. Reports 1988*, at p. 98, para. 73.
81 *Arbitral Award case King of Spain, I.C.J. Reports 1960*, at p. 203.
82 *Gulf of Maine case, I.C.J. Reports 1984*, at p. 286, para. 75.
83 *Nicaragua case, I.C.J. Reports 1984*, at p. 183, paras. 33 and 34 (US).
84 *Nicaragua case, I.C.J. Reports 1986*, at p. 145, para. 291 (emphasis added).
85 *Gabcikovo case, I.C.J. Reports 1997*, at p. 49, para. 64 and at p. 53, para. 73.
86 *Ibid.*, at p. 65, para. 107.
87 *Ibid.*, at p. 66, para. 107.
88 *Ibid.*
89 *Ibid.*

The Court may come to the conclusion that in a post-adjudicatory phase 'no progress has been made in implementing the Special Agreement following the 1982 Judgment', and this on the basis of 'what has been brought to the attention of the Court by the two Parties in the present proceedings'.[90]

Although a Court assessment that *no progress* has been made is based on material brought by the parties, it could also be able to come to that conclusion on the basis of its own awareness and knowledge of reports in the public domain about the state of the process.

Accusations of Bad Faith

When an Applicant is blaming the Respondent for the failure of a proposal because of the conditions laid down for its acceptance, the Court does not feel obliged to deal with this particular attempt for attribution, and it may limit itself to observing that the proposal 'was not put into effect, however, because the Parties failed to agree on how it should be implemented'.[91]

The Court may, in reviewing the facts of the case, limit itself to indicate (the) various reasons for the failure of the negotiations, such as a change of government and an ensuing further deterioration of the relations between the parties.[92]

The mere fact that a process of negotiations did not result in the conclusion of an agreement could reasonably but in our view not necessarily lead to the question whether the parties did negotiate in good faith. In light of the Court's case law, however, it might be fully justified to raise doubt about the parties' compliance with their respective and mutual obligation to negotiate in good faith.[93]

Accusations of bad faith during prior negotiations may be exchanged during the proceedings. According to one party the bad faith displayed 'either ruined any hope of reaching a new agreement or removed in advance the value of any agreement which might have been arrived at'. The argument continues that the party that is responsible for the impasse in negotiations 'cannot take advantage of its own wrongful behaviour' in order 'to prevent' the other party 'from achieving full and final settlement of the dispute between the two States by bringing the matter before this Court'.[94]

With regard to a process of negotiations involving the UN, the Court may explicitly observe that the UN 'undoubtedly conducted the negotiations in good faith'.[95] This benevolent approach may create the perception that this does not imply good faith behaviour on the part of the other *party*, especially since the Court added that '[t]hese proposals were rejected by South Africa'.[96]

From comments made by the Court one cannot possibly infer that they apply more to one party because it is the Respondent.[97] This applies more generally when the Court is pronouncing itself on the failure of negotiations, for instance without identifying the State responsible for the state of affairs.

As Judge Higgins has poignantly observed, a reminder to parties of their duty to negotiate in the reasoning of the judgment does not entail 'a determination that one party had acted contrary to international law when no such determination on that point of law had been sought by the other party in its final submission'.[98]

Having regard to the requirements formulated earlier in its case law as to the conduct of parties during a process of negotiations rejection of proposals tabled by the other party does not always have to be considered as a sign of bad faith, but only when the proposals are being rejected out of hand.

One of the other factors potentially contributing to the lack of progress or deadlock of a process of negotiations may be found in the (alleged) violation by one of the parties of its obligation to abstain from acts

---

90 *Revision and Interpretation of the 1982 Continental Shelf Judgment, I.C.J. Reports 1985*, at p. 229, para. 67.

91 *Request for Interpretation of the 1962 Temple of Preah Vihear Judgment, I.C.J. Reports 2011*, at p. 549, para. 48 (Cambodia) and at pp. 550–51, para. 53.

92 *Territorial and Maritime Dispute between Nicaragua and Honduras, I.C.J. Reports 2007*, at p. 677, para. 48.

93 *Kosovo Advisory Opinion, I.C.J. Reports 2010, Declaration by Judge Tomka*, at p. 463, para. 29.

94 *Land and Maritime Boundary case, I.C.J. Reports 2002*, at p. 423, para. 243 (Cameroon).

95 *Namibia Advisory Opinion, I.C.J. Reports 1971*, at p. 44, para. 84.

96 *Ibid.*

97 *DRC v. Rwanda Case, I.C.J. Reports 2002*, Separate opinion by Judge *ad hoc* Dugard, at p. 271, para. 13.

98 *Oil Platforms case, I.C.J. Reports 2003*, Separate opinion by Judge Higgins, at pp. 228–9, para. 14 (*mutatis mutandis*).

calculated to frustrate the object and purpose of a bilateral treaty. The circumstances of the case may require an examination of the course of the negotiations in order to establish such a breach of the treaty.

Whether the actions taken by one of the parties inevitably also constitute a breach of 'its obligation to negotiate in good faith', and were of such a nature 'as to frustrate the negotiations' and meant 'that the negotiations were not meaningful', will depend on the course of the negotiations and the contributions the parties made to the process.[99]

In such circumstances the exact sequence of events is crucial; indeed, an action undertaken by one party after the other party has already expressed its view that the negotiations have failed, consequently 'cannot be seen as frustrating the negotiating process'.[100]

The view may be held that engaging in good faith in negotiations does not rule out a party taking 'preparatory steps to ensure that it is ready to proceed' with a project whatever the outcome of the process of negotiations; the taking of such preparatory steps 'is not, *in itself*, contrary to the duty to negotiate in good faith'.[101]

In order for such preparatory steps to qualify as breaches of the obligation to negotiate in good faith it will also be necessary that the record 'shows that the party concerned did not intend to engage in meaningful negotiations'.[102]

But also in this approach to the question one should duly take into account that the parties, being aware of some action taken prior to the start of the process, did not consider them as precluding meaningful negotiations.[103] Furthermore, one should differentiate between such actions as just mentioned and those which are not related to the controversy which is the subject-matter of the treaty and of the negotiating process.[104]

As to judicial consequences that may be attached to an eventual Court assessment that one of the parties has clearly and undoubtedly negotiated in bad faith, not much can be put forward because relevant and straightforward case law is not yet available. One small indication could be found when in a dissenting opinion the Court is blamed for seemingly having rewarded parties who negotiated in bad faith.[105]

An additional question that may be raised is related to the case-law based presumption of good faith that a State will not repeat a wrongful act once established by the Court. There is no particular reason to put aside this presumption if the Court were to conclude that one of the parties had been engaged in negotiations in bad faith.[106]

Has a Deadlock Been Reached?

Diplomatic exchanges may not only disclose the existence of a dispute between the parties but also that negotiations have reached a deadlock.[107]

Although negotiations may extend over a long period of time, such as 13 years, in practice, according to the Court, 'the actual length of negotiations is no test whether the possibilities of agreement have been exhausted; it may be sufficient to show that an early deadlock was reached and that one side adamantly refused compromise'. In fact the deadlock 'had patently been reached' long before, for instance, the United Nations 'finally abandoned its efforts to reach agreement'.[108]

---

99 *Pulp Mills case, I.C.J. Reports 2010*, Separate opinion by Judge Keith, at p. 127, para. 17; at p. 128, para. 18; and at p. 130, para. 24. Determining the moment when the process was deadlocked is relevant for establishing state responsibility in connection with the obligation to negotiate in good faith.

100 *Ibid.*, at p. 131, para. 25.

101 *Ibid.*, Separate opinion by Judge Greenwood, at p. 227, para. 16 (emphasis added).

102 *Ibid.*

103 *Ibid.*, at p. 228, para. 20.

104 *Ibid.* at p. 228, para. 21.

105 *Ibid.*, Dissenting opinion by Judge *ad hoc* Vinuesa, at p. 272, para. 20.

106 *Ibid.*, at pp. 67–8, para. 149 and at p. 105, para. 278 with a strong dissent by Judge *ad hoc* Vinuesa, at pp. 274–5, para. 35.

107 *Right of Passage case, I.C.J. Reports 1957*, at p. 149.

108 *Namibia Advisory Opinion, I.C.J. Reports 1971*, at pp. 44–5, para. 85.

Referring to the case law, a Respondent may however argue that in its jurisprudence the Court has taken several factors into account when evaluating whether negotiations have reached deadlock, 'such as the duration of the negotiations and the authenticity of efforts to reach a negotiated settlement'. The review of the case law may lead to the conclusion 'that whatever form they may take, substantially, negotiations are an exchange of points of view on law and facts, of mutual compromises in order to reach an agreement'.[109]

Negotiations may reach an 'early deadlock' which then may be assessed by the Court.[110]

Even 'a cursory examination of the views, propositions and arguments consistently maintained by the two sides' may convince the Court that an impasse was reached prior to the instituting of the proceedings and that it continued to exist.[111]

The Court's assessment is not limited to the process prior to the start of the proceedings; it also includes the situation during the course of the proceedings.

An Application nicely divided in two sets of subparagraphs containing the respective positions of the parties[112] may make it clear that the two governments had maintained their respective positions during the diplomatic negotiations.[113]

Although the Court is not expressing itself on it, maintaining your positions during the negotiations is contrary to the judicial guideline not to keep inflexibly your position, and is of course the direct cause for the deadlock and ultimately for the filing of the Application.

On the other hand it has to be admitted that in relation to diametrically opposed entitlement claims there is probably not that margin for real and genuine negotiations.

The chances of a process of negotiations becoming successful are substantially reduced, perhaps even non-existent, when the parties involved 'are at odds to the fundamental basis on which the process rests'.[114] This would be the case when both parties are not prepared to go beyond a number of elements, or agreements that do not involve a number of elements.[115] In the *Namibia case* Judge Dillard observed that 'without impugning the good faith of South Africa, its reiterated insistence on negotiating from a position that denied the reasonable basis on which the General Assembly's negotiating posture rested added weight to the General Assembly's determination' on South Africa's performance under the Mandate system.[116]

Judge Gros went further when he stated that it 'is necessary to determine which party has been misusing its legal position in this controversy on the extent of the obligation to negotiate'.[117] He affirmed that negotiations 'for the conclusion of a trusteeship agreement never began, and for that South Africa was responsible'. Judge Gros added that the 'rule infringed herein is the obligation to negotiate in good faith'. Hence, the General Assembly could legitimately 'have taken note of the deadlock and demanded South Africa's compliance with its obligation to negotiate'.[118]

The Court may not have been persuaded that the Respondent had been prejudiced as a result of the instituting of proceedings instead of pursuing negotiations which, 'moreover, were deadlocked when the Application was filed'.[119] Given the Court's general approach to the functional interaction the absence of deadlock would not have led to a different judicial assessment.

---

109 *CERD case, I.C.J. Reports 2011*, at pp. 130–31, para. 150.

110 *Fisheries Jurisdiction (Federal Republic of Germany v. Iceland), I.C.J. Reports 1974*, at p. 201, para. 68; *Fisheries Jurisdiction (United Kingdom v. Iceland), I.C.J. Reports 1974*, at p. 32, para. 76.

111 *South West Africa cases, I.C.J. Reports 1962*, at p. 345.

112 *Aegean Sea Continental Shelf case, I.C.J. Reports 1978*, at pp. 6–7, para. 12.

113 *Ibid.*, at pp. 36–7, para. 87.

114 *Namibia Advisory Opinion, I.C.J. Reports 1971*, Separate opinion by Judge Dillard, at p. 160.

115 *International status of SWA, I.C.J. Reports 1950*, Separate opinion by Judge Read, at p. 171.

116 *Namibia Advisory Opinion, I.C.J. Reports 1971*, Separate opinion by Judge Dillard, at p. 161.

117 *Ibid.*, Dissenting opinion by Judge Gros, at p. 344, para. 43.

118 *Ibid.*, at pp. 344–5, para. 43.

119 *Land and Maritime Boundary case, I.C.J. Reports 1998*, at p. 304, para. 58.

7.7 The Functional Interaction at Work: Should There Be Consistency between Positions Taken during Negotiations and Arguments Invoked before the Court?

As part of its strategy of non-appearance a Respondent may decide not to use the possibility of consulting records in the Registry of the Court as they had been deposited by the Applicant, the Court obviously not being able to take cognizance of any similar record on the Respondent side.[120]

Parties obviously can rely on records of negotiations, but their records have to support their contentions. As a result, original drafts ultimately not having been accepted cannot be relied on.[121]

The question may be raised whether estoppel could also be applicable in general to positions taken in the course of negotiations.[122]

The principle of preclusion:

> operates to prevent a State contesting before the Court a situation contrary to a clear and unequivocal representation previously made by it to another State, either expressly or impliedly, on which representation the other State was, in the circumstances, entitled to rely and in fact did rely, and as a result that other State has been prejudiced or the State making it has secured some benefit or advantage for itself.[123]

Would this principle operate with regard to the (non-)inclusion of positions taken during negotiations as argument during the proceedings?

First of all 'there can be no legal obligation for a party to a dispute to transpose, for the settlement of that dispute, a particular solution previously adopted by it in a different context'.[124] The Court thus reaffirms if need be the singularity and particularity of each case before it, not only *vis-à-vis* other judicial proceedings but also towards solutions arrived at during diplomatic negotiations on similar questions. The fact that there are certain common elements 'is of no more than formal weight'.[125]

Secondly, a detailed examination by the Court of the negotiations through minutes that have been signed brings to the surface the real respective objectives the parties were trying to achieve, and this judicial interpretation may conflict with arguments put forward by (one of) the parties.[126]

Thirdly, questions raised during prior negotiations are almost inevitably bound to come up again and extensively in the pleadings and hearings on the merits.[127]

Fourthly, although one of the aims of prior negotiations is to make more precise the nature and scope of the dispute the parties are willing to bring before the Court, it is clear that the dispute the Court will be called upon to adjudicate will be further and clearly defined by the parties in their written and oral pleadings.[128]

Fifthly, parties must bear in mind that although prior negotiations and diplomatic exchanges may provide the prospective Applicant with considerable information about the opposing legal position, it can expect in case of instituting proceedings before the Court[129] – another aspect of the functional interaction – that any initial advantage that either side might obtain would be neutralized, in the long run, by the scope of the Court's process.[130]

A non-invocation clause may have an impact on the willingness of the parties to make concessions during the prior negotiations.

---

120 *Fisheries Jurisdiction (United Kingdom v. Iceland), I.C.J. Reports 1974*, Dissenting opinion by Judge Gros, at p. 129, note 1.

121 *Ambatielos case, I.C.J. Reports 1952*, at p. 45.

122 *North Sea Continental Shelf case, I.C.J. Reports 1969*, at p. 26, para. 30.

123 *Temple of Preah Vihear case, I.C.J. Reports 1962*, Dissenting opinion by Judge Spender, at pp. 143–4.

124 *Jan Mayen case, I.C.J. Reports 1993*, at p. 76, para. 85.

125 *Ibid.*, at p. 77, para. 86.

126 *North Sea Continental Shelf case, I.C.J. Reports 1969*, at p. 26, para. 31 and *Fisheries Jurisdiction (United Kingdom v. Iceland), I.C.J. Reports 1974*, at p. 33, para. 77.

127 *Fisheries Jurisdiction (United Kingdom v. Iceland), I.C.J. Reports 1974*, at p. 20, para. 43.

128 *Guardianship Convention case, I.C.J. Reports 1958*, p. 55 at p. 62.

129 *Barcelona Traction case, I.C.J. Reports 1964*, at p. 25. For a fine example of the sequence of 'diplomatic representations' in the exercise by various States of their diplomatic protection see *Barcelona Traction case, I.C.J. Reports 1970*, Separate opinion by Judge Jessup, at pp. 170–82, paras. 19–37.

130 *Barcelona Traction case, I.C.J. Reports 1964*, at p. 25.

On the other hand, such a clause 'is only likely to be important when negotiations have been prolonged, or when criteria of reasonableness or acceptability are expected to play a significant part at the judicial stage'.[131]

Sixthly, in delimitation cases maps may show lines representing approximately the boundaries one of the parties would have wished to obtain in the course of the prior negotiations.[132]

Finally, the previous history of the dispute as demonstrated by positions taken during negotiations may render a new claim inconsistent.[133]

With regard to negotiations taking place within the UN, it is not surprising that members 'adopt very different positions, according to the political requirements of the case under discussion. Not only have some delegations adopted differing points of view, but the same delegations have often put forward one argument in one case and a contrary argument in another.'[134]

7.8 The Functional Interaction under Threat: Could or Should Positions Taken during Negotiations (Not) Be Invoked during the Proceedings?

Parties may beforehand agree not to use arguments from negotiations during the proceedings before the Court, as the *Gulf of Maine case* has demonstrated. Such an exclusion may have been part of a draft Special Agreement, but as a result of objection by one of the parties it may finally not have been included in the final text, in spite of the importance attached to it by the other party.[135]

The question of the propriety of recourse to the record of negotiations was raised some 20 years ago, when the Court did recognize the continued existence of the rule of customary international law in this domain as defined by its predecessor.

Indeed, it is established jurisprudence that it is not open to the Chamber or the Court for that matter to 'take account of declarations, admissions or proposals which the Parties may have made in the course of direct negotiations which have taken place between them, declarations which, moreover, have been made without prejudice in the event of the points under discussions forming the subject of judicial proceedings', when the negotiations in question have not led to an agreement between the parties.[136]

The Chamber considered the 'without prejudice practice' – 'whereby the parties to a dispute, having each advanced their contentions in principle, which thus define the extent of the dispute, proceed to venture suggestions for mutual concessions, within the extent so defined, with a view of reaching an agreed settlement. If no agreement is reached, neither party can be held to such suggested concessions' – not only to be 'common and laudable' but indeed 'of the essence of negotiations'.[137]

In the case at hand the Chamber could not take account 'of any negotiating concessions which might have been made as to the *position*' of the limit between two islands, but it was entitled 'to take account of the shared view' of the parties in a distant past 'as to the basis and extent of their dispute'.[138] So the Court will look very carefully on which aspects there was a common understanding between the parties and on which other issues there was no agreement between them.

The without prejudice practice may also arise in case of unspecific references to the unacceptability of a particular position and without allusion to particular legal arguments as both elements are 'sufficient to prevent the position' of a party being prejudiced.[139]

131 J. Merrills, *International Dispute Settlement*, at p. 21.

132 *North Sea Continental Shelf case, I.C.J. Reports 1969*, at p. 14, para. 5.

133 *Land, Island and Maritime Frontier Dispute, I.C.J. Reports 1992*, at pp. 547–8, para. 312.

134 *Admission of a State to the United Nations (Charter, Art. 4), Advisory Opinion, I.C.J. Reports 1948*, p. 57, Dissenting opinion by Judge Zoricic, at pp. 102–3.

135 *Case between Qatar and Bahrain, I.C.J. Reports 1995*, at pp. 125–6, para. 40.

136 *Factory at Chorzow case, P.C.I.J. Series A, No. 9*, p. 19; F*actory at Chorzow case (Claims for Indemnity), Merits, P.C.I.J. Series A, No. 17*, pp. 51, 62–3; *Land, Island and Maritime Frontier Dispute, I.C.J. Reports 1992*, at pp. 405–6, para. 73.

137 *Land, Island and Maritime Frontier Dispute, I.C.J. Reports* 1992, at pp. 405–6, para. 73.

138 *Ibid.*, at pp. 406–7, paras. 73 and 76.

139 *Jan Mayen case, I.C.J. Reports 1993*, at pp. 55–6, para. 38.

While a Respondent may invite the Court to take into account examination by the Frontier Commission of 'proposals aimed at the delimitation of maritime spaces', the Applicant may express reservations 'at this recourse to matters raised during negotiations' since 'any approaches of its delegates' were 'purely by way of conciliation and did not prejudice its legal position'.[140]

As far as the Court is concerned the question whether a party may invoke those positions 'expressed by the parties' on a particular question during a diplomatic conference for the adoption of a multilateral convention is separate from the question whether a decision of the Court may be based 'on such positions'[141] – a question to which we turn later. Furthermore, the Court may draw *inferences* from such positions, as we will discuss shortly.

In case parties have included their negotiations positions in their written proceedings, the Court is able to reproduce them.[142]

Silence is Not Always Golden

During negotiations a party may make it clear to the other party that it would raise a particular objection, for instance of non-exhaustion of local remedies. However, evidence to that effect should be supplied to the Court.[143]

But the 'absence of a riposte' cannot amount to an estoppel when 'the matter was still being pursued at the diplomatic level',[144] another manifestation of the functional interaction at work. In certain circumstances estoppel could arise from a silence 'when something ought to have been said', but 'there are obvious difficulties in constructing an estoppel from a mere failure to mention a matter at a particular point in somewhat *desultory* diplomatic exchanges'.[145]

It is interesting to note that this view can have an impact on the conduct of parties during negotiations, since the mere failure to mention a matter will not without difficulty amount to an estoppel.

It has been argued that keeping silent for more than 15 years on the subject of an alleged claim which had been raised that long ago in the course of negotiations 'makes it inappropriate for the Court to entertain it'.[146]

The Court attributed force to a Respondent's contention that the Applicant did fail 'to follow up on the issues raised' in 'timely manner' when the record shows that the matter had only been taken up again on the diplomatic level 14 years later.[147]

It may happen that following a call to 'submit to the International Court of Justice all such information and documents as may be needed to clarify' the questions posed three States continue 'before the Court the discussion' over a legal question which had been dividing them, and 'on which they had embarked in the General Assembly'.[148]

From the above case law it becomes clear that positions taken by the parties during negotiations may perform a different *function* in the course of judicial proceedings. They cannot be invoked by the parties either because parties beforehand agreed not to allow it or, alternatively, in the absence of an explicit agreement or understanding to that effect between the parties, as common and laudable practice.

As far as the Court is concerned, it will not take note of positions taken by the parties during the negotiations given the common and laudable without prejudice practice which is the essence of negotiations, in case the process has not produced an agreement. Moreover, only '[w]eighty circumstances are required to establish that a party intended abruptly to abandon a position long held by it'.[149]

---

140 *Land, Island and Maritime Frontier Dispute, I.C.J. Reports 1992*, at p. 586, para. 379.

141 *Jan Mayen case, I.C.J. Reports 1993*, at p. 56, para. 39.

142 *Nicaragua case, I.C.J. Reports 1986*, at p. 77, para. 139; *Frontier Dispute (Burkina Faso/Mali), I.C.J. Reports 1986*, at p. 632, para. 147; *Territorial Dispute (Libyan Arab Jamahiriya/Chad), I.C.J. Reports 1994*, at p. 27, para. 55.

143 *ELSI case, I.C.J. Reports 1989*, at p. 41, para. 46 (Italy).

144 *Ibid.*, at p. 44, para. 54.

145 *Ibid.* (emphasis added).

146 *Nauru case, I.C.J. Reports 1993*, Dissenting opinion by Judge Oda, at p. 324, para. 28.

147 *Case concerning Maritime Dispute(Peru v. Chile), I.C.J. Reports 2014*, para. 142.

148 *Western Sahara Advisory Opinion, I.C.J. Reports 1975*, Separate opinion by Judge Petren, at p. 112.

149 *Case between Qatar and Bahrain, I.C.J. Reports 1995*, Dissenting opinion by Judge Sahabuddeen, at p. 57.

7.9 Negotiations Finding their Way into the Judicial Reasoning

It is one thing to observe and to note the functional impact of the matters discussed during prior negotiations on the extent and scope of the Court's jurisdiction, and their clear and more direct impact on the scope and interpretation by the Court (and by the parties obviously) of the subject-matter of the dispute; but it does not necessarily ensue that negotiations may find their way in the judicial reasoning which in general terms is quite a different matter altogether.

In performing its function the Court may take account of materials which have been used in the negotiating process as well as materials not having formed part of that process.

Long-standing jurisprudence has made it clear that 'the operative part of a judgment is difficult to separate from the essential reasons upon which it is directly based and of which it constitutes a synthesis'.[150]

As within the context of judicial economy the Court 'retains the freedom to select the ground upon which it will base its judgment, and is under no obligation to examine all the considerations advanced by the Parties if other considerations appear to it to be sufficient for its purpose',[151] this naturally may have an impact on the way the Court is dealing with negotiations between the parties prior to and during the proceedings.

One should bear in mind Judge Lauterpacht's well-known observation that considerations of judicial economy 'are not, for this Court, the only legitimate factor in the situation'.[152] On the other hand, Hersch Lauterpacht's both doctrinal and judicial view was shared by Judge Jessup in the *Barcelona Traction case*, 'that there are compelling considerations of international justice and of development of international law which favour a full measure of exhaustiveness of judicial pronouncements of international tribunals'.[153]

The *nec plus ultra petita* rule of judicial settlement law means that 'it is the duty of an international tribunal "not only to reply to the questions as stated in the final submissions of the parties, but also to abstain from deciding points not indicated in those submissions"'.[154]

On the other hand, while 'a judicial organ is obliged to pass upon all the formal submissions made by a party, it is not obliged, in framing its judgment, to develop its reasoning in the form of a detailed examination of each of the various heads of claim submitted'.[155]

The *framing* of its judgment may imply that the Court in the course of its deliberations may very well, in order to find a (large) majority, perform such a detailed examination of the various heads of claim submitted. The decisive benchmark has to be that 'a tribunal may employ direct or indirect reasoning, and state specific or merely implied conclusions, provided that the reasons on which the judgment is based are apparent'.[156] The way prior negotiations may then find their way into the Court's reasoning will be explored in more detail in the next paragraphs.

7.10 Judicial Inferences from Positions Taken during Negotiations

Within the wide range of their multifunctionality as described earlier, the main objective of negotiations is of course to achieve a peaceful and final settlement of the dispute.

In case of a successful and comprehensive conclusion of the process, the dispute comes to an end and the judicial part of the functional interaction does not come into operation.

---

150 Ph. Couvreur, 'The Effectiveness', p. 103, note 49 with further reference to relevant case law. On the distinction between 'inseparable' and 'essential' reasons see more recently *Request for the Interpretation of the Judgment of 15 June 1962 in the Case* concerning the Temple of Preah Vihear (Cambodia v. Thailand) *(Cambodia v. Thailand), Judgment, I.C.J. Reports 2013*, p. 281, Joint declaration by Judges Owada,Bennouna and Gaja, at pp. 320–21, paras. 1–2.

151 *Guardianship Convention Case, I.C.J. Reports 1958*, p. 55 at p. 62.

152 *Certain Norwegian Loans case, I.C.J. Reports 1957*, Separate opinion by Judge Lauterpacht, at p. 36.

153 *Barcelona Traction case, I.C.J. Reports 1970*, Separate opinion by Judge Jessup, at p. 161.

154 *Application for Review of Judgment No. 158 of the United Nations Administrative Tribunal, Advisory Opinion, I.C.J. Reports 1973*, at pp. 207–8, para. 87.

155 *Ibid.*, at pp. 210–11, para. 95.

156 *Ibid.*

In case of a partial or complete failure of the process (one of) the parties may decide to cross the Rubicon and to argue its case before the Court.

The process of negotiations having come to a deadlock or having been suspended for the time being, the question arises how the Court should and could deal with the positions taken earlier by the parties, assuming that the records of the negotiations are available and accessible and that the parties have not explicitly excluded the invocation of their positions during the process of negotiations.

In fact the options for the Court are twofold: either it can allow positions taken by the parties to play a role in its treatment of the arguments or it can keep the two processes separate. By adopting such a clear-cut distinction and division the Court substantially reduces the potential role of functional interaction.

Some Doctrinal Views

The international judge is hesitant to attach legal effects to positions taken by the parties during the process of negotiations,[157] exception made for a clearly articulated view or in other cases lack of response towards such an articulated view by the other party.[158]

However, in cases where 'insufficient evidence is available' the Court may use 'judicial presumptions' as a 'judicial tool of reasoning',[159] for instance with regard to a State's approach, involvement and conduct during negotiations, even with regard to a previous stage of the process.[160]

An inference also 'indicating a relationship between two facts, is permissive', while a presumption is mandatory.[161] Inferences must 'leave *no room* for reasonable doubt'.[162]

One would be tempted to argue that by agreeing beforehand not to use positions taken during prior negotiations parties may render unnecessary the use of judicial presumptions. However, a general rule has developed in international jurisprudence that international courts and tribunals 'will not consider evidence consisting of statements, admissions or proposals made in the course' of settlement negotiations between the parties, 'so that the information or documents generated can not be used against the parties in any pending or future litigation'.[163]

In case only one party has submitted *its* records of negotiations the Court 'must have more recourse to indirect evidence, inferences and presumptions'.[164]

In general terms two kinds of inference could be made: a negative one that a party is not opposing a particular position or proposal; or a rather positive one that the absence of its opposition equals its acceptance.

Would it be reasonable and justified just to apply this dual approach to the attitude of the parties during all kinds of negotiations as a general principle? The standard rule appears to be that judicial caution is called for when the Court feels the need to make inferences from the positions taken by the parties during prior or parallel negotiations, or from their conduct during that process.

The Judicial Approach: Drawing Inferences

The case law provides us with the following scenarios and modalities of judicial inferences from positions taken by parties during negotiations.

The submissions of the parties in many cases will flow, to a varying extent of course, from positions they have been taking during the negotiations. This does not necessarily mean that the functional interaction operates in such a way that judicial inferences have an (in)direct link with positions taken prior to the seisin of the Court. Indeed, it is 'a sound principle of judicial procedure that, unless the provisions of the Statute

157 J.-P. Cot, 'La bonne foi', 146.
158 J-P. Cot, 'La bonne foi', 147.
159 A. Riddell and B. Plant, *Evidence*, p. 100.
160 A. Riddell and B. Plant, *Evidence*, p. 106.
161 A. Riddell and B. Plant, *Evidence*, p. 112.
162 A. Riddell and B. Plant, *Evidence*, p. 113.
163 A. Riddell and B. Plant, *Evidence*, p. 154.
164 A. Riddell and B. Plant, *Evidence*, p. 121.

or other cogent legal considerations make that impossible, the judgment of the Court should attach to the submissions of the Parties a *purpose*, though not necessarily *an effect*, which the Parties attached to them'.[165]

Although the positions of the parties during a process of negotiations and involving 'a disagreement on a point of law or fact, a conflict of legal views or interests, or the positive opposition of the claim of one party by the other need not necessarily be stated *expressis verbis*',[166] in most cases they will be explicitly formulated.

The apparent absence of such a requirement until the *CERD case* may have an impact not only on the conduct of the parties during negotiations, but also on the Court's assessment of that conduct. Indeed, in 'the determination of the existence of a dispute, as in other matters, the position or the attitude of a party can be established by inference, whatever the professed view of that party'.[167]

In fact, the failure of a party to 'invoke a particular argument throughout the whole period of bilateral negotiations' may lend support to a particular presumption.[168]

Meanwhile previous agreements concluded between the parties 'provide an important part of the context in which the statements which the Parties invoke were made'.[169]

In case the Court is called to address issues related to or arising out of an implicit or tacit agreement the intentions and terms of which it infers from the conduct of the parties, there is every reason for great caution. Evidence 'of a tacit legal agreement must be *compelling*'.[170] Its existence 'is not easily to be presumed'[171] and 'must be firmly established'.[172] It may happen that a later agreement between the parties 'cements the tacit agreement reached earlier' even without giving any 'indication of the nature of the maritime boundary'.[173]

The Intentions of the Parties

Although judicial inferences from the positions taken by the parties are most likely to occur in contentious cases, the Court may also turn to them in advisory proceedings. Indeed, for the reply to the question submitted to be pertinent and effective, complete and not misleading, the Court 'must first ascertain the meaning and full implications of the question in the light of the actual framework of fact and law in which it falls for consideration'.[174]

Past and eventually ongoing negotiations are part of that framework of reference for the Court. The Court may recall the circumstances in which, for instance, an arbitration agreement had been drawn up 'in order to assess the weight' of a particular line of argument.[175]

Diplomatic correspondence may indeed reveal the objectives the parties were attempting to achieve, but if the difference consists of a claim by one party that the other party would terminate a particular action which it refuses to halt, there is not much of a subject-matter to have negotiations in a proper sense about.[176]

Although diplomatic correspondence may lead up to the conclusion of a Special Agreement 'whereby the dispute which had arisen between the two Governments was referred to the Court',[177] such correspondence between parties does not necessarily form part and parcel of negotiations going on between them, as they may very well serve the purpose of expressing a government's determination to uphold for instance the

165 *Certain Norwegian loans case, I.C.J. Reports 1957*, p. 9, Separate opinion by Judge Lauterpacht, at p. 35 (emphasis added).

166 *Land and Maritime Boundary case, I.C.J. Reports 1998*, at p. 315, para. 89.

167 *Ibid.*

168 *Sovereignty case between Malaysia and Singapore, I.C.J. Reports 2008*, at p. 79, para. 219.

169 *CERD case, I.C.J. Reports 2011*, at p. 88, para. 39.

170 *Case concerning Maritime Dispute (Peru v. Chile), I.C.J. Reports 2014*, para. 91.

171 *Territorial and Maritime Dispute between Nicaragua and Honduras in the Carribean sea (Nicaragua v. Honduras), I.C.J. Reports* 2007 (II), at p. 735, para. 253.

172 *Sovereignty case between Malaysia and Singapore, I.C.J. Reports 2008*, Dissenting opinion by Judge *ad hoc* Dugard, at p. 148, paras. 38 and 39.

173 *Case concerning Maritime Dispute (Peru v. Chile), I.C.J. Reports 2014*, paras. 91 and 92.

174 *Interpretation Agreement between the WHO and Egypt, Advisory Opinion, I.C.J. Reports 1980*, at p. 76, para. 10.

175 *Arbitral Award case, I.C.J. Reports 1991*, at p. 71, para. 53.

176 *Nuclear Tests (Australia v. France) I.C.J. Reports 1973*, at p. 104, para. 25.

177 *Asylum case, I.C.J. Reports 1950*, at p. 273.

independence of its judiciary,[178] while one month of negotiations just prior to the instituting of the proceedings by Application held after such a long period of diplomatic correspondence may not bear fruit and not lead to an agreement.[179]

With regard the positions taken during negotiations which have led to the conclusion of a Special Agreement, it should be duly noted that the intention of the parties when drafting a Special Agreement should not be interpreted as reflecting their will only to submit part of the dispute to the Court, if such interpretation would run counter to a reasonable interpretation of the actual wording of the agreement and its coherence, especially in a case where they had recommended that 'the whole dispute should be decided by the Court'.

Giving effect to such an assumed intention of the parties would not only result in the dispute not being finally decided; it would also not give full effect to the resolution of the Security Council, but more importantly it 'would leave open the possibility of a further dispute'.[180]

Reluctance, Caution and Assurance

In order to comply with Article 32, para. 2 of the Rules of Court, even unsuccessful negotiations will not only allow the Applicant State to specify the provision on which to base the jurisdiction of the Court but also to state the precise nature of its claim and the grounds on which it is based.[181] That seems to be the judicial limit for the functional use of those prior negotiations.

Indeed, in case prior negotiations have not led 'to a complete agreement' the Court 'cannot take into account declarations, admissions or proposals which the Parties may have made during direct negotiations between themselves'.[182]

The Court is particularly prudent not to infer from declarations made and '*taken in the aggregate*' too far-reaching inferences.[183]

On the other hand there is the unambiguous affirmation by the Court with regard to the potential legal value and effect to be attached to a unilateral act 'even though not made within the context of international negotiations'.[184] This clearly implies that such unilateral binding declarations are most frequently made within that context, of course on condition of the intention to be bound, 'as not all unilateral acts imply obligation'.[185]

A definite offer to negotiate for the purpose of reaching a settlement or of concluding a Special Agreement certainly testifies to the good will of the party extending such an invitation. It is certainly a unilateral act, entailing legal consequences; but the question is to what extent?

For present purposes it is important for any party to a dispute to be well aware of the Court's reassurance in this regard. Indeed, such an offer cannot be interpreted as 'consent to participate' or 'actual participation', or as implying 'the abandonment of any defence' or 'acceptance of any claim' unless this has been clearly expressed or follows indisputably from the attitude adopted by that party.[186]

The reasoning behind the Court's pronouncement is particularly relevant for the functional interaction: indeed, the Court considered that it could not possibly be otherwise because then the use of the means of settlement recommended by Article 33 of the UN Charter would be seriously hampered. Indeed, such an interpretation would constitute an obstacle to the opening of any negotiations at all.[187]

---

178 *Ibid.*, at p. 285.

179 *Nuclear Tests (New Zealand v. France), I.C.J. Reports 1974*, at p. 464, para. 25.

180 *Corfu Channel case, I.C.J. Reports 1949*, at p. 26.

181 *The Northern Cameroons case, I.C.J. Reports 1963*, at p. 28.

182 *Nuclear Tests (New Zealand v. France), I.C.J. Reports 1974*, at p. 476, para. 57 and *Frontier Dispute, I.C.J. Reports, 1986*, at p. 632, para. 147, citing *Factory at Chorzow (Merits), P.C.I.J. Series A, No. 17*, p. 51.

183 *North Sea Continental Shelf case, I.C.J. Reports 1969*, at p. 27, para. 32 (emphasis added).

184 *Nuclear Tests (New Zealand v. France), I.C.J. Reports 1974*, at p. 472, para. 46.

185 *Ibid.*, at p. 472, para. 47.

186 *Nottebohm case, I.C.J. Reports 1955*, at p. 20.

187 *Ibid.*, at p. 19.

Inequality of Power

Would the Court be allowed or perhaps even obliged – in assessing the positions taken by the parties during negotiations in order to draw inferences from them – to take into account their respective power position?

In a territorial dispute an Applicant may use the argument with regard to its negotiations with the Respondent's former colonial power that it 'lacked the experience to engage in difficult negotiations with a Power enjoying the benefit of long international experience'.[188] The Libyan negotiators wished to 'leave outside the question of frontiers' as they needed more time to 'study the subject', but the French delegation said that it was not possible to 'conclude the treaty without an agreement on the frontiers'.[189]

In fact the Court did not deal with this argument as part of the circumstances of the conclusion of the Treaty because the Applicant 'has not however taken this argument so far as to suggest it as a ground for invalidity of the Treaty itself'.[190]

This seems to imply that if the Applicant had put forward this argument the Court would have been obliged to look at the respective power positions during negotiations in order to accept or dismiss the argument as not a solid ground for invalidating the treaty.

In the *Corfu Channel case* Judge Krylov did not accept the argument in support of Albania's cognizance of the minelaying based on inaccuracies and contradictions in the diplomatic correspondence of that government, as it was 'a new Government without experience in the conduct of international affairs and without the assistance of experts in questions of international law'.[191] Judge Badawi Pasha also referred to the difference in 'strength, culture, history, position and a multitude of other circumstances' between the two parties.[192]

Admissions Made during Negotiations

Looking more closely at the Court's handling of what has been tabled by the parties during their bilateral talks, the following deserves to be duly noted.

Although the perusal of diplomatic exchanges between two governments may bring to the surface a note containing an admission by one party, the Court rejected the argument that such an admission could not be invoked against that party 'as it was made in the course of negotiations which did not result in agreement'.[193] The Court held the view that it was not a proposal or a concession made during negotiations but a statement of facts, without reservation whatsoever and which must be considered to represent the official view of that party.

Draft treaties prepared by one party and submitted as an official proposal within the framework of a regional peace process and which had been submitted with that party's Application 'do not constitute an admission' of a wrongful act, but 'simply make provision for the future in the context of the inter-American system'.[194]

For purposes of finding a state responsible the 'Court may take into account any statements made by either party that appear to bear upon the matters in issue, and have been brought to its attention',[195] and 'it may accord to them such legal effect as appropriate'.[196]

Conversely, a waiver of claims can also take place during negotiation,[197] although it does not necessarily follow inference from a party's conduct during the negotiation that 'the party definitively waived' a particular claim.[198]

---

188 *Territorial Dispute, (Libyan Arab Jamahiriya/Chad), I.C.J. Reports 1994*, at p. 20, para. 3 (Libya).

189 *Ibid.*, at pp. 27–8, paras. 55–6.

190 *Ibid.*, at p. 22, para. 41 and at p. 20, para. 36.

191 *Corfu Channel case, I.C.J. Reports 1949*, Dissenting opinion by Judge Krylov, at p. 69.

192 *Ibid.*, Dissenting opinion by Judge Badawi Pasha, at p. 64.

193 *The Minquiers and Ecrehos case, Judgment of 17 November 1953, I.C.J. Reports 1953*, p. 7 at p. 71.

194 *Nicaragua case, I.C.J. Reports 1986*, at p. 77, para. 139 and at p. 86, para. 159.

195 *Nuclear Tests (Australia v. France), I.C.J. Reports 1974*, at pp. 263–7, paras. 30–41.

196 *Bosnian Genocide case, I.C.J. Reports 2007*, at p. 199, para. 378.

197 *Nauru case, I.C.J. Reports 1993*, at p. 247, para. 13.

198 *Application for Revision of the Judgment of 11 September 1992 in the Case concerning the* Land, Island and Maritime Frontier Dispute (El Salvador/Honduras: Nicaragua intervening) *(El Salvador v. Honduras), Judgment, I.C.J. Reports 2003*, p. 392, Dissenting opinion by Judge *ad hoc* Paolillo, at p. 419, para. 20.

Partially Successful Negotiations

Would it be possible to infer that the Court might take into account such declarations, admissions and proposals in case the parties had reached a partial agreement?

The importance of dividing points of agreement and remaining outstanding issues during partially successful negotiations has been aptly illustrated in the case law. Indeed, an Applicant can argue that during the process there may be a 'last point on which there was agreement between the parties in the delimitation of their maritime boundary'[199] but it certainly was 'not the last point on which there were negotiations'[200] which 'even if they proved to be unfruitful' were in fact intense and 'from the outset, focused on the entire maritime boundary'.[201]

The fact that a partial failure of negotiations may have led to submission of the whole boundary dispute, even on those parts where an agreement had been reached, would seem to bring the process of negotiations as far as judicial inferences are concerned within reach of the Court's approach indicated earlier.

Although in case parties have conducted negotiations which have been partially successful, the Court may pay 'particular attention' to an argument based 'on the conduct' of the other party 'during negotiations which led to agreements being concluded' for the delimitation of kilometres of frontier 'which are no longer in dispute',[202] the Court did consider the approach adopted by one party in the course of negotiations of 'little significance' when it has to weigh 'the legal force of the respective evidence submitted by the Parties for its appraisal' when fixing the frontier line.[203]

7.11 (Un)(successful) Negotiations *as Part of* the Basis for the Court's Decision

We have just examined one aspect of the functional interaction. Now we turn to the other side of the coin, namely the way in which elements coming out of a successful or unsuccessful process of negotiations could influence the judicial settlement of the dispute by becoming *part of* the basis for the Court's decision.

The Court's General Approach

As the Court has the power 'to take into consideration all relevant elements in administering justice between the parties',[204] these elements do include negotiations conducted during the course of the proceedings and their eventual outcome.

Although it may be common ground between the parties where the *fons et origo* of the dispute has to be situated,[205] the Court will have regard to material submitted and considerations put forward by the parties 'only to such extent as it may find in them reasons for the decision it has to give in order to settle the dispute'.[206]

This also applies to negotiations conducted by the parties prior to the start of the proceedings. A party may advance prior negotiations as one of the reasons why the Court should decide in its favour, but when they are being advanced as part of the submissions the Court has the power to exclude them, when necessary, insofar as they do not indicate what the party is asking the Court to decide.[207]

199 *Land and Maritime Boundary case, I.C.J. Reports 2002*, at p. 423, para. 243 (Cameroon).

200 *Ibid.*

201 *Land and Maritime Boundary case, I.C.J. Reports 2002*, at p. 423, para. 243 (Cameroon) and *I.C.J. Reports 1998*, at p. 322, para. 110.

202 *Frontier Dispute, I.C.J. Reports 1986*, at p. 570, para. 34.

203 *Ibid.*, at p. 575, para. 42.

204 *Fisheries Jurisdiction (United Kingdom v. Iceland), I.C.J. Reports 1974*, at p. 22, para. 48.

205 *Temple of Preah Vihear case, I.C.J. Reports 1962*, at p. 16.

206 *Ibid.*, at p. 14.

207 *Nuclear Tests (New Zealand v. France), I.C.J. Reports 1974*, at p. 466, para. 30.

The Court's well-established jurisprudence requires that the *petitum* has to be 'a precise and direct statement of a claim'. Negotiations, however, may also turn about 'definitions, principles, or rules to justify certain contentions'; as such they may find their way in *the reasoning* of the Court to support its decision.[208]

As far as the time element is concerned, the fact that a Convention has only been in force for one year when negotiations broke down plays a role in the Court's assessment on the alleged emergence of a new rule of customary law on the matter.[209]

When the Applicant invoked the rule that 'proposals and statements made in the course of or at the commencement of unfruitful negotiations are not to be taken into account in defining the legal rights of the Parties' the Chamber stated that 'this rule should not be given too extended an interpretation, being primarily intended to ensure that legal rights are not prejudiced by offers of compromise designed to lead to a negotiated settlement, but which are not successful'.[210]

The position taken by one of the parties during the negotiations may be upheld by the Court in the absence of 'any reasoned contention' by the other party in favour of a different line with respect to a different sector of the line.[211] The Chamber thus not only reaffirmed the existence of the rule but also attempted to play down its potential dysfunctional use having regard to the rule's primary objective.

The Chamber's approach was rather cautious and nuanced, as it held that unratified delimitation may be used in conjunction with equity *infra legem* as there 'is nothing in the records' of the negotiations 'to suggest that there was a fundamental disagreement between the Parties on that line'.[212]

In the process of reaching its decision the Court may note that a particular criterion for the delimitation problem has been invoked by both parties during the negotiations.[213]

In drawing the line of a maritime frontier the Chamber might consider it material that the 'line was agreed – if only *ad referendum* – in 1934, probably in view of its practical merits, and the provisional agreement was so long left unchallenged'.[214] This example illustrates how even the provisional outcome of negotiations is taken by the Court as the basis for its decision.

An agreed delimitation is 'binding' and 'to be respected in the delimitation operation carried out by the Court'.[215] A Respondent may persuasively argue that the principle of *pacta sunt servanda* and the principle of stability of 'boundaries prevent any attempt to invite the Court to redraw a boundary that has already been agreed'.[216]

A party may consider it appropriate and useful to request the Court to 'include into the operative part of its Judgment the line of the common frontier in the two sectors on which the Parties have agreed, so as to endow this line with the force of *res judicata*'.[217]

Parties may request the Court to 'note the existence' of such an agreement and 'to place it on record for them'; but a request to include its content in the operative part of the Court's decision would not only, in the circumstances of a case, exceed the jurisdictional limits placed upon the Court by the Special Agreement, but it would also fall outside the Court's judicial function.[218]

The reason for such an unprecedented request arguably was that then 'the two Parties will indisputably be bound in accordance with their agreement (*entente)* on those two sectors, in the same way that they will be

208 *Anglo-Norwegian Fisheries case, I.C.J. Reports 1951*, at p. 126.

209 *North Sea Continental Shelf case, I.C.J. Reports 1969*, at p. 43, para. 74.

210 *Land, Island and Maritime Frontier Dispute, I.C.J. Reports 1992*, at p. 485, para. 204.

211 *Ibid.*, at p. 552, para. 321.

212 *Ibid.*, at p. 514, para. 262 and at pp. 514–15, para. 263.

213 *Aegean Sea Continental Shelf case, I.C.J. Reports 1978*, at p. 36, para. 86.

214 *Land, Island and Maritime Frontier Dispute, I.C.J. Reports 1992*, at p. 422, para. 101; see also at p. 408, para. 79 and at pp. 421–2, paras. 99–101.

215 H. Thirlway, 'The Law and Procedure of the International Court of Justice 1960–1989 Supplement, 2007: Parts Four, Five and Six' (2007) LXXVIII *British Yearbook of International Law* 17–175, at 114, note 387.

216 *Case concerning Maritime Dispute (Peru v. Chile), I.C.J. Reports 2014*, para. 23 and para. 182 (Chile).

217 *Frontier Dispute between Burkina Faso and Niger, I.C.J. Reports 2013*, at p. 66, para. 37 (request by Burkina Faso).

218 *Ibid.*, at p. 66, para. 37; at p. 68, para. 39; at p. 69, paras. 43 and 44. Writing prior to this decision and discussing the feasibility of such a decision and the limits upon the Court in taking it: R. Kolb, *The ICJ*, pp. 751–4.

bound with regard to the frontier line which the Court will determine with regard to the sector that remains in dispute'.[219]

The other party may categorically dispute the need for such an inclusion, and take the view that the Court 'should note the agreement in question in the reasoning of its Judgment and settle the only remaining dispute between the Parties'.[220] Such a request in the final submissions in a case where the only basis for the Court's jurisdiction is the Special Agreement has to remain within the jurisdictional limits as defined by that Special Agreement.[221]

The Court drew a sharp distinction between noting the 'existence of an agreement between the Parties and to place it on record for them' on the one hand, and the 'quite different matter to appropriate the content of that agreement in order to make it the substance of a decision of the Court itself' on the other.[222]

Even if such a request were to fall within the jurisdictional limits, the Court would still have to verify 'that the object of this request falls within the Court's judicial function, as defined by its Statute'.[223]

Since the existence of a dispute is the primary condition for the Court to exercise its judicial function, a pre-existing agreement between the parties on two sectors of the line for their common frontier 'signifies that there is no longer any dispute between them on the subject-matter of that agreement'.[224] Moreover, the requested *res judicata* authority 'would not reinforce the binding character of that delimitation'.[225]

The situation would have been different if the agreement had been reached as result of resumed negotiations conducted during the course of the proceedings,[226] as the case law of its predecessor makes clear.[227]

The way the Court handled this particular request once more illustrates that parties should not attempt to impose upon the Court a mode of dysfunctional interaction between prior negotiations and adjudication as methods of peaceful settlement.

In case of negotiations which have been partially unsuccessful but where the parties 'intended that all boundary issues between them, whether on land or on sea, be resolved in a comprehensive way',[228] the Court's 'judgment will thus substitute for the non-existent agreement between the Parties on the delimitation of the continental shelf and the exclusive economic zones and shall resolve all such matters which have not been settled by the Parties'.[229]

The Parties' Approach

Parties may decide to introduce into the proceedings proposals made during negotiations towards a maritime boundary settlement not only by using them in their pleadings but also even beforehand by laying down in their Special Agreement the result of those negotiations.

Then the question arises whether the result of those negotiations is binding on the Chamber.[230] The Chamber in fact concluded that it 'must conform to the terms by which the Parties have defined' its task because if 'it did not do so, it would overstep its jurisdiction'.[231]

Parties may also have reserved the right to negotiate and to exclude from the case before the Court a dispute related to that one.[232]

219 *Frontier Dispute between Burkina Faso and Niger, I.C.J. Reports 2013*, at p. 66, para. 37 (request by Burkina Faso).

220 *Ibid.*, at p. 68, para. 39 (Niger). The reference in the Special Agreement to the previous agreement on the two sectors had only been accepted in order to allow the Court to be seised: at p. 68, para. 39.

221 *Ibid.*, at pp. 68–9, para. 42.

222 *Ibid.*, at p. 69, para. 43.

223 *Ibid.*, at p. 69, para. 45.

224 *Ibid.*, at p. 70, para. 50.

225 *Ibid.*, at p. 71, para. 53.

226 *Ibid.*, at p. 72, para. 55.

227 *Ibid.*, at p. 72, paras. 56–7.

228 *Maritime Delimitation in the Black Sea, I.C.J. Reports 2009*, at p. 73, para. 28.

229 *Ibid.*, at p. 74, para. 29.

230 *Gulf of Maine case, I.C.J. Reports 1984*, at p. 265, para. 19.

231 *Ibid.*, at p. 266, para. 23.

232 *Ibid.*, at pp. 265–6, para. 20; at p. 266, para. 21. and paras. 22–3; and at p. 277, para. 56.

Parties may disagree about the (dys)functional interaction when they debate whether and if so to what extent principles they have recognized in an earlier agreement could be applicable to both 'diplomatic negotiations between the two States and for the purpose of any eventual settlement of the dispute by the Court'.[233]

One view is that in the relevant provision 'no distinction is made between, on the one hand, the negotiations and, on the other hand, the other procedures to which the Parties might have recourse to solve the problem of delimitation'.[234]

The opposite view consists in keeping separate and distinct the process of negotiations and the current proceedings during which the Court is obliged to decide in accordance with Article 38 of the Statute.[235] Indeed, the principles enunciated in the agreement 'were to form the basis on which the Parties were to negotiate a delimitation agreement, but they were not agreed by the Parties as applying to the subsequent judicial proceedings'; some principles may be relevant to the Court as part of established rules, 'but not as part of any bilateral agreement'.[236]

The Court's position was clear: given the *chapeau* of those principles, '"shall *negotiate*" ... suggests that these principles were intended by the Parties to be taken into account in their negotiations ... but do not constitute the law to be applied by the Court'.[237]

In a clear attempt to arguably *optimalize* the functional interaction, parties may in their Special Agreement request the Court to 'place on record the Parties' agreement' on 'the results of the work of the Joint Technical Commission on Demarcation' with regard to particular sectors of their boundary.[238]

Parties are free to submit together with their Special Agreement an Exchange of Notes embodying their agreement on the delimited sectors of the frontier.[239] However, a request by one of the parties to include such in the operative paragraphs so as to endow the line agreed with *res judicata* authority – in order that the parties will be bound by that agreement 'in the same way that they will be bound with regard to the frontier line which the Court will determine with regard to the sector that remains in dispute' (the need for such inclusion being contested by the other Party) – [240] will not be granted by the Court, as such a request exceeds 'the limits of the Court's jurisdiction as defined by the Special Agreement'.[241]

In a clear attempt to *minimalize* the functional interaction, parties may have taken precautions 'to ensure that, if necessary, they will be free to negotiate on the boundary laid down by the decision'.[242]

7.12 (Potential) Impact of Judicial Settlement on Ongoing Negotiations

The dispute perhaps dividing the parties for decades has in most cases been the subject of a long process of intensive negotiations before, in light of lack of progress or a real deadlock; and in spite of all genuine attempts displayed by both parties, the decision has been taken to turn to the Court for a judicial settlement. The case as it has been brought before the Court may cover the whole dispute or some or various more controversial aspects of the dispute. Events at home and abroad may contribute to (one of) the parties' growing conviction that after the institution of the proceedings, and certainly after the delivery of the judgment, a resumption of the process of negotiations is called for and is no longer considered to be futile or rather unlikely.

In such circumstances both the parties and the Court have to safeguard the potential functional interaction between the two mechanisms while at the same time being aware of the risk of a dysfunctional interaction in case of a negative impact of the judicial settlement on ongoing or future negotiations.

---

233 *Maritime Delimitation in the Black Sea, I.C.J. Reports 2009*, at p. 75, para. 33 (Romania).
234 *Ibid.*, at p. 76, para. 34 (Romania).
235 *Ibid.*, at p. 77, paras. 36 and 37 (Ukraine).
236 *Ibid.*, at p. 77, para. 37 (Ukraine).
237 *Ibid.*, at p. 78, para. 41.
238 *Frontier Dispute between Burkina Faso and Niger, I.C.J. Reports 2013*, at p. 50, para. 2, Article 2 (2).
239 *Ibid.*, at p. 65, para. 33.
240 *Ibid.*, at p. 66, para. 37 (Burkina Faso) and at p. 68, para. 39 (Niger).
241 *Ibid.*, at p. 66, para. 37 (Burkina Faso) and at p. 69, para. 43.
242 *Gulf of Maine case, I.C.J. Reports 1984*, Dissenting opinion by Judge Gros, at p. 362, para. 4.

Such negotiations may develop and be conducted between the parties, but also between (one of) the parties and a third State.

Which lessons can be learned from the Court's case law in this regard?

In the fully fledged exercise of its contentious jurisdiction – that is to say when the Court delivers a judgment on the merits of a case – the *potential* impact on *ongoing negotiations* has until now only played a rather negligible role both in the arguments put forward by the parties and in the Court's reasoning, not to mention its operative paragraphs.

It is in fact in the *Arrest Warrant case* that the view was expressed that the judicial upholding of the Belgian arrest warrant would interfere with the ongoing negotiations to end the armed conflict in the region of the Great Lakes.[243]

In the exercise of its advisory jurisdiction, a first aspect to be noted is the Court's position – that the eventual effect the Court's finding might have, for instance, in respect of the further process of decolonization of a territory – is not being considered as an issue 'having a preliminary character', but to 'constitute part of the substance of the case'.[244]

In considering the propriety of responding to or declining a request for an advisory opinion, the Court regularly has to examine the alleged potential impact its Opinion could have on ongoing or future negotiations. The Court's Opinion could arguably undermine 'progress already made or being made on this sensitive subject and therefore, (would be) contrary to the interests of the United Nations Organization' and 'might adversely affect disarmament negotiations'.[245]

The Court took a clear and firm position in this regard. It was convinced that its conclusions 'would have relevance for the continuing debate on the matter in the General Assembly and would present an additional element in the negotiations on the matter', thereby stressing the positive functional interaction; but beyond that 'the effect of the opinion is a matter for speculation'.[246]

However, one could not fail to observe that also the potential positive functional interaction could be, although perhaps to a lesser and debatable extent, a matter for speculation – as the Court seems to realize when it added that it heard contrary positions advanced on this and it could not prefer one assessment to the other as there were no evident criteria to do so. Finally, the Court could not 'regard this factor as a compelling reason to decline to exercise its jurisdiction'.[247]

Anticipated dysfunctional interaction could even be invoked as an argument against the mere adoption by the General Assembly of a request for an advisory opinion, i.e. the functional propriety of submitting a request could situate itself at the heart of the debate.[248]

Judge Oda would have liked the Court to decline for reasons of judicial propriety and judicial economy.[249] A number of hypothetical questions in the future carry the risk of affecting the Court's main function, namely to settle international disputes on the basis of law.[250] This position refers the subject-matter of the request back to the international negotiating table in order to preserve intact the judicial part of the functional interaction.

According to the opposite view, whatever the Court's opinion on the matter of the request it 'would clarify the steps which the international community needs to take towards removing the obstacles along the path to the attainment' of total nuclear disarmament.[251] This position maintains the operation of the functional interaction, whatever in fact the potential impact on the ongoing negotiations.

---

243 *Arrest Warrant case, I.C.J. Reports 2000,* Dissenting opinion by Judge *ad hoc* Bula-Bula, at p. 234, para. 22 and *I.C.J. Reports 2002*, Dissenting opinion by Judge *ad hoc* Bula-Bula, at p. 129, para. 88.

244 *Western Sahara Advisory Opinion, I.C.J. Reports 1975*, at p. 17, para. 12.

245 *Nuclear Weapons Advisory Opinion, I.C.J. Reports 1996*, at p. 236, para. 15 and at p. 237, para. 17. It could be noted in passing that the Review Conference on the NPT was of the opinion that insufficient progress had been made.

246 *Ibid.*, at p. 237, para. 17.

247 *Ibid.*

248 *Ibid.*, Dissenting opinion by Judge Oda, at pp. 338–9.

249 *Ibid.*, at p. 372, paras. 52 and 53.

250 *Ibid.*, at p. 372, para. 53.

251 *Nuclear Weapons in Armed Conflict Advisory Opinion, I.C.J. Reports 1996*, Dissenting opinion by Judge Weeramantry, at p. 160. 'The whole process' of nuclear weapons negotiations is 'a search for referent principles and then for implementing details': W. Zartman, 'Negotiations: Theory and Reality', 73, writing about the Strategic Arms Limitation Talks (SALT).

One of the parties at the centre of a legal controversy, using the *Eastern Carelia* precedent, has made reference to the fact that the 'parties repeatedly agreed that these issues are to be settled by negotiation, with the possibility of an agreement that recourse could be had to arbitration'.[252] In doing so the parties concerned obviously have opted for a successive functional interaction.

Also other States and entities appearing before the Court have argued that the Court's opinion 'could impede a political, negotiated solution to the Israeli-Palestinian conflict … could complicate the negotiations envisaged in the "Roadmap"'.[253]

One participant argued that if the Court were to give a response it 'should in any event do so keeping in mind' – as part of the 'two key aspects of the peace process' – 'the fundamental principle that permanent status issues must be resolved through negotiations',[254] an unambiguous call for a rather close functional interaction between the two mechanisms.

The Court was conscious that the 'roadmap' which was endorsed by the SC in Resolution 1515 (2003) constitutes a negotiating framework for the resolution of the Israeli–Palestinian conflict. It is not clear, however, what influence the Court's Opinion might have on those negotiations: 'participants in the present proceedings have expressed differing views in this regard. The Court cannot regard this factor as a compelling reason to decline to exercise its jurisdiction.'[255]

Recently the Court again included its *Nuclear Weapons* observation that 'there are no evident criteria by which it can prefer one assessment to another'.[256] In describing the factual background to the request the Court recalled Security Council support for the Secretary-General's intention to start a political process to determine the future status of Kosovo.[257]

7.13 A (Dys)Functional Role for Actual or Potential Future Negotiations with Third States in the Judicial Settlement of the Pending Dispute?

A Request for Intervention Has Been Made

Article 62 of the Statute of the Court 'provides the major procedural device by which the interests of States not party to proceedings before the ICJ are protected by the Court'.[258]

Before an application to intervene can be made there is no need for a dispute between the would-be intervener and (one of) the original parties to have been identified through a process of prior negotiations.

The functional objectives of an application to intervene under Article 62 are twofold: to press a claim and/or to inform the Court.[259]

The functional interaction between negotiations and adjudication may be of a rather indirect nature, for instance when, as we have seen in the previous chapter, the Court in considering a request for intervention is aware of its usefulness for third States with a view to forthcoming negotiations or disputes with either one of the parties or with third States.[260]

A State asking for permission to intervene has to prove its assertions,[261] such as for instance being involved in negotiations with one or both of the parties. *The right to enter into negotiations* with one or

252 *Wall Advisory Opinion, I.C.J. Reports 2004*, at p. 157, para. 46.

253 *Ibid.*, at p. 159, para. 51.

254 *Ibid.*, at p. 160, para. 52.

255 *Ibid.*, at p. 160, para. 53. In comparison with the *Nuclear Weapons Advisory Opinion*, the Court's approach might seem similar with regard to the different views expressed as to the potential impact of its Opinion on the process of negotiations, but notably without the addition that the Court cannot choose one or the other assessment given the absence of a clear criterion.

256 *Kosovo Advisory Opinion, I.C.J. Reports 2010*, at p. 418, para. 35.

257 *Ibid.*, at p. 430, para. 64.

258 C. Chinkin, 'Article 62', at p. 1530, MN 1;and p. 1332, MN 1.

259 H. Thirlway, 'The Law and Procedure of the International Court of Justice 1960–1989: Part Thirteen' (2003) LXXIV *The British Yearbook of International Law* 7–114, at 37–40 and 40–43.

260 *Continental Shelf (Tunisia/Libya), I.C.J. Reports 1981*, at p. 8, para. 12.

261 *Indonesia/Malaysia case, I.C.J. Reports 2001*, at p. 587, para. 29.

both of the parties to settle a particular claim may allegedly constitute, according to the requesting State, an interest of a legal nature, distinct from the territorial claim itself which will become the subject-matter of future negotiations.[262]

A requesting State may not only ask the Court not to delimit a maritime boundary between the parties beyond a certain point, but in addition not 'to express an opinion which could prejudice' its interests 'in the context of (its) maritime boundary negotiations' with its neighbours.[263] The Court must then, in fixing the maritime boundary between the parties, 'ensure that it does not adopt any position which might affect the rights' of the requesting State.[264]

However, the Court ruled that the potential impact of its decision or reasoning in the case on future negotiations in which different instruments (from the ones before the Court) will be relevant between the requesting State and one or both of the parties 'is simply too remote for purposes of Article 62'.[265]

A non-party intervener might later invoke a favourable decision as *res judicata* against the original parties, for instance in negotiations, while in case of an unfavourable decision for the non-party intervener the original parties cannot invoke it conclusively.[266]

A Request for Intervention Has Been Denied

The concept of good administration of justice 'may be related not only to the management of a case but also to the rights of the parties'.[267] It may also be used by the Court to 'reject a request for permission to intervene', and this 'besides the conditions laid down in Article 62(1)'.[268]

The rejection for that particular reason may have an impact on the (un)willingness of the parties concerned to embark upon or restart a trilateral process of negotiations.

In case a request for intervention is being denied by the Court, it follows in line with Article 59 of the Statute 'that no conclusions or inferences may legitimately be drawn from those findings or that reasoning with respect to rights or claims of other States not parties to the case'.[269]

Although this general principle applies to all third States that are looking for conclusions or inferences with respect to their own rights or claims within the context of current or subsequent negotiations, it is clear that a judgment in delimitation cases '*will also be a guide* in other similar controversies to help States *settle by negotiation* or other peaceful means of their own choice, their eventual differences in this respect'.[270]

One way the functional interaction works finds its source in Article 59 of the Statute, which provides a dual guarantee for the *freedom of negotiations with and for the third States*.[271]

Although 'a declaration of the parties whereby they do not consider themselves bound by the Court's judgment cannot be allowed being contrary' to Article 59,[272] this does not take away parties' freedom to depart in the post-adjudicative negotiations from the operative part of the judgment.

262 *Ibid.*, at p. 589, para. 38 (emphasis added).

263 *Land and Maritime Boundary case, I.C.J. Reports 2002*, at pp. 329–30, para. 29 (Equatorial Guinea).

264 *Ibid.*, at p. 421, para. 238 and at p. 424, para. 245.

265 *Indonesia/Malaysia case, I.C.J. Reports 2001*, at p. 604, para. 83. In the *Continental Shelf case between Tunisia and Libya* Malta's application to intervene was based on its fear that the Court's reasoning would have a prejudicial effect on the future settlement of its own continental shelf boundaries with the parties. However, although the potential impact on future negotiations was allegedly more direct and clear, that was not 'a pertinent factor in deciding whether or not to allow Malta to intervene': *I.C.J. Reports 2001*, at p. 597, paras. 51 and 52.

266 *Territorial and Maritime Dispute (Nicaragua v. Colombia), Application by Honduras to intervene, I.C.J. Reports 2011*, Dissenting opinion by Judge Donoghue, at p. 483, para. 30.

267 H. Sakai, '*La Bonne Administration de la Justice*', 116.

268 H. Sakai, '*La Bonne Administration de la Justice*', 120.

269 *Continental Shelf case between Tunisia and Libya, I.C.J. Reports 1981*, at p. 20, para. 35.

270 *North Sea Continental Shelf case, I.C.J. Reports 1969*, Separate opinion by Judge Padilla Nervo, at p. 99 (second emphasis added).

271 *Continental Shelf case between Libya and Malta, I.C.J. Reports 1984*, at p. 15, para. 22.

272 *Free Zones case, P.C.I.J., Series A/B, No. 46*, p. 161.

A judgment 'will be *res inter alios acta*' and 'cannot be creative or [have] more rights or obligations' for that third State than any delimitation resulting from direct negotiations.[273]

The other way functional interaction works finds its expression in the failed argument that the role of prior negotiations in establishing a dispute should apply *a fortiori* to a 'comparable application to intervene in proceedings commenced by agreement, and pending between two States',[274] such a reasoning obviously not applying in proceedings instituted by unilateral application.

As a matter of principle, in a maritime dispute, the Court will protect the interests of a third State which 'needs a protection that is not provided by the relative effect of decisions of the Court under Article 59 of the Statute',[275] interests which will not be affected by the operation itself of taking into account all coastal and coastal relationships as a geographical fact for the purpose of effecting an eventual delimitation between the parties before it.[276]

At the stage of the determination of the relevant area, third party entitlements cannot be affected,[277] although 'some awareness of the actual and potential claims of third parties is necessary'.[278]

As far as the actual delimitation is concerned, 'the Court has always taken care not to draw a boundary line which extends into areas where the rights of third States may be affected'.[279] Given Article 59 of the Statute, the boundary line is 'without prejudice to any claim of a third State or any claim which either Party may have against a third State'[280] and which may be the subject of previous or future negotiations.

Judge Xue would have preferred the Court using the arrow pointing technique for the time being given third State's maritime entitlements in the area and which neither the principle *res inter alios acta* nor Article 59 of the Statute could properly protect.[281]

Also the potential outcome of future negotiations on the maritime delimitation between the Applicant and its adjacent neighbours should play a role.[282] The States concerned should be allowed enough space 'to first draw up their respective boundaries and then readjust their maritime relations'.[283]

It 'is a truism' nowadays 'that judicial or arbitral maritime delimitations, except in geographical circumstances where only two States could possibly have rights over the area, tend to be *handled bilaterally*, but have to be *conceived multilaterally*'; and various devices, including the 'directional arrow', much discussed in recent cases, 'have had to be devised to square this particular circle'.[284]

Parties themselves could delimit overlapping entitlements without prejudicing 'the interests of third States in the area beyond national jurisdiction'.[285]

Judge Donoghue maintained her position that the Court should have allowed the request for intervention by Honduras: the Court's judgment on the merits, while taking into account the interests of both Honduras and Costa Rica, 'had the potential to affect at least one interest of a legal nature pertaining to Honduras'.

273 *Continental Shelf case between Libya and Malta, I.C.J. Reports 1984*, at p. 17, para. 26 (Malta).

274 *Ibid.*, at p. 17, para. 25 (Malta; the discussions with the would-be intervener were held but with regard to a different area).

275 *Territorial and Maritime Dispute (Nicaragua v. Colombia), Application Costa Rica to Intervene, I.C.J. Reports 2011*, at p. 372, paras. 86 and 87.

276 *Land, Island and Maritime Frontier Dispute, I.C.J. Reports 1990*, at p. 124, para. 77.

277 *Maritime Delimitation in the Black Sea, I.C.J. Reports 2009*, at p. 100, para. 114.

278 *Territorial and Maritime Dispute (Nicaragua v. Colombia), Judgment, I.C.J. Reports 2012*, p. 624, at p. 685, para. 162. Whereas the 'relevant area' is 'a legal concept' (*Maritime Delimitation in the Black Sea, I.C.J. Reports 2009*, at p. 99, para. 110) which should 'be taken into account as part of the methodology of maritime delimitation' (at p. 99, para. 110), the Court duly admitted that such determination 'does not purport to be precise and is approximate' (at p. 100, para. 111) as referred to by G. Giraudeau, *Les différends territoriaux*, at pp. 366 and 367.

279 *Territorial and Maritime Dispute (Nicaragua v. Colombia), Judgment, I.C.J. Reports 2012*, at p. 707, para. 228.

280 *Ibid.*

281 *Ibid.*, Declaration of Judge Xue, at pp. 749–50, paras. 12–13.

282 *Ibid.*, at p. 750, para. 14.

283 *Ibid.*, at p. 750, para. 15.

284 H. Thirlway, 'The Law and Procedure of the International Court of Justice 1960–1989 Supplement, 2011: Parts Eleven, Twelve and Thirteen', at 126–7 (emphasis added).

285 *Territorial and Maritime Dispute (Nicaragua v. Colombia), I.C.J. Reports 2012*, Separate opinion by Judge Donoghue, at p. 757, para. 22.

Indeed, the 'steps that the Court followed in arriving at the final boundary illustrate why the Court should have concluded' that Honduras did fulfil the requirements of Article 62.[286]

The two judges *ad hoc* in the case shared the view that 'the rights and interests of third States are affected by the Judgment', in particular because of the bilateral agreements concluded in the area.[287] A bilateral maritime dispute 'falls within a wider and very specific geographical framework'.[288]

To succeed with a request for permission to intervene in a maritime dispute the would-be intervener has to show that 'its interest of a legal nature in the maritime area bordering the area in dispute' between the parties before the Court 'needs a protection that is not provided by the relative effect of decisions of the Court under Article 59 of the Statute'.[289]

No Request for Intervention Has Been Made

The question which concerns us now – apart from the use of Articles 62 and 63 of the Statute of the Court and having *due regard* to the interests of third States – is whether and which role is reserved, within the framework of functional interaction, by actual or potential negotiations with third States in the judicial settlement of the pending dispute.

A third State 'is not obliged to have recourse to intervention to protect its interests; it may simply sit back and watch the proceedings, relying on Article 59 of the Statute for substantive legal protection, and on the Court's self-declared duty of restraint for protection against any overly extensive judgment'. However, intervention has the advantage 'of ensuring that the Court is fully aware of the point at which the judgment would become excessive'.[290]

Pursuant to Article 59:

> the legal rights of third States are in no way affected by a judgment of the Court. Such a judgment may however, if the Court is incautious or misguided, be so worded as to *appear* to affect the rights of a third State; and while those rights are not in fact affected, the legal *interests* of the third State are involved, since it will have to assert the principle of *res inter alios acta* in negotiation with the parties in order to protect its rights.[291]

The Court's self-restraint not to render an overly extensive judgment may in cases where no request for intervention has been made or where it has denied the request allegedly result in judicial action *infra petita.*[292]

In case no request to intervene has been made, the nature of the dispute, its complexity for geographical or other reasons may bring (one of) the parties to draw the Court's attention to legal interests of other States and to which arguably the Court may have 'due regard' in reaching its decision.[293]

Multiparty negotiations may also occur prior to the proceedings covering a wider range of subject-matters than the core of the dispute and on which no bilateral negotiations have been possible.[294] The considerable tension between two parties were linked to the problems and difficulties those multiparty negotiations may encounter.[295]

---

286 *Ibid.*, at pp. 760–61, paras. 34–6.

287 *Ibid.*, Declaration by Judge *ad hoc* Mensah, at p. 766, para. 13 and Declaration by Judge *ad hoc* Cot, at p. 769, para. 9.

288 *Ibid.*, Declaration by Judge *ad hoc* Cot, at p. 768, para. 3.

289 *Territorial and Maritime Dispute (Nicaragua v. Colombia), Costa Rica Application to Intervene, I.C.J. Reports 2011*, at p. 372, para. 87.

290 H. Thirlway, 'The Law and Procedure of the International Court of Justice 1960–1989: Part Thirteen', at 52.

291 H. Thirlway, 'The Law and Procedure of the International Court of Justice 1960–1989: Part Thirteen', at 52–3.

292 R. Kolb, 'General Principles', in A. Zimmermann, C. Tomuschat and C. Tams (eds), *The Statute of the International Court of Justice: A Commentary* (Oxford, 2006), at p. 817 MN 42.

293 *Fisheries Jurisdiction (United Kingdom v. Iceland), I.C.J. Reports 1974*, at p. 6, para. 11 (b) and p. 7, para. 11 (e); see also at p. 34, para. 79 (4), (c).

294 *Fisheries Jurisdiction (Spain v. Canada), I.C.J. Reports 1998*, Dissenting opinion by Judge *ad hoc* Torres Bernardez, at p. 594, para. 35; at p. 595, para. 39; and at p. 598, para. 45.

295 *Ibid.*, at p. 599, para. 48.

Previous and successful negotiations between one of the parties and a third State could constitute the very subject-matter of a dispute before the Court and the core of the submissions of the Applicant, the *East Timor case* being the textbook example in this regard.

Interesting to note is that the Applicant's claim was *inter alia* not only directed at negotiations the Respondent had been conducting but was still continuing to conduct on the delimitation of the continental shelf[296] considered by the applicant to be a violation, but also its exclusion from negotiations on a related matter (exploration and exploitation).[297]

In line with its previous submissions the Applicant may then request the Court to adjudge and declare that the Respondent is bound 'to refrain from any negotiation … with any other State concerning the delimitation, exploration and exploitation of the continental shelf'.[298]

In the Court's contentious case law this is the only example where the Applicant is requesting the Court to impose on the Respondent such a duty of abstention to negotiate with any other State on a particular subject-matter.

The circumstances of the dispute provide the explanation for what otherwise would certainly be an *unexpected functional link* between negotiations and judicial settlement: the Court not recommending or ordering the parties to negotiate towards a peaceful solution in the post-adjudicative phase, but instead obliging one of them to abstain from negotiations with a third State.

The position taken by a Respondent and reflected in its submissions in a case on maritime delimitation that its territorial sea would not extend beyond a certain point should have been upheld by the Court in order to prevent 'the overlapping of the maritime areas of the Parties' and to eliminate 'a potential source of future conflict'.[299]

A delimitation reaching beyond (a trilateral) point not only risks affecting the rights of third States but, moreover, 'amounts implicitly to take a position on a dispute which is not the subject of the present case'.[300]

It has been rightly observed in doctrine that 'le statut de certains tiers devant les juridictions internationales découle peut-être cette fois-ci d'un principe général embryonnaire de respect des droits des tiers'.[301]

7.14 Negotiations as Part of the Operative Paragraphs: The Court Leading the Parties from the Adjudicative into the Post-adjudicative Phase

In case the Court orders the parties to negotiate within a particular legal framework, 'the autonomy and flexibility that negotiation originally possessed are lost', but instead 'negotiation becomes objective'.[302]

From a functional interaction perspective it has to be noted that the Court considers such a decision to be part of its facilitative functions mentioned earlier,[303] while the judicial indication of the framework for the post-adjudicative process makes the negotiations 'conditional' in contrast to the pre-adjudicative negotiations or those taking place during the proceedings which are rather 'unconditional'.[304]

The Court ordering the parties to negotiate 'should be valuated as an appropriate use of a new judicial function',[305] and it also illustrates another aspect of the functional interaction. By providing the parties with a

296 *East Timor case, I.C.J. Reports 1995*, at p. 94, para. 10 (2); see also at p. 98, para. 19.

297 *Ibid.*, at p. 94, para. 10 (3).

298 *Ibid.*, at p. 95, para. 10 (5).

299 *Territorial and Maritime Dispute between Nicaragua and Honduras, I.C.J. Reports 2007*, Separate opinion by Judge Koroma, at pp. 778–9, paras. 20–21.

300 *Ibid.*, Dissenting opinion by Judge *ad hoc* Torres Bernardez, at p. 825, para. 158.

301 E. Jouannet, 'Quelques perspectives théoriques: incertitudes sur le tiers et désordres de la justice internationale' in *Le tiers à l'instance devant les juridictions internationales* (Paris, 2005), pp. 255–63 at 261. See also generally on some aspects of international judicial procedure and practice relating to these elements S. Torres Bernardez, 'Bilateral, Plural and Multilateral Elements in International Judicial Settlement' in N. Ando, E. McWhinney and R. Wolfrum (eds), *Liber Amicorum Judge Shigeru Oda* (2 vols, The Hague, 2002), vol. 2, pp. 995–1007.

302 S. Sakamoto, 'Revaluation', 3.

303 S. Sakamoto, 'Revaluation', 20.

304 S. Sakamoto, 'Revaluation', 31.

305 S. Sakamoto, 'Revaluation', 31.

legal framework for the process they are obliged to embark upon, the negotiations will depend on normative factors and less on the respective power positions of the parties, while the resulting agreement will be a normative one.[306]

On the other hand, the very nature of such a Court decision makes it more likely that 'interpretation surrounding the execution of the decision is requested' later by (one of) the parties,[307] which then constitutes one of the scenarios to be dealt with in Chapter 9.

The Court ordering the parties to negotiate may be based on the Special Agreement, but it may also be based upon a unilateral request by one party. A judicial order to negotiate has a substantive part 'concerning the content of the agreement' to be reached and a rather 'procedural part related to the form of negotiation' – namely to negotiate in good faith.[308]

One important aspect of the functional interaction is how precise the judgment should be and what should be left for the parties to negotiate later on, or whether there is perhaps nothing left for them other than just to apply automatically, with no margin of appreciation or discretion in the post-adjudicative phase what the Court has decided.

We have already emphasized the crucial importance for the parties of clearly formulating, for instance during the negotiations leading up to a Special Agreement, what they are asking the Court to deliver. In practice, after having concluded a Special Agreement to submit a dispute to the Court parties may, in spite of having conducted successful negotiations, find themselves in disagreement about what exactly they are asking the Court to do. This dispute may relate to 'the degree of precision of the judgment of the Court, and the corresponding extent or absence of freedom of the Parties and their experts' in the post-adjudicative stage.[309]

Parties may take opposing views as to the interpretation of the Special Agreement. According to one view they would, after the delivery of the judgment, only have the 'technical task of application', and this would leave 'no room for any difficulty to arise' between the delegations;[310] meanwhile the other view holds that the Court's task is 'to indicate the additional considerations and factors which have to be taken into account and balanced' by the parties themselves after the delivery of the judgment.[311]

In such a situation the Court may very well come to the conclusion that 'there is no fundamental difference of opinion' between the parties, 'only' a 'difference of emphasis as to the respective roles of the Court and of the experts of the two countries', and that in fact the whole controversy is 'of minor importance'.[312]

The Court has to be 'as precise as to what it decides' because providing the parties with mere 'guidance' would run counter to Article 59 and 60 of the Statute and Article 94, para. 1 of the Rules of Court.[313] However the Court may, depending on the circumstances of the case and of course the submissions of the parties, provide them with directions for post-adjudicative negotiations either to implement the judgment it will deliver or to settle outstanding issues.

Moreover, given the provisions of a Special Agreement to that effect, 'there will be no need for further negotiation between experts of the Parties regarding the factors to be taken into account in their calculations, since the Court will have determined the matter'.[314]

The Court's interpretation of the Special Agreement is in line with its view on the extent of its judicial function: to settle the dispute between the parties in such a final and decisive way that the risk of further difference and tension between them after the delivery of the judgment are reduced to a strict minimum.

What is left for the parties to do is the technical task 'of making possible the drafting of the treaty incorporating the result of the work by the experts'.[315]

---

306 S. Sakamoto, 'Revaluation', 33.
307 S. Sakamoto, 'Revaluation', 34.
308 S. Sakamoto, 'Revaluation', 31.
309 *Continental Shelf case between Tunisia and Libya, I.C.J. Reports 1982*, at p. 39, para. 26.
310 *Ibid.*, at p. 39, para. 27 (Tunisia).
311 *Ibid.*, at p. 39, para. 28 (Libya).
312 *Ibid.*, at pp. 39–40, para. 29.
313 *Ibid.*, at p. 40, para. 29; see also Dissenting opinion by Judge *ad hoc* Evensen, at p. 279.
314 *Ibid.*, at p. 40, para. 30.
315 *Ibid.*

This case once more illustrates how important it is for the functional interaction that the Court determines and identifies, in the light of the prior negotiations and the arguments put before it during the proceedings, the essential issues in dispute; otherwise bringing a dispute before the Court may end up, after the delivery of the judgment, in increased tension and difficulties between the parties.

In case the parties have reserved for themselves post-adjudicative negotiations in order to reach agreement on for instance delimitation, the Court 'will discharge its task in such a way' as to provide them 'with the requisite directions'.[316]

A decision which would refer the parties back to negotiate an agreement 'which would attribute each of them an equitable share of the continental shelf' would 'not have satisfied the letter of the Special Agreements any more than the spirit thereof'.[317]

The suspension of negotiations 'in the face of difficulties which had been encountered, in order to be re-opened and completed in the light of the indications to be given by the Court'[318] succinctly reflects the functional interaction. The fact that the parties decide to present the matter to the Court may be based upon their conviction that the lack of agreement in the negotiation was not conclusive.[319]

However, the Court will not substitute itself for the parties by 'means of a detailed indication of the methods to be followed and the factors to be taken into account' during that process:[320] Nevertheless the Court may still give 'some degree of indication' as to the possible ways in which a particular rule may be applied in a case, although the parties are free to agree upon another method.[321]

Although there is in fact no limit to the considerations the parties may wish to take into account during the post-adjudicative negotiations on a delimitation in order to reach an equitable result, the circumstances will determine the relative weight to be given to different considerations.[322]

The Court may indicate which various aspects *must* be taken into account in the balancing act the parties will have to perform after the delivery of the judgment.[323]

Finally, the Court may not only determine the end result of the post-adjudicative negotiations, but it may also provide the parties with a non-exhaustive list of factors they have to take into account in the course of the negotiations.[324]

A request for the indication of a provisional measure may be prompted by acts of sovereignty by the Respondent which allegedly prejudge not only the judgment on the merits to be given by the Court but also 'the maritime delimitation to be effected subsequently between the States'.[325]

Here the functional interaction stretches well into the post-adjudicative phase as perceived and presented by one of the parties.

Given the functional interaction, it is not surprising that prior negotiations may have a direct impact on the Court's decision on the merits of the case.

In determining the framework for the post-adjudicative negotiations, the Court is taking into consideration the positions adopted by the parties during the negotiations.[326] During those post-adjudicative negotiations parties are under an obligation 'to consider, within the context of the 1977 Treaty, in what way the multiple objectives of the treaty can best be served, keeping in mind that all of them should be fulfilled';[327] moreover, objectives have to be 'pursued in a joint and integrated way'.[328]

316 *North Sea Continental Shelf case, I.C.J. Reports 1969*, at p. 46, para. 84.
317 *Ibid.*, Separate opinion by Judge Ammoun, at p. 145.
318 *Ibid.*, at p. 147.
319 *Ibid.*, Separate opinion by Judge Padilla Nervo, at p. 98.
320 *Ibid.*, at p. 46, para. 84.
321 *Ibid.*, at p. 50, para. 92.
322 *Ibid.*, at p. 50, para. 93.
323 *Ibid.*, at p. 50, para.94.
324 *Ibid.*, at p. 53, para. 101 (C) and (D).
325 *Arbitral Award case, I.C.J. Reports 1990*, at p. 67, para.15 (Guinea-Bissau).
326 *Gabcikovo case, I.C.J. Reports 1997*, at p. 77, para. 138.
327 *Ibid.*, at p. 77, para. 139.
328 *Ibid.*, at p. 78, para. 141.

This is a clear example of the Court identifying in more detail the parameters of the negotiations to come: by ruling that all of the objectives of the treaty should be fulfilled, the Court excludes freedom of the parties to select some of the objectives to the detriment of some others.

Furthermore, the Court determined not only that the negotiations should be conducted on a purely bilateral basis – as trilateral talks did not succeed because the parties maintained diametrically opposed positions – but also that the process should be embarked upon 'without pre-conditions'.[329]

The Court is thus ruling out the setting of any pre-conditions whatsoever by any of the parties: at the same time the negotiations have to take place at the bilateral level, in accordance with Article 5 of the compromis, but 'Parties can benefit from the assistance and expertise of a third party'.[330] According to the Court third party involvement 'may be helpful and instrumental in finding a solution, provided each of the Parties is flexible in its position'.[331]

The now traditional and judicially supported condition of flexibility during negotiations is thus paramount for the successful outcome of the new process of negotiations.

In a departure from a literal interpretation of Article 5 of the Special Agreement, the Court considered some third party involvement; by determining in a strict way the contours of those non-conditional negotiations still to come the Court has made an attempt to substantially reduce the risk of another failure.

Dismissal of the main claim and a counterclaim 'could obviously give rise to the criticism that' a pre-existing deadlock would continue after the close of the proceedings[332]

A refusal of the Court to intervene in any way based upon the *Monetary Gold* rule, in spite of the governments concerned having turned to the Court 'asking it to give them guidance', may 'well give rise to a deadlock or aggravate the difficulties'.[333]

Such judicial outcome implies dysfunctional interaction. Moreover, the rights and obligations of a third State may (have) constitute(d) the subject-matter of prior, ongoing or even future negotiations between that State and (one of) the parties to the case.

---

329 *Ibid.*, at p. 79, para. 143.

330 *Ibid.*

331 *Ibid.*, at p. 68, para. 113.

332 *Asylum case, I.C.J. Reports 1950*, Dissenting opinion by Judge Read, at p. 357.

333 *Case of the Monetary Gold removed from Rome in 1943 (Preliminary Question), Judgment of 15 June 1954: I.C.J. Reports 1954*, p. 19, Dissenting opinion by Judge Carneiro, at p. 45.

PART III
Negotiations during the Post-Adjudicative Phase

Introduction

Challenges for the Functional Interaction

We have already identified and reviewed the various modes of operation of the functional interaction during the pre-adjudicative and the adjudicative phases. Should we expect the interaction to take on different modes in the post-adjudicative phase as a result of the judicial intervention through the delivery of a judgment on the merits of a case or in relevant circumstances the Court's advisory opinion?

The functional interaction faces several challenges in the post-adjudicative phase, as various questions seem to indicate.

In case, for instance, the Court declares itself without jurisdiction are the parties then finding themselves back to square one as a result?

When the Applicant has in vain turned to the Court as a last resort, does the general obligation to peacefully resolve a dispute which has already proven to constitute a threat to international peace and security revive, or is there no point and perhaps no real obligation to use once more a negotiation process as it was provided for in the relevant compromissory clause or in a communiqué in which provision had been made for further meetings on substantive issues, and which the Court has considered not to furnish a valid basis for establishing its jurisdiction?

The Court may leave it to the parties to see what role 'if any, is to be given to the Joint Communiqué in their further efforts to arrive at an amicable settlement of their dispute'.[1] The Court may almost invite the parties to come back before it with the dispute 'if and when the conditions for establishing its jurisdiction are satisfied'.[2]

During the post-adjudicative phase a close form of functional interaction is bound to operate in different ways and modalities. Indeed, the advisory opinion or the judgment had been delivered or rendered, which, in principle and in theory, puts an end to this mechanism to settle the dispute, as the objective of the declaratory part of a claim may be precisely to avoid further legal differences[3] and post-adjudicative negotiations play an important role in restoring friendly relations between the parties.

The process is multifunctional, as it may be embarked upon in order to implement the judgment; to prevent the dispute reappearing in the not too distant future; or to keep under control issues that were not settled in a satisfactory way either during previous stages of negotiations or, as the case may be, by the judgment delivered.

Negotiations between the parties may find their way not only into the judicial reasoning, through the provisional measures the Court could indicate, but ultimately also into the judgment's or advisory opinion's operative paragraphs where the Court may – depending on the submissions and the circumstances of the case – not limit itself to oblige the parties to (re)negotiate in the post-adjudicative phase, but may also provide

1 *Aegean Sea Continental Shelf case, I.C.J. Reports 1978*, at p. 44, para. 108.

2 *Ibid.* As indicated earlier this procedural failure can well be cured through negotiations following the judgment in which the Court did find that it had no jurisdiction. Such post-adjudicative negotiations then in fact start to fulfil the functional role the prior negotiations between the parties should have performed in the first place.

3 *Fisheries case, Order of 9 November 1949, I.C.J. Reports 1949*, at p. 233.

them with directions for that process. In some cases it may be up to individual judges to suggest to the parties to resume or start negotiations.

The normal way the post-adjudicative phase is brought about is by the delivery of a judgment or an advisory opinion; but also discontinuance inevitably has the same effect, the difference being of course that the dispute has not been solved through judicial means. Does this entail that the negotiation process can fully reclaim its functional role?

Also the follow-up to be given to an advisory opinion may require post-adjudicative negotiations within a multilateral framework. The Court may not only make it clear that a negotiated solution should be based on international law, but it may also identify the international legal parameters for those negotiations.[4]

The follow-up may not only imply negotiations for instance between the UN and one of its member States, the 'relational dimension' of the implementation,[5] but also real action as such by the IO's organs, the 'institutional dimension'.[6]

Requests for interpretation or revision of a judgment clearly belong to the post-adjudicative phase. When the non-implementation of a judgment is allegedly due to its lack of clarity, should the parties then first attempt to remove this obstacle through negotiations so that a *new* dispute can arise before either of them is entitled to submit a request for interpretation?

In the post-adjudicative phase problems of various natures may arise. In their Special Agreement parties may give themselves a period of time after the delivery of the judgment, for instance, to start the work of demarcation and provide that in case of difficulty of execution of the judgment either of them can come back on the basis of Article 60 of the Statute,[7] the assumption being that problems of implementation would be caused by issues of interpretation and not by bad faith of either of them.

Should parties first have in good faith attempted to implement the judgment by way of negotiations and then to jointly or separately indicate the points of difference before a request for interpretation can be filed, even unilaterally?[8]

It is with regard to territorial disputes that most problems of compliance and implementation do arise.[9]

By the nature of things all proceedings before the Court possess a *retrospective component* arising from the history and causes of the dispute, and in most cases following a process of prior negotiations. There is by the nature of things also always the *future-oriented aspect* through the *res judicata* authority of the Court's ruling on the merits of the case. Those two components are present irrespective of the way of seisin of the Court.

The Obligation of Compliance and of Implementation

Parties to a case have both a customary and a conventional obligation to implement the Court's judgments[10] expressed through Article 59 of the Statute and Article 94 , para. 1 of the Charter, this obligation being the

---

4 *Wall Advisory Opinion, I.C.J. Reports 2004*, at p. 201, para. 162: 'to achieving as soon as possible, on the basis of international law, a negotiated solution to the outstanding problems and the establishment of a Palestinian State, existing side by side with Israel and its other neighbours, with peace and security for all in the region'.

5 L. Boisson de Chazournes and A. Angelini, 'Between Saying and Doing: The Diplomatic Means to Implement the International Court of Justice's *Iuris Dictum'* in L. Boisson de Chazournes, M. Kohen and J. Vinuales (eds), *Diplomatic and Judicial Means of Dispute Settlement* (Leiden, Boston, 2013), pp. 155–85 at p. 182.

6 *Wall Advisory Opinion, I.C.J. Reports 2004*, at p. 202, para. 163 (E); L. Boisson de Chazournes and A. Angelini, 'Between Saying and Doing', p. 177.

7 *Frontier Dispute between Benin and Niger, I.C.J. Reports 2005*, at p. 96, para. 2, Article 7. A similar arrangement was made in the Special Agreement between Burkina Faso and Niger: *Frontier Dispute between Burkina Faso and Niger, I.C.J. Reports 2013*, at pp. 51–2, para. 2, Article 7 (2) and (3).

8 As Libya argued in the *Revision and Interpretation of the 1982 Continental Shelf Judgment case, I.C.J. Reports, 1985*, Separate opinion by Judge Ruda, at pp. 232–5, paras. 4–13.

9 H. Tourard, 'Le champ opératoire: nouvelles perspectives ?' in C. Apostolidis (ed.), *Les arrêts de la Cour internationale de Justice* (Dijon, 2005), pp. 11–20 at p. 16.

10 A. Azar, *L'Exécution des décisions de la Cour Internationale de Justice* (Brussels, 2003), p. 29.

corollary of the parties' consent to seise the Court.[11] As a matter of law, the 'equality of legal obligations embraces also the obligations in the post-adjudicative phase'.[12]

Given the terms of Article 94, para. 1 of the UN Charter it is correct to point out that a State 'cannot accept an obligation and then withhold the means of performing the obligation'[13] such as entering into a process of post-adjudicative negotiations if so required as a result of the judgment rendered by the Court. Article 94 of the Charter is actually based on the premise that implementation of a judgment does not necessarily take place on a consensual basis.[14]

In a relatively limited number of compromissory clauses States Parties make it explicitly clear that they will comply with the decision of the Court. In a number of Special Agreements parties have taken care to provide for post-adjudicative negotiations to start – immediately or as soon as possible – after the delivery of the judgment on the modalities of its implementation, a process which should be concluded within sometimes a rather short period of time.

In case no agreement would be forthcoming due to difficulties in that implementation parties refer to the option under Article 60 of the Statute or provide for the possibility of an additional judgment to determine the modalities for executing the Court's judgment.

'The process by which the decision of the Court is implemented … consists in the main of a succession of political decisions',[15] but within the new legal framework put in place by the Court's judgment.

Doctrine has recently and rightly so pointed out that implementation of a Court judgment or advisory opinion covers more than acts or conduct that necessarily end in compliance as parties' or third subjects' conduct may still relate to the post-adjudicative phase.[16] Compliance has been described as consisting in 'acceptance of the judgment as final, and reasonable performance in good faith of any binding obligation'.[17]

---

11 A. Azar, *L'Exécution*, p. 47.

12 S. Rosenne, *Intervention*, p. 110.

13 *Right of Passage case, I.C.J. Reports 1960*, Dissenting opinion b y Judge Armand-Ugon, at p. 79.

14 On the general question see for instance A. Tanzi, 'Problems of Enforcement of Decisions of the International Court of Justice and the Law of the United Nations' (1995) 6 *European Journal of International Law* 4, 539–72. On the role of the Security Council under Article 94 see also S. Rosenne, *The Law and Practice*, vol. 1, pp. 244–9; K. Oellers-Frahm, 'Article 94' in B. Simma, D.-E. Kahn, G. Nolte and A. Paulus (eds), *The Charter of the United Nations: A Commentary*, 3rd edn (Oxford, 2012), pp. 1957–71; and A. Pillipech, 'Article 94' in J.-P. Cot, A.Pellet and M.Forteau (eds), *La Charte des Nations Unies. Commentaire article par article*, 3rd edn (2 vols, Paris, 2005), vol. 2, pp. 1987–98.

It is sufficient here to observe that it 'seemed possible' for the SC 'to recommend something other than the full execution of a judgment': R. Kolb, *The ICJ*, p. 56. Furthermore, the SC may abstain from action under Article 94, para. 2 'for the purposes of reaching a satisfactory solution of the dispute, for example if direct negotiations between the parties were under way with the promise of an adequate outcome, and one of the parties, for tactical reasons, sought at a difficult moment in those negotiations, to embarrass the other by taking the matter to the Security Council': R. Kolb, *The ICJ*, p. 849. Moreover, in ' highly exceptional circumstances' the SC, while doing 'everything possible not to damage the force of *res judicata'*, may recommend the 'winning party' 'to drop its demand that the judgment be executed now, in part or in full', the recommendation having to 'relate solely to the modalities of execution': R. Kolb, *The ICJ*, p. 851. Also the freezing of the execution of a judgment, for reasons of international peace and security, by a binding decision of the SC 'can never be more than a temporary matter': R. Kolb, *The ICJ*, p. 852.

15 S. Rosenne, *The Law and Practice of the International Court*, 2nd edn (Dordrecht, 1985), p. 115.

16 L. Boisson de Chazournes and A. Angelini, 'Between Saying and Doing', p. 157.

17 C. Paulson, 'Compliance with Final Judgments of the International Court of Justice since 1987' (2004) 98 *American Journal of International Law* 3, 434–61 at 435–6. See more generally also Y. Shany, 'Compliance with Decisions of International Courts as Indicative of their Effectiveness: A Goal-Based Analysis' in J. Crawford and S. Nouwen (eds), *Select Proceedings of the European Society of International Law* (Oxford and Portland, 2012), pp. 229–41. For an overview of non-compliance and defiance problems in five post-Nicaragua cases in relation to the manner the Court was seised see A. Llamzon, 'Jurisdiction and Compliance in Recent Decisions of the International Court of Justice' (2008) 18 *European Journal of International Law* 5, 815–52. For a selection of (non)compliance cases see also S. Rosenne, *The Law and Practice*, vol. 1, pp. 249–70. On the post-adjudicative phase of advisory opinions see *inter alia* S. Rosenne on the 'reception' by the requesting organ: *The Law and Practice*, vol. 1, pp. 304–16 and L. Boisson de Chazournes and A. Angelini, 'Between Saying and Doing', pp. 177–84.

We will not enter into the debate on how to measure compliance and whether in most cases the Court's judgments have been complied with by the parties.[18] It is sufficient here to note that 'decreased hostility towards judgments rendered by virtue of compulsory jurisdiction is perceptible',[19] that non-compliance may be 'a matter of increment and degree', whereas defiance 'involves wholesale rejection of the judgment as invalid coupled with a refusal to comply'.[20]

In case of allegations by one party of misconduct by the other, repeated failure of demarcation agreements and continuing border problems may suggest that the Respondent 'may not be completely fulfilling its obligations to execute the judgment reasonably and in good faith'. However, 'because most of the problems of implementation stem from failure to negotiate, perhaps it is more accurate to say that mutual non-compliance or failed good faith negotiations persist'.[21]

One should be cautious in considering that the implementation of a decision is to apply its operative part as the Court stated in the *Interhandel case*,[22] and one should pay due regard 'to the precise terms of the operative part'.[23]

As the PCIJ has stated, 'all the parts of a judgment concerning points in dispute explain and complete each other and are to be taken into account in order to determine the precise meaning and scope of the operative portion'.[24] Moreover, one should acknowledge that the enormous variety of contentious cases which have led to a Court judgment and which have been implemented by the parties 'ne permet pas de conclure à une théorie générale de l'exécution'.[25]

It is evident that 'compliance for the time being with the decision in a case does not in itself furnish any continuing guarantee that the problem out of which the case arose is solved or that the decision will not be frustrated or negated by further developments'.[26] Indeed, 'the conflict, which underlies the dispute, is not

18 C. Schulte, *Compliance*. It is sufficient to note that recently a former President of the Court referred to 'the impressive compliance rate with the legal solutions the Court indicates': R. Higgins, 'Shabtai Rosenne and the International Court of Justice', at 169.

19 A. Llamzon, 'Jurisdiction', 820.

20 A. Llamzon, 'Jurisdiction', 823. *The Question of the Delimitation of the Continental Shelf between Nicaragua and Colombia beyond 200 Nautical miles from the Nicaraguan Coast (Nicaragua v. Colombia)* is a case in point. In its Application, dated 16 September 2013, Nicaragua contends that any possibility for a bilateral negotiation is precluded by Colombia's reaction to the Court's judgment of 19 November 2012 which Colombia has declared inapplicable and Nicaragua considers not to have determined the question of the delimitation of the continental shelf in the area beyond 200 nautical miles: p. 5, para. 7 and p. 6, para. 10 (text available on the Court's website).

Another case in point concerns *Alleged violations of Sovereign Rights and Maritime spaces in the Caribbean Sea (Nicaragua v. Colombia)*. In its Application, dated November 2013, Nicaragua contends that it has declared itself willing to discuss issues relating to the implementation of the same Judgment of 19 November 2012 in which the Court has declared its rights and maritime zones while the Respondent has 'rejected the dialogue'. The Applicant invokes as basis for the Court's jurisdiction Article XXXI of the Pact of Bogota – which the Respondent had denounced with effect on the following day – and alternatively the Court's 'inherent power to pronounce on the actions required by its Judgments': Press Release No. 2013/36 of 27 November 2013 (text available on the Court's website).

For a detailed account of events and decisions in post-adjudicative phases in general during the 1987–2004 period see *inter alia* C. Paulson, 'Compliance', where full implementation of the judgments has taken an average of two and a half years: 452, note 221. See also generally on events and possible actions during the post-adjudicative phase S. Rosenne, *Interpretation, Revision and Other Recourse from International Judgments and Awards* (Leiden and Boston, 2007).

21 A. Llamzon, 'Jurisdiction', 828.

22 *Interhandel Case, I.C.J. Reports 1959*, at p. 28.

23 S. Rosenne, *The Law and Practice* (2nd edn), p. 115, note 1.

24 As cited by Judge De Castro in his dissenting opinion to the *Namibia Advisory Opinion, I.C.J. Reports 1971*, at p. 294.

25 A. Azar, *L'Exécution*, p. 22.

26 C. Jenks, *The Prospects of International Adjudication* (London and New York, 1964), p. 665. See for instance the case concerning *Certain Activities carried out by Nicaragua in the Border Area (Costa Rica v. Nicaragua), Joinder of Proceedings, Order of 17 April 2013, I.C.J. Reports 2013*, p. 166, at pp. 166–7, para. 1.

necessarily settled by a judgment of the Court'.[27] Indeed, although the Court's decisions are binding, 'the result can be that the dispute *seems* to be resolved, but in fact is not'.[28]

Implementation is 'neither theoretically nor practically the same as compliance' and thus 'comprises those acts which go beyond or diverge from compliance but contribute to the resolution of a dispute not fully resolved, whether because of the Court's limited jurisdiction or because of its reluctance to address some of the aspects relevant *in casu*'.[29]

One should add that 'compliance with a judgment of the Court has an *erga omnes* character and consequently all States have the duty and not merely the right to assist in bringing about the performance of the obligations required by the Court's judgment'.[30]

Non-compliance by the losing party illustrates that 'the reach of the shadow of the Court which can work in the bargaining process between States is extremely (relatively) limited in international society'.[31]

The obligation to implement the Court's judgment is an autonomous legal obligation; it manifests the legal links between the parties and the Court[32] and it imposes itself upon the parties from the moment the judgment is rendered. Parties have to carry out this obligation unconditionally.[33]

However, compliance within a reasonable period of time may bring into operation either an approach to merely delay the exercise or to spread it over a period of time.[34] Although it is an obligation 'aux moyens de réalisation flexibles',[35] it is an obligation of result for both parties.

Assessing the Effectiveness of the Court's Performance

There is only one criterion to assess the effectiveness of the Court's judicial performance: when the Court is asked to decide a case, it is not simply applying international law; it is not a sort of seminar – it is actually being asked *to settle a dispute*.[36]

Although this is not the focus of Part III , it is clear that judicial settlement of a dispute by the Court does not offer any guarantee that the dispute, as it had been submitted , is finally over. Indeed, a judgment 'does not by itself resolve – and is not intended to resolve – all the difficulties between the parties.[37] The judicial function is not 'inherently retrospective' and a judgment of the Court 'must be capable of execution'.[38] This is an important aspect of any assessment of the way the Court did perform its judicial function.

---

27 O. Yasuaki, 'The ICJ: An Emperor Without Clothes? International Conflict Resolution, Article 38 of the ICJ Statute and the Sources of International Law' in N. Ando, E. McWhinney and R. Wolfrum(eds), *Liber Amicorum Judge Shigeru Oda* (2 vols, The Hague, 2002), vol. 1, pp. 191–212 at p. 194.

28 R. Kolb, *The ICJ*, p. 334.

29 L. Boisson de Chazournes and A. Angelini, 'Between Saying and Doing', p. 158.

30 O. Schachter as cited by R. Bilder, 'International Dispute Settlement', at 147, note 35 in connection with Article 94, para. 2 of the UN Charter. On the implementation of (quasi-)judicial decisions in particular branches of international law see most recently G. Marceau and J. Hamaoui, 'Implementation of Recommendations and Rulings in the WTO System'; M. Langer and E. Hansbury, 'Monitoring Compliance with the Decisions of Human Rights Courts: The Inter-American Particularism' and J. Vinuales and D. Bentolia', The Use of Alternative (Non-Judicial Means to Enforce Investment awards against States' in L .Boisson de Chazournes, M. Kohen and J. Vinulaes (eds), *Diplomatic and Judicial Means of Dispute Settlement* (Leiden and Boston, 2013), respectively pp. 187–212, pp. 213–46 and pp. 247–80.

31 O. Yasuaki, 'The ICJ', p. 198 (emphasis added).

32 A. Mansour, *La mise en* œuvre *des arrêts et sentences des juridictions internationales* (Brussels, 2011), p. 99.

33 A. Mansour, *La mise en* œuvre, pp. 83–100.

34 Fonction dilatoire et fonction d'étalement dans le temps: J.-M. Thouvenin, 'Le délai raisonnable', pp. 114 and 116.

35 A. Mansour, *La mise en* œuvre, p. 101.

36 Observation made by Ian Brownlie during the Nijmegen Conference 40 Years UN, on file with the author. The main factors on which the effectiveness of international courts depend are 'the quality of the men and women who ascend to the bench' (D. Terris, C. Romano and L Swigart, *The International Judge*, p. 15) and for another substantial part on the litigation strategy of the parties before them, including high-quality advocacy, and including the functional role they wish the negotiation process between them to play prior to, during and after the proceedings before the Court.

37 *Nicaragua case, I.C.J. Reports 1984*, at p. 437, para. 100 (Nicaragua).

38 Ibid.

Part III will consist of two chapters. In Chapter 8 we will address the distinctive way in which the functional interaction operates in the post-adjudicative phase, whereas Chapter 9 will be devoted to the particular situation when (one or both of) the parties feel(s) the need to return to the Court.

It is worth noting that States Parties can commit themselves in a compromissory clause that during the proceedings they shall abstain from any action capable of having an adverse influence on the execution of the Court's decision, a fine example of functional interaction operating prior, during and after the proceedings.

Chapter 8
Functional Interaction in the Post-Adjudicative Phase

Introduction

The functional interaction already became operational during the period prior to the instituting of the proceedings before the Court, as we reviewed in Part I. Once the parties found themselves willingly or unwillingly in the Great Hall of Justice that interaction was not necessarily suspended, as indicated in Part II. After the delivery of the judgment or the advisory opinion there is no compelling reason to assume that the functional interaction would come to an abrupt or inevitable standstill or complete end. How it actually operates during the post-adjudicative phase is the focus of this chapter.

8.1 Some Distinctive Features of Post-Adjudicative Negotiations

The nature of the process of negotiations may be said to be different depending on the moment in time it actually takes place.

Prior negotiations are multifunctional, their main objective being to actually settle the dispute once and for all, and by doing so to prevent the need to resort to adjudication. Negotiations on the merits during the course of proceedings are part of a double track strategy, oscillating between the two means of peaceful settlement of dispute; post-adjudicative negotiations 'are designed to create positive relations' *inter alia* through the proper implementation of the judgment rendered by the Court.[1]

The Court's basic assumption with regard to the post-adjudicative phase is that of good faith on the part of the parties: the judgment will be implemented, and in appropriate cases there will be, for instance, no recurrence of wrongful acts, eventually coupled with parties' assurances and guarantees of non-repetition. The essence of the obligation to implement the judgment in good faith is 'that it does not permit either party to impose a *unilateral* solution'.[2]

The Court may have found it necessary to consider the parties' readiness to accept assistance from third parties during the post-adjudicative negotiations as an indication of their good faith.[3] According to one authoritative commentator, this was a 'remarkable' and 'unprecedented attempt by the Court to interfere' in the post-adjudicative phase of the case and 'difficult to reconcile with the principle' that the Court 'will be slow to accuse a party of bad faith'.[4]

Perhaps the Court's pronouncement has to be viewed rather as a kind of judicial warning to the parties. Moreover, Article 94 of the Charter entails 'a duty of compliance that must be read as involving compliance in good faith' and 'bad faith will not be presumed'.[5] However, '[t]his is not, of course, to say that the parties, *by agreement*, might act otherwise than in compliance with a judgment of the Court, which does not of itself create rules of *ius cogens*'.[6]

---

1 W. Zartman, 'Looking Forward and Looking Backward', p. 297.

2 *Request for the Interpretation of the Judgment of 15 June 1962 in the Case concerning the* Temple of Preah Vihear (Cambodia v. Thailand*) (Cambodia v. Thailand), Judgment, I.C.J. Reports 2013*, at p. 316, para. 99(emphasis added).

3 *Gabcikovo case, I.C.J. Reports 1997*, at p. 79, para. 143.

4 H. Thirlway, 'The Law and Procedure of the International Court of Justice 1960–1989 Supplement, 2006: Part Three', at 14, note 52.

5 H. Thirlway, The Law and Procedure of the International Court of Justice 1960–1989 Supplement, 2005: Parts One and Two', at 16. See also *Fisheries Jurisdiction (Spain v. Canada), I.C.J. Reports 1998*, Dissenting opinion by Judge *ad hoc* Torres Bernardez, at p. 654, para. 198.

6 H. Thirlway, The Law and Procedure of the International Court of Justice 1960–1989 Supplement, 2005: Parts One and Two', at 17, note 62.

Although post-adjudicative negotiations may be perceived as sharing a number of common features with the process of prior negotiations and negotiations during the course of proceedings – such as for instance the Permanent Court's ruling that 'an obligation to negotiate does not imply an obligation to reach an agreement'[7] – the judicial intervention performed with *res judicata* authority brings about a fundamental change in the operation of the functional interaction.

Resuming the prior negotiations where they were left is then in fact and also in law ruled out. The (new) rights and obligations, rules and principles as confirmed or pronounced by the Court will hence and in principle provide the legal framework for the parties' conduct, although they are still free to depart, in whole or to a certain extent, from the Court's finding, except when in their Special Agreement they committed themselves unreservedly to implement the Court's decision through a process of negotiations during which the parties may take the judgment also merely as a source of inspiration.[8]

The fundamental change of factual and legal circumstances brought about by the Court's judgment on the merits of the case means that the parties do have to be reasonably inspired by the convergence of interests[9] such as they may have found expression in their Special Agreement providing for post-adjudicative negotiations or in a compromissory clause providing for post-adjudicative negotiations in *tempore non suspecto*.[10]

The absence in principle of an obligation to reach an agreement can of course be remedied either through a Court ruling to that effect or by way of a *pactum de contrahendo* between the parties. Parties may also make a declaration before the Court during the proceedings that they will embark upon a (new) process of negotiations in the post-adjudicative phase.

In contrast to negotiations taking place during the course of the proceedings – for instance to find common ground on issues of a procedural nature, to establish an interim arrangement or indeed to reach an out of court settlement, and thus where the process is less multifunctional compared to prior negotiations – post-adjudicatory negotiations, as their pre-adjudicative counterpart, are potentially more multifunctional. Indeed, they may be called for either to implement the judgment, as the Court may order the parties to do in the operative paragraphs of its decision; to work towards a negotiated solution of those remaining aspects of the dispute which may not have been submitted to the Court or which the Court, in the opinion of (one of) the parties, has not resolved in a satisfactory way; or to resume the process of prior negotiations which may have been *suspended* until the Court's judgment, but this time in light of the Court's final decision.

The subject-matter and hence the function of post-adjudicative negotiations may be twofold. Parties may be compelled by their Special Agreement and/or by the actual content of the operative paragraphs to embark upon a process of negotiations about the *modalities of implementation* of the judgment. This process consists of 'des négociations nécéssaires',[11] whose first object may very well be to persuade a recalcitrant party to accept the judgment.[12]

In case of the parties having submitted only part of their dispute to the Court, post-adjudicative negotiations will then not only relate to the implementation of the judgment but also to resolving the outstanding issues of the dispute.[13]

When bringing a case before the Court on the question of the delimitation of the continental shelf beyond 200 nautical miles, an Applicant may refer to the absence of an agreement in this regard with a neighbouring country: 'any possibility for a bilateral negotiation' may arguably have 'been precluded' by the

7 *RailwayTraffic Advisory Opinion, P.C.I.J.Series A/B, No. 42*, p. 116 as referred to by the Court for instance in the *Pulp Mills case, I.C.J. Reports 2010*, at p. 68, para. 150.

8 Pablo Sandonato, 'Diplomatic and Judicial Means', p. 83.

9 P. Reuter, 'De l'obligation de négocier', 723.

10 See in this regard Libya's contention – that the final delimitation could only 'be established by an agreement, so that the findings communicated by the Court are merely 'guidance' as referred to by judge Gros in his dissenting opinion and 'which goes to the heart of the Court's judicial role': *Continental Shelf case between Tunisia and Libya, I.C.J. Reports 1982*, at p. 145, paras. 4 and 5. In Judge Gros' view the Court should not have kept silent in the face of this, and the option of (one of) the parties when concluding the Special Agreement that they 'reserved for them wholly or partly to modify the Court's jurisdictional act'.

11 A. Azar, *L'Exécution*, p. 98.

12 A. Azar, *L'Exécution*, p. 100.

13 A. Azar, *L'Exécution*, p. 102.

Respondent's 'widely publicized' reaction to a previous judgment of the Court and which 'is well known to the international community'.[14]

Depending on their (respective) submissions and the nature of the dispute, alternatively or partly in combination with the first function, parties may agree to work towards an agreement *departing in whole or in part* from the Court's decision. This process of negotiations may produce 'des résultats contrastés'.[15]

In case of a dispute over state responsibility the negotiations may relate to the question of reparation.

In case of a boundary dispute the negotiation may relate to a delimitation different from the one issued by the Court.[16]

However, the margin of appreciation for the parties – the scope of which is determined by the degree of precision of the operative paragraph within the limits of the Court's jurisdiction – is limited by the principle of good faith[17] and by the concept of implementation within a reasonable period of time.[18] This in turn evidently depends on the kind of action required from (one of) the parties[19] and may be extended in case co-operation between the parties is required,[20] for instance in order to establish a Commission of Demarcation[21] or a commission entrusted with the implementation of the judgment.[22]

A reasonable interpretation of post-adjudicative agreements departing from the Court's decisions is to accept that the *res judicata* is also realized when the Court's decision plays a role in or influences the negotiations which bring the parties to a definitive settlement of the dispute,[23] which is the ultimate touchstone for assessing the implementation of the judgment.[24]

In several cases implementation agreements were concluded relatively smoothly[25] and have 'proved possible also in the lack of a pre-agreed framework for implementation'.[26] On the other hand, since 'most of the problems of implementation stem from failures of negotiations, this result may amount to mutual noncompliance or *simply failed good faith negotiation*',[27] although Slovakia's request for an additional judgment was aiming at a Court declaration that Hungary had not been negotiating in good faith.[28]

When implementation 'requires close cooperation between the parties, it will be difficult to attribute clear responsibility for the failure of negotiations'.[29]

By the nature of things parties have to negotiate on the modalities of implementation of the judgment and on the timing of this implementation exercise.

Negotiations manifest themselves as an indispensable complement to the purely judicial solution given by the Court. In case one party rejects the Court's judgment and so refuses to implement it, only negotiations can bring about the ultimate acceptance by the reluctant party.[30]

---

14 Application of the Republic of Nicaragua dated 16 September 2013 instituting proceedings against the Republic of Colombia regarding the question of the delimitation of the continental shelf between Nicaragua and Colombia beyond 200 nautical miles from the Nicaraguan coast, paras. 6 and 7(text available on the Court's website).

15 A. Azar, *L'Exécution*, p. 103.

16 A. Mansour, *La mise en œuvre*, pp. 129–30.

17 A. Mansour, *La mise en œuvre*, p. 134.

18 A. Mansour, *La mise en œuvre*, p. 142.

19 A. Mansour, *La mise en œuvre*, p. 145.

20 A. Mansour, *La mise en œuvre*, p. 147.

21 A. Mansour, *La mise en œuvre*, pp. 475–92

22 A. Mansour, *La mise en œuvre*, pp. 493–9.

23 A. Azar, *L'Exécution*, p. 105.

24 A. Azar, *L'Exécution*, p. 107.

25 See for more details L. Boisson de Chazournes and A. Angelini, 'Between Saying and Doing', p. 163, note 23.

26 L. Boisson de Chazournes and A. Angelini, 'Between Saying and Doing', p. 164 and for more details note 27.

27 C. Paulson, 'Compliance', 439 (emphasis added), an example probably being the post-adjudicative negotiations in the *Gabcikovo case* p. 449 and A. Llamzon, 'Jurisdiction', 834–5.

28 A. Llamzon, 'Jurisdiction', p. 833.

29 C. Schulte, *Compliance*, p. 29.

30 J.-L. Amougou, 'La négociation dans l'exécution des arrêts de la CIJ', (2006) 31 *Revue de la Recherche juridique. Droit prospectif* 1, 1515–39, at 1525.

8.2 The Functional Interaction between the Pre-adjudicative and the Post-adjudicative Phase

As it is up to the parties to submit a dispute to the Court, either unilaterally or jointly, it is in the first place also up to them to bring into play a functional interaction between the pre-adjudicative and the post-adjudicative phase.

As it has been pointed out with regard to arbitration the success of resorting to the Court depends 'on a certain amount of goodwill between the parties in drawing up the compromis' as well as 'actually enforcing' the judgment 'subsequently made'.[31]

Although the 'extensive negotiations aimed at solving the dispute that preceded many of the cases' during a particular period 'did not appear to affect compliance',[32] it does not obscure the fact that in more than the majority of those cases extensive prior negotiations had indeed taken place.

Close relations, cultural similarities and values as well as a common conception of the dispute as a legal one and a genuine common commitment to settle it through adjudication, as expressed in the Special Agreement, may have been relevant factors in the pre-adjudicative phase and the transition to the adjudicative phase, but they are also factors contributing to the success of post-adjudicative negotiations.[33]

Conversely, 'hostile relations and mutual suspicions between the parties' and a Respondent's 'initial opposition to judicial settlement and unwillingness to reconcile during the proceedings' which have been characterizing the pre-adjudicative phase may later on help to explain the difficulties encountered by the parties during the post-adjudicative phase,[34] although these factors 'are not necessarily fatal to successful implementation'.[35]

In fact, there are 'many indications to suggest that defiance is less likely where States have given their specific consent to proceedings before the Court'.[36]

In case of unilateral seisin and depending on the submissions, the Court may have to refrain from establishing or suggesting a 'particular set of measures to be taken in order to actually implement the judgment', for instance to avoid a future pollution of a boundary river.[37]

An 'express reference to implementation before adjudication can mitigate some of the hurdles potentially looming over the horizon'.[38]

Indeed, in their Special Agreement parties may have taken care to explicitly request the Court to determine 'the legal consequences, including rights and obligations for the Parties, arising from its Judgment'.[39] Such a provision makes it possible for the Court to impose upon the parties an obligation to negotiate in the post-adjudicative phase, as it later turned out to be the case in the operative paragraphs of this judgment.[40]

The parties may determine the object and purpose of those *immediate* post-adjudicative negotiations as exclusively oriented towards the execution of the judgment. In case of failure of the process within a self-imposed time limit of six months, either party could be entitled to request an additional judgment 'to determine the modalities for the execution of the judgment'.[41]

In some cases the Court may interpret its task under the Special Agreement in such a way that post-adjudicative negotiations are being reduced to a strict minimum.[42] Margin for these negotiations are being limited by the requirement of accordance with the decision of the Court.

31 M. Shaw, 'Settling territorial disputes', p. 268.
32 C. Paulson, 'Compliance', 460.
33 C. Schulte, *Compliance*, pp. 132, 140 and 178.
34 C. Schulte, *Compliance*, p. 136.
35 C. Schulte, *Compliance*, p. 141.
36 C. Schulte, *Compliance*, p. 406.
37 P. Sandonato, 'Diplomatic and Judicial Means', p. 84; on the course of the post-adjudicative negotiations in the *Pulp Mills case* see in more detail pp. 84–5.
38 L. Boisson de Chazournes and A. Angelini, 'Between Saying and Doing', p. 160.
39 *Gabcikovo-Nagymaros Project (Hungary/Slovakia), Order of 14 July 1993, I.C.J. Reports 1993*, p. 319, at p. 320.
40 *Gabcikovo case, I.C.J. Reports 1997*, at p. 83, para. 155 (2), B.
41 *Ibid.*, at p. 12, para. 2, Article 5 (2) and (3).
42 *Continental Shelf case between Libya and Malta, I.C.J. Reports 1984*, at p. 10, para. 4 (Article III).

Although considerations made to provide 'guidance to the Parties for further conduct and place their mutual relations in a wider perspective' may reflect 'the rules and principles of international law, referred to in the Special Agreement', they 'can merely focus on the undertakings of the Parties entered into in the context of their efforts to settle the dispute peacefully and on their *present and future relations*'.[43]

A fruitful and commendable form of functional interaction may be expressed in the pre-adjudicative phase when parties have committed themselves to continue their co-operation in respect of, for instance, boundary rivers 'whatever the terms of the judgment rendered by the Chamber'.[44]

Whatever the legal basis for post-adjudicative negotiations – an operative paragraph, a provision in the compromis, the inherent need for such a process in order to implement the judgment – a return to the negotiating table may eventually fail and bring the parties back to the Court, a problem to be addressed in the next chapter.[45]

However, a return before the Court may also be the result of prior negotiations not having taken care – intentionally or not – of all relevant legal issues of the dispute, thereby having limited the scope of the Court's task and of corresponding submissions then resulting in a partial judicial settlement of the dispute .

8.3 The Functional Interaction between the Adjudicative and the Post-adjudicative Phase

The Role of the Parties

What is valid for the conduct of parties following the publication of a conciliation report equally and one would say almost *a fortiori* applies to the post-adjudicative phase: parties should (endeavour) not to give into pressure of public comments as this is 'unlikely to be helpful to those negotiations'.[46] On the other hand, 'a diplomatic effort to solve the dispute' may explicitly take into account 'the timing of the judgment' and use 'it as an opportunity to bring the parties together'.[47]

The fact that the parties have to regulate an issue not touched upon by the Court because it was not part of their submissions, and this in order to reach 'a comprehensive solution', could be the reason for the delay in concluding an agreement implementing the judgment.[48]

Provisions made in the Special Agreement for the post-adjudicative phase are rightly so considered to be a positive factor for the compliance with the Court's judgment. On the other hand, if the Court is not more precise than formulating or reaffirming 'an obligation of both sides to negotiate, particularly if the very reason the parties had seized the Court had been their inability to find a negotiated solution', it is not surprising that difficulties or delays on the implementation of the judgment do arise.[49]

In its Application a State may not only ask the Court to adjudge and declare the existence of a particular obligation for the Respondent, but additionally also to declare that the dispute is one which is suitable for submission for judicial settlement, arbitration or conciliation under the conditions the Court has to determine.[50]

Negotiations as a mechanism to settle the dispute did not figure among the possible choices for the obvious reason that prior negotiations had not been successful. As a result the Court is not being called upon to declare that the dispute is one which is fit for another round of negotiations.

---

43 *Case between* Botswana *and Namibia, I.C.J. Reports 1999*, Separate opinion by Judge Kooijmans, at p. 1148, paras. 23 and 24 (emphasis added).

44 *Frontier Dispute (Benin/Niger), I.C.J. Reports 2005*, Dissenting opinion by Judge *ad hoc* Bennouna, at p. 163, para. 49.

45 It has to be noted that it is 'not appropriate for a court to send back a case to states instead of filling gaps in the law for the sake of the solution of the dispute': A. Paulus, 'International Adjudication', p. 222.

46 D. Bowett, 'Developments', 187.

47 L. Boisson de Chazournes, M. Kohen and J. Vinuales, 'Introduction', p. 5.

48 C. Schulte, *Compliance*, p. 223.

49 C. Schulte, *Compliance*, p. 274.

50 *Interhandel Case (interim measures of protection), Order of 24 October 1957: I.C.J. Reports 1957*, p. 105 at p. 106.

In its submissions an Applicant may request the Court to declare that the parties have a legal duty to negotiate for the establishment of a particular regime[51] or on how a right which is in dispute between the parties and which it also asked the Court to declare shall be guaranteed.[52]

This may also be the result of a counterclaim on reparation[53] or of the acceptance during the hearings by (one of) the parties of the need for direct bilateral post-adjudicative negotiations to solve problems arising from the Court upholding either of the submissions.[54]

Non-appearance may be quite 'indicative of a lack of any readiness to compromise and a bad sign for the prospects for compliance'.[55] In addition to this factor, an amicable resolution of the dispute may also be seriously hampered by 'ultimatums from both sides, coupled with the impossibility of face-to-face negotiations'.[56]

The Role of the Court

A basic condition for this mode of functional interaction to operate properly is not only that the Court 'should make its legal assessments and conclusions comprehensible and thereby acceptable to litigant States', but moreover that the judgment is seen by both parties 'as logical and fair in its historical, political and social dimensions'.[57]

President Owada's point that it is 'not the enforceability of the decision but rather the legitimacy and persuasiveness based on the reasonableness of the proposition given by the Court'[58] which ensures the adherence of the parties, applies to all orders and judgments of the Court with regard to post-adjudicative negotiations. Hence the impact of the quality of the Court's pronouncements on the success or failure of post-adjudicative negotiations should certainly not be underestimated.

Clarifying statements on how and under what conditions the new obligations flowing from the operative part of the judgment should be implemented in the post-adjudicative phase are necessary[59] also in order to reduce the risk of ensuing difficulties which may then bring (one of) the parties to invoke Article 60 on interpretation.

Finally, the Court has 'no power to pronounce upon the failure of a party to discharge the obligations flowing from a judgment unless such failure has led to the institution of new proceedings'.[60] Hence 'diplomatic means remain, for better or for worse, the last resort to guarantee the outcome of third-party adjudication', although sometimes it is only following negotiations after several judgments of the Court that a solution to the dispute has been found.[61]

The Impact of the 'Nature' of the Court's Judgment

In general terms one can only agree that:

---

51 *Fisheries Jurisdiction (United Kingdom v. Iceland), I.C.J. Reports 1974*, at p. 7, para. 11 (e).

52 *Great Belt case, I.C.J. Reports 1991*, at p. 14, para. 6 (d) (Finland).

53 *Germany v. Italy case, I.C.J. Reports 2010*, p. 312, para. 3 *in fine*.

54 *Case between Qatar and Bahrain, I.C.J. Reports 2001*, Dissenting opinion by Judge *ad hoc* Torres Bernardez, at p. 272, para. 32.

55 C. Schulte, *Compliance*, p. 155.

56 C. Schulte, *Compliance*, p. 169.

57 *Case between the DRC and Uganda, I.C.J. Reports 2005*, Separate opinion by Judge Kooijmans, at p. 307, para. 4.

58 *Request for Interpretation of the Judgment of 15 June 1962 in the Case concerning The* Temple of Preah Vihear (Cambodia v. Thailand) *(Cambodia v. Thailand), Provisional Measures, Order of 18 July 2011, I.C.J. Reports 2011*, Dissenting opinion by Judge Owada, at p. 561, para. 16.

59 *Avena and Other Mexican Nationals (Mexico v. United States of America), Judgment, I.C.J. Reports 2004*, p. 12, Dissenting opinion by Judge *ad hoc* Sepulveda, at p. 121, para. 64.

60 M. Hudson, *The Permanent Court*, at p. 595.

61 Judge Bernardo Sepulveda-Amor, 'Opening Remarks' in L. Boisson de Chazournes, M. Kohen and J. Vinuales (eds), *Diplomatic and Judicial Means of Dispute Settlement* (Leiden and Boston, 2013), p. 9.

la nature transactionnel d'une decision ne constitue pas une garantie de mise en oeuvre, mais elle reste toutefois la plus à même de satisfaire les Etats et de permettre *la résolution défintive du ltige*, ce qui explique en partie la tendance des juridictions à préférer des résultats de cette nature.[62]

The functional interaction carries with it that the nature of the Court's judgment will have factual and legal consequences on the post-adjudicative negotiations.

A judgment in which the Court upholds a preliminary objection to its jurisdiction may have an impact on the willingness to and unfolding of post-adjudicative negotiations.

A judgment in which the Court upholds a preliminary objection to the admissibility of the claim may also have an albeit probably different impact on the willingness to and unfolding of post-adjudicative negotiations.

Although it can be maintained, as a matter of principle, that a judgment on preliminary objections 'does not create legal obligations *stricto sensu* which the parties ... are required to comply with',[63] '[s]ome elements of *res judicata* attaches to' the findings of the Court that the parties are in a legal dispute the subject-matter of which it has objectively determined.[64]

It is another matter altogether to draw the conclusion that a party that sees its preliminary objection rejected by the Court 'does not suffer any legal consequences'.[65] Indeed, in its reasoning the Court's pronouncements on, for instance, the format and the subject-matter of the prior negotiations may have an impact on both parties' positions during the post-adjudicative negotiations. This impact may occur whether the Court outright declines jurisdiction or declares the Application inadmissible because the compromissory condition of prior negotiations had not been fulfilled. It is not completely unlikely in the latter case once the judgment has begun influencing in a calming and positive way the relations between the parties, that the former Applicant may decide to properly start the process of negotiations.

Of course, 'lack of jurisdiction does not in itself indicate that the dispute is not justiciable, nor does it relieve the parties of their duty to pursue peaceful settlement on the basis of international law'. The interaction fully certainly reclaims its functional role when the Court calls upon the parties to settle their dispute in a situation where 'all attempts at pursuing other peaceful means were rejected by the Respondent State before the case was brought before the Court'.[66]

Judicial calls for negotiations can be made explicit and binding, less explicit and non-binding or rather implicit. In the latter case parties 'preserve their entire freedom in the implementation of the judgment, within the limits of the judgment itself, yet with more clear and concrete elements upon which to develop diplomatic means'.[67]

Such calls or recommendations could be part and parcel of the Court's judicial strategy 'either to prevent new differences arising or to somehow remedy the Court's inability to address and resolve certain important aspects of the dispute, be that because of its limited competence or because the applicable law was in flux'.[68]

Such a judicial recommendation 'creates *some* legal obligation which, however rudimentary' and imperfect it might be, 'is nevertheless a legal obligation': although the State concerned is 'not bound to accept' it, that State 'is bound to give it due consideration in good faith'.[69]

Both the source of the duty to negotiate and the objective of the forthcoming process of post-adjudicative negotiations being identified by the Court thus acquire a *judicial imprimatur*.

---

62 G. Giraudeau, *Les différends territoriaux*, p. 141 (emphasis added).

63 *Bosnian Genocide case, I.C.J. Reports 2007*, Dissenting opinion by Judge *ad hoc* Kreca, at pp. 468–9, para. 17.

64 *Certain Property case, I.C.J. Reports 2005*, Dissenting opinion by Judge *ad hoc* Berman, at p. 81, para. 28.

65 *Bosnian Genocide case, I.C.J. Reports 2007*, Dissenting opinion by Judge *ad hoc* Kreca, at p. 469, para.17.

66 *Aerial Incident between Pakistan and India, I.C.J. Reports 2000*, Dissenting opinion by Judge Al-Khasawneh, at p. 48, para. 2 and at pp. 48–9, para. 3.

67 P. Sandonato, 'Diplomatic and Judicial Means', p. 83.

68 L. Boisson de Chazorunes and A. Angelini, 'Between Saying and Doing', p. 173. For two opposite views on the use by the Court of this technique see J. d'Aspremont, 'The Recommendations Made by the International Court of Justice' (2007) 56, *International and Comparative Law Quarterly*, 185–97. Thirlway observed that invitations to negotiate can be found in separate opinions of individual judges: 'The Recommendations', 155, note 24.

69 *South-West Africa – Voting procedure, Advisory Opinion of 7 June 1955: I.C.J. Report 1955*, p. 67, Separate opinion by Judge Lauterpacht, at pp. 118–19 (*mutatis mutandis* on a recommendation by the GA).

What is stated in the rulings, pronouncements in the operative paragraphs is 'thus established with the full weight of the Court's judicial authority'[70] but a judicial prescription that 'certain behaviour (such as post-adjudicative negotiations) is obligatory in the future' has only binding force if it is done in the operative part of the judgment.[71] Moreover, there is no doubt that post-adjudicative developments in the relevant branch of international law may 'virtually' displace 'the Court's orders regarding negotiations'.[72]

Traditionally, a distinction is drawn between requests for a declaratory judgment and a judgment which requires one of the parties or both of them to take action which may certainly include an obligation to negotiate.[73]

Even when the ultimate objective of the litigation is to 'obtain the termination of certain conduct' which the Applicant considers to be illegal, a request for a declaratory judgment is normally sufficient[74] because 'in contentious proceedings involving a genuine dispute' its fundamental purpose is 'to clarify and stabilize the legal relations between the parties'.[75]

However, it should be noted that the operative paragraphs of a judgment may contain both declaratory and prescriptive parts, as illustrated for instance by the *Gabcikovo case*,[76] although a Respondent may argue that the 'relief available to the Applicant State in these proceedings … is limited to the rendering of a declaratory judgment'.[77]

Declaratory judgments which 'die bestehende Rechtslage zwischen den Parteien bloss festellen, die aber weder in diese Rechte im Sinne einer anderung eingreien noch konkrete Verhaltensordnungen enthalten', and hence 'nicht vollstreckbar sind',[78] still do possess a strong preventive function.[79]

Moreover, as it does interfere much less with the freedom of conduct and decision of the parties than prescriptive judgments, it is up to the parties to elaborate between themselves the concrete implementation of the judgment.[80] Post-adjudicative negotiations may depart from the Court's pronouncements in such declaratory judgments,[81] leaving them much room for their diplomatic negotiations.[82]

Examples of declaratory judgments are jurisdictional judgments, decisions on admissibility, and decisions on applications to intervene.[83]

The fact that a judgment is purely of a declaratory nature does not necessarily rule out of course the parties feeling the need for a process of post-adjudicative negotiations. Indeed, a declaratory judgment endowed with *res judicata* force 'may provide the basis for diplomatic negotiations',[84] during which the parties have to respect what the Court has said 'with regard to the legal issues that were in issue'.[85]

A judgment on the merits creates legal duties for the parties, so that 'neither party can by unilateral means free itself from its obligation under international law to carry out the judgment in good faith'.[86]

---

70 *Bosnian Genocide case, I.C.J. Reports 2007*, at p. 94, para. 123.

71 R. Bernhardt, 'Article 59' in A. Zimmermann, C. Tomuschat and C. Tams (eds), *The Statute of the International Court of Justice: A Commentary* (Oxford, 2006), p. 1242, MN 35; and C. Brown, 'Article 59' in A. Zimmermann, C. Tomuschat and K. Oellers-Frahm (eds), *The Statute of the International Court of Justice: A Commentary* (Oxford, 2012), pp. 1416–46, at p. 1431, MN 41.

72 C. Murphy, 'The World Court', 565.

73 *Nuclear Tests (New Zealand v. France), I.C.J. Reports 1974*, at p. 466, para. 30.

74 *Nuclear Tests (Australia v. France), I.C.J. Reports 1974*, Joint dissenting opinion by Judges Oneyama, Dillard, Jimenez de Arechaga and Waldock, at p. 314, para. 8.

75 *Ibid.*, at p. 321, para. 21.

76 *Gabcikovo case, I.C.J. Reports 1997*, at pp. 82–4, para. 155.

77 *Bosnian Genocide case, I.C.J. Reports 2007*, at p. 73, para. 66 (Serbia and Montenegro).

78 S. Wittich, 'Das Feststellkungsurteil im Verfahren vor dem Internationalen Gerechsthof' (2006) 44 *Archiv des Völlkerrechts* 1, 1–32 at 5.

79 S. Wittich, 'Das Feststellungsurteil', 13.

80 S. Wittich, 'Das Feststellungsurteil', 14

81 S. Wittich, 'Das Feststellungsurteil', 15.

82 S. Wittich, 'Das Feststellungsurteil', 30.

83 S. Wittich, 'Das Feststellungsurteil', 10.

84 *The Northern Cameroons case, I.C.J. Reports 1963*, Dissenting opinion by Judge *ad hoc* Beb a Don, at p. 196.

85 R. Kolb, *The ICJ*, p. 836.

86 *Bosnian Genocide case, I.C.J. Reports 2007*, Dissenting opinion by Judge *ad hoc* Kreça, at p. 469, para. 15 referring to the *Socobel case* of the PCIJ.

The Court's judgment may reaffirm 'important obligations of a continuing character', including the duty to co-operate.[87]

Dissenting judges may hold a different view as to the need, feasibility, the basis and the legal framework of the post-adjudicative negotiations following their position taken with regard to the Court's decision on the merits of the case.[88]

The Court may indicate provisional measures 'so as to maintain the peace that is necessary to such negotiations as the Parties have contemplated or might be contemplating, and the execution of the judgment that the Court might hand down in the case'.[89]

Already at the stage of the indication of provisional measures the Court's decision may be aiming at contributing to an atmosphere conducive to ongoing negotiations or to post-adjudicative negotiations required to implement the judgment still to come.[90]

Although the binding force of the measures comes to an end on the day of the delivery of the judgment, and even if their content is not reaffirmed in the operative part of the judgment on the merits, the Court's Order may not only have influenced the readiness and progress of (resumed) negotiations during the proceedings, but it may also have a similar impact on the post-adjudicative phase.

In the *Fisheries Jurisdiction case* between Germany and Iceland the parties did not enter into a provisional agreement. However, the Court made it clear that they 'are not at liberty to conduct their fishing activities in the disputed waters without limitation'. Indeed, both parties were ordered by the Court in its judgment to negotiate in good faith, involving 'in the circumstances of the case an obligation upon the Parties to pay reasonable regard to each other's rights and to conservation requirements pending the conclusion of the negotiations'.[91] This can:

> leave the impression of a tendency to preserve the substance of the interim measures indicated and extend their practical effects beyond the date of the delivery of the final judgment – with replacement of the order by the prescribed duty to negotiate as a new basis for the continued interim protection of the 'respective rights of either party.[92]

Protecting the Position of Third States

As far as the position of third States is concerned, especially maritime, and to a lesser extent territorial delimitation cases bring to the fore some of the difficulties the functional interaction between adjudication and post-adjudicative negotiations might encounter. A negative decision on a request to intervene obviously cannot 'limit or nullify its ability to establish the (potential) merits of its claims in due course',[93] and this may happen for instance in the process of post-adjudicative negotiations with (one of) the parties.

In one of the most recent cases Judge Abraham persuasively pointed to the paradoxical situation that although the object of intervention is precisely to enable the Court in cases of maritime delimitation to follow its practice of not fixing the end point until it 'meets the area in which a third State has rights', the Court may refuse intervention 'on the pretext' that 'the information provided in the proceedings for permission to intervene is sufficiently complete':[94] clarification on rights claimed by third States is paramount in this regard.

According to Judge Gaja it 'seems paradoxical that, in case of maritime delimitation, the only way for a third State to submit information about its interest of a legal nature which may be affected by a decision of the Court would be to make an application that the Court considers inadmissible'. Hence, the Court

87 *Pulp Mills case, I.C.J. Reports 2010*, Separate opinion by Judge Greenwood, at pp. 231–2, para. 29.

88 *Bosnian Genocide case, I.C.J. Reports 2007*, Dissenting opinion by Judge Oda, at pp. 167–8, paras. 31–2 and Dissenting opinion by Judge Herczeg, at pp. 202–3.

89 *Land and Maritime Boundary case, I.C.J. Reports 1996*, Declaration by Judge *ad hoc* Mbaye, at pp. 33–4.

90 *Ibid.*

91 *Fisheries Jurisdiction case (FRG. v. Iceland), I.C.J. Reports 1974*, at p. 202, para. 70.

92 J. Sztucki, *Interim Measures*, p. 205.

93 *Territorial and Maritime Dispute (Nicaragua v. Colombia), Costa Rica Application to Intervene, I.C.J. Reports 2011*, Dissenting opinion by Judge Abraham, at p. 387, para. 11.

94 *Ibid.*, at p. 387, para. 12.

'should establish a new procedural mechanism short of intervention that would allow third States to submit information which they consider useful in order to protect their interests of a legal nature'.[95]

The functional interaction operates in a particular way when the would-be intervener has signed a maritime delimitation treaty with one of the parties and its the ratification has been suspended pending the proceedings and is applied on a provisional basis in common agreement.[96]

The actual outcome of the judgment, without the intervention being granted, and in line with the Court's practice not to fix the maritime boundary in a way which might affect the rights of third States, but letting prevail the Applicant's claim in a particular area, would not only 'extinguish the essential basis' of that treaty but it would also 'require new delimitation' between the would-be intervener and its new neighbour.[97] This is an example of a quite distorting impact of a judicial decision on the functional interaction with post-adjudicative negotiations.[98]

The Court declining to set a final endpoint and deciding 'that the boundary line continues until it reaches 'the area in which the rights of third State may be affected' does happen whether or not raised in intervention proceedings.[99]

In maritime delimitation cases the Court has been facing a dilemma in order to protect the rights of third States.[100]

When the Court has localized a tripoint, the parties to the case will rely on this decision *vis-à-vis* a third State in order to refuse any concession as far the determination of this tripoint is concerned.[101]

When the Court is looking for a balance between the legal interests of the parties before it and those of third States, and which is satisfactory to all parties concerned, it is more like an exercise of conciliation rather than a judgment decided in accordance with international law.[102]

Perhaps the principle of the protection of the rights of a third party is maybe not a fundamental principle of the international legal system[103] as it stands today, and situates itself within the context of a more institutionalized justice, whereas applying the *Monetary Gold* rule belongs to the more traditional contractual approach to justice.[104]

In delimitation cases an individual judge may attach sketch-maps in the hope that his view of equity in the drawing of a boundary 'may in future assist governments in their negotiations with neighbouring States',[105] or the judge may formulate 'some observations which could provide guidance to the Parties for further conduct'.[106]

---

95 *Ibid.*, Declaration by Judge *ad hoc* Gaja, at pp. 417–18, paras. 4–5.

96 *Ibid.*, Dissenting opinion by Judge Abraham, at p. 388, para. 13.

97 *Territorial and Maritime Dispute (Nicaragua v. Colombia), Costa Rica Application to Intervene, I.C.J. Reports 2011*, Joint dissenting opinion by Judges Cançado Trindade and Yusuf, at p. 409, para. 18.

98 Without an assessment of 'the point at which a third State may have an interest of a legal nature' the Court 'risks placing a directional arrow within a area which is subject to claim by a third State'. Such an approach could be seen to have prejudged subsequent delimitation negotiations in the post-adjudicative phase: *Territorial and Maritime Dispute (Nicaragua v. Colombia), Costa Rica Application to Intervene, I.C.J. Reports 2011*, Dissenting opinion by Judge Donoghue, at pp. 416–17, para. 7.

99 *Territorial and Maritime Dispute (Nicaragua v. Colombia), Honduras Application to Intervene, I.C.J. Reports 2011*, Dissenting opinion by Judge Donoghue, at pp. 477–9, para. 19.

100 For a succinct but incisive view of the relevant cases and the ingenious way the Court has sought to solve the problem see E. Jouannet, 'L'impossible protection des droits du tiers par la Cour internationale de Justice dans les affaires de delimitation maritime', *La mer et son droit. Mélanges offerts à Laurent Luchini et Jean-Pierre Quéneudec* (Paris, 2003), pp. 315–41.

101 E. Jouannet, 'L'impossible', p. 330.

102 E. Jouannet, 'L'impossible', p. 331.

103 E. Jouannet, 'L'impossible', p. 333.

104 E. Jouannet, 'L'impossible', pp. 340–41.

105 *Case between Qatar and Bahrain, I.C.J. Reports 2001*, Separate opinion by Judge Oda, at p. 142, para. 41.

106 Case *between Botswana and Namibia, I.C.J. Reports 1999*, Separate opinion by Judge Kooijmans, at p. 1148, para. 23.

8.4 Disagreement between the Parties on the Court's Precise Role and on the Room for and Scope of Post-adjudicative Negotiations

Disagreement between the parties on the precise scope of the Court's task and on the room for and scope of their post-adjudicative negotiations, as reflected in their respective submissions, is bound to have a functional impact on the object and unfolding purpose of the post-adjudicative negotiations.

The adoption by the Court of submissions 'framed in such broad and general terms that their acceptance would still have left wide room for substantive negotiations and for substantial disagreement between the Parties ... would not have advanced the settlement of the dispute to any great extent'.[107] Moreover, such an approach 'would in fact have made the implementation of the Court's judgment depend upon the subsequent agreement of the Parties'.[108]

Indeed, one party may be holding the view that the judicial intervention should be limited to the Court determining the starting point of a maritime delimitation which from that point onwards should be agreed between the parties on the basis of an arbitral award, while the other party may request the Court to declare what the single maritime boundary is.[109] It is only in the first scenario that the ruling of the Court would function as one of the bases for the post-adjudicative negotiations.[110]

By handing down its judgment on the merits of a case, the Court, in the proper exercise of its judicial function, inevitably and substantially changes the factual and legal relations between the parties. That in the process of post-adjudicative negotiations as in the pre-adjudicative phase and during the proceedings parties may propose 'some possible methods' for implementation, followed by a decision of the other party not to pursue those possibilities,[111] is part of a genuine process of negotiations and does not necessarily manifest a dispute over the meaning or scope of the relevant obligations as pronounced by the Court.

In maritime and territorial delimitation disputes the distinction between delimitation and demarcation is of utmost importance for the functional role of post-adjudicative negotiations, i.e. the ensuing need or absence of it for real negotiations to be conducted.[112]

Demarcation consists of an exercise to determine how a line of delimitation is to be given expression on the ground or in the maritime area: it is a task 'of a technical nature, and not within the judicial field which belongs to the Court'.[113] Demarcation involves 'correction of a number of "minor defects" in the instruments, the elimination of various uncertainties and the solution of any existing geographical difficulties' to be settled by the parties in light of the Court's decision 'on the delimitation of the boundary as a whole',[114] and thus becoming part of the subject-matter of the post-adjudicative process of negotiations.[115]

A boundary line as established by instruments and which is not being disputed by the parties may not be modified by the Court; hence it would be up to the parties to find a solution to any resultant problems. The Court, already taking into account the possible need for post-adjudicative negotiations, also and in the same vain determines the purpose of such a process, namely 'with a view to respecting the rights and interests of the local population'.[116]

Parties may have included in their Special Agreement that a special Demarcation Commission would begin the demarcation within three months of the delivery of the judgment, and this until completion.[117] When,

107 *Continental Shelf case between Tunisia and Libya, I.C.J. Reports 1982*, Separate opinion by Judge *ad hoc* Jimenez de Arechaga, at pp. 100–101, para. 3.

108 *Ibid.*, at pp. 101–2, para. 6.

109 *Territorial and Maritime Dispute between Nicaragua and Honduras, I.C.J. Reports 2007*, at p. 666, para. 17 and at p. 668, para. 18.

110 *Ibid.*, at p. 763, para. 321 (4).

111 *Request for the Interpretation of the Avena judgment, I.C.J. Reports 2008*, Joint dissenting opinion by Judges Owada, Tomka and Keith, at p. 345, para. 14.

112 *Land and Maritime Boundary case, I.C.J. Reports 2002*, at p. 343, para. 54; see also at pp. 359–60, paras. 84 and 85 for the difference according to the Court.

113 *Temple of Preah Vihear case, I.C.J. Reports 1962*, Dissenting opinion by Judge Moreno Quintana, at p. 69.

114 *Land and Maritime Boundary case, I.C.J. Reports 2002*, at p. 358, para. 80 (Cameroon).

115 G. Giraudeau, *Les différends territoriaux*, at p. 94.

116 *Land and Maritime Boundary case, I.C.J. Reports 2002*, at p. 374, para. 123.

117 *Land, Island and Maritime Frontier Dispute, I.C.J. Reports 1992*, at p. 358, para. 4, Article 6, 1.

however, parties disagree as to the respective role of the special Demarcation Commission and the Chamber they also disagree on the scope of the post-adjudicative negotiations.[118]

There is, however, no margin for further negotiations between the parties within the context of that Commission when the Chamber considers it its duty to give such indications as to enable the Commission 'to demarcate it by a [merely] technical operation'.[119]

The Court may reject the argument that its task would be limited to just declaring 'the basis of delimitation' and thus leaving 'the precise articulation (or demarcation) of the alignment to negotiation between the parties',[120] as that 'would not be a complete discharge of its duty to determine the dispute'. Delimitation should be defined by the Court 'in such a way' that 'any questions which might still remain' would be 'matters strictly relating to hydrographic technicalities which the Parties, with the help of their experts, can certainly resolve'.[121]

In the Court's view the functional interaction comes to an end with the delivery of its judgment; as for the remaining questions of a purely technical nature the parties can rely on their experts, meaning that no real political discussion would then be needed.

In a different case the Court may have been 'addressing the task of States in negotiation' as a result of the terms of the compromis.[122]

8.5 The Potential Reach and Limits of the Court's Multifunctional Role with Regard to Post-adjudicative Negotiations

The Freedom Left for the Parties

Once the Court has delivered its judgment (endowed with *res judicata* authority) the parties – whether they have participated willingly or unwillingly in the proceedings – regain their pre-adjudicatory freedom of action, but this time subject of course not only to Article 94 of the UN Charter but also to the (new) rights and obligations contained in the judgment's operative paragraphs because *res judicata* entails an authority which 'réside dans l'acceptation du pouvoir hiérarchique du tribunal *vis-à-vis* des parties'.[123]

How far can the parties go in their negotiations without putting in jeopardy the principle of *res judicata*?[124] This regained but limited freedom of action entails that the *res judicata* authority of the Court's judgment may be affected by the impact of national interests on the implementation process.[125] The prominence of the diplomatic component in the post-adjudicative phase 'stresses the relativity of the *res judicata* whose content can be modified by the parties either fully consensually or as the result of a pragmatic accommodation of interests imposed by one party's rejection of the pronouncement'.[126]

The parties cannot 'claim to modify the legal findings of the judgment itself' which 'as a judicial act, must, therefore, be distinguished from the disputes issues to which it relates' and which the parties can resolve 'in any way they wish'.[127]

The parties' determination to put an end to their dispute may bring them to depart from the actual terms of the judgment or to defer its implementation.[128] However, post-adjudicative negotiations cannot affect the

---

118 *Ibid.*, at p. 385, para. 39.

119 *Ibid.*, at p. 386, para. 39. In such a situation there is a dual functional link between the task of the Chamber and that of the special Demarcation Commission as provided in Article 5 of the Special Agreement : at p. 390, para. 47 and at p. 385, para. 39.

120 *Jan Mayen case, I.C.J. Reports 1993*, at p. 56, para. 41 (Norway).

121 *Ibid.*, at p. 78, para. 89.

122 *Ibid.*, at p. 63, para. 57.

123 L. Brant, 'L'autorité des arrêts de la Cour internationale de Justice' in C. Apostolides (ed.), *Les arrêts de la Cour internationale de Justice* (Dijon, 2005), pp. 141–68, at p. 168.

124 J.-L. Amougou, 'La négociation', p. 1520.

125 J.-L. Amougou, 'La négociation', p. 1527.

126 L. Boisson de Chazournes and A. Angelini, 'Between Saying and Doing', p. 166.

127 R. Kolb, *The ICJ*, p. 774.

128 J.-L. Amougou, 'La négociation', p. 1528.

meaning and scope of a judgment, for instance when a request pursuant to Article 60 of the Statute is made.[129] The mode of seising the Court will inevitably influence the smooth or difficult implementation as such.

To the extent that the *res judicata* authority is considered not to be limited to the proper implementation of a judgment but as a judicial contribution to the final settlement of the dispute, the *res judicata* authority may be strengthened by post-adjudicative negotiations.[130] This certainly applies to cases where the parties resorted to the Court merely to receive indications for their post-adjudicative negotiations on the merits of the dispute.[131]

In case there is no post-adjudicative agreement departing from the operative paragraphs, the Court's judgment will be definitive and binding.[132]

Given the perhaps narrow formulation of the submissions, or because of other circumstances such as *lacunae* in the international legal order, the Court may not have 'definitively settled the dispute'; but the Court's findings may have left 'the parties with a clearer understanding of their respective rights and obligations' under a particular Convention, 'thereby facilitating negotiations'.[133]

A pronouncement by the Court on the rights and duties of the parties under existing international law in a way which could have a forward reach would be compatible with its judicial function. Declaring the law as it might be at a later time such as the expiration of an interim agreement would go beyond the powers of any tribunal.[134]

This also means that, given that 'the possibility of the law changing is ever present',[135] the greater the lapse of time between the delivery of a judgment containing directions to the parties with regard to the post-adjudicative negotiations and the actual start of this process, the greater the potential margin of freedom left to the parties.[136]

During 'fresh' post-adjudicative negotiations 'Parties will have the benefit of the judicial appraisal of their respective rights, and of certain guidelines defining their scope', that is in case the Court also gives the contours of the rights the parties have to take into account: their own respective rights and the rights of other States concerned.[137]

A judgment of the Court 'obviously cannot preclude the Parties from benefitting from any subsequent developments in the pertinent rules of international law'.[138]

The 'modficiation of judgments in light of changing circumstances is not, in fact, a judicial function. It is for the parties – they alone are the *domini negotii*, and it is they who have the primary competence when it comes to implementing a judgment'.[139]

It was rightly noted that the Court could not take notice 'of future events, contingencies or situations that may arise consequent on the holding or withholding of negotiations'[140] and that in case of post-adjudicative problems parties could always request the Court for an interpretation of the judgment rendered.[141]

129 *Request for the Interpretation of the Judgment of 15 June 1962 in the Case concerning the* Temple of Preah Vihear (Cambodia v. Thailand*) (Cambodia v. Thailand), Judgment, I.C.J. Reports 2013*, at p. 306, para. 75.

130 J.-L. Amougou, 'La négociation', p. 1530.

131 J-L. Amougou, 'La négociation', p. 1536.

132 *Application for Revision and Interpretation of the Judgment of 24 February 1982 in the Case concerning the* Continental Shelf (Tunisia/Libyan Arab Jamahiriya*) (Tunisia v. Libyan Arab Jamahiriya), Judgment, I.C.J. Reports 1985*, at pp. 218–19, paras. 47–8 and at p. 229, paras. 67–8.

133 C. Schulte, *Compliance*, p. 107.

134 *Fisheries Jurisdiction (United Kingdom v. Iceland), I.C.J. Reports 1974*, at p. 19, para. 40.

135 *Ibid.*

136 As far as negotiations in general are concerned it has to be recognized that 'with the passage of time – certain provisions may gain or lose in importance in a way not foreseen in the negotiations': *Aerial Incident between Pakistan and India, I.C.J. Reports 2000*, Dissenting opinion by Judge Al-Khasawneh, at p. 59, para. 36.

137 *Fisheries Jurisdiction (United Kingdom v. Iceland), I.C.J. Reports 1974*, at p. 33, para. 78.

138 *Ibid.*, at p. 33, para. 77.

139 R. Kolb, *The ICJ*, p. 808.

140 *Fisheries Jurisdiction (United Kingdom v. Iceland), I.C.J. Reports 1974*, Declaration by Judge Singh, at p. 43.

141 *Ibid.*, Separate opinion by Judge Waldock, at p. 125, para. 46.

Judicial Determination of the Legal Framework for the Negotiations: Functional Interaction Operates Both Ways

The Court may in rendering its judgment provide the parties with its 'assistance juridictionnelle',[142] which may be immediate or may take place at a later stage.

The Court may merely invite or recommend the parties to negotiate. Alternatively, and depending on the submissions, the Court may indicate to the parties the direction for the process of negotiations.

In case post-adjudicative negotiations are not successful, the Court may be called upon to play a further role, as we will review in Chapter 9. Although they made provision for such a process, the parties may disagree about the content and scope of the first round of post-adjudicative negotiations. According to one party there is an obligation to enter into negotiations in order to produce the result as required by a 1976 Convention,[143] while the other party was of the view that the process could include 'such amendments as might be made to it [the 1977 Treaty] by agreement between the Parties, further to future negotiations'.[144]

The Court's task was to determine 'what the *future* conduct of the Parties should be'. This part of the judgment 'is prescriptive rather than declaratory because it determines what the rights and obligations of the parties' are going to be.[145]

By ruling that the parties 'will have to seek agreement on the modalities of the execution of the judgment in the light of this determination, as they agreed'[146] in the relevant provision of the Special Agreement, the Court in fact and in law determined the framework of rights and obligations of the parties within which the negotiations would have to be conducted.

The functional interaction which is certainly operating in one direction when in determining this framework the Court is taking into consideration the positions adopted by the parties during the negotiations[147] also reaches its limits because during the post-adjudicative negotiations parties are under an obligation 'to consider, within the context of the 1977 Treaty, in what way the multiple objectives of the treaty can best be served, keeping in mind that all of them should be fulfilled',[148] something parties failed to observe during the process of prior negotiations .

The Court is here identifying in more detail the parameters of the negotiations to come, in this way that all of the objectives of the treaty should be fulfilled; the freedom of the parties to select some of the objectives to the detriment of some other is here being excluded.

Moreover, these objectives have to be 'pursued in a joint and integrated way'.[149] The functional interaction operates in a nuanced way as, while determining the legal parameters for the process, it is not up to the Court to also determine 'what shall be the final result of these negotiations'.[150] On the other hand, it is 'for the parties themselves to find an agreed solution that takes account of the objectives of the treaty, which must be pursued in a joint and integrated way, as well as the norms of international environmental law and the principles of the law of international watercourses'.[151]

Although the Court is indeed not determining with judicial authority the final outcome of the negotiations, it is adding international environmental law and the law on international watercourses as part of the legal framework for the process. The agreed solution has to be found by the parties 'within the cooperative context of the Treaty'.[152] Indeed, 'the survival of the Treaty' provides '*a specific framework, for the wishes of the two*

142 A. Azar, *L'Exécution*, p. 114.

143 *Gabcikovo case, I.C.J. Reports 1997*, at p. 73, para. 125 (Hungary).

144 *Ibid.*, at p. 74, para. 128 (Slovakia). This ruling was constitutive of a *pactum de contrahendo*; no such precedent existed at the time of writing (1974) by L. Marion, 'La notion', 365.

145 *Gabcikovo case, I.C.J. Reports 1997*, at pp. 75–6, para. 131.

146 *Ibid.*, at p. 76, para. 131.

147 *Ibid.*, at p. 77, para. 138.

148 *Ibid.*, at p. 77, para. 139.

149 *Ibid.*, at p. 78, para. 141.

150 *Ibid.*

151 *Ibid.*

152 *Ibid.*, at p. 78, para. 142.

States in negotiation' which 'will thus be channelled in order to avoid undesirable excesses, or conversely, any reluctance, by either Party'.[153]

One of the parties returning to the Court arguing that the other party failed to comply with that post-adjudicative obligation brings to the fore whether the Court is equipped to evaluate the parties' conduct in the realization of that judicially imposed *pactum de contrahendo*,[154] the main stumbling block being the unwillingness of international jurisprudence in general 'de ne pas pénétrer dans les intentions des Etats'.[155]

In other circumstances, although the Court may have determined that (some) islands fall with the sovereignty of the Respondent, that State may be under an obligation to negotiate with the other party 'towards a mutually acceptable joint regulatory regime' regarding certain matters. Such post-adjudicative negotiations have to take place 'within the framework of principles set out' in a particular Convention.[156]

Views of Individual Judges

The opinions held by individual judges on this aspect of the Court's multifunctional role cover a wide range of possibilities and modalities.

On the one hand, it 'is not beyond the range of [the Court's] function to indicate the nature of the legal rights involved and to provide guidelines in order to facilitate the *better* resolution of the dispute as was done in the *Continental Shelf* cases'.[157]

On the other hand, 'it would not only be improper but quite out of the question for a court of law to direct negotiations in every case or even to contemplate such a step when the circumstances did not justify the same'.[158]

Moreover, 'a *duty* to negotiate does not imply that the parties *must* immediately or later engage in negotiations'.[159] And then 'one of the parties would need to initiate them when it considered that circumstances so required. The duty to respond would then lie with the other party'.[160]

Sometimes (dissenting) judges would have preferred the Court instead of recalling certain principles to the parties to recall 'a further obligation': 'the conclusion of an agreement, the terms of which it would be for the Parties themselves to prescribe'; it should have instructed the parties 'to endeavour to reach an equitable solution through negotiations'.[161]

In 'describing the practical method to be employed for the delimitation between the Parties' the Court may '*suggest*' a particular line for a certain segment.[162]

The question has been raised whether an indication by the Court of the factors to be taken into account in the course of the negotiations is simply a suggestion to assist the parties or whether it amounts to a determination of law?[163]

When the Court refuses to examine whether a provision of a Special Agreement is in conformity with the Charter and with the Statute 'it leaves the Parties in confusion, and the supposed negotiations without any certain limits'.[164]

---

153 *Ibid.*, Dissenting opinion by Judge Bedjaoui, at p. 138, para. 65.

154 L. Marion, 'La notion', 386.

155 L. Marion, 'La notion', 389 and 392. The most far-reaching approach staying well within this limit could be found in a summary of negotiations referring to the numerous political difficulties that had caused a delay in the process of negotiations: L. Marion, 'La notion', 390, note 100.

156 *Case between Botswana and Namibia, I.C.J. Reports 1999*, Dissenting opinion by Judge Weeramantry, at p. 1195, para. 116.

157 *Fisheries Jurisdiction (United Kingdom v. Iceland), I.C.J. Reports 1974*, Separate opinion by Judge Dillard, at p. 66 (first emphasis added).

158 *Ibid.*, Declaration by Judge Singh, at p. 41.

159 *Ibid.*, Separate opinion by Judge Dillard, at p. 67.

160 *Ibid.*

161 *Case between Qatar and Bahrain, I.C.J. Reports 2001*, Joint Dissenting opinion, at p. 201, para. 180.

162 *Continental Shelf case between Tunisia and Libya, I.C.J. Reports 1982*, Dissenting opinion by Judge Oda, at p. 268, para. 177 and para. 179 (emphasis added).

163 *Jan Mayen case, I.C.J. Reports 1993*, Separate opinion by Judge Oda, at p. 105, para. 60.

164 *Continental Shelf case between Tunisia and Libya, I.C.J. Reports 1982*, Dissenting opinion by Judge Gros, at p. 147, para. 7.

The Conduct of the Parties during the Process

The recommended practice that talks in order to draft a Special Agreement should be held only 'following suitable preparation'[165] applies to all kind of negotiations, whatever their timing or subject-matter. One aspect of this preparation would certainly be that the two governments 'do everything in their power to reduce the present tensions in the area so that the negotiating process may be facilitated'[166] as they may have been urged by the Security Council in the exercise of its role under Chapter VI of the Charter.

The evident precondition for any round of negotiations to be potentially successful is that the parties have to take the necessary measures in order to create a climate that is conducive to the holding of these negotiations, whatever the phase of the functional interaction during which they are taking place.

In case of post-adjudicative negotiations based on the judgment by the Court the degree of preparations will then also depend on the preciseness of the directions given by the Court.

Once a State has made a commitment to enter into negotiations, 'it is not the Court's function to contemplate that it will not comply with it'.[167] This equally applies to post-adjudicative negotiations either on the initiative of the parties or as result of the judgment delivered by the Court obliging the party to negotiate.

The Court's directions as to how parties should conduct themselves during a process of negotiations have acquired more general applicability[168] also to post-adjudicative negotiations.

In case prior negotiations have not satisfied these conditions, the Court may make it clear to the parties that 'fresh negotiations are to take place on the basis of the present Judgment'.[169]

The Security Council also aligned itself with the general principles on negotiations as pronounced by the Court by insisting that the States should not just go through the formal process of negotiations but 'do everything within their power that this results in mutually acceptable solutions'.[170]

The Court does not hesitate to remind the parties that the principle of good faith obliges them 'to apply it in a reasonable way and in such a manner that its purpose can be realized'.[171] The fundamental and important aspect is that the 'renegotiation must be seen as a strict obligation, exactly like the good faith conduct it implies'.[172]

Moreover, the negotiations 'without pre-conditions' should be bilateral, in accordance with the Special Agreement, although the Court wisely added that, given the history of the prior negotiations, parties 'can benefit from the assistance and expertise of a third party',[173] another mode of functional interaction.

The fact that the parties may have been unable to conclude a provisional arrangement does not mean that they are at liberty 'to conduct their fishing activities in the disputed waters without limitation' given *inter alia* a catch-limitation fixed by the Court in an Order indicating provisional measures. The negotiations in good faith which the Court may order in its judgment may involve an obligation for the parties, pending the conclusion of the negotiations, to pay reasonable regard to each other's rights and to conservation requirements.[174] This may be a self-evident principle, but the Court may have found it necessary to reaffirm it.

Particular Category of Disputes May Require Different Modes of Functional Interaction

An Application filed in a delimitation case may be considered inappropriate, as delimitation 'is inherently unsuitable' for such cases 'unless there is some form of agreement on the part of the Respondent as to the

165 *Aegean Sea Continental Shelf case, I.C.J. Reports 1978*, at p. 41, para. 101 (Greece).
166 *Ibid.*, at p. 12, para. 38.
167 *Nuclear Tests (New Zealand v. France), I.C.J. Reports 1974*, at p. 477, para. 63.
168 *North Sea Continental Shelf case, I.C.J. Reports 1969*, at p. 47, para. 85.
169 *Ibid.*, at p. 48, para. 87.
170 *Aegean Sea Continental Shelf case, I.C.J. Reports 1976*, at p. 12, para. 38.
171 *Gabcikovo case, I.C.J. Reports 1997*, at p. 79, para. 142.
172 *Ibid.*, Dissenting opinion by Judge Bedjaoui, at p. 140, para. 69.
173 *Ibid.*, at p. 79, para. 143. As already indicated, in the operative paragraphs of its judgment the Court left no doubt that the parties' post-adjudicative freedom is limited to the modalities for the achievement of the objectives of the 1977 Treaty: at p. 83, para. 155, 2 (B).
174 *Fisheries Jurisdiction (Federal Republic of Germany v. Iceland), I.C.J. Reports 1974*, at p. 202, para. 70.

role and powers of the Court'[175] Virtually 'all celebrated cases on maritime delimitation were submitted to the Court on the basis of a Special Agreement between the parties'.[176]

Maritime and territorial delimitation are by nature matters between States which they have to resolve primarily and foremost by a process of negotiations. In case prior negotiations have not been successful (one of) the parties may take the alternative road to The Hague. Recourse to the Court may provide an opportunity for the functional interaction to actually become operational in various modes. On the one hand the Court's decision on the status of a particular maritime area may be 'an essential prerequisite to the process of delimitation which can then be negotiated on a realistic basis',[177] while on the other hand interaction is limited of course as the Court is bound to leave it to the parties (and to third States) to negotiate to reach an agreement on particular aspects outside the subject-matter of the dispute.[178]

The Court's view on the functional interaction found a clear expression when it considered a pre-existing additional agreement between the parties not as establishing a boundary 'but rather a process for arriving at one, which is reaching its culmination in these proceedings'.[179]

Although the Court thus rightly presents both negotiations and judicial proceedings as processes, judicial proceedings are seen as the culmination of the overall process.

An agreement between the parties may contain 'detailed provisions regarding factors to be taken into account during negotiations'.[180] The Respondent may view the pre-existing agreement as setting 'the framework for future negotiations to conclude a delimitation agreement'.[181]

One compromis may leave 'the Parties a margin for negotiations leading to a treaty' but 'in accordance with the decision of the Court', whereas another subsequent compromis with another party may 'simply provide for experts to apply the decision of the Court'.[182]

Difficulties arising in post-adjudicative negotiations may find their source in a Special Agreement submitting a delimitation dispute to the Court. Parties, while reserving for themselves the actual process of delimitation,[183] may request the Court not only to determine the applicable principles and rules of international law, but also to 'specify the practical way' in which they apply in the particular situation so that in the post-adjudicative stage experts can carry out the delimitation without any difficulties.[184]

Parties may include provisions to the effect that 'there will be no need for further negotiation between experts of the Parties regarding the factors to be taken into account in their calculations, since the Court will have determined the matter'.[185]

Indeed, after having concluded a Special Agreement to submit a dispute to the Court parties may, in spite of having conducted successful negotiations, find themselves in disagreement about what exactly they are asking the Court to do: this dispute may relate to 'the degree of precision of the judgment of the Court, and the corresponding extent or absence of freedom of the parties and their experts' in the post-adjudicative stage.[186]

From the perspective of the functional interaction the question is how precise the judgment should be and what should be left for the parties to negotiate later on, or would there be nothing left for them other than just to apply automatically, with no margin of appreciation or discretion in the post-adjudicative phase.

According to one view the parties would, after the delivery of the judgment, only have 'technical task of application' and this would leave 'no room for any difficulty to arise' between the delegations,[187] while the

175 *Jan Mayen case, I.C.J. Reports*, Separate opinion by Judge Ajibola, at p. 281, citing Norway's argument.

176 *Ibid.*, Separate opinion by Judge Ajibola, at p. 281.

177 *Land, Island and Maritime Frontier Dispute, I.C.J. Reports 1992*, at p. 603, para. 409 (El Salvador).

178 *Ibid.*, at pp. 608–9, para. 420.

179 *Maritime Delimitation in the Black Sea, I.C.J. Reports 2009*, at p. 87, para. 70.

180 *Ibid.*

181 *Ibid.*, at p. 124, para. 194 (Romania).

182 *Continental Shelf case between Libya and Malta, I.C.J. Reports 1984*, at p. 10, para. 14 (Article III) and at p. 14, para. 20.

183 *Continental Shelf case between Tunisia and Libya, I.C.J. Reports 1981*, at p. 10, para. 15.

184 *Continental Shelf case between Tunisia and Libya, I.C.J. Reports 1982*, at p. 21, para. 2 (Article 1).

185 *Ibid.*, at p. 21, para. 2, Articles 1 and 2 and at p. 40, para. 30.

186 *Ibid.*, at p. 39, para. 26.

187 *Ibid.*, at p. 39, para. 27 (Tunisia).

other view is that the Court's task is 'to indicate the additional considerations and factors which have to be taken into account and balanced' after the delivery of the judgment by the parties themselves.[188]

In such a situation the Court may very well come to the conclusion that 'there is no fundamental difference of opinion' between the parties – 'only' a 'difference of emphasis as to the respective roles of the Court and of the experts of the two countries' – and consider the whole controversy as 'of minor importance'.[189]

The Court has to be 'as precise as to what it decides'; providing the parties with mere 'guidance' would run counter to Article 59 and 60 of the Statute and Article 94, para. 2 of the Rules of Court.[190]

Although it is then not part of the 'function conferred upon the Court', this 'does not prevent the Court from indicating the boundary which, in its view, would result from the application of such method as the Court may choose for the Parties to achieve the relevant determination'.[191]

What is left for the parties to do is the technical task 'of making possible the drafting of the treaty incorporating the result of the work by the experts'.[192] In such cases the Court interprets its task under the Special Agreement in such a way that post-adjudicative negotiations are being reduced to a strict minimum.

This interpretation of the Special Agreement is in line with the Court's view on the extent of its judicial role within the functional interaction – namely to determine and identify, in the light of the prior negotiations and the arguments put before it during the proceedings, the essential issues in dispute. This is the essential prerequisite for the Court to perform its duty: to settle a dispute between the parties in such a final and decisive way that the potential of further difference and tension between them in the aftermath of its judgment are substantially reduced, without overstepping the limits of the task the parties have been willing to confer upon it.

In the operative paragraphs of its judgment the functional interaction operates in a balanced way as the Court identified and determined 'the principles and rules of international law for the delimitation, to be effected by agreement in implementation'of the judgment[193] while also giving a non-exhaustive list of the 'relevant circumstances' which are to be taken 'into account in achieving an equitable delimitation'.[194]

Although there is still a margin for the parties to take into account other circumstances, and which may then be the subject of a round of negotiations, on the other hand they are under a legal obligation to take into account the circumstances listed by the Court.

Parties may also have agreed differently when jointly submitting their dispute to the Court. Indeed, 'without difficulty' necessarily 'entails the indication by the Court of the method or methods which it considers to result from the proper application of the appropriate rules and principles'. Depending on the method there will be no (equidistance line) margin for the parties or in case of another method, 'less automatic in their operation', the Court may have to give 'more detailed indications of the criteria' to be used later by the parties.[195]

With regard to the post-adjudicative phase as required by the submissions the delimitation has 'to be effected by agreement *in implementation of the present Judgment*'.[196]

In its operative paragraphs the Court gives a limitative list of circumstances and factors that the parties will have to take into account.[197] The formulation leaves no room for interpretation or doubt: they are decisive for the parties; hence the margin for negotiations is limited or may be even reduced to none.

In cases introduced by unilateral Application the Court, having 'defined the course of the maritime boundary', may *expect* the parties to determine the precise geographical co-ordinates, which the Court had 'not been asked to do … in the Parties' final submissions', and to carry out this exercise 'in accordance' with the Judgment, 'in the spirit of good neighbourliness'.[198]

---

188 *Ibid.*, at p. 39, para. 28 (Libya).
189 *Ibid.*, at pp. 39–40, para. 29.
190 *Ibid.*, at p. 40, para. 29.
191 *Ibid.*, at p. 78, para. 108.
192 *Ibid.*, at p. 40, para. 30.
193 *Ibid.*, at pp. 92–3, para. 133 (A).
194 *Ibid.*, at p. 93, para. 133 (B).
195 *Continental Shelf case between Libya and Malta, I.C.J. Reports 1985*, at p. 24, para. 19.
196 *Ibid.*, at p. 56–7, para. 79 (A).
197 *Ibid.*, at p. 57, para. 79 (B).
198 *Case concerning Maritime Dispute (Peru v. Chile), I.C.J.Reports 2014*, para. 197.

A pactum de negotiando and *de contrahendo* included in a Special Agreement will become operational upon the delivery of the judgment.[199]

Although reserving for themselves the task of delimiting the further boundaries, the parties guarantee a legally binding transition of the pre-adjudicative functional interaction through the adjudicative phase – as the agreement will be concluded 'on the basis of, and in accordance with, the principles and rules of international law found by the Court to be applicable'[200] – into the post-adjudicative phase. In such cases the Court 'will discharge its task in such a way' as to provide them 'with the requisite directions'.[201] However, the Court will not substitute itself for the parties by 'means of a detailed indication of the methods to be followed and the factors to be taken into account' during that process.[202]

Once again the functional interaction operates in a restrained but balanced way as the Court may still give 'some degree of indication' as to the possible ways in which a particular rule may be applied in a case, although the parties are free to agree upon another method.[203]

Although there is in fact no limit to the considerations the parties may wish to take into account during the post-adjudicative negotiations on a delimitation in order to reach an equitable result, the circumstances will determine the relative weight to be given to different considerations.[204]

The Court may indicate which various aspects must be taken into account in the balancing act the parties will have to perform after the delivery of the judgment.[205]

Finally, the Court may determine the end result of the post-adjudicative negotiations.[206] The Court also provides the parties with a non-exhaustive list of factors they have to take into account in the course of the negotiations.[207]

The Particular Nature of the Rights Involved May Increase or Limit the Functional Interaction

When a State claims a right against another State 'it must be a right which should be enforceable. It must be a right which if conceded by the Court, could be given effect to by the defendant State.' If an Applicant fails 'to formulate any legal right' which can be asserted against the Respondent, it is then 'only by negotiations which may result in a treaty that the modalities' can be settled. It goes without saying that the 'Court cannot be called upon to draft a treaty between' the parties.[208]

In some branches of international law the legal basis for the obligation to negotiate is (implicitly) to be found in the preferential nature of the rights at stake, such as those involved in the exercise of fisheries jurisdiction: the very nature of those rights entails that States should reach an agreement by negotiations in order to make it possible for the holder to exercise those rights and in 'order to define or delimit the extent of those rights'.[209]

The preferential nature of the rights involved also affect the functional interaction because, as 'the obligation to negotiate thus flows form the very nature of the respective rights of the Parties', it would be a proper exercise of its judicial function for the Court in such a case to direct them to negotiate.[210] Moreover, this also corresponds to the principles and provisions of the UN Charter on PSD.[211]

In proceedings instituted on a unilateral basis the Applicant may request the Court to provide the parties with some guidance as to the principles which they should take into account in their negotiations.[212]

199 *North Sea Continental Shelf case, I.C.J. Reports 1969*, at p. 6.
200 *Ibid.*, at p. 13, para. 2.
201 *Ibid.*, at p. 46, para. 84.
202 *Ibid.*, at p. 46, para.84.
203 *Ibid.*, at p. 50, para. 92.
204 *Ibid.*, at p. 50, para. 93.
205 *Ibid.*, at pp. 50–51, para. 94.
206 *Ibid.*, at p. 53, para. 101 (C), (1).
207 *Ibid.*, at p. 53, para. 101 (D).
208 *Right of Passage case, I.C.J. Reports 1957*, Dissenting opinion by Judge *ad hoc* Chagla, at p. 175.
209 *Fisheries Jurisdiction (United Kingdom v. Iceland) I.C.J. Reports 1974*, at p. 32, para. 74.
210 *Ibid.*, at p. 32, para. 75.
211 *Ibid.*
212 *Fisheries Jurisdiction (Federal Republic of Germany v. Iceland), I.C.J. Reports 1974*, at pp. 201–2, para. 68.

In proceedings commenced on the basis of a Special Agreement and pursuant to which the Court is requested to specify precisely the practical way of application of principles and rules of international law to be determined by it with regard to the delimitation of the continental shelf, mere 'guidance' does not define 'the requirement of what the Court should specify'.[213]

Although the Court may thus be called upon or take it upon itself to provide the parties with directions as to the post-adjudicative negotiations, it would 'meet with difficulties if it were itself to attempt to lay down a precise scheme for an equitable adjustment of the rights involved', as the relevant information and expertise is mainly in the possession of the parties.[214]

Moreover, the continuous *nature of the obligation to (re)negotiate* clearly stems from the fundamental objective of the primary rules involved aiming at the protection of especially vulnerable (non-)renewable resources, and this in light of ever changing scientific information.[215]

In the process of examining together 'the measures required for the conservation and development, and equitable exploitation' of fishery resources the parties have to take into account not only pre-existing agreements in force between them, but also 'such other agreements as may be reached in the matter in the course of further negotiations'.[216]

In case of preferential rights the functional interaction fundamentally determines the extent and the scope of this inherent obligation to negotiate, as the existence of an interim arrangement concluded during the course of the proceedings after the indication of provisional measures does not affect the duty of the parties 'to regulate their relations in accordance with the terms of the judgment' as soon as the interim regime ceases to be in force.[217] Moreover, the judgment 'may provide a basis for the negotiation of arrangements to follow those contained in the Interim Agreement',[218] a fine example of a rather comprehensive and integrated interaction indeed.

The Court's judgment will then constitute *a* (not *the)* basis for the negotiations in the post-adjudicative phase.

In the Court's view the 'most appropriate method for the solution of the dispute is clearly that of negotiation'.[219] In accordance with the particular subject nature of international maritime law, the Court may determine the objective of such post-adjudicative negotiations, building on its pronouncements at the stage of the indication of provisional measures.[220]

In declaring or reaffirming this obligation for the parties the Court may indicate that they have to make use of a particular institutional machinery or 'such other means as may be agreed upon as a result of international negotiations'.[221]

The intrinsic value of this case for our study situates itself at the constant functional interaction between negotiations between the parties leading to the conclusion of an interim arrangement and the subsequent judicial endorsement of what the parties have already achieved.

Parties may of course through their prior negotiations agree to include in their Special Agreement a provision according to which they would have the possibility of extending a maritime boundary to be drawn by the Court, and this by 'agreement of the parties or by recourse to third party settlement procedures'. In case they are unable to agree on the terms of such a submission, each of them 'may submit the question of the seaward extension of the maritime boundary to the Chamber'.[222]

The particular nature of the rights involved may in particular circumstances have a *limiting* effect on the functional interaction when, indeed, a duty of non-recognition, albeit expressed in a Court's advisory

213 *Continental Shelf case between Tunisia and Libya, I.C.J. Reports 1982*, at p. 40, para. 29.
214 *Fisheries Jurisdiction (United Kingdom v. Iceland) I.C.J. Reports 1974*, at p. 32, para. 73.
215 *Ibid.*, at p. 34, para. 79, (4), (e).
216 *Ibid.*, at p. 31, para. 72.
217 *Ibid.*, at p. 19, para. 39 (UK).
218 *Ibid.*
219 *Ibid.*, at p. 31, para. 73.
220 *Ibid.*
221 *Ibid.*, at p. 35, para. 79 (4) (e).
222 *Gulf of Maine case, I.C.J. Reports 1982*, at p. 8, para. 8 (4) and *I.C.J. Reports 1984*, at p. 255.

opinion, could not be so rigid 'as to preclude *all* intergovernmental dealings under all circumstances ... Under particular circumstances a limited measure of intercourse is essential'.[223]

With regard to a boundary river, certain needs for non-commercial purposes 'do not translate into rights. The Parties should reach an arrangement on the subject on their own terms. It is not for the Court to do so on their behalf', whereas relating to fishing riparian 'Parties should co-operate in making sure that this practice does not cross the threshold of fishing for commercial purposes'.[224]

8.6 Third State Intervention and Post-adjudicative Negotiations: The Diversity of the Potential Functional Interaction

The Diversity of the Functional Interaction if Intervention Has (Not) Been Requested or Has (Not) Been Granted

Both an intervening State and a third State whose application to intervene has been rejected by the Court (can) have an interest in compliance with the judgment through post-adjudicative negotiations between the original parties.

As already indicated, a request for and the granting by the Court of intervention may be useful for third States with a view to forthcoming negotiations or disputes with either of the parties or with third States, although its object is 'not to obtain from the Court by way of intervention any form or ruling or decision concerning' those negotiations or disputes.[225] The object of a formal request for intervention is to ensure that the Court's decision does not affect the third State's legal rights and interests.[226]

However, such an interest 'has to be the object of a real and concrete claim of that State, based on law, as opposed to a claim of a purely political, economic or strategic nature'.[227] This apparently rules out, at least in the Court's view, as a possible ground for a request of intervention the potential impact on future negotiations when these do not (yet) involve such a claim.

However, although the Court 'has not ruled directly upon what it regards as an improper purpose for intervention',[228] the view that the Court would be 'justified in rejecting the claim on the grounds that the request was not made in good faith' in case intervention had been requested 'for an ulterior purpose' such as 'to use these claims in conjunction with other diplomatic steps against one or more of the parties'[229] appears rather far-fetched.

On the other hand, it 'is clear that Article 62 is not intended to open the door to "political intervention" (whatever that expression could mean in the context of international litigation)'.[230]

Part of the direct costs (for a third State) of participating in a negotiation may 'involve the *disclosure of information* which may be exploited by the counterpart in future action'.[231] Unsurprisingly a would-be intervener will have to bear the same direct cost.

Although viewed from a positive perspective, Judge Gaja persuasively observed that the only way to submit information for the third State is to request intervention. Hence the Court 'should establish a new

223 *Namibia Advisory Opinion, I.C.J. Reports 1971*, Separate opinion by Judge Dillard, at p. 166.

224 *Dispute regarding Navigational and Related Rights, I.C.J. Reports 2009*, Separate opinion by Judge Skotnikov, at p. 286, para. 14 and at p. 289, para. 20.

225 *Continental Shelf case between Tunisia and Libya, I.C.J. Reports 1981*, at p. 8, para. 12 (Malta) and dissenting opinion by Judge Ago, at p. 123, para. 14.

226 *Territorial and Maritime Dispute (Nicaragua v. Colombia), Costa Rica Application to Intervene, I.C.J. Reports 2011*, at p. 354, para. 12 and at p. 357, para. 19, and *Territorial and Maritime Dispute (Nicaragua v. Colombia), Honduras Application to Intervene, I.C.J. Reports 2011*, at p. 426, para. 12 and at p. 428, para. 16.

227 *Territorial and Maritime Dispute (Nicaragua v. Colombia), Costa Rica Application to Intervene, I.C.J. Reports 2011*, at p. 358, para. 26.

228 C. Chinkin, *Third Parties*, p. 172.

229 C. Chinkin, *Third Parties*, p. 172.

230 S. Rosenne, *Intervention*, p. 32.

231 G. Blum and R. Mnookin, 'When *Not* to Negotiate', p. 105.

procedural mechanism short of intervention that would allow third States to submit information which they consider useful in order to protect their interest of a legal nature'.[232]

In this regard it could be observed that a third State having a legal interest in a case may, without having to request intervention, always inform the Court about its views by submitting documents to the Court.[233]

In case the Court rejects the intervention, taking account of the would-be intervener's submission 'gives rise to a *de facto* means of third State participation that is not currently a feature of the Statute or the Rules of Court'.[234] Alternatively, 'it might be possible to develop another mechanism for the submission of third-state views'.[235]

The request by several States, pursuant to Article 53, para. 1 of the Rules of Court to be furnished with copies of the pleadings and documents annexed in a case, serves multiple functional objectives: not only to enable them to assess whether or not to request intervention but also to assess the potential impact of the arguments used by the parties in the case and its possible outcome on future (post-adjudicative) negotiations with one or both of the parties or with one or more of (the) other (requesting) States.[236]

Delimitation requiring 'the involvement of, and thus of negotiations with a third State' as parties to a case may admit, does not mean that it would be 'proper or reasonable to "compel" that third State to expose its views and its position by means of an intervention under Article 62 even before the negotiations with the neighbouring States have begun'.[237] The third State may always opt to request intervention even before such negotiations have begun, and specifically with the aim of influencing those subsequent negotiations.

Given the proper scope of Article 62 of the Statute, the fact a would-be intervener had no prior negotiations 'with the original parties leading to a solution' does not constitute one of the grounds for rejecting a request for intervention.[238]

A distinct aspect of the functional interaction manifests itself when the Court grants a request for intervention in such a situation: it would force the parties to the case 'to go directly in to judicial proceedings without previous negotiations to define the dispute, and without even determining whether a dispute in fact existed' with the third State.[239]

On the other hand, a geographical limitation on the scope of a case, could 'exclude the possibility of any compensations and trade-offs which the Parties might exchange in the course of diplomatic negotiations'.[240]

Moreover, as tripoints 'are the most difficult and delicate issues in any delimitation' it is arguable that 'their establishment by a judicial decision would predetermine the outcome of subsequent negotiations' between a would-be intervener and each of the original parties.[241]

From the functional interaction perspective it should certainly not be overlooked that a judgment providing guidelines for assigning to one of the parties areas claimed by a would-be intervener 'would have more force than the agreement' between the parties, 'since its authority could be invoked in diplomatic negotiations' and in a subsequent 'litigation it might be difficult for the Court to reach different conclusions'.[242]

A request for intervention may be 'founded on the view that a decision of the Court relating to the specific features of the area would inevitably bind' the requesting State in its relations with both original parties 'simply as a statement of law'.[243]

---

232 *Territorial and Maritime Dispute (Nicaragua v. Colombia), Costa Rica Application to Intervene, I.C.J. Reports 2011*, Declaration by Judge *ad hoc* Gaja, at pp. 417–18, paras. 4–5.

233 *Barcelona Traction case, I.C.J. Reports 1970*, Separate opinion by Judge Gros, at p. 281.

234 *Territorial and Maritime Dispute (Nicaragua v. Colombia), Honduras Application to Intervene, I.C.J. Reports 2011*, Dissenting opinion by Judge Donoghue, at p. 491, para. 57.

235 *Ibid.*, at p. 492, para. 59.

236 *Ibid.*, at p. 426, para. 8 and *Territorial and Maritime Dispute (Nicaragua v. Colombia), Costa Rica Application to Intervene, I.C.J. Reports 2011*, at p. 354, paras. 7 and 10.

237 *Land and Maritime Boundary case, I.C.J. Reports 1998*, Separate opinion by Judge Kooijmans at p. 361, para. 21.

238 *Continental Shelf case between Libya and Malta, I.C.J. Reports 1984*, Dissenting opinion by Judge Oda, at p. 108, para. 34.

239 *Ibid.*, Separate opinion by Judge *ad hoc* Jimenez de Arechaga, at p. 63, para. 25.

240 *Ibid.*, at p. 65, para. 30.

241 *Ibid.*, at p. 67, para. 33.

242 *Ibid.*, at p. 69, para. 38.

243 *Continental Shelf case between Libya and Malta, I.C.J. Reports 1981*, Separate opinion by Judge Schwebel, at p. 39.

'What is key is the probability, or at any rate the possibility', that the parties 'are seeking the Court's support for positions which, if sustained (whether in the *dispositif* or other passages of the Court's Judgment), may actually affect' the requesting State's 'particular legal interests', despite the fact that it did not submit claims against the parties.[244]

One way to save the objective of the functional interaction in such a situation would indeed consist in the Court deciding that only one of the parties 'is called upon, by geographical or other relevant circumstances, to negotiate a delimitation' with the would-be intervener or with other third States 'along certain lines or in certain sectors of the area in dispute'.[245]

Such a judgment would, despite its relative effect, 'project its consequences *erga omnes* and would constitute a most useful and significant contribution' to the resolution of the dispute between the original parties.[246]

'A virtue of this better course' – namely to grant the permission to intervene – 'would have been that, while [its] claims would of course remain', the requesting State 'would know with which other claimant to negotiate or adjudicate them'.[247]

The functional interaction does not, as far as the legal interests of third States are concerned, necessarily and in all cases result in a request for intervention. Indeed, it 'is up to the State to apply to intervene, even though the Court may, in the course of a particular case, draw the attention of third States to the possible impact that its future judgment on the merits may have on their interests'.[248]

This way the Court may contribute to the third States starting negotiations with (one of) the parties to the case before it or to the third States starting separate proceedings. A State may have decided not to intervene; in the absence of a jurisdictional ground existing between one of the parties and the third State, it 'seems quite unreal to suppose' that one of the parties would agree upon a Special Agreement for submitting the third State's claim.[249]

In case of a request for a *non-party intervention* the functional interaction operates in such a way that the intervener, after the judgment in which its rights have not been affected, then initiates negotiations with (one of) the parties on the basis of the judgment which is *res judicata* for the original parties or institutes proceedings, whereas the object of intervention *as a party* is to also 'bind the original parties to it and thus to *affect its interests of a legal nature* quite directly'.[250] As no 'State has yet been admitted to intervene as a party' this 'regime of intervention has not yet been fully worked out'.[251]

Here the impact of the functional interaction because of the *res judicata* effect is that there is no need and no possibility either for the intervener to institute proceedings against (one of) the parties afterwards. The only option under the functional interaction open to the intervener, and the original parties to the case for that matter, is to embark upon a process towards the actual implementation of the judgment. Moreover, attempting to add, through intervention as a party, a new dispute (the issue of the location of a 'tripoint' between the three States concerned) to the pending one[252] would maximize the functional interaction through the *res judicata* authority the would-be intervener would have wished for.

---

244 *Ibid.*

245 *Continental Shelf case between Libya and Malta, I.C.J. Reports 1984*, Separate opinion by Judge *ad hoc* Jimenez de Arechaga, at p. 70, para. 41.

246 *Ibid.*

247 *Continental Shelf case between Libya and Malta, I.C.J. Reports 1985*, Dissenting opinion by Judge Schwebel, at p. 178.

248 *Territorial and Maritime Dispute (Nicaragua v. Colombia), Honduras Application to Intervene, I.C.J. Reports 2011*, at p. 433, para. 34, as indeed it did in the *Land and Maritime Boundary case, I.C.J. Reports 1998*, at p. 324, para. 116.

249 *Barcelona Traction case, I.C.J. Reports 1970*, Separate opinion by Judge Jessup, at p. 185, s 43.

250 *Territorial and Maritime Dispute (Nicaragua v. Colombia), Honduras Application to Intervene, I.C.J. Reports 2011*, Dissenting opinion by Judge Donoghue, at p. 482, para. 27.

251 H. Thirlway, 'The Law and Procedure of the International Court of Justice 1960–1989 Supplement, 2011: Parts Eleven, Twelve and Thirteen', at p. 129.

252 *Territorial and Maritime Dispute (Nicaragua v. Colombia), Honduras Application to Intervene, I.C.J. Reports 2011*, Dissenting opinion by Judge Donoghue, at p. 489–90, para. 54.

The Court's Role in this Diversity of Potential Functional Interaction

Potential functional interaction does not affect the exercise by the Court of its jurisdiction to deal with the case before it. Indeed, when negotiations with a third State are underway, or become necessary after a judgment in a case between two other parties, that is not a reason not to deal with a case. Article 62 of the Statute 'impliedly' considers 'continuance of the proceedings in the absence of a State whose "interests of a legal nature" might be "affected"'.[253] It is up to the third State to make its rights being considered by the Court through intervention.

On the other hand, negotiations already taking place during the course of the proceedings by one of the parties with a third State with a view to determining the frontier [254] could have an impact on the (later) decision of the Court.

The decision granting permission to intervene 'can be understood as a *preventive* one' enabling the intervening State 'to contribute to the protection of such an interest throughout the main proceedings'.[255] It is of course in principle and mainly for the Court to ensure the protection of that legal interest through the dispositif and the reasoning of its judgment

The third State has in fact to make a choice at one of the many crossroads of the functional interaction: either 'to institute principal proceedings, which would enable it to ensure the *recognition* of its legal interests going beyond their mere *protection*';[256] or to be reassured through its intervention, as the Court repeatedly has reminded States, that the 'protection afforded by Article 59 of the Statute may not always be sufficient'.[257]

When the State decides in favour of intervention, one of the other aspects of functional interaction becomes relevant again. Indeed, one of the reasons why a State is 'not obliged, at the current stage of the proceedings, to set forth in full every argument that it will made in the subsequent stage'[258] may be found in subsequent, possibly post-adjudicative negotiations with one of the parties: in case intervention having been denied the third State should not be compelled to give away arguments during judicial proceedings which then later may be used during the negotiations.

The Court does not seem to agree with the argument drawn from the distinction between the two stages of the proceedings, as the evidence to convince the Court of the existence of a legal interest 'cannot be described as restricted or summary at this stage of the proceedings'.[259]

The Applicant in such a case may vehemently deny that the 'mere fact' of being neighbours and the 'absence of a lateral maritime delimitation line' would be enough to justify the existence of a relevant legal interest,[260] whereas the requesting State may consider its legal interest to be established by referring to the fact that such interest is established in reference to the 'hypothetical delimitation scenario' between itself and the Applicant[261] which can only result from post-adjudicative negotiations.

In order to qualify for intervention the third State has to 'show that its interest of a legal nature in the maritime area bordering the area in dispute' between the original parties 'needs a protection that is not provided by the relative effect of decisions of the Court under Article 59 of the Statute'.[262]

The *protection* the Court is bound to accord in cases of maritime delimitation 'to any third State, whether intervening or not', is to stay clear 'of any area where third party interests could become involved',[263] if

253 *Land, Island and Maritime Frontier Dispute, I.C.J. Reports 1990*, at pp. 115–16, para. 55.

254 *Frontier Dispute, I.C.J. Reports 1986*, at p. 563, para. 16.

255 *Territorial and Maritime Dispute (Nicaragua v. Colombia), Costa Rica Application to Intervene, I.C.J. Reports 2011*, at p. 359, para. 27 and at p. 360, para. 33 (emphasis added).

256 *Ibid.*, at p. 361, para. 40 (emphasis added).

257 *Land and Maritime Boundary case, I.C.J. Reports 2002*, at p. 421, para. 238; *Territorial and Maritime Dispute (Nicaragua v. Colombia), Costa Rica Application to Intervene, I.C.J. Reports 2011*, at p. 361, para.41 and at p. 371, para. 85.

258 *Territorial and Maritime Dispute (Nicaragua v. Colombia), Costa Rica Application to Intervene, I.C.J. Reports 2011*, at p. 362, para. 46 (Costa Rica).

259 *Ibid.*, at p. 363, para. 49.

260 *Ibid.*, at p. 365, para. 58 (Nicaragua).

261 *Ibid.*, at p. 364, para. 54 (Costa Rica).

262 *Ibid.*, at p. 372, para. 87.

263 *Maritime Delimitation in the Black Sea, I.C.J. Reports 2009*, at p. 100, para. 112.

necessary by ending 'the line in question before it reaches an area in which the interests of a legal nature of third States may be involved'.[264]

The interest of a third State may arise out of its 'involvement in the facts' of the case because, for instance, of its geographical location *vis-à-vis* the parties. The Court's reasoning may contain 'substantive elements that in content' must or may have inevitably 'an impact upon subsequent relations' with the parties to the case.[265]

The interest of a legal nature concerns 'rather the potential implications of reasons which the Court might give in its decision in the present case on matters in issue as' between the requesting state and one or both of the parties.[266]

The fear of the requesting State may be that the reasoning of the Court 'may afterwards have a prejudicial effect on' the state's 'own legal interests in future settlement' with the parties or with other States.[267] This post-adjudicative impact may occur either by way of a judicial settlement or through an out-of-court one as result of a process of negotiations with the parties in the case.

The requesting State may argue that correspondence with one of the parties relating to respective claims and the existence of a Special Agreement with one of the parties concerning their claims being brought before the Court are further indications of its legal interest.[268]

The possibility of later appearance before the Court as a principal party in parallel proceedings against one or both of the parties should allegedly not affect the pertinence of a request for intervention, as any decision in that case would come considerably later.[269] This argument equally applies with regard to the potential impact of the decision in the case on subsequent negotiations.

Because of subsequent delimitation negotiations with (one of) the parties and/or third States, a third State could claim that its legal interests might be affected; but as an exercise of delimitation frequently 'involves taking into account of a coast of a third State', taking into account 'all coasts and coastal relationships' as 'a geographical fact for the purpose of effecting an eventual delimitation as between two riparian States', this 'in no way signifies that by such an operation itself the legal interest of a third riparian State' may be affected.[270]

This may happen anyway, but not necessarily so and not in all cases.

In a case of maritime delimitation two States may disagree whether the matter of the entire sea boundary between them has been finally and conclusively settled by a previous judgment[271] or whether there is still a 'dispute over the delimitation line between the endpoint of the boundary' fixed by that judgment and 'the tripoint boundary line' in a maritime delimitation treaty.[272]

The requesting State may define the object of its intervention primarily *as a party* 'to settle the maritime boundary between itself and the two States parties to the case', and 'to achieve a final settlement of the dispute between itself' and one of the parties.[273]

The State requesting intervention may argue that because in the previous judgment in a case involving itself and the Applicant the Court did not rule on a bilateral maritime delimitation treaty, 'a matter that the Court was not asked to address', as a result 'there still exists uncertainty to be resolved in regard to the respective sovereign rights and jurisdiction of the three States in the area',[274] and the '*res judicata* in principle only applies to the *dispositif* of the Judgment'.[275]

---

264 *Territorial and Maritime Dispute (Nicaragua v. Colombia), Costa Rica Application to Intervene, I.C.J. Reports 2011*, at p. 372, para. 89; *Territorial and Maritime Dispute (Nicaragua v. Colombia), Honduras Application to Intervene, I.C.J. Reports 2011*, Dissenting opinion by Judge Donoghue, at p. 477, para. 19.

265 *Continental Shelf case between Tunisia and Libya, I.C.J. Reports 1981*, at p. 9, para. 13 (Malta).

266 *Ibid.*, at p. 12, para. 19.

267 *Ibid.*, at p. 17, para. 29.

268 *Ibid.*, at p. 18, para. 30 (Malta).

269 *Ibid.*, at p. 10, para. 14 (Malta).

270 *Land, Island and Maritime Frontier Dispute, I.C.J. Reports 1990*, at p. 124, para. 77.

271 *Territorial and Maritime Dispute (Nicaragua v. Colombia), Application Honduras to Intervene, I.C.J. Reports 2011*, at p. 428, para. 16 and at p. 438, para. 54 (Nicaragua).

272 *Ibid.*, at p. 438, para. 16

273 *Ibid.*, at p. 429, para. 18 and at pp. 430–31, para. 22.

274 *Ibid.*, at p. 436, para. 49.

275 *Ibid.*, at p. 437, para. 52.

If in such a case the Court refuses to grant the permission to intervene as a party, it actually reminds the requesting State of the functional interaction by either sending the would-be intervener and the party appearing before it back to the negotiation table, for instance if they already have gone through such a process prior to the request, or alternatively inviting the would-be intervener to start new proceedings on the merits with the other party.

When the Court in fact notes the requesting State's assertion that 'these issues, if not answered, would certainly affect the finality and stability of the legal relations between the two Parties' (Honduras and Nicaragua),[276] this could indeed be interpreted as making it clear to the parties that the (re)opening of negotiations may be necessary in order to solve these issues.

When several States involved in situations and disputes of maritime delimitation decide to embark upon the necessary negotiations – either prior to, during or after the judicial proceedings – they have to take duly into account the Court's reminder that although they 'may conclude maritime delimitation treaties on [a] bilateral basis ... under the principle *res inter alios acta*' these treaties 'neither confer rights upon a third State, nor impose any duties on it', meaning that whatever 'concessions one State party has made to the other shall remain bilateral and bilateral only, and will not affect the entitlements of the third State'.[277]

Article 59 of the Statute Provides (In)Sufficient Protection

'Article 59 relates to the obligation arising out of the judgment and binding on the parties to that case; it does not affect the quality of the judgment as a judicial decision stating what the law is on that date' because the 'standing and weight of a judgment is a matter of general international law'.[278]

The Court has repeatedly reminded States that the 'protection afforded by Article 59 of the Statute may not always be sufficient', particularly 'in the case of maritime delimitation where the maritime areas of several States are involved', not even from the indirect effects of a judgment affecting their legal rights,[279] for instance in future post-adjudicative negotiations with (one or both of) the parties before the Court.

That factor must allegedly play a role in the exercise of its jurisdiction by the Court,[280] and as a result the Court cannot extend the equidistance line 'beyond a point where it might affect rights' of the intervening State[281] and it can 'do no more than indicate the general direction'.[282]

In their Special Agreement parties may commit themselves that they 'shall enter into negotiations for determining the area of their respective continental shelves and for concluding an agreement for that purpose' during the post-adjudicative phase under the self-imposed margin to do so 'in accordance with the decision of the Court'.[283]

The purpose of a request for intervention may be that that the Court will give 'every needful indication' to the parties for their post-adjudicative negotiations 'to ensure that they do not' include 'any areas which, on account of the existence of rights possessed' the would-be intervener ought to be subject of subsequent delimitation agreements.[284]

As the aim of the Special Agreement is that the parties would be able in the post-adjudicative phase to delimit their areas of continental shelf without difficulty, the Court would 'be in a better position to give the Parties such indications' if it were 'fully enlightened as to the claims and contentions' of that third State.[285]

276 *Ibid.*, at p. 440, para. 62.

277 *Ibid.*, at p. 444, para. 72.

278 S. Rosenne, *The Law and Practice of the International Court of Justice, 1920–1996*, 3rd.edn (4 vols., The Hague, 1997), vol. 3, p. 1633.

279 *Land and Maritime Boundary case, I.C.J. Reports 2002*, at p. 421, para. 238.

280 *Ibid.*

281 *Ibid.*, at p. 443, para. 292.

282 *Ibid.*, at p. 448, para. 307.

283 *Continental Shelf case between Libya and Malta, I.C.J. Reports 1984*, at p. 10, para. 14, Article III.

284 *Ibid.*, at p. 12, para. 17 and at p. 21, para. 33 (Italy).

285 *Ibid.*, at p. 25, para. 40.

Because of particular provisions in the compromis, the Court directly brings those interests within the legal framework for the post-adjudicative phase negotiations between the parties, in a way that the parties themselves would most probably not be willing to do and did not anticipate.[286]

This is a fine example of how the interests of a third party may have an impact on the scope and outcome of post-adjudicative negotiations between the parties to a case. It also illustrates that, apart from the protective role of intervention as an institution with regard to the interests of third States, 'considerations of the effectiveness of judicial action may add a dimension to the question' of intervention in general.[287]

On the other hand Article 59 of the Statute of the Court firmly limits the scope of the functional interaction, as it not only guarantees for instance freedom of negotiations for and with third States, but moreover the 'principles and rules of international law found by the Court to be applicable' to a particular delimitation cannot be 'relied on by the Parties against any other States'.[288] Obviously they can be invoked and referred to as authoritative pronouncements on the applicable principles and rules, thus providing the framework for those subsequent negotiations.[289]

In case a request for intervention is being denied by the Court, it follows in line with Article 59 of the Statute 'that no conclusions or inferences may legitimately be drawn from those findings or that reasoning with respect to rights or claims of other States not parties to the case'.[290]

Subject to the modern interpretation of Article 38, para. 1 (d) of the Court's Statute, this applies to all other States who are looking for conclusions or inferences with respect to their own rights or claims within the context of subsequent negotiations.

Another aspect of the functional interaction having in mind post-adjudicative negotiations between the would-be intervener and (one of) the parties is that the protection offered by Article 62 is 'of a different nature and operates in a different manner' from that flowing from Article 59. Article 62 gives the Court 'powers of an essentially procedural and preventative nature'.[291]

The object of a non-party intervention might be to submit to the Court information about the intervener's claim to help the Court set a final point in such a way as not to prejudice the claims of the intervener.[292] This is also part of the functional interaction if the intervener after the judgment in which its rights have not been affected then initiates negotiations with (one of) the parties on the basis of the judgment which is *res judicata* for the original parties or institute proceedings.

The observation that given the insufficient protection offered by Article 59 of the Statute 'a State that is concerned about the possible impact of a judicial maritime delimitation in progress between two of its neighbours will nevertheless not improve its position in law by intervening under Article 62 of the Statute 'as a non-party'[293] does, in our view, not necessarily apply in all circumstances.

8.7 Multiparty Involvement in Post-adjudicative Negotiations

During the pre-adjudicative phase parties may have in vain tried to solve their dispute through a process of negotiations on a purely bilateral basis. Perhaps assistance by third States or by an International Organization may not have guaranteed a successful outcome on the merits either, although it may have resulted in the

286 *Ibid.*, at p. 25, para. 41.

287 H. Thirlway, 'The Law and Procedure of the International Court of Justice 1960–1989 Supplement, 2011: Parts Eleven, Twelve and Thirteen', at 127.

288 *Continental Shelf case between Libya and Malta, I.C.J. Reports 1984*, at p. 26, para. 42.

289 See generally M. al-Qahtani, 'The Status of Would-be Intervening States before the International Court of Justice and the Application of *Res Judicata*' (2003) 2 *The Law and Practice of International Courts and Tribunals* 2, 269–4.

290 *Continental Shelf case between Tunisia and Libya, I.C.J. Reports 1981*, at p. 20, para. 35.

291 *Territorial and Maritime Dispute (Nicaragua v. Colombia), Application of Costa Rica to Intervene, I.C.J. Reports 2011*, Dissenting opinion by Judge Al-Khasawneh, at p. 377, para. 11.

292 *Territorial and Maritime Dispute (Nicaragua v. Colombia), Application of Honduras to Intervene, I.C.J. Reports 2011*, Dissenting opinion by Judge Donoghue, at p. 482, para. 26.

293 H. Thirlway, 'The Law and Procedure of the International Court of Justice 1960–1989 Supplement, 2011: Parts Eleven, Twelve and Thirteen', at 133.

parties concluding a Special Agreement. During the proceedings before the Court the functional role of third parties may have been limited, for instance in helping the parties find common ground towards an interim arrangement pending the delivery of the judgment.

Whether the Court, in imposing upon the parties a bilateral obligation to negotiate concerning 'respective' rights of a bilateral character when one of the parties has accepted 'a multilateral obligation to negotiate on much wider bases' in international institutions beyond the Court's jurisdiction, has made a useful contribution to the settlement of the dispute may have been doubted by individual judges.[294]

Judge Petren voiced the same doubts but on the different ground that the Court, in his view, avoided answering the question of the legal status of the fishing waters in dispute, a reply on this point being a prerequisite for a successful process of negotiations.[295]

Once the Court has rendered its judgment parties are obliged to accept and carry it out in good faith and to take the necessary measures for its implementation. This aspect will be addressed in the next chapter.

Here we will look at the way the parties or the Court already anticipate or indicate elements of multiparty involvement in that process.

The Exercise of the Court's Contentious Jurisdiction and Multiparty Post-adjudicative Negotiations

International organizations are 'well-positioned to provide a framework for negotiation and cooperation, as well as to offer practical support for States engaged in implementation',[296] a clear example of functional interaction at the level of an international organization between the adjudicative and the post-adjudicative phase.

The judgment in the *Land and Maritime Boundary case* was handed down in 2002, and the Greentree Agreement was concluded in 2006, mainly as a result of the efforts of the UN Secretary-General, who had already 'called the two leaders to ask if they would be prepared to meet with' him to 'discuss the decision of the Court which was going to be released in three months'.[297] The process took three years to get to an agreement, and during that period the possibility of referring the matter to the Security Council was considered by the Applicant.[298]

A debate within a multilateral framework like the General Assembly of the UN can be characterized as a process of real negotiations during which, for instance, it is possible for a State to waive one of its claims or positions, although the Applicant did not wish to make the issue 'a matter for United Nations discussions'.[299] The Court may point out that the question 'was on several occasions discussed in the various competent United Nations bodies'.[300]

For debates within the Security Council to be considered as a form of proper negotiations the first requirement here is of course that both parties, after having failed to settle the matter bilaterally, treat the dispute as (still) negotiable.[301]

A deadlock in a process of multiparty negotiations taking place within the framework of an international organization – the fact that the process was taking place may be denied by a Respondent[302] – may not always be so much on matters of substance as resulting from conditions and restrictions placed upon the process by

294 *Fisheries Jurisdiction (United Kingdom v. Iceland), I.C.J. Reports 1974*, Dissenting opinion by Judge Gros, at p. 121, para. 24.

295 *Fisheries Jurisdiction case (FRG v. Iceland), I.C.J. Reports 1974*, Dissenting opinion by Judge Petren, at p. 241.

296 L. Boisson de Chazournes and A. Angelini, 'Between Saying and Doing', p. 168. Examples of the various ways international organizations have been involved can be found in the rather detailed accounts at pp. 169–71.

297 N. Michel, 'Two Cases in Perspective: Boundary Delimitation in the Bakassi Peninsula and Criminal Accountability in Kenya', Interview of H.E. Kofi Annan, in L. Boisson de Chazournes, M. Kohen and J. Vinuales (eds), *Diplomatic and Judicial Means of Dispute Settlement* (Leiden and Boston, 2013), pp. 281–90, at p. 282.

298 N. Michel, 'Two Cases in Perspective', p. 283.

299 *Nauru case, I.C.J. Reports 1993*, at p. 248, para. 17 (Australia) and at p. 250, para. 19 (Nauru).

300 *Ibid.*, at p. 251, para. 24.

301 A. Lall, *Modern International Negotiation*, p. 24. Under the constitutional structure of the UN there is functional interaction between the ICJ which in its jurisprudence has dealt with the way the Council has been performing its functions. See *inter alia* K. Wellens, 'The Legal Significance Given to the Security Council in the Court's Jurisprudence since Lockerbie' (2013) 55 *Japanese Yearbook of International Law*, 134–75.

302 *South West Africa cases, I.C.J. Reports 1962*, at p. 344 (South Africa).

one of the parties.[303] In case of (such) a deadlock the Court may find itself compelled to consider the question what the chances are of success for further negotiations[304] in the post-adjudicative phase. Taking into account one party's doubts in light of new terms of reference of an organ of the UN – within the framework of which negotiations were held – and the confirmation of the deadlock by the arguments put before the Court by the parties may bring the Court to the conclusion that there is no real probability that further negotiations would lead to a settlement.[305] Such a negative judicial reply then would bring the pre-existing functional interaction to an end with the delivery of the judgment.

It is relevant to note, as the Court did, that behind one dispute between two parties there may be another one, dealing with identical questions, between one of the parties before the Court and the United Nations.[306]

Looking forward to the post-adjudicative phase, an Applicant may already express its conviction that it should be possible, within the framework of a regional specialized intergovernmental organ, to come to a multilateral arrangement with all nations concerned.[307]

A diplomatic note inviting the other party to enter into multilateral negotiations may from the outset identify the legal framework for the negotiations proposed, as the aim of such multilateral negotiations should be 'to bring about an agreement that would take into account "the principles of international law" and "the historic interests of all nations concerned"'.[308]

The same although more detailed approach may be found in one of the submissions of another party in a parallel case.[309]

Are parties entitled 'to know whether the Court would consider itself competent to continue to deal with their dispute in the event that the negotiations did not take place or were unsuccessful' before the expiry of an interim agreement between them?[310]

By deciding not to join the parallel cases instituted by two States the Court deprived 'itself of the possibility of prescribing joint negotiations between them' and the Respondent.[311]

The Exercise of the Court's Advisory Jurisdiction and Multiparty Post-adjudicative Negotiations

In Chapters 2 and 5 we have already referred to the particular ways the functional interaction could operate when the Court is exercising its advisory jurisdiction.

The involvement of an International Organization may situate itself at the *relational* or *institutional* dimension or require a combination of both.

The institutional dimension may concern 'relations between political organs, between a political and an administrative organ and, finally, between a political and a judicial organ'.[312]

Practice reveals varying degrees of mutual support, disguised avoidance, failure to act and successful involvement.[313]

As to the relational dimension, practice may indicate that 'piecemeal efforts at implementation, which are more concerned with the immediate interests of the parties, can risk undermining the pronouncement itself'.[314]

303 *Ibid.*, at p. 344 (Ethiopia and Liberia).

304 *Ibid.*

305 *Ibid.*, at p. 345.

306 *Ibid.*

307 *Fisheries Jurisdiction (Federal Republic of Germany v. Iceland), I.C.J. Reports 1974*, at p. 186, para. 28.

308 *Ibid.*, at p. 57, para. 19 (FRG).

309 *Fisheries Jurisdiction (United Kingdom v. Iceland) I.C.J. Reports 1974*, at pp. 5–6, para. 8 (b); at p. 6, para. 11 (b); and at p. 7, para. 11 (e) (UK).

310 *Ibid.*, Dissenting opinion by Judge Petren, at p. 153.

311 *Ibid.*, at p. 154. In this respect it should be noted that a proposal made during the proceedings by the FRG to have tripartite negotiations was not accepted by the Respondent: *Fisheries Jurisdiction (Federal Republic of Germany v. Iceland), I.C.J. Reports 1974*, Dissenting opinion by Judge Gros, at p. 234, para. 1.

312 L. Boisson de Chazournes and A. Angelini, 'Between Saying and Doing', p. 177.

313 For more details see the cases analysed by L. Boisson de Chazournes and A. Angelini, 'Between Saying and Doing', pp. 177–81.

314 L. Boisson de Chazournes and A. Angelini, 'Between Saying and Doing', p. 183.

Within the context of advisory proceedings it is only natural that as far as the post-adjudicatory phase is concerned, a functional role may be reserved for the requesting and other organs within the UN system having at their disposal various options such as 'for instance with regard to consultations between the interested parties'.[315]

An absolute refusal by the States concerned 'to take part, in any manner whatsoever, in the procedure provided for in the dispute clauses' of applicable Treaties may even be maintained in the post-adjudicative phase, and this notwithstanding the Court having declared in its advisory opinion that the governments have the obligation to carry out the peaceful settlement of provisions.[316] Notwithstanding the non-binding nature of its advisory opinion and the Court's function to assist the requesting organ and not the States concerned, this is an example of a clear reprimand by the Court.

When ruling that there is an urgent need for the UN 'as a whole to redouble its efforts to bring the Israeli–Palestinian conflict, which continues to pose a threat to international peace and security, to a speedy conclusion – thereby establishing a just and lasting peace in the region'[317] – the Court makes it clear that this should be done through negotiations, which it considers only to have been 'initiated' so far.[318]

With regard to the post-adjudicative phase, the impact of the Court's ruling is undeniable as it considers it its duty not only to draw the attention of the General Assembly to the need 'for these efforts to be encouraged', but also in the same vain to remind all parties concerned of the international legal parameters for the process.[319]

The further action referred to by the Court in the operative paragraphs certainly implies, among other modalities, negotiations between the UN and Israel on the matter.[320]

315 *Western Sahara Advisory Opinion, I.C.J. Reports 1975,* at p. 37, para. 72.
316 *Interpretation of Peace Treaties (second phase), Advisory Opinion, I.C.J. Reports 1950*, p. 221, at p. 228.
317 *Wall Advisory Opinion, I.C.J. Reports 2004*, at p. 200, para. 161.
318 *Ibid.*, at p. 201, para. 162.
319 *Ibid.*
320 *Ibid.*, at p. 202, para. 163 (E).

Chapter 9
Failed Post-Adjudicative Negotiations and Returning to the Court

Introduction

Although as indicated in Chapter 6 discontinuance may also trigger this new phase, in most cases once the Court has performed its judicial function – as it had been determined by the parties through their Application or Special Agreement and their submissions – and has rendered its judgment on the merits of the case, a new phase of functional interaction commences. Pursuant to Articles 59 and 60 of the Statute the judgment is binding, final and without appeal for the parties in respect of that particular case; they have the Charter-based obligation under Article 94, para. 1 to comply with the decision of the Court.

The 'element of factual unpredictability of endeavours of peaceful settlement' – applicable in general terms on any process of negotiations, and to a lesser extent on judicial intervention – is certainly to be reckoned with as far as post-adjudicative negotiations are concerned.[1] The extent to which this process is influenced by the judgment rendered will be the focus of this chapter.

The pendulum of the functional interaction then swings back to the parties and to the means they are expected to turn to in order to carry out the judicial decision. A (renewed) process of negotiations may be necessary for a variety of reasons, as indicated in the introduction to this Part of the study.

As a result of the judicial settlement of the dispute – or its absence in case of discontinuance or a negative jurisdictional decision – the legal framework for this post-adjudicative process has completely changed, and this factor inevitably has an impact on various aspects of the unfolding of these negotiations: the (un) willingness of (one of) the parties to embark, perhaps one last time, upon this exercise; the complexity and the comprehensiveness or partiality of the subject-matters to be discussed; the chances of success or failure; and, ultimately, also the (remote or real) possibility or need of returning to the Court.

The difficulties and challenges parties are to encounter may have to do, for instance, with a question of reparation for the wrongful act the Court had established; the correct reading of the judgment and common understanding of its actual scope; the occurrence of new facts; or the mere fact that no final judgment on the merits has been rendered.

This chapter attempts to clarify these issues through the Court's relevant case law, which could provide us with indications whether perhaps a distinction imposes itself between negotiations as (a)/(the) means required to comply with the judgment ; negotiations as (one of)/(the) means to finally settle the dispute following the judicial ruling; and negotiations in case the Court recommended/obliged the parties to do so.

Perhaps also a different distinction has to be made between a post-adjudicative phase which starts after discontinuance, resulting or not from a (partial) out-of-court settlement; after a lack of jurisdiction judgment; in case of a judgment on the merits either on the whole of the dispute or on parts of it which had been submitted by the parties; in case one of the parties does not accept the judgment and fails to perform the obligations incumbent upon it under the judgment.

The latter situation is governed by Article 94, para. 2 of the Charter, which 'is not a provision for enforcement of a judgment per se'[2] and will not be addressed any further in this study. It is sufficient to add here that one modality of the post-adjudicative phase could consist in the Security Council recommending negotiations between the parties towards compliance with the jugdment.

---

1 *Request for Interpretation of the 1962 Temple of Preah Vihear Judgment, I.C.J. Reports 2011*, Separate opinion by Judge Cançado Trindade, at p. 567, para. 3.

2 Judge Owada, President of the International Court of Justice before the UN Security Council on 27 October 2010, p. 5 (text available on the Court's website).

The Court may have upheld an objection to its jurisdiction, thereby making the performance of its adjudicatory function on the merits impossible, sometimes only for the time being. If however it would at the same time decide 'an important issue of fact or law, forming part of the merits, against the applicant state', then 'grave injustice' would be done to that State. Indeed:

> The effect of the refusal to permit adjudication … would be to remit the applicant and respondent States to other measures, legal or political, for the settlement of the dispute. Neither the applicant nor the respondent should be prejudiced, in seeking an alternative solution to the dispute, by the decision of any issue of fact or law that pertains to the merits.[3]

9.1 Provisions Made by the Parties or by the Court for Post-Adjudicative Negotiations

When at the end of pre-adjudicative negotiations parties have been able to conclude a Special Agreement they may have anticipated the post-adjudicative phase through the inclusion of a *pactum de negotiando* or a *pactum de contrahendo*. Such a provision may have been accompanied by more precise indications about the real subject-matter of that process which, moreover, may be restricted in time by a self-imposed deadline.

Parties may also have foreseen the revival of the functional interaction in case of failure of those negotiations. For instance, *a pactum de contrahendo* to conclude a treaty incorporating the work of experts in a dispute concerning maritime delimitation may be subject to a rather limited deadline of a renewable period of three months.

In case of failure of those negotiations the parties will come back together to the Court to request 'such explanations or clarifications as may facilitate the task of the delegations',[4] thereby already considering the real possibility of a request for interpretation under Article 60 of the Statute. In other cases parties may have given themselves six months[5] or a year to bring those post-adjudicative negotiations to a successful outcome.[6]

Parties may also have requested the Court, for instance, to nominate experts who will assist the parties in their post-adjudicative task of demarcation, a request to which the Court may have responded by an Order issued after the delivery of its judgment on the merits of the case.[7]

Responding to a similar request, the Court may 'having regard to the circumstances' of the case be of the opinion that it 'is inappropriate at this juncture to make the nominations' and to postpone its decision to ascertain 'the view of the Parties, particularly as regards the practical aspects of the exercise by the experts of their functions'.[8]

During the adjudicative phase a request for the indication of provisional measures may be prompted by acts of sovereignty which prejudge 'not only the judgment on the merits to be given by the Court' but also 'the maritime delimitation to be effected subsequently between the States' in the post-adjudicative phase.[9]

In proceedings instituted unilaterally the Court itself may decide in its judgment on jurisdiction and admissibility to 'afford the Parties the opportunity to ensure the submission to the Court of the entire dispute', provided this process 'of negotiations' is completed within five months and results in the conclusion of a Special Agreement.[10]

---

3 *Anglo-Iranian Oil Case, I.C.J. Reports 1952*, Dissenting opinion by Judge Read, at p. 149.

4 *Continental Shelf case between Tunisia and Libya, I.C.J. Reports 1982*, at p. 22, para. 2, Article 3. In his dissenting opinion Judge Gros criticized the Court for not having pronounced itself on the compatibility of this provision with Article 60 of the Statute of the Court: at p. 146, para. 6.

5 *Gabcikovo case, I.C.J. Reports 1997*, at p. 12, Article 4 (3).

6 *Frontier Dispute, I.C.J. Reports 1986*, at p. 558, Article V.

7 *Frontier Dispute, Nomination of Experts, Order of 9 April 1987, I.C.J. Reports 1987*, p. 7, at p. 8.

8 *Frontier Dispute between Burkina Faso and Niger, I.C.J. Reports 2013,* at p. 92, para. 113. On 12 July 2013 the Court did nominate the experts: *Frontier Dispute (Burkina Faso/Niger), Order of 12 July 2013, Nomination of Experts, I.C.J. Reports 2013*, p. 226, at pp. 227–8.

9 *Arbitral Award case, I.C.J. Reports 1990*, at p. 67, para. 15 (Guinea-Bissau).

10 *Case between Qatar and Bahrain, I.C.J. Reports 1994*, at p. 125, para. 38 and at p. 127, para. 41 (3).

On the very day of this 1994 judgment the Respondent invited representatives of the Applicant 'to a meeting at the earliest possible opportunity in order to work towards the signing of a joint submission'. The Applicant was willing to discuss whether 'it would be possible to act jointly so as to ensure that the whole of the dispute is placed before the Court'.[11]

After several meetings following this interlocutory judgment – and during which no progress was made, since both parties tabled successive draft joint acts which were then rejected by the other party – the Respondent finally informed the Applicant that 'it seemed pointless to hold another meeting'.[12]

In a subsequent development the Applicant, given 'the absence of an agreement between the parties to act jointly', submitted the whole of the dispute to the Court,[13] whereas in its report on the implementation of the 1994 judgment the Respondent held that the submission of the whole of the dispute must be 'be consensual in character, that is a matter of agreement between the parties',[14] and this 'on the basis of new and agreed terms of reference'. Following the breakdown of these post-adjudicative negotiations the Respondent had withdrawn the last draft joint act.[15]

From the start of the process – as happens in various other circumstances also to be dealt with shortly – parties held different views on the object and scope of the post-adjudicative negotiations, as they disagreed as to the scope of the commitment they had made back in 1987.[16]

In its judgment on the merits the Court may then recall that the parties had an opportunity to submit either jointly or separately the whole of the dispute within a time limit fixed by the Court, but that they failed to do it jointly.[17]

After the Court rendered its judgment the parties let it be known to the Court that judicial settlement by the Court 'was the only way of resolving by peaceful means' (Qatar) this long-standing dispute (Qatar) which 'has divided our two nations for almost a century' (Bahrain). The Applicant expressed the hope that 'following the rendering of the Court's judgment, the two sisterly States can enter upon a new phase of good relations'.[18]

In their submissions in a case instituted on a unilateral basis (one of) the parties may consider the possibility of post-adjudicative negotiations on the question of reparation and judicial determination of it in case of failure of that process.

The normal course of the procedure might have been modified in case an Application was replaced 'by a kind of novation in the Special Agreement' signed during the course of the proceedings, putting 'an end to the proceedings instituted by unilateral Application (and) intended to replace it',[19] and which may, moreover, limit 'the effect of the Court's decision to the main fact of recognition of responsibility, and regarding essentially the purpose of international justice as being to declare the right'.[20]

Also when filing a counterclaim alleging wrongful acts, the party filing it may submit that 'the amount of reparation due therefore, if not agreed between the parties within six months of the date of the judgment, [is] to be determined by the Court in a further judgment'.[21]

Sometimes the maximum inference that can be drawn from both a treaty preamble and the general principle of law is an obligation for States to embark upon negotiations in order to solve a particular set of problems.[22]

---

11 *Case between Qatar and Bahrain, I.C.J. Reports 1995*, at p. 12, para. 18.

12 *Ibid.*, at pp. 12–14, paras. 19–21 and at p. 14, para. 21.

13 *Ibid.*, at p. 9, para. 12.

14 *Ibid.*, at p. 10, para. 13.

15 *Ibid.*

16 *Ibid.*, at pp. 15–16, para. 26.

17 *Case between Qatar and Bahrain, I.C.J. Reports 2001*, at p. 45, paras. 8 and 10.

18 Letters sent to the Registrar on respectively 19 and 27 March 2001.

19 *Corfu Channel case, I.C.J. Reports 1949*, Dissenting opinion by Judge Winiarski, at p. 57.

20 *Ibid.*, Dissenting opinion by Judge Azevedco, at pp. 96 and 97.

21 *Land and Maritime Boundary between Cameroon and Nigeria, Order of 30 June 1999, I.C.J. Reports 1999*, p. 983, at p. 985. I.*C.J. Reports 2002*, at p. 323, para. 26 (7); at p. 325, para. 26 (6); and at p. 329, para. 27 (6).

22 *Dispute regarding Navigational and Related Rights, I.C.J. Reports 2009*, Declaration by Judge *ad hoc* Guillaume, at p. 300, para. 19, qualifying this reasoning of the Court 'as extremely weak'.

9.2 The Question of Reparation and Post-Adjudicative Negotiations: The Respective Role of the Parties and of the Court

Negotiation scholars have identified 'the *erasure of damage*' as part of a combined backward- and forward-looking negotiation strategy involving 'acknowledgment of responsibility' and 'request for a pardon and response to forgiveness', elements resembling to some extent aspects of the state responsibility regime.[23] It goes without saying that in this process diplomacy plays an important role.[24]

'A *contentieux* on reparations does not have a "subsidiary" nature in relation to the *faits générateurs* of the international responsibility of States. It has a dynamics of its own'.[25] The duty of reparation is not at all 'a secondary obligation ... because it is a *fundamental* obligation'.[26]

The Role of the Parties

The right to reparation and the related issue of its modalities may be separated by (one of) the parties either in their Special Agreement, their Application and subsequent submissions, or indeed in their counterclaims; they may indeed reserve the latter issue for the post-adjudicative negotiations.

When 'a Special Agreement confers on the Court the power to determine whether compensation is due, this also means that the Court has the power to decide upon the amount of compensation'[27] or to order parties to negotiate. The Respondent may dispute the Court's jurisdiction on this question and make, to no avail, repeated calls to the Applicant to negotiate directly.[28]

One possible technique to overcome a deadlock situation by utilizing time is 'to set aside [a] thorny issue, moving it to a more favourable moment in the negotiation' and 'leaving it to be managed at the stage of agreement implementation'.[29]

Parties have resorted to such a technique when with regard to the issue of reparation they have jointly made provision that in case of failure of post-adjudicative negotiations within a certain time limit it will be for the Court to decide the matter, although individual judges may consider such a provision resembling 'an arbitral rather than a truly judicial procedure', particularly given the fact that the handling of the case itself took 12 years.[30]

The same option is open to any Applicant who may choose to give the functional interaction an opportunity to operate properly by requesting the Court to deliver a judgment which will be of a mainly declaratory nature while leaving open the possibility for the Court to settle the amount of reparation – reserving, for instance, the determination of the amount 'failing agreement between the Parties'[31] and 'if necessary' to assess 'the nature and the amount of reparation' in a separate phase of the proceedings.[32]

When 18 months after the delivery of a judgment on the merits of the case the Applicant had to inform the Court that no agreement had been reached 'as to the form and amount of the reparation', it may request the Court 'to make the necessary orders for the conduct of the case'.[33]

23 W. Zartman, 'Looking Forward and Looking Backward', p. 299.

24 See for instance H. Moser, 'Restitution Negotiations'.

25 *Germany v. Italy case, I.C.J. Reports 2010*, Dissenting opinion by Judge Cançado Trindade, at p. 367, para. 96.

26 *Ahmadou Sadio Diallo (Republic of Guinea v. Democratic Republic of the Congo), Compensation, Judgment, I.C.J. Reports 2012*, p. 324, Separate opinion by Judge Cançado Trindade, at p. 362, para. 40.

27 M. Bedjaoui, 'An International Contentious Case on the Threshold of the Cold War', in K. Bannelier, T. Christakis and S. Heathcote (eds), *The ICJ and the Evolution of International Law: The Enduring Impact of the Corfu Channel Case* (London and New York, 2012), pp. 3–20 at p. 15.

28 A. Constantinides, 'The *Corfu Channel* Case in Perspective: The Factual and Political Background' in K. Bannelier, T. Christakis and S. Heathcote (eds), *The ICJ and the Evolution of International Law: The Enduring Impact of the Corfu Channel Case* (London and New York, 2012), pp. 41–59 at p. 53.

29 G. Faure, 'Deadlocks', p. 48.

30 *Diallo case, I.C.J. Reports 2010*, Separate opinion by Judge Cançado Trindade, at p. 797, paras. 200–201.

31 *Nicaragua case, I.C.J. Reports 1986*, at p. 149, para. 292 (15).

32 *Certain Property case, I.C.J. Reports 2005*, at p. 11, para. 10 and at p. 12, para. 11, 2 (Liechtenstein).

33 *Military and Paramilitary Activities in and against Nicaragua (Nicaragua v. United States of America), Order of 18 November 1987, I.C.J. Reports 1987*, p. 188, at p. 189.

In a slight variation, an Applicant may also request the Court's authorization to submit 'an assessment of the compensation due to it', and this 'in the event that the two Parties should be unable to agree on the amount thereof within a period of six months following the delivery of the Judgment'.[34]

An Applicant may also express its intention 'to claim damages, at a later date, through the diplomatic channel or otherwise, in the event of a favourable decision furnishing it with a declaration of illegality'.[35] Also the Respondent, having submitted a counterclaim when formulating its submissions,[36] may request that in the absence of an agreement between the parties the Court would settle the question of reparation.[37]

It is possible that 'the Court may be required to enter the final stage of the case and determine the appropriate reparations in accordance with the Judgment, as the Judgment required the Court to do in the event that the Parties are unable to come to a negotiated settlement'.[38] The Special Agreement, the Application, the counterclaim and the submissions of the parties of course determine the Court's precise role in this regard.

It is for the parties to decide whether in their submissions they would leave room for such a process of negotiations or rather put aside the post-adjudicative diplomatic component of the functional interaction in this regard and leave the question of reparation for the Court to determine in a subsequent phase of the proceedings. This may be seen as an indication of unwillingness by (one or both of) the parties to enter into a process of negotiations, at least until the Court has delivered its judgment on the merits in the first phase of the proceedings.[39]

Could the first approach be considered to be 'in accordance with existing international jurisprudence' as it has been argued under reference in particular to *Nicaragua*?[40]

The case law has not established that the parties should negotiate in an attempt to find an agreement on reparation/compensation, and that only in case of failure would it be for the Court to decide at a later stage of the proceedings.

The Court may note the Applicant's intention 'to seek initially to resolve the issue of reparation by way of direct negotiations' and to submit the question to the Court only 'failing agreement between the parties'. Hence the functional interaction returns to the parties, at least on a temporary basis; and thus it is 'not for the Court to determine the final result of these negotiations to be conducted by the Parties'.[41]

The functional interaction reappears not only because the Court, providing the substantive legal framework within which those negotiations have to take place, instructs the parties that in those negotiations they 'should seek in good faith an agreed solution based on the findings of the present Judgment'[42] – the Court's findings thus forming the basis for the post-adjudicative process – but also because, failing an agreement between the parties, the question of reparation due to both parties shall be settled by the Court.[43]

The Role of the Court

In case the Court has made its judicial assessment of for instance 'intersecting wrongs' by both parties the Court may observe 'that the issue of compensation could satisfactorily be resolved in the framework of an overall settlement if each of the Parties were to renounce or cancel all financial claims and counterclaims', leaving the parties free to agree otherwise.[44]

---

34 *Diallo case, I.C.J. Reports 2010*, at p. 648, para. 13; at p. 650, para. 14 (Republic of Guinea); and at p. 691, para. 162.

35 *Nuclear Tests (Australia v. France), I.C.J. Reports 1974*, Joint dissenting opinion by Judges Oneyama, Dillard, Jimenez de Arechaga and Waldock, at p. 318.

36 *Case between the DRC and Uganda, I.C.J. Reports 2005*, at p. 256, para. 258 (DRC).

37 *Ibid.*, at p. 282, paras. 345, 14.

38 Judge Owada, President of the International Court of Justice, speech before the UN Security Council on 29 October 2009 (text available on the Court's website).

39 *Croatian Genocide case, I.C.J. Reports 2008*, at p. 419, para. 21 (d) (Croatia).

40 *Case between the DRC and Uganda, I.C.J. Reports 2005*, at pp. 256–257, para. 258 (DRC).

41 *Ibid.*, at p. 257, para. 261.

42 *Ibid.*

43 *Ibid.*, at p. 281, para. 345 (6) and at p. 282, para. 34 (14).

44 *Gabcikovo case, I.C.J. Reports 1997*, at p. 81, para. 153 and at p. 83, para. 155, 2 (D).

The Court may rule that 'the Parties should indeed engage in negotiation in order to agree on the amount of compensation'.[45] Should those negotiations not bear fruit within six months, 'the question of the compensation due' would be settled by the Court, which 'reserves for this purpose the subsequent procedure in this case'.[46] The view was also expressed that given the circumstances of the case, 'the Court could and should have proceeded, *ex offico, sponte sua*, to the determination of the reparations due'.[47]

Individual judges may look in more detail into the various aspects of the reparation as part of the post-adjudicative negotiation process.[48] For grave breaches of human rights and international humanitarian law the regime of reparation 'would exhaust itself at the inter-State level', although 'individuals are titulaires of the right to reparation'.[49]

The question had already been raised whether and to what extent this feature influences the functional interaction between the objective judicial determination of a wrongful act of a State and the eligibility of the matter of reparation to become and remain a matter for negotiators.

In case this last question receives a positive response, the individual cannot be left 'at the end without any reparation and at the mercy of the entire discretion of the wrongdoing State'[50] and the conclusion may then be drawn that in such circumstances the obligation to negotiate is an obligation of result.

As the 'centrality of the position of victims, as justiciables, has implications for the approach to distinct forms of reparation',[51] and which for instance 'as part of restorative justice' cannot 'be disrupted by undue invocation of state sovereignty or state immunity',[52] there certainly has to be an impact on the legal framework of the negotiations still to be conducted.

A time limit fixed by the Court may expire without an agreement having been reached between the parties on the question of compensation.[53] The view was also expressed that apparently no real negotiations took place undoubtedly because of the too wide divergence between the parties on the amount of the compensation, the parties blaming each other for this failure.[54]

9.3 Compliance with the Judgment through Post-Adjudicative Negotiations: The Respective Roles of the Parties and of the Court

The focus of this Part of the study is, as already indicated, not on the downstream line of compliance with judgments in the sense of what has been the result of post-adjudicative negotiations – it is sufficient here to note that in a number of cases what we find in the post-adjudicative phase is *sub-optimal compliance* or *approximate judgment implementation* – but on the functional interaction between the two mechanisms for peaceful settlement of disputes.

Should the ICJ 'consider ways to design the adjudication process so it encourages voluntary compliance? Or does inviting voluntary compliance instead of traditional enforcement mechanisms threaten' its authority or legitimacy?[55]

45 *Diallo case, I.C.J. Reports 2010*, at p. 691, para. 163.

46 *Ibid.*, at p. 693, para. 165 (8). A submission along the same lines may be formulated but without a time limit for the process: *Case between Djibouti and France, I.C.J. Reports 2008*, at p. 185, para. 17 (10) (Djibouti).

47 *Ahmadou Sadio Diallo (Republic of Guinea v. Democratic Republic of the Congo), Order of 20 September 2011, I.C.J. Reports 2011*, p. 635, Declaration by Judge Cançado Trindade, at p. 638, para. 4.

48 *Gabcikovo case, I.C.J. Reports 1997*, Dissenting opinion by Judge Oda, at pp. 168–9, para. 34.

49 *Germany v. Italy Case, I.C.J. Reports 2012*, Dissenting opinion by Judge Cançado Trindade, at p. 269, para. 252.

50 *Diallo case, I.C.J. Reports 2012*, Separate opinion of Judge Cançado Trindade, at p. 361, para. 36.

51 *Ibid.*, at p. 369, para. 57.

52 *Belgium v. Senegal case, I.C.J. Reports 2012*, p. 422, Separate opinion by Judge Cançado Trindade, at p. 554, para. 170 and at p. 533, para. 119.

53 *Diallo case, I.C.J. Reports 2012*, at p. 329, para. 8.

54 *Ibid.*, Separate opinion by Judge *ad hoc* Mahiou, at p. 396, para. 1.

55 A. Spain, 'The International Judicial Function', p. 17.

The Freedom of the Parties

The freedom of the parties to make any kind of arrangements with regard to the way they wish the functional interaction to operate is subject to the peremptory provisions of the Court's Statute.[56]

Post-adjudicative negotiations have to be distinguished from 'the subsequent approval of the Parties' of the validity if the judgment, which would be incompatible with the Statute and with the position of the Court as a Court of Justice.[57]

It is also important to note from the start the Court's approach that 'the use which the successful party makes of the judgment is a matter which lies on the political and not on the judicial plane'.[58]

A party losing a case may graciously concede defeat and congratulate the other party; however, sometimes not without downplaying the importance of the victory, 'a strip of land or less is of no importance when it is a question of good relations between two sister nations'.[59]

It is beyond doubt that, if successful, post-adjudicative negotiations, sometimes requiring multiparty involvement, could play an important role in restoring friendly relations between the parties.

The action that may be taken by one or both parties after the delivery of the judgment may be retroactive or prospective, or it may be an avoidance of any action.[60] This may imply the resumption of prior negotiations; the actual start of a distinct process of post-adjudicative negotiations; or, in case the judgment does not really require any negotiations at all, its straightforward implementation.

In case an Applicant requests the Court to oblige the Respondent to provide guarantee of non-repetition of the wrongful acts, this could be done in the post-adjudicative phase either by a unilateral act or be the subject of negotiations between the parties.[61]

The Court's General Approach

Although the Court 'neither can nor should contemplate the contingency of the judgment not being complied with',[62] it does not solve the problem whether the chances of compliance with the judgment by the losing Party should/could be taken into account by the Court when sending the parties back to the negotiating table.

It should also be recalled that the Court has drawn a distinction between it considering the 'manner of compliance with its Judgment, or the likelihood of compliance, and, on the other hand, considering whether the judgment, if rendered, would be susceptible of any compliance or execution whatever, at any time in the future'.[63]

Because in the particular circumstances of a case it might be highly desirable 'that the elements of a dispute that were not settled' by an arbitral award 'be resolved as soon as possible, as both Parties desire,' the Court may decide not to refer the parties back to the negotiating table in spite of the declaration by the Respondent that it wishes to negotiate on one aspect of the dispute because of the Application's relation to all maritime territories.[64]

In another case the Court may not only observe that the implementation of its judgment 'will afford the Parties a beneficial opportunity to co-operate', but it may in addition identify some of the sectors where post-adjudicative negotiations would be required.[65]

---

56 See in this regard also the dissenting opinion by Judge Gros in the *Continental Shelf case between Tunisia and Libya, I.C.J. Reports*, at p. 147, para 7.

57 *Free Zones case, P.C.I.J. Series A/B, No. 46*, p. 161 as cited in the *Northern Cameroons case, I.C.J. Reports 1963*, at p. 29.

58 *The Northern Cameroons case, I.C.J. Reports 1963*, at p. 37.

59 *Arbitral Award case King of Spain, I.C.J. Reports 1960*, at p. 210: reaction Nicaragua to Honduras after the award had been handed down by the King of Spain.

60 *The Northern Cameroons case, I.C.J. Reports 1963*, at pp. 37–8.

61 *Breard case, I.C.J. Reports 1998*, at p. 251, para. 5 (Paraguay's submission).

62 *Nicaragua case, I.C.J. Reports 1984*, at p. 437, para. 101.

63 *The Northern Cameroons case, I.C.J. Reports 1963*, at p. 37.

64 *Arbitral Award case, I.C.J. Reports 1991*, at p. 75, para. 68.

65 *Land and Maritime Boundary case, I.C.J. Reports 2002*, at p. 452, para. 316.

Functional Interaction between the Court's General Approach and the Freedom of the Parties

The aim of the parties in concluding a Special Agreement and in coming to the Court may well be to achieve later a delimitation without difficulty by agreement, whereas in other cases the parties may have reserved for themselves 'a margin for negotiations leading to a treaty'.[66]

Moreover, the provision in the Special Agreement with regard to a post-adjudicative treaty to implement the judgment and to contain the final delimitation 'is not a bare *pactum de contrahendo*. The Parties have undertaken not merely to conclude a treaty, but in doing so to apply the rules and principles indicated by the Court in its 1982 Judgment.'[67]

The question may be raised whether this would apply to all kind of post-adjudicative negotiations to implement a judgment or only when the parties have explicitly requested the Court to indicate the rules and principles which they *should* apply when later concluding the agreement.

The Court made it clear that the parties 'may of course still conclude a mutual agreement upon a delimitation that does not correspond to that decision'.[68] Is it a tenable position that negotiations as a means for settlement of a dispute regain their full force and weight as part of the functional interaction after the delivery of the judgment? Is this a tenable position even following their explicit request to the Court when bringing the case?

The Court unreservedly affirmed that if they depart from the Court's decision as a result of their post-adjudicative negotiations 'their accord will constitute an instrument superseding their Special Agreement'.[69] Failing such mutual agreement, 'the terms of the Court's Judgment are definitive and binding'.[70]

These Court pronouncements further clarify the content, scope and limits of the functional interaction at work. Indeed, limitations placed on the role of the Court by a Special Agreement are unable to reduce specific indications found in an earlier judgment to nothing more 'than approximations' or 'guidance', a view the Court already rejected in its 1982 judgment.[71]

On the other hand, 'the opposite presumption would also be false: it is not to be supposed that all figures used in the judgment would have to be regarded as absolute'.[72]

'Each such reference must be read in its context, to establish whether the Court intended it to be a precise statement, an approximation for working purposes, or a simple indication subject to variation.'[73] This is exactly one of the factors which render difficult any process of post-adjudicative negotiations.

The degree and success or not of the Court's facilitative performance depends to a large extent on the preciseness of the indications it includes in its judgment.

When it is impossible to apply the criteria adopted by the Court simultaneously there is need for clarification 'as regards the hierarchy' between them.[74]

When the Court has given 'coordinates' in the judgment with regard to the post-adjudicative negotiations, do they then only have a binding character when they are repeated in the operative paragraphs?[75]

The Court, referring to its 1982 judgment, made it clear that if it were to leave room for extensive disagreement between the (experts of the) parties by employing a particular criterion, and which 'would not necessarily be capable of final resolution', that would not 'be a proper discharge of its duty to indicate

66 *Continental Shelf case between Libya and Malta, I.C.J. Reports 1982*, at p. 554. See also *Revision and interpretation of the 1982 Continental Shelf judgment, I.C.J. Reports 1985*, at p. 224, para. 58 and *Continental Shelf case between Libya and Malta, I.C.J. Reports 1984*, at pp. 14–15, para. 20, leaving the parties 'a margin for negotiations'.

67 *Revision and Interpretation of the 1982 Continental Shelf Judgment, I.C.J. Reports 1985*, at p. 219, para. 48.

68 *Ibid.*

69 *Ibid.*

70 *Ibid.*

71 *Ibid.*, at p. 219, para. 49.

72 *Ibid.*

73 *Ibid.*

74 *Ibid.*, at p. 219, para. 50. (Tunisia in its Application).

75 *Ibid.*, at p. 222, para. 54.

the practical method of delimitation' so 'as to enable the experts to effect the delimitation "without any difficulties"'.[76]

This pronouncement of the Court is of a more general importance for a proper understanding and thus also assessment of the judicial function. The ultimate and compelling objective for the Court is to discharge its function in such a way as to minimize the room for extensive disagreement between the parties during the negotiations on the implementation of the judgment, subject of course to the *non ultra petita* rule in cases where it had not been requested to provide the parties with indications as to, for instance, a practical problem of delimitation.

Even a decision by the Court in its earlier judgment to leave the exact coordinates of the most westerly point to the experts 'is covered by the force of *res judicata*'.[77]

In case parties are facing difficulties in the process of implementing the judgment rendered, they could thus come back to the Court asking for its help, on condition they have successfully negotiated an agreement to do so. Indeed, 'the force of *res judicata* is such as (not) to prevent the Parties returning to the Court to present a joint request that it should order an expert survey ... But they would have to do so by means of an agreement'.[78]

'Whether, and in what circumstances, the Court might in the future give effect to a request to appoint an expert submitted by one party only, does not fall to be considered at the present time.'[79]

On the other hand it may not be excluded *a priori* that a unilateral request for the Court's assistance in the implementation of the judgment through post-adjudicative negotiations may be considered admissible, for instance if the other party has not been really cooperating in good faith during that process, provided of course the Court's jurisdiction can be established.

As judging by what has been brought before to its attention the Court may come to the conclusion that 'no progress has been made in implementing the Special Agreement following' a judgment,[80] the parties may find themselves still under the obligation 'to carry out the Special Agreement to the very end, and to have' the judgement 'implemented so that the dispute is finally disposed of'.[81]

This is exactly where the functional interaction almost finds its culmination when the Court is reaffirming that implementation of the judgment would finally dispose of the dispute, at least as far as it had been brought before it. Hence, parties must 'ensure that their experts and representative[s] engage in a sincere exercise involving a genuine effort'.[82]

Implementing Arbitral Awards

The problem of compliance presents itself not only with regard to orders issued and judgments rendered by the Court, but also in case of arbitral awards, which then may bring into operation a particular post-adjudicative mode of the functional interaction.

A challenge to the validity and the binding nature of an arbitral award may give rise to a dispute, following a series of exchanges leading to a proposal relating to the demarcation of a certain part of the boundary in accordance with part of the operative clause of the award.[83]

Not giving effect to an arbitral award rendered more than half a century ago constitutes a breach of an international obligation which a State may bring before the Court in order to have a declaratory judgment as well as the judicial determination of any measures to achieve that purpose.[84]

As a disagreement over the validity of an arbitral award because of alleged obscurities and contradictions making its execution impossible is not a matter that can be settled by negotiations, there is no real need to

76 *Ibid.*, at p. 224, para. 58.
77 *Ibid.*, at p. 228, para. 66.
78 *Ibid.*
79 *Ibid.*, at p. 229, para. 67.
80 *Ibid.*
81 *Ibid.*, at p. 229, para. 68.
82 *Ibid.*, at p. 229, para. 69.
83 *Arbitral Award case King of Spain, I.C.J. Reports 1960*, at p. 203.
84 *Ibid.*, at p. 195 (Honduras).

follow that path; there is no room to solve this controversy by way of negotiations to find a compromise. Instead a party accused of non-compliance may express its readiness to submit to arbitration or mediation the disagreement over the award's validity.[85]

And it may ask the Court to adjudge and declare that, 'as all phases of the disagreement have not been settled by the Judgment of the Court, the Parties are bound' – as provided for in a resolution of an International Organization – 'to conclude an additional agreement within a period of three months from the date of the delivery of the judgment, with a view to submitting the disagreement concerning their frontier to the arbitral procedure provided for' by a regional agreement, i.e. the Pact of Bogota.[86]

9.4 Disagreement between the Parties over the Implementation of the Judgment

One important aspect of the functional interaction should never be underestimated. Indeed, the scope of the claim and submissions may evidently limit or broaden the nature and complexity of the issues (to be) left to the parties to regulate in the post-adjudicative phase through negotiations.

A claim has to be defined with sufficient precision to enable the Court to pass upon it, even if the day-to-day exercise of the right, with correlative obligations for the other party, may give rise to delicate question of application[87] and which have to be solved through post-adjudicative negotiations.

Disagreement between the parties over (the modalities of) the implementation of the judgment rendered by the Court may have multiple causes and origins. A party which has been unwilling to participate in the proceedings in the first place and has exhausted all procedural means to delay a judicial decision on the merits of the dispute may be easily tempted afterwards to invoke a series of legal arguments leading to a disagreement about the judgment's implementation. They may relate to the scope of the operative paragraphs as compared with the submissions, the alleged lack of clarity of the Court's ultimate decision as contained in those paragraphs or of the judicial reasoning leading to it.

It should be added that joint submission of a dispute or part of it does not necessarily offer any guarantees for a smooth transition to and unfolding of the post-adjudicative phase and ensuing negotiations, as illustrated by the *Gabcikovo case*.

The party returning to the Court, because 'of the unwillingness' of the other party 'to implement the Judgment delivered by the Court' – a 'series of negotiations' have been conducted 'on the modalities for executing' the judgment, leading to a draft Framework Agreement which the other party has disavowed – may request it to determine that party's 'responsibility for the failure so far to agree on' those modalities but also that the parties 'shall resume their negotiations in good faith so as to expedite their agreement on the modalities for achieving the objectives of the Treaty of 16 September 1977'.[88]

Whereas the object and purpose of the post-adjudicative negotiations as provided for in the Special Agreement was the execution of the judgment still to be rendered – and in this sense relatively open-ended subject to the *petita* of the parties and the Court's judgment – the objective of the new and second round of post-adjudicative negotiations was entirely different, given the judgment of the Court and the failure of the first process of post-adjudicative negotiations.

After the rendering of an arbitral award the execution of which gave rise to a dispute between the parties, a multiparty consultative body may deal with it, leading to the conclusion of a Special Agreement for submission of the dispute to the ICJ.[89] The Agreement may contain in separate Appendices a statement by each party with 'such facets of the matter in disagreement as it deems pertinent'.[90]

---

85 *Ibid.*, at p. 197 (Nicaragua).

86 *Ibid.*, at pp. 197–8 (Nicaragua).

87 *Right of Passage case, I.C.J. Reports 1960*, at p. 37.

88 Request for an additional judgment filed by Slovakia on 3 September 1998: Press release ICJ, 98/28. The case has been dormant ever since.

89 *Arbitral Award case King of Spain, I.C.J. Reports 1960*, at p. 203.

90 *Ibid.*

The parties may leave no doubt that the reference to their position is of a general nature and does not constitute the definition or limitation of the matter to be submitted to the Court.[91]

When the parties are unable to agree on how to give effect to the previous judgment it is only at first glance that is within the discretion of each party to determine that the post-adjudicative negotiations have failed;[92] ultimately of course this determination has to be made by the Court.

The day after the Court has rendered a judgment declaring inadmissible a request for the interpretation of a previous judgment concerning the same dispute, the time may have come to carry out the judgment. The initial Respondent may come back to the Court for a declaratory judgment in its favour.[93]

By giving effect to submissions by both parties asking the Court how the previous judgment should be executed[94] the Court would depart from its judicial function.[95] The choice to be made among the various courses open to the parties to carry out their obligation to comply with the first judgment is for the parties alone, based 'only on considerations of practicality or of political expediency'.[96]

In this particular case the Court did not send the parties without any guidance at all: after the clarification of their mutual legal relations by the Court, the Court was rather confident that the parties would be able to find 'practical and satisfactory solution'.[97]

Negotiations should thus be conducted between the parties aiming at a solution, not based on the Court's ruling but on 'considerations of courtesy and good-neighbourliness'.[98]

9.5 Post-Adjudicative Negotiations and Requests for Interpretation

The function and the objective of judicial proceedings are to settle in a final and binding way the dispute between the parties.

One of the various problems in the post-adjudicative phase which may give reason for concern with one or both of the parties may be the alleged lack of clarity in the judgment, leading to a request for interpretation. Indeed, a judgment may contain 'gaps of such a nature as to render its execution impossible'.[99]

A request for interpretation may be solely motivated by the requesting State's determined will to conform to it.[100] A request for interpretation can be the reason for or result from incapacity-based non-compliance (allegedly) due to the lack of clarity of the judgment.[101] It has been rightly pointed out that the:

> relief sought in the proceedings for interpretation does not in principle consist in the requirement that the respondent State take any particular action, nor even (or not necessarily) a judicial statement that that State is under any particular obligation: the Court is simply asked to say what was meant by a particular provision in its earlier decision.[102]

91 *Ibid.*, at p. 204 (Honduras). It should be noted that the post-adjudicative negotiations which have led to such an agreement did not produce much in terms of clarification of the respective positions in such a way as to clearly define the legal issues the Court was called upon to adjudge.

92 *Haya de la Torre case, I.C.J. Reports 1951*, at p. 4.

93 *Ibid.*, at pp. 72–3.

94 *Ibid.*, at pp. 75–6.

95 *Ibid.*, at p. 83.

96 *Ibid.*, at p. 79.

97 *Haya de la Torre case, I.C.J. Reports 1951*, at p. 83.

98 *Ibid.*

99 *Request for Interpretation of the Judgment of 20 November 1950 in the Asylum case (Colombia/Peru), Judgment of 27 November 1950: I.C.J. Reports 1950*, p. 395, at p. 397, § 3.

100 *Ibid.*, at p. 399, para. 15.

101 On the distinction between capacity-based and incapacity-based non-compliance see J. Cogan, 'Noncompliance and the International Rule of Law' (2006) 31 *Yale Journal of International Law*, 189–210, at 194.

102 H. Thirlway, 'The Law and Procedure of the International Court of Justice 1960–1989 Supplement, 2011: Parts Eleven, Twelve and Thirteen', at 64.

Post-adjudicative negotiations by their nature and purpose possibly provide the main context within which facts subsequent to the delivery of the judgment gave 'rise to different views advanced by the contending parties',[103] although a letter sent to the President of the Security Council may already have manifested the point of view of one of the parties;[104] and as long 'as this difference of interpretation persists and remains unresolved, there is unlikely to be any prospect of achieving a mutually agreed solution *within the framework of bilateral negotiations*'.[105]

The interpretation given by the Court 'could then serve as a basis for a final resolution of this dispute through negotiation or any other peaceful means'.[106]

When making a request for the interpretation of a judgment – for instance as a result of difficulties arising during the post-adjudicative negotiations to implement the judgment – a party has, pursuant to Article 98, para. 2 of the Rules of Court, to indicate 'the precise point or points in dispute as to the meaning or scope of the judgment'.[107]

The Scope of Application of Article 60 of the Statute

Although States are probably right in holding the view that they 'do not have to apply' judgments on jurisdiction, but that 'they only have to take note of it',[108] such judgments can also be the 'object of a request for interpretation'.[109]

The 'admissibility of requests for interpretation of the Court's judgments needs particular attention because of the need to avoid impairing the finality, and delaying the implementation, of these judgments'.[110]

Parties may disagree for instance whether *res judicata* authority only applies to the dispositif of the judgment[111] or whether it extends also 'to the reasoning in so far as it is inseparable from the operative part'.[112]

The Court in fact made it clear that the reasoning in a number of paragraphs of its 2007 judgment 'was an essential step leading to the dispositif of the Judgment' and 'with this reasoning, the decision made by the Court in its 2007 Judgment leaves no room for any alternative interpretation'.[113]

The Time Factor

For the varied multifunctionality of negotiations to operate properly, the time factor is important not only for a dispute to arise, for a dispute to crystallize, but also for negotiations to succeed as at least some duration of the process seems to be required before an assessment of failure can be made.

There is no particular reason to take a different approach to the time factor in case of post-adjudicative negotiations, except of course when the parties themselves or the Court have determined a deadline in this regard.

Article 60 jurisdiction 'has unusual indelibility and durability'.[114] This means that the post-adjudicative phase is in principle and under the Statute of unlimited duration. So even when post-adjudicative negotiations

---

103 *Request for the Interpretation of the 1962 Preah Vihear Judgment, I.C.J. Reports 2011*, Separate onion by Judge Cançado Trindade, at p. 579, para. 38.

104 *Ibid.*, Request by Cambodia, para. 16.

105 *Ibid.*, para. 17 (emphasis added).

106 *Ibid.*, para. 31.

107 *Request for the Interpretation of the Avena judgment, I.C.J. Reports 2009*, at p. 15, para. 38.

108 *Request for Interpretation of the Judgment of 11 June 1998 in the Case concerning the* Land and Maritime Boundary between Cameroon and Nigeria (Cameroon v. Nigeria), Preliminary Objections *(Nigeria v. Cameroon), Judgment, I.C.J. Reports 1999*, p. 31, at p. 35, para. 9 (Cameroon).

109 *Ibid.*, at p. 35, para. 10.

110 *Ibid.*, at p. 36, para. 12.

111 *Territorial and Maritime Dispute (Nicaragua v. Colombia), Application Honduras to Intervene, I.C.J. Reports 2011*, at p. 437, para. 52 (Honduras).

112 *Ibid.*, at p. 438, para. 54 (Nicaragua).

113 *Ibid.*, at p. 443, para. 70.

114 *Request for Interpretation of the 1962 Temple of Preah Vihear Judgment, I.C.J. Reports 2011*, Dissenting opinion by Judge Donoghue, at p. 615, para. 7.

to implement the judgment have been concluded successfully there always may rise a problem during the implementation process itself, over which the Court has no power of oversight.[115]

Article 60 of the Statute 'does not impose any time limit on requests for interpretation' and hence 'such a dispute can, in itself, certainly arise from facts subsequent to the delivery of that judgment',[116] for instance the failure of post-adjudicative negotiations aiming at its implementation caused by an alleged lack of clarity. However, a 'failure to comply with a judgment does not in itself signal a dispute as to its 'meaning and scope'.[117]

A particular feature of (dys)functional interaction arises however in case provisional measures are being requested in view of 'threatened non-compliance' – e.g. refusal to resume negotiations as imposed by the Court – with the judgment concerned. Since 'in the context of interpretation proceedings' the Court has no power to declare such a non-compliance to have occurred, and to draw appropriate legal conclusions, it is questionable whether it would have the power to indicate measures which would oblige the other party to resume the process of negotiations.[118]

The 'greater the lapse of time since the delivery of the impugned judgment, the heavier the burden of proof on the requesting party to show that the dispute really is one as to its meaning or scope'.[119]

Although one would reasonably expect the parties first to embark upon a careful reading of the judgment before entering into the process of post-adjudicative negotiations aiming at its implementation, Article 60 does not rule out that the request for interpretation is made on the very day of the delivery of the judgment, and thus without careful study of the judgment[120] or any round of negotiations at all.

According to the party submitting such a request the disagreement about the clarity of the judgment, i.e. its meaning and scope, gave rise to a new dispute between them.[121]

As the divergence of views should be on definite points, as required by Article 79, para. 2 of the (old) Rules of Court,[122] it could be inferred that for a dispute to arise as required by the Court there is an element of time to be considered.

Only three weeks after the delivery of an interpretative judgment one party may already file an Application as the parties 'were unable to come to an agreement on the manner in which effect should be given to the said judgments' concerning the surrender of the refugee Victor Raul Haya de la Torre.[123]

In another case three days after the rendering of the arbitral award one party asked the King of Spain for clarifications in order to avoid possible difficulties in its interpretation, as the award allegedly contained contradictory concepts.[124] In case this clarification would not be forthcoming, that party would make 'a friendly approach to' the other party 'to settle "these final details"'.[125]

During the course of the proceedings requests may be made by either of the parties for an extension of particular time limits, and this in order to resume negotiations. Such a request may also accompany a request for the interpretation of an earlier judgment.[126] A request for interpretation introduces a new case but it 'cannot in itself suffice to justify the extension of a time-limit', but here it has been granted 'given the circumstances of the case'.[127]

115 *Ibid.*, at p. 615, para. 8.

116 *Ibid.*, at p. 546, para. 37.

117 H. Thirlway, 'The Law and Procedure of the International Court of Justice 1960–1989 Supplement, 2011: Parts Eleven, Twelve and Thirteen', at 163.

118 H. Thirlway, 'The Law and Procedure of the International Court of Justice 1960–1989 Supplement, 2011: Parts Eleven, Twelve and Thirteen', at 168–9.

119 H. Thirlway, 'The Law and Procedure of the International Court of Justice 1960–1989 Supplement, 2011: Parts Eleven, Twelve and Thirteen', at 157.

120 *Request for Interpretation of the 1950 Asylum case judgment, I.C.J. Reports 1950*, at p. 396 and p. 400.

121 *Ibid.*, at p. 401.

122 *Ibid.*, at p. 403.

123 *Haya de la Torre case, Order of 3 January 1951: I.C.J. Reports 1951*, p. 4.

124 *Arbitral Award case King of Spain, I.C.J. Reports 1960*, at p. 211.

125 *Ibid.*

126 *Land and Maritime Boundary between Cameroon and Nigeria, Order of 3 March 1999, I.C.J. Reports 1999*, p. 24, at p. 25.

127 *Ibid.*, (Cameroon) and at p. 26.

The Conditions for the Application of Article 60 of the Statute: Failure of Post-adjudicative Negotiations on the Meaning of the Judgment?

From a functional interaction perspective it is worth observing that prior and post-adjudicative negotiations have in common that in case of failure they must at least enable the parties to indicate the precise points of difference in their original Application to institute proceedings or in their request for interpretation.

It is worth noting that, because there is a duty for the Court 'to abstain from deciding points not included' in the submissions, it is irrelevant for the Court's decision on the admissibility of a request for interpretation that a qualification made by an ambassador 'had given rise to discussions between the two Governments through a diplomatic correspondence' *before* the 'proceedings in Court in the principal case'.[128]

For the purposes of Article 60 of the Statute it is not required that the *dispute* should have manifested its existence in a specific manner, such as through a process of post-adjudicative negotiations.[129]

The Court found the legal basis for its position in the wider scope of the term *contestation* compared to the term *différend* of Article 36, para. 2 of the Statute, not requiring the same degree of opposition,[130] which, moreover, does not have to manifest itself in a formal way and which may concern the question whether a particular point has been decided with binding force or not.[131] The distinction between 'contestation' and 'dispute' (not in the English text) has consequences in terms of procedural requirements.

From our perspective it is interesting to note that a State introducing a request for interpretation 'is not obliged to exhaust all diplomatic channels beforehand'.[132]

The existence of a dispute in the sense of Article 60 of the Statute 'does not require the same criteria to be fulfilled as those determining the existence of a dispute under Article 36, § 2 of the Statute'.[133]

Through their joint submission of a dispute parties may have utilized the Court's facilitative function with the aim of concluding a delimitation agreement following post-adjudicative phase negotiations to be conducted in accordance with the Court's judgment. The Special Agreement may further provide that if no agreement has been reached through that process of negotiations, both parties could go back to the Court and request 'any explanations or clarifications which would facilitate the task of the two delegations',[134] the parties in doing so calling once more upon the facilitative function of the Court.

Through such provisions in a Special Agreement parties may thus make the functional interaction operate twice with regard to two successive and separate disputes separating them. Such a commitment for post-adjudicative negotiations to implement the judgment 'presupposes' that both parties 'would have made a good faith effort to implement' the judgment and that 'if they were not successful, they would have been obliged to indicate the precise points of difference to be included in the reference to the Court'; it then may be contended that the other party 'has neither endeavoured in good faith to implement' nor 'indicated the precise points of difference' in its unilateral approach to the Court.[135]

One party may argue that the procedure provided for in the Special Agreement implies an 'evident obligation for them first to exhaust the remedy of seeking explanations and clarifications', otherwise a request for interpretation under Article 60 of the Statute of the Court is inadmissible.[136]

---

128 *Request for Interpretation of the 1950 Asylum case judgment, I.C.J. Reports 1950*, p. 395, at p. 402.

129 *Revision and Interpretation of the 1982 Continental Shelf Judgment, I.C.J. Reports 1985*, at p. 218, para. 46; *Request for the Interpretation of the Avena judgment, I.C.J. Reports 2008*, at pp. 325–6, para. 54.

130 *Request for the Interpretation of the Avena judgment, I.C.J. Reports 2008*, at p. 325, para. 53. See also *Request for Interpretation of the Avena judgment, I.C.J. Reports 2009*, at p. 9, para. 17.

131 *Request for Interpretation of the 1962 Temple of Preah Vihear Judgment, I.C.J. Reports 2013*, at p. 296, para. 33 and at p. 301, para. 48.

132 *Request for Interpretation of the 1962 Temple of Preah Vihear Judgment, I.C.J. Reports 2011*, Dissenting opinion by Judge *ad hoc* Cot, at p. 630, para. 14.

133 *Ibid.*, at p. 542, para. 22.

134 *Application for Revision and Interpretation of the Judgment of 24 February 1982 in the Case concerning the* Continental Shelf (Tunisia/Libyan Arab Jamahiriya) *(Tunisia v. Libyan Arab Jamahiriya), Judgment, I.C.J. Reports 1985*, at p. 214, para. 41.

135 *Ibid.*, at p. 215, para. 41 (Libya).

136 *Ibid.*, at p. 215, para. 42 (Libya).

The other party allegedly has not made a *bona fide* attempt to agree on points of explanation or clarification for the purpose of a joint request under the relevant article of the Special Agreement.

The Court did not accept this argument. The exercise of the right of one party to seek an interpretation under Article 60 'would be effectively blocked by the other party, if that party chose not to co-operate' and 'it is not likely to be presumed that a State would renounce or fetter its right under Article 60 of the Statute to request an interpretation unilaterally'. Hence, the right of the Applicant to file a request for interpretation is not 'affected by the existence of Article 3 of the Special Agreement'.[137]

The view that as long as a 'difference of interpretation of a previous judgment' persists – in the sense of a dispute or 'contestation'[138] – 'and remains unresolved, there is unlikely to be any prospect of achieving a mutually agreed solution within the framework of bilateral negotiations'[139] does not only seem to be applicable more generally, but it also refers to the functional interaction between the two mechanisms.

Except when the conditions for a request for revision are fulfilled, no fact posterior to a judgment rendered could have the effect to change either the judgment or its legal consequences, and the binding nature of the judgment has to be considered as a permanent obligation without time limit.[140]

The object and purpose of the procedure of Article 60 of the Statute is to address a situation when difficulties arise putting in danger the respect for an obligation directly arising from the judgment, or constitute an obstacle to its implementation, and when these difficulties result directly from a dispute between the parties on the meaning and scope of the judgment; then there is the procedure of Article 60.[141]

In spite of normal and peaceful relations between neighbours having been established, steps taken in the post-adjudicative phase to initiate a bilateral process could have led to the establishment of a stable situation which would have made possible the judgment's implementation. The possibility of a new dispute would have been avoided if the process had been conducted to its final stage with success.[142]

The functional interaction operates as it normally also does in the pre-adjudicatory phase: one party may come to the conclusion that there is no realistic chance that the process of negotiations in progress can be brought to a successful conclusion without a renewed judicial intervention interpreting a previous judicial performance in order to 'preserve or re-establish the legal situation resulting from the judgment itself'.[143] The party requesting interpretation will be looking for an explanation by the Court of 'the real meaning of the sense and scope of the' previous judgment and which 'could then serve as a basis for a final resolution of this dispute through negotiation or any other peaceful means'.[144]

Although doubts may be expressed about the use of Article 41 of the Statute in Article 60 proceedings,[145] provisional measures in Article 60 proceedings which are triggered by a dispute arising from post-adjudicative negotiations to implement a judgment could freeze positions of the parties defined during those negotiations or could favour the positions taken by one of them – even if later not confirmed in the interpretative judgment; and they may still impact on the resumption of post-adjudicative negotiations in light of the future interpretation still to be given by the Court.

A *caveat* has been rightly formulated that:

> there is reason to suppose that the object of the request may have been less to obtain the resolution of a difficulty over the meaning of the text of the judgment than to set proceedings in motion before the Court that could be used as a vehicle for a request for the indication of provisional measures.[146]

137 *Ibid.*, at p. 216, para. 43.

138 *Request for Interpretation of the 1962 Temple of Preah Vihear Judgment, I.C.J. Reports 2011*, Application Cambodia, at pp. 17–23, paras. 21–5.

139 *Ibid.*, at p. 17, para. 17.

140 *Ibid.*, at p. 11, para. 11 and at pp. 24–5, para. 28.

141 *Ibid.*, at p. 25, para. 28.

142 *Ibid.*, at p. 25, para. 30.

143 *Ibid.*, at p. 25, paras. 30 and 28.

144 *Ibid.*, at p. 27, para. 31.

145 *Ibid.*, Dissenting opinion by Judge Donoghue, at pp. 616–19, paras. 10–16.

146 H. Thirlway, 'The Law and Procedure of the International Court of Justice 1960–1989 Supplement, 2011: Parts Eleven, Twelve and Thirteen', at 152.

And 'even if the basis of jurisdiction in the original case lapses, the Court, nevertheless, by virtue of Article 60 of the Statute, may entertain a request for interpretation provided that there is a "dispute as to the meaning or scope" of any judgment rendered by it'. The Court will indicate provisional measures 'only if it is satisfied that there appears *prima facie* to exist a "dispute" within the meaning of Article 60 of the Statute' because at that stage the Court 'need not satisfy itself in a definitive manner that such a dispute exist[s]'.[147]

The disagreement between the parties may in particular centre on the question whether the obligations derived from the operative clauses of a judgment are of a general and continuing character.[148] The answer depends on the nature of obligations specified in the operative clause, except of course for the permanent obligation to comply in general with the judgment – i.e. not to frustrate the object and purpose of the judgment rendered which was to settle the dispute as submitted by the parties.

9.6 Post-Adjudicative Negotiations and an Application for Revision of a Judgment

The duty to inform itself is part of certain requirements normal diligence entails when a State is sending a delegation to a process of negotiations.[149] Non-fulfilment of that duty is bound to have an impact on the admissibility of a subsequent request for revision of the judgment rendered.[150]

The *Request for an Examination of the Situation in Accordance with Paragraph 63 of the Court's judgment of 20 December 1974 in the* Nuclear Tests (New Zealand v. France) case may just be mentioned as a unique case distinct from a normal request for interpretation and application for revision.

In an Application for revision the Respondent may first intend to request the Court to 'make the admission of the proceedings in revision conditional on previous compliance with the judgment' – which, because of the necessary post-adjudicative negotiations would have again brought into operation the functional interaction – but then decide not to do so and thus 'not to ask the Chamber to require prior compliance with the terms of the judgment'.[151]

The Chamber reminded States that 'paragraph 3 of Article 61 of the Statute and paragraph 5 of Article 99 of the Rules of Court afford the Court the possibility at any time to require previous compliance with the terms of the judgment whose revision is sought, before it admits proceedings in revision',[152] thereby recalling the institutional blessing of this aspect of functional interaction.

The 1922 and 1936 Rules 'made specific reference to the Court's power to make the admission of the application conditional upon previous compliance'.[153]

The Court can, pursuant to Article 61, para. 3 of the Statute, 'make compliance with the terms of a judgment a condition for admitting proceedings in revision, a provision never applied thus far'.[154]

The invocation of Article 61 cannot always, *per se* and necessarily, be regarded as a delaying strategy with regard to the process of post-adjudicative negotiations to implement the judgment rendered.

---

147 *Request for Interpretation of the 1962 Temple of Preah Vihear Judgment, I.C.J. Reports 2011*, at p. 542, para. 21.

148 *Ibid.*, at p. 543, para. 28 (Cambodia) and at p. 544, para. 31.

149 *Application for Revision and Interpretation of the Judgment of 24 February 1982, I.C.J. Reports 1985*, at p. 206, para. 27.

150 *Ibid.*, at p. 207, para. 28.

151 *Application for Revision of the Judgment of 11 September 1992 in the Case concerning the* Land, Island and Maritime Frontier Dispute (El Salvador/Honduras: Nicaragua intervening) *(El Salvador v. Honduras), judgment, I.C.J. Reports 2003*, p. 392, at p. 399, para. 22.

152 *Ibid.*, at p. 399, para. 22.

153 A. Zimmermann and R. Geiss, 'Article 61' in A. Zimmermann, C. Tomuschat, C. Tams and K. Oellers-Frahm (eds), *The Statute of the International Court of Justice: A Commentary* (Oxford, 2012), pp. 1497–1528, p. 1052 atMN 12.

154 C. Schulte, *Compliance*, p. 38 and S. Rosenne, *Interpretation, Revision and Other Recourse*, at p. 174. In the case of the Application for revision of the 1992 judgment in the case of the Land, island and Maritime frontier dispute Honduras 'at first asked the Court to apply' the paragraph, 'but in the end it withdrew that request': *I.C.J. Reports 2003*, at p. 399, para. 22 referred to by R. Kolb, *The ICJ*, p. 822. 'The Court, for its part did not consider it necessary to require Article 61, paragraph 3 to be applied *proprio motu*': R. Kolb, *The ICJ*, p. 822.

Conclusions
Revisiting the Functional Interaction between Negotiations and Judicial Settlement by the International Court of Justice

General Picture

The fundamental mission of international law may be described as twofold: the creating and implementation of primary rules; and the peaceful settlement of disputes which may originate from both violation of such rules and particular other claims States might put forward in their mutual relations.

Our study has delineated the scope, advantages and limits of the functional interaction between two modes of PSD, negotiations between parties and adjudication by the Court. The questions and issues raised in this study about the functional interaction can be said to 'lie at the heart of the Court's ability to respond as efficaciously as possible to its clientele'.[1]

Time has come now to revisit the functional interaction interplay between the diplomatic and judicial settlement of inter-state disputes in light of the Court's jurisprudence spreading over more than six decades.

The analysis carried out in this study now enables us to identify a number of *trends* – 'A "trend" implies movement, development; not every judicial decision is by definition evolutionary'[2] – in the case law as a reflection of a discernible judicial *policy*[3] with regard to the challenges and directions of the exercise of the respective role of both modes of PSD and to their ultimate functional interaction.

If such a judicial policy can be detected it is an important tool for a tentative *functional impact assessment* and it would constitute an important building block for the international law of dispute settlement consisting of cooperational duties for both the Court and the parties.[4]

The case law analysis has confirmed that a number of the standards and benchmarks – which negotiation scholars still did consider in the mid-1960s as *incipient trends* and what an authoritative commentator has recently described as 'ethics of dispute management' requiring 'at least a minimum of good-will which is indispensable in the international society of today'[5] – have indeed been brought into the realm of law and have developed into *legal principles* of general applicability with regard to state conduct during negotiations outside and within the context of PSD, throughout the three successive phases.

The growing importance of the functional interaction, in its infinite variety, between these complementary methods of PSD is nowadays – both in state practice and in the Court's case law – undeniable and well established, as is their respective *processual* nature.

From the perspective of the parties, the richness and complexity of the functional interaction is based *inter alia* on the history of a particular dispute; its subject-matter; past and present relations between the parties; their changing perceptions of each other's attitudes and positions taken during both processes; the strategy chosen – *una via selacta* or double track – and the appropriate moment in time to cross the Rubicon into the Peace Palace; and the real impact of this major political decision during and after the proceedings in The Hague.

---

1 *A Dialogue at the Court*, at p. 2.

2 H. Thirlway, 'Some Observations on Recent Trends', 7.

3 In the narrow sense as described by P.-M. Dupuy, *Judicial Policy*, p. 62.

4 Various cases can indeed be considered to have been landmark cases in the (progressive) development of such a judicial policy, the most relevant ones being *Fisheries Jurisdiction cases* of the 1970s, the *Aegean Continental Self case*, the *Central American cases* involving Article XXXI of the Pact of Bogota and the *CERD case*.

5 K. Oellers-Frahm, 'Nowhere to Go', 451.

From the Court's perspective all these factors and elements also play their role – in addition to the collegiate exercise of its judicial function – comprising both an evident and *primordial settlement of dispute component* and a subordinated but potentially equally effective *facilitative role* – when it has been called by (one of) the parties to properly intervene.

Parties may decide to follow the *una via selecta* or double track strategy.

Functional interaction is in most cases still rather remote when prior negotiations perform their *more substantive function*, i.e. to actually settle (part of) the dispute; parties may indeed not even consider the prospect of adjudication. Functional interaction is actually brought into operation when prior negotiations perform their more *albeit not exclusively procedural function*, i.e. to conclude a Special Agreement in order to submit the dispute to the Court – parties having been unable between them to settle it.

A jointly undertaken double track strategy could potentially reinforce that functional interaction, although not necessarily without ensuing difficulties, as the *Aegean Sea Continental Shelf case* has demonstrated. A separately undertaken double track strategy simply suspends the functional interaction from becoming fully operational until the moment is considered to be right by the party concerned.

The role of negotiations within and outside the context of PSD is multifunctional, both from an international relations and from an international law perspective; and although stability has been identified as one of the primary objectives of frontier negotiations,[6] in general the aim is to bring to an end a state of tension inevitably flowing from a dispute between States.

The first major political decision States have to take is to recognize that they have a (potential) dispute at their hands for the solution of which they are under a general legal obligation to negotiate, a process which is not necessarily the only way towards settlement.[7] Both a positive or negative decision at this preliminary crossroad already has an impact on the potential role of functional interaction.

If and when the decision to start the process produces a (partial) settlement, the negotiation component has (even temporarily) fulfilled its role, putting aside the need for fully fledged adjudication to come into play, although the mere prospect of judicial intervention may have functioned as an extra incentive for the parties to reach such an agreement.

A refusal to embark upon the process or an unsuccessful outcome may bring forward the unilateral or joint transition from the pre-adjudicative into the adjudicative phase, thereby activating the functional interaction.

A closer look at the practice of optional clauses has revealed some varied forms and degrees of (potential) functional interaction. The potential for parties to follow a unilateral double track strategy is substantially reduced when both of them have accepted the Court's jurisdiction under Article 36, para. 2 of the Statute, but excluding the invocation of a declaration made or ratified less than 12 or six months prior to the filing of an Application. The functional impact of such an exclusion on the progress and outcome of prior negotiations is uncertain.

Conversely, the parties' willingness to negotiate prior to the start of proceedings may be expressed through the inclusion of disputes with regard to which they have agreed upon a *modus vivendi* pending the final decision of the Court or by committing themselves, in a separate bilateral agreement, to a three-year moratorium not to invoke a reservation in this declaration or to initiate proceedings regarding matters governed by treaties in force between them.

As general international law does not require prior negotiations – to perform a substantive or rather procedural function – as a precondition for the judicial component to be brought into action, their important role is still to enable the Court to determine the existence and subject-matter of the dispute, as well as the critical date.

All actors in the adjudicative phase have to assess a refusal to enter into the prior process of negotiations, its deadlock or, in most cases, the (partial) failure of it.

The judicial assessment of the compliance with a conventional prior negotiation clause – opening the door to the Great Hall of Justice only when the dispute cannot or has not been settled – entails an examination that a genuine attempt in good faith to settle by negotiations has been made and that there is no reasonable probability that continuation or resumption of the process would turn out to be successful.

6 *Temple of Preah Vihear case, I.C.J. Reports 1962*, at p. 34.
7 A. Lall, *Modern International Negotiation*, at pp. 35 and 46.

Once the Rubicon has been crossed parties and Court find themselves under cooperational duties aiming at a proper and good administration of justice.

In a departure from a common and laudable practice and provided the case file allows this mode of functional interaction to work, the Court as well as the parties could be called on to handle and interpret positions previously held during negotiations.

In its assessment of the scope, nature and state of progress of a process of negotiations the Court in relevant cases carries out an examination of the views of the parties. Provided the records of these discussions are part of the case file, and depending on the degree of their completeness, the Court may have to limit itself to to a 'cursory examination' indeed.[8]

Interim arrangements reached during the proceedings do not only demonstrate the continuum between the two components of functional interaction; they also reflect the general duties for parties flowing from the principles of judicial process.

Resumed substantive negotiations stretching beyond the objective of temporary arrangements have a clear and distinct impact on the Court's procedural decisions, and of course on decisions by Court and/or parties to discontinue the proceedings altogether, putting an end to the attempts to settle the dispute by adjudication.

A two-way street has come to light as far as requests and indication of provisional measures is concerned.

The Court's freedom to bring prior negotiations into its *judicial reasoning, to draw inferences* from parties' positions taken during negotiations and to use their outcome *as part* of its ultimate decision is limited by the subject-matter of the dispute, the way it has been presented and the *petita*.

The 1970s *Fisheries Jurisdiction cases* are fine examples of a constant functional interaction between negotiations leading to the conclusion of an interim arrangement and the subsequent judicial endorsement, without any request to that end, of what the parties had already achieved.

Together with the particular nature of the dispute and the rights involved, and the actual occurrence or judicial refusal of third State intervention, pre-adjudicative or negotiations during the proceedings co-determine the Court's precise post-adjudicative role and the room for and scope of post-adjudicative negotiations to implement the judgment and/or to solve outstanding issues.

Failed post-adjudicative negotiations may, sometimes unexpectedly, reactivate the functional interaction when (one of) the parties feels the need to either request the Court to interpret its judgment or to apply for its revision .

Functional interaction works both ways.

There is a discernable impact *of* negotiations on the performance of the judicial function prior to (jurisdiction) during the course and after the proceedings, although 'a tribunal should not be *over-influenced* in the exercise of its functions by the course followed by the other mode, that of negotiation'.[9]

There is a potential impact *on ongoing or future* negotiations between the parties and between (one of) the parties and third States of the performance of the judicial function, although this issue only played a rather negligible role both in the arguments put forward by the parties and in the Court's reasoning, not to mention the operative clauses of its decision.

The case law has not indicated that the traditional judicial approach of the importance and chances of success of diplomatic negotiations as a relative question has changed.

In order for functional interaction to properly operate during any of the successive phases parties should at all times openly and clearly state their respective objectives and positions. This goes for both processes of PSD, be it with regard to the existence and subject-matter of the dispute or the precise task the Court is called upon to perform.

---

8 T. Bernardez, 'Are Prior Negotiations', p. 515, para. 29.

9 *Fisheries Jurisdiction case, I.C.J. Reports 1974,* Dissenting opinion by Judge Gros, at p. 308 (emphasis added).

Main Findings in the Case Law as to the Prolegomena to the Functional Interaction: The Pre-Adjudicative Phase

Negotiations scholars have rightfully stressed the functional importance of the pre-negotiation phase, referred to by the Court as 'exploratory discussions'[10] during which litigation may already be considered as an alternative, in case of failure or deadlock, of the negotiation process to follow.

As to the prerequisites for any process of negotiations, the Court has implied a certain duty for States to conduct themselves in such a way as to contribute to a situation which is conducive to the conduct of fruitful negotiations.

When allegations of improper conduct outside the strict negotiation forum are being voiced as not contributing to the required climate of tranquillity for a process of negotiations the Court – in contrast to positions sometimes taken by individual judges – has never explicitly ruled on this important precondition for fulfilling the good faith requirement.

Raising a claim that another State is in breach of substantive treaty obligations does not necessarily, and in all circumstances, entail the initiating of the governing settlement of dispute provisions,[11] but it is the first necessary step to producing legal effects with regard to the functional interaction. The situation is no different in case of territorial or maritime claims detached from any allegations of treaty violations.

An offer to negotiate may be seen by the Court as marking the critical date, whereas acceptance of the invitation does not necessarily have the same legal effect in the absence of conflicting claims being raised. An offer to negotiate does not amount to an unequivocal consent to participate in the process, but once a State has made a commitment to enter into negotiations 'it is not the Court's function to contemplate that it will not comply with it'.[12] Indeed, a clear and unambiguous expression of the intention to enter into pre-negotiation may be considered as forming part of the good faith requirement governing any process of negotiations.

A refusal to even enter into a process of negotiations because allegedly there is no dispute or there are no issues to be discussed may put an early end to the negotiation component, potentially destroying *in limine* any question of a consensual resort to adjudication. Later on the Court may then decide that as a result of such a refusal there undoubtedly exists a dispute which has not or could not be settled by negotiations.

What Constitutes Negotiations in the Case Law of the Court?

Because the process has to develop and unfold and can consist of several successive stages, such as to start with 'exploratory discussions', there is an inherent element of time in the overarching notion of negotiations.

Cases brought have enabled the Court to progressively follow an almost winding road towards its own judicial approach of the definitional aspect of the negotiation component of the functional interaction and to finally address it more fully, at least in *its procedural aspect* in its jurisdictional judgment in the *CERD case*.

The pending case between Bolivia and Chile will compel the Court to examine more closely and for the first time in its history *the substantive aspects* of the diplomatic component of the functional interaction.

The *CERD case* indicates that not all statements by an Applicant may be considered as genuine attempts to negotiate relevant matters although accusations and replies on relevant issues attest to the existence of a dispute between the parties on a subject-matter capable of falling under a compromissory clause, but they may fail to demonstrate a (genuine) attempt to negotiate these relevant matters.

Although parties may disagree, already during the process prior to proceedings and well after the Court has been seised, about the nature of the discussions they had, it is, as the *CERD case* has demonstrated, ultimately for the Court to determine whether or not a genuine attempt has been made by (one of) the parties to engage in serious discussions with each other.

---

10 *Fisheries Jurisdiction case UK v. Iceland, I.C.J. Reports 1974*, at p. 14, para. 28.

11 *CERD case, I.C.J. Reports 2011*, at p. 102, para. 69.

12 *Nuclear Test case, I.C.J. Reports 1974*, at p. 47, para. 63.

The Obligation to Negotiate in Good Faith

In case the Court has determined that a wrongful act has been committed, good faith is being presumed as to the possible repetition of that act.[13] The case law points to the Court also presuming that parties have been negotiating in good faith until the opposite is claimed and proven before it.

Unless obliged to do so pursuant to the terms of an Application or counterclaim, the Court has seen no need to explicitly ascertain in its reasoning and determine with judicial authority in the operative clause whether and to what extent particular conduct by (one of) the parties could be considered to have significantly contributed to or perhaps even decisively caused the failure of a process of negotiations.

The case law does not seem to imply that the importance of progress – and the (alleged) lack of it – in the negotiations could be used as a benchmark for assessing compliance with the good faith requirement. Individual or collective judicial calls or recommendations addressed to the parties to continue or resume their negotiations efforts, in case of temporary deadlock, could however be interpreted as the first signs of a possible different trend in this regard.

As far as a *double track strategy* in its successive formats is concerned, the *principle of good faith* does not offer any relief to a Respondent claiming that the Applicant while negotiating was preparing for the instituting of a procedure before the Court, given the absence in general international law of an obligation for one State to inform the other party to a dispute of its intention to bring proceedings.

We are facing here the outer limits of the potential reach of the functional interaction: it does not stretch that far.

When, after the breakdown of a series of bilateral negotiations, a party is said to have 'finally' abandoned its efforts to reach an agreement, this carries with it the judicial presumption that the determined continuance of the process can be regarded as a sign of good faith.

When considering its jurisdictional decision the Court may, as it did in the *Belgian Senegal case*, explicitly blame the Respondent for lack of progress in a process of negotiations which did not and could not lead to a settlement.

The question whether one party or the other could be blamed for the fact that diplomatic negotiations have not been pursued may be irrelevant when the Court is assessing the admissibility of a (counter) claim.

Even when *accusations of bad faith* during the pre-adjudicative phase are voiced, the Court in almost all cases has refrained from attributing the failure to one of the parties. Only an explicit request in that regard brings the Court to pronounce itself upon the conduct raised, although individual judges occasionally have been less reluctant and have explained their position in this regard.

The *Pulp Mills case* has demonstrated the difficulty of a judicial assessment of actions allegedly constituting a breach of the obligation to negotiate in good faith.

The fact that 'tribunals have imposed good faith negotiations on States in situations where disputes have become protracted and acrimonious, i.e. where the parties had clearly not negotiated in good faith', has been called 'intriguing'.[14] However, such a judicially imposed obligation should not surprise at all, as the Court has both in fact and in law no other option than to reaffirm a pre-existing general and/or conventional obligation to negotiate.

The Functional Interaction Operates in a (Not) Entirely Different Way When the Court Exercises its Advisory Jurisdiction

Except in the quasi-contentious cases arising under the UN Privileges and Immunities Conventions, at first glance the general context and overall situation is entirely different when the Court is required to deliver an advisory opinion pursuant of Article 96 of the UN Charter.

As a matter of principle there is no inter-state dispute being brought by parties before the Court. This does not mean however, as the study has demonstrated, that there is no room for functional interaction.

13 *Pulp Mills case, I.C.J. Reports 2010*, at p. 105, para. 278.

14 C. Hutchinson, 'Duty to Negotiate', 121.

In advisory proceedings functional interaction operates as a two-way street: prior negotiations may have taken place and will co-determine the timing, the appropriateness of requesting the Court's opinion and of course the actual formulations of the request.

The Court's advisory opinion may in turn have a certain impact on the post-adjudicative process of negotiations, a question which does not concern the Court except when explicitly asked to express itself on it. In this respect the functional interaction is thus entirely different from its operation in contentious cases. The delivery of the opinion may bring the functional interaction, which is already different in both nature and scope, to a final and definitive end. On the other hand, functional interaction clearly claims its role and place.

Whereas in contentious cases the existence of a dispute is an absolute condition for the Court to exercise its jurisdiction, in advisory proceedings the very existence of a dispute between two States may constitute a compelling reason for the Court to decline to exercise its jurisdiction. Prior negotiations within a multilateral framework are important indications in this regard.

Negotiations of a bilateral or multilateral nature may form part of events the Court may have been informed about since the request was made.

Functional interaction does not come to an end by the submission of a request.

The alleged potential impact of the Court's opinion on ongoing or future negotiations has not been a compelling reason for the Court, in an act of negative interaction, to decline to respond to a request.

The Court stressed the positive functional interaction by viewing its opinion as potentially becoming an additional element in the negotiations, irrespective of whether it has identified the legal parameters for subsequent negotiations. On one occasion the Court has expressed its view that a framework approved by the Security Council constitutes only an offer to *initiate* negotiations.

Functional Interaction in Case of a Conventional Prior Negotiation Clause

In the absence of a general principle or rule requiring prior negotiations, such a condition 'may, however, be explicitly or implicitly imposed by the title of jurisdiction'.[15] Prior negotiations clauses in optional clauses and compromissory clauses are undoubtedly to be considered to constitute a reasonable condition or reservation.

That within the optional clause regime 'the significance of the commitment is likely to lie as much in the incentive it provides to try to avoid going to Court, as in the number of cases actually litigated'[16] equally applies to negotiation clauses.

Although the question whether customary international law contains a rule according to which prior negotiations are a mandatory precondition for seisin has been answered in the negative by the Court, this reply does not diminish both the *factual and legal functional importance* of prior negotiations, for instance as being part *of the context* for the interpretation of compromissory clauses, and more prominently of course to establish between the parties and for the Court to evaluate the very existence of a legal dispute and to clarify the respective legal claims of the parties.

The Court's Statute does not contain a prior exhaustion of diplomatic negotiations rule precisely in order to prevent dysfunctional interaction which would occur if a party were allowed successfully to invoke some hope of a settlement by negotiations just to avoid the Court's jurisdiction.

As a brief review has demonstrated, the functional interaction has been institutionalized by the drafting of compromissory clauses, the conclusion of Special Agreements and by the depositing of facultative declarations containing a precondition clause *ratione pre-adjudicatory conduct*, i.e. prior negotiations as a precondition.[17]

The case law does not seem to indicate that the Court has been interpreting a prior negotiation condition more flexibly or rather strictly depending on whether it was included in a Special Agreement, an optional or a compromissory clause.

15 S. Rosenne, *The Law and Practice of the International Court of Justice* (1965), vol. 2, p. 513, as cited by Torres Bernardez, 'Are Prior Negotiations', p. 511, para. 15.

16 J. Merrills, 'Does the Optional Clause Still Matter?', p. 453.

17 The degree of institutionalization has been particularly high in the 1975 Statute which was at the heart of the *Pulp Mills case*.

Moreover, if a conventional precondition of prior negotiations is considered to be of a merely procedural nature, any defect in that respect could be – a number of surrounding circumstances permitting – (relatively) easily cured by *joint action* after the start of the proceedings. Viewed as a precondition of a more substantive nature, that defect would become harder or even impossible to cure.

Does the conventional prior negotiation clause impose a *legal obligation* upon the parties or is it *merely a matter of fact* later to be *objectively* assessed by the Court? This question was at the heart of the *CERD case*.

Even if the parties would merely *contemplate* a resumed or new process of negotiations, functional interaction would come closer when the Court would consider that to suffice to fulfil the prior negotiation condition, as it did in the *Border and Transborder Armed Actions case*.

The case law analysis has definitely demonstrated that the functional interaction certainly has a general impact when and in the way the Court exercises its judicial function, and this from the moment the Court examines prior negotiations as a precondition for the existence of a dispute and the clarification of its subject-matter – both fundamental prerequisites for a proper exercise of jurisdiction – and when it has to decide whether the seisin is admissible.

Judicial awareness and recognition of the respective functions and limitations of both mechanisms of PSD reinforce the Court, stressing the need that parties should ensure through prior negotiations, method of seisin and submissions its precise role within the context of the functional interaction.

The analysis of the case law leaves no doubt that in order to be able to properly perform its judicial task the Court is determined to examine and assess the format, scope and extent of the process of prior negotiations in order to be able to determine that, in light of the circumstances, the threshold for the existence of a dispute has been reached.

A compromissory clause providing an alternative way for prior negotiations and recourse to a treaty-monitoring body certainly reinforces the autonomous character of negotiations within the context of invoking it and seising the Court.

In case of a *conventional prior negotiation clause* the task of the Court is twofold: to establish whether the facts of the record show that the parties 'engaged in negotiations'; and 'if the Parties did engage in such negotiations, to determine whether those negotiations failed, therefore enabling the Court to be seised of the dispute'.[18] Parties may

> disagree as to the interpretation or application *in casu* of the prior negotiations clause or proviso concerned. In such cases, the Court reserves for itself the determination of whether or not the prior negotiation condition has been fulfilled, bearing in mind generally the wording of the clause or the proviso in question and the arguments of the parties thereon, as well as their actual conduct before and after the filing of the case, so as to establish the existence at the date of the application of a real possibility of settling the dispute through diplomatic or direct negotiations between the parties.[19]

Indeed, 'the very fact that proceedings have been instituted and that the said determination of the Court is made thereafter are circumstances which militate powerfully against the conclusion that the dispute could have been solved by prior negotiations as prescribed'.[20] There can thus be no doubt that with regard to those two important preliminary questions the Court is the key holder.

Is it possible to discern a *certain judicial trend* with regard to the varied formulations used: when a dispute *cannot be settled, has not been settled* and *failure to refer to particular treaty provisions*?

A Dispute which Has Not Been Settled

Prior to the *DRC Rwanda case* the Court's case law was characterized by a certain flexibility with regard to the interpretation of this requirement, especially when, in the absence of a treaty-monitoring body, an attempt to negotiate did not receive any positive response by the other party.

18 *CERD case, I.C.J. Reports 2011*, at pp. 135–6, para. 169.
19 Torres Bernardez, 'Are Prior Negotiations', p. 525, para. 62.
20 Torres Bernardez, 'Are Prior Negotiations', p. 525, para. 63.

Torres Bernardez observation that '[i]n practice and *as things stand*, the possibility that the Court might disclaim jurisdiction or declare a given application inadmissible from want of fulfilment of a precondition of negotiations in the particular title of jurisdiction concerned, as generally drafted, would appear very remote indeed'[21] has been overtaken by the Court's decision in the *CERD case*.

In the course of the unfolding of the proceedings in the *CERD case*, the operation of the functional interaction underwent a drastic change: at the stage of the indication of the provisional measures, admittedly when assessing its *prima facie* jurisdiction, the Court did not interpret Article 22 as suggesting that formal negotiations did constitute a precondition to be fulfilled prior to the seisin. The provision only *suggests* that *some attempts* should have been made.

The joint dissent to the Court's 2008 Order was followed by a strong disagreement between the parties in their arguments before the Court on the question whether the provision contained a legal obligation or merely a statement of fact, and at the stage of its jurisdictional decision, by a diametrically opposed approach by the majority, when it considered prior negotiation to be a legal precondition.

The way in which the Court elaborated and applied the various constituent elements of this precondition have significantly reduced the potential functional interaction which at first glance may have seemed to be maximized.

In spite of genuine attempts which must have been made, the Court's assessment must be that there was no *reasonable probability* that further negotiations would lead to a settlement, the latter conclusion being based *inter alia* on the fact that owing to the Respondent's position no progress was made as a result of the lack of change in the respective positions of the parties. The Court's reasoning clearly illustrates the close functional interaction between the prior negotiations and the judicial proceedings.

The Court's judgment in the *Belgium Senegal case* – delivered just over a year after the judgment in the *CERD case* and explicitly citing the precondition approach taken in that case – does not contribute to alleviating the concerns expressed by the joint dissent and by doctrine regarding the potential impact of that judgment on both prospective parties and the Court regarding the further development of the relevant case law from the perspective of the functional interaction.

A Dispute which Cannot Be Settled

In order to have *bona fide* negotiations the parties' 'irreducible minimum objectives' must 'not be totally incompatible'.[22]

If the transactional is considered also to be present in non-territorial disputes, could it then be assumed to be more contributable to the definitive settlement of the dispute? Or is the transactional perhaps excluded in non-territorial disputes by the nature of the dispute and the submissions of the parties?

The analysis has certainly *not* provided us with a *general* transactional trend in the judicial component, whereas it is clearly almost inherently present in the negotiation part of the functional interaction.

This brings us back to the issue that with regard to a number of rights and duties of States negotiations cannot take place (non-negotiable) prior to the proceedings, and that as a result there is no room either for the transactional in the Court's dealing with the case; those disputes *cannot be settled by negotiations*.

Disputes involving allegations of violations of human rights by their very nature do fall outside the diplomatic component of the functional interaction, and consequently are only suitable for either non-forcible countermeasures or adjudication.

'Respect for human rights by its very essence is non-negotiable; human rights are either respected or they are not.'[23]

Functional interacting would operate to its maximum potential if and when the Court's assessment that the dispute cannot possibly be settled by negotiations refers to the time when the Application was filed, although

21 Torres Bernardez, 'Are Prior Negotiations', p. 512, para. 20.

22 A. Lall, *Modern International Negotiation*, p. 54.

23 P. Kooijmans, 'Inter-State Disputes Settlement in the Field of Human Rights' (1990) 3 *Leyden Journal of International Law* 3, 87–98, at 90. Writing a few months prior to the adoption of the 1966 Covenants, A. Lall could still hold that all international disputes are 'at one stage or another negotiable': *Modern International Negotiation*, pp. 54 and 131.

the appreciation of that impossibility may very well refer to (much) earlier moments in time. Arguably the inference could be drawn that parties would be obliged to continue their attempts to settle the dispute until the very moment of the transition from the pre-adjudicatory to the adjudicative phase.

The continuous nature of the obligation to negotiate has been reflected in two general duties for the parties: to conduct themselves in such a way as not to render the performance of the Court's task more difficult or impossible; and not to aggravate the dispute – entailing, perhaps, in *statu nascendi*, a corollary positive duty to continue negotiations and to resume the process which previously had failed.

As far as the Court is concerned the conclusion of an interim arrangement during the proceedings does not exhaust the obligation to negotiate, although it clearly terminates when the exchanges become futile.

The overall, objective and judicial appreciation of this state of affairs, subsequent to a political assessment made by each party, is bound to take into consideration various factors such as the complexity of the subject-matter, the pre-existing and traditional relations between the parties, the controversy being part of a larger conflict and so on.

For the functional interaction to properly operate it is necessary for the Court to examine whether – in spite of genuine attempts to negotiate having been made – a deadlock or a refusal by one of the parties did occur, in order to determine whether 'further negotiations became futile and showed no *reasonable probability* that they could result in a settlement of the dispute'.[24]

Whether negotiations have been going on in collective format within the context of conference diplomacy or by way of direct talks does not really matter according to the Court for its assessment of failure or success, as what is really important are 'the attitude and the views of the Parties on the substantive issues of the question involved'.[25]

The Potential or Actual Role of Third States in the Functional Interaction during the Pre-Adjudicative Phase

Functional interaction also operates in the shadow of the legal interests of third States, a bystander as a silent witness, a potential intruder, facilitator or actual intervener.

Mainly depending on the subject-matter of a dispute the parties have to make, possibly already during the pre-negotiation phase, the decision whether or not to include into the process third States whose (legal) interests might come into play.

Such a decision, which in itself is capable of co-determining the success or failure of the process, will inevitably also have consequences on both components of the functional interaction once the bilateral dispute has been brought before the Court.

Main Findings in the Case Law as to the Functional Interaction during the Adjudicative Phase

Whereas negotiations are being used by the parties primarily to (attempt to) settle their dispute, and in a subordinated way to (attempt to) manage it, the functional interaction becomes fully operational when the parties turn to the Court as 'producer of a settlement'.[26]

Changing attitudes and positions, their respective evolving dispute-settlement driven strategies, the impact of the time factor co-determine the way the functional interaction works in the transition from pre-adjudicative negotiations towards the adjudicative phase, which may have been triggered by a so-called functional deadlock. In this latter case judicial intervention may have been resorted to by (one of) the parties to bring the prior negotiations process back on track.

---

24 *Belgium Senegal case, I.C.J. Reports 2012*, Separate opinion by Judge Yusuf, at pp. 650–61, paras. 4 and 6 (emphasis added) and Separate opinion by Judge Setubinde, at p. 594, para. 13.

25 *SWA cases, I.C.J. Reports 1962*, at p. 346.

26 H.Thirlway, 'The International Court of Justice 1989–2009', p. 355.

When the mere proposal of bringing a case before the Court has resulted in a successful outcome or prior negotiations, this could in retrospect be regarded as a particular form of functional interaction.

In case the process has not resulted in settling the dispute, seisin triggers the comprehensive *potential* of the functional interaction. Seisin changes the very nature of the factual and legal relations between the parties and between the Court and the parties – and in appropriate circumstances third States – which now find themselves subject to the mostly imperative rules of the Statute and Rules of Court. Moreover, new cooperational duties impose themselves upon all the actors involved in the adjudicative phase.

The *Qatar Bahrain case* has amply demonstrated that the functional interaction may result in complex problems from the very start of the proceedings.

The Court's *primary judicial function to settle the dispute* in accordance with international law and within the limits of the *petita* will, however, not prevent it from *also performing its facilitative function* in order to assist the parties in eventually reaching an (interim) arrangement during the course of the proceedings.

Under their cooperational duties to bring the adjudicatory component to a successful and durable conclusion, the Court has to ensure it provides good administration of justice which will *inter alia* require whatever procedural decision necessary, while parties must conduct themselves *in foro* and out of Court in such a way as to make that possible.

Double Track Strategy during the Proceedings

'A formalized procedure, in which at a certain point during the litigation it is mandatory to step aside and to reconsider the possibility that there may be a basis for a settlement without proceeding to a final award or judgment, could be a helpful facility in many cases'.[27]

The double-track strategy during the proceedings, on a voluntary basis, could also perform that function, eventually resulting in discontinuance. There can be no question, as far as double-track strategy is concerned, 'of the incompatibility of negotiations with judicial settlement at any stage in the course of the dispute'.[28]

The functional interaction may be curtailed by the overarching *proper administration of justice*, for instance when long duration of proceedings in cases where an individual is the ultimate beneficiary does not seem to justify allowing the parties another period of time to negotiate an agreement on reparation instead of having that question settled by the Court itself.

Welcoming any negotiation between the parties with a view to achieving a direct and friendly settlement, the Court made it perfectly clear that the functional interaction can continue to operate both ways after the start of the proceedings, because the ultimate objective of the functional interaction still remains the final settlement of the dispute, *in foro* and/or out of court. Hence the freedom of the parties to resume negotiations is preserved, provided the process does not result in aggravating the dispute or rendering in any other manner the exercise by the Court of its judicial task more difficult or impossible.

Resumed negotiations do have a definite influence on the Court's performance of its judicial duties, which in turn may have, for instance, contributed to the parties' readiness in the first place to restart the process which came to a (temporary) end as result of the seisin and which, moreover, may also be influenced by the final submissions.

Resumption of negotiations may lead the functional interaction to operate through *its more procedural component* – requests for extension of time-limits as a result of or as a condition for resumed negotiations, or a request for postponement of hearings in order to give the resumed process a real chance or to put additional pressure on the parties to achieve provisional or full and final settlement, or a *request* for the indication of provisional measures – or *more substantial component*: no aggravation of the dispute, *indication* of provisional measures, interim arrangements agreed between the parties.

Indeed, nothing prevents the parties, and the final settlement of the dispute may sometimes even require the parties, pending the proceedings, still to use (once more) the process of negotiations and, in case of success, to decide to discontinue the proceedings, thus bringing to an end, perhaps for the time being, both components of the functional interaction

27 V. Lowe, 'The Function of Litigation', 222.

28 *Aegean Sea Continental Shelf case, I.C.J. Reports 1978*, Separate opinion by Judge Singh, at p. 48.

An explicit and clear manifestation of the full impact of functional interaction has been found in the limiting effect of the general principles as to the judicial process on the freedom of parties to negotiate after seisin: at the time the Court takes its decision the dispute must still continue to exist and the facts have to be those occurring up to the close of the oral proceedings.

In the actual judicial settlement of the dispute *by the Court* the functional interaction operates in various modes and under diverse appearances.

Both the dispute settlement and facilitative function of the Court influence the judicial significance it wishes to attach to negotiations.

The functional interaction is most limited when the Court in the narrative of the facts of a case *merely reports* that a process of negotiations has taken place.

The Court has *reviewed* negotiations in order to judicially qualify their nature, scope and purpose, and only rarely to discover the reason why the process has broken down.

A judicial finding that the Court does not posses jurisdiction may at first glance put an end to the judicial component of the functional interaction.

However, its potential impact does not stop there because some elements of *res judicata* attaches to its findings about the existence of a legal dispute and its subject-matter.

In its *judicial reasoning* the Court has sometimes merely reported, while in other cases it has, albeit cautiously, *drawn inferences* from the parties' views expressed during negotiations – provided the quality of the material allows the Court to consider it as conclusive – and from their conduct during that process.

The Court has used the partially (un)successful, even provisional, outcome of negotiations as *part of the basis* for its ruling, together of course with the parties' arguments *in foro*.

The functional interaction stretches well into the post-adjudicative phase when upon request or pursuant to a provision of the Special Agreement the Court provides a judicial basis for the parties' continuous duty to negotiate; and in taking its decision on the merits, albeit to a limited extent and in appropriate circumstances, taken into account the potential impact of its decision on forthcoming negotiations for which it may provide parties with directions.

As far as the parties are concerned the functional interaction is very limited, if not almost non-existent, when they have agreed beforehand to implement a *non-invocation clause* during the proceedings. In order to find a political solution parties may, during negotiations, refrain from claiming rights which they later could assert before the Court.

The common and laudable practice of non-invocation of concessions made and positions held is intended to preserve the relative autonomy of both processes, which in turn could increase the chances of both methods succeeding.

The Potential or Actual Role of Third States in the Functional Interaction during the Adjudicative Phase

A controversial application of the *Monetary Gold* rule accompanied by a Court refusal to intervene may entail dysfunctional interaction, perhaps also aggravating a trilateral dispute.

Negotiations by (one of) the parties with a third State has a potential impact on the exercise of its judicial function by the Court. The Court may indeed assess the progress made during that process, although it may not always feel the need to do so.

Requests by third States to be furnished with copies of the written pleadings may be related to either or both of the components of the possible future functional interaction: to assist them in forthcoming negotiations and/or to consider invoking Article 62 of the Statute.

Although an interest of a legal nature may very well come to the fore in negotiations with (one of) the parties prior to the proceedings, Article 62 does not require such prior negotiations; and also the Court has made it clear that there is no requirement for the third State to define a dispute in prior negotiations in order to apply for intervention under Article 62. Such an interest of a legal nature may however still have to appear in forthcoming negotiations during or after the adjudicatory phase, provided it is the object of a real and concrete claim.

The right to enter into negotiations with one or both of the parties to settle a particular claim may only constitute an interest of a legal nature, distinct from the territorial claim itself which may become the subject-matter of future negotiations, provided the same instrument will be as relevant as the ones already before the Court, as the *Indonesia Malaysia case* has demonstrated:

The possibility of later appearance before the Court as a principal party in parallel proceedings against one or both of the parties should not affect the pertinence of a request for intervention as any decision in that case would come considerably later.[29]

This argument equally applies with regard to the potential impact of the decision in the case on subsequent negotiations.

The potential role of third States in both negotiations with (one of) the parties and the ongoing proceedings has tested the very limits of the functional interaction, especially in maritime delimitation cases.

In case a request for intervention has been denied and the Court has thus preserved the bilateral nature of the functional interaction, or no request for intervention has been made and it is the third State which has left untouched the bilateral nature of the proceedings, *judicial awareness* of even potential claims of third States has come into play at the stage of determining the relevant area in maritime delimitation cases, whereas with regard to the actual delimitation the Court provides protection going beyond Article 59.

Main Findings in the Case Law as to the Functional Interaction during the Post-Adjudicative Phase

'The lawyers can go home at the end of an international case; but the parties usually have to continue to live with another. Anything that helps them to find their own way of doing that can only enhance the utility of international litigation.'[30]

Both the dispute settlement and the facilitative part of the Court's functioning have played their role in this regard.[31]

Judicial deference – i.e. sending the parties back to the negotiating table – has to be properly situated within the functional interaction as a result of the way the parties have, during the pre-adjudicatory phase, limited the jurisdiction of the Court, which in turn has not only interpreted in a more liberal or strict way those limits but moreover has scrupulously examined the exact content and scope of the parties' submissions as developed during the proceedings.

It has been rightly argued that the function of implementing a judgment is perhaps more important 'for the prevention of future disputes' than 'for the resolution of the existing dispute'. Moreover, it is for the parties 'to decide the place' that the 'judicial component' should have in their dispute 'according to what process is feasible and appropriate under their existing political relationship'.[32]

When the Court orders the parties to negotiate in the operative part of its judgment, thereby leading the parties from the adjudicative into the post-adjudicative phase, the functional interaction enters into largely unchartered waters, although the Court may tailor 'its judgment to the practical needs of further negotiations',[33] particularly in territorial and maritime delimitation disputes.

The broader or stricter limits of the submissions, formulated in light of prior negotiations or the lack thereof – resulting in a Special Agreement or in an Application as the case may be – are decisive for the parties'margin of freedom subsequent to the Court's decision.

Accordingly, the Court has in appropriate cases not only determined the end result of those negotiations but it has also provided the parties with requested directions and a non-exhaustive list of factors to be taken

29 *Continental Shelf case between Tunisia and Libya, I.C.J. Reports 1981*, at p. 10, para. 14 (Malta).

30 V. Lowe, 'The Function of Litigation', 222.

31 V. Lowe, *The Interplay*, p. 246.

32 L. Boisson de Chazournes and A. Angelini, 'After "The Court Rose": The Rise of Diplomatic Means to Implement the Pronouncements of the International Court of Justice', (2012) 11 *The Law and Practice of International Courts and Tribuna*ls 1–46, at 8 and 10.

33 C. Murphy, *The World Court*, 561.

into account. A limited list entails a less balanced and more exclusively judicial operation of the functional interaction in this category of cases.

The negotiation part of the functional interaction fully reclaims its role once the judicial component has provided a binding settlement of the dispute as it had been submitted – or discontinuance has taken place – subject to the obligation to implement the judgment rendered and within the new legal framework laid down by the Court in the prescriptive part of its judgment.

In case negotiations have not fulfilled the now classical conditions as established by the Court's jurisprudence, the Court has, within the limits of its jurisdiction, made it clear that fresh negotiations are to take place on the basis of its decision on the merits.[34]

Post-adjudicative negotiations may be necessary to implement the judgment, if need be to settle remaining issues left out of the task given to the Court; to resume negotiations in the absence of a judgment on the merits; and in appropriate cases jointly to depart in whole or in part from the Court's decision.

An Order indicating provisional measures may influence the readiness of the parties and the progress of (resumed) negotiations both during and after the proceedings, while a purely declaratory judgment may provide the basis for negotiations.

In the post-adjudicative phase the pendulum of the functional interaction clearly swings back, although not necessarily irreversibly, from the adjudicatory settlement by the Court to the process of negotiation between the parties either to implement the judicial decision for the expected positive impact of which they may have suspended that process in the first place and/or to resume negotiations to solve outstanding issues.

Our study has demonstrated the inevitable functional interaction between the pre-adjudicative and adjudicative phases and between the adjudicative and the post-adjudicative phases, in terms both of negotiation between the parties and the Court's performance of its task.

Provisions made by the parties during the pre-adjudicative phase – for instance in an attempt to minimalize the functional interaction by agreeing beforehand to ensure their freedom to negotiate on for instance the boundary laid down by the Court's decision or the absence thereof, leaving the Charter-based obligation of Article 94 of the Charter to operate without any prearranged surrounding modalities or by interlocutory decisions taken by the Court and potential disagreement between the parties during either of the three phases – are bound to have a conducive or more rarely complicating impact on that process.

Parties' decisions to allow the functional interaction to operate in various modes with regard to compliance with the judgment and for instance also on the important question of reparation are already an indication of their (un)willingness to enter into a process of negotiation relating to this particular issue.

The Court has to discharge its task in such a way – respecting the *non ultra petita* rule and fully aware of the *res judicata* authority of its decision – that the room for disagreement between the parties as to the implementation of its judgment is reduced as far as possible.

Among the various factors co-determining the successes or failure of these negotiations, both the quality of the Court's pronouncements and the nature of the Court's decisions are important. In practical terms this means a clear and articulate judicial reasoning, convincingly supporting precisely formulated operative clauses, also to avoid the need for parties to come back to The Hague and make requests for interpretation.

The request for the interpretation of the 1962 judgment in the *Temple of Preah Vihear case* has clearly pointed to the sometimes potentially unlimited duration of the post-adjudicative phase.

Although in both post-adjudicative scenarios a certain element of time is involved for any such request to be submitted,there is a reasonable expectation that the parties should, after a careful reading of the judgment, first at least make a genuine attempt to agree on the proper understanding of the Court decision, in spite of Article 60 not requiring the parties to do so. Pre-adjudicatory arrangements between the parties may have made provision for such a course of action, before submitting a request pursuant to Article 60.

The Court has made it clear that previous compliance with its judgment may be required in case of an Application for revision under Article 61, hence reinforcing the expectation of post-adjudicatory negotiations preceding such an Application.

34 *North Sea Continental Shelf case, I.C.J. Reports 1969*, at p. 48, para. 87.

The Potential or Actual Role of Third States in Functional Interaction during the Post-Adjudicative Phase

Although the Court has occasionally drawn the attention of third States to the possible impact that its future judgment may have on their interests, it has be duly noted that the freedom for parties and for third States to negotiate *inter sese* is guaranteed by Article 59 of the Statute.

A rejection of a request for permission to intervene may amount to a reminder to the requesting State of the functional interaction by either sending the would-be intervener and (one of) the parties back to the negotiating table or inviting that State to start new proceedings.

(Dys)Functional Interaction

Dysfunctional interaction may be described as the phenomenon where, intentionally or unexpectedly, the prospective autonomy of both modes of PSD is preserved, restored or maximized, or where the desired positive impact of functional interaction is being jeopardized, distorted.

Providing information on the scope or state of progress of negotiations to the Court will enable it to determine for instance whether parties have agreed to suspend functional interaction initially envisaged, by excluding recourse to the Court for the duration of the process of negotiations.

Dysfunctional interaction occurs in case the parties are locking themselves into needless continuation of litigation; but it may also be the result, for instance, when the Court refuses to indicate provisional measures while at the same time welcoming further negotiation, or when its decision on the merits is likely to ensue in a hardening of the parties' bargaining positions in the adjudicative or post-adjudicative phase, and this in spite of the endeavours of the parties and the Court to safeguard the functional interaction's potential.

The Court almost formulated an indication in general to States to explicitly address the question of the potential impact of ongoing negotiations on the prospective exercise of its jurisdiction. In particular circumstances the perception may arise that exercising or declining jurisdiction, both in contentious or advisory proceedings, is not the most conducive judicial contribution to an ultimately successful settlement of the dispute.

A perceived risk of future dysfunctional interaction may underlie the argument that judicial intervention would effectively decide the main dispute, thereby removing the other parties' readiness to continue negotiations, as the *Interim accord case* has demonstrated.

Functional interaction may also *in limine* be preventive, both *in fact and in law*, when the particular nature of the rights – such as for instance of a humanitarian character, disagreement over which constitutes the subject-matter of the dispute – renders it *impossible* to be settled by negotiations.

As a result of its irreversible and ever-increasing humanization, the present state of the international legal order has revived the perennial debate about justiciable and non-justiciable disputes, in the sense that if the subject-matter is considered to be non-negotiable because of the inherent nature of the rights at hand, it is only for the Court to decide such a dispute.

Dysfunctional interaction may occur at various stages of its *normal trajectory*: for instance when a prospective Respondent, although not willing to negotiate in good faith, nevertheless prolongs negotiations in an artificial way with the mere intention of avoiding the judicial component of the interaction (yet) to become operational; or for instance when a claim is being asserted for the first time in a Memorial without such a claim (allegedly) ever having been put forward during a process of prior negotiations.

Good administration of justice does not allow a *dysfunctional use* of the interaction when one party's argument that no proper process of negotiations had ever taken place does not withstand judicial scrutiny, or when the alleged responsibility of one party for a failure of negotiations has not been included in the *petita*.

The functional interaction is potentially also being distorted as a result of a litigation strategy consisting in splitting up an overall conflict into separate cases by way of serial Applications.

The argument that the continuation of proceedings as part of a jointly chosen double track strategy is not very conducive towards the creation of a favourable climate for the resumed process of negotiations is the expression of an attempt at dysfunctional interaction. Another example is the argument which repeatedly has been rejected by the Court that there cannot be a dispute between the parties while negotiations are continuing.

In contrast to a request by parties to place on record a potential agreement they have reached in order to optimalize the functional interaction, the *Frontier Dispute between Burkina Faso and Niger* has demonstrated that an attempt to impose upon the Court a mode of dysfunctional interaction by a request to include in the operative clauses the content of a limited delimitation agreement in order to endow it with the force of *res judicata* was bound to fail as exceeding the limits of the Court's judicial function.

Dysfunctional interaction will not arise, however, when principles formulated in an agreement become relevant to the Court as part of established rules it has to apply pursuant to Article 38, para. 1 of its Statute.

The (Dys)Functional Role of Prior Negotiation Clauses

The Court has consistently held that there 'is no obligation of the exhaustion of negotiations or any other diplomatic means before instituting proceedings'; case law 'also shows' in case of such a conventional prior negotiation condition that the Court 'finds quite easily that this condition has been met'.[35] The latter part of that assessment was valid until the Court's decision in the *CERD case*.

The *CERD case* first of all has, perhaps temporarily and not without strong dissent, brought to an abrupt end the relative absence of a judicial policy with regard to a liberal or rather strict interpretation of the scope of compromissory clauses. How the Court's handling of that condition in the *CERD case* is going to affect state practice on prior negotiations as a precondition remains largely to be seen.

The Court's approach in its 2011 jurisdictional decision risks having serious repercussions on the future operation of both components of the functional interaction. Indeed, there is not only the fully justified fear that States will as a result adapt their prior negotiation strategy,[36] but also a State's access 'could be barred unless it follows new procedural requirements', which that States with limited resources and lacking experience before the Court 'will not find in the text of the treaty, the Statute or the Rules of Court'.[37]

Furthermore, the view has been persuasively been put forward that a particular Court order or a judgment 'will not enhance the Court's scope to contribute to the peaceful resolution of disputes', but 'instead [will] chill the appetite of States to consent even in a limited way to the Court's jurisdiction e.g. in a special agreement, through a compromissory clause or through a declaration that contains some limitations'.[38]

Such a scenario would strongly direct the functional interaction towards increasing the pre-existing trend of States towards negotiations to the detriment of judicial intervention.

Adaptation of negotiation strategy might involve greater reluctance by (one of) the parties to interrupt the process permanently and to postpone such a decision if it ultimately turns out to be inevitable as long as possible so that neither of them is led to give up hope of reaching a negotiated settlement.

Viewed form the perspective of PSD such an adaptation potentially, it could be argued, might improve the chances of those modes of settlement to succeed. However, it might also provoke a functional deadlock, bringing forward the resort to adjudication because the Court will also assess whether the Applicant has pursued the negotiations as far as possible, before determining that the process actually failed or became futile.

In a strange and almost contradictory way the functional interaction may lead to surprising and perhaps also undesirable results because of their post-adjudicative impact on the chances to resume negotiations when, in case of prior negotiations coming to an end after the start of the proceedings, the Court should decline jurisdiction.

On the other hand, functional interaction seems to be maximized when an Applicant has without success genuinely attempted to settle the dispute when it still seemed reasonably possible to do so, and subsequently

35 M. Kohen, *Interaction*, p. 23.

36 *CERD case, I.C.J. Reports 2011*, Dissenting onion by Judge Cançado Trindade, at p. 298, para. 138.

37 *Ibid.*, Separate opinion by Judge Donoghue, at p. 339, para. 25.

38 *Request for the interpretation of the 1962 Temple of Preah Vihear Judgment, I.C.J. Reports 2011*, Dissenting opinion of judge Donoghue, at p. 624, para. 28. In this context one should note that 'states today are much less willing to conclude new compromissory clauses', but that 'they are more willing than before to invoke existing ones': C. Tams, 'The Continued Relevance', 487.

seising the Court presented itself as the only feasible option and the Court funds jurisdiction because there is no longer a reasonable prospect of a negotiated settlement.

Only an explicit provision could require the parties to carry out their general obligation to continue prior negotiations to a point where it is no longer reasonably possible – the case law seems to point to endeavours having been made within reasonable limits indeed – to pursue them and they become futile.

When in a case such as *CERD* the Court finds it lacks jurisdiction, are parties finding themselves then back to square one?

It does not seem reasonable, when parties have in vain turned to the Court as a last resort, to expect them to use again the dispute settlement mechanisms of a treaty in case for instance the dispute has already proven to constitute a threat to international peace and security.

A compromissory clause may provide that for instance putting into operation the judicial component is only admissible until such time as a special procedure has been concluded.

A standstill situation such as to leave no prospect of the process being continued or resumed appears to suffice. However, such a judicial assessment may be made in light of subsequent negotiations taking place during the proceedings which then allegedly may be regarded as to ensure the continuation of the initial process without interruption.

Whether the functional interaction would present itself in a particular fashion as a result of such an approach by both parties would depend of course on the Court's assessment of the respective object and nature of both processes.

Although the Court does not normally go into that area, it is difficult to say, but it would be surprising if the Court were to carry out its judicial assessment of the performance of the obligation to negotiate in a different way depending on whether it was of a conventional general or judicial origin.

The Requests for and the Indication of Provisional Measures

The case law leaves no doubt that the Court, in exercising its powers under Article 41 of the Statute, firmly endorses the functional interaction and has provided a number of examples of the functional interaction operating as a two-way street as far as requests for and the indication of provisional measures are concerned.

The climate favourable to resumption of negotiations can only benefit from compliance with the measures indicated, whereas the non-indication by the Court may negatively influence parties' readiness in that respect.

Parties' perception in light of the exchange of written pleadings that, in spite of an earlier deadlock, a chance exists for a resumption of negotiations may make such resumption the very essence of a request for provisional measures.

The Court takes into account the scope, nature and (lack of) progress of the pre-adjudicative negotiations, which is not surprising given the functional link between prior negotiations and the measures.

The fact that the Applicant is not providing the Court with details on the scope or state of progress of negotiations is one of the considerations the Court takes into account when examining its *prima facie* jurisdiction to indicate provisional measures.[39]

In case the conciliatory spirit of pending negotiations is sufficiently reassuring, the Court may reject a request, whereas in general interim protection does not, as a matter of principle, depend on the prospect or progress of that process.

In case the chances of successful negotiations are rather remote, the Court, in rejecting a request, may decisively limit the functional interaction to its judicial component.

The functional interaction entails that instructions given by the Court will affect the parties' freedom of negotiation, while the Court will also monitor compliance by the parties, thus introducing a compatibility test.

In order not to distort the delicate balance between the parties in the operation of the functional interaction, recommendations accompanying a rejection of a request should not imply legal evaluations of the relevant facts.[40]

39 *Arrest Warrant case, I.C.J. Reports 2000*, at p. 200, para. 66.

40 H. Sakai, 'New Developments', 278.

Unsuccessful outcome of negotiations ordered by the Court may bring the functional interaction to a new level when subsequently the Court indicates in its decision on the merits what should have been the outcome of the negotiations.

There is no in inherent reason why functional interaction would rule out the conclusion of interim arrangements in combination with interim measures of protection.

Both the adjudicative phase in its ultimate moment of the delivery of the judgment and the post-adjudicative phase may build on the outcome of negotiations towards such an interim arrangement. The Court may also limit the temporal scope of its provisional measures until the parties have concluded such an interim arrangement.

Albeit somewhat contradictory discontinuance of proceedings may constitute an attempt to create circumstances that would be conducive for future negotiations.

The object and purpose of *discontinuance* is to actually restore the pre-adjudicative situation, subject of course to the factual and legal changes which the proceedings may have brought as a result of resumed negotiations following acts of judicial intervention.

In some cases resumption of negotiations may have been made conditional upon discontinuance of the proceedings, a kind of rather reversed functional interaction.

Deadlock of the Process of Negotiations

Deadlock does not always result form a mere refusal to continue the process; it may also be caused by the 'inability' of one party to give way.

Resumption of negotiations does not always guarantee a successful outcome, particularly when prior discussions were of such a nature as to render this attempt *superfluous*.

Representations may continue to remain unilateral in nature, resulting in a final offer for negotiations towards the conclusion of a Special Agreement.

When called on to exercise its powers and competences under Chapter VI, the Security Council has insisted that the parties should do everything within their power to ensure that the formal process of negotiations results in a *mutually acceptable solution*; this has to be considered as an implicit given within the requirements determined by the Court and governing the conduct of the parties during any process of negotiations.

In assessing whether a deadlock has been reached the Court does not limit itself to the pre-adjudicative phase, and it will look very carefully on which aspects there was a common understanding between the parties and on which other issues there was no agreement at all.

The functional interaction does not go as far as to require consistency between respective positions taken during negotiations and arguments the parties invoke before the Court, albeit alone, because under its established jurisprudence the Court *does not take account* of these positions, even admissions made, under the without prejudice practice – unless the positions have been properly reaffirmed in the written and oral pleadings – if the process has not produced an agreement.

However, this does not apply when the Court has been able to find shared views of the parties, or the records do not suggest a fundamental disagreement about a particular point and such a suggestion has not been contradicted by the arguments in the pleadings.

Moreover, such a requirement would seriously jeopardize the essence of negotiations as a mechanism of PSD.

By keeping in those circumstances the two processes separate, the Court intentionally and for reasons of good administration of justice substantially reduces functional interaction.

Although according to Lall 'disparity of power' may 'militate against resort to negotiate' to settle the dispute,[41] the Court would take the impact of the respective power position of States into account only provided the argument has been taken so far as to suggest being a ground for invalidity of the treaty which was concluded.

41 A. Lall, *Modern International Negotiation*, p. 150.

Outlook

In order to enhance the potential of the functional interaction within the *optional clause* regime, Waldock's suggestion of an 'insertion at the end of Article 36, para. 2 of a proviso' in order to put an end to the anomaly of joining the system and instantly institute proceedings has *mutatis mutandis* still some value today: 'Provided that for a period of two years after the date when any such declaration comes into force it shall not have effect with respect to a dispute concerning matters which were the subject of *negotiations* between the parties during the two years immediately preceding that date.'[42]

The particular circumstances of each case have required the Court to utilize a more or less flexible approach towards the functional interaction at work, but the study has not led us to believe that in doing so the Court has seriously undermined its role as a *forum for dispute resolution.*[43]

Although whether the way the Court has been dealing with the functional interaction is conducive to a more efficient and more sharply durable solution-focused use of negotiations by parties to a dispute is largely speculative, a few remarks can be made here.

The reaffirmation and progressive refinement by the Court of its judicial requirements of the way States should carry out their obligation to negotiate in good faith will continue to govern state conduct.

Is there an evolution or perhaps a pendulum movement in the case law from a flexible, less formalistic approach to negotiation to a stricter, more or even excessively formalistic approach in light of the *CERD case*?

A question raised by Thirlway with regard to a particular case whether 'the judgment is perhaps less helpful than it might have been'[44] is of more general importance as it is directly related to the adjudicatory/facilitative dichotomy of the Court's function.

Although the assessment of the Court's' performance under both these aspects has been outside the scope our study, we can however safely say that the answer to that question for each and every contentious case is decisively dependent on the way functional interaction has been properly operating throughout the three successive phases.

Although one of the possible collateral impacts of the Court's handling of the *CERD case* is that only future will tell whether after 'moving away from negotiation towards more judicialization of international disputes, the pendulum might start to swing back towards negotiated settlements',[45] it is certain that negotiations 'will continue to have in the future a vital role to play' as a method of settlement of disputes; negotiations can be 'useful both before and in conjunction with other methods'.[46]

'The cause of peace may well depend in part upon the explicit recognition by the world community of a duty to negotiate in good faith.'[47]

In light of the case law one should still duly acknowledge that finally 'even the best dispute settlement techniques or institutions cannot substitute for general attitude of cooperativeness, accommodation and good neighbourliness between or among the nations involved, or for their will to settle problems by peaceful means and in good faith'.[48]

The analysis in our study has certainly not put in doubt the general observation that '*It Does Not Follow from the Growth of International Courts and Tribunals that Judicial Means will Replace Diplomatic Means of Dispute Settlement*'.[49]

---

42 H. Waldock, 'Decline', 286 (change added).

43 A. Riddell and B. Plant, *Evidence*, p. 412.

44 H. Thirlway, 'The Law and Procedure of the International Court of Justice 1960–1989. Supplement, 2009: Parts Seven and Eight', 31 (concerning the *Sovereignty case between Malaysia and Singapore*).

45 A. Schneider, 'Bargaining in the Shadow of (International) Law: What the Normalization of Adjudication in International Governance Regimes Means for Dispute Resolution' (2008–09) 41 *New York University Journal of International Law and Politics*, 789–822, at 790.

46 H. Darwin, 'Negotiation', p. 82.

47 T. Hassan, 'Good Faith', 481.

48 R. Bilder, 'An Overview', 28.

49 L. Reed, 'Observations on the Relationship', p. 292 (emphasis original).

Although the 'diplomatic and legal process can sometimes work in harmony and sometimes in opposition',[50] international adjudication 'is likely to set the pace of the interactions between diplomatic and judicial means'.[51]

It is true that the Court's judicial function 'is not incompatible with that of rendering in its judgments peace to the spirit, particularly in the case of sovereign States; *Pax est justitia*',[52] but if the Court, within its limited strategic space, does not really manage to resolve the dispute in a case where it could have done so given the scope of its jurisdiction and the submissions of the parties, then its peacemaking function as the principal judicial organ of the UN has not been properly fulfilled.[53]

50 J. Merrills, 'The Mosaic', p. 393.

51 L. Boisson de Chazournes, M. Kohen and J. Vinuales, 'Concluding Observations' in L. Boisson de Chazournes, M. Kohen and J. Vinuales (eds), *Diplomatic and Judicial Means of Dispute Settlement*, pp. 335–33è, at p. 337.

52 *Arbitral Award case, I.C.J. Reports 1960*, Declaration by Judge Moreno Quintana, at p. 218.

53 One has also to acknowledge that a 'list of withdrawn cases, or cases that did not go past the provisional measures stage, may be a sign of a vigorous and creative tribunal finding an optimal role in the complex business of settling international disputes': V. Lowe, 'The Interplay', p. 247.

Index

For Product Safety Concerns and Information please contact our EU representative GPSR@taylorandfrancis.com
Taylor & Francis Verlag GmbH, Kaufingerstraße 24, 80331 München, Germany

www.ingramcontent.com/pod-product-compliance
Ingram Content Group UK Ltd.
Pitfield, Milton Keynes, MK11 3LW, UK
UKHW052054230926
475702UK00031B/2783
* 9 7 8 1 1 3 8 7 0 0 7 5 8 *